FIVE HUNDRED YEARS
OF CHAUCER CRITICISM
AND ALLUSION
1357–1900

VOLUME II
CONTAINING
PARTS II AND III

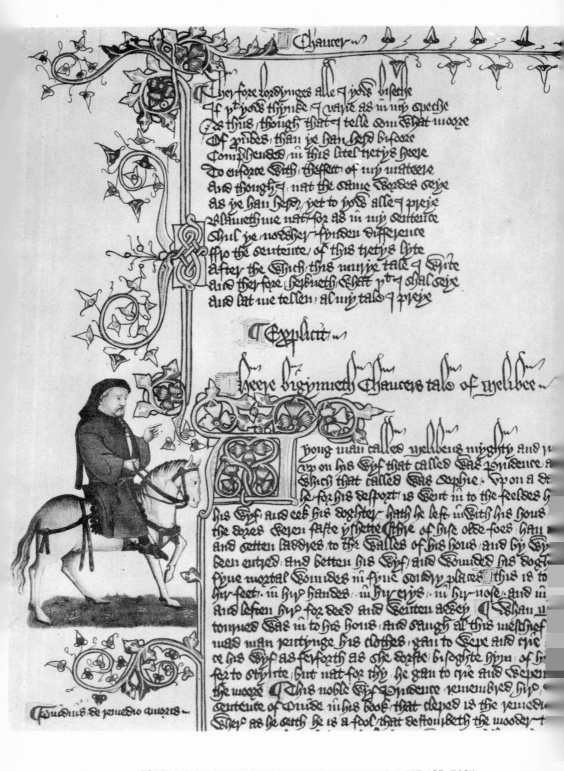

Ther fore lordynges alle I yow biseche
If þt yow thynke I varie as in my speche
As this, though that I telle som what moore
Of þuides, than ye han herd bifoore
Compiehended in this litel tretys heere
To enforce with, theffett of my mateere
And though I nat the same wordes seye
As ye han herd, yet to yow alle I preye
Blameth me nat, for as in my sentence
Shul ye nowher, fynden difference
Fro the sentence, of this tretys lyte
After the which, this mirie tale I wryte
And ther fore herkneth, what þt I shal seye
And lat me tellen, al my tale I preye

¶ Explicit

Heere bigynneth Chaucers tale of Melibee

Yong man called Melibeus myghty and
vp on his wyf that called was Prudence a
which that called was Sophie. vp on a day
for his despoort is went in to the feeldes h
his wyf and eek his doghter hath he left in with his hous
the dores weren faste yshette thre of hise olde foes han
and setten laddres to the walles of his hous and by the
been entred and betten his wyf, and wounded his doghter
fyue mortal woundes in fyue sondry places this is to
hir feet, in hise handes in hir erys, in hir nose, and in
and lefien hir for deed and wenten awey ¶ Whan M
torned was in to his hous, and saugh al this meschief
was man rentynge his clothes, gan to wepe and crie
re his wyf as ferforth as she dorste bisoghte hym of h
fer to stynte but nat for thy he gan to crie and wepen
the moore ¶ This noble wyf Prudence remembred hir
sentence of Ovyde in his book, that cleped is the remedi
Love, as he seith he is a fool that destourbeth the moder t

Prudencia de remedio amoris

PORTRAIT OF CHAUCER, ELLESMERE MANUSCRIPT, LEAF 157 BACK

FIVE HUNDRED YEARS OF CHAUCER CRITICISM AND ALLUSION

1357–1900

By

CAROLINE F. E. SPURGEON

DOCTEUR DE L'UNIVERSITÉ DE PARIS; HON. LITT.D. MICHIGAN;
HILDRED CARLILE PROFESSOR OF ENGLISH LITERATURE IN THE
UNIVERSITY OF LONDON

WITH
TWENTY-FOUR
COLLOTYPE ILLUSTRATIONS
INTRODUCTION, NOTES, APPENDICES
AND GENERAL INDEX

IN
THREE VOLUMES
VOLUME II

New York
RUSSELL & RUSSELL
1960

FIVE HUNDRED YEARS OF CHAUCER
CRITICISM AND ALLUSION: 1357–1900
appeared as Series 48–50, 52–56 of The Chaucer Society publications in 1908–1917. Subsequently, the sections were gathered into three volumes and published in 1925 by Cambridge University Press. The present edition is published by Russell & Russell, Inc., in 1960 by arrangement with Cambridge University Press.

PRINTED IN THE U. S. A.

CONTENTS

LIST OF ILLUSTRATIONS

Vol. II

PART II

(1801–1850)

1801. Aikin, John. *General Biography, or Lives, critical and historical, of the most eminent persons. . . .* vol. ii, pp. 647/2 to 649/2 Chaucer, Geoffrey.

[The life is taken from the Biographia Britannica ; Tyrwhitt's edition and theories are referred to, and the ' true poetical character ' of Chaucer's work is insisted upon.]

1801. Ellis, George. *Specimens of the Early English Poets, To which is prefixed An Historical Sketch of the Rise and Progress of the English Poetry and Language ;* 3 vols. [This " Historical Sketch," in which nearly all the references occur, is not in first edn., 1790.]

[Vol. i : Language, pp. 2, 7, 40, 85 *n.*, 86 *n.*, 126, 131, 229, 390 ; " King Horn " in *Sir Thopas,* 106 ; Chaucer's satire of the Romances and Love-Songs in *Sir Thopas,* 111 , Edward III. and Chaucer, 172–4 ; Gower and Chaucer, 177–9, 261 ; Lydgate and Chaucer, 273–6 ; quotation from *Troilus* (ll. 1793–8), 10, 130 ; *Gamelyn* and *Beryn,* 346–7 ; *Compleynt of Venus,* 174–9 ; *Hous of Fame,* 406 ; chapter viii, pp. 199–224 is on Chaucer, gives some facts based on Tyrwhitt, and quotes from *Court of Love, Canterbury Tales, Parlement of Foules, Legend of Good Women, Complaint of the Black Knight, Troilus, Rom. Rose ;* respect felt for Chaucer in the sixteenth century, 132. Other references, pp. 144, 147, 158, 169 and *n.,* 225, 226, 231, 266, 293 *n.,* 298, 299–300 *nn.,* 305, 315–16, 320–1, 341, 349, 361, 385 ; vol. ii, pp. 2–3, vol. iii, pp. 176, 409.]

1801. Leyden, John. *The Complaynt of Scotland,* ed. J. Leyden, Edinburgh.

[*Testament of Love* quoted as Chaucer's, p. 80 ; quotation from John de Irlandia mentioning the moral influence of the works of Chaucer and Gower, p. 86 ; *Orisoune of Chaucer* quoted, pp. 87–93 ; quotation from the *Parlement of Foules* " attributed to Chaucer," p. 104 ; mention of the vigorous description of a sea-fight in *Legend of Good Women* (Cleopatra), reference and quotation, pp. 114, 115 ; *Nonne Prestes Tale* mentioned as anterior to Cockleby's Sow, p. 134 *n. ;* passing references to musical instruments in Chaucer, pp. 153–5 ; brief mention of *Canterbury Tales,* p. 236 ; Arthur in the Romaunt, p. 237 ; references to *The Maying of Chaucer,* p. 245 ; source of *Frankeleyns Tale,* quotation from Tyrwhitt's edition, p. 262 ; the "Kingis note " (*Milleres Tale*), p. 277 ; authorship of the *Orisoune of Chaucer,* p. 289.]

1801. Strutt, Joseph. *Glig-Gamena Angel-þeod, or the Sports and Pastimes of the People of England . . . from the earliest period to the present time.*

[English mediæval setting of the Knight's Tale, p. vi; Court entertainments in *Hous of Fame,* p. xxiii; Chaucer's attitude to the monks who loved hunting (in this connection the *Ploughman's Tale* is mentioned as Chaucer's), p. 8; brief mention of Sir Thopas as a hunter and archer, pp. 22, 40; quotation from description of the Yeoman in the Prologue, ll. 103–8, p. 47; wrestling, quotation from Chaucer's description of the knight and the miller, p. 64; description of miracles as represented in Chaucer's day; reference in footnote to Wife of Bath's Prologue, p. 117; significance of 'Tragedy' as used by Chaucer illustrated by quotation from Prologue to the Monk's Tale, p. 122; brief reference and quotation concerning jesters, p. 137; references given to tregetours and joggleurs in Chaucer, pp. 153, 154, 156; brief reference, p. 158; brief mention of hoppesteres, p. 173; tymbesteres in Chaucer's translation of Le Roman de la Rose, reference and quotation, p. 177; brief mention of dancing in Chaucer, p. 222; brief mention in footnote of swinging, p. 226. Other references, mostly slight, pp. 30, *Testament of Love* quoted as Chaucer's, 142, 144, 233 *n.,* 262 *n.,* 275 *n.,* 298 *n.*]

1801. Unknown. *Note* [to the article entitled] Remarks on the Genius and Writings of Allan Ramsay, [in] The Edinburgh Magazine or Literary Miscellany, New Series, April 1801, p. 261. [A cutting of this article is included by Joseph Haslewood in his Collections for the Lives of the English Poets, *c.* 1833, vol. iii, p. 817, *q.v.*]

[Almost as much difference in language between *Christ's Kirk on the Green* and *The Gaberlunzie Man* as between Chaucer and Spenser.]

1801. Wordsworth, Dorothy. *Journal,* ed. W. Knight, 1897, 2 vols., vol. i, pp. 67–9, 73–4.

Friday, 4th [Dec. 1801]. . . . Wm. translating *The Prioress's Tale.*

Saturday, 5th. . . . Wm. finished *The Prioress's Tale,* and after tea, Mary and he wrote it out. . . .

Sunday, 6th. . . . Wm. worked a while at Chaucer, then [p. 68] we set forward to walk into Easedale. . . . In the afternoon we sate by the fire: I read Chaucer aloud . . .

[p. 69] *Monday Morning, 7th.* . . . William at work with Chaucer, *The God of Love.*

Tuesday, 8th Dec. 1801. . . . Wm. at work with Chaucer. . . . William worked at *The Cuckoo and the Nightingale* till he was tired.

Wednesday Morning, 9th December. . . . I read *Palemon* [*sic*] *and Arcite.* . . . William writing out his alteration of Chaucer's *Cuckoo and Nightingale.* . . .

[p. 73]   *Tuesday, 22nd* [Dec.]. . . . We sate snugly round the fire. I read to them the Tale of Constance and the Syrian Monarch, in the *Man of Lawe's Tale,* also some of the *Prologue.* . . .

Wednesday, 23rd. . . . Mary wrote out the Tales from Chaucer for Coleridge. . . .

Thursday, 24th. Still a thaw. Wm., Mary, and I sate comfortably round the fire in the evening, and read Chaucer. . . .

[p. 74]   *Saturday, 26th.* After tea we sate by the fire comfortably. I read aloud *The Miller's Tale.*

1801. Wordsworth, William. *Selections from Chaucer modernised. The Prioress's Tale (from Chaucer). The Cuckoo and the Nightingale (from Chaucer)* [by Clanvowe, not Chaucer]. *Troilus and Cressida (from Chaucer)* [bk. v, ll. 519–686]. (Poetical works, ed. W. Knight, 1896, 8 vols, vol. ii, pp. 238–69.)

[A prefatory note to the *Prioress's Tale* reads :]

In the following Piece I have allowed myself no farther deviations from the original than were necessary for the fluent reading, and instant understanding, of the Author : so much however is the language altered since Chaucer's time, especially in pronunciation, that much was to be removed, and its place supplied with as little incongruity as possible. The ancient accent has been retained in a few conjunctions, such as *alsō* and *alwāy,* from a conviction that such sprinklings of antiquity would be admitted, by persons of taste, to have a graceful accordance with the subject. The fierce bigotry of the Prioress forms a fine background for her tender-hearted sympathies with the Mother and Child ; and the mode in which the story is told amply atones for the extravagance of the miracle.

[Of these modernizations, which were all (with the *Manciple's Tale,* which has never been published) written in 1801, the first was published in 1820 (*Poems,* 1815–20, vol. iii [*The River Duddon, etc.*], pp. 173–86), and the second and third in 1841 (in the *Poems of Geoffrey Chaucer Modernised,* by Horne, etc.). The *Prioress's Tale* is preceded by Milton's lines :

> Call up him who left half told
> The story of Cambuscan bold.

Compare Wordsworth's remarks on his modernizations with those of Leigh Hunt, printed before his *Death and the Ruffians,* 1855, below. Two further letters from Wordsworth, 1840 and 1841, and Horne's Introduction to *Chaucer Modernised,* 1841, are printed below.]

1802. Drake, Nathan. *Canterbury Tales.*

[Four Tales of Terror, in the style of Mrs. Radcliffe, with no connexion whatever with Chaucer except in title.]

1802. Malcolm, James Peller. *Londinium Redivivum,* 4 vols, 1802–7, vol. i, p. 149.

[Description of Chaucer's tomb.]

1802. Planta, Joseph. *Catalogue of the Cottonian Library.* Note on Caligula, A. ii, Article 19, p. 42, col. 2.

Emaré, an old romance.

> Beg : Ihu : that ys kyng in trone
> As that I hoope bothe sone and mone.

Chaucer appears to have been indebted to this romance for his Man of Law's Tale.

[Cot. Calig. A. ii, the Romance of Emaré, was edited for the E.E.T. Soc. by Edith Rickert, 1908 ; her conclusion alone, p. xxviii, that 'the absence of archaic forms suggests a post-Chaucerian date, and 1400 is probably nearer the fact than is 1350,' nullifies Planta's surmise.]

1802. [Ritson, Joseph.] *Bibliographia Poetica.* List of editions and poems of Chaucer, pp. 19–23 ; Chaucer and Gower, pp. 24–5 *n.* ; dedication of Troilus and Cressida, p. 38 ; references in life of Occleve, pp. 60–3 ; in life of Lydgate, pp. 67, 70, 79, 88, 90 ; brief mention of La Belle dame sans mercie, generally ascribed to Chaucer, but really by Ros, p. 95 ; Scogan, pp. 97–8 ; the Mylner of Abington, p. 136 ; Brigham, p. 144 ; Robinson's Reward of Wickedness [*q. v.* above, [1574.] vol. i, p. 109], pp. 225–6 *n.*, 312 ; [Note to p. 19,] 403 ; brief references, pp. 8, 25, 102, 174, 347.

1802. Ritson, Joseph. *Ancient Englesh Metrical Romances.* Advertisement, vol. i, p. ii ; Dissertation on Romance and Minstrelsy, pp. vi (note), lxxix, lxxxi, lxxxvii, xcv, xcvi, xcvii, cxliii, clx, clxi, cxcii, ccv (note), ccvi (and note). Notes on Ywaine and Gawin, vol. iii, p. 239 ; Notes on Lybeaus Disconus, pp. 254, 259, 260, 263 ; Notes on the Geste of Kyng Horn, pp. 265, 267, 268, 281 ; Emaré, pp. 323 and *n.*, 327, 328, 329 ; Sir Orpheo, p. 336 ; Le bone Florence of Rome, pp. 340, 341 ; The Squyr of Lowe Degre, pp. 345, 346, 347, 350, 352.

1802. Seward, Anna. *Letter to Sir Walter Scott,* dated July 10, 1802, [in] Letters of Anna Seward, 6 vols., Edinburgh, 1811, vol. vi, p. 35. Letter vii.

[Letter to Scott on his inclusion of her *Rich Auld Willie's Farewell* in his *Scottish Minstrelsy,* mentioning that the ancient Scotch dialect seemed more pleasing than the phraseology of Chaucer and his contemporaries.]

1802. Sibbald, James. *Chronicle of Scottish Poetry.* **4** vols.

[Reprints of selected Scottish poems arranged in periods. The pieces with Chaucerian reference are :—

Vol. i, pp. 157–77. Henrysoun's "Testament of Faire Creseide."
„ pp. 253–63. Dunbar's "Goldin Targe."
Note on "Chaucer's Cuckowe and Nightingale," vol. i, p. 183 ; reference to Wife of Bath, vol. i, p. 240 ; Jack Upland, described as Chaucer's, ii, 31 ff. ; glossarial and metrical notes, i, 209, 229–30, 271–2, 323, 380 ; ii, 6, 19, 170, 371, 390 ; iv, xlvi–xlviii, lii–liv, and many in glossary.]

1802. Unknown. *Critique* on *The Complaynt of Scotland,* from the *British Critic,* July 1802. Reprinted in *Critiques by* **Mr.** *David Herd and others upon the new edition of the Complaynt . . .* 1829, p. 18. [John de Irlandia attributed the "Orisoun to the Virgin" to Chaucer ; it was more probably composed by Lydgate. *See* Leyden, 1801, above.]

1802. Unknown. *The English Encyclopædia.* 10 vols., vol. ii, pp. 366/2–367/2 ; vol. v, p. 401/2.

[The Chaucer and Lydgate articles are exact reprints of these articles as they appeared for the first time in the *Encyclopædia Britannica,* 2nd edn., 1778, *q.v.* above, vol. i, p. 452.]

1802. Wordsworth, Dorothy. *Journal,* ed. W. Knight, 2 vols., 1897, vol. i, pp. 113–4, 155.

Wednesday, 28th April. . . . I copied *The Prioress's Tale*
[p. 114] . . . I . . . wrote out *The Manciple's Tale* . . . When we came in we corrected the Chaucers, but I could not finish them to-night.
[p. 155] *Saturday, 30th October. . . .* After tea, S. [Stoddart] read Chaucer to us.

[a. 1803.] Thomson, Alexander. *MS. Criticism on the Howlat,* p. 16, [printed in] The Buke of the Howlat, by Holland, ed. D. Laing, Bannatyne Club, 1823, p. xvi.

To the character of an original inventor the author of the *Houlate* has but a slender claim ; for besides having taken the story of his poem from the fable of the Jackdaw with borrowed feathers, he is indebted to *Chaucer's Assemble of Foules* for some of its principal decorations. The catalogue of birds, and the personification of Nature are, both of them, imitations of *Chaucer ;* but the former is inferior, in every respect, to the characteristic sketches of his master; and the latter is so little suited to the situation in which it stands, as clearly shews it to have been exotic, transplanted from a much more poetic soil.

[The MS. was apparently lent to Laing by Dr. Robert Anderson, Thomson's friend, after the latter's death in 1803; *see* p. xi. It is not now known where it is.]

1803. **Aikin,** John. *General Biography* . . . vol. iv, pp. 479/2, 480/1 [article on Gower; for Chaucer article *see* above, 1801].

[1803 ?] Boucher, Jonathan. *Proposals for printing by subscription in two volumes . . . Linguæ Anglicanæ Veteris Thesaurus, or a Glossary of the Ancient English Language . . . by . . .* Jonathan Boucher, pp. 4, 12. [In a collection of prospectuses, 1796–1842, in Brit. Mus. (11902. bbb. 23), in 3 vols, 1 and 2 lettered *Collectio Prospectuum*, vol. i, pp. [in MS.] 49 *b*, 53 *b*.]

[p. 12] [A specimen is given of the dictionary under the word Achates, or Acates, Victuals; and a quotation from the Prologue,

> A gentil manciple was there of a temple,
> Of which achatour mighten take ensemple . . . [to]
> That he was aye before in his estate.]

[This glossary was not published until 1832, and was then edited by J. Hunter and J. Stevenson. Boucher died in 1804, *see* below, *a.* 1804.]

1803. **Coleridge,** Samuel Taylor. *Letter to Southey,* [dated] Keswick, July, 1803. (Letters of S. T. Coleridge, 1895, vol. i, p. 425.)

[Coleridge sketches the plan of a *History of British Literature* for Southey to write, and says :] The first half of the second volume should be dedicated to great single names, Chaucer and Spenser, Shakespeare, Milton and Taylor, Dryden and Pope.

1803. **Godwin,** William. *Life of Geoffrey Chaucer,* 2 vols, London, 1803.

[Vol. i. ch. xv, pp. 277–297, a long analysis of *Troilus and* [p. 298] *Creseide*.] From this analysis of the poem, it is not difficult to infer the degree of applause to which its author is entitled. It has already been observed by one of the critics upon English poetry [Warton, vol. i, sect. 14], that it is " almost as long as the Æneid." Considered in this point of view, the Troilus and Creseide will not appear to advantage. It is not an epic poem.

[p. 299] . . . It is merely a love-tale. It is not the labour of a man's life ; but a poem which, with some previous knowledge of human sentiments and character, and a very slight preparation of science, the writer might perhaps be expected to complete in about as many months, as the work is divided into books. . . .

It is . . . considerably barren of incident. There is not enough in it of matter generating visible images in the reader, and exciting his imagination with pictures of nature and life. There is not enough in it of vicissitudes of fortune. . . . Add to which, the catastrophe is unsatisfactory and offensive. . . .
[p. 300] Dryden thoroughly felt this defect in the poem of Chaucer, and has therefore changed the catastrophe when he fitted the story for the stage, and represented the two lovers as faithful, but unfortunate.

But, when all these deductions have been made from the claims of the Troilus and Creseide upon our approbation, it will still remain a work interspersed with many beautiful passages, passages of exquisite tenderness, of great delicacy, and of a nice and refined observation of the workings of human sensibility. Nothing can be more beautiful, genuine, and unspoiled by the corrupt suggestions of a selfish spirit, than the sentiments of Chaucer's lovers. While conversing with them, we seem transported into ages of primeval innocence. Even Creseide is so good, so ingenuous and affectionate, that we feel ourselves as incapable as Troilus, of believing her false. Nor are the scenes of Chaucer's narrative . . . drawn with that vagueness of manner, and ignorance of the actual emotions of the heart, which, while we read them, we nauseate and despise. On the contrary, his personages always feel, and we confess the truth of their feelings.
[p. 301] Pandarus himself comes elevated and refined from the pen of Chaucer: his occupation loses its grossness, in the disinterestedness of his motive, and the sincerity of his friendship. In a word, such is the Troilus and Creseide, that no competent judge can rise from its perusal without a strong impression of the integrity and excellence of the author's disposition, and of the natural relish he entertained for whatever is honourable, beautiful and just. . . .

The poem will appear to be little less than a miracle, when

we combine our examination of it, with a recollection of the times and circumstances in which it was produced. [The "languid
[p. 302] and perishing" state of the English tongue in Chaucer's time.] . . . [Chaucer] surprised his countrymen with a poem, eminently idiomatic, clear and perspicuous in its style, as well
[p. 303] as rich and harmonious in its versification. . . . The loves of Troilus and Creseide scarcely retain any traces of the preposterous and rude manners of the age in which they were delineated.

This poem therefore, as might have been expected, long fixed upon itself the admiration of the English nation. . . . [It] was probably, more than any of his other works, the basis of his fame, and the foundation of his fortune.[1]

[vol. ii, p. 572] This Canterbury Tales is [*sic*] the great basis of the fame of Chaucer, and indolent men have generally expressed themselves with contempt of the rest of his works as unworthy of attention. . . . He indeed who wishes to become personally acquainted with Chaucer, must of necessity have recourse to his minor pieces. The Canterbury Tales are too full of business, variety, character and action, to permit the writer in any great degree to show himself. . . . The Troilus and Creseide in particular, that poem of which Sir Philip Sidney speaks with so much delight, though deficient in action, cannot be
[p. 573] too much admired for the suavity and gentleness of nature which it displays. . . . All the milder and more delicate feelings of the soul are displayed . . . and displayed in a manner which none but a poet of the purest and sweetest dispositions, and at the same time of the greatest discrimination, could have attained.

The Canterbury Tales is certainly one of the most extraordinary monuments of human genius . . .

What infinite variety of character is presented to us in the Prologue to the Canterbury Tales ! It is a copious and extensive review of the private life of the fourteenth century in England.

This has usually, and perhaps justly, been thought the most conspicuous excellence of Chaucer ; his power of humour, of delineating characters, and of giving vivacity and richness to comic incidents.

⁎   ⁎   ⁎   ⁎   ⁎   ⁎   ⁎

[1 For Charles Lamb's remarks upon this criticism, see below, 1803.]

[p. 582]   His best works, his Canterbury Tales in particular, have an absolute merit, which stands in need of no extrinsic accident to show it to advantage, and no apology to atone for its concomitant defects. They class with whatever is best in the poetry of any country or any age. Yet when we further recollect that they were written in a remote and semi-barbarous age, that Chaucer had to a certain degree to create a language, or to restore to credit a language which had been sunk in vulgarity and contempt by being considered as a language [p. 583] of slaves, . . . the astonishment and awe with which we regard the great father of English poetry must be exceedingly increased . . .

1803. H., D.   *Letter,* [in] The Gentleman's Magazine, vol. lxxiii, part i, p. 129.

. . . Where is Mr. Johnes likely to find the *supposed* interview between Petrarch and Chaucer? It is rightly said to be *supposed ;* and what Englishman's researches can keep pace with a Frenchman's suppositions?

[A reply to a previous letter signed 'Z': *see* below.]

1803–10. Johnes, Thomas.   *Sir John Froissart's Chronicles.* Newly translated from the best French editions . . . by Thomas Johnes, At the Hafod Press, 1803–10, 4 vols.

[Motto on Title-pages, vols. 1–4 :]
Who so shall telle a tale after a man . . . [to]
Or feinen thinges, or finden wordes newe.
—Chaucer's Prologue [ll. 731–36].

1803. Lamb, Charles.   *Letter* to Thomas Manning, [dated] Feb. 19, 1803. (The Works of Charles and Mary Lamb, ed. E. V. Lucas, 1903–5, 7 vols., vol. vi, pp. 258–9.

[p. 258]   For God's sake don't think any more of "Independent Tartary." . . . I am afraid 'tis the reading of Chaucer has [p. 259] misled you; his foolish stories about Cambuscan and the ring, and the horse of brass. Believe me there's no such things, 'tis all the poet's *invention ;* but if there were such *darling* things as old Chaucer sings, I would *up* behind you on the Horse of Brass and frisk off for Prester John's Country.

1803. Lamb, Charles.   *Two Letters to William Godwin,* [dated] Nov. 8 [and] Nov. 10, 1803. (Works of Charles and Mary Lamb, ed. E. V. Lucas, 1903–5, 7 vols, vol. vi, pp. 281–2.)

Nov. 8, 1803.

MY DEAR SIR,—I have been sitting down for three or four days successively to the review [of Godwin's *Life of Chaucer*], which I so much wished to do well, and to your satisfaction. But I can produce nothing but absolute flatness and nonsense. My health and spirits are so bad, and my nerves so irritable, that I am sure, if I persist, I shall teaze myself into a fever. . . .

You will give me great satisfaction by sealing my pardon and oblivion in a line or two, before I come to see you, or I shall be ashamed to come.

Your, with great truth,

C. LAMB.

Nov. 10, 1803.

DEAR GODWIN,—You never made a more unlucky and perverse mistake than to suppose that the reason of my not writing that cursed thing was to be found in your book. I assure you most sincerely that I have been greatly delighted with Chaucer. I may be wrong, but I think there is one considerable error runs through it, which is a conjecturing spirit, a fondness for filling out the picture by supposing what Chaucer did and how he felt, where the materials are scanty. So far from meaning to withhold from you (out of mistaken tenderness) this opinion of mine, I plainly told Mrs. Godwin that I did find a *fault*, which I should reserve naming until I should see you and talk it over. This she may very well remember, and also that I declined naming this fault until she drew it from me by asking me if there was not too much fancy in the work. I then confessed generally what I felt. . . . I remember also telling Mrs. G. (which she may have *dropt*) that I was by turns considerably more delighted than I expected. . . . I even had conceived an expression to meet you with, which was thanking you for some of the most exquisite pieces of criticism I had ever read in my life. In particular I should have brought forward that on "Troilus and Cressida" and Shakespear, which it is little to say delighted me, and instructed me. . . . All these things I was preparing

to say, and bottling them up till I came . . . when lo ! this
deadly blight intervened.

I certainly ought to make great allowances for your mis-
understanding me. You . . . cannot conceive of the desultory
and uncertain way in which I (an author by fits) sometimes
cannot put the thoughts of a common letter into sane prose.
[Lamb enlarges upon his utter inability to write at times.] I
wrote such stuff about Chaucer, and got into such digressions,
quite irreducible into $1\frac{1}{5}$ column of a paper, that I was perfectly
ashamed to show it you.   However, it is become a serious
matter that I should convince you I neither slunk from the
task through a wilful deserting neglect, or through any (most
imaginary on your part) distaste of Chaucer; and I will try
my hand again, I hope with better luck. My health is bad
and my time taken up, but all I can spare between this and
Sunday shall be employed for you, since you desire it: and
if I bring you a crude, wretched paper on Sunday, you
must burn it, and forgive me; if it proves anything better
than I predict, may it be a peace-offering of sweet incense
between us.

C. LAMB.

[Lamb's review of Godwin's *Life of Chaucer* has not been identified. Perhaps it
was never completed, or perhaps Godwin burnt it when they met on the Sunday.
See Letter 202, and notes, Lucas's edn., vol. i, p. 463, vol. iii, p. 473, and vol. vi,
pp. 450, 451-2, where Lamb tells Wordsworth that his review of the *Excursion* was
the first review he ever wrote.]

1803. Leyden, John. *Scenes of Infancy.* *See* below, App. A.

1803. Malcolm, James Peller. *Londinium Redivivum,* **4** vols., 1802-7,
vol. ii, 1803, pp. 11, 329-30.

[p. 330]   [A note (from Stowe) that Richard Chaucer was usually
considered father to the poet, and citation of Granger (*q.v.*
above, 1769, vol. i, pp. 431-2) that his verse, musical to his contemporaries, was unsuited to the ears of the present age. Then
follows a notice of the portrait in Hoccleve.]

1803. Southey, Robert. *Letter* to C. W. W. Wynn, dated June 9,
1803. (Life and Correspondence of Robert Southey, 1850, vol. ii,
p. 212.)

[Southey says he has just been reading Scott's Border
Ballads.] Scott, it seems, adopts the same system of metre
with me, and varies his time in the same stanza from iambic
to anapæstic *ad libitum.* In spite of all the trouble that
has been taken to torture Chaucer into heroic metre, I have

no doubt whatever that he wrote upon this system, common to all the ballad writers. Coleridge agrees with me upon this. The proof is, that, read him thus, and he becomes everywhere harmonious; but expletive syllables, en's and y's and e's, only make him halt upon ten lame toes. I am now daily drinking at that pure well of English undefiled, to get historical manners, and to learn English and poetry.

1803. [**Southey,** Robert.]   *Review* of Ritson's *Ancient English Romances*, [in] The Annual Review, vol. ii, art. ii, pp. 516, 523.

[p. 516]   When the race of little men had succeeded, they were for improving everything. Dryden . . . could perceive that Chaucer was a poet, but his old gold seemed to him to want scouring, and he thought it was reserved for him to make it shine. [A similar reference to Pope's versions follows.]

1803. Southey, Robert. *Review* of Godwin's *Life of Chaucer*, [in] The Annual Review, vol. ii, art. ii, pp. 462–73.

     [A scathing review, pointing out the disproportion and
[p. 463] irrelevance of the work ; in this method :] Chaucer was born in London, 1328, . . . therefore the first chapter . . . is a
[p. 464] history . . . of the city of London ! . . . When the poet was a young man he must have heard the minstrels : so Chaucer and the minstrels are the fifth chapter. . . . Chaucer must have seen castles and cathedrals and palaces : so the eighth chapter is upon Gothic architecture. . . .
[p. 472] By attempting too many things in this work, the author has failed in all. [The merits of the work are : a good account is given of the reign of Richard II, much light is thrown upon the minor poems of Chaucer, and some facts respecting his life have been recovered from public records.]

1803. [**Southey,** Robert.]   *Review* of Ellis's *Specimens of the Early English Poets,* [in] The Annual Review, vol. ii, art. iv, pp. 548, 549.

     [A long passage from Ellis on Chaucer's language and style quoted approvingly ; the language of Chaucer, says Southey, is] a subject which should have been investigated by his late biographer [Godwin].

1803. Unknown. '*Amadis de Gaul,*' *by Southey and by Rose,* [in] The Edinburgh Review, Oct. 1803, vol. iii, pp. 135–6.

[p. 135] The avowed model upon which Mr. Rose has framed his Amadis, is the translation of Le Grand's *Fabliaux,* by Mr. Way, and it is but justice to state, that, in our opinion, he has fully attained what he proposed. . . . The following passage is a successful imitation of Chaucer :

[p. 136]   ' To tell, as meet, the costly feast's array,
    My tedious tale would hold a summer's day :
    I let to sing who mid the courtly throng
    Did most excel in dance or sprightly song ; ' [etc.]

1803. Unknown. *Letter,* [in] The Gentleman's Magazine, vol. lxxiii, part i, pp. 207–8.

[A modernization of part of the "Legende of Ariadne of Athens," prefaced by remarks :]

[p. 207] The ear accustomed to harmonious numbers will derive little pleasure from them, on account of the want of variety in the cæsura of each verse. He may, however, excuse it when he is acquainted with the intention of the writer; whose object was not to attend to variety in the cæsura, but to adhere studiously to the form of the original; trying, by this method, and an alteration of the obsolete into more modern language, if some of the simple manner of the original would not be preserved; and Chaucer still be himself, although in a new dress . . .

[The modernization runs :]
    Of those false lovers poison be the bane !
    To Ariadne will I turn again.
    Tir'd with the voyage in grateful sleep she lies ;
    With deepest sorrow doom'd, alas ! to rise.
    Too soon the dawning light dispells the charm,
    And hopeful o'er the bed she spreads her arm,
    But no one finds.   Alas ! She said, the morn,
    Alas ! the fatal hour that saw me born.
    I am betray'd—her lovely tresses rent,
    Barefoot in haste along the shore she went,
    And cried in vain—" Theseus, my heart's desire,
    Where art thou ? where, my love, dost thou retire ?
    Ah fled me ! left by cruel beasts to die " . . .
[and so on, for 27 lines.]

1803. Unknown. *Review* of Godwin's *Life of Chaucer*, [in] The Gentleman's Magazine, vol. lxxiii, pp. 1141–50, 1229–35.

[This review consists almost entirely of copious extracts from the book ; the only critical opinion is in the last paragraph, which runs as follows:]

p.1235] That the present Biographer of Chaucer has cleared up some points in his history, will not be disputed : that his partiality has been well supported by his imagination ; and that much of the contemporary history is introduced to form a book, and to set off the writer ; whence it may be inferred, that the Life of Chaucer might have been compressed into smaller compass.

1803. Wordsworth, Dorothy. *Journal* (ed. W. Knight, 2 vols., 1897, vol. i, pp. 158, 181).

[p. 158] [*Tuesday, Jan. 11th.*] Mary read the Prologue to Chaucer's Tales to me in the morning. . . . Read part of *The Knight's Tale* with exquisite delight . . .

[p. 181] [*Friday, August 19th.*] There were two beds in recesses in the wall ; above one of them I noticed a shelf with some books :—it made me think of Chaucer's Clerke of Oxenforde :—

Liever had he at his beds head
Twenty books clothed in black and red.

1803. Z. *Letter,* [in] The Gentleman's Magazine, vol. lxxiii, part i, p. 8.

Mr. Tyrwhitt laments that the author of "Mémoires pour la Vie de Pétrarque" never indulged the publick with his promised account of the (supposed) interview between Petrarch and Chaucer. May we not hope that the deficiency which Mr. T. regrets will be supplied by the researches of Mr. Johnes ?

[The reference is to Johnes' translation of Froissart, published in 5 vols., 1803–10. *See* Johnes above, 1803, and also H., D., above, 1803.]

1804. Aikin, John. *Letters to a Young Lady on a Course of English Poetry,* pp. 22–6, 269.

[Dr. Aikin describes Dryden's *Knight's Tale,* "taken from Chaucer." He then goes on to "The Cock and the Fox," of which he speaks precisely as if Dryden were the original author, and Chaucer is not mentioned. For instance, "Dryden . . . seems to have thought the character of that kind of fiction termed *fable,* sufficiently preserved, if the actions belong to the animals which are the personages of the story, while the language and sentiments are those of human beings. . . . Dryden's Cock and Hen have all the knowledge which he himself possessed, and quote fathers and schoolmen just as in his Hind and Panther," etc.   He also speaks of the Good Parson without reference to Chaucer.]

[a. 1804.] **Boucher**, Jonathan.   *Boucher's Glossary of Archaic and Provincial Words.   A Supplement to the Dictionaries of the English Language, particularly those of Dr. Johnson and Dr. Webster* . . . edited jointly by Joseph Hunter and Joseph Stevenson, 1832, Introduction, pp. vii, xix, xxxii, xl, xli and note, xlv, xlvi note, lvi, and continual references in the Glossary.

[Boucher devoted fourteen years to this Glossary, and left it uncompleted when he died, in 1804.   In 1803, he had issued proposals for printing it (*see* above, 1803); the part including letter A was published in 1807, and finally, in 1832, Hunter and Stevenson brought out the Introduction to the whole work as prepared for the press by Boucher, and the Glossary A to Blade.

It was not successful, and Mr. W. P. Courtney says (*see* article Boucher in *D. N. B.*) that it is understood that most of the materials passed into the hands of the proprietors of Webster's English Dictionary.   Besides the references to Chaucer in the introduction, his poems are quoted on almost every page, and often there are 6 or 8 quotations from him on a page.   On the first page (really only half a page), on the letter A, there are 15 references to or quotations from Chaucer.   But this is unusually many.   In the first 20 pages there are in all 69 Chaucer references and quotations.]

1804. **Coleridge**, Samuel Taylor.   *Letter to Sir George Beaumont*, Feb. 1, 1804, [printed in] Memorials of Coleorton, ed. W. Knight, 1887, vol. i, p. 46.   [This letter is not printed in the (select) Letters of S. T. Coleridge, 1895.]

One fortnight in each month I shall . . . devote to poetry, and the other fortnight to Essays . . . The first, on the Genius and Writings of Chaucer.

1804. **Irving**, David.   *Lives of the Scotish Poets*, 2 vols.   Vol. i, Barbour and Chaucer, pp. 253, 259, 265–7 ; James I and Chaucer, pp. 303, 325 ; Henry the Minstrel compared, pp. 353, 358 ; Dunbar compared, pp. 405, 415, 418, 437–8 ; Henryson and *Troilus*, pp. 378, 380, 385–6 ; vol. ii, Gavin Douglas and Chaucer, pp 27, 43, 60, 64 ; Allan Ramsay, a competitor with Chaucer and Boccaccio as a comic poet, p. 328.

1804. Robinson, Thomas. *Letter* to Henry Crabb Robinson, [dated] May 6th, 1804. (Crabb Robinson Letters [unpublished], in Dr. Williams' Library, Gordon Square, W.C.)

Since I wrote to you I have been considerably interested by reading the first vol. of Godwin's "Life of Chaucer." [Here follows a detailed description of that work, not flattering to Godwin, concluding :] I have received many new ideas and been highly delighted by some beautiful passages which are pointed out in works of the poet, and which I was capable of relishing in spite of the obsoleteness of the language.

1804. Scott, Sir Walter. *Review* of Ellis's *Specimens of the Early English Poets*, [in] The Edinburgh Review, vol. iv, p. 156. (Miscellaneous Prose Works of Sir Walter Scott, Edinburgh, 1834–71, 30 vols., vol. xvii., pp. 6, 9, 11.)

[p. 9]   The epoch from which English may be considered as a classical language, may be fixed in the reign of Edward III, the age of Gower and of Chaucer, in which it was no longer confined to what the latter has called "the drafty riming" of the wandering minstrel.

1804. Scott, Sir Walter. *Review* of the *Works of Thomas Chatterton*, [in] The Edinburgh Review, April, 1804, vol. iv, pp. 228–9. (Miscellaneous Prose Works of Sir Walter Scott, 30 vols., Edinburgh, 1834–71, vol. xvii, pp. 237–8.)

[p. 237]   An instance of a curious mistake committed by Chatterton occurs in these excerpts from the Pseudo-Rowley prose writings. In a MS. in Chatterton's handwriting, in the Museum, there occur several excerpts from Chaucer, apparently culled to bolster out some intended imitations. Among others we [p. 238] find the two lines respecting the mormal on the leg of the pilgrims' cook—

> " But great harm was yt, as it thought me,
> That on his skinne a mormall had he."

Skinne is here miscopied for *shin*. This mistake, and another more whimsical, we can trace into the ' Rolle of Seyncte Bartholæmeweis Priorie,' printed in Barret's History of Bristol, to whom it was communicated by Chatterton. Among a list of medical books . . . we find . . . Johan Stowe *of the cure of mormalles and the waterie leprosie: the rolle of the blacke mainger.* In a note on these two last articles, we are told, "Chaucer says, on his skin a mormalle had he and a blacke manger." Now, in the first place Chatterton, adhering to his erroneous transcript from Chaucer, of *skinne* for *shinne*, has made Johan Stowe lecture on the cure of mormalles as if they were, like the leprosy, a cutaneous distemper, and not a cancer on the bone. But, besides, he has so far mistaken his author as to take *blanc-manger*, a dish of exquisite cookery, which is pronounced by Chaucer to be the cook's masterpiece of skill, for *blacke manger*, some strange and nondescript disease . . . Chaucer's words are—

> " But gret harme was it, as it thoughte me,
> That on his shinne a mormal hadde he,
> For *blanc-manger* that made he with the best."

1804. Scott, Sir Walter. *Review* of Godwin's *Life of Chaucer,* [in] The Edinburgh Review, vol. iii, Jan. 1804, art. xvi, pp. 437–52. (Miscellaneous Prose Works of Sir Walter Scott, 30 vols., Edinburgh, 1834–71, vol. xvii, pp. 55–80.)

[p. 55] The perusal of this title excited no small surprise in our critical fraternity. The authenticated passages of Chaucer's life may be comprised in half a dozen pages ; and behold two voluminous quartos !

. . . .

[p. 56] The reader will learn, with admiration, that Mr. William [p. 57] Godwin's two quarto volumes contain hardly the vestige of an authenticated fact concerning Chaucer, which is not to be found in the eight pages of Messrs. Thomas Tyrwhitt and George Ellis. The researches into the records have only produced one or two writs, addressed to Chaucer, while clerk of the works ; the several grants and passports granted to him by Edward III and Richard II which had been referred to by former biographers; together with the poet's evidence in a court of chivalry, a contract about a house, and a solitary receipt for half a year's salary. These, with a few documents referring to John of Gaunt, make the Appendix to the book, and are the only original materials brought to light by the labours of the author.

. . . .

[p. 65] The public are indebted to Mr. Godwin for the recovery of [p. 66] Chaucer's evidence in a question about bearing arms, occurring

CHAUCER CRITICISM.—II.

betwixt Scrope and Grosvenor * ; but the manner in which it is narrated, is a good illustration of the strained inferences concerning Chaucer's temper and disposition, deduced by his biographer from the most common and trivial occurrences.

.   .   .   .

[p. 68]   Some particular passages of the life, are less fancifully and more correctly delineated. Mr. Godwin combats, and in our opinion successfully, the opinion of those who deny the honourable claim of Thomas Chaucer, to call the poet father: and he has vindicated the relation, which the Dreme of Chaucer unquestionably bears to the History of John of Gaunt.

The critical dissertations upon Troilus and Creside, and Chaucer's other poems, have considerable merit. They are the production of a man who has read poetry with taste and feeling ; and we wish sincerely, that instead of the strange [p. 69] farrago which he calls the life of Chaucer, he had given us a correct edition of the miscellaneous poetry of the author, upon the same plan with Mr. Tyrwhitt's admirable Canterbury Tales.

.   .   .   .

We were much surprised to find, that the Canterbury Tales, [p. 70] the most important, as well as the most exquisite, of Chaucer's productions, have attracted so little of Mr. Godwin's attention. He might have displayed, in commenting upon poems as varied in subject as in beauty, his whole knowledge of the manners of the middle ages, were it ten times more extensive. But Mr. Godwin, beginning probably to write before he had considered either the nature of his subject, or the probable length of his work, had exhausted both his limits and materials ere he came to the topic upon which he ought principally to have dwelt. The characters, therefore, of the several pilgrims, so exquisitely described, that each individual passes before the eyes of the reader, and so admirably contrasted with each other ; their conversation and manners, the gallantry of the Knight and Squire, the affected *sentimentality* of the Abbess, the humour of mine Host, and the Wife of Bath ; the pride of the Monk, the humility of the Parson, the learning and

---

* We hold this to be the only circumstance of importance, which Mr. Godwin's researches have brought to light ; and so far our thanks are due to him.

poverty of the Scholar, with the rude but comic portraits of the inferior characters, are, in the history of the life and age of Chaucer, of which they form a living picture, passed over in profound silence, or with very slight notice. The truth is, Mr. Godwin's speed and strength were expended before he came within sight of the goal, and he saw himself compelled with a faint apology to abandon that part of his subject which must have been universally interesting. The few remarks which he has made upon the Canterbury Tales, induce us to believe that he has seen and regretted his error; but it is a poor excuse, after writing a huge book, to tell the reader that it is but "superficial work," because the author "came a novice to such an undertaking."

.   .   .   .

[p. 79] But, upon the whole, the Life of Chaucer, if an uninterest-
[p. 80] ing, is an innocent performance; and were its prolixities and superfluities unsparingly pruned (which would reduce the work to about one fourth of its present size), we would consider it as an accession of some value to English literature.

1804. Scott, Sir Walter. *Sir Tristrem,* a Metrical Romance . . . by Thomas of Ercildoune, edited by Walter Scott, title-page and pp. xxviii, xliv, xlviii, lvi, lviii, lxi, lxviii, lxxxiv*n.*

[Quotation on title-page :]

Now, hold your mouth, pour charitie,
Both Knight and Lady fre, . . .
　　[to]
Anon I wol you tel. —CHAUCER.

[*Sir Thopas,* ll. 180–5.]

[p. xxviii] Saxon, although spoken chiefly by the vulgar, was gradu-
ally adopting, from the rival tongue, those improvements and changes, which fitted it for the use of Chaucer and Gower.
[p. xliv] [Chaucer's "French of Stratford atte Bowe" alludes to the difference between proper French and Anglo-Norman.]
[p. lvi] [The 'sotherne' Persones 'rim ram ruf' points to alliteration as then being a characteristic of northern poetry.]
[p. lxi] The romance of *Wade,* twice alluded to by Chaucer, but now lost, was probably a border composition. The castle of this hero stood near the Roman Wall.

1804. Southey, Robert. *Letter* to John Rickman, dated Jan. 20, 1804. (Life and Correspondence of Robert Southey, 1850, vol. ii, p. 251.)

This vile reviewing still birdlimes me ; I do it slower than anything else . . . Yesterday Malthus received, I trust, a mortal wound from my hand ; to-day I am at the Asiatic Researches—Godwin's Life of Chaucer is on the road to me.

[There is an apparent discrepancy of date here, as Southey's review of Godwin's Chaucer is in The Annual Review for 1803, *q.v.* above. But the volume did not appear until April 1804, so that Southey doubtless did not write the review until February 1804. He alludes to his expectation of the arrival of Godwin's life of Chaucer in two other letters (1) to John King, dated Keswick, Nov. 19, 1803, and (2) to Miss Barker, dated Keswick, 1804 (Selections from the letters of Southey, ed. J. W. Warter, 1856, vol. i, pp. 245, 254).]

1804. Southey, Robert. *Letter* to S. T. Coleridge, dated Feb. 1804. (Life and Correspondence of Southey, 1850, vol. ii, pp. 266, 267, 268.)

I am not sorry that you gave Godwin a dressing . . . I daresay he deserved all you gave him ; in fact I have never forgiven him his abuse of William Taylor, and do now regret, with some compunction, that, in my reviewal of his Chaucer, I struck out certain passages of well-deserved severity.

1804. Unknown. *Review* of Godwin's *Life of Chaucer*, [in] The European Magazine and London Review, vol. xliv, pp. 441–6 ; vol. xlv, pp. 44–8, 121–30, 201–11, 281–93.

[A running commentary, in which the writer has " most painfully and anxiously endeavoured " to compress the evidence on Chaucer's life, manners, habits, the features of his mind, and the principal traits of his character [xlv, 292]. The main point made in the criticism is that Godwin did not seem well to understand the difference between biography and general history, and that he discoursed too largely on contemporary affairs, not mentioning Chaucer for chapters together.]

1804. Unknown. *On the Use of the words " Shall " and " Will,"* [in] The Literary Magazine and American Register, Philadelphia, Feb. 1804, vol. i, p. 356.

In Chaucer "*the faithe I shall* to God " means the faith I owe to God ; thence it [*shall*] became a sign of the future tense.

1804. Unknown. *Character of Chaucer, by Godwin,* [in] The Literary
Magazine and American Register, Philadelphia, April, May, 1804,
vol. ii, pp. 48–53, 121–6.

[Quotation, from Godwin, of biographical statement and
literary estimate—"a sort of recapitulation of the work."]

1804. Unknown. *Godwin and Malthus,* [in] The Literary Magazine
and American Register, Philadelphia, August 1804, vol. ii, p. 361.

[Note that in his *Life of Chaucer,* Godwin seemed to have
renounced the principles of policy and government raised in
his *Political Justice.*]

1804. Unknown. *The Squire's Tale, imitated from Chaucer,* [in] The
Poetical Register and Repository of Fugitive Poetry for 1804,
London, 1806, pp. 275-92.

> Where wide the plains of Tartary extend,
> And Sarra's towers in glittering pomp ascend,
> A monarch reigned, who made proud Russia yield
> Beneath his arm, in many a bloody field :
> Cambuscan was the mighty hero's name,
> Of yore unrivall'd in the list of fame !

. . . .

1804. Unknown. *Review* of *Ellis's Specimens of Early English
Poetry,* [in] The Edinburgh Review, April, 1804, vol. iv, pp. 154,
156-8.

[p. 154]   To this specimen of Saxon poetry [Ode on Æthelstan's
victory] Mr. Ellis has subjoined a translation of it into the
English of the age of Chaucer, which we recommend to our
readers as one of the best executed imitations that we have
ever met with. It was written by a friend of Mr. Ellis
(Mr. Frere, if we mistake not) while at Eton School, and
struck us with so much surprise, that we are obliged to
extract a passage . . .

> 'The Mercians fought I understond,
> There was gamen of the hond ' [etc.]

[*See* Ellis, above, 1801. The translation as given in George
Ellis's *Specimens of the Early English Poets,* London, 1801,
vol. i, pp. 32–4, is not there noted as Chaucerian.]

1804-5. Wharton, Richard. *Fables: consisting of Select parts from Dante, Berni, Chaucer, and Ariosto, imitated in English Heroic Verse,* by Richard Wharton, 2 vols.

Vol. i, pp. 70–99. [The Franklein's Tale from Chaucer.]
Vol. ii, pp. i–xvi, 1–199. Fables, containing Cambuscan, an Heroic Poem in six books, founded upon and comprising a free imitation of Chaucer's fragment on that subject, 1805.

[Wharton's version of the celebrated lines on love may serve as a specimen of his modernization :]

[vol. i, p. 78]
> Gentles, who hear the tale, learn this from me,
> *Love cannot bloom beneath authority.*
> That union best endures where each receives
> A little grace, and each a little gives ;
> For Love, if either strive to rule alone,
> Extends his wings and farewell ! he is gone.
> Love is a thing as any spirit free
> Lost by restraint and gained by liberty.

    .   .   .   .

Mr. Pope's imitation,

> Spreads his light wings and in a moment flies,

however beautiful in the structure of the verse, is weaker than the original,

> Beateth his wings and farewell, he is gone—

the active *flies* not conveying the idea of the immediate effect of authority so forcibly as the passive, *is gone.* Perhaps this may seem too fine a criticism ; but it has induced me to preserve as much of Chaucer's line as was consistent with modern idiom.

[vol. ii, p. iv]
[Introductory Advertisement. The author defends his use of Dryden's heroic couplet :] Chaucer, had he lived at a later period, though he would have preserved his nice discrimination of character, and the forcible style which brings action before the reader's eye, would have enriched his poems with all the graces which Time, Taste, and Learning have interwoven into the originally coarse fabric of his native tongue. To copy the turn of thought, the boldness of figure, and the animation of Chaucer's poems, is to copy Chaucer : to preserve his hobbling cadences and obsolete phrases is to copy the baldness of our language at the period when he lived. Had Chaucer lived in the seventeenth century, he would have given us *his* Palamon and Arcite, as Dryden has dressed it . . .

[p. v] I shall acquit myself more to the satisfaction of the critical world by keeping in mind the language and numbers in which Dryden has told some of the Canterbury Tales, than by sedulously imitating the dryness of the original poems: the expression of Chaucer being, indeed, strong and quaint; but very inadequate to convey either *his* ideas or Dryden's.

1804. Ω. *Review* of Godwin's *Life of Chaucer*, [in] The Literary Journal, January and February, 1804, vol. iii, coll. 11–19, 64–79.

[p. 15] . . . We cannot but be startled at the first sentence of the preface; "The two names which do greatest honour to the annals of English Literature, are those of Chaucer and of Shakspeare." That Chaucer was a wonderful poet when we consider the times in which he lived, no man will dispute; but to enthrone him above Milton and all the other splendid geniuses who have adorned our literature . . . is an hyperbole of rather inauspicious aspect at the commencement of a work.

[p. 69] . . . In Chaucer we find some happy expressions, many striking images and many traits of genuine humour; but to suppose that these can convey equal pleasure to the reader in the uncouth and antiquated style in which they are expressed, as when we find them in the finely-turned versification of the reign of Queen Anne, is an idea which could be entertained for a moment, only by the blindest enthusiasm.

[p. 70] Mr. G. must also know that Pope and Dryden will continue to be read with delight by all their countrymen; while his "*popular book in modern English*" will never be able to rescue Chaucer from the cabinets of the antiquaries. That poet was indeed admirable in his day; and had he been destined to write in a later age, his works would still have been read with delight.

1805–6. Cary, Henry Francis. *The Inferno of Dante Alighieri* . . . with a translation in blank verse, notes . . . by the Rev. Henry Francis Cary, 2 vols. Notes, vol. i, pp. 66 [quotation from the non-Chaucerian *Chaucer's Dream*], 251 [Ser Brunetto's *Tesoretto* 'is a curious work, not unlike the writings of Chaucer in style and numbers']; vol. ii, pp. 260 [quotation from the *Squieres Tale*, for Achilles' spear], 281 [Genilon, in Nonne Preestes Tale, and 'Peter of Spaine,' in Monkes Tale].

[For Cary's complete translation of the Divina Commedia, with these and additional Chaucer references in the notes, which are there printed together at the end of each volume, *see* below, 1814.]

1805. Drake, Nathan. *Essays Biographical, Critical and Historical,
Illustrative of the Tatler, Spectator and Guardian,* 3 vols., London,
1805 ; vol. i, p. 306–7 ; vol. ii, pp. 66, 69, 169, 261–2, 294–300,
305 ; vol. iii, pp. 85, 89, 108.

[vol. i,   [On Addison's remarks on Chaucer in the *Account of the
pp. 306– *Greatest English Poets* :]
307]

    Chaucer is distinguished merely by his powers of exciting
merriment, a most inadequate representation of this fine
old poet, whose vein of description and pathos is remark-
ably rich and pure.

vol. ii,   [Quotation from Dryden's Preface to the *Fables.*]
pp. 66–9] [Quotations from *Il Penseroso* and Warton.]
[pp.   [On Chaucer's debt to the *Decameron* in the framework of
261–2] the *Canterbury Tales ;* the contrast of the pilgrims, p. 296 ;
[pp. Chaucer's "intimate acquaintance with Arabian literature
294–300]and fable" in the *Squieres Tale.* Chaucer's debt to the Italians,
with quotation from Godwin.]

1805. Edgeworth, Maria. *The Modern Griselda, a Tale,* pp. 39–40,
43–55.

    [This is not based on *The Clerkes Tale,* to which, however,
the authoress owes some suggestion.
[p. 39]   Mention of the *Clerkes Tale,* which is read at a "reading
party" (Chap. iv)—in the heroic couplets of Ogle [*q. v.* above,
1739 and 1740, vol. i, pp. 384, 389], and one passage,
corresponding to *Clerkes T.,* is quoted thus :—

> "Swear, that with ready will and honest heart,
> Like or dislike, without regret or art ;
> In presence or alone ; by night or day,
> All that I will you fail not to obey," etc.

These words produce a lively discussion. "Had Chaucer
lived in our enlightened times, he would doubtless have
drawn a very different character," says Mr. Granby ; and
another speaker cites the usual statement on "the times in
which he wrote."
    This book was quoted the same year in America, and
was translated with the *Clerkes Tale* into French in 1813.
See Appendix B, 1813.]

1805. Ellis, George. *Specimens of Early English Metrical Romances,*
edited by George Ellis, in three volumes. Vol. i, p. 124, Chaucer
and Wade ; vol. ii, p. 5, *Sir Guy* mentioned by Chaucer as a
romance of price ; brief reference, vol. i, p. 125.

1805. Scott, Sir Walter. *Letter to George Ellis*, [in] Lockhart's Memoirs of the Life of Sir Walter Scott, ed. 1900, 5 vols, vol. i, p. 408.

As for the British Poets, my plan was greatly too liberal to stand the least chance of being adopted by the trade at large, as I asked them to begin with Chaucer.

1805. Todd, Henry John. *The Works of Edmund Spenser*, 8 vols. [A variorum edn., with life, new notes, and glossary by Todd.] Vol. i, [Life of Spenser], pp. clvi [Spenser buried by Chaucer at his own desire, epitaphs on him], clvii *n*, quotation from Sir John Davies' Orchestra, 1596 [*q. v.* above, vol. i, p. 140], clix *n* [quotation from Don Zara del Fogo, 1656, *q. v.* above, vol. i, p. 232]. [Also notes on the text throughout, mainly parallels for the use of words.]

1805. Whitaker, Thomas Dunham. *History and Antiquities of . . . Craven in the County of York*, pp. 195, 227, 286, 289, 307, 335, 336–9, 345–8, 350–2, 362, 423, 424. [The references in the second edition, 1812, are pp. 207, 254, 326, 329 (wrongly numbered 366), 348, 394, 395, 396, 397, 405–7, 412 (the reference to *lytel Lowys* being excised), 493–4. In the third edition, ed. A. W. Morant, 1878, the references are, pp. 269, 325, 399, 401, 419, 464, 473–5 (with the suppression noted above), 496, 574, 575.]

[p. 195 *n.*] [Reference to *gore* in *C. Tales.*]

[p. 227] [Reference to "the canon's yeoman in Chaucer, whose tale is perhaps the finest satire upon chemical jugglers to be found in any language."]

[p. 286] [Quotation from *Milleres Tale*, ll. 134–5, on *waget*.]

[p. 289 *n.*] [References to *Knight's Tale.*]

[p. 335 *n.*] [Quotation from *Knight's Tale.*]

[p. 336 *n.*] [Quotation from *Legend of Good Women.*]

[p. 345] The English language underwent no very considerable change from the reign of Edward the Third to that of Edward the Fourth. The style of Gower is not materially different from that of Lydgate. Of Langland and Chaucer I say nothing. The great Poet wrote the language of no age; the rude Satyrist that of an age long prior to his own.

[A footnote to this reads:] Skinner's remark on the elder Bard is well known : "Integra verborum plaustra invexit."

[Whitaker then proceeds to quote from a MS. at Bolton, which he ascribes to the Canons, and which begins :

Why artt thow soo poure man, and I ame soo ryche?

The quotation is given "as a commentary on some parts of the Chanones Yeman's Tale, in order to shew with what

exactness Chaucer copied, while he derided the jargon of that pretended science." Extracts follow, pp. 347–8.]

[pp. 350–2] [Whitaker gives an excerpt from a Latin treatise on astronomy, ascribed to the same source, and proceeds :]

This treatise is evidently one of those *many conclusions* on the subject of Astronomy spoken of by Chaucer as extant in his time, *which the Latin folk had in Latin ;* but when the Canons of Bolton lectured their illiterate pupil and patron [Henry, Lord Clifford the Shepherd], they must have imitated the condescension of that Bard to *lytel Lowys*, in shewing hym *wonder lyght Rules, and naked Wordes in Englysh, for Latyn ne canst thou but smale, my sonne.*

[p. 362] [Quotation from *Legend of Good Women.*]

[p. 423] [Reference to the *Romaunt of the Rose.*]

[p. 424] [Quotation from *Reeves Tale* with remarks which imply that the two scholars of Soleres Hall (of a town highte Strother) came from Longstrother, their dialect "being precisely the modern dialect of Craven."]

1805. Wordsworth, William. *Letter* to Walter Scott, Nov. 7, 1805, [in] Letters of the Wordsworth Family, ed. Knight, 3 vols., 1907, vol. i, p. 208. [Also printed in] J. G. Lockhart's Memoirs of the Life of Sir Walter Scott, 1837, vol. ii, p. 81. (Library of English Classics, edited by A. W. Pollard, 1900, vol. i, ch. xiv, p. 434.)

. . . I do not mean to say there is nothing of this [poetical language in the highest sense, language of the imagination, or the intense passions] in Dryden, but as little, I think, as is possible, considering how much he has written. You will easily understand my meaning, when I refer to his versification of Palamon and Arcite, as contrasted with the language of Chaucer.

1805. Wordsworth, William. *Prelude,* Book III, ll. 278–81. (The Poetical Works of William Wordsworth, ed. W. Knight, 1896, vol. iii, p. 176.)

Beside the pleasant Mill of Trompington
I laughed with Chaucer in the hawthorn shade ;
Heard him, while birds were warbling, tell his tales
Of amorous passion.

1806. Cary, Henry Francis. *Letter to Miss Seward,* dated Aug. 16, 1806, [in] Memoir of the Rev. F. H. Cary . . . by his Son, 1847, 2 vols., vol. i, pp. 227, 238.

[p. 227] Your opinion of Dante himself I do not attempt to controvert . . Together with Chaucer and Spenser, it will ever be to you, as " caviare to the multitude," and as Ossian to me.

[p. 238] [Miss Seward " was not to be silenced." She says, in the course of a very long letter, that there is more reason to suppose the " coldness of a poetic mind " to the beauty and sublimity of Madoc is " the result of prejudice," than " to fancy any sensibility of the real faults of Chaucer, Spenser, and Dante a sort of unhallowed irreverence for crude and easy composition."]

1806. Chalmers, George. *Notes* to *Poetical Works of Sir David Lyndsay* . . . *with a life* . . . *dissertation, and* . . . *glossary,* 3 vols.

[Vol. i (Life and Dissertation): statement that there were 12 edns. of Chaucer between 1475 and 1602, and that none was printed out of England ; Chaucer master of Scots and English Poets, pp. 90, 99; citation from *The Flyting of Montgomery and Polwart*: " Fra Lyndsay thou *tuik,* thou'rt Chaucer's cuik," p. 102; Chaucer and the Scots poets, pp. 123, 127, 131 ; Chaucer and James I, pp. 134–6 ; Chaucer and Lydgate, p. 189 *n.* ; versification, pp. 180–2 ; language, pp. 138, 141, 144–53, 155–9, 165, 168–179, 180–2, 190 *n.* Many other references in the notes and glossary.]

[p. 172] It is apparent, from this minute examination, that, of Lyndsay's words, about 1, in 24, is obsolete ; and of Chaucer's 1, in 20 ; yet, the languages of the two poets are the same English . . . and yet Chaucer died in 1400, and Lyndsay in 1557.

1806. Fox, Charles James. *Record* of Fox's veneration for Chaucer and reading of Dryden's *Palamon and Arcite. See* below, 1811, Trotter. For a letter to Charles Grey referring to Chaucer's love of birds, *see* below, App. A., 1800.

1806. Lamb, Charles, *Letter* to William Wordsworth, [dated] Feb. 1, 1806. (The Works of Charles and Mary Lamb, ed. E. V. Lucas, 1903–5, 7 vols., vol. vi, Letters, p. 333.)

We have made some alterations in the Editions since your sister's directions. . . . The Spencer [*sic*] and the Chaucer, being noble old books, we did not think Stockdale's modern volumes [of Shakespeare] would look so well beside them. . . . The state of the purchase then stands thus,

Urry's Chaucer	.	.	.	.	£1 16 —
Pope's Shakespeare	.	.	.	.	2 2 —

Spenser [*sic*] . . . ∘ .		14	—
Milton	1	5	—
Packing Case, &c.		3	6
	6	—	6

1806. **Mitford**, Mary Russell (Mother of Miss Mary R. Mitford). *List of Books read January* 1806. [This is a list of books, made by her mother, which Miss Mary R. Mitford read during the above month.] The Life of Mary Russell Mitford . . . ed. Rev. A. G. L'Estrange. 1870, vol. i, p. 30.

List of Books read January 1806.   vols.

Fourth Volume of Canterbury Tales   .   .   1

[The edition must be Tyrwhitt's, 1775.]

1806. **Seward**, Anna. *Letter to the Rev. Robert Fellowes*, dated May 31, 1806 [referring to Chaucer's meeting and conversation with Petrarch].
    Letter to Mrs. Jackson, dated June 3, 1806. (*Letters of Anna Seward*, 6 vols., Edinburgh, 1811, vol. vi, pp. 257, 268–70, Letters XLVI and XLVII.)

[p. 268]   [Reference to Godwin's *Life*, on which the writer continues:]
[p. 269]   This author is insanely partial to the poetic powers of Chaucer, whose compositions, allowing for the disadvantage of obsolete language, have so little good which is not translation, and so much that is tedious, unnatural, conceited, and obscure. Amid scenes and circumstances, so much more interesting than any which appertain to Chaucer, the poet pops up his nose at intervals, like a wooden buoy, floating, sinking, and rising, amongst a throng of gallant boats and vessels, on the billows of the ocean.

1806. [**Southey**, Robert.] *Review* of Chalmers' *Poetical Works of Sir David Lyndsay*, [in] The Annual Review, vol. v, art. i, p. 494.

Happy are the Scotch Poets, for they shall find editors. Is it not disgraceful, that of all Chaucer's works, only the Canterbury Tales have been well edited?

1806. [**Southey**, Robert.] *Review* of Lord Holland's *Account of Lope de Vega*, [in] The Annual Review, vol. v, art. xvi, p. 401.

[The Latin rhymes] into which Sir Francis Kynaston translated part of Chaucer's Troilus and Cressida, strange as they at first appear, are exceedingly beautiful.

1806. Unknown. *Review of Hoare's 'Giraldus Cambrensis,'* [in] The Edinburgh Review, July, 1806, vol. viii, p. 403.

> Girald has collected all the vituperative reflections upon the fair sex which either sacred or profane authors afforded, with an industry only exceeded by the fifth husband of the Wife of Bath, who compiled the treatise,
> " Where divers authors (whom the Devil confound) . . . [to] And Venus sets ere Mercury can rise."

1806. Wordsworth, William. *Letter to Lady Beaumont,* [printed in] Letters of the Wordsworth Family, ed. W. Knight, 3 vols, 1907, vol. i, p. 280.

> Out of this alley . . . should be a small blind path leading to a bower, such as you will find described in the beginning of Chaucer's poem of *The Flower and the Leaf,* and also in the beginning of the *Assembly of Ladies.*

1807. Poetical Works of Chaucer, 16°.

[No copy of this has been found in a public library, nor is it mentioned by Miss Hammond in *Chaucer, a bibliographical manual.* The title is taken from a dealer's list.]

1807. Beloe, William. *Anecdotes of Literature.* For vol. ii, *see* below, App. A., 1807 ; for vol. vi, below, 1812.

1807. Byron, George Gordon, Lord. *List of the different Poets, dramatic or otherwise, who have distinguished their respective languages by their productions,* [in Byron's memorandum-book, dated Nov. 30, 1807]. Life and Works of Byron, ed. Moore, edn. 1835, 17 vols., vol. i, pp. 147–8 ; Murray's 1-vol. Life, by Moore, 1908, p. 49.

[This was first printed in Moore's *Letters and Journals of Lord Byron,* 1830, vol. i, pp. 100–1.]

> In my list of English, I have merely mentioned the greatest; —to enumerate the minor poets would be useless, as well as tedious. Perhaps Gray, Goldsmith, and Collins, might have been added, as worthy of mention, in a *cosmopolite* account. But as for the others, from Chaucer down to Churchill, they are 'voces et præterea nihil';—sometimes spoken of, rarely read, and never with advantage. Chaucer, notwithstanding the praises bestowed on him, I think obscene and contemptible :—he owes his celebrity merely to his antiquity, which he does not deserve so well as Pierce Plowman, or Thomas of Ercildoune.

1807. Cockloft, Pindar, *pseud.* [**Irving**, Washington.] *To Lancelot Langstaff. Esq.*, [in] Salmagundi, Feb. 1807. (Irving's Works, 27 vols., 1880–3, vol. xvi, p. 68.)

> O, 'twould do your heart good,
> Launce, to see my mill grind
> Old stuff into verses and poems refined :—
> Dan Spenser, Dan Chaucer, those poets of old,
> Though covered with dust, are yet true sterling gold ;
> I can grind off their tarnish, and bring them to view,
> New-modell'd, new-mill'd, and improved in their hue.

1807. Coleridge, Samuel Taylor. *Letter to Sir H. Davy*, Sept. 11, 1807. (Letters of S T. Coleridge, 1895, vol. ii, pp. 515–16.)

[Coleridge is sketching a series of lectures.] 2. On Spenser, including the metrical romances, and Chaucer, though the character of the latter as a manner-painter I shall have so far anticipated in distinguishing it from, and comparing it with, Shakespeare.

1807. Dibdin, Thomas Frognall. *The Director; A Weekly Literary Journal*, 2 vols. ; vol. i, pp. 126–8, 345 ; vol. ii, pp. 207, 280.

[p. 126] *Royal Institution.* The fourth lecture of the Rev. Mr. Dibdin, *on the rise and progress of English literature*, was devoted entirely to the life and writings of Chaucer.
[p. 127] [Doubts as to Gower's chronological priority to Chaucer; events of Chaucer's life ; his works discussed, especially the
[p. 128] ' Canterbury Tales ' ; the testimony of English authors, from Ascham to Warton, in praise of Chaucer ; and the need of an improved edition of his poems.]

[Dibdin's Lectures appear never to have been published in full.]

1807. D'Israeli, Isaac. *Curiosities of Literature*, 5th edn., 2 vols., 1807, vol. i, pp. 172–3 (14th edn., 3 vols., 1849, vol. i, p. 115).

Chaucer was more facetious in his tales than in his conversation, and the Countess of Pembroke used to rally him by saying that his silence was more agreeable to her than his conversation.

[*See also* below, 7th edn., 1823, and 9th edition, 1834. The 1st edn. appeared in 1791, in one vol., and contained only one Chaucer reference, on p. 503 ; the 2nd series appeared in 1823 ; the author revised the book continually until the 12th and last edn. of his lifetime, 1841.]

1807. Douce, Francis. *Illustrations of Shakespeare and of Ancient Manners,* 2 vols.; vol. i, pp. 2, 15, 43, 48, 109, 134, 177, 183, 188–9, 203–6, 215, 223, 232–3, 246, 301, 350, 407, 415–16, 474, 487, 506 ; vol. ii, pp. 7, 60, 64, 67–8, 151, 153–4, 180, 183, 213, 228, 253–4, 276, 281, 285, 351, 363, 420, 450–1.

[vol. i, p. 15] [Quotation from "Chaucer's *Testament of Creseid,*" describing the Man in the Moon.]

[p. 109] [Quotation from Troilus, Bk. iii, ll. 1366–72.]

[p 183] [Tyrwhitt quoted to the effect that "the Pluto and Proserpine of Chaucer were the true progenitors of Oberon and Titania."]

[p. 189] [Quotation from "Chaucer's *Flower and the Leafe*" for the word henchman.]

[p. 204] [Quotation from Wife of Bath's Tale, ll. 863–74, to illustrate fairies in Midsummer Night's Dream :] The other quotation which Mr. Steevens has given, is not to the present purpose. The *fairies' blessing* was to bring *peace* upon the house of Theseus ; the *night-spell* in the *Miller's Tale,* is pronounced against the influence of elves, and those demons, or evil spirits, that were supposed to occasion the nightmare.

[vol. ii, p. 64] [Chaucer probably borrowed the plot of Troilus and Cressida from Boccaccio's Filostrato ; what Dryden said of Lollius entirely destitute of proof.]

[p. 68] Such part of our play as relates to the loves of Troilus and Cressida was most probably taken from Chaucer, as no other work, accessible to Shakespeare, could have supplied him with what was necessary.

[Most of the other references are parallel quotations from Chaucer and illustrate the vocabulary of the plays.]

[p. 281] [On the anachronisms and some other incongruities of Shakespeare :] From the time of Chaucer to that of Shakespeare, there is scarcely an author to be found who is not implicated in this accusation . . .

[p. 285] [Footnote.] Mr. Stothard, the most unassuming of men, but with every claim to superior talent, has recently finished a painting of the procession of Chaucer's Canterbury Pilgrims, which may be classed amongst the choicest morsels of its kind. The attention to accuracy of costume which it displays has never been exceeded, and but very seldom so well directed.

1807. Hoppner, John. *Letter to Richard Cumberland*, dated **May 30,** 1807, [printed in] *Critical Description of . . . Chaucer's Pilgrims . . . by Thomas Stothard*, by William Carey, 1808 [*q.v.* below], pp. 12, 13.

[The letter is a critical description of Stothard's painting of Chaucer's pilgrims. The painter, says Hoppner, in delineating the pilgrims, shows that he has] studied the human heart with as much attention, and not less successfully, than the Poet.

[There follows praise of the landscape, the freshness of the spring morning, of which we see the influence on] the cheeks of the Fair Wife of Bath, and her rosy Companions, the Monk and Friar.

[The picture has a further peculiarity] that it bears no mark of the period in which it was painted, but might very well pass for the work of some able artist of the time of Chaucer.

1807. Pindar, Peter, *pseud.* [**Wolcot**, John.] *Lines addressed to Chaucer*, [in] The Monthly Magazine, Feb. 1, 1807, vol. xxiii, p. 59.

> Old jocund bard, I never pass
> The Tabard, but I take a glass,
>   To drink a requiem to thy ghost;
> Where once the pious pilgrims met,
> Companions boon, a jovial set,
>   And midst the bands a jovial host.
>
> Methinks I see them on the road
> To Becket's miracle-abode,
>   That cleans from Satan's soot the soul;
> Methinks I hear their comic tale,
> Delighting lanes, and hills, and dales,
>   And bidding time more gayly roll.
>
> .   .   .   .
>
> Shall Shakespeare boast his Jubilee,
> And, Chaucer, nought be done for thee,
>   The father of our British lays?
> Oh bards, and bardlings, fie! oh fie!
> And Southwark folks to you I cry,—
>   How are ye mute in Geoffry's praise?
>
> Is it reserved for me alone
> To boast how Chaucer's merits shone
>   On dark unclassic ground?

How well he touched the British lyre,
And kindled high the Muse's fire,
   When not a sparkle gleamed around ?

Oh then be formed a club of fame
To hail thy venerable name ;
   And let me join the choral throng.
For stanzas I'll invoke the Muse,
And, consequently [I] will chuse
   My old friend Shield to set the song.

Ah ! what though, obsolete, thy phrase
No more delights our modern days,
   I love thy genius in each line ;
Like thee I strive to charm our isle ;
Like thee I court the Muse of Smile ;
   And wish to leave a name like thine !

Though obsolete, alas ! thy line,
And doomed in cold neglect to shine,
   By me shall Chaucer be rever'd ;
Whose art a new Parnassus rais'd,
That midst barbaric darkness blaz'd,
   A sun where not a star appear'd !

1807. Seward, Anna. *Two Letters*, dated respectively Jan. 29 and April 17, to Sir Walter Scott. (Letters of Anna Seward, 6 vols., Edinburgh, 1811, vol. vi, pp. 330, 333, 336. Letters LIX and LX.)

[p. 330] [Jan. 29.] He [Dryden], Spencer, and Chaucer, have, in my opinion, been overpraised. On a balance of their beauty and deformity, not one of them equals yourself or Southey.

[p. 333] [April 17. The writer differs from Scott's opinion that "modern poetic talent [was] in a state of dwarfism, from the days of Chaucer, Spencer, and Dryden."]

[p. 336] From the writers of Spencer's period, I have gathered that it was the fashion to speak degradingly of his powers in comparison with those of Chaucer.

1807. Southey, Robert. *Specimens of the Later English Poets, with preliminary notices*, by Robert Southey, London, 1807. In three volumes, vol. i, pp. xiii–xix.

[p. xiii] V. The classification of our Poets into schools is to be objected to, because it implies that we have no school of our

CHAUCER CRITICISM.—II.

own ; a confession not to be admitted, till the prototypes and masters of Chaucer, Shakspeare, and Milton are produced. . . .

[p. xiv] The first imported fashion was the Provençal, or Lemosin. Chaucer composed his complimentary poems in this style. . . . The Romance of the Rose . . . he must have translated for its reputation, and not for its merit . . . it is impossible not to regret, that the time bestowed upon this long and wearying rigmarole, had not been employed upon the Canterbury Tales. . . .

[p. xv] It is not easy to understand Chaucer's system of versification, whether it was metrical or rhythmical. . . . Avoiding the harshness and obscurity of alliterative rhythm on the one hand, and on the other the frequent recurrence and intricate intertexture of rhymes which are found in some of the romances ; he preferred forms less rude than the one, less artificial than the other ; less difficult, and therefore more favourable to perspicuity than either. Chaucer, therefore, became the model of succeeding Poets ; the ten-syllable couplet, [p. xvi] in which his best poems are composed, has become our most usual measure ; and even when rhyme is disused, that length of line which he considered as best adapted for narrative, is still preferred for it.

Petrarca, Dante, and Chaucer, are the only Poets of the dark ages whose celebrity has remained uninjured by the total change of manners in Europe. . . . To attempt any comparison between three writers, who have so little in common, would be ridiculous ; but . . . Chaucer displays a versatility of talents, which neither of the others seem to have possessed : in which only Ariosto has approached, and only Shakspeare equalled him. Few, indeed, have been so eminently gifted with all the qualifications of a Poet, essential or accidental. [p.xvii] He was well versed in all the learning of his age, even of the abstrusest kind ; he had an eye and an ear, for all the sights and sounds of nature ; humour to display human follies, and feeling to understand, and to delineate human passions. As a painter of manners, he is accurate as Richardson ; as a painter of character, true to the life and spirit, as Hogarth . . . his fame will stand. The more he is examined, the higher he will rise in estimation. Old Poets in general, are only valuable because they are old ; on the contrary, nothing but his age prevents Chaucer from being universally ranked

among the greatest Poets of his country : far indeed below
Shakspeare and Milton ; perhaps below Spenser, for his mind
was less pure and his beauties are scattered over a wider and
more unequal surface,—but far above all others.

VI. The *ornate* style originated in Chaucer ; he has just left
specimens enough to shew that he had tried the experiment,
and did not like it. . . .

[p. xix]   VII. From Chaucer to the days of Henry VIII, no progress
was made in literature. . . .

1807. Wordsworth, William. *Note* to the second poem *To the Daisy*
(1802). [Dated 1807 by Prof. Knight.] (Poetical Works, ed. W.
Knight, 1896, vol. ii, p. 357 *n.*)

[Resemblance to Mr. Montgomery's poem entitled " A Field
Flower " :]

Mr. Montgomery will not think any apology due to him ; I
cannot, however, help addressing him in the words of the
Father of English Poets :

> " Though it happe me to rehersin—
> That ye han in your freshe songis saied
> Forberith me, and beth not ill apaied,
> Sith that ye se I doe it in the honour
> Of Love, and eke in service of the Flour."
>
> [Prologue to Legende of Good Women, ll. 78–82.]

1808. Carey, William (Picture Dealer). *Critical Description of the
Procession of Chaucer's Pilgrims to Canterbury,* painted by Thomas
Stothard.

[This is a pamphlet of 77 pp., prefaced by a letter from Carey
to John Leigh Philips, and followed by a critical description
of the picture, which gives a detailed account of each pilgrim.
There are Chaucer allusions all through the pamphlet; the
following are the most interesting:]

[p. 9]   [Opening of the ' Critical Description.']

Many have expressed a surprise that the *Procession of
Chaucer's Pilgrims* was not earlier selected by some of our
distinguished Artists. But difficulties exist in the subject
sufficient to deter the generality of minds from the undertaking. [Difficulty of grouping a number of figures *all form-
ally directed one way.*]

[p. 11]   From Chaucer's minute description, the Artist has drawn
each as a Portrait in the English costume of the 14th century.

[Here follows a letter from Hoppner to Richard Cumberland, 1807, *q. v.* above.]

[p. 15] [The Miller that '*for* dronken *was* all pale' is next described,
[p. 16] and his dogs; the Host with quotation from the Prologue
[p. 18] describing him, and so on.]

[p. 24]   It cannot be denied that Chaucer's description of the Knight is very marked in all its details, and very perfect. It unites the minute accuracy of Albert Durer's *St. Hubert* with the fine colouring and dignity of Holbein in his most *Tizianesque* portraits. . . .

[p. 30]   [Description of the Squire.]

Chaucer, when in *Italy*, was introduced to *Petrarch*, the friend of Contemporary Art. But whether the British Bard ever took up the pencil, or acquired any interest in the works of others, is a question.

Nevertheless, on reading Chaucer's life, a supposition arises, that . . . he drew the character of the Squire from what he was himself when he wrote his "*Court of Love.*" [To draw their own portraits is a common practice among painters and poets.]

[pp. 43–4] [Carey does not agree with Tyrwhitt when he says that the Yeoman belongs to the Knight, and not to the Squire, as Chaucer would never have given the son an attendant when the father had none. The Yeoman was young, and so probably the Squire's attendant, possibly his foster-brother. But even if it were an error to assign the servant to the son, he cannot
[p. 45] agree with Tyrwhitt,] unless we are to suppose that *Chaucer was above error* in the design or invention of his characters, . . . Chaucer's acknowledged judgment, and his rich invention, did not lift him above the commission of error and oversight in composition.

[p. 57]   [Description of Chaucer.]

The countenance of Chaucer is designed from that in the British Museum, *painted* by Thomas Occleve, the Poet's scholar. I think that I have somewhere read the life of this Thomas Occleve. *But I had sent, to a distant part of the kingdom, all my books and works of art, some days before I thought of commencing this essay.* I have now nothing to refer to but the Bible, Johnson's Dictionary, Montgomery's Poems, and Chaucer's Works : . . . and I have not been able to discover any mention of this Painter or Picture in Chaucer

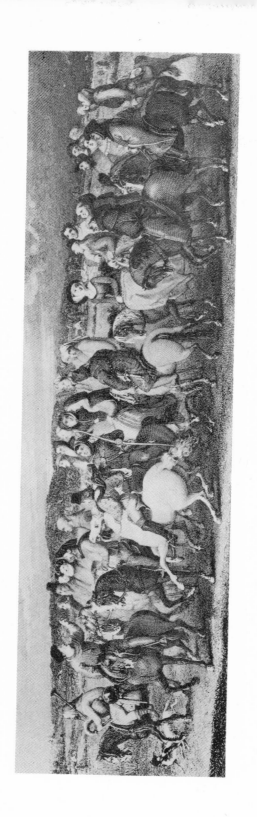

THE PROCESSION OF CHAUCER'S PILGRIMS TO CANTERBURY
BY THOMAS STOTHARD
Engraved by Schiavonetti 1808

. . . It appears to me, however, an interesting question : Who taught Thomas Occleve to paint?

[This pamphlet was re-issued in 1818 with the addition of dedicatory and other letters, in which there are further brief but unimportant references to Chaucer.]

[1808.] **Coleridge,** Samuel Taylor. *Notes* written in Lamb's copy of "The Poetical Works of Mr. Samuel Daniel," 2 vols., 1718, [printed in] Notes and Queries, Aug. 7, 1852, vol. vi, p. 118. [Also quoted by E. V. Lucas, Life of Charles Lamb, vol. ii, pp. 316–7.]

[Note on 4th fly-leaf :]

Is it from any hobby-horsical love of our old writers (and of such a passion respecting Chaucer, Spenser, and Ben Jonson, I have occasionally seen glaring proofs in one the string of whose shoe I am not worthy to unloose), or is it a real Beauty, the interspersion I mean (in stanza poems) of rhymes from polysyllables—such as Eminence, Obedience, Reverence?

1808. [**Cromek,** Robert Hartley ?] *The Procession of Chaucer's Pilgrims to Canterbury. Proposals for publishing, by subscription, a print, from the well-known cabinet picture on that subject, by Thomas Stothard, Esq., R.A., to be executed . . . by Louis Schiavonetti, etc.,* [appended to Blair's] The Grave, Cromek, 1808.

[The reputation of Chaucer as the reformer of the English language, etc., justifies the Proprietor in presenting all the characters of the Canterbury Tales, the most pleasing of his works.

Description of the picture, giving a few words to each character. The Ploughman is called the *Old Ploughman,* and the Squire the *Fop of Chaucer's Age;* a Goldsmith is introduced. *See,* for criticism of all this, Blake's Descriptive Catalogue, below, 1809. It is claimed that "the costume of each Person is correct with an antiquarian exactness," Douce's *Illustrations of Shakespeare* being quoted is support of the statement ; also a note states that the portrait of Chaucer is painted from that by Occleve in the British Museum. Appended is a letter from John Hoppner to Richard Cumberland, *q.v.* above, 1807.]

1808. **Jamieson,** John. *An Etymological Dictionary of the Scottish Language:* illustrating the words in their different Significations by Examples from Ancient and Modern Writers . . . Edinburgh, 2 vols.

[There are a certain number of Chaucer references and quotations all through the Dictionary ; there are 13 such references in the first 20 pages.]

1808. L., G. W.   *Chaucer's Tomb*, [in] The Gentleman's Magazine, Nov. 1808, vol. lxxviii, p. 974.

From the mutilated state of that [the tomb] of our first Poet Chaucer, very few know the spot where he was interred; indeed the inscription is almost defaced, and the Monument itself has suffered much through neglect. It is the only one hereabouts which accords with the building in which it is placed; yet, as if that were a defect, it has been made the supporter of another, which (not to say anything of the striking discordance) absolutely appears as if it had casually *perched* on it! Notwithstanding these disadvantages, many may be pleased by having this Monument pointed out to them. On entering the aile [*sic*] it is the fourth on the right hand from the door, and is between those of Cowley and Phillips. The slab appears to be of Petworth marble; and the canopy over it, having a rich pendent roof, is supported by pillars, the sculpture on which forms a kind of lozenge or chequer-work. The Latin inscription and other particulars, may be found by referring to Weever, who closes his survey of the tombs in the Abbey with an account of this [*q. v.* above, 1631, vol. i, p. 204].

1808. Lamb, Charles.   *Specimens of English Dramatic Poets.*   Footnote to Middleton's *Women Beware Women*. (The Works of Charles and Mary Lamb, ed. E. V. Lucas, 1903–5, 7 vols., vol. iv, p. 129.)

This is one of the scenes which has the air of being an immediate transcript from life. Livia the " good neighbour " is as real a creature as one of Chaucer's characters. She is such another jolly Housewife as the Wife of Bath.

1808. Pratt, Samuel Jackson.   *The Cabinet of Poetry, containing the best entire pieces to be found in the works of the British Poets.* Introductory Essay on Poetry, 6 vols., vol. i, pp. xl, li, lxxi.

[The pieces include nothing from Chaucer, but " Dryden's Character of a Good Parson " is given.]

[p. xl]   This charm of individuality was in some of their poems eminently possessed by Chaucer, and other of our elder bards.

[p. lxxi]   The passion for allegory, so long the characteristic of the Italian school, was by Chaucer rendered as prevalent in England as it had previously been on the continent.

1808. Scott, Sir Walter. *Works of John Dryden,* 18 vols., vol. i, Life
of John Dryden, pp. 171, 427, 430, 441, 444, 494–96, 498–503, 505.
   Notes to Troilus and Cressida, vol. vi, pp. 228, 229, 230.
   Notes to Preface to the Fables, vol. xi, pp. 215, 216, 217, 220, 221,
222, 223, 226, 230, 232, 233, 235.
   Notes to Palamon and Arcite, vol. xi, pp. 243 [a long note on the
origins of the Knight's Tale, with critical remarks on Chaucer's
treatment of it], 245, 246, 255, 256, 267, 280, 286, 287, 289, 303,
309, 311, 312.
   Notes to The Cock and the Fox, vol. xi, pp. 326 [critical remarks
on Chaucer's treatment], 333, 339, 343, 350, 352.
   Notes to The Flower and the Leaf, vol. xi, pp. 354, 372.
   Notes to The Wife of Bath, vol. xi, pp. 376 [critical remarks on
Chaucer's tale], 378, 382.
   Note on Good Parson, vol. xi, p. 394.

[Vol. i,   The "Knight's Tale," the longest and most laboured of
p. 494] Chaucer's stories, possesses a degree of regularity which might
satisfy the most severe critic. [The honour of this, says
Scott, is due to Chaucer. Passages follow on Dryden's treatment of the Knight's Tale.]

        .   .   .   .

[p. 498]   With Chaucer, Dryden's task was more easy than with
Boccacio.   Barrenness was not the fault of the Father of
English poetry ; and amid the profusion of images which he
presented, his imitator had only the task of rejecting or
selecting.   In the sublime description of the temple of Mars,
painted around with all the misfortunes ascribed to the influence of his planet, it would be difficult to point out a single
idea, which is not found in the older poem.   But Dryden has
judiciously omitted or softened some degrading and some disgusting circumstances ; as the "cook scalded in spite of his
long ladle," the "swine devouring the cradled infant," the
"pick-purse," and other circumstances too grotesque or
ludicrous, to harmonize with the dreadful group around them.
Some points, also, of sublimity, have escaped the modern
poet.   Such is the appropriate and picturesque accompaniment
of the statue of Mars :

> A wolf stood before him at his feet
> With eyen red, and of a man he eat.

In the dialogue, or argumentative parts of the poem, Dryden
has frequently improved on his original, while he falls something short of him in simple description, or in pathetic effect.

Thus, the quarrel between Arcite and Palamon is wrought up with greater energy by Dryden than Chaucer, particularly by the addition of the following lines, describing the enmity of the captives against each other :

> Now friends no more, nor walking hand in hand,
> But when they met, they made a surly stand
> And glared like angry lions as they pass'd,
> And wish'd that every look might be their last.

But the modern must yield the palm, despite the beauty of his versification, to the description of Emily by Chaucer ; and may be justly accused of loading the dying speech of Arcite with conceits for which his original gave him no authority.

.   .   .   .

[p. 501]   [The French element in Chaucer's language.]

[p. 502]   Upon the whole, in introducing these romances of Boccacio and Chaucer to modern readers, Dryden has necessarily deprived them of some of the charms which they possess for those who have perused them in their original state. . . . To antiquaries Dryden has sufficiently justified himself, by declaring his version made for the sake of modern readers, who understand sense and poetry as well as the old Saxon admirers of Chaucer, when that poetry and sense are put into words which they can understand. Let us also grant him that for the beauties which are lost, he has substituted many which the original did not afford ; that, in passages of gorgeous description, he has added even to the chivalrous splendour [p. 503] of Chaucer, and has graced with poetical ornament the simplicity of Boccacio ; that, if he has failed in tenderness, he is never deficient in majesty.

.   .   .   .

[Vol. xi, p. 245]   The "Knight's Tale," whether Chaucer's or Dryden's version, is one of the finest pieces of composition in our language. . . . The work of Chaucer cannot, however, properly be termed a translation ; on the contrary, the tale has acquired its most beautiful passages under the hand of the English bard. He abridged the prolix, and enlarged the poetical, parts of the work ; compressed the whole into one concise and interesting tale ; and left us an example of a beautiful heroic poem.

.   .   .   .

[p. 326]   [Note before "The Cock and the Fox."]   Tyrwhitt
detected the original of this fable in the translation of "Æsop,"
made by Marie of France into Norman-French . . . But the
hand of genius gilds what it touches; and the naked Apologue,
which may be found in Tyrwhitt's "Preliminary Discourse,"
was amplified by Chaucer into a poem, which, in grave, ironical
narrative, liveliness of illustration, and happiness of humorous
description, yields to none that ever was written.

[p. 376]   [Note before "The Wife of Bath."] . . . What was a mere
legendary tale of wonder in the rhime of the minstrel, and a
vehicle for trite morality in that of Gower, in the verse of Chaucer
reminds us of the resurrection of a skeleton, reinvested by a
miracle with flesh, complexion, and powers of life and motion.
Of all Chaucer's multifarious powers, none is more wonderful
than the humour, with which he touched upon natural frailty,
and the truth with which he describes the inward feelings of
the human heart; at a time when all around were employed in
composing romantic legends, in which the real character of
their heroes was as effectually disguised by the stiffness
of their manners as their shapes by the sharp angles and
unnatural projections of their plate armour.

[p. 394]   [Note before "The Character of a Good Parson."]   This
beautiful copy of a beautiful original makes us regret, that
Dryden had not translated the whole Introduction to the
"Canterbury Tales," in which the pilgrims are so admirably
described. Something might have been lost for want of the
ancient Gothic lore, which the writers of our poet's period did
not think proper to study; but when Dryden's learning
failed, his native stores of fancy and numbers would have
helped him through the task.

[In Cochrane's Catalogue of the Abbotsford Library, 1838, notices of Chaucer's works
in the Collection will be found at pp. 42, 154–5, 172, 185, 190, 239.]

1808. Unknown.   A Catalogue of the Harleian Manuscripts in the
British Museum, 4 vols., 1808–12, vol. ii, pp. 673, 675, 682, vol. iii,
pp. 97, 526.   [Vol. iv only is dated 1812.]

[vol. i,
p. 217]   372. [Anelida and Arcite.]
[vol. ii,
p. 673]   2376. [Note on the colophon to Piers Plowman.]   At the
end is this Note, "Hic explicit visio Wilelmi de Petro Plowman."   Now among the several persons to whom the Poems

of Piers Plowman have been ascribed, I remember not any William; so that if Geffrey Chaucer was the man, he disguised his name for fear of the Clergy, who are bitterly inveighed against in these Poems.

[p. 675] 2382 (5, 6). [Prioress's and Second Nun's Tales.]

[p. 682] 2392. [Troilus and Cressida.]

[vol. iii, p. 97] 3943. [Troilus and Cressida.]

[p. 526] 7333 (6–27). [Canterbury Tales.] (29) [Parliament of Foules.] (30) A part of his Complaint of Mars & Venus, with the unusual title "The Broche (?) of Thebes, as of the love of Mars and Venus." (31) [Anelinda [*sic*] and Arcite.] (35) Ballads by Chaucer . . . and other small poems.

[p. 526.] 7334. [Canterbury Tales.]

7335. An old and imperfect copy of Chaucer's Canterbury Tales.

1808. Unknown. *Review of Lectures on the Truly Eminent English Poets,* by Percival Stockdale, 1807, [in] The Edinburgh Review, April, 1808, vol. xii, pp. 63, 64.

[p. 63] The series of Mr. Stockdale's Eminent Poets commences with Spencer . . . one who, if Chaucer be called the day-star, may certainly be pronounced the sun-rise of our poetry.

1808. Unknown. *Review* of Scott's *Dryden,* [in] The Edinburgh Review, Oct. 1808, vol. xiii, p. 135.

In this edition of Dryden, we would have curtailed the life, . . . omitted many of the notes, the original fables from Chaucer and Boccace, the reply of Stillingfleet to Dryden's controversy.

1809. Blake, William. *Sir Jeffery Chaucer and the nine and twenty Pilgrims on their Journey to Canterbury,* [in] A Descriptive Catalogue of Pictures, Poetical and Historical Inventions Painted by William Blake in water colours, London, 1809, pp. 7–34. [Printed in *Life of William Blake,* by Alex. Gilchrist, enlarged edition, 1880, vol. ii, pp. 142–52.]

[For Lamb's appreciation of this article, *see* p. 49 below, 1810, H. Crabb Robinson.]

[p. 9] The characters of Chaucer's Pilgrims are the characters which compose all ages and nations : as one age falls, another rises, different to mortal sight, but to immortals only the same ; for we see the same characters repeated again and again, in animals, vegetables, minerals, and in men ; nothing new occurs [p. 10] in identical existence : Accident ever varies, Substance can never suffer change nor decay.

Of Chaucer's characters, as described in his Canterbury
Tales, some of the names or titles are altered by time, but the
characters themselves for ever remain unaltered, and consequently they are the physiognomies or lineaments of universal
human life, beyond which Nature never steps. Names alter,
things never alter. I have known multitudes of those who
would have been monks in the age of monkery, who in this
deistical age are deists. As Newton numbered the stars, and
as Linneus [*sic*] numbered the plants, so Chaucer numbered
the classes of men. . . .

[p. 11]   The Knight and Squire with the Squire's Yeoman lead the
procession, as Chaucer has also placed them first in his prologue.
The Knight is a true Hero, a good, great, and wise man; his
whole-length portrait on horseback, as written by Chaucer,
cannot be surpassed. He has spent his life in the field; has
ever been a conqueror, and is that species of character which in
every age stands as the guardian of man against the oppressor.
His son is like him with the germ of perhaps greater perfection
still, as he blends literature and the arts with his warlike
studies. . . . The Squire's Yeoman is also a great character, a
man perfectly knowing in his profession:

"And in his hand he bare a mighty bow."

Chaucer describes here a mighty man; one who in war is
the worthy attendant on noble heroes.

[p. 12]   The Prioress follows these with her female chaplain. . . .
This Lady is described also as of the first rank; rich and
honoured. She has certain peculiarities and little delicate
affectations, not unbecoming in her, being accompanied with
what is truly grand and really polite; her person and face,
Chaucer has described with minuteness; it is very elegant,
and was the beauty of our ancestors, till after Elizabeth's
time, when voluptuousness and folly began to be accounted
[p. 13]   beautiful. . . . The Monk is described by Chaucer, as a man
of the first rank in society, noble, rich, and expensively
attended: he is a leader of the age, with certain humorous
accompaniments in his character, that do not degrade, but
render him an object of dignified mirth, but also with
accompaniments not so respectable.

The Friar is a character also of a mixed kind.

" A friar there was, a wanton and a merry; "

but in his office he is said to be a "full solemn man:" elo-
[p. 14] quent, amorous, witty, and satyrical; young, handsome and
rich; he is a complete rogue; with constitutional gaiety enough
to make him a master of all the pleasures of the world . . .

It is necessary here to speak of Chaucer's own character,
that I may set certain mistaken critics right in their conception
of the humour and fun that occurs on the journey.

Chaucer is himself the great poetical observer of men, who
in every age is born to record and eternize its acts. This he
does as a master, as a father, and superior, who looks down on
their little follies from the Emperor to the Miller; sometimes
with severity, oftener with joke and sport.

Accordingly Chaucer has made his Monk a great tragedian,
[p. 16] one who studied poetical art. . . . Though a man of luxury,
pride and pleasure, he is a master of art and learning, though
affecting to despise it. . . .

For the Host who follows this group, and holds the center
of the cavalcade, is a first-rate character, and his jokes are no
trifles; they are always, though uttered with audacity, and
equally free with the Lord and the Peasant, they are always
substantially and weightily expressive of knowledge and
experience; Henry Baillie, the keeper of the greatest Inn, of
the greatest City; for such was the Tabarde Inn in Southwark,
near London: our Host was also a leader of the age. . . .

[p. 17] But I have omitted to speak of a very prominent character,
the Pardoner, the Age's Knave, who always commands and
domineers over the high and low vulgar. This man is sent
in every age for a rod and scourge, and for a blight, for a
trial of men, to divide the classes of men, he is in the most
holy sanctuary, and he is suffered by Providence for wise ends,
and has also his great use, and his grand leading destiny.

His companion the Sompnour, is also a Devil of the first
magnitude, grand, terrific, rich and honoured in the rank of
[p. 18] which he holds the destiny. The uses to society are perhaps
equal of the Devil and of the Angel; their sublimity, who can
dispute . . .

The principal figure in the next groupe is the Good Parson;
an Apostle, a real Messenger of Heaven, sent in every age for
its light and its warmth. This man is beloved and venerated
by all, and neglected by all: He serves all, and is served by
none; he is, according to Christ's definition, the greatest of his

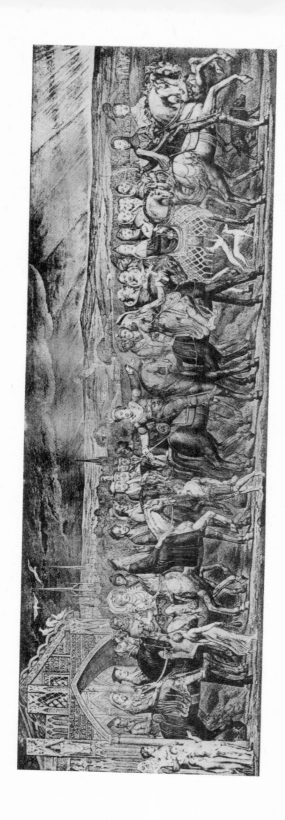

SIR JEFFERY CHAUCER AND THE NINE AND TWENTY PILGRIMS ON THEIR JOURNEY TO CANTERBURY
BY WILLIAM BLAKE
Engraved 1810

age. Yet he is a Poor Parson of a town. Read Chaucer's description of the Good Parson, and bow the head and the knee to him, who, in every age sends us such a burning and a shining light. . . .

[p. 19] Chaucer's characters live age after age. Every age is a Canterbury Pilgrimage ; we all pass on, each sustaining one or [p. 20] other of these characters; nor can a child be born, who is not one of these characters of Chaucer. The Doctor of Physic is described as the first of his profession ; perfect, learned, completely Master and Doctor in his art. Thus the reader will observe, that Chaucer makes every one of his characters perfect in his kind, every one is an Antique Statue ; the image of a class, and not of an imperfect individual.

[p. 20] . . . The Franklin is one who keeps open table, who is the genius of eating and drinking, the Bacchus ; as the Doctor of Physic is the Esculapius, the Host is the Silenus, the Squire is the Apollo, the Miller is the Hercules, &c. Chaucer's characters are a description of the eternal Principles that exist in all ages. The Franklin is voluptuousness itself most nobly pourtrayed . . . .

[p. 21] The Plowman is simplicity itself, with wisdom and strength for its stamina. Chaucer has divided the ancient character of Hercules between his Miller and his Plowman. Benevolence is the Plowman's great characteristic, he is thin with excessive labour, and not with old age, as some have supposed. . . . Visions of these eternal principles or characters of human [p. 22] life appear to poets, in all ages. . . . The Plowman of Chaucer is Hercules in his supreme eternal state, divested of his spectrous shadow ; which is the Miller, a terrible fellow, such as exists in all times and places, for the trial of men. . . .

[p. 24] The characters of Women Chaucer has divided into two classes, the Lady Prioress and the Wife of Bath. Are not these leaders of the ages of men ? The lady prioress, in some ages, predominates ; and in some the wife of Bath, in whose character Chaucer has been equally minute and exact ; because she is also a scourge and a blight. I shall say no more of her, nor expose what Chaucer has left hidden ; let the young reader study what he has said of her : it is useful as a scarecrow. There are of such characters born too many for the peace of the world.

I come at length to the Clerk of Oxenford. This character

varies from that of Chaucer, as the contemplative philosopher varies from the poetical genius. There are always these two classes of learned sages, the poetical and the philosophical. The painter has put them side by side, as if the youthful [p. 25] clerk had put himself under the tuition of the mature poet. Let the Philosopher always be the Servant and Scholar of inspiration and all will be happy.

[The rest of the section is devoted to a critical examination of Stothard's rival picture and the prospectus of Schiavonetti's engraving (*q.v.* above, p. 37, 1808), and Blake gives examples of how carelessly Stothard has read Chaucer and how little he has understood him. He calls the Squire a fop, which he is not; he puts in three Monks instead of one; he places the Reeve between the Knight and the Squire although Chaucer says

"And ever he rode hinderest of the rout."

He makes the Wife of Bath a blooming damsel, and the Plowman old, and he introduces a character that Chaucer has not, namely a Goldsmith. "All is misconceived, and its mis-execution is equal to its misconception."]

1809. Brydges, Sir Samuel Egerton. *Censura Literaria,* Containing Titles, Abstracts and Opinions of Old English Books, etc., vol. ix, art. ix, *Hawking*, pp. 61 and *n.*, 260, 264, 368–9, 371.

[p. 260]　　Chaucer has a pretty Episode of the Falcon rehearsing a tale of forsaken love to the Princess Canace.

1809–10. Byron, George Gordon Noel, Lord. *Childe Harold.* Note on Canto I, stanza ix, l. 5, in the original MS., on Chaucer's use of *lemman.* (Poetical Works, ed. E. Hartley Coleridge, 1899, etc., vol. ii, p. 22.)

1809. Dibdin, Thomas Frognall. *Bibliomania. See* below, App. A, 1809.

1809. Drake, Nathan. *Essays, Biographical, Critical, and Historical, illustrative of the Rambler, Adventurer, and Idler,* 2 vols., London, 1809–10 ; vol. i. pp. 160, 166–8, 429, 433, 435 *n.*, 445, 448, 449 *n.*; vol. ii, pp. 143, 190, 200, 204, 205.

[vol. i, p. 160]　[Drake quotes the list drawn up by Dr. Johnson of various literary undertakings projected by him, but not carried out. Of these No. 5 is "Chaucer, a new edition of him, from manuscripts and old editions" etc. (*see* above, [*c.* 1750?], vol. i, p. 401). Upon this Drake remarks :]

[p. 166]　　No. 5. Of this proposed edition of *Chaucer,* a part has been well executed in the elaborate edition of the Canterbury Tales, by Mr. Tyrwhitt, and in the copious life of the poet, [p. 167] by Mr. Godwin; but there still remains the greater portion of his works untouched by any skilful editor; for neither Speght nor Urry can be deemed at all competent to the task which [p. 168] they undertook. By the indefatigable industry of our literary antiquaries, much light has lately been thrown upon the state of our language anterior to the age of Chaucer; its mutations have been traced, its history ascertained, its poetry commented upon, and of course the diction and versification of Chaucer, their merits and defects, better understood and defined. The application of these resources to a new edition of the entire works of the venerable bard, would, there is little doubt, be well received by the public.

1809. Godwin, William. *Essay on Sepulchres:* or, a Proposal for Erecting some Memorial of the Illustrious Dead in all Ages on the Spot where their Remains have been Interred, p. 82.

I pity the being of slender comprehension, who lives only with George the Third, and Alexander of Russia, and Wieland, and Schiller, and Kant, and Jeremy Bentham, and John Horne Tooke, when if the grosser film were removed from his eyes, he might live and sensibly mingle with Socrates, and Plato, and the Decii, and the Catos, with Chaucer, and Milton, and Thomas Aquinas, and Thomas à Becket, and all the stars that gild our mortal sphere.

1809. Hamper, William. *Letter,* [in] The Gentleman's Magazine, June 1809, vol. lxxix, p. 512.

[On Tyrwhitt's Chaucer, with suggestions as to obscure passages.]

1809. Scott, Sir Walter. *Reliques of Burns . . . collected and published by R. H. Cromek,* [in] The Quarterly Review, vol. i, pp. 35–6. (Miscellaneous Prose Works of Sir Walter Scott, Edinburgh, 1834–71, 30 vols. vol. xvii, p. 266.)

We know not whether the family of the poet will derive any advantage from this publication of his remains. If so, it is the best apology for their being given to the world; if not, we have no doubt the editor, as he is an admirer of Chaucer, has read of a certain pardoner, who

—" with his *relics* when that he fond
A poor persone dwelling up on lond,
Upon a day he gat him more moneie
Than that the persone got in monethes tweie."

1809. Unknown. *Review* of *Partonopex of Blois, a Romance, freely translated from the French of M. Le Grand . . . by William Stewart Rose*, [in] The Edinburgh Review, Jan., 809, vol. xiii, p. 422.

We can hardly conceive that a motley dialect of Chaucer, Spenser, and other old ballads, grafted on a modern versification, could be familiar to any one's understanding . . .

Child . . . never occurs in Chaucer . . .

1809. Unknown. *Review* of *Extractos em Portuguez e em Inglez*, 1808, vol. i, [in] The Quarterly Review, May 1809, vol. i, p. 273.

[Comparison of early Portuguese poets with Chaucer and Dante, showing the superiority of the latter two, and mentioning the pre-eminence of Shakspere and Milton.]

1809. Unknown. *Review* of *Jamieson's Etymological Dictionary*, [in] The Edinburgh Review, April 1809, vol. xiv, pp. 127, 130, 133, 138. [*See* above, 1808, Jamieson.]

[References to the use of various words by Chaucer; *and* for *if, bybill, fordo, quod.*]

1810. The Works of Geoffrey Chaucer, vol. i [of] The Works of the English poets from Chaucer to Cowper, ed. by Alexander Chalmers, 21 vols.

[This edition contains a life of Chaucer by Chalmers, *q. v.* below, and besides the works, some pseudo-Chaucerian pieces : the Complaint of the Black Knight, the Court of Love, the Flower and the Leaf, the Cuckow and the Nightingale, and Chaucer's Dream (the Isle of Ladies).]

1810. Brayley, Edward Wedlake. *Beauties of England and Wales*, vol. x, pt. ii, p. 413.

Chaucer's Monk who ' bore a Sheffield whittle in his hose' is generally admitted as a proof of the early manufacture of knives in England.

[*See* above, 1727, Defoe, vol. i, p. 368, and below, 1848, Macaulay. It is not the Monk, but the Reve's Miller who has the whittle (Reve's Tale, l. 13).]

1810. Brydges, Sir Samuel Egerton. *The British Bibliographer*, vol. i, pp. 28, 29–30 [Bibliotheca Critica], pp. 106, 285, 297 [Clark's, or rather Covell's, reprint of Polimanteia, 1595, *q. v.* above, vol. i, p. 141], p. 375 [reprint of Simon Smel-knaue [1591 ?], *q. v.* above, vol. i, p. 134]. [For vols. ii and iii *see* below, 1812.]

1810. Chalmers, Alexander. *The Life of Chaucer*, prefixed to The Works (*q. v.* above), pp. iii–xv.

[A fairly critical biography, resting largely on Tyrwhitt;

but the Court of Love is cited as Chaucer's (and is included in the text); Godwin's *Life* is not mentioned.]

1810. Dibdin, Thomas Frognall.   *Typographical Antiquities . . .* begun by Joseph Ames and augmented by William Herbert, and now enlarged with copious notes, vol. i, p. vii, Preliminary Disquisition; pp. cix, cxvi, Life of Caxton; pp. 291-301, The Book of the Tales of Caunterburye; pp. 303-15, 327.

[The additions are mainly bibliographical and of little Chaucerian interest.   For vols. ii, iii, and iv *see* below, 1812, 1816, and 1819.   For Ames's original edn. of 1749, *see* above, vol. i, p. 398; for Herbert's intermediate edn. *see* above, vol. i, 1785, p. 477; 1786, p. 483; 1790, p. 491.]

1810. Haslewood, Joseph.   *Introduction and notes* [to] *The Book containing the Treatises of Hawking, Hunting* [etc.] by *Juliana Berners*, 1496, p. 59.   [Quotes Chaucer for the word 'mountance.']

[c. 1810.] Richman, Henry John.   *Sequel to the Canterbury Tales.*

[Richard Warner, in his *Literary Recollections*, 1830, vol. i, pp. 141-2, says: 'He himself [Richman] has frequently told me, that in early manhood, he had written a sequel to Chaucer's Canterbury Tales, which (as I have been informed by a competent judge, who then perused them) breathed much of the spirit, style, and diction, of the venerable bard.   But of this work I could never obtain a sight.   He always declined permitting his friends to peruse it, upon the principle, that the levity of such compositions, was inconsistent with the decorum of the clerical character.'   The work is apparently still unpublished.   Richman graduated at Oxford in 1802.   For Warner *see* below, p. 180.]

1810. Robinson, Henry Crabb.   *Conversation* with Lamb, [reported in] Diary, Reminiscences and Correspondence of Henry Crabb Robinson, 3 vols., 1869, vol. ii, p. 380 (under 1852).

[Speaking of Blake's drawing and description of the Canterbury Pilgrims, *q.v.* above, p. 42:]
When, in 1810, I gave Lamb a copy of the Catalogue of the paintings exhibited in Carnaby Street, he was delighted, especially with the description of a painting afterwards engraved [Blake's Canterbury Pilgrims]. . . . Stothard's work is well known; Blake's is known by very few.   Lamb preferred the latter greatly, and declared that Blake's description was the finest criticism he had ever read of Chaucer's poem.

[*c.* **1810.**] **Southey**, Robert. *Common-Place Book*, third series, edited by John Wood Warter, London, 1850, p. 227.

[The Abbé Goujet had said in his *Bibliothèque Françoise, ou Histoire de la Littérature Françoise*, tome 7e, p. 340 :
'George Chaucher, que l'on a surnommé l'Homère de l'Angleterre, l'avait traduit [the *Teseide* of Boccaccio] en vers Anglois dès l'an 1400.'
Southey quotes and adds the comment : 'Good !']

1810. Todd, Henry John. *Illustrations of the Lives and Writings of Gower and Chaucer.*

[Introduction, i–xlvii, discussing Chaucer, Gower (principally biography), and Thynne, Speght, Tyrwhitt, Ellis, Godwin, Plowman's Tale, Flower and the Leaf, and Testament of Love.

No. 1. Reprint, Thynne's Animadversions (above, p. 149), 3–83.
     2. Testamentum Johannis Gower, 87.
     3. Account of valuable MSS. of Gower and Chaucer, 95.
     4. Extracts from Confessio Amantis, Berthelet, 1532, 135.
     5. Extracts from Prologue to Tales, Tyrwhitt's edn., 171 ; Floure and Leafe, Speght's edn., 203 ; Notes on these, 227–292.
     6. Poems supposed to be written by Chaucer during his imprisonment (Lord Stafford's MS.), 295–309.
     7. Glossary, 317–394.]

1810. Unknown. *Review* of Milner's *History of Winchester*, [in] The Quarterly Review, May 1810, vol. iii, p. 366.

The writings of the two satiric poets, Langland and Chaucer, both Catholics, and one an ecclesiastic, led to this irresistible conclusion, that the lives of religious votaries, both male and female, were even then greatly deflected from their original rule.

1810. Unknown. *Review* of *Select Poems from Herrick, Carew, etc.,* [in] The Quarterly Review, Aug. 1810, vol. iv, p. 176.

. . . . Where the orthography of a poet influences his rhyme, as Chaucer's and Spenser's does every moment, the whole ought to be sacred ; but where that is not the case, we can see no reason why our present improved and fixed system of orthography should not be adopted.

1810. Unknown. *Review* of Southey's *History of Brazil*, Part the First, [in] The Quarterly Review, Nov. 1810, vol. iv, p. 456.

[Passing reference to Chaucer's knowledge of Brazil dye.]
But Chaucer, when he mentions the red dye of Brazil in

the same breath with the graine of Portingale,[1] displays a premature knowledge of its produce which is very perplexing . . . because we cannot find any sufficient authority to prove that the wood existed in the ancient hemisphere, or that Brazil has a meaning in any Eastern or European language.

> [1] Him needeth not his colour for to dien
> With Brazil or with graine of Portingale.
> Nonnes Preest's Tale.   [Epilogue, ll. 4648–9.]
> [The country was named from the dye, not the dye from the country. *See* Skeat's *Works of Chaucer*, vol. v, p. 258.]

1810. Wilkes, John. *Encyclopædia Londinensis*, vol. iv, 1810, p. 130, Chaucer; vol. xiii, 1815, pp. 530, 549–50, Chaucer's tomb, 819–20, Lydgate.

[vol. iv, p. 130] [New Chaucer article in the main, but the last paragraph of the *Encyclopædia Britannica* article is reprinted (*q.v.* above, 1778, vol. i, p. 452).]

[vol. xiii, p. 819] [Lydgate an imitator of Chaucer.]

1810. Wordsworth, Christopher (Master of Trinity Coll., Camb.). *Ecclesiastical Biography*, vol. i, pp. 168 *n.* [quotation of Prol. ll. 766–76, to illustrate the singing of songs on pilgrimages], 307–10 [extract from Foxe, Acts and Monuments, *q.v.* above, vol. i, p. 104]. [In fourth edn., 1853, vol. i, pp. 311, 312 *n.*, vol. ii, pp. 35, 414–16.]

[1810 ?] Wordsworth, William. *The Country Churchyard, and Critical Examination of Ancient Epitaphs.* (Prose Works, ed. W. Knight, 1896, vol. ii, p. 150.)

> Farwel my Frendys, the tyd abydeth no man,
>   I am departed hens, and so sal ye,
> But in this passage the best song I can
>   Is *Requiem Eternam*, now Jesu grant it me,
> When I have ended all myn adversity
> Grant me in Paradys to have a mansion
> That shedst Thy bloud for my redemption.

This epitaph might seem to be of the age of Chaucer, for it has the very tone and manner of the Prioress's Tale.

[Wordsworth says he quotes 'from an old book' (? Camden or Weever).   The Essay upon Epitaphs is in two parts, the first from *The Friend*, Feb. 22, 1810, the second from the author's MSS.   Grosart first printed the latter.   See his note on the contents page of vol. ii.   I date *The Country Churchyard* [1810 ?]: this was the year in which the *Friend* article was published, and in which the translation of the Chiabrera epitaphs was made.]

1810. Wordsworth, William. *Article* [on Christopher North's article signed 'Mathetes,' in] The Friend, no. 20, Jan. 4, 1810, p. **305.** (Prose Works, ed. W. Knight, 2 vols., 1896, vol. i, p. 91.)

Happy moment was it for England when her Chaucer, who has rightly been called the morning star of her literature, appeared above the horizon!

1811. Brydges, Sir Samuel Egerton. *Desultoria: or, Comments of a South-Briton on Books and Men,* Lee Priory, no. 1 [dated Sept. 8, 1811], pp. 3–4.

I look around my library, and task my recollection whether the standard works which now fill its shelves, obtained for their authors, during life, the same credit they now possess.
[p. 4] I see Erasmus, and Bacon; Chaucer, Spenser, Shakespeare, Milton, Cowley, Dryden, Pope, and Swift: Clarendon, Burnet, Temple, Bolingbroke, and Middleton! Their own age bowed to their ascendant talents, and posterity have ratified the pre-eminence.

1811. Byron, George Gordon, Lord. *Hints from Horace,* ll. **79–82,** 423–36. (Poetical Works, ed. by E. H. Coleridge, 1898–1904, vol. i, pp. 395, 420.)

[ll. 79-82]   New words find credit in these latter days,
If neatly grafted on a Gallic phrase;
What Chaucer, Spenser did, we scarce refuse
To Dryden's or to Pope's maturer Muse.

.   .   .   .

[ll. 423-36]   Ye, who seek finished models, never cease,
By day and night, to read the works of Greece.
But our good Fathers never bent their brains
To heathen Greek, content with native strains.
The few who read a page, or used a pen,
Were satisfied with Chaucer and old Ben;
The jokes and numbers suited to their taste
Were quaint and careless, anything but chaste;
Yet, whether right or wrong the ancient rules,
It will not do to call our Fathers fools!
Though you and I, who eruditely know
To separate the elegant and low,
Can also, when a hobbling line appears,
Detect with fingers—in default of ears.

1811. Collier, John Payne. *Extract* from *Diary* for Oct. 29, 1811, [in] Lectures and Notes on Shakspere and Milton . . . by Samuel Taylor Coleridge, now first collected by T. Ashe (Bohn's Standard Library), 1883. Introductory, p. 15.

Coleridge told us . . . that he means very soon to give a series of lectures at Coachmakers' Hall mainly upon Poetry . . . [They] would, necessarily, embrace criticisms on Shakspere, Milton, and all the chief and most popular poets of our language, from Chaucer, for whom he had great reverence, down to Campbell, for whom he had little admiration.

[For Notes of Coleridge's Lectures, *see* below, 1818.]

1811. Douce, Francis. *Preface* to The Customs of London, otherwise called Arnold's Chronicle, p. x.

In an anonymous, but by no means incurious, Liliputian volume, published about the year 1763, and intitled, 'A short account of the first rise and progress of Printing, with a compleat list of the first books that were printed,' is the following confused and extraordinary passage—The author is speaking, though most inaccurately, of Arnold's Chronicle.— 'In this the Nut-brown Maid, supposed by Chaucer as Skelton confirms, by having had a copy given him by Lidgate, Monk of Bury. Mr. Prior has made a paraphrase on it, and has also printed it from the old English, but knew not that it was by Chaucer; . . . The author . . . seems to quote this unaccountable jargon from 'Lord Pembroke's manuscript notes before his Book of St. Albans' . . . Adopting, probably, the mistake of the above writer, the editor of a work intitled, 'Mêlanges de poésie Angloise,' 1764, 12°, has given a very dull prose translation of Prior's beautiful version, which he calls 'Poème imité de la Belle Brune, de Chaucer.' So much for French accuracy !

[*See* below, App. A. [1763], for the 'Short Account,' and below, end of App. B., for the 'Mêlanges.']

[1811.] Dyer, George. *On the Connection and Mutual Assistance of the Arts and Sciences, and the Relation of Poetry to them all,* [in] The Reflector, vol. i, no. ii, art. vii, p. 358.

. . . Chaucer, the first of our poets, on reference to the change of our language from the Saxon, of much account, was well acquainted with all the literature of his time, and with something better.

1811. { **Field**, Barron.
 Hunt, James Henry Leigh. } *Is it justifiable to reprint the Pruriencies of our Old Poets?—The Question discussed in a Dialogue* [in] The Reflector, vol. i, no. 2, art. x, pp. 366, 371.

[Discussion on Chalmers's edition of the English Poets. Difficulty of old orthography in reading Chaucer, p. 366. Indecencies of Chaucer not of a seductive kind, p. 371.]

1811. **Lamb**, Charles. *The Genius and Character of Hogarth*, [in] The Reflector, No. iii, 1811. (The Works of Charles and Mary Lamb, ed. E. V. Lucas, 1903–5, 6 vols., vol. i, p. 77 [text from Works, 1818].)

There remains a very numerous class of his [Hogarth's] performances, the object of which must be confessed to be principally comic. But in all of them will be found something to distinguish them from the droll productions of Bunbury and others. They have this difference, that we do not merely laugh at, we are led into long trains of reflection by them. In this respect they resemble the characters of Chaucer's *Pilgrims*, which have strokes of humour in them enough to designate them for the most part as comic, but our strongest feeling still is wonder at the comprehensiveness of genius which could crowd, as poet and painter have done, into one small canvas so many diverse yet co-operating materials.

1811. **Malcolm**, James Peller. *Anecdotes of the Manners and Customs of London from the Roman Invasion to the Year 1700*, pp. 110–11, 468.

[Quotations from *Chanouns Yemannes Prol.*, on alchemy, and from *Wife of Bath's Prol.*, as a specimen of versification.]

1811. **Robinson**, Henry Crabb. *Diary, Reminiscences, and Correspondence*, 3 vols., 1869, vol. i, p. 324.

March 30th.—At C. Lamb's. Found Coleridge and Hazlitt there . . . In apology for Southey's review of Godwin's " Life of Chaucer " Coleridge ingeniously observed that persons who are themselves very pure, are sometimes on that account *blunt* in their moral feelings.

1811. **Sherwen**, John. *On the Authenticity of Rowley's Poems*, [in] The Gentleman's Magazine, May, vol. lxxxi, p. 428 ; June, pp. 515–16.

[Note on Chaucerian ' graythe ' and ' ay ' (egg) and Rowleian ' gratche,' controverting Tyrwhitt.]

1811. Sherwen, John. *Review of Jamieson's Etymological Dictionary,* [in] The Gentleman's Magazine, July 1811, pp. 26–7; Oct. 1811, pp. 324–5 ; Suppl. to vol. lxxxi, p. 612.

A modern Scotticism is an antient Anglicism . . . Whoever has a doubt of this . . . let him put a volume of Chaucer . . . into the hands of an intelligent Scotch gardener, who will have little occasion for a glossary to explain the real old English words and phrases, though he may frequently require it for the affected Frenchified ones. Chaucer has been censured by Verstegan as a corrupter, rather than an illuminator of the English tongue : [Quotation; see above, vol. i, p. 176.]

The testimony of Mr. Rymer, in a fanciful panegyric on Chaucer, confirms the censure of Verstegan. 'Chaucer threw in Latin, French, Provençal, and other languages, like *new stum*, to raise a fermentation.'   See his 'Short View of Tragedy' [*q.v.* above, vol. i, p. 265].   This may be pretty as a simile, but as an argument it is ridiculous; for Sir Hugh Evans and Dr. Caius might have been equally entitled to the compliment. . . .

[p. 27]   . . . The impracticability of rooting out the language of a country is visible in the necessity that Chaucer was under of writing in English, in order to be generally understood.

[p. 234]   'Araced, *part.* rubbed, hurt.'

'The shippes and the stockes *arraced* with the flode, moten assemblen,' etc. Chaucer's Boethius, p. 396. [Boethius, book iii, Prose xi, l. 165, ed. Skeat.]

Chaucer's meaning is neither '*rubbed*' nor '*hurt*,' but carried away by the flood.

[p. 325]   [*Bargain* synonymous in Chaucer with battle. Rom. of the Rose, ll. 2549–51 quoted.]

[p. 612]   [Drouery or Droorie connotes a pledging of truth. Sir Thopas, l. 184, and Rom. of the Rose, ll. 5051–64 quoted.]

1811. Southey, Robert. *Letter to Walter Savage Landor.* (Life and Correspondence, ed. C. C. Southey, 1850, vol. iii, p. 295.)

Your abhorrence of Spencer is a strange heresy. I admit that he is inferior to Chaucer (who for variety of power has no competitor except Shakspeare), but he is the great master of English versification. . . . Surely Chaucer is as much a poet as it was possible for him to be when the language was in so rude a state.

1811. Trotter, John Bernard. *Memoirs of the latter years of the Right Honourable Charles James Fox*, pp. 395, 425.

[p. 395]   Among the ancient English poets he [Fox] entertained a sincere veneration for Chaucer, a poet in tenderness and natural description, resembling Euripides.

[p. 425]   The days and evenings were now [1806] devoted to reading [aloud to Fox] *Palamon and Arcite* improved by Dryden, Johnson's lives of the poets,—the Æneid,—and Swift's Poetry.

[*See also* below, App. A., 1800.]

[*n.b.* **1811.**] **Unknown.** *Chaucer's Canterbury Tales, with the Tales of Gamelyn and Beryn, modernized* (unpublished).

[Specimen from the *Prioresses* Tale :]
> Among these children was a widow's son,
> A little sprout of clerkship, seven years old,
> Whose daily joy it was to school to run ;
> And if he chanced an image to behold
> Of Christ's blest mother, as he had been told
> He ought, he never failed to kneel and say
> An Ave Maria as he past the way.

[Vol. ii of the MS. of this modernization came into the possession of Prof. Dowden in 1880. Dr. Furnivall wrote to the Academy (*q. v.* below, 1880) to inquire if anything was known of the author or of vol. i, but, as far as is known, without result. The watermark of the paper is dated 1811.]

1811. Warton, Joseph, and **Warton,** John. *The Poetical Works of John Dryden, with notes by the late Rev. Joseph Warton, D.D., and the Rev. John Warton, M.A., and others,* vol. iii, notes.

[Notes on Palamon and Arcite, the Flower and the Leaf, and the Wife of Bath's Tale ; The Reeve's, Miller's, Shipman's, Merchant's and Sumnour's Tales, and the Wife of Bath's Prologue, are omitted from this edition.

Dr. Joseph Warton : pp. 55 ('Chaucer more than 60 years old, and Dryden 70, when they wrote Palamon'), 172–3 (quotes Dr. Akenside's lines to be placed under Chaucer's statue at Woodstock), 211 (strange that Dryden does not mention The Flower and The Leaf among his modernizations from Chaucer).

Rev. John Warton : pp. 61, 72, 75, 77, 78, 81, 89, 92, 106, 112, 113, 118, 119, 122, 127, 135, 138, 147, 155, 161, 211, 214, 219, 233, 251 ; these are nearly all quotations from Chaucer's original text.]

1812. The Prologue and Characters of Chaucer's Pilgrims, selected from his Canterbury Tales ; intended to illustrate a particular design of Mr. William Blake, which is engraved by himself, and may be seen at Mr. Colnaghi's.

[Text from Speght, 1687 ; translation from Ogle, 1741, pp. iv, 61.]

1812. Beloe, William. *Anecdotes of Literature and Scarce Books,* vol. vi (1812), pp. 49, 50, 221 [quotation from Brathwaite's *Commentary,* 1665, *q. v.* above, vol. i, p. 242].

[For vol. ii, *see* below, App. A., 1807.]

1812. Brydges, Sir Samuel Egerton. *The British Bibliographer,* 4 vols., 1810–14, vols. ii, iii, 1812 ; vol. ii, pp. vi, 1–10, 94, 200, 272, 628; vol. iii, pp. 6, 95, 180, 202 *n.*, 205 *n.*, 268 *n.*, 305, 317, 376, 383.

[The references are nearly all contained in the pieces by old writers reprinted in *The British Bibliographer,* and will be found under their authors above, in vol. i, and below, in App. A. For vol. i of *The British Bibliographer see* above, 1810; vol. iv contains no Chaucer reference.]

[vol. ii,　[Reprint of articles on Gower and Chaucer from Leland's
pp. 1–10.　*Commentarii de Scriptoribus Britannicis.*]
[vol. iii,
p. 180.]　[Chaucer and Masuccio probably indebted to some one earlier fabulist for the plot of *The Milleres Tale.*

1812. Crabbe, George. *Preface* to *Tales in Verse.* (The Life and Poetical Works of George Crabbe, by his Son, 1901, pp. 273–4.)

[p. 273]　It may probably be remarked, that Tales, however dissimilar, might have been connected by some associating circumstances to which the whole number might bear equal affinity, and that examples of such union are to be found in Chaucer, in Boccace, and other collectors and inventors of Tales. . . . To imitate the English poet, characters must be found adapted to their several relations, and this is a point of great difficulty and hazard : much allowance seems to be required even for Chaucer himself ; since it is difficult to conceive that on any occasion the devout and delicate Prioress, the courtly and valiant Knight, and 'the poure good Man the persone of a Towne,' would be the voluntary companions of the drunken Miller, the licentious Sumpnour, and 'the Wanton Wife of Bath,' and enter into that colloquial and travelling intimacy which, if a common pilgrimage to the shrine of St. Thomas may be said to excuse, I know nothing beside (and certainly nothing in these times) that would produce such effect. . . . To have followed the method of Chaucer might have been of use, but could scarcely be adopted, from its difficulty.

[p. 274]　That those poets should so entirely engross the title as to exclude those who address their productions to the plain sense and sober judgment of their readers, rather than to their fancy and imagination, I must repeat that I am unwilling to admit . . . All that kind of satire wherein character is skilfully delineated must (this criterion being allowed) no longer

be esteemed as genuine poetry . . . A considerable part of
the poems, as they have hitherto been denominated, of
Chaucer, are of this naked and unveiled character : and there
are in his Tales many pages of coarse, accurate, and minute,
but very striking description.

1812. **Dibdin,** Thomas Frognall. *Typographical Antiquities* . . . begun
by Joseph Ames and augmented by William Herbert, and now
enlarged with copious notes, vol. ii, pp. 514, 515-20 [Chaucer's
Works, 1526], 521-5 [The Canterbury Tales, Pynson, n.d.].
[For vol. i, *see* above, 1810 ; for vols. iii and iv, below, 1816 and
1819. For Ames' original edn. of 1749 *see* vol. i, p. 398 ; for
Herbert's intermediate edn. *see* vol. i, 1785, p. 477 ; 1786, p. 483 ;
1790, p. 491.]

1812. **D'Israeli,** Isaac. *Calamities of Authors,* 2 vols., vol. i, pp. 61, 99 ;
vol. ii, p. 46. [In the edition by the Earl of Beaconsfield, 1867,
the references are pp. 28, 41, 130.]
[i, 61. Reference to Stowe's labours on Chaucer.]
[i, 99. Cowley's ashes deposited between those of Chaucer and
Spenser.]
[ii, 46. Quotation from Harvey's *Foure Letters: q.v.* above,
vol. i, p. 134.]

1812. **Ellis,** Sir Henry. *Preface* to *A Catalogue of the Lansdowne
MSS. in the British Museum,* Part i, p. xi.

In poetry . . . is a very fair and perfect copy, also on
vellum, of the Canterbury Tales of Chaucer [No. 851], written
about the reign of Henry the Fifth, in the initial letter of
which is a full-length portrait of the author.

[For the entry for this manuscript, which occurs in Part ii of the Catalogue, *see*
below, 1819.]

1812. **Galt,** John. *Life and Administration of Cardinal Wolsey,* pp.
191 *n.,* 194 *n.*

[p. 191 *n.*] I have never been able to bring myself to entertain any
feeling approximating to respect for the works of Chaucer,
Gower, and Lydgate, and the other tribe of rhymers that preceded the reign of Henry VIII. They seem to me to have
acquired their fame before the nation knew anything of poetry,
and to have remained famous when their works are no longer
read. There is a little sprinkling here and there of *naïveté* in
Chaucer, but his lists and catalogues of circumstances are anything but poetry. Lydgate is bare naked prose. . . .

1812. [Hunt, James Henry Leigh.]   *The Feast of the Poets,* [in] **The** Reflector, vol. ii, no. 4, p. 322.

> I must mention, however, that during the wine,
> The mem'ry of Shakspeare was toasted with nine;
> To Chaucer were five, and to Spenser one more,
> And Milton had seven, and Dryden had four. . . .

[For the book-editions of this, *see* below, 1814 and 1815.]

1812. P.   *Tabard Inn,* [in] The Gentleman's Magazine, Sept., p. **217.** *See* below, App. A.

1812. Southey, Robert.   *Omniana,* vol. i, pp. 192, 254-6.

[p. 254]   [No. 135, *Early English Metre.*] Mr. Weber observes upon the passage [from 'Octouian Imperator,' with rhyme 'Jame' and 'fra me'] that 'this singular rhyme strongly supports the opinion of Wallis and Tyrwhitt in his Essay on the versification of Chaucer, that the final *e* which is at present mute, was anciently pronounced obscurely like the *e* feminine of the French. . . .' [Quotation from *Troilus and Creseide,* i, 1–5, follows.]

[p. 255]   [136. *Troilus and Creseide.*]

It is evident from the first stanza of this poem (just quoted), when the narrator says 'er that I part froy,' that Chaucer intended it for one of his Canterbury Tales, and this seems to be confirmed by the 65th stanza of the first book.

> For aie the nere the fire the hotter is,
> *This (trow I) knoweth all this companie.*

I do not know whether this has been observed before. A compleat and faithful edition of the works of this great father of English poetry, with an accurate verbal index, as well as glossary, is much to be desired.

1812. Unknown.   *Review* of Galt's *Life of Cardinal Wolsey,* [in] The Quarterly Review, September, 1812, vol. viii, p. 170.

[Galt says] 'I have never been able to bring my self to entertain any feeling approximating to respect for the works of Chaucer, Gower, or Lydgate, and the other tribe of rhymers that preceded the reign of Henry VIII.' If Mr. Galt came into the world without faculties to understand or an heart to feel the sublimity and pathos, or even the wit and humour, of Chaucer, or to distinguish those qualities from the tame mediocrity of Gower, and the tedious insipidity of Lydgate, who can help it?

[For Galt, *see* above, 1812.]

1813. Brand, John [or **Ellis,** Sir Henry ?]. *Observations on Popular Antiquities* (revised by Henry Ellis), 2 vols., vol. i, pp. 47 *n.*, 65 *n.*, 114 *n.*, 215 *n.*, 418 *n.*, 428–9 *n.*, 473 *n.* ; vol. ii, pp. 61–2 *n.*, 100, 116 *n.*, 136 *n.*, 139, 290, 296, 322–3 *n.*, 342–3 *n.*, 673 [mostly illustrative quotations from Chaucer].

1813. Thurlow, Edward Hovell, Lord. *Sylva,* [in] *Poems on Several Occasions* . . . Second edition, p. 148. [Not in 1st edition (also of 1813).]

> Who have been great, in this our mortal clime,
> Begirt around by the loud-voiced sea ?
> Why sacred Chaucer, that, in homely rhyme,
> First held the lamp up to Posterity :
> Then Spenser, in whose rich Virgilian strain
> The moral Virtues are disposed fair :
> Then glorious Milton, who surpass'd his reign
> In depths of Hell and in th' Olympick air :
> But, most of all, and to our wond'ring eyes,
> And to the eyes of all futurity,
> Great Shakspeare stands, that was by Nature wise,
> And made a spoil of his posterity ;
> When he was born, great Nature did her most,
> And when he died, the World's delight was lost !

1813. Whitaker, Thomas Dunham. *Visio Willī de Petro Plouhman,* Introduction, pp. vi, vii, xxxvi, xliii, xlvi, xlvii–xlviii, and several references in notes and glossary.

[p. vi]   His contemporaries, Chaucer and Gower, repose beneath magnificent tombs, but Langland (if such were really his name) has no other monument than that which, having framed for himself, he left to posterity to appropriate.

[p. vii]   Under the refining hand of Chaucer, indeed, it [English] became almost a new language.

[p. xxxvi]   The æra of this Vision is now ascertained to have preceded the great work of Chaucer by twenty years.

[p. xliii]   [Note on Tyrwhitt's suggestion that Spenser meant to allude to the *Ploughman's Tale* rather than to *Piers Plowman* in the Epilogue to the *Shepherd's Calendar.*]

[p. xlvi]   [Quotations from Warton's Observations on Spenser, mentioning Gower and Chaucer in connexion with *Piers Plowman.*]

[pp. xlvii–xlviii]   [Long note, wherein Whitaker defends his position that the author of the Visions must be considered the first English poet. The fact that the *Canterbury Tales* were not published (according to Tyrwhitt) till 1381, and that Chaucer was 34 years old in 1362, is Whitaker's main evidence that *Piers Plowman* negatives his right to be termed first of English Poets.]

1814. Berington, Joseph. *A Literary History of the Middle Ages,* book vi, pp. 447–457 [biographical notice and critical appreciation].

[p. 450] Our Chaucer is read, not as a poet—who delights by the richness of his imagery, or the harmony of his numbers—but as a writer who has pourtrayed with truth, the manners, customs, and habits of the age. Such . . . was my own judgment, at least, when, some years ago, I was prevailed upon to peruse him.

[p. 452] His works, of which the *Canterbury Tales* form the most original portion, are in every one's hands : but I would willingly learn by how many they have been read ; and particularly by how many with the feeling of delight.

1814. Cary, Henry Francis. *The Vision . . . of Dante,* translated by H. F. Cary. 3 vols., 1814. [First complete edition.] Vol. i, notes, pp. 156, 157, 160, 179, 182, 211, 214, 216 ; vol. ii, notes, pp. 159, 172, 174, 194, 212 ; vol. iii, notes, pp. 157, 158, 187, 190, 202. [Mainly illustrative quotations from Chaucer ; for the earlier edition of the Inferno alone (with the Italian text) *see* above, 1805–6.]

1814. Dunlop, John Colin. *The History of Fiction,* ed. 2, 1816 (first in B.M.), 3 vols., vol. ii, pp. 143–4, 146, 220, 228, 235–7, 248, 300–1, 319–20, 335–6, 342–4, 349, 352, 382–4, 488. (Ed. 1888, 2 vols., vol. i, pp. 131, 440–1 ; vol. ii, pp. 20, 50, 56, 60, 68, 109–10, 122–5, 135, 140–1, 146, 148, 207, 240.)

[vol. ii, p. 146] Some writers have considered the Sir Thopas of Chaucer as a prelude to the work of Cervantes. It may be much to the honour of the English poet that he so early discerned and ridiculed the absurdities of his contemporary romancers, but it cannot be conceived that Sir Thopas had any effect in discrediting their compositions.

[p. 220] [The outline of the *Pardoneres Tale* taken from the *Cento Novelle,* 82.]

[p. 236] If the frame in which Boccaccio has set his Decameron be compared with that in which the Canterbury Tales have been enclosed by Chaucer, who certainly imitated the Italian novelist, it will be found that the time chosen by Boccaccio is infinitely preferable to that adopted by the English poet. The pilgrims of the latter relate their stories on a journey, though they are on horseback, and are twenty-nine in number; and it was intended, had the author completed his plan, that this rabble should have told the remainder of their tales in an abominable tavern at Canterbury. On the other hand, the Florentine assembly discourse in tranquillity and retirement . . . But then the frame of Chaucer afforded a much greater opportunity of displaying a variety of striking and dramatic characters, and thence of introducing characteristic tales. His assemblage is mixed and fortuitous, and his travellers are distinguished from each other both in person and character. Even his serious pilgrims are marked by their several sorts [p. 237] of gravity, and the ribaldry of his low characters is different. 'I see,' says Dryden, 'every one of the pilgrims in the Canterbury Tales as distinctly as if I had supped with them.' All the company in the Decameron, on the other hand, are fine ladies and gentlemen of Florence, who retire to enjoy the sweets of select society, and who would scarcely have tolerated the intrusion of such figures as the Miller or the Sompnour.

[pp. 300–1] [Boccaccio's Fra Cipolla (Decam. vi, 10) compared with Chaucer's Pardoner, and quotation of Prol. ll. 701–4.]

The incidents in the novel of Boccaccio [Decam. vii, 9] concerning the pear-tree . . . have . . . some resemblance to the Merchant's Tale in Chaucer, and by consequence to Pope's January and May.

[p. 342] This story of Boccaccio [Decam. x, 5] is the origin of the Frankelein's Tale of Chaucer, in which the circumstances are precisely the same as in the Decameron, except that the impossible thing required of the lady is, that her lover should remove the rocks from the coast of Britany [*sic*]: a similar tale, however, according to Tyrwhitt, occurs in an old Breton lay, from which he conceives the incidents may have come immediately to the English poet . . .

[p. 343] The tale of Boccaccio is supposed by the editor of Beaumont and Fletcher to be also the origin of the Triumph of Honour . . . but it is more probable that these dramatists [p. 344] took their plot from the Frankelein's Tale in Chaucer, as the impossible thing required in the Triumph of Honour, by

Dorigen from her lover Martius, is that a mass of rocks should be converted into 'a Champain field.'

[p. 349]   [The Clerkes tale derived from Boccaccio (Decam. x, 10) through Petrarch.]

1814. Hazlitt, William.   *On Posthumous Fame,* [in] The Examiner, May 22, 1814.   [Reprinted in the 'Round Table,' 1817.]   (Collected Works of William Hazlitt, ed. Waller and Glover, 1902–6, 13 vols., vol. i, p. 23.)

Chaucer seems to have derived his notions of fame more immediately from the reputation acquired by the Italian poets, his contemporaries, which had at that time spread itself over Europe.

1814. Hazlitt, William.   *Why the Arts are not Progressive?*   [A fragment composed of articles from the Morning Chronicle and the Champion, Jan. 11 and 15, and Sept. 11, 1814.   Reprinted in the 'Round Table,' 1817.]   (Collected Works of William Hazlitt, ed. Waller and Glover, 1902, 13 vols., vol. i, pp. 161–3.)

[p. 161]   Homer, Chaucer, Spenser [and a list of others] all lived near the beginning of their arts—perfected, and all but created them.

[p. 162]   Nature is the soul of art . . . It was the same trust in nature that enabled Chaucer to describe the patient sorrow of Griselda ; or the delight of that young beauty in the Flower and the Leaf, shrouded in her bower, and listening, in the morning of the year, to the singing of the nightingale. . . .

1814. Hunt, James Henry Leigh.   *Essay on Washerwomen,* [in] The Seer, p. 42.   [Reprinted in 1841, also in the 'Round Table,' by W. Hazlitt and Leigh Hunt, 1817, vol. ii, p. 181.]

The greatest master of detached portrait is Steele ; but his pictures too form a sort of link in a chain.   Perhaps the completest specimen of what we mean in the English language is Shenstone's *School-Mistress,* by far his best production . . . But what?   Are we leaving out *Chaucer?*   Alas, we thought to be doing something a little original, and find it all existing already, and in unrivalled perfection, in his portraits of the Canterbury Pilgrims!   We can only dilate, and vary upon his principle.

1814. Hunt, James Henry Leigh. *The Feast of the Poets, with Notes . . . by the Editor of the Examiner*, p. 19, [Notes] pp. 121, 122.

[p. 19]   'Twould be tedious to count all the names as they rose,
But none were omitted you'll eas'ly suppose,
Whom Fancy has crown'd with one twig of the bay,
From old father Chaucer to Collins and Gray.

[Notes] [pp. 121, 122]   Of the studious disposition of all our greatest poets we have complete evidence.   Chaucer's eagle in the House of Fame accuses him of being so desperate a student, that he takes no heed of anybody, and reads till he looks stupid ;
[Here follows a quotation, beginning :]
. . . No tidinges comin to the, . . .
[and ending]   And al so dombe as any stone
Thou sittest at anothir boke,
Tyl fully dasid is thy loke.   [v. 140.]
Chaucer however, was too true a poet not to read nature as well as books, as his writings abundantly testify, both in character and description.   Milton and Spenser were both men of learning, and, what is rarer for poets, men of business ; and so indeed was Chaucer . . . Chaucer revels in morning scenery.

[Compare with this the text as printed in the *Reflector*, 1812, above, and in the second edition, 1815, below.]

1814. Manning, Owen, and **Bray**, William. *The History and Antiquities of the County of Surrey. . . .* Begun by the late Rev. Owen Manning . . . enlarged and continued to the year 1814, by William Bray of Shire, 3 vols., 1804–14, vol. iii, p. 551, Southwark.

This being the great thoroughfare for all persons passing to *London* from *Kent, Surrey*, and *Sussex*, has been always noted for a number of inns to accommodate travellers.   That mentioned by *Chaucer*, as the place from which he set out with the pilgrims whose stories he relates in his *Canterbury Tales*, has had so much said of it by different authors, that it is unnecessary to say more here, than that the sign was then the *Tabard ;* that is, a military or herald's coat without sleeves ; but that it was long ago converted into that of a dog, which by corruption of the original name, has since been known by the name of a Talbot, and is designated by a spotted dog. This name it still bears.   On the frieze of the beam whereon the sign hung, till removed on forming the new pavement, about 1767, was inscribed, 'This is the Inne where Sir *Jeffrey Chaucer* and the nine and twenty pilgrims lay in their journey to *Canterbury anno* 1383.' An inscription to this purport is still in the yard. It is near St. *Margaret's Hill.* . . .

1814. [**Peacock**, Thomas Love.] *Sir Proteus: a Satirical Ballad,* by P. M. O'Donovan, Esq., stanza i. (Works of Thomas Love Peacock, ed. Cole, 1875, vol. iii, p. 117.)

> Oh ! list to me : for I'm about
>   To catch the fire of *Chaucer,*
> And spin in doleful measure out
>   The tale of Johnny Raw, sir.

1814. Scott, Sir Walter. *Essay on Border Antiquities.* [Introduction to] Border Antiquities of England and Scotland. (Miscellaneous Prose Works of Sir Walter Scott, Edinburgh, 1834–71, 30 vols., vol. vii, pp. 32–3.)

The northern minstrels' . . . earliest attempts at poetry were . . . formed on alliteration ; and as late as the time of Chaucer it was considered as the mark of a northern man to 'affect the letter.'

[p. 33]   [Reference in footnote to 'rom ram ruf,' Parson's Prol., ed. Skeat, ll. 42–4.]

1814. Scott, Sir Walter. *Memoirs of Jonathan Swift, D.D.* (Miscellaneous Prose Works of Sir Walter Scott, Edinburgh, 1834–71, 30 vols., vol. ii, pp. 305 *n.*, 414.)

[p. 305 *n.*] [Reference to, and quotation from, an imitation of Chaucer by Dr. Arbuthnot in 'Critical Remarks on Captain Gulliver's Travels,' *q.v.* below, App. A. 1735, Arbuthnot.]

[p. 414]   Chaucer appears also to have been his favourite, for I observe among his papers a memorandum of the oaths used in the Canterbury Tales, classed with the personages by whom they are used.

[Footnote] 'Mr. Walter Scott informs us (Life of Swift, p. 465) that Chaucer was a favourite of Swift, and that he had observed among his papers a Memorandum of the oaths used in the Canterbury Tales. Mr. Scott was so obliging as to transmit to me an imitation, but by no means a successful one, of the style of this early English poet. The attempt was in the handwriting of Swift, I have been so unfortunate as to have lost . . . the document' . . . Monck Mason.
[*See* below, App. A., *a.* 1740, Swift.]

1814. Southey, Robert. *Notes* for a series of Inscriptions in honour of English Poets, [printed in] Preface, by Herbert Hill, to Southey's *Oliver Newman*, 1845, pp. x–xi.

Tuesday, 6th Sept. 1814. Inscriptions for the Poetical Ground of these Kingdoms ; *i. e.* a tribute of respect to all those poets who deserve it. This, I think, would be a worthy task.

Chaucer—at Woodstock ? Blenheim will become an empty name, and that palace a pile of ruins, while he remains.

1814. [**Southey,** Robert ?] *Review* of Chalmers' *English Poets,* [in] The Quarterly Review, July 1814, vol. xi, pp. 482–4 ; Oct., vol. xii, pp. 61, 64, 65, 67. 69, 73, 82–4.

[The passage on Chaucer's rejection of the ornate style at the end of the following extract echoes Southey's words in his *Specimens,* q.v. above, 1807, closely enough to warrant the provisional attribution of this review to him.]

[vol. xi,   Chaucer himself was a star of the first magnitude : no
p. 482]   man ever did so much with a language in so rude a state, and only Shakespeare has surpassed him in his intuitive know-ledge of human character, and the universality of his genius. Mr. Chalmers indeed, with that comfortable self-satisfaction which he derives from flourishing in the nineteenth century, when the world has the advantage of being enlightened by lectures on poetry, assures us that Chaucer's popularity is gone by :—it may be so with those ladies and gentlemen who conceive poetry to be ' the art of pleasing,' and believe that nothing which requires thought can possibly give pleasure. Chaucer has not written for critics and readers of this nature :
. . . the rank which the father of English poetry holds in literature has not been assigned by caprice, or fashion, or superstition. He whom Spenser called his master, and whom Milton referred to as to his great and immortal prede-cessor, is justly placed with them in the first class of poets, and his fame, like theirs, is for ever. It is a reproach to our literature that the Canterbury Tales should be the only portion of his works which have been edited with any degree of care or ability.

[vol. xii,   He [the author of *The Cid*] built with rubbish and
p. 64]   unhewn stones ; Dante and Petrarca with marble. Chaucer's materials more resembled those of the Spaniard than of the Italian poets. This has been in some degree unfortunate for himself, inasmuch as the progressive improvement of our

tongue has at length rendered him obsolete, (or rather caused him to be thought so,) and thus deprived him of that extensive and pre-eminent popularity which he long and deservedly enjoyed. . . .

[p. 65]   Chaucer drew much from the French and Italian poets, but more from observation and the stores of his own wealthy and prolific mind. Strong English sense, and strong English humour characterize his original works. He caught with a painter's hand the manners and features of the age ; he beheld the objects of external nature with a poet's eye, and he penetrated with a poet's intuition into the recesses of the human heart. Dante holds a higher place in literature because he wrought with materials which were capable of displaying and preserving his exquisite skill. Dante may be classed above all other poets for strength and severity of style : Nothing can be worse than the plan of the Divina Commedia ; the matter is sometimes puerile, sometimes shocking, frequently dull, but the style is uniformly perfect. Here Chaucer falls short of him, but only here, where, from the state of the English language, it was impossible that he should prove his equal : in extent and variety of power he is greatly his superior.

[During the 15th century] there could be little encouragement for poetry, and what was produced chiefly consisted either of dull translations, or vapid imitations of Chaucer. The 'style ornate' had been introduced, and was sanctioned by Chaucer's name : of the poems in that style which are printed as his, many are of questionable authority ; few traces of it are to be found in his greater and better works ; and it seems probable that he just tried the experiment, and convinced himself of its unfitness.

1814. Thurlow, Edward Hovell, Lord. *Moonlight, a Poem, with Several Copies of Verses,* p. 21. [There is another edition of this poem, also of 1814 ; the title runs differently—'Moonlight, the Doge's Daughter, Ariadne,' etc.]

[The author asks his Muse : Where are now the great poets of Italy ?]

> Or, if we turn to England in our thought,
> Tell me where Chaucer may be found ? or where
> Sweet Spenser, that from rebels fled to death,
> His heart quite broken with the faulty time ? . . .

1814. Unknown. *Review* of Ginguené's *Histoire Littéraire d'Italie*, and Sismondi's *De la Littérature du Midi de l'Europe*, [in] The Quarterly Review, April 1814, vol. xi, p. 22.

To the English reader it [the Theseide] presents the additional interest, of being the model of the ' Knight's Tale ' of Chaucer, and the origin therefore of one of the noblest poems in our language, the ' Palamon and Arcite ' of Dryden.

1814. Unknown. *Review* of Mathias's edition of Mason's *Life and Writings of Gray*, [in] The Quarterly Review, July 1814, vol. xi, p. 315.

[Comparison is made between a line in Gray, and a line from the Reve's Prologue :

" Even in our ashes live their wonted fires."
Gray, Mason's ed. p. 67.
" Even in our ashen cold is fire ywreken."
Chauc. Reve's Tale, ed. Tyrwhitt, l. 3180.]

[For this old comparison *see* above, vol. i, p. 465, 1782, Dodsley.]

1814. Unknown. *Review* of Dunlop's *History of Fiction*, [in] The Edinburgh Review, Nov. 1814, vol. xxiv, p. 46.

[With a few exceptions] by far the best fictitious narratives in existence are poems. And a history of Mathematics which should exclude Archimedes and Newton, would not be more extraordinary than a history of Fiction which excludes Homer, Hesiod, Virgil, Lucian, Ariosto, Tasso, Chaucer, Spenser, Milton, Scott, Campbell and Byron.

1814. Wordsworth, William. *Second Tour in Scotland ; Yarrow visited,* [in] Memoirs of William Wordsworth, by Christopher Wordsworth, 1851, 2 vols., vol. ii, p. 30. (Poetical Works, ed. W. Knight, 1896, 8 vols, vol. vi, p. 36.)

The old man [Dr. Anderson, the editor of the British Poets] was passionately fond of poetry, though with not much of discriminating judgment, as the volumes he edited sufficiently show. . . . Through these volumes I became first familiar with Chaucer.

1815–16. Brydges, Sir Samuel Egerton. *Restituta,* 4 vols., 1814–16, vol. i, Preface [dated March 28, 1815], p. x. ; vol. ii, pp. 138, 140, 508 ; vol. iv, pp. 29, 168, 199 [quotations on Chaucer from old writers].

But such is the brilliance of primary genius, that even the darkest ages will not repress the appearances of its true character. What vivid pictures does Chaucer give us ! What a selection of circumstances! What animation of manner, and language! How does he bring out the prominent traits in the characters which he so happily draws in his *Canterbury Tales*; while we see the whole merry group on their journey, as if we were accompanying them along the Kentish road!

1815. **Dibdin**, Thomas Frognall. *Bibliotheca Spenceriana*, 4 vols., 1814–15; vol. iv, 1815, pp. 288–319, 426–31.

[Lengthy bibliographical descriptions, with extracts and facsimiles, of Caxton's editions of the Canterbury Tales; ed. 1, pp. 288–92, No. 868; ed. 2, pp. 292–309, No. 869, with facsimiles of the cuts of the characters; Boecius, pp. 310–12, No. 870; Book of Fame, pp. 312–19, No. 871; Troylus, p. 319, No. 872; of Pynson's ed. of the Canterbury Tales, pp. 426–31, No. 917.]

1815. **G[riffiths]**, A[cton] F[rederick]. *Bibliotheca Anglo-Poetica;* or a descriptive catalogue of a rare and rich collection of Early English Poetry in the possession of Longman, Hurst, Rees, Orme and Brown, etc. [formerly Park's collection], pp. 36–40, 431–2, nos. 84–96, 898–901.

[No. 84, Canterbury Tales, Pynson, n.d., imperfect at beginning, £25; the portrait of Chaucer is reproduced. No. 85, Works, Bonham, n.d., £7 7s.; Ritson is quoted for the date 1542 for this edn., and Tyrwhitt for the spuriousness of the Plowman's Tale, which first appeared in it. Nos. 86, 87, Works, 1598, £3 10s. and £2 12s. 6d. No. 88, Works, 1602, £4 4s. No. 89, Works, ed. Urry, 1721, £1 15s. No. 90, item, large paper, £3 3s.; "The Coke's Tale of Gamelyn" and "The Merchant's Second Tale, or the History of Beryn," included in this edn., non-Chaucerian, but praised by Ritson. No. 91, Canterbury Tales, ed. Tyrwhitt, 1775–8, £6 16s. 6d. No. 92, item, with proof prints from Bell's edn. and portraits of Chaucer and Tyrwhitt, £8 8s.; a note in praise of the edn. follows. No. 93, Canterbury Tales, ed. Tyrwhitt, 1798, £2 10s. No. 94, Canterbury Tales, Ogle's modernized edn., 1741, £1 11s. 6d. No. 95, item, £2 6s. No. 96, The assemble of foules, Wynkyn de Worde, 1530, £50. The book unique; reference to Dr. Billam's letter to Herbert [*see* above, vol. i, p. 483, 1786]; a general note on Chaucer follows, and a quotation of Warton's well-known passage beginning "I consider Chaucer as a genial day in an English Spring." (Supplement.) No. 898, Canterbury Tales, Pynson, 1526, imperfect, £25. No. 899, Works, R. Toye, n.d. (another issue of no. 85), £6 6s. No. 900, Works, Reynes, 1542, £7 7s. No. 901, Works, 1561, £5 5s.]

1815. Hazlitt, William. *On the Ideal,* [in] The Champion, Jan. 8, 1815. (Collected Works of William Hazlitt, ed. Waller and Glover, 1902–6, 13 vols., vol. xi, p. 226.)

Are the admirable descriptions of the kings of Thrace and Inde in Chaucer's Knight's Tale, less poetical, or historical, or ideal, because they are distinguished by traits as characteristic as they are striking ; in their lineaments, their persons, their armour, their other attributes, the one black and broad, the other tall, and fair, and freckled, with yellow crisped locks that glittered as the sun ? The four white bulls, and the lions which accompany them are equally fine, but they are not fine because they present no distinct image to the mind. The effect of this is somehow lost in Dryden's Palamon and Arcite, and the poetry is lost with it.

1815. Hazlitt, William. *Essay on Manners,* [in] The Examiner, Sept. 3, 1815. (Collected Works of William Hazlitt, ed. Waller and Glover, 1902–6, 13 vols., vol. xi, pp. 269–272, 274.)

[p. 269] Nothing can be more striking than the difference of style or manner, where the *matter* remains the same, as in paraphrases and translations. The most remarkable example which occurs to us is in the beginning of the *Flower and Leaf* by Chaucer, and in the modernisation of the same passage by Dryden. . . .

[pp. 270, 271] [Six stanzas of the *Flower and the Leaf* and Dryden's modernization of the same passage are quoted, and the inferiority of Dryden's version is pointed out.]

[p. 272] Compared with Chaucer, Dryden and the rest of that school were merely *verbal poets.* They had a great deal of wit, sense and fancy ; they only wanted truth and depth of feeling.

1815. Hazlitt, William. *Queries relating to the Essay on Population,* [no. 23 of the Round Table series in] The Examiner, Oct. 29, 1815. (Collected Works of William Hazlitt, ed. Waller and Glover, 1902–6, 13 vols., vol. iii, p. 385.)

[Query] 18. Lastly, whether the whole of the reverend author's management of the principle of population and of the necessity of moral restraint, does not seem to have been copied from the prudent friar's advice in Chaucer ?

' Beware therefore with lordes for to play,
　Singeth Placebo :—
　To a poor man men should his vices tell,
　But not to a lord, though he should go to hell.'

1815. Hazlitt, William. *Review* of Sismondi's *Literature of the South,* [in] The Edinburgh Review, June 1815, vol. xxv, pp. 54, 59, 60, 62. (Collected Works of William Hazlitt, ed. Waller and Glover, 1902-6, 13 vols., vol. x, pp. 69, 73-7).

[p. 73] We cannot go on with this splendid catalogue of foreigners without feeling ourselves drawn to the native glories of two of our own writers . . . —we mean Chaucer and Spenser—who are now, we are afraid, as little known to the ordinary run of English readers as their tuneful contemporaries of the South . . .

[There follows, pp. 74-6, a short but good and fresh appreciation of Chaucer, which Hazlitt elaborated and illustrated with quotations in the Lectures of 1818, but leaving some passages unaltered. *See* below, 1818.]

1815. Hunt, James Henry Leigh. *The Descent of Liberty;* a masque, p. 60. [Issued in 1819 as part of vol. i (with date 1816) of Leigh Hunt's Poetical Works.]

Three Gothic seats, in which are enthroned the shapes of Chaucer, Shakespeare, and Milton, crowned with laurel, and holding globes in their hands—the first a terrestrial, the third a celestial, and the second a double one of both.

1815. Hunt, James Henry Leigh. *The Feast of the Poets,* . . . second edition, amended and enlarged, p. 23, Notes [identical as regards the Chaucer reference with those in 1st edition], pp. 120, 121. [Issued in 1819 as part of vol. ii. of Leigh Hunt's Poetical Works; the original title page is dated 1815. *See* above, 1812 and 1814.]

I must mention, however, that during the wine,
The mem'ry of Shakspeare was toasted with nine;
When lo, as each poet was lifting his cup,
A strain of invisible music struck up :—

.   .   .   .

The next name was Chaucer,—and part of the strain
For the glorious old boy was play'd over again.
Then, "Milton!" they cried, with a solemner shout,
When bursting at once in its mightiness out,
The organ came gathering and rolling its thunder.

.   .   .   .

Last followed my Spenser (I wish I'd been there).

1815. Macaulay, Thomas Babington, Lord. *Letter* to his Mother, [dated] Aug. 23, 1815, [in] The Life and Letters of Lord Macaulay by . . . George Otto Trevelyan, 1876. (New ed., 1883, 2 vols., vol. i, p. 59.)

Hear and wonder! I have . . . read Boccaccio's Decameron . . . he is always elegant, amusing, and . . . strikingly delicate and chastised. I prefer him infinitely to Chaucer.

1815. Marsh, Herbert. *Horæ Pelasgicæ*, Part the First, p. 23.

[The Pelasgi spoke] the same *language* with Thucydides himself, though the *form* of it, as used by the Pelasgi, might bear to the form of it in the writings of Thucydides a relation similar to that, which the English of Chaucer bears to the English of Pope.

[This passage is quoted in a review of Marsh's book in the Quarterly Review July, 1815, vol. xiii, p. 346.]

1815. Mitford, Mary Russell. *Letter to Sir William Elford*, July 7, *Life of Mary Russell Mitford*, edited by A. G. L'Estrange, 3 vols., 1870, vol. i, pp. 311, 312.

I have been to see Donnington Castle, the classic ground where Chaucer certainly resided and perhaps wrote some of those exquisite tales which, while they are among the earliest specimens of our language, will undoubtedly endure to the last. Are you an enthusiast for this venerable bard? My admiration for him is very ardent. His poetry seems to me so healthy, so vigorous, so much in the thought, and so little in the expression; his powers are so various, so pliable, ranging at will from the thrilling pathos of Griselda to the wild fancy of 'Cambuscan bold.' . . . Setting Milton and Shakespeare aside, I am not sure that I don't prefer him to almost any writer in the circle of English poetry. I speak, of course, of his best works, and not of his poems *en masse;* but two or three of his " Canterbury Tales," and some select passages from his other productions, are worth all that the age of Queen Anne, our Augustan age as it has been called, ever produced.

[Enclosed in this letter was the following Sonnet :]

On visiting Donnington Castle, said to have been the latest Residence of Chaucer, and celebrated for its Resistance to the Army of the Parliament during the Civil Wars.

Oh for some sprite to lead the ivy band,
High-seated Donnington, around thy towers!
Oh for some sprite to wipe from Chaucer's bowers
The lingering trace of War's deforming hand!

Nature herself hath banished from the land
Such signal.   Here the trench no longer lours,
But, like a bosky dell, bedecked with flowers
And garlanded with May, it seems to stand
A very spot for youthful poet's dreams
In Spring's fair hour : Griselda's mournful lay,
The 'half-told' tale would sound still sweeter here.
Oh for some sprite to hide with ivy spray
War's ravages, and chase the meaner themes
Of King and State, Roundhead and Cavalier.

[See below, 1852, for a passage in Miss Mitford's *Recollections*.]

1815–16. Nott, George Frederick.   *The Works of Henry Howard Earl of Surrey and of Sir Thomas Wyatt the Elder,* 2 vols.

Dissertation on the state of English Poetry before the sixteenth century, vol. i, pp. cxxxvii–clxxvi, clxxxvi *note*, clxxxviii–cxciii, cxc, cxcvi, cxcix, ccxxxi–ii, ccxxxv–vi, ccxliii–vi, ccxlii–vi, ccxlix–li, cclxvii, cclxix–xx, cclxxxv. [In the Notes to the poems there are many references to Chaucer, pointing out passages and lines where Surrey has imitated him.] Notes to Surrey's Poems, vol. i, pp. 234, 236, 238–41, 243, 246–47, 249–50, 252, 257, 259–60, 263–66, 276, 278, 282, 284, 287, 289, 291, 295–97, 302–3, 306–7, 315–16, 318–24, 326, 329–30, 334–35, 337–39, 341, 348–49, 351–52, 356–57, 359, 361, 369, 372–73, 375, 380, 383, 387–88, 398, 401–11, 413, 417, 421, 424–25.

Vol. ii [Wyatt], pp. xxxii, xxxiii and *note*, lxxxvi, cliii and *note*, clix and *note*, clx.   Notes to Wyatt's poems, vol. ii, pp. 538–41, 545–50, 552–53, 555–56, 558, 560–66, 568–72, 574–75, 577, 581–82.

[vol. i, p. clviii] Sect. IV. *Of Chaucer's versification—that his verses were Decasyllables, but rhythmical—of the use and importance of the cæsura in rhythmical versification.*

It seems certain then that our versification anterior to Chaucer, whether the lines were Alexandrine, Octosyllabic, or Alliterative, was uniformly rhythmical.   It now remains to ascertain what were the alterations which Chaucer made. First, he rejected alliteration. . . .   Secondly, he established the practice of always changing the rhyme with the couplet. . . . Thirdly, he introduced the Heroic stanza of seven lines, . . .; a stanza, which for many centuries after was used as the system of verse best suited to serious and elevated subjects. . . .

But the chief improvement introduced by Chaucer into our versification was that of dropping altogether the use of the Alexandrine line, and substituting the line of ten syllables in its stead. . . .

But though Chaucer reduced our verse to ten syllables, he suffered it to retain in other respects the properties of the old Alexandrine verse. Like that it was divided by the old cæsura into hemistichs; had the pause at the end, and was recited rhythmically. It was still what Lydgate called "the verse of Cadence." It is true that many of Chaucer's lines [p.clix] have the appearance of being pure Iambic Decasyllables. This however was the effect of accident. For accent and quantity, which are not of necessity the same, would sometimes coincide, and when they did, a pure Iambic Decasyllable was unavoidably the result. It was the frequent occurrence of these fortuitous Iambic lines that led Mr. Tyrwhitt, and before him Mr. Urry, and the learned Mr. Morell, to believe that Chaucer's system of versification was altogether metrical. But an impartial consideration of the subject, and a reference to good MSS. must I think lead us to conclude that Chaucer had not a metrical system of numbers in contemplation; but that, on the contrary, he designed his verses to be read, like those of all his contemporaries, with a cæsura and rhythmical cadence.

Should it be asked why so many Iambic lines are to be found in Chaucer, the answer is obvious. Our language had become more compressed. Most of the words in common use had dropped their final syllables, and monosyllables were multiplied. This could not but produce a corresponding effect on our versification, and lines of ten syllables would insensibly be written instead of lines of twelve or fourteen. . . .

[Here follow some instances from Manning's, or Robert of Brunne's, continuation of Langtoft's Chronicle, of the mixture of the Alexandrine with verses of ten syllables.]

.   .   .   .

[p. clx]   Manning's use of the Decasyllabic verse, therefore, was partial and accidental. The case was otherwise with Chaucer. He used it uniformly, and upon system. This admits of no doubt. I am not aware that a single instance of the Alexandrine verse occurs in all Chaucer's works; for I fully agree with Mr. Tyrwhitt that the Tale of Gamelyn was not written by Chaucer.

[p. clxi]   To give the reader a clear notion of what I conceive to have been Chaucer's system of versification, I will transcribe the opening lines of the Canterbury Tales, marking as well the cæsura in the middle of each verse as the pause at the end, and also the strongly accented syllables, to shew in what manner rhythmical Decasyllabic verses were, I apprehend, recited.

> Whēn thăt Aprìl ‖ wīth hĭs shōurĕs sòote |
> Thĕ droūght ŏf Màrch ‖ hăd piērcĕd tŏ thĕ ròote |
> And bāthĕd ĕvĕry vèin ‖ ĭn sūch lĭquŏur |
> Of whīch vīrtùe ‖ ĕngēndĕrĕd ĭs thĕ flòur |
> [&c., &c.]

.   .   .   .

That I may not be thought to assume too much in this point without proof, I will adduce some reasons why I consider Chaucer's verses, though Decasyllabic, to have been rhythmical, and not metrical.

First, because a large proportion of them cannot be read as Iambic Decasyllables, without doing the utmost violence to our language ; all which verses are harmonious as verses of cadence, if read with the cæsura rhythmically.   And further, because all those verses might easily by a slight transposition have been made pure Iambic Decasyllables, had Chaucer either known that mode of versification, or intended to have adopted it : as in the following instance.

[p. clxii]   In her is high beauty withouten pride.

Cant. Tales. 4522.

Unless this line be read rhythmically, it has no principle of harmony at all ; but when so read, it has all the harmony that sort of versification aspires to.

In hèr ĭs hìgh bĕautè ‖ wĭthòutĕn prīde.

Had the Iambic Decasyllabic measure been intended, the line with the transposition of a single word, might have been made a perfect Iambic Decasyllable.   We cannot suppose this would have escaped Chaucer's notice.

In her high beauty is, withouten pride.

The above observations apply to a large number of lines of a similar construction, occurring in almost every page of Chaucer's works.

Again ; the incessant recurrence of defective and redundant verses seems to me wholly inconsistent with the notion of a regular system of metrical versification, but not so with rhythmical versification. . . .

* * * * * * * * *

Another, and I conceive a conclusive reason for believing Chaucer's verses to have been rhythmical verses, or verses of cadence, may be drawn from the Manuscripts themselves in which his poems are preserved. [Nott here goes on to show that in all the MSS. either the cæsura, or the pause at the end of the line is marked, and that sometimes both are carefully marked, and that all the MSS. agree in fixing the cæsura in every line, with hardly any variation, at the same place ; pointing to the fact that Chaucer not only meant his verses to be rhythmical, but did all he could to settle what their rhythm should be.]

* * * * * * * * *

Sect. VIII. *Of the nature and importance of Poetic Ornament, and of the defects of our early English Poets in Point of Poetic Diction.* . .

[p. clxxxviii] Chaucer did much towards refining our poetic diction, but he left it indefinite : and therefore open to subsequent innovation and experiment. Indeed he was not consistent in the use of one uniform style. In his Canterbury Tales what he seems to have particularly aimed at was simplicity of construction and a not over-curious selection of words. By these means he obtained a sort of natural dignity, and simple elegance of style which rose often into sublimity, and enabled him to present his thoughts in a manner singularly clear and distinct. In his Troilus and Cressida, which is evidently his most laboured composition, he aimed at something like involution, and affected a greater nicety of terms.

* * * * * * * *

[p. cxcii] Another defect in Chaucer, and in all our early poets, was the little attention paid by them to their system of Rhyming.
[p. cxciii] . . . We find him [Chaucer] constantly admitting double rhymes, which in grave and heroic subjects cannot be allowed, as they carry with them an air of lightness inconsistent with the dignity of heroic composition. He rhymed also not only on feeble words, but on such as in themselves were mean and trivial. The following rhymes occur in the Knights' Tales,

[*sic*] one of his most elevated pieces : *us, after, shall, ah, thus, her, other, þan, merry, ladle, cradle, shirt.* His rhymes are likewise often unpleasing by being formed of words, either purely French, or of English words distorted, it should seem arbitrarily, to rhyme with them, by being made to bear a strong and heavy accent on the last syllable. . . . I know that this evil prevailed before Chaucer's time, and I am willing to believe he did something to correct it. Still we find him rhyming on the following words, *semblaùnt, variaùnt, plesaùnce, chevisaùnce,* [&c., &c.] . . .

.   .   .   .

Sect. XIII. *Of the vague and diffuse Style used by our early Poets.* . . .

[p. ccxxxv] [Remarks on the diffuseness and tautology of the early poets, and an example of this is given from Chaucer, Complaint of Mars, fol. ccclxx, ed. 1532, beginning :]

It seemeth Love hath to lovers enmity.]

.   .   .   .

[p. ccxli, note a.] [Nott says our early poets often debased fine passages by the introduction of mean circumstances, or trivial and ignoble words, and as an example of this, he says :]

In Chaucer's complaint of Mars and Venus, we find this very spirited description of Mars arming himself.

He throweth on his helm of hugie weight,
    And girt him with his sword ; and in his hand
[p. ccxlii]   His mighty spear, as he was wont to fight
He shaketh so, that it almost to-wonn'd.

Thus far all is general and beautiful : but Chaucer cannot forbear adding a circumstance which proves he had a Man at Arms of the 14th century in his imagination.

Full heavy was he to walken over lond.

[p. ccxlii] Sect. XV. *Of the want of skill in all our early Poets in translating and imitating other writers, and Surrey's excellence in this particular.*

.   .   .   .

Chaucer was incomparably the best and noblest of all our early writers. Yet even Chaucer was unacquainted with the art of imitating or translating with spirit and originality. [Here follow several examples of translated passages :

(1) Troilus, Bk. ii, v. 1030, beginning :

> For though the best // harper upon live
> Would on the best // sowned joly harp . . .

which lines, says Dr. Nott, are 'an imperfect imitation of two passages from Horace' in which Chaucer comprehends his author's meaning, and applies it to his subject with considerable skill; but we look in vain for the point and terseness of the original.

[p. ccxliii] (2) Translation from Petrarch's Sonnet 102, in Troil. and Cress., Bk. i, ed. 1532 :

> If no love is, oh God ! // what feel I so, &c.

in which the words are so ill chosen where the version is close; and where it is paraphrastic the circumstances added are selected with so little taste, and expressed with so little elegance, that the spirit of the original is lost.]

.   .   .   .

[p. ccxliv] A still more striking proof of Chaucer's want of taste in translation occurs in his Canterbury Tales, where he attempts a version of Dante's famous story of Ugolino. . . . With what prosaical tameness and meanness of circumstance does he paraphrase the . . . lines, in which Ugolino describes how his suspicion was excited as to the fate which awaited his unfortunate family and himself.

Sect. XVI. *Of the further improvements made by Surrey in our Poetry* . . .

[p. ccxlvii] All our poets previous to Surrey wrote as if no other manners, ideas, or modes of life ever had existed, or ever could exist than those with which they themselves were conversant. . . .

[p. ccxlix] That limited taste . . . pervaded the whole of Chaucer's Knight's Tale. Who must not feel the first principles of good taste violated, when he is told that Dan Arcite was a 'lusty bachelor,' chamberlain and squire principal to Duke Theseus ; that the said Duke found Arcite and Palamon in the woods when he went thither himself 'amaying;' and that he learnt Arcite's passion by hearing him sing a Roundel in praise of love, and talk of purgatory ?

.   .   .   .

[p. ccl]   The same confusion arising from an absurd use of particular instead of general ideas and sentiments in points of feeling, reigns throughout the whole of the Troilus and Cressida. Indeed were the names of the personages altered, that poem would not only become a tale of chivalry, but would gain beauty as well as propriety by the change.

.   .   .   .

[p. cclvi]   How much inferior, on this account [*i. e.* incongruity and confusion of ideas] is Palamon and Arcite, one of Chaucer's most finished works, to his Squire's Tale, which even in its imperfect state remains the most vigorous effort of his fancy. The reason of the inferiority is this.   In the Squire's Tale every thing is of a piece; the subject, the figures, the ideas, the machinery, are all purely Gothic, with a certain mixture of eastern imagery which gave, at the time of the Crusades, a peculiar colouring to our northern romances. . . But in the Knight's Tale we are sensible at every page that the principal rules of good taste are violated; we feel the absurdity of combining manners of periods so remote from each other as the time of Theseus, and the reign of Edward the Third; and even when we are most pleased we tremble lest some strange incongruity should arise, to destroy the effect of all that has preceeded.

.   .   .   .

[p. cclxix] Sect. XX.   *Of the authors whom Surrey studied; of Chaucer, Dante . . .*

As for Chaucer his name is in every one's mouth; and is always mentioned with praise. Nor could it well be otherwise. We could not but speak with respect of the author whom Spencer had declared to have been his poetic father, whom so many subsequent writers had called 'the Well-head of English undefiled,' and whom Dryden had commended in terms of filial reverence.   Still Chaucer is little read, and his merits are imperfectly understood.   He was a poet of as large and comprehensive a mind as almost any whom this, or any other country can boast.   He was a great and an universal scholar. This praise cannot be denied to him who was master of all the learning of his times.   His memory was stored with images collected from all the sources of information then open to enquiry. . . Had the Squire's Tale been finished . . . I am persuaded that Chaucer would have left us the noblest

specimen of romantic imagination to be found within the
compass of modern literature. But Chaucer's chief merit
consists in his knowledge of human nature and in his
power of delineating character. In humorous and satiric
portraits, we meet with the nicest touches of discrimination
between vice and foible that can well be imagined : and
in his heroic characters we find him constantly preserving
gradations of excellence even in those points where there is a
general resemblance. The Knight and the Squire, Palamon
[p. and Arcite, Demetrius of Inde, and Lycurgus of Thrace, are
cclxx] all brave and enterprising ; but each of them is an individual
of himself. Courage is the one common attribute of all.
But there are the same shades of difference in the courage of
each that Homer has been so often admired for preserving
in the characters of Ulysses and Antilochus ; Diomed and
Patroclus ; Ajax and Achilles. I know of no writer in
modern times, Shakespeare excepted, who can be compared
with Chaucer for masterly discrimination of character.

[Vol. ii,   . . . For though it is evident that he [Wyatt] had read
p. cliii] Chaucer, and admired him, his imitations are neither frequent,
nor of a description to make us suppose that he took him as
his master, or considered him to be 'the well-head of English
undefiled.'

1815. **Turner**, Sharon. *History of England*, vol. ii.

[Part V, containing five chapters, is a "History of English
Poetry, from the twelfth century to the middle of the fifteenth."
Of these chapters, no. iv (pp. 499–538) concerns the "Life and Poems
of Chaucer," and is based principally on Godwin and a study of the
text.   There are many quotations, principally from the Testament,
Dream, Legende, Troilus, Assemble of Fowles, Complaint of the
Black Knight. A general account of the works is given. Other
references are :—

Chaucer's borrowings from Dante and Boccaccio, p. 480 and *n.*
Chaucer and Gower, pp. 481, 483, 488 *n.*, 498 *n.*
Chaucer and Lydgate, pp. 540, 541, 545–8, 552, 555. Turner
considers Lydgate's versification superior to Chaucer's, p. 545.]

1815. **Unknown.** *Chaucer's Dying Ode,* [Flee from the prees . . .
"attempted in modern English," in] The Monthly Repository,
May, vol. x, no. cxiii, p. 309.

[The text of Chaucer is given, followed by the modernization, of which the first stanza will serve for a specimen :]

Fly from the crowd, and be to virtue true,
Content with what thou hast tho' it be small,
To hoard brings hate; nor lofty thoughts pursue,
He who climbs high endangers many a fall.
Envy's a shade that ever waits on fame,
And oft the sun that raises it will hide;
Trace not in life a vast expansive scheme,
But be thy wishes to thy state ally'd.
Be mild to others, to thyself severe;
So truth shall shield thee or from hurt or fear.

1815. Wilkes, John. *Encyclopædia Londinensis,* vol. xiii, 1815. *See* above, 1810.

1815. Wordsworth, William. *Essay, Supplementary to the Preface to the Edition of the Poems,* 1815. (Prose Works of William Wordsworth, ed. W. Knight, 2 vols., 1896, vol. ii, pp. 247–8.)

[On Johnson's *Lives* :]

We open the volume of Prefatory Lives, and to our astonishment the *first* name we find is that of Cowley !—What is become of the morning-star of English poetry ? Where is the bright Elizabethan constellation ? Or, if names be more acceptable than images, where is the ever-to-be-honoured Chaucer ? where is Spenser ?

1815. Wordsworth, William. *Notes* to the second poem *To the Daisy.* (Poetical Works, ed. W. Knight, 1896, vol. ii, p. 356 *n.*)

See, in Chaucer and the elder Poets, the honours formerly paid to this flower.

1816. Dibdin, Thomas Frognall. *Typographical Antiquities . . .* begun by Joseph Ames and augmented by William Herbert, and now enlarged with copious notes, vol. iii, pp. 62–5 [Chaucer's Works, Godfray, 1532], 269–270 [Chaucer's Works, 1542], 514 [Chaucer's Works, Petit, etc., n.d.], 575 *n.*, 586. [For vols. i, ii, *see* above, 1810, 1812 ; for vol. iv, below, 1819 ; for Ames' original edn. of 1749, *see* vol. i, p. 398 ; for Herbert's intermediate edn., *see* vol. i, 1785, p. 477, 1786, p. 483, 1790, p. 491.]

1816. Hazlitt, William. *On Pedantry,* [in] The Round Table. (Collected Works of William Hazlitt, ed. Waller and Glover, 1902–6, 13 vols., vol. i, pp. 84–5.)

Chaucer has drawn a beautiful picture of a true scholar in his Clerk of Oxenford. [Prol. 285–308, is then quoted.]

1816. [**Hazlitt**, William ?] *Review* of Leigh Hunt's *Rimini*, [in] The Edinburgh Review, June 1816, vol. xxvi, p. 476.

[This poem] unquestionably bears a still stronger resemblance to Chaucer than to his immediate followers in Italy. [The descriptions, diction and characterization resemble Chaucer's.]

[For the evidence for Hazlitt's authorship of this review, *see* Collected Works of William Hazlitt, ed. Waller and Glover, 1902–6, 13 vols., vol. x, p. 407.]

1816. Hunt, James Henry Leigh. *Preface to The Story of Rimini*, pp. x, xi, xiv–xvii. (Poetical Works, 1819, vol. i.)

[p. x]   The romance of Launcelot of the Lake, upon the perusal of which the principal incident turns, is little known at present, but was a great favourite all over Europe, up to a late period. Chaucer, no long time after the event itself, mentions it, in [p. xi] his significant way, as a work held in great estimation by the ladies. The Nun's Priest, speaking of the Tale of the Cock and the Fox, which he is relating, says to his hearers,

> This story is al so trewe, I undertake,
> As is the book of Launcelot du Lake
> That women holde in ful gret reverence.
>
>   Cant. Tales, v. **15147.**

The great father of our poetry, by the way, is a little ungrateful with his jokes upon chivalrous stories, of which he has left such noble specimens in the Palamon and Arcite, and in the unfinished story of Cambuscan, which Milton delighted to remember ; but both he and the Italian poets appear to have laughed at them occasionally, as lovers affect to do at their mistresses.

[p. xiv]   The great masters of modern versification are, Dryden for common narrative . . . —Spenser, who was musical from pure taste,—Milton, who was learnedly so,—Ariosto, . . . — [p. xv] Shakspeare, . . . —and, though the name may appear singular to those who have not read him with due attention to the nature of the language then existing,—Chaucer,—to whom it sometimes appears to me, that I can trace Dryden himself.

[p. xvi]   The poet should therefore do as Chaucer or Shakspeare did, —not copy what is obsolete or peculiar in either, any more than they copied from their predecessors—but use as much as [p. xvii] possible an actual, existing language,— . . . Of the style, to

which I allude [*i. e.* that which is most beautiful], exquisite
specimens, making allowances for what is obsolete, are to be
found in the Canterbury Tales of Chaucer, and his Troilus
and Cressida.

1816. **Hunt**, James Henry Leigh. *Epistles. To the Right Honourable Lord
Byron on his departure for Italy and Greece* [dated on p. lxxvii]
Hampstead, April 1816, [in] Foliage, or Poems Original and
Translated, 1818, pp. lxxiii, lxxiv. [Cf. The Feast of the Poets,
by Leigh Hunt, ed. 1832.]

> But all the four great masters of our song,
> Stars that shine out amidst a starry throng,
> Have turned to Italy for added light,
> As earth is kissed by the sweet moon at night ;—
> Milton for half his style, Chaucer for tales,
> Spenser for flowers to fill his isles and vales
> And Shakspeare's self for frames already done
> To build his everlasting piles upon.

1816. **Jeffrey**, Francis, Lord. *Letter to Thomas Moore,* [dated] Edinburgh, May 28, 1816, [in] Memoirs, Journals, and Correspondence
of Thomas Moore, ed. by the Right Hon. Lord John Russell, M.P.,
1853, vol. ii, p. 100.

It [Leigh Hunt's Rimini] is very sweet and very lively in
many places, and is altogether piquant, as being by far the
best imitation of Chaucer and some of his Italian contemporaries that modern times have produced.

1816. **Jeffrey**, Francis, Lord. *Review of Scott's edition of Swift,* [in]
The Edinburgh Review, Sept. 1816, vol. xxvii, pp. 3, 4. (Francis
Jeffrey's Contributions to the Edinburgh Review, 1853, pp. 74, 75.)

[p. 3]   Our first literature consisted of saintly legends, and
[p. 4] romances of chivalry,—though Chaucer gave it a more
national and popular character by his original descriptions of
external nature, and the familiarity and gaiety of his social
humour.

1816.   **Scott**, Sir Walter. *Old Mortality* (Tales of my Landlord), vol. iv.
ch. xv. [ed. 2, the first in B.M.]. (Border Edition, ed. Andrew
Lang, 1893, vol. ii, ch. xxiii, p. 286.)

[Chapter Heading.]
Yet could he not his closing eyes withdraw
[and four following lines].

[Dryden's] *Palamon and Arcite.*

1816. Scott, Sir Walter. *The Antiquary,* 3 vols, vol. i, ch. iii, p. 56, ch. x, pp. 213–15, vol. iii, ch. v, p. 114. (Border edition, ed. Andrew Lang, 1893, vol. i, ch. iii., p. 31, chap. x, pp. 120–1, vol. ii, chap. xiii, p. 165.)

[Vol. i, p. 31]   It was chiefly on his books that he [Mr. Oldbuck] prided himself, repeating, with a complacent air, as he led the way to the crowded and dusty shelves, the verses of old Chaucer—

> For he would rather have, at his bed-head,
> A twenty books, clothed in black or red,
> Of Aristotle, or his philosophy,
> Than robes rich, rebeck, or saltery.
>
> [Prol., ll. 293–6.]

This pithy motto he delivered, shaking his head and giving each guttural the true Anglo-Saxon enunciation, which is now forgotten in the southern parts of this realm . . .

Vol. i, pp. [The room] was hung with tapestry . . . It seemed as if 120–1] the prolific and rich invention of old Chaucer had animated the Flemish artist with its profusion, and Oldbuck had accordingly caused the following verses from that ancient and excellent poet, to be embroidered in Gothic letters, on a sort of border which he had added to the tapestry :—

> Lo ! here be oakis grete, streight as a lime

[and six following lines, The Flower and the Leaf, ll. 29–35].

And in another canton was the following similar legend :—

> And many a hart, and many a hind

[and five following lines, Book of the Duchesse, ll. 427–32].

[Vol. ii, p. 165]   [Another brief reference to the above lines.]

1816. Unknown. *Encyclopædia Perthensis,* vol. v, pp. 259–60, Chaucer, vol. xiii, p. 486, Lydgate. [Both articles are taken from edn. 2 of the Encyclopædia Britannica (*q.v.* above, 1778, vol. i, p. 452), slightly altered in phrasing only.]

1816. Unknown. *Illustrations of Westminster Abbey,* No. xvii, [in] The British Lady's Magazine, no. 21, vol. iv, Sept. 1, 1816, pp. 186–7.

These specimens [*i. e.* the modernized tales of Dryden, Pope, etc.] are quite enough to open the mind to the genius of Chaucer, who, however far himself a translator from the Italian, was a prodigy for his age, and, contending, as he did, with an unformed language, an uncommon instance of ability and industry united. . . .

1816. Unknown. *Review* of *Works of Howard and Wyatt,* ed. G. F. Nott, [in] The Edinburgh Review, Dec. 1816, vol. **xxvii**, pp. 405, 412, 413, 415–19, 422.

[p. 412]   [Chaucer the only old poet who makes reference to his sources.   Debt to Boccaccio in ' Palamon and Arcite.']

[pp.415-419]   [Stating the difference of opinion between Tyrwhitt and Nott on Chaucer's versification (pronunciation of final *e,* etc.), and Nott's dictum that Chaucer wrote rhythmically rather than metrically, the reviewer concludes that, though there was much rhythmical verse in Chaucer's and even in Surrey's time, this type is quite distinct from Chaucer's. Various quotations from Chaucer (description of the ' Lawyer ' from the *Prologue,* etc.) are given in illustration.]

[p. 422]   . . . If we see not the slightest ground for depriving Chaucer, in one respect, of his title of Father of English Poetry, we are heartily ready to allow that Surrey well deserves that of the Eldest Son, however he was surpassed by the brothers that immediately followed him.

[For Nott's edn. of Surrey and Wyatt, *see* above, 1815–16.]

1817. Coleridge, Samuel Taylor. *Biographia Literaria,* 2 vols., 1817, vol. i, pp. 21, 22, 32, 38, 55, 203, 205 ; vol. ii, pp. 97, 79, 104.

[ch. i, pp. 21-22]   In my defence of the lines running into each other, instead of closing at each couplet, and of natural language, . . . I had continually to adduce the metre and diction of the Greek Poets . . . and still more of our elder English poets from Chaucer to Milton.

.   .   .   .

[ch. ii, p. 32]   Through all the works of Chaucer there reigns a chearful-ness, a manly hilarity, which makes it almost impossible to doubt a correspondent habit of feeling in the author himself. [Cf. *Table Talk,* below, 1834.]

.   .   .   .

[p. 38]   In the days of Chaucer and Gower, our language might (with due allowance for the imperfections of a simile) be compared to a wilderness of vocal reeds, from which the favourites only of Pan or Apollo could construct even the rude Syrinx ; and from this the *constructors* alone could elicit strains of music.

.   .   .   .

[p. 55]   Having announced my intention to give a course of lectures on the characteristic merits and defects of English poetry in its different eras; first, from Chaucer to Milton; second, from Dryden inclusive to Thomson; and third, from Cowper to the present day; I changed my plan and confined my disquisition to the two former eras.

[ch. x, p. 203] I received as many lessons in the Gothic of Ulphilas as sufficed to make me acquainted with its grammar, and . . . I read through . . . the most important remains of the Theotiscan, or the transitional state of the Teutonic language from the Gothic to the old German of the Swabian period . . . (the polished dialect of which is analogous to that of our Chaucer). . .

[p. 205] In Pindar, Chaucer, Dante, Milton, and many more, we have instances of the close connection of poetic genius with the love of liberty and of genuine reformation.

    .   .   .   .

[Vol. ii, p. 79] [Defence of the use of mythological personages by the older poets.] Nay, even at this day what scholar of genial taste will not so far sympathise with them, as to read with pleasure in Petrarch, Chaucer, or Spenser, what he would perhaps condemn as puerile in a modern poet?

[Vol. ii, ch. xx, p. 97] In truth our language is, and from the first dawn of poetry ever has been, particularly rich in compositions distinguished by this excellence [*i. e.* a natural style and an apt expression of thought, combined with the rhyme and metre of poetry]. The final *e*, which is now mute, in Chaucer's age was either sounded or dropped indifferently. . . . Let the reader, then, only adopt the pronunciation of the poet and of the court, at which he lived, both with respect to the final *e* and to the accentuation of the last syllable: I would then venture to ask, what even in the colloquial language of elegant and unaffected women (who are the peculiar mistresses of " pure English and undefiled ")—what could we hear more natural, or seemingly more unstudied, than the following stanzas from Chaucer's Troilus and Creseide?

    " And after this forth to the gate he wente,
      Ther as Creseide out rode a ful gode paas :
    And up and doun there made he many a wente," &c.,
      [42 lines quoted, bk. v, stanzas 87–91, 93.]

[Wordsworth included this latter passage in his ' Selections from Chaucer modernised,' written 1801.]

[p. 164]   [Heading to Chap. xx.]   The neutral style, or that common to Prose and Poetry, exemplified by specimens from Chaucer, Herbert, &c.   [There are no specimens from Chaucer.]

1817. Dibdin, Thomas Frognall. *The Bibliographical Decameron,* 3 vols., vol. ii, pp. 346 *n*, 383, 437 *n*, 446-8, 517-18 ; vol. iii, pp. 27, 58-9, 75, 100, 127, 227 and *n*, 318, 404, 420, 434, 467.

[vol. ii, p. 3]   [Footnote. The two Chaucers (*i. e.* the first and second edns. of the Canterbury Tales) among the Caxtons at Spencer House.]

[p. 446]   [The binding of books in velvet noticed by Chaucer. "Bokes clothed in black or red" meant bound in velvet. Chaucer's works bound in leather in the sixteenth century ; quotation from Copland, *q. v.* above, 1530, vol. i, p. 76.]

[vol. iii. p. 58-9]   [Sale at the Roxburghe sale of a MS. of Chaucer for £357, and of Troilus, 1517, for £43.]

[p. 100]   [Sale at the Towneley sale of Chaucer, 1532, for £5. 5. 0, and of Caxton's edn. of Troilus for £252.]

[p. 127]   [Sale at the Edwards sale of Troilus, 1517, for £39. 18. 0.]

[p. 227]   [Bradwardine mentioned by Chaucer; quotation from the Nun's Priest's Tale, ll. 414-22.]

[p. 318]   [Hunterian Library contains Canterbury Tales, 1526, Troilus, n. d., House of Fame, n. d., all by Pynson, in one volume ; Canterbury Tales, Pynson, n. d. (Ratcliffe's copy).]

[p. 404]   [The Wentworth Collection contains first edn. of Chaucer (Ratcliffe's copy).]

[p. 420]   [Boethius (Caxton) in Ripon Cathedral Library.]

[p. 434]   [Troilus, n. d., and Canterbury Tales, 2nd edn., in St. John's College Library, Oxford (Dibdin's own College).]

[p. 467]   [Reference to, and quotation from, Chaucer's Ballade to his Empty Purse.]

1817. Gregson, Matthew. *Portfolio of Fragments, relative to the History and Antiquities of the County Palatine of the Duchy of Lancaster* . . . Liverpool, 1817, p. 6.

[John of Gaunt and Catherine Swinford and Chaucer's marriage and pension.]

1817. Hazlitt, William. *Characters of Shakespear's Plays.* (Collected Works of William Hazlitt, ed. Waller and Glover, 1902-6, 13 vols., vol. i, pp. 224-7, 332, 358.)

[pp. 224-5] [Comparison of the characters in Chaucer's Troilus and in Shakspere's :] The difference of the manner in which the subject is treated arises less from intention, than from the different genius of the two poets. There is no *double entendre* in the characters of Chaucer : they are either quite serious or quite comic . . . We see Chaucer's characters as they saw themselves, not as they appeared to others or might have appeared to the poet. He is as deeply implicated in the affairs of his personages as they could be themselves . . . There is little relief, or light and shade in his pictures . . . Shakespear never committed himself to his characters . . . His genius was dramatic, as Chaucer's was historical . . .

[p. 226]   Chaucer attended chiefly to the real and natural, that is, to the involuntary and inevitable impressions on the mind in given circumstances ; Shakespear exhibited also the possible and the fantastical—not only what things are in themselves, but whatever they might seem to be, their different reflections, their endless combinations. He lent his fancy, wit, invention, to others, and borrowed their feelings in return. Chaucer excelled in the force of habitual sentiment ; Shakespear added to it every variety of passion, every suggestion of thought or accident. Chaucer described external objects with the eye of a painter, or he might be said to have embodied them with the hand of a sculptor, . . . Shakespear's imagination threw over them a lustre

" Prouder than when blue Iris bends."

Every thing in Chaucer has a downright reality. . . . In Shakespear the commonest matter-of-fact has a romantic grace about it ; or seems to float with the breath of imagination in a freer element. No one could have more depth of feeling or observation than Chaucer, but he wanted resources of invention to lay open the stores of nature or the human heart with the same radiant light, that Shakespear has done. However fine or profound the thought, we know what is coming, whereas the effect of reading Shakespear is " like the eye of vassalage at unawares encountering majesty." Chaucer's mind was consecutive, rather than discursive. He arrived at truth through a certain process ; Shakespear saw everything by intuition. Chaucer had a great variety of power, but he could do only one thing at once. He set himself to work on a particular subject. His ideas were kept separate, labelled, ticketed and parcelled out in a set form, in pews and compartments by themselves. They did not play into one another's hands. They did not re-act upon one another. . . . There is

something hard and dry in them. What is the most wonderful
thing in Shakespear's faculties is their excessive sociability,
and how they gossiped and compared notes together.

[Passages from each poet are cited and compared.]

1817. Hunt, James Henry Leigh. *The Round Table:* by William
Hazlitt [and Leigh Hunt], 2 vols., 1817, vol. i, pp. 15–16 [Intro-
duction], p. 186 [Essay on the Poetical Character].

[p. 15] It must not be concealed, that both Shakespeare and
Milton have owed a great part of their reputation of late years
to causes which . . . have been unconnected with a direct
poetical taste . . . Milton still remains unknown to the
better classes, . . . and Chaucer and Spenser, the two other
great poets of England, . . . are scarcely known at all . . .
Chaucer is considered as a rude sort of poet, who wrote a vast
while ago, and is no longer intelligible . . . Chaucer is
nothing but *old* Chaucer or honest Geoffrey . . .

[p. 186] It is not one of the least curious instances of the native
spirit of this country, that three out of its four greatest poets
—Chaucer, Spenser, and Milton—have been men of busy
action in the political world,—that two out of the three were
unequivocally on the side of freedom, and helped to procure
us our present enjoyments. . . . Thomson was of a cheerful
temperament . . . and so was Chaucer, till he got into prison
in his old age.

1817. Hunt, James Henry Leigh. *On Chaucer,* [Essay No. xvi, in] *The
Round Table:* by William Hazlitt [and Leigh Hunt], 2 vols.,
vol. i, pp. 124–41.

[Leigh Hunt discusses the possibility of a modern poet being
able to complete Chaucer's Squire's Tale. He thinks it would
be difficult to find any one capable of doing it satisfactorily.
He goes on to deal with what appears to him the best method
of modernizing Chaucer, which is little more than a change of
spelling, and he gives examples of this from the Squire's Tale.]

1817. Keats, John. *Sonnet;* written on a blank space at the end of
Chaucer's Tale of "The Floure and the Lefe." [This transcript is
from Keats's holograph in Cowden Clarke's Chaucer, and gives
his punctuation and use of capital letters. First printed in The
Examiner, March 16, 1817.] (Complete Works of John Keats, ed.
H. Buxton Forman, 1900–1, 5 vols., vol. ii, pp. 175–6.)

This pleasant Tale is like a little copse
    The honied Lines do freshly interlace
    To keep the Reader in so sweet a place

So that he here and there full-hearted stops
And oftentimes he feels the dewy drops
    Come cool and suddenly against his face
    And by the wandering Melody, may trace
Which way the tender-legged Linnet hops.
O what a Power hath white Simplicity !
    What mighty Power has this gentle Story
    I that for ever feel athirst for glory,
Could at this Moment be content to lie
    Meekly upon the Grass as those whose sobbings
    Were heard of None beside the mournful Robins.

[It is agreed now that *The Floure and the Lefe* is not by Chaucer. The edition Keats used, and in which this sonnet is written, belonged to Charles Cowden Clarke, and is The Poetical Works of Geoffrey Chaucer, in 14 vols., in Bell's edn. of the Poets of Great Britain, 109 vols, Edinburgh, 1782–3, vol. xii, 1783, pp. 104–5. It is now in the British Museum, MS. Add. 33516.]

1817. Keats, John. *Letter to Messrs. Taylor and Hessey,* [dated] Margate, 16 May, 1817. (Complete Works of John Keats, ed. H. Buxton Forman, 1900–1, 5 vols., vol. iv, p. 23.)

This evening I go to Canterbury, having got tired of Margate . . . At Canterbury I hope the remembrance of Chaucer will set me forward like a Billiard Ball.

1817. Keats, John. *Motto* [at the head of] *Sleep and Poetry.* (Complete Works of John Keats, ed. H. Buxton Forman, 1900–1, 5 vols., vol i, p. 51.)

        " As I lay in my bed slepe full unmete

    [to]
            Than I, for I n'ad sickness nor disese."
                              Chaucer.

[This is from the non-Chaucerian poem, the Flower and the Leaf, ll. 17–21.]

1817–18. Keats, John. *Endymion,* bk. i, ll. 131–4. (Complete Works of John Keats, ed. H. Buxton Forman, 1900–1, 5 vols., vol. i, pp. 75, 104, 105 *n.* Works, ed. E. de Sélincourt, 1907, p. 56.)

[p. 75]   But let a portion of ethereal dew
              Fall on my head, and presently unmew
              My soul ; that I may dare, in wayfaring,
              To stammer where old Chaucer us'd to sing.

    .   .   .   .

[p. 104]   Yet, in our very souls, we feel amain
             The close of Troilus and Cressid sweet.

[p. 105] [Buxton Forman, in a footnote, says that Woodhouse records that Keats by 'close' in the line above meant 'embrace.' He also says, " This allusion I apprehend is to Chaucer's, and not to Shakespeare's work under this title." Buxton Forman thinks the reference is to Shakespeare. For much valuable discussion on Keats's debt to Chaucer, *see* Professor de Sélincourt's edition of Keats's poems.]

304 THE FLOURE AND THE LEAFE.

Madam, quod I, although I left worthy,
||Unto the Lefe I owe mine obfervaunce.
That is, quod fhe, right well done certainly,
And I pray God to honour you advaunce,
And kepe you fro the wickid remembraunce
Of Malébouch and all his cruëltie,
And all that gode and well-condition'd be; 581

For here I may no lengir now abide,
But I muft follow the grete company
That ye fhay fe yondir before you ride;
And forthwith as I comb moft humily
I toke my leve of her, and fhe gan hie
Aftir them as faft as evir fhe might,
And I drow homeward, for it was nigh night, 588

And put all that I had fene in writing,
Undir fupport of them that luft it rede.
O little boke! thou art fo unconning,
How darft thou put thy felf in prees for drede?
It is wondir that thou wexift not rede,
Sith that thou woft fall lite who fhall behold
Thy rude langage full boyftoufly unfold. 595

Finis.

This pleasant Tale is like a little copfe:
The honied lines fo frefhly interlaces,
To keep the reader in fo fweet a place,
So that he here and there full hearted ftoops;
And oftentimes he feels the dewy drops
Come cool and fuddenly againft his face,
And, by the wandering melody may trace
Which way the tender-legged linnet hops.
O! what a power has white fimplicity!
What mighty power has this gentle ftory!
I, that do ever feel athirft for glory,
Could at this moment be content to lie
Meekly upon the grafs, as thofe whofe fobbings
Were heard of none befide the mournful robins.

J. K. Feby 1817.

THE COURT OF LOVE.

WITH timerous herte and trembling hand of drede,
Of cunning nakid, bare of eloquence,
Unto the flour of port in womanhede
I write, as he that none intelligence
Of metris hath ne flouris of fentence,
Sanfe that me lift my writing to convey
In that I can to plefe her high nobley. 7

The blofomes frefh of Tulius gardin fote
Prefent thei not, my mattir for to borne,
Poemes of Virgile takin here no rote,
Ne crafte of Galfride may not here fojourne;
Why n'am I cunning? o'wel maie I mourne
For lacke of fcience, that I can nat write
Unto the princes of my lyfe aright! 14

No termes are digne unto her excellence,
So is fhe fprónge of noble ftripe and high;
A world of honour and of reverence
There is in her, this wil I, teftifie:
Caliope, thou liftir wife and fly,
And thou Minerva! guide me with thy grace,
That fangrage rude my mattir not deface. 21

The Court of Love] This book is an imitation of The Romaunt of the Rofe, fhewing that all are fubject to love, what impediments foever to the contrary, containing alfo thofe 20 ftatutes that are to be obferved in The Court of Love, &c.

1817. Lockhart, John Gibson. *See* below, Z.

1817. Reynolds, John Hamilton. *Sonnet to Keats,* dated Feb. 27,
1827, on reading his Sonnet written in Chaucer (in Woodhouse's
Commonplace Book). (Complete Works of John Keats, ed. H.
Buxton Forman, 1900–1, 5 vols., vol. ii, p. 176 *n.*)

Thy thoughts, dear Keats, are like fresh-gathered leaves,
  Or white flowers pluck'd from some sweet lily-bed ;
They set the heart a-breathing, and they shed
  The glow of meadows, mornings and spring eves,
Over the excited soul. .   .   .   .   .

    .   .   .   .

Go on ! and keep thee to thine own green way,
  Singing in that same key which Chaucer sung ;—
Be thou companion of the Summer day,
  Roaming the fields and olden woods among :—
So shall thy muse be ever in her May ;
  And thy luxuriant Spirit ever young.
[For Keats's sonnet, *see* above, 1817.]

1817. Scott, Sir Walter. *Ivanhoe,* 1819 [references to 2nd edn., 1820],
pp. xix–xx, Dedicatory Epistle [dated 1817], 20, 130, 157, 174,
234, headings to chapters ii, viii, ix, x and xii, (or rather xiii,
ch. x being duplicated and the subsequent numbers wrong in the
early edns.). (Border Edition, ed. Andrew Lang, 1893, vol. i,
pp. xlviii–ix, 14, 86, 104, 159.)

Dedicatory Epistle.

[p. xlviii] He who first opens Chaucer, or any other ancient poet,
is so much struck with the obsolete spelling, multiplied consonants, and antiquated appearance of the language, that he is
apt to lay the work down in despair, as encrusted too deep
with the rust of antiquity, to permit his judging of its merits
or tasting its beauties. But if some intelligent and accom-
[p. xlix] plished friend points out to him, that the difficulties by which
he is startled are more in appearance than reality, if, by reading aloud to him, or by reducing the ordinary words to the
modern orthography, he satisfies his proselyte that only about
one-tenth part of the words employed are in fact obsolete, the
novice may be easily persuaded to approach the " well of
English undefiled," with the certainty that a slender degree of
patience will enable him to enjoy both the humour and the
pathos with which old Geoffrey delighted the age of Cressy
and of Poictiers.

[p. 14]   [Chapter ii is headed with a quotation from the Prologue,

" A Monk ther was, a fayre for the maistrie," &c. (ll. 165–
172). The description of the Monk in chapter ii is based
on Chaucer:] He was obviously an ecclesiastic of high
rank . . . In defiance of conventual rules . . . the sleeves
of this dignitary were lined and turned up with rich furs ; his
mantle secured at the throat with a golden clasp. . . .

This worthy churchman rode upon a well-fed ambling
mule, whose furniture was highly decorated, and whose bridle,
according to the fashion of the day, was ornamented with
silver bells.   In his seat he had nothing of the awkwardness
of the Convent, but displayed the easy and habitual grace of a
well-trained horseman. [Cf. Prologue, ll. 165–172 ; 193–196.]

[Chapters viii and ix are headed by quotations from
Dryden's Palamon and Arcite ; chapter x from the Flower and
the Leaf (modernized) ; chapter xiii from the Knightes Tale,
ll. 1741–1752, " The heralds left their pricking up and
down," &c.]

1817. Southey, Robert. *Preface* and *Notes* to *The Byrth, Lyf and
Actes of King Arthur*, vol. i, pp. i, lvi.

[p. i]   [The English tongue was] stampt for immortality by
Chaucer.

[p. lvi]   I believe all the poems with a French title which are
printed with Chaucer's works are translations from that
language.

1817. Southey, Robert. *Letter to Chauncey Hare Townshend*, [dated]
Oct. 31, 1817. (Life and Correspondence of Southey, 1850, vol. iv,
p. 284.)

[Southey is speaking of Heaven, and the many intimacies
he has made among the dead.] As for us poets . . . we shall
find one another out, and a great many questions I shall have
to ask of Spenser and of Chaucer.   Indeed, I half hope to get
the whole story of Cambuscan bold.

1817. Unknown. *Life of Robert, Hermit of Knaresborough*, [in] The
Gentleman's Magazine, vol. lxxxvii, Dec. 1817, p. 509.

In Speght's Life of Chaucer, I find ' Thomas Chaucer (son
of Geffrey [*sic*]) Constable of Knaresborough Castle, and the
Forest of Knaresborough, during life.'   From the style of the
composition, might not this [the Life of Robert] be the production of Chaucer? which seems possible, by the following
extract from the *Prologue* to the Poem :

And howe he lyffed in yat cave,
After the konnynyg yat I have
Yat treuly whilk I to me toke
Enformed als I was by a boke
That was sentt me by a frere
Fray Sayntt Robert to me here
After that boke sall I say
Wott I p[ur]pose for to pray
To Cryst yat he wald sped my penne
Yan to say ylk men—Amen '

The probability of the Poet being with his son at Knaresborough, strengthens this conjecture.   Speght, in his edition
of Chaucer, also observes, 'John Gower, the lawyer and the
poet, a Yorkshire man borne, was his familiar friend.'

1817. Unknown. *Review* of Stewart's *Dissertation*, [in] The Quarterly
Review, April 1817, vol. xvii, p. 56.

[Chaucer's intimate acquaintance with human nature.]

[n.a. 1817.] Webb (or Webbe), Cornelius. *[Satire on the 'Cockney
School,'* quoted in] Blackwood's Edinburgh Magazine, **vol. ii,**
pp. 38, 194.

Our talk shall be (a theme we never tire on)
Of Chaucer, Spenser, Shakespeare, Milton, Byron,
(Our England's Dante)—Wordsworth—HUNT and KEATS,
The Muses' son of promise ; and of what feats
He yet may do.

[For the quotation of this in *Blackwood's Edinburgh Magazine, see* below, 1817, Z.]

1817. Z [i.e. **Lockhart,** John Gibson.] *On the Cockney School of
Poetry,* [signed 'Z,' in] Blackwood's Edinburgh Magazine, vol. ii.
pp. 38, 39, 40, 194.

[For Lockhart's authorship of this, *see* Colvin, Keats, 1918, pp. 308–9.]

[Parts i and ii of the article both begin with the quotation
from Cornelius Webb (or Webbe) given above.]

[p. 39]   He [Leigh Hunt] pretends, indeed, to be an admirer of
Spenser and Chaucer, but what he praises in them is never
what is deserving of praise—it is only that which he humbly
conceives, bears some resemblance to the more perfect productions of Mr. Leigh Hunt.

1818. B., C. *General Remarks upon the Peculiar Styles and Excellences of the best British Poets,* [in] The Gentleman's Magazine, October, vol. lxxxviii, pp. 294-6.

[A very fair criticism, pointing out Chaucer's gift for describing the 'real manners of ordinary life'—as shown in the Canterbury Tales. The description of the Temple of Mars (Knight's Tale) is quoted, and then :]

[p. 295] Those who by Poetry simply mean the melody of numbers, will perhaps find little to admire in the rough phraseology of this quotation. The whole poem has been elegantly translated into more modern language by Dryden. . . .

[p. 296] The language and the numbers of our old Poet, though certainly quaint and rough, appear to have been far superior to those of any of his predecessors or contemporaries. . . .

The state of our language at so distant a period as 400 years would not permit much harmony in composition ; nor had at that time much attention been paid to the rules which govern verse. Hence it arises that Chaucer is often harsh, and sometimes lame in his numbers.

[Here follow the usual remarks on his versification, and debate as to what sort of heroic metre he wrote. For this we are referred to Tyrwhitt's essay.]

But I have a worse fault to alledge against Chaucer ; and it is one that his admirers would in vain excuse or soften down : on too many occasions we find his pages sullied with disgusting obscenity, and the lowest ribaldry, conveyed in the most direct and coarse terms. . . .

As a Poet, Chaucer possessed a most minute observation, a fertile invention, a happy vein of humour, and an ear susceptible of harmony.

But his genius was not of the highest class, nor can all the hyperbolical praises of the illustrious Dryden prove that he was gifted with one spark of the sublime spirit of the Grecian Bard.

1818. Brayley, Edward Wedlake. *The History and Antiquities of the Abbey Church of St. Peter, Westminster, . . . illustrated by John Preston Neale,* vol. i, supplement [An Historical Account of King Henry the Seventh's Chapel], p. 5. [For vol. ii *see* below, 1823.]

It seems probable . . . that a part of the site [of Henry VII's Chapel] had been once occupied by the Poet Chaucer, to whom 'a Tenement in a garden,' adjoining to St. Mary's Chapel, was leased by Robert Harmodesworth, Chaplain, in 1399, for fifty-three years, at the yearly rent of fifty-three shillings and sixpence, with liberty to distrain for a fortnight's arrears.[1]

[1] A copy of the original lease was engraved by the direction of Dr. Rawlinson in 1752 [*q. v.* below, App. A.; for the original lease, *see* above, 1399, vol. pp. 13–14].

1818. Cary, Henry Francis. *Letter to the Rev. Walter Birch*, [dated] April 8, 1818, [in] Memoir of the Rev. H. F. Cary . . . by his Son, 1847, 2 vols., vol. ii, p. 24.

Then, for myself, I have read . . . for the first time Chaucer regularly through, except one tale, Patient Grisilde, which I know so well that I passed it. This, I think, is all the heavy artillery I can bring into the field, if it is not insulting pleasant old Geoffrey to speak thus of him.

1818. Coleridge, Samuel Taylor. *Notes of Lectures* [of the course of 1818]. (Literary Remains of S. T. Coleridge, 1836–9, 4 vols, vol. i, pp. 83, 88, 89, 231–3, 238.)

[p. 83]   I dare make none [no excuse] for the gross and disgusting licentiousness, the daring profaneness, which rendered the Decameron of Boccaccio the parent of a hundred worse children, fit to be classed among the enemies of the human race ; . . . which interposes a painful mixture in the humour of Chaucer.

[p. 88]   [Lecture III. The Troubadours—Boccaccio—Petrarch— Pulci—Chaucer—Spenser.] . . Chaucer must be read with an eye to the Norman-French Trouveres, of whom he is the best representative in English. He had great powers of invention. As in Shakspere, his characters represent classes, but in a different manner; Shakspere's characters are the representatives of the interior nature of humanity, in which some element has become so predominant as to destroy the health of the mind;

[p. 89] whereas Chaucer's are rather representatives of classes of manners. He is therefore more led to individualize in a mere personal sense. Observe Chaucer's love of nature ; and how happily the subject of his main work is chosen. When you reflect that the company in the Decameron have retired to a place of safety from the raging of a pestilence, their mirth provokes a sense of their unfeelingness ; whereas in Chaucer nothing of this sort occurs, and the scheme of a party on a pilgrimage, with different ends and occupations, aptly allows of the greatest variety of expression in the tales.

[p. 231] [On Style.] As an instance equally delightful and complete, of what may be called the Gothic Structure as contradistinguished from that of the Greeks, let me cite a part of our famous Chaucer's character of a parish priest as he should be. Can it ever be quoted too often?

> A good man thér was of religioun

[and forty-five following lines].

[p. 233] Such change as really took place in the style of our literature after Chaucer's time, is with difficulty perceptible, on account of the dearth of writers, during the civil wars of the fifteenth century . . .

[p. 238] It is, indeed, worthy of remark that all our great poets have been good prose writers, as Chaucer, Spenser, Milton; and this probably rose from their just sense of metre.

[The remarks on Chaucer's prose are reported at greater length in the Tatler, vol. ii, no. 224, May 23, 1831, p. 893.]

1818. Coleridge, Samuel Taylor. *Note on Troilus and Cressida.* (Literary Remains of S. T. Coleridge . . . 4 vols., 1836-9, vol. ii, p. 129.)

[Coleridge quotes the note in Stockdale's 1807 edn. of Shakespeare : " Mr. Pope (after Dryden) informs us, that the story of Troilus and Cressida was originally the work of one Lollius, a Lombard ; but Dryden goes yet further ; he declares it to have been written in Latin verse, and that Chaucer translated it."]

1818. Gifford, William. *Review* of *Hazlitt's Lectures on the English Poets,* [in] The Quarterly Review, London, July 1818, vol. xix, pp. 430, 432.

[p. 430] The following extract is still more exquisite. ". . . The characteristic of Chaucer is intensity ; of Spenser, remoteness ; of Milton, elevation ; of Shakspeare, everything." The whole passage is characteristical of nothing but Mr. Hazlitt.

.   .   .   .   .   .

[p. 432] The following lines from Chaucer are very pleasing :—

> '——Emelie that fayrer was to sene

.   .   .   .   .   .

> I n'ot which was the finer of hem two.'

But surely the beauty does not lie in the last line, though it is with this that Mr. Hazlitt is chiefly struck.

[Hazlitt answers this criticism in his Letter to William Gifford, 1819 ; *see* below. For Hazlitt's Lectures *see* below, 1818.]

1818. Hallam, Henry. *View of the State of Europe during the Middle Ages*, 2 vols, vol. ii, pp. 607–8. [In the edition of 1819 the references are vol. iii, pp. 575–7.]

[p. 607] But the principal ornament of our English literature was Geoffrey Chaucer, who, along with Dante and Petrarch, fills up the triumvirate of great poets in the middle ages. . . . I cannot, in my own taste, go completely along with the eulogies that some have bestowed upon Chaucer, who seems to me to have wanted grandeur, where he is original, both in conception and in language. But in vivacity of imagination and ease of expression, he is above all the poets of the middle time, and comparable perhaps to the greatest of those who have followed. He invented, or rather introduced from France, and employed with facility the regular iambic couplet; and though it was not to be expected that he should perceive the capacities latent in that measure, his versification, to which he accommodated a very licentious and arbitrary pronunciation, is uniform and harmonious. [Footnote here referring to Tyrwhitt's essay, and Nott's disagreement with it (*q. v.* above, 1775, vol. i, p. 442, and 1815–16).] It is chiefly, indeed, as a comic poet, and a minute observer of manners and circumstances, that Chaucer excels. In [p. 608] serious and moral poetry he is frequently languid and diffuse; but he springs, like Antæus from the earth, when his subject changes to coarse satire or merry narrative. Among his more elevated compositions, the Knight's Tale is abundantly sufficient to immortalize Chaucer. . . . The second place may be given to Troilus and Creseide, a beautiful and interesting poem, though enfeebled by expansion. But perhaps the most eminent, or at any rate the most characteristic testimony to his genius will be found in the Prologue to his Canterbury Tales; a work entirely and exclusively his own, which can seldom be said of his poetry, and the vivid delineations of which perhaps very few writers but Shakspeare could have equalled.

1818. Hazlitt, William. *Lectures on the English Poets*, pp. 25-6, 27, 41-85, 88, 90, 91, 99, 102, 135, 161, 162. (Collected Works of William Hazlitt, ed. Waller and Glover, 1902-6, 13 vols., vol. v, pp. 13, 19-46, 50-52, 68, 82, 99, 129, 146. *See* also Blackwood's Edinburgh Magazine, February, 1818, vol. ii, pp. 558-60.)

Lecture II.   On Chaucer and Spenser.

[p. 19]   . . . I shall take, as the subject of the present lecture, Chaucer and Spenser, two out of four of the greatest names in poetry, which this country has to boast.   Both of them, however, were much indebted to the early poets of Italy, and may be considered as belonging, in a certain degree, to the same school.   .   .   .   .

[Here follows a short biography of Chaucer.]

[p. 20]   There is . . . an obvious similarity between the practical turn of Chaucer's mind and the restless impatience of his character, and the tone of his writings.   Yet it would be too much to attribute the one to the other as cause and effect : for Spenser, whose poetical temperament was as effeminate as Chaucer's was stern and masculine, was equally engaged in public affairs, and had mixed equally in the great world. . . . For while Chaucer's intercourse with the busy world, and collision with the actual passions and conflicting interests of others, seemed to brace the sinews of his understanding, and gave to his writings the air of a man who describes persons and things that he had known and been intimately concerned in ; the same opportunities, operating on a differently con-stituted frame, only served to alienate Spenser's mind the more from the ' close-pent up' scenes of ordinary life. . . .

It is not possible for any two writers to be more opposite in this respect.   Spenser delighted in luxurious enjoyment ; Chaucer, in severe activity of mind.   As Spenser was the most romantic and visionary, Chaucer was the most practical of all the great poets, the most a man of business and the world. His poetry reads like history.   Everything has a downright reality ; at least in the relator's mind.   A simile, or a sentiment, is as if it were given in upon evidence.   Thus he describes Cressid's first avowal of her love.

' And as the new abashed nightingale, . . .
That stinteth first when she beginneth sing,
     .   .   .   .   .   .
Right so Cresseide, . . .' [etc., one stanza].
                              [Troilus, Bk. iii, ll. 1233-9.]

This is so true and natural, and beautifully simple, that the two things seem identified with each other. Again, it is said in the Knight's Tale—

[p. 21]
'Thus passeth yere by yere, and day by day [etc., to]
I n'ot which was the finer of hem two.'

[Knight's Tale, ll. 175-81.]

This scrupulousness about the literal preference, as if some question of matter of fact was at issue, is remarkable.[1] I might mention that other, where he compares the meeting between Palamon and Arcite to a hunter waiting for a lion in a gap ;—

'That stondeth at a gap with a spere,'
[etc., four lines],
[Knight's Tale, ll. 781-4.]

or that still finer one of Constance, when she is condemned to death—

'Have ye not seen somtime a pale face ?'
[etc., one stanza].
[Man of Law's Tale, ll. 547-53.]

The beauty, the pathos here does not seem to be of the poet's seeking, but a part of the necessary texture of the fable. He speaks of what he wishes to describe with the accuracy, the discrimination of one who relates what has happened to himself, or has had the best information from those who have been eye-witnesses of it. The strokes of his pencil always tell. He dwells only on the essential, on that which would be interesting to the persons really concerned: yet as he never omits any material circumstance, he is prolix from the number of points on which he touches, without being diffuse on any one ; and is sometimes tedious from the fidelity with which he adheres to his subject, as other writers are from the frequency of their digressions from it. The chain of his story is composed of a number of fine links, closely connected together, and riveted by a single blow. There is an instance of the minuteness which he introduces into his most serious

[1 *See* Gifford's criticism of this passage, 1818, above, and Hazlitt's answer below, 1819.]

descriptions in his account of Palamon when left alone in his cell :

> 'Swiche sorrow he maketh that the grete tour
> Resouned of his yelling and clamour,
> The pure fetters on his shinnes grete
> Were of his bitter salte teres wete.'

[Knight's Tale, ll. 419–22.]

[p. 22]   The mention of this last circumstance looks like a part of the instructions he had to follow, which he had no discretionary power to omit or introduce at pleasure. He is contented to find grace and beauty in truth. He exhibits for the most part the naked object, with little drapery thrown over it. His metaphors, which are few, are not for ornament, but use, and as like as possible to the things themselves. He does not affect to show his power over the reader's mind, but the power which his subject has over his own. The readers of Chaucer's poetry feel more nearly what the persons he describes must have felt, than perhaps those of any other poet. His sentiments are not voluntary effusions of the poet's fancy, but founded on the natural impulses and habitual prejudices of the characters he has to represent. There is an inveteracy of purpose, a sincerity of feeling, which never relaxes or grows vapid, in whatever they do or say. There is no artificial, pompous display, but a strict parsimony of the poet's materials, like the rude simplicity of the age in which he lived. His poetry resembles the root just springing from the ground, rather than the full-blown flower. His muse is no 'babbling gossip of the air,' fluent and redundant; but, like a stammerer, or a dumb person, that has just found the use of speech, crowds many things together with eager haste, with anxious pauses, and fond repetitions to prevent mistake. His words point as an index to the objects, like the eye or finger. There were none of the common-places of poetic diction in our author's time, no reflected lights of fancy, no borrowed roseate tints; he was obliged to inspect things for himself, to look narrowly, and almost to handle the object, as in the obscurity of morning we partly see and partly grope our way; so that his descriptions have a sort of tangible character belonging to them, and produce the effect of sculpture on the mind. Chaucer had an equal eye for truth of nature and discrimination of character; and his interest in what he saw gave new distinctness and force to his power of observation. The picturesque and the dramatic are in him closely blended together, and hardly distinguishable ; for he principally describes external appearances as indicating character, as symbols of internal sentiment. There is a meaning in what he sees ; and it is this which catches his eye by sympathy. Thus the costume and dress of the Canterbury Pilgrims—of the Knight—the Squire—the Oxford Scholar—the Gap-toothed Wife of Bath, and the rest, speak for themselves. . .

[Quotation, Prol. ll. 118–29, 136–55, 165–207, 321–2, 449–52.]

[p. 24]　　Chaucer, it has been said [by Blake, *q. v.* above, 1809], numbered the classes of men, as Linnæus numbered the plants. Most of them remain to this day : others that are obsolete . . . still live in his descriptions of them. Such is the Sompnoure :

　　'A Sompnoure was ther with us in that place,
　　That hadde a fire-red cherubinnes face '
　　[and following twenty-five lines, Prol. ll. 623–69, 688].

[p. 25]　　It would be a curious speculation (at least for those who think that the characters of men never change, though manners, opinions, and institutions may) to know what has become of this character of the Sompnoure in the present day; whether or not it has any technical representative in existing professions ; into what channels and conduits it has withdrawn itself, where it lurks unseen in cunning obscurity, or else shows its face boldly, pampered into all the insolence of office, in some other shape, as it is deterred or encouraged by circumstances. *Chaucer's characters modernised*, upon this principle of historic derivation, would be an useful addition to our knowledge of human nature. But who is there to undertake it ? . . .

　　　　[Quotation, Knight's Tale, ll. 1270–1328.]

[p. 26]　　Chaucer's descriptions of natural scenery possess the
[p. 27] same sort of characteristic excellence, or what might be termed *gusto*. They have a local truth and freshness, which gives the very feeling of the air, the coolness or moisture of the ground. Inanimate objects are thus made to have a fellow-feeling in the interest of the story ; and render back

the sentiment of the speaker's mind. One of the finest parts in Chaucer is of this mixed kind. It is the beginning of the Flower and the Leaf, where he describes the delight of that young beauty, shrowded in her bower, and listening, in the morning of the year to the singing of the nightingale.

[Quotation, Floure and the Leaf, ed. Skeat, ll. 36–42, 78–133.]

[p. 28]   It was the same trust in nature, and reliance on his subject, which enabled Chaucer to describe the grief and [p. 29] patience of Griselda ; the faith of Constance ; and the heroic perseverance of the little child, who, going to school through the streets of Jewry,

' Oh *Alma Redemptoris mater,* loudly sung,' [1]

and who after his death, still triumphed in his song. Chaucer has more of this deep, internal, sustained sentiment, than any other writer, except Boccaccio. In depth of simple pathos, and intensity of conception, never swerving from his subject, I think no other writer comes near him, not even the Greek tragedians. . . . I will take the following from the Knight's Tale. The distress of Arcite, in consequence of his banishment from his love, is thus described :

' Whan that Arcite to Thebes comen was,
Ful oft a day he swelt and said Alas,
For sene his lady shall he never mo. . . . '
[and fourteen following lines, Knight's Tale, ll. 497–513].

This picture of the sinking of the heart, of the wasting away of the body and mind, of the gradual failure of all the faculties under the contagion of a rankling sorrow, cannot be surpassed. Of the same kind is his farewel to his mistress, after he has gained her hand and lost his life in the combat :

Alas the wo ! alas the peines stronge . . .
[and eight following lines, Knight's Tale, ll. 1913–21].

[p. 30]   The death of Arcite is the more affecting, as it comes after triumph and victory, after the pomp of sacrifice, the solemnities of prayer, the celebration of the gorgeous rites of chivalry. The descriptions of the three temples of Mars,

[1 This line, which has two syllables too many, does not occur in the *Prioresses Tale.*]

of Venus, and Diana, of the ornaments and ceremonies used
in each, with the reception given to the offerings of the
lovers, have a beauty and grandeur, much of which is lost in
Dryden's version. . .

[Quotation, Knight's Tale, ll. 1109–22.]

. . . The story of Griselda is in Boccaccio ; but the Clerk of
Oxenforde, who tells it, professes to have learnt it from
Petrarch. . . . In spite of the barbarity of the circumstances,
which are abominable, the sentiment remains unimpaired and
unalterable.   It is of that kind, ' that heaves no sigh, that
sheds no tear ' ; but it hangs upon the beatings of the heart ;
it is a part of the very being ; it is as inseparable from it as
the breath we draw.   It is still and calm as the face of death.
Nothing can touch its ethereal purity : tender as the yielding
flower, it is fixed as the marble firmament.   The only remon-
strance she makes, the only complaint she utters against all
the ill-treatment she receives, is that single line where, when
turned back naked to her father's house, she says,

' Let me not like a worm go by the way.'

[p. 31]   The first outline given of the characters is inimitable :

'Nought fer fro thilke paleis honourable'
[ten stanzas, Clerkes Tale, ll. 141–89, 218–38].

.   .   .   .

[p. 32]   The story of the little child slain in Jewry, (which is told
by the Prioress, and worthy to be told by her who was 'all
conscience and tender heart,') is not less touching than that
of Griselda.   It is simple and heroic to the last degree.   The
poetry of Chaucer has a religious sanctity about it, connected
with the manners and superstitions of the age.   It has all
the spirit of martyrdom.

It has also all the extravagance and the utmost licentiousness
of comic humour, equally arising out of the manners of the
time.   In this too Chaucer resembled Boccaccio that he excelled
in both styles, and could pass at will 'from grave to gay,
from lively to severe ;' but he never confounded the two
styles together (except from that involuntary and unconscious
mixture of the pathetic and humorous, which is almost always
to be found in nature), and was exclusively taken up with
what he set about, whether it was jest or earnest.   The

[p. 33] Wife of Bath's Prologue (which Pope has very admirably modernised) is, perhaps, unequalled as a comic story. The Cock and the Fox is also excellent for lively strokes of character and satire. January and May is not so good as some of the others. Chaucer's versification, considering the time at which he wrote, and that versification is a thing in a great degree mechanical, is not one of his least merits. It has considerable strength and harmony, and its apparent deficiency in the latter respect arises chiefly from the alterations which have since taken place in the pronunciation or mode of accenting the words of the language. The best general rule for reading him is to pronounce the final *e*, as in reading Italian.

It was observed in the last Lecture that painting describes what the object is in itself, poetry what it implies or suggests. Chaucer's poetry is not, in general, the best confirmation of the truth of this distinction, for his poetry is more picturesque and historical than almost any other. But there is one instance in point. . . . It is the story of the three thieves who go in search of Death to kill him, and who meeting with him, are entangled in their fate by his words, without knowing him. . . . The moral impression of Death is essentially visionary; its [p. 34] reality is in the mind's eye. . . . Death is a mighty abstraction, like Night, or Space, or Time. He is an ugly customer, who will not be invited to supper, or to sit for his picture. He is with us and about us, but we do not see him. . . . Chaucer knew this. He makes three riotous companions go in search of Death to kill him, they meet with an old man whom they reproach with his age, and ask why he does not die, to which he answers thus:

> Ne Deth, alas! ne will not han my lif
> [and eleven following lines, Pardoner's Tale, ll. 399–410].

They then ask the old man where they shall find out Death to kill him, and he sends them on an errand which ends in the death of all three. We hear no more of him, but it is Death that they have encountered!

.   .   .   .

[p. 46] The four greatest names in English poetry are almost the four first we come to—Chaucer, Spenser, Shakespeare, and Milton. There are no others that can really be put in competition with these. The two last had justice done them by the voice of common fame. Their names are blazoned in the very firmament of reputation; while the two first (though "the fault has been more in their stars than in themselves that they are underlings") either never emerged far above the horizon, or were too soon involved in the obscurity of time. The three first of these are excluded from Dr. Johnson's Lives of the Poets (Shakespeare indeed is so from the dramatic form of his compositions). . . . In comparing these four writers together, it might be said that Chaucer excels as the poet of manners, or of real life . . . Chaucer most frequently describes things as they are. . . . As poets, and as great poets, imagination, that is, the power of feigning things according to nature, was common to them all; but the principle, or moving power, to which this faculty was most subservient in Chaucer, was habit, or inveterate prejudice. . . . The characteristic of Chaucer is intensity . . .

[p. 50]   Chaucer's characters are sufficiently distinct from one another, but they are too little varied in themselves, too much like identical propositions. They are consistent, but uniform; we get no idea of them from first to last; they are not placed in different lights, nor are their subordinate *traits* brought out in new situations; they are like portraits or physiognomical studies, with the distinguishing features marked with inconceivable truth and precision, but that preserve the same unaltered air and attitude. . . . Chaucer's characters are narrative. . . . That is, Chaucer told only as much of his story as he pleased, as was required for a particular purpose. He answered for his characters himself. . . . In Chaucer we perceive a fixed essence of character . . .

[p. 52]   Nearly all those [dialogues] in Shakespeare, where the interest is wrought up to its highest pitch, afford example of this dramatic fluctuation of passion. The interest in Chaucer is quite different; it is like the course of a river, strong, and full, and increasing.

[On Dryden and Pope.]

[p. 82]   . . . His [Dryden's] alterations from Chaucer and Boccaccio show a greater knowledge of the taste of his readers and power of pleasing them, than acquaintance with the genius of his authors. He ekes out the lameness of the verse in the former, and breaks the force of the passion in both. The Tancred and Sigismunda is the only general exception, in which, I think, he has fully retained, if not improved upon, the impassioned declamation of the original. The Honoria has none of the bewildered, dreary, preternatural effect of Boccaccio's story. Nor has the Flower and the Leaf any thing of the enchanting simplicity and concentrated feeling of Chaucer's romantic fiction. Dryden, however, sometimes seemed to indulge himself as well as his readers, as in keeping entire that noble line in Palamon's address to Venus :

Thou gladder of the mount of Cithæron !

His Tales have been, I believe, the most popular of his works ; and I should think that a modern translation of some of the other serious tales in Boccaccio and Chaucer, as that of Isabella, the Falcon, of Constance, the Prioress's Tale, and others, if executed with taste and spirit, could not fail to succeed in the present day.

[p. 146] I cannot say I ever learnt much about Shakespeare or Milton, Spenser or Chaucer, from these professed guides [some of the poets of the day] ; for I never heard them say much about them. They were always talking of themselves and one another.

1818. **Hazlitt**, William. *Lectures on the Comic Writers.* On the Works of Hogarth, etc. Delivered in 1818. (Collected Works of William Hazlitt, ed. Waller and Glover, 1902–6, 13 vols., vol. viii, pp. 144, 151.)

[p. 144] [The contradictory faculties of embodying the serious and ludicrous combined in Chaucer, Shakspere and Hogarth.]

1818. **Hazlitt**, William. *A View of the English Stage*, p. 239. (Collected Works, ed. Waller and Glover, 1902–6, 13 vols., vol. viii, p. 284, 371.)

p. 284] Chaucer spoke of the Monks historically, Shakespear poetically.

[These theatrical criticisms appeared first in the *Morning Chronicle, Champion, Examiner* and *Times,* 1813–17.]

1818. **Hazlitt**, William. *Review* of *Letters of Horace Walpole,* [in] The Edinburgh Review, Dec. 1818, vol. xxxi, p. 92. (Collected Works, ed. Waller and Glover, 1902–6, 13 vols., vol. x, p. 171.)

The author is exceedingly amusing in his attempt at tracing his descent from Chaucer.

[This refers to Walpole's letter to George Montagu, of Aug. 11, 1748, *q.v.* above, vol. i, p. 898.]

1818. Keats, John. *Robin Hood; to a Friend.* (Complete Works of John Keats, ed. H. Buxton Forman, 5 vols., 1900–01, vol. ii, p. 118, vol. iv, p. 73 [in a letter to J. H. Reynolds of 3 Feb. 1818].)

> Gone, the merry morris din;
> Gone the song of Gamelyn;
> Gone, the tough-belted outlaw
> Idling in the "grenè shawe."

[*Cf.* "Where ridestow under this grene shawe," *Freres Tale,* line 88. Similarly Keats uses the phrase "Ah! hertè mine" in a letter (11 Oct. 1819, Works, vol. v, p. 129). This occurs *passim* in *Troilus,* but is common in old poetry.]

1818. Keats, John. *Letter* to John Hamilton Reynolds, [dated] Teignmouth, May 3, 1818. (Complete Works of John Keats, ed. H. Buxton Forman, 5 vols. 1900–1, vol. iv, p. 106.)

We will have some such days upon the heath like that of last summer—and why not with the same book? or what say you to a black-letter Chaucer printed in 1596 [*sic*] . . . Aye, I've got one huzza! I shall have it bound in gothique —a nice sombre binding—it will go a little way to unmodernize.

[There is no Chaucer of 1596. Keats probably meant Speght's edn. of 1598.]

1818. Keats, John. *Poem* in Letter to Thomas Keats, July 17, 1818. (Complete Works of John Keats, ed. H. Buxton Forman, 1900–1, 5 vols., vol. ii, p. 231, vol. iv, p. 139.)

> And as this is the summum bo-
> num of all conquering,
> I leave "withouten wordes mo"
> The Gadfly's little sting.

[Prol. l. 808.]

1818. Scott, Sir Walter. *Chivalry,* [in] Supplement to Encyclopædia Britannica, vol. iii, pp. 121, 124, 128, 130, 132, 140. (Miscellaneous Prose Works of Sir W. Scott, 30 vols., Edinburgh, 1834–71, vol. vi, pp. 27–8, 42, 56–7, 65, 74–5, 107.)

[p. 27]　Chaucer, when he describes the assembly of the knights
[p. 28]　who came with Arcite and Palemon to fight for the love of the fair Emilie, describes the manners of his age in the following lines :—

> For every knight that loved chivalry
> .　　.　　.　　.　　.
> It were a lusty sight for to see.
> .　　.　　.　　.　　.

[p. 42] The *Canterbury Tales* of Chaucer contain many narratives, of which, not only the diction, but the whole turn of the narrative, is extremely gross. Yet it does not seem to have occurred to the author, a man of rank and fashion, that they were improper to be recited, either in the presence of the Prioress or her votaries, or in that of the noble Knight who

> ——of his port was meek as is a maid,
> And never yet no villany he said.

And he makes but a light apology for including the disasters of the *Millar of Trompington*, or of *Absalom the Gentle Clerk*, in the same series of narrations with the *Knight's Tale*.

[p. 56] In the words of Chaucer, describing the Character of the Squire—

> Curteis, he was, lowly and servisable,
> And carf before his fader at the table.

> .   .   .   .   .   .

Chaucer's Squire, besides that he was " singing and fluting all the day "—

> Could songs make and well indite
> Joust, and eke dance, and well pourtray and write.

[p. 57] Unquestionably, few possessed all these attributes; but the poet, with his usual precision and vivacity, has given us the picture of a perfect esquire. . . .

[p. 74] Chaucer has enumerated some of these varieties [of Knights' armour] :—

> With him ther wenten Knights many on.
> Some wol ben armed in an habergeon

[p. 75]   [and eight following lines].

1818. Scott, Sir Walter. *Rob Roy*, 3 vols., vol. ii, chap. vi, p. 122, ch. xii, p. 242. (Border Edition, ed. Andrew Lang, 1893, vol. ii, ch. ii, p. 21, ch. viii, p. 93.)

[Vol. ii, p. 21] We alighted at the door of a jolly hostler-wife, as Andrew called her, The Ostelere of old father Chaucer, by whom we were civilly received.

[Chapter heading.]

[Vol. ii, p. 93] So stands the Thracian herdsman with his spear
         [and five following lines].
         [Dryden's] Palamon and Arcite.

1818. Todd, Henry John. *Johnson's Dictionary*, ed. by the Rev. H. J. Todd, 4 vols., vol. i, pp. liv, lxx *n.*, lxxvi–vii.

[p. liv] [Quotation from *Sir Thopas*, giving the "romaunces of pris."]

[p. lxiii] [Johnson says that "Gower calls Chaucer his disciple." On this Todd says :] Dr. Johnson is mistaken in saying that Gower calls Chaucer *his* disciple ; for it is Venus whom Gower describes, at the close of his Confessio Amantis, claiming Chaucer as *her scholar and bard.* That Gower is to be placed before Chaucer is unquestionable. He was born before Chaucer. Authors both historical and poetical, in the century after the decease of these poets, usually coupling their names and describing their accomplishments, place Gower before Chaucer ; not intending precedence in respect to talents, but merely to seniority. John Fox observes, that "he (Chaucer) and Gower were both of one time ; although it seemeth that *Gower was a great deale his ancient."*

[p. lxx n.] Dr. Johnson has copied both the poetry and prose of Chaucer from the edition of Urry in 1721, which Mr. Tyrwhitt, the last accomplished editor of the poet's Canterbury Tales, pronounces most incorrect. This may be abundantly seen even by the comparison of so much of the Prologue, as Dr. Johnson took from Urry, with the text as now adopted from the excellent edition of Tyrwhitt. With the text of the remaining poems we must be content, till an elaborate and correct edition of the poet's works, which we greatly want, be given. Perhaps some little help is afforded towards such an important undertaking, in Illustrations of Gower and Chaucer, published in 1810 [by Todd, *q.v.* above] ; an account of several manuscripts of Chaucer, containing hitherto unemployed materials, being there given. . . . Of the prose of Chaucer there has been less corruption.

[p. lxxvii] [John Walton of Oseney's praise of Chaucer quoted ; *see* above, 1410, vol. i, pp. 20–21.]

1818. Unknown. *Notice of Hazlitt's 2nd Lecture on English Poetry— Chaucer and Spenser—*[in] Blackwood's Edinburgh Magazine, vol. ii, February, pp. 558–60. [For Hazlitt *see* above, 1818.]

[The Notice is a general account of Hazlitt's lecture, devoid of any real critical examination.]

[*a.* **1819. Southey**, Robert.] *The Doctor*, [published] 1834, vol. i, p. 48, vol. ii, pp. vi, 24, vol. iii, p. x, vol. v, p. 157, vol. vii, p. 87 note.

[Vol. i,   The persons who?—
p. 48]
                  I maie not tell you all at once ;
                  But as I maie and can, I shall
                  By order tellen you it all.
          So saith Chaucer. [A reminiscence of *B. of the Duchesse*, ll.
          216–18 ?]

[Vol. ii,   [Heading to chapter xxxv.]
pp. vi
and 24]   Why I should I sowen draf out of my fist
          When I may sowen wheat, if that me list ?
                              Chaucer [Parson's Prol., ll. 35–6].

[Vol. iii,   Prelude of Mottoes.
p. x]
                  Out of the old fieldes, as men saith
          [and four following lines, Assemble of Foules, st. 4].
                                              Chaucer.

[Vol. v,   [Wordsworth has 'very skilfully' modernised one of
p. 157]   Chaucer's poems.]

[Vol. vii, p. 87]   We . . . sat doun, an' grat.*

          [Note] * *i. e.* wept, from the old word *greet*, common to all the
          northern languages. Chaucer, Spenser, etc., use it.

          [*The Doctor*, though not published till 1834, was begun in 1813, and Cuthbert
          Southey says (Life and Correspondence of Southey) that the greater part of the book
          was written before he was born, *i. e.* before 1819.]

1819. Byron, George Gordon, Lord. *Letter to Mr. Murray*, Jan.
          20, 1819 [printed in the Works of Byron, ed. T. Moore, 1832–5,
          vol. iv, p. 138, letter 324]. (Letters and Journals, ed. Rowland
          E. Prothero, 1900, vol. iv, pp. 276.)
              The opinions which I have asked of Mr. H[obhouse] and
          others were with regard to the poetical merit, and not as to
          what they may think due to the *Cant* of the day, which still
          reads the *Bath Guide, Little's Poems*, Prior, and Chaucer, to
          say nothing of Fielding and Smollett.

1819. Campbell, Thomas. *Specimens of the British Poets*, vol. i.
          References to Chaucer's language, p. 14 ; metre, p. 59 ; Sir Thopas,
          p. 60 ; Chaucer and Langland, pp. 62–3 ; Court of Love, p. 70 ;
          romance, pp. 70–71 ; Hous of Fame, p. 71 ; Flower and Leaf,
          p. 72 ; Gower, p. 73 ; Chaucer and his successors, pp. 79, 87–88 ;
          vol. ii., pp. 3–49 [biographical notice, followed by Prol., ll. 1–714],
          50, 59–60, 67–9 [Scottish Poetry], 76, 77.

              [The edition consists of an Essay on English Poetry, vol. i, pp.
          3–271, and a general index in the same vol., followed by extracts
          from the principal poets, each preceded by a biographical notice.
          The preliminary Essay was published separately, Boston, 1819,
          and, with the Biographical Notices, edited by Peter Cunningham,
          in 1848. The Chaucer references in the latter are, pp. 7, 9 *n.*,
          23, 26, 27, 28, 29, 31–34, 37, 47 and *n.*, 52, 53 *n.*, 104 and *n.*,
          108 *n.*, 117 *n.*, 120–36, 138, 163, 303 *n.*, 396 *n.*]

[vol. i,
pp. 70-
2]   Chaucer was probably known and distinguished as a poet anterior to the appearance of Langlande's Visions. Indeed if he had produced nothing else than his youthful poem, "the Court of Love," it was sufficient to indicate one destined to harmonise and refine the national strains. But it is likely, that before his thirty-fourth year, about which time Langlande's Visions may be supposed to have been finished, Chaucer had given several compositions to the public.

[Campbell continues that the simple old narrative romance had become too familiar to invite Chaucer, and the poverty of English had obliged him to seek models in Latin and foreign tongues. Ovid, Claudian, Statius and Boethius were the favourite Latins, by the allegory of the last two of whom he was influenced, as by the French allegorical romances. The dreams, emblems, etc., of this last visionary school proved too light and playful for his strong genius, though in this work, too, his peculiar grace and gaiety are conspicuous. The Hous of Fame and Flower and Leaf are examples. His similar poems, even the most fantastic in design, are relieved by fresh and joyous descriptions of nature. . . . Chaucer was subsequently drawn to the style of Boccaccio.]

   .   .   .   .

[vol. ii,
pp. 13,
14]   [Tyrwhitt had vindicated Chaucer from the charge brought against him by Verstegan, etc., of having adulterated English with French words. Such revolutions in language are not wrought by individuals; and Chaucer's style will compare with that of Gower, Wyclif and Mandeville.]

   .   .   .   .

[p. 15]   . . . He has a double claim to rank as the founder of English poetry, from having been the first to make it the vehicle of spirited representations of life and native manners, and from having been the first great architect of our versification, in giving our language the ten syllable, or heroic measure, which, though it may sometimes be found among the lines of more ancient versifiers, evidently comes in only by accident. This measure occurs in the earliest poem that is attributed to him, The Court of Love. . . . It is a dream, in which the poet fancies himself taken to the Temple of Love, introduced to a mistress, and sworn to observe the statutes of the amatory
[p. 16] god. As the earliest work of Chaucer, it interestingly exhibits the successful effort of his youthful hand in erecting a new and stately fabric of English numbers. As a piece of

fancy, it is grotesque and meager [*sic*]; but the lines often flow with great harmony.

His story of Troilus and Cresseide was the delight of Sir Philip Sydney ; and perhaps, excepting the Canterbury Tales, was, down to the time of Queen Elizabeth, the most popular poem in the English language.   It is a story of vast length and almost desolate simplicity, and abounds in all those glorious anachronisms which were then, and so long after, permitted to romantic poetry : such as making the son of King Priam read the Thebais of Statius, and the gentlemen of Troy converse about the devil, justs and tournaments, bishops, parliaments, and scholastic divinity.

The languor of the story is, however, relieved by many touches of pathetic beauty.   The confession of Cresseide in the scene of felicity, when the poet compares her to the " new abashed nightingale, that stinteth first ere she beginneth sing," is a fine passage, deservedly noticed by Warton.   The grief of Troilus after the departure of Cresseide is strongly portrayed in Troilus's soliloquy in his bed.

. . . .

[p 17]   The sensations of Troilus, on coming to the house of his faithless Cresseide, when, instead of finding her returned, he beholds the barred doors and shut windows, giving tokens of her absence, as well as his precipitate departure from the distracting scene, are equally well described.

. . . .

The two best of Chaucer's allegories, The Flower and the Leaf, and The House of Fame, have been fortunately per-
[p. 18] petuated in our language ; the former by Dryden, the latter by Pope.   The Flower and the Leaf is an exquisite piece of fairy fancy. . . . Pope had not so enchanting a subject in The House of Fame ; yet, with deference to Warton, that critic has done Pope injustice in assimilating his imitations of Chaucer to the modern ornaments in Westminster Abbey, which impair the solemn effect of the ancient building.   The many absurd and fantastic particulars in Chaucer's House of Fame will not suffer us to compare it, as a structure in poetry, with so noble a pile as Westminster Abbey in architecture. Much of Chaucer's fantastic matter has been judiciously omitted by Pope, who at the same time has clothed the best ideas of the old poem in spirited numbers and expression.

Chaucer supposes himself to be snatched up to heaven by a large eagle, who addresses him in the name of St. James and the Virgin Mary, and, in order to quiet the poet's fears of being carried up to Jupiter, like another Ganymede, or turned into a star like Orion, tells him, that Jove wishes him to sing of other subjects than love and "blind Cupido," and has therefore ordered, that Dan Chaucer should be brought to behold the House of Fame. In Pope, the philosophy of [p. 19] fame comes with much more propriety from the poet himself, than from the beak of a talkative eagle.

It was not until his green old age that Chaucer put forth, in the Canterbury Tales, the full variety of his genius, and the pathos and romance, as well as the playfulness of fiction. In the serious part of those tales he is, in general, more deeply indebted to preceding materials, than in the comic stories, which he raised upon slight hints to the air and spirit of originals. . . .

Chaucer's design . . . though it is left unfinished, has definite boundaries, and incidents to keep alive our curiosity, independent of the tales themselves. At the same time, while the action of the poem is an event too simple to divert the attention altogether from the pilgrims' stories, the pilgrimage itself is an occasion sufficiently important to draw together almost all the varieties of existing society, from the knight to the artisan, who, agreeably to the old simple manners, assemble in the same room of the hostellerie. The enumeration of those [p. 20] characters in the Prologue forms a scene, full, without confusion; and the object of their journey gives a fortuitous air to the grouping of individuals, who collectively represent the age and state of society in which they live.

. . . .

[p. 21] Chaucer's forte is description; much of his moral reflection is superfluous; none of his characteristic painting. His men and women are not mere ladies and gentlemen, like those who furnish apologies for Boccaccio's stories. They rise before us minutely traced, profusely varied, and strongly discriminated. Their features and casual manners seem to have an amusing congruity with their moral characters. He notices minute circumstances as if by chance; but every touch has its effect to our conception so distinctly, that we seem to live and travel with his personages throughout the journey.

1819. Cary, Henry Francis. *The Life of Dante*, prefixed to *The Vision
. . . of Dante* translated by H. F. Cary, 2nd edition, 1819, 3 vols.,
vol. i, pp. xxxix, xliii, note [many notes additional to those in
1st edition of 1814, *q. v.*]. Notes on the text, pp. 12,* 13, 18,
21,* 32, 37, 43,* 44,* 47,* 60,* 99,* 112, 127, 264, 265, [a note
from Warton's Hist. of Eng. Poetry] 269, 281, 283, 287, 292 ;
vol. ii, pp. xi, 4, 64, 78, 168,* 193, 201,* 207,* 247,* 255,* 305,
309 * ; vol. iii, pp. 4, 7, 9,* 81,* 127, 131,* 148, 171, 172, 204,
215,* 226,* 237,* 280,* 290,* 291.*

[* Not in 1st edition.]

1819. [Clarke, William.] *Repertorium Bibliographicum; or, some
account of the most celebrated British Libraries*, 2 vols., vol. i,
pp. 35, 37, 76, 116–7, 142, 166–7, 183, 198, 233, 256, 280–1 ; vol. ii,
pp. 351–2, 362, 389, 441, 449, 481, 521, 534, 553, 602, also index,
pp. 616–7, 619, 670, 672.

[Brief accounts of the libraries, with lists of notable volumes
under each. The Chaucers are entered alternatively under
either Caxton, Wynkyn de Worde, or the author.]

1819–28. Coleridge, Samuel Taylor. *Note on Milton and Shakespeare*,
[in] Anima Poetæ, ed. Ernest Hartley Coleridge, 1895, p. 296.

[p. 296] Found Mr. G[illman] with Hartley in the garden, attempting
to explain to himself and to Hartley a feeling of a something
not present in Milton's works, that is, in "Paradise Lost,"
"Paradise Regained," and "Samson Agonistes," which he *did*
feel delightedly in the "Lycidas." . . . And this appeared to
me to be the *poet* appearing and wishing to appear as the poet,
and likewise as the man, as much as, though more rare than,
the father, the brother, the preacher, and the patriot. Compare
with Milton, Chaucer's "Fall of the Leaf" [*sic*] and Spenser
throughout, and you cannot but *feel* what Gillman meant to
convey.

1819. Dibdin, Thomas Frognall. *Typographical Antiquities* . . . begun
by Joseph Ames and augmented by William Herbert, and now
enlarged with copious notes, vol. iv, pp. 371 *n.*, 469–70 [Chaucer's
Works, 1561].

[For vols. i, ii, and iii, *see* above, 1810, 1812 and 1816. For Ames's original edn.
of 1749, *see* vol. i, p. 398 ; for Herbert's intermediate edn. *see* vol. i, 1785, p. 477 ;
1786, p. 483 ; 1790, p. 491.]

1819. Ellis, Sir Henry. *Remarks* on *Lansdowne MS. 851*, and *Vol. XLIV. of Bishop Kennett's Collections:* consisting of Biographical Memoranda, (many of them relating to the English clergy) from A.D. 1500 to A.D. 1521, [in] *A Catalogue of the Lansdowne MSS. in the British Museum*, 1812–19, part ii, 1819, pp. 210, 239, Lansdowne MSS. 851, 978.

851. folio.

[pp. 210-11]   A very fair, perfect, and well preserved copy of Chaucer's Canterbury Tales, elegantly written on vellum about the reign of Henry the Fifth.   It contains,

1. "Vita Galfridi Caucer [sic orig.] ex Scriptorum Britanniæ Centuria Septima Cap. XXIIII," fo. 1.

This is only a modern transcript from Bale.

2. The general Prologue.   fo. 2 [followed by the Tales, concluding with]

48. "Sermo" Rectoris.   fo. 230 *b.*

In the initial letter to this volume there is a small and neatly executed whole length portrait of Chaucer, with a book in his hand and a knife suspended from his neck.   He is dressed in a long greyish gown, with red stockings, and a kind of sandals.   His head is uncovered, and the hair rather closely shorn.   This miniature, though a little damaged, may be of considerable use to an artist.   Many of the other pages and letters are painted and gilt in the usual style of the time.

The manuscript formerly belonged to Mr. Philip Carteret Webb, and was consulted by Mr. Tyrwhitt and cited by him under the letter W.   See his admirable edition of "The Canterbury Tales," vol. i, p. xxiii. edit. 1775, in 8vo.

[See the print of the MS. in the Chaucer Society's Six-Text and separate issues.]

[p. 239]   They [Bishop Kennett's Collections] relate to—
1. Geoffrey Chaucer.   fo. 1.

1819. Hazlitt, William. *A Letter to William Gifford, Esq.* (Collected Works of William Hazlitt, ed. Waller and Glover, 1902–6, 13 vols., vol. i, pp. 384, 399, 400, 401.)

[p. 400]   You observe, that "Some lines I have quoted from Chaucer, are very pleasing—

——"Emilie that fayrer was to sene
Than is the lilie upon his stalke grene
And fresher than the May with floures newe:
For with the rose-colour strove hire hewe;
I not which was the finer of hem too." . . .

"But surely the beauty does not lie in the last line, though it is with this that Mr. Hazlitt is chiefly struck. 'This scrupulousness,' he observes, 'about the literal preference, as if some question of matter of fact were at issue, is remarkable.'"

That is, I am not chiefly struck with the beauty of the last line, but with its peculiarity as characteristic of Chaucer. The beauty of the former lines might be in Spenser: the scrupulous exactness of the latter could be found nowhere but in Chaucer. I had said just before, that this poet 'introduces [p. 401] a sentiment or a simile, as if it were given in upon evidence.' I bring this simile as an instance in point, and you say I have not brought it to prove something else.

[For Hazlitt's original criticism and Gifford's comment upon it, *see* above, 1818.]

1819. Hunt, James Henry Leigh. *Pleasant recollections connected with various parts of the Metropolis,* [in] The Indicator, Oct. 27, 1819, pp. 20, 24.

[References to the monument in St. Saviour's church in the Borough to Gower, 'Chaucer's contemporary'; to the Tabard Inn, the site of which is "pointed out by a picture and inscription"; and to the French of Stratforde-atte-Bowe.]

[1819–20. Irving, Washington.] *The Sketch Book of Geoffrey Crayon, Gent.,* London, 1820, 2 vols., vol. i, pp. 129, 177, 183–4, 189, 271–2 *n*, 282 ; vol. ii, p. 415. (Works, Geoffrey Crayon edn., [1880-83], 27 vols., vol. ii, pp. 96–7, 125, 130, 134, 185–6 *n*, 193, 522.)

[The papers composing the Sketch Book were written in England and published serially in America in 1819–20. The first edition in B.M. is that to which references are given above.]

Rural life in England.

[pp. 96–7] [Reference to the *Flower and the Leaf* as Chaucer's.]

A Royal Poet.

[p. 125]   [King James I of Scotland read Chaucer's translation of [p. 130] Boethius in prison ; compared to Palamon and Arcite ; his [p. 134] admiration for Chaucer ; traces of similarity in their writings.]

The Mutability of Literature.

[p. 185 *n*.] [Quotation from "Chaucer's Testament of Love."]

[p. 186 *n*.] Holinshed, in his Chronicle, observes, "Afterwards also, by diligent travell of Geffry Chaucer and John Gowre, in the time of Richard the Second, and after them of John Scogan and John Lydgate, Monke of Berrie, our said toong was brought to an excellent passe." [Holinshed's Chronicles, 1808, 6 vols., vol. i, p. 24 ; *see* below, App. A, 1577.]

[p. 193]   The setting may occasionally be antiquated, and require now and then to be renewed, as in the case of Chaucer; but the brilliancy and intrinsic value of the gems continue unaltered.

Motto to Envoy.

[p. 522]   Go, little Booke, God send thee good passage
[and four following lines].
Chaucer's [or rather Ros's] *Belle Dame sans Mercie.*

1819. **Jeffrey**, Francis. *Review* of Campbell's *Specimens of the British Poets*, [in] The Edinburgh Review, March 1819, vol. **xxxi**, p. 474. (Contributions to the Edinburgh Review, 1853, p. 365.)

The following sketch of Chaucer, and of the long inter-regnum that succeeded, is likewise given with great grace and spirit.

[Here follows a quotation from Campbell's Essay on English Poetry, pp. 71–3, 79–84, *q. v.* above, 1819.]

1819. **Keats**, John. *Letters.* (The Complete Works of John Keats, ed. H. Buxton Forman, 1900–1, vol. v, pp. 31, 67, 93, 121, 133.)

[p. 31]   [To George and Georgiana Keats. March, 1819.] Besides this volume of Beaumont and Fletcher—there are on the table two volumes of Chaucer. . . .

[p. 67]   [To B. R. Haydon. June 17, 1819.] My purpose is now to make one more attempt in the Press—if that fail, " ye hear no more of me " as Chaucer says.

[p. 93]   [To J. H. Reynolds. Sept. 22.] I always somehow associate Chatterton with autumn. . . . He has no French idiom or particles, like Chaucer.

[p. 121]   [To George and Georgiana Keats. September 17.] . . . The purest English, I think—or what ought to be the purest—is Chatterton's. The language had existed long enough to be entirely incorrupted of Chaucer's Gallicisms, and still the old words are used.

[p. 133]   [To John Taylor. Nov. 17, 1819.] Wonders are no
wonders to me. I am more at home amongst Men and
women. I would rather read Chaucer than Ariosto.

1819. Mitford, Mary Russell. *Letter from Miss Mitford to Sir William
Elford, Jan. 9,* 1819, [in] *The Life of Mary Russell Mitford,* ed.
Rev. A. G. L'Estrange, 1870, vol. ii, p. 49.

Considering my doleful prognostications, you will like to
know, my dear friend, that I have outlived the ball, so I
must write. It's a thing of necessity. Yes, I am living and
" lifelich," as Chaucer says.

1819. Moore, Thomas. *Diary* for April 14, 1819, [in] *Memoirs, Journals
and Correspondence of Thomas Moore,* ed. by the Rt. Hon. Lord
John Russell, M.P., 8 vols., 1853-6, vol. ii, p. 290.

Walked to Bowood to see the Lansdownes ... [Lord Lans-
downe] told me that Murray had offered Stewart Rose £2,000
for a translation of " Ariosto." . . . We all acknowledged the
convenience of such a thing. . . . I could [not] sympathise
with the world in some of its admirations, but thought it
better to be silent in these cases, than risk an impeachment of
my own taste in questioning that of others. Chaucer, for
instance, in what terms some speak of him! while I confess I
find him unreadable. Lord L. said he was glad to hear me
say so, as he had always in silence felt the same.

1819. Ormerod, George. *The History of the County Palatine and
City of Chester,* 3 vols., vol. iii, p. 84, and *n.*

[Chaucer and the Scrope-Grosvenor suit. The passage is
the same in the second edition of the book, revised by Thomas
Helsby, 1882, vol. iii, p. 146.]

1819. Rees, Abraham. *The Cyclopædia,* vol. vii, *Chaucer, Geoffrey;*
vol. xxi, *Lydgate, John.*

[vol. vii]   CHAUCER, Geoffrey ... the earliest English classic poet ...
[here follows life]. . . . His works are numerous: his fame
ranks high as an original poet. . . . He enriched his native
language by new forms of diction and versification; but there

is nothing in which he excels his contemporaries more than in possessing that true poetical character of which they were almost wholly void.

In many of his tales are to be found fine figures and splendid imagery displayed in glowing and elegant language . . .

The Canterbury Tales have been handsomely published by Mr. Tyrwhitt . . . but the editions of Chaucer's other works do no credit to the lovers of ancient English poetry.

1819. [Reynolds, John Hamilton.]   *Preface* to *Peter Bell, a Lyrical Ballad*, p. v.

[Footnote.] A favourite flower of mine [*i. e.* the daisy]. It was a favourite with Chaucer, but he did not understand its moral mystery as I do.

[This travesty of Peter Bell was published anonymously before the actual appearance of Wordsworth's poem of that name ; the above footnote was quoted in a review by John Keats, which appeared in the Examiner, April 25, 1819.]

1819. Sanford, Ezekiel. *Select Poems of Geoffrey Chaucer.* With a life of the author, by E. Sanford, [in] Works of the British Poets, Philadelphia, 1819-23, 50 vols., vol. i, Chaucer, etc., Preface, pp. vii–ix, Life and Poems, pp. 1–216, and vol. ii, pp. 7, 15.

[Vol. i contains a Life of Chaucer by Sanford, which consists largely of criticism, explicit or implicit, of Godwin and other biographers of Chaucer for their guesses and irrelevancies. The select poems are from the *Canterbury Tales* with the *Flower and Leaf.* Gower, Skelton, Wyatt, Surrey and Gascoigne complete the volume.]

1819. Scott, Sir Walter. *The Bride of Lammermoor*, vol. i, ch. xi, p. 289. (Border Edition, ed. Andrew Lang, 1893, vol. i, ch. xii, p. 166.)

[Chapter heading.]

" Now dame," quoth he, " Je vous dis sans doute [and five following lines].

Chaucer, *Sumner's Tale* [ll. 130–5].

1819. Scott, Sir Walter. *Ivanhoe. See* above, 1817.

[1819 ?] Unknown. *Childe Harold in the Shades, an infernal Romaunt.* [Not in B. M. The extract given below is taken from a review in The Gentleman's Magazine, April, 1819, vol. lxxxix, pp. 336–7.]

The Noble Shade . . . also vieweth the shades of Dr. Johnson and Dan Chaucer . . .

The father of English Poetry is more kindly treated [than Dr. Johnson] :

> In antique vest arrayed stands Chaucer there,
> Telling quaint stories to a listening throng ;
> Maid, widow, wife, old, young, ill-favoured, fair,
> Cruel and yielding, in his motley song
> Together flowed : unpolished, rough, but strong,
> And full of fire the merry notes he used ;
> Rightly to him our earliest bays belong,
> Though much by modern copyists abused,
> Who imitate the faults the age in him excused.

1819. Unknown. *Review* of *Campbell's Specimens of English Poetry*, [in] Blackwood's Edinburgh Magazine, March 1819, vol. iv, pp. 698, 702–4. [For Campbell, *see* above, 1819.]

[Quotations from Campbell's passages on Chaucer, with the comment, p. 704 :]

The existence of the works of Chaucer changes, it may be said, to our apprehension, the whole character of the age— raising up to our mind an image of thoughtful, intellectual cultivation, and of natural and tender happiness in the simplicity of life, which would otherwise be wanting in the dark stern picture of warlike greatness and power.

1819. Unknown. *Review* of Crabbe's *Tales of the Hall*, [in] The Gentleman's Magazine, July, vol. lxxxix, p. 46.

Ever since " The Canterbury Tales " of Chaucer, poets who have dealt much in narrative have generally been anxious to string together their tales by some connecting chain, however slight. The " Tales of the Hall " are in this respect quite dramatic.

[For Crabbe on this point, *see* above, 1812.]

[a. 1819.] Watt, Robert. *Bibliotheca Britannica;* in Two Parts :— Authors and Subjects. Edinburgh, 1824, volume i.—Authors, p. 218 *d–t*, Chaucer, Jeffery ; volume iii.—Subjects, sign. 2 J 2 : Chaucer, Jeffery.

[Watt died 12th March, 1819, when only a few sheets had been printed off. The book appeared in parts, Glasgow, 1819–20, and the complete work has title-pages dated 1824. *See* D.N.B.]

1819. Webb (or Webbe), Cornelius. *Sonnet: To Italy,* [in] Sonnets, Amatory, Incidental, and Descriptive, by Cornelius Webb, 1820, p. 15.

XXV.—*To Italy.*

On C——S L——H's (*i.e.* Chandos Leigh's) Visit to Rome in 1819.

Old Chaucer loved thee [Italy] for Boccaccio's stories—

[1820 ?] Chaucer's Canterbury Tales and Other Poems, published by John Cumberland, 2 vols.

[*See* E. P. Hammond, *Chaucer*, pp. 136–7. This edn. is not in the Douce Collection, as Miss Hammond states, nor in the Bodleian, nor the B. M.]

1820. Collier, John Payne. *The Poetical Decameron, or, Ten Conversations on English Poets and Poetry, particularly of the Reigns of Elizabeth and James I,* 2 vols., vol. i, pp. xxi, 81, 297 ; vol. ii, pp. 165, 166.

[vol. i, p. xxi.]
"For out of the old fields, as men saith,
    Cometh all this new corn fro year to year,
  And out of old books, in good faith,
    Cometh all this new science that men lere ; "

is the language of Chaucer in his "Assembly of Foules' [*Parlement of Foules*, ll. 22–5], and if it were true at the time he wrote how much more likely is it to be true at the time when we are speaking ?

. . . .

[p. 81] MORTON. There is a passage in Ascham's Schoolmaster, which expressly alludes to the admirers and imitators of Petrarch . . . "Some (he says) that make Chaucer in English, and Petrarch in Italian, their gods in verses, . . . would needs be counted like unto him." [*See* vol. i, pp. 97, 98, above.]

. . . .

[p. 297] MORTON. Chaucer, in his Man of Law's Tale, I remember, has a pretty passage in praise of a good woman :

"In her is hie beautie, without pride . . .
  Her honde minister of fredome & almes."

[ll. 162-3.]

BOURNE. But that is by no means equal to his description of a good and obedient wife, and the comfort to be derived from her, in his Merchant's Tale :

> " A wife ! ah saint Mary benedicite !
> How might a man haue any aduersitie
> That hath a wife."—

And so on for about ten lines farther, but my memory does not serve me to repeat them.

     ELLIOT. I recollect it goes on thus—

[p. 298]   ———— " Certes I can not say
> The blisse that is betwixt hem twey."—

But the wife of Bath could have told him.

     MORTON. You have a knack of finding out ambiguities never dreamt of by the pure simplicity of the author :

         —— *Ævo rarissima nostro*
         Simplicitas.

     BOURNE. Chaucer's "pure simplicity," as you call it, upon those subjects is very questionable.

.   .   .   .

[vol. ii,   BOURNE . . . Did you ever hear of a separate printed poem
p. 165] by William Painter; I mean unconnected with "the Palace of Pleasure?"

     MORTON. Certainly never.

     BOURNE. Yet such a poem, or rather collection of poems,
[p. 166] was shown me not long since . . . The title page is wanting, but the running-title is "Chaucer painted:" why it is so called I cannot guess, as in the cursory view I had of the book I saw nothing that had any relation to Chaucer: the greater portion was proverbs strung together in four-line stanzas. Towards the end was a poem lamenting the degeneracy of shepherds, and an anagram on the mother of the author, *Jone Clark.* [*See* above, 1623, vol. i, p. 198.]

[*c.* 1820.] Emerson, Ralph Waldo.   *Journal.* [Quoted in the Biographical Sketch in his Works, Centenary Edition, 1903, vol. i, p. xvi.]

     [Alluding to himself in his Journal, he writes of] the youth who has no faculty for mathematics and weeps over the impossible analytical geometry, to console his defeats with Chaucer and Montaigne, with Plutarch and Plato at night.

1820. H., R.   *On the Connexion between the Character and Poetry of Nations,* [in] The London Magazine, Oct., 1820, pp. 423–4.

     [The works of Gower, Chaucer, and Langlande are strongly

[p. 424] characteristic of their times; love and arms being their principal occupations, form the basis of their poetry, which seldom aims at more than the amusement of the reader.]

We may fairly take Chaucer as the poet of the age we are now describing, and we shall find all the ingredients of the character of that age collected in his works: his Canterbury Tales are full of broad but not deep feeling—replete with humour and waggery, and thus well calculated to attract the attention of a people whose simplicity was full of archness. Let us suppose that the works of Collins had been put into the hands of one of Chaucer's cotemporaries, and that his eye rested on that immortal 'ode on the Poetical Character;' how completely unintelligible it must have been to him.

1820. Hazlitt, William. *Lectures, chiefly on the Dramatic Literature of the Age of Elizabeth.* (Collected Works of William Hazlitt, ed. Waller and Glover, 1902–6, 13 vols., vol. v, pp. 190, 195, 196, 239, 240, 261, 289, 296.)

[p. 195] [Ferrex and Porrex, or, Gorboduc.] There seems a reference to Chaucer in the wording of the lines—

> " Then saw I how he smiled with slaying knife
> Wrapp'd under cloke, then saw I deep deceit
> Lurk in his face, and death prepared for me." [1]

	.	.	.	.	.	.	.

[p. 196] The Induction to the Mirrour for Magistrates . . . sometimes reminds one of Chaucer.

[p. 239] [Brief reference to " patient Grizzel."]

[p. 240] Deckar is more like Chaucer or Boccaccio; as Webster's mind appears to have been cast more in the mould of Shakespear's. . . .

[p. 261] [Chaucer's " Palamon and Arcite," especially the latter part, is more powerfully dramatic than the Two Noble Kinsmen.]

	[1] "The smiler with the knife under his cloke."—*Knight's Tale.*

1820. Hunt, James Henry Leigh. *A Few Thoughts on Sleep,* [in] The Indicator, Jan. 12, 1820, pp. 107–8.

Chaucer has drawn the cave of the same God [Morpheus] with greater simplicity [than Spenser]; but nothing can have a more deep and sullen effect than his cliffs and cold running waters. It seems as real as an actual solitude or some quaint

old picture in a book of travels in Tartary. He is telling the
Story of Ceyx and Alcyone in the poem called his Dream
[*i. e. The Book of the Duchesse.* Quotation, ll. 153–69].

1820. Hunt, James Henry Leigh. *Seamen on Shore,* [in] The Indicator,
March 15, 1820, pp. 182-3.

[p. 182]   Chaucer, who wrote his " Canterbury Tales " about four
hundred and thirty years ago, has among his other characters
in that work a *Shipman,* who is exactly of the same cast as the
modern sailor—the same robustness, courage, and rough drawn
virtue, doing its duty, without being very nice in helping
itself to its recreations. There is the very dirk, the complexion, the jollity, the experience, and the bad horsemanship.
The plain, unaffected ending of the description has the air of
a sailor's own speech; while the line about the beard is
exceedingly picturesque, poetical, and comprehensive. [23
lines quoted from the *Prologue* (ll. 388-410) and 4 (ll. 1187–
90) from the *Shipman's Prologue.*]

1820. Hunt, James Henry Leigh. *Spring and Daisies,* [in] The
Indicator, April 19, 1820, pp. 219–21.

[Reference to and quotation from Chaucer's ' beautiful poem
of the *Flower and the Leaf,*' and also quotation from the
passage in the *Legend of Good Women* [ll. 29–53] where ' he
says that nothing but the daisied fields in spring could take
him from his books.' Lines 178–84 are further quoted, and
Hunt then states in a footnote that it is not generally known
that Chaucer was four years in prison in his old age for the
freedom of his opinions].

1820. Hunt, James Henry Leigh. *Mayday,* [in] The Indicator, April
26, 1820, pp. 228–31.

But when morning pleasures are to be spoken of, the lovers
of poetry who do not know Chaucer, are like those who do not
know what it is to be up in the morning. He has left us two
exquisite pictures of the solitary observance of May, in his
" Palamon and Arcite." They are the more curious inasmuch
as the actor in one is a lady, and in the other a knight. How
far they owe any of their beauty to his original, the " Theseide "
of Boccaccio, we cannot say. . . . To begin, as in duty

bound, with the lady. How she sparkles through the antiquity of the language, like a young beauty in an old hood !

> Thus passeth yere by yere, and day by day,
> Tille it felle ones in a morrowe of May,
> That Emelie—

But we will alter the spelling where we can, as in a former
instance, merely to let the reader see what a notion is in his
way if he suffers the look of Chaucer's words to prevent his
enjoying him.

> Thus passeth year by year, and day by day,

[and 29 more lines, ending]

> There as this Emily had her playning.
> Bright was the sun, and clear that morwèning—

> *[Knightes Tale,* ll. 1033-62.]

How finely, to our ears at least, the second line of the
couplet always rises up from this full stop at the first !

> Bright was the sun, and clear that morwèning

[and seven more lines].

Sir Walter Scott, in his edition of Dryden [*q. v.* above,
1808], says upon the passage before us, and Dryden's version
of it, that 'the modern must yield the palm to the ancient,
in spite of the beauty of his versification.' We quote from
memory, but this is the substance of his words. For our parts
we agree with them, as to the consignment of the palm, but
not as to the exception about the versification. With some
allowance as to our present mode of accentuation, it appears
to us to be touched with a finer sense of music even than
Dryden's. It is more delicate, without any inferiority in
strength, and still more various.

[A comparison of Chaucer's and Dryden's descriptions of
Arcite follow—both passages are quoted and Dryden's
declared inferior. The passage ends :]

There was as much difference between him and his original,
as between a hot noon in perukes at St. James's, and one of
Chaucer's lounges on the grass, of a May morning.

1820. Hunt, James Henry Leigh. *La Belle Dame sans Mercy,* [in]
The Indicator, May 10, 1820, pp. 246-7.

[p. 246] Among the pieces printed at the end of Chaucer's works,

and attributed to him, is a translation, under this title, of a
poem of the celebrated Alain Chartier, secretary to Charles
the Sixth and Seventh. It was the title which suggested to
a friend the verses at the end of our present number [Keats's
' Belle Dame sans Mercy,' signed ' Caviare '] . . .

[p. 247]   We know not in what year Chartier was born, but he must
have lived to a good age and written the poem in his
youth if Chaucer translated it; for he died in 1449, and
Chaucer, an old man, in 1400. The beginning, however, as
well as the goodness of the version, looks as if our countryman had done it, for he speaks of the translation having been
enjoined him by way of penance. And the Legend of Good
Women was the result of a similar injunction in consequence
of his having written some stories not so much to the credit
of the sex! He who, as he represents, had written infinite
things in their praise ! But the Court-ladies, it seems, did not
relish the story of Troilus and Cressida. The exordium,
which the translator has added, is quite in our poet's manner.
He says that he rose one day, not well awaked ; and thinking
how he should best enter on his task, he took one of his
morning walks,

> Till I came to a lusty green vally

[and four following lines].

1820. [**Hunt**, James Henry Leigh ?] *Death and the Drunkards* [*the
Pardoneres Tale*] *modernized from Chaucer*, [in] Ollier's Literary
Miscellany, No. 1 [and last], pp. 48-53.

[p. 53]   [Appended is the following note :] The above is a prose
modernisation of one of the Canterbury Tales of Chaucer. The
reader, who has been deterred from the pages of this great
poet, in consequence of the vulgar opinion that they are insur-
mountably obsolete and difficult, will perhaps be struck with
the grand and simple power shown here ; and when he learns
that the words are Chaucer's own, he may get rid of his
timidity and go at once to the original works where he will
be richly rewarded for a little preliminary trouble. This is
the only aim of the above; for every alteration of Chaucer is
an injury.

[This is attributed here to Leigh Hunt on account of its similarity to parts of the
passage from his *Mayday*, of the same year ; some of which is quoted above.]

1820. [**Lamb,** Charles.] *Oxford in the Vacation,* signed 'Elia,' [in] The London Magazine, Oct. 1820, p. 366. (Published in Elia, 1823. The Works of Charles and Mary Lamb, ed. E. V. Lucas, 7 vols., 1903–5, vol. ii, Elia [no. 2], p. 9.)

The walks at these times are so much one's own,—the tall trees of Christ's, the groves of Magdalen ! The halls deserted, and with open doors, inviting one to slip in unperceived. . . . Then, to take a peep in by the way of the butteries, and sculleries, redolent of antique hospitality : the immense caves of kitchens, kitchen fireplaces, cordial recesses ; ovens whose first pies were baked four centuries ago ; and spits which have cooked for Chaucer ! Not the meanest minister among the dishes but is hallowed to me through his imagination, and the Cook goes forth a Manciple.

1820. **Lamb,** Charles. *Review* of Keats's *Lamia and other Poems,* [in] The New Times, July 19, 1820. (The Works of Charles and Mary Lamb, ed. E. V. Lucas, 1903–5, 7 vols., vol. i, p. 201.)

Like the radiance, which comes from those old windows upon the limbs and garments of the damsel [in the Eve of St. Agnes], is the almost Chaucer-like painting, with which this poet illumes every subject he touches. . . . The finest thing in the volume is the paraphrase of Boccaccio's story of the Pot of Basil. . . . Her [Isabella's] avowal at it [the grave] and digging for the body, is described in the following stanzas, than which there is nothing more awfully simple in diction, more nakedly grand and moving in sentiment, in Dante, in Chaucer, or in Spenser :

She gazed into the fresh-thrown mould [etc.].

1820. **Mitford,** Mary Russell. *Letter to Sir William Elford,* Aug. 24, 1820, [in] The Life of Mary Russell Mitford, ed. Rev. A. G. L'Estrange, 1870, vol. ii, p. 108.

I have as yet only seen some extracts from Mr. Keats's new poems. Those extracts seem to me finer than anything that has been written these two hundred years—finer than Wordsworth even—more Dantesque, a compound of Chaucer and the old Florentine. I hope and trust he will live to answer his barbarous critics by many such works.

1820. **Scott,** Sir Walter. *The Abbot,* 3 vols., vol. iii, ch. i, p. 9. (Border Edition, ed. Andrew Lang, 1893, vol. ii, ch. vii, p. 108.) [Brief reference to Chaucer's Pardoner. For references added in Introduction and notes to later edns., *see* below, 1831.]

1820. Scott, Sir Walter. *The Monastery*, 3 vols., vol. i, ch. x, p. 302 ; vol. ii, ch. i, pp. 9–10 and *n.* ; vol. iii, ch. iv, pp. 94–5. (Border edition, ed. Andrew Lang, 1894, vol. i, ch. xi, p. 132 ; ch. xiii, p. 154 ; vol. ii, ch. xii, p. 164.) [For an additional reference in the introduction to later edns., *see* below, 1830.]

[vol. i, p. 132.] It is an old proverb, used by Chaucer, and quoted by Elizabeth, that "the greatest clerks are not the wisest men"; and it is as true as if the poet had not rhymed or the Queen reasoned on it.

[For other references by Scott to Queen Elizabeth's quotation of this line, *see* below, 1821, *Kenilworth*, and 1828, *Tales of a Grandfather*.]

[vol. i, p. 154] But then a miller should always be of manly make, and has been described so since the days of Chaucer and James I.[1]

[vol. ii, p. 164] [Brief reference to Chaucer's Knight, and quotation of *Prol.* l. 69.]

[1] The verse we have chosen for a motto, is from a poem imputed to James I. of Scotland. As for the Miller who figures among the Canterbury Pilgrims, besides his sword and buckler, he boasted other attributes, all of which, but especially the last, shew that he relied more on the strength of the outside than of the inside of his skull.

> The miller was a stout carl for the nones,
> Full big he was of brawn, and eke of bones ;
> That proved well, for wheresoe'r he cam,
> At wrestling he wold bear away the ram ;
> He was short-shoulder'd, broad, a thick gnar ;
> There n'as no door that he n'old heave of bar,
> Or break it at a running with his head, &c.   [*Prol.*, ll. 545–51.]

1820. Unknown. *Ancient State of the Jews in England*, [in] The London Magazine, May, pp. 505, 509 and *n.*

Chaucer, who so clearly shews us the minutest peculiarities, as well as the deepest feelings of his times, gives us, in the Prioresses Tale, the feeling of the pious as to the motives of this toleration of princes.

> There was in Asie in a gret citee

[and four following lines.]

[*Prioresses Tale*, ll. 36–40.]

[p. 509] Chaucer, who used the poet's licence of supporting any fable, however mischievous, from which he might produce a striking effect, alludes, in the beautiful tale which we have already quoted,—and which is as powerful in the expression of devout implicit faith, as 'the story of Cambuscan bold' or the Knight's tale, is in romantic or chivalrous feeling,—to the story of Hugh of Lincoln, and puts in the mouth of the Prioress an excellent reason for her belief in it ;—

> O Young Hew of Lincoln ! slain also
> With cursed Jews, as it is notable
> *For it n' is but a litel while ago,*
> Pray else for us, we sinful folks unstable, etc.
>
> [*Prioresses Tale*, ll. 232–5.]

This 'little while ago' was about 130 or 140 years, so that the Prioress of Chaucer must have had as accurate a personal knowledge of the fact, as we have of the young Pretender's being conveyed into the bed of James the Second's Queen, in a warming pan, in the year 1688.

1820. Unknown. *Manners of the Athenians,* [in] The Quarterly Review, May, 1820, vol. xxiii, p. 267 *n.*

In his [Aristophanes'] Birds, the sycophant, more bold than Chaucer's summoner, whom he there resembles in vocation, announces his trade and justifies it by reasoning. [Brief quotation, *Freres Tale*, ll. 1393–4.]

1820. [Wainewright, Thomas Griffiths ?] *Modest Offer of Service from Mr. Bonmot to the Editor of the "London Magazine,"* [in] The London Magazine, Jan., 1820, pp. 22, 24. [Ascribed to Wainewright conjecturally and reprinted in Essays and Criticisms by T. G. Wainewright, 1880, pp. 2, 9.]

[The 'modest offer' in the form of a letter is followed by twelve stanzas, which, says the editor, "We believe we owe to Mr. Bonmot's goodness." One stanza alludes to Chaucer :]

> I'm glad to find there is a doubt
> From what trunk Chaucer was a sprout ;—
>   A noble one some say :
> But whispers go, that Chaucer's father
> A vintner was—or cobbler rather—
>   Hence his French name—*Chaucier.*

1820. [Wainewright, Thomas Griffiths.] *Sentimentalities on the Fine Arts,* by Janus Weathercock, Esq., nos. ii, iii, [in] The London Magazine, March and April, pp. 285, 287, 402–3. (Essays and Criticisms, 1880, pp. 23, 29, 38.)

[p. 23]   [Quotation for heading :
> Through the trees the Sunné shone [to]
> Ne in all the welkin was no cloud.

[p. 29]   [Quotations, Prol., l. 81, and Rom. Rose, l. 826.]

[p. 38]   [Quotation, Legend of Good Women, ll. 31 *sqq.*]

1820. Wordsworth, Dorothy. *Journal of a Tour on the Continent,* [in] the Journals of Dorothy Wordsworth (ed. W. Knight, 2 vols., 1897, vol. ii, pp. 179, 186).

[p. 179] *Cologne, Saturday, July 22nd.*—. . . We turned our backs upon the cathedral tower of Cologne, an everlasting monument . . . of sublime designs unaccomplished—remaining, though not wholly developed, sufficient to incite and guide the dullest imagination,—

> Call up him who left half-told
> The story of Cambuscan bold !

[p. 186]   Mayence [no date] . . . Last night, in reading Chaucer's Prologue to the *Canterbury Tales*, mine host of the *Tabard* recalled to my memory our merry master in the dining room at Mayence.

> A seemly man our Hoste was withalle
> To han bene a Marshal in an Halle ;
> A large man he **was**—bold of his speech.

1820. Wordsworth, William. *Seathwaite Chapel* : sonnet xviii [in the River Duddon series]. (Poetical Works, ed. W. Knight, 1896, 8 vols., vol. vi, p. 249, 269–70 [Notes].)

> In those days
> When this low pile a Gospel Teacher knew,
> Whose good works formed an endless retinue :
> Such Priest as Chaucer sang in fervent lays.

[The revised text of 1845 reads :

> " A Pastor such as Chaucer's verse portrays."]

[p. 269]   [Note on the above lines following an extract from parish register of Seathwaite Chapel concerning the burial of the Rev. Robert Walker :]

[p. 270]   This individual is the Pastor alluded to, in the eighteenth Sonnet, as a worthy compeer of the Country Parson of Chaucer.

1820–21. [**Hazlitt,** William.] *The Plain Speaker.* Vol. i. On the Pleasure of Hating, p. 321. Vol. ii. On Reading Old Books, p. 78. On Personal Character, p. 111. On Antiquity, p. 147. On the Difference between Writing and Speaking, p. 183. On a Portrait of an English Lady, p. 208. (Collected Works of William Hazlitt, ed. Waller and Glover, 1902–6, 13 vols., vol. vii, pp. **133–4,** 227, 240, 255, 270, 280.)

[Some of the Essays appeared, as " Table Talk," in the London Magazine, 1820-21.]

[On the Pleasure of Hating.]

[p. 133]   To cry up Shakespeare as the God of our idolatry, seems
like a vulgar national prejudice ; to take down a volume of
Chaucer, or Spencer, or Beaumont and Fletcher, or Ford, or
Marlowe, has very much like the look of pedantry and
egotism.

.   .   .   .

[On Antiquity.]

[p. 255]   When Chaucer, in his Troilus and Cressida, makes the
Trojan hero invoke the absence of light, in these two lines—

> Why proffer'st thou light for me to sell?
> Go selle it them that smallé seles grave !

he is guilty of an anachronism ; or at least I much doubt
whether there was such a profession as that of seal-engraver in
the Trojan war.

1821. Byron, George Gordon, Lord. *The Vision of Judgment*, Preface
[signed "Quevedo Redivivus"]. (The Works of Lord Byron,
Poetry, ed. E. Hartley Coleridge, 1899, etc., vol. iv, p. 484 ; one
volume ed., 1905, p. 517.)

The whole action passes on the outside of heaven ; and
Chaucer's *Wife of Bath*, Pulci's *Morgante Maggiore*, Swift's
Tale of a Tub, . . . are cases in point of the freedom with
which saints, etc., may be permitted to converse in works not
intended to be serious.

[The Allusion is to the Ballad, *q.v.* above, vol. i, p. 288, and below, App. A., c.
1600. The Vision of Judgment was finished on October 4, 1821. The Preface,
though written at the same time, was not published with the poem in the Liberal
(no. 1, Oct. 15, 1822), *see* Works, Poetry, ed. E. H. Coleridge, vol. iv, p. 478.]

1821-4. [Cary, Henry Francis.] *The Early French Poets*, [in] The
London Magazine, Dec. 1821, vol. iv, pp. 588, 591 ; March 1822,
vol. v, p. 231 ; Jan. 1823, vol. vii, p. 44 ; May, 1823, vol. vii,
p. 554 ; Sept. 1823, vol. viii, pp. 305-6 *n* ; April 1824, vol. ix,
pp. 402-3. (Volume edn., 1846, pp. 3-4, 12, 51, 185, 212, 232-4 *n*,
271, 273, 275.)

[pp. 3-4]   [Marot's Temple of Cupid worthy of Chaucer.]

[p. 12]   It may be seen from this view of one of his poems (the
Temple of Cupid) how strong a resemblance Marot bears to
Chaucer. He has the same liveliness of fancy ; the same
rapidity and distinctness of pencil ; the same archness ; the
same disposition to satire : but he has all these generally in a

less degree. His language does not approach much nearer to
the modern than old Geoffrey's, though his age is so much
less remote from ours.

[p. 51]   When we consider, that . . . the Father of English poetry
used to refresh himself largely at the same fountain [French
poetry], we cannot but look upon it as a source of hallowed
waters.

[p. 212]   [Ros's translation of " La Belle Dame sans Merci," mis-
takenly attributed to Chaucer.]

1821. De Quincey, Thomas. *Confessions of an English Opium-Eater,*
pt. ii, [in] The London Magazine, Oct. 1821, p. 364. (Works,
1862–71, vol. i, p. 218.)

Here I take the liberty of an Eclectic philosopher, and I
look out for some courteous and considerate sect that will
condescend more to the infirm condition of an opium-eater ;
that are " sweet men," as Chaucer says, " to give absolution,"
and will show some conscience in the penances they inflict,
and the efforts of abstinence they exact, from poor sinners
like myself.
[In the later editions " sweet men, &c." was replaced by
" pleasant men and courteous, such as Chaucer describes, to
hear confession or to give absolution . . ."]

1821. Hazlitt, William. *Pope, Lord Byron, and Mr. Bowles,* [in] The
London Magazine, June 1821, pp. 605–6. (Collected Works of
William Hazlitt, ed. Waller and Glover, 1902–6, 13 vols., vol. xi,
pp. 505–6.)

[p. 605]   Natural interests are those which are real and inevitable, and
are so far contradistinguished from the artificial, which are
factitious and affected. If Lord Byron cannot understand the
difference, he may find it explained by contrasting some of
Chaucer's characters and incidents with those in the Rape of
the Lock, for instance. Custance floating in her boat on the
wide sea, is different from Pope's heroine,

'Launched on the bosom of the silver Thames.'

·   ·   ·   ·   ·   ·   ·

[p. 606]   Griselda's loss of her children, one by one, of her all, does
not belong to the same class of incidents, nor of subjects for
poetry, as Belinda's loss of her favourite curl . . . There is

more true, unfeigned, unspeakable, heartfelt distress in one
line of Chaucer's Tale just mentioned [The Clerkes Tale],

> ' Let me not like a worm go by the way,'   [l. 880]

than in all Pope's writings put together; and we say it without any disrespect to him too.

1821. Markland, James Heywood. *Some Remarks on the early use of
Carriages in England,* read February 22, 1821, [in] Archæologia,
vol. xx (1824), pp. 445, 452.

[p. 445]   Our female ancestors despised both distance and weather;
and the Wife of Bath, whose praise it was that, " *girt with
a pair of sporres sharpe,*" " *upon an ambler esily she sat,*"
would doubtless have felt herself insulted had a carriage been
selected for her use.

1821. Scott, Sir Walter. *The Pirate,* 3 vols., vol. iii, ch. xv, p. 339.
(Border Edition, ed. Andrew Lang, 1893, vol. ii, chap. xxii, p. 331.)
Enveloped in the vain occult sciences which she [Norna]
pretended to practise, her study, like that of Chaucer's physician, had been " but little in the Bible."

1821. Scott, Sir Walter. *Kenilworth,* 3 vols., vol. i, ch. i, p. 4, ch. xi,
p. 265; vol. ii, ch. xii, p. 312; vol. iii, ch. vi, p. 92. (Border
Edition, ed. Andrew Lang, 1893, 2 vols. vol. i, ch. i, p. 2, ch. xi,
p. 173; vol. ii, ch. vii, pp. 109-10, ch. xiv, pp. 185-6.)

[vol. i,   Since the days of old Harry Baillie of the Tabbard [*sic*] in
p. 2]   Southwark, no one had excelled Giles Gosling in the power
of pleasing his guests of every description.

[vol. i,   [Heading to Chapter II.]
p. 173]   I say, my lord can such a subtilty
[and six following lines].
          The Canon's Yeoman's Prologue [ed. Skeat, ll. 620–26].

[vol. ii,   " O, she is well attended, Madam," replied the dame whom
p. 109]   she addressed, who from her jolly and laughter-loving demeanour, might have been the very emblem of the wife of Bath.

[vol. ii,   " I doubt," she [Queen Elizabeth] said, "this same poetical
p. 185]   Master Tressillian . . . may be one of those of whom
Geoffrey Chaucer says wittily, the greatest clerks are not the
wisest men."

[For other references by Scott to Queen Elizabeth's quotation of this line *see*
above, 1820, *The Monastery,* and below, 1823, *Tales of a Grandfather.*]

1821. Shelley, Mary Wollstonecraft. *Journal,* [printed in] Shelley and Mary, 4 vols. [privately printed, 1882], vol. iii, p. 716.

Shelley reads Chaucer's "Flower and the Leaf," and then Chaucer's "Dream" to me.

[Chaucer's "Dream" may be either the Book of the Duchess or the non-Chaucerian Isle of Ladies.
Mary Shelley says of Shelley (perhaps referring only to his earlier years), in her note to Queen Mab (Poetical Works, 1908, ed. T. Hutchinson, p. 828), "Our earlier poetry was almost unknown to him."]

1821. Shelley, Percy Bysshe. *A Defence of Poetry.* (The Works of P. B. Shelley in Verse and Prose, ed. H. Buxton Forman, 1880 [1876—80], vol. vii, pp. 130, 134.)

[The *Defence of Poetry* was written in 1821, and was intended to be published in *Ollier's Literary Miscellany,* as an answer to Peacock's *Four Ages of Poetry,* but it only appeared posthumously in 1840 in *Essays and Letters.*]

[p. 130]   The age immediately succeeding to that of Dante, Petrarch and Boccaccio, was characterised by a revival of painting, sculpture and architecture. Chaucer caught the sacred inspiration, and the superstructure of English literature is based upon the materials of Italian invention. . . .

. . . .

[p. 134]   But it exceeds all imagination to conceive what would have been the moral condition of the world, if neither Dante, Petrarch, Boccaccio, Chaucer, Shakspeare, Calderon, Lord Bacon, nor Milton had ever existed; if Raphael and Michael Angelo had never been born; if the Hebrew poetry had never been translated; if a revival of the study of Greek literature had never taken place; if no monuments of ancient sculpture had thus been handed down to us; and if the poetry of the religion of the ancient world had been extinguished together with its belief.

1821. Unknown. *Mad. de Genlis—Pétrarque et Laure,* [in] The Quarterly Review, vol. xxiv, p. 542.

[Similitude in scheme of the *Dream, Flower and Leaf,* and *Hous of Fame,* with the *Trionfi* of Petrarch.]

1821. Unknown. *Chaucer and Don Juan,* [in] Blackwood's Edinburgh Magazine, Oct. 1821, vol. x, pp. 295-8.

[An article claiming that Chaucer introduced the serio-comic style into English Literature long before Byron, and criticising Godwin, especially for his estimate of *Troilus,* from which extracts are given.]

1821. Unknown. *Criticism of Poems, Songs and Sonnets . . . by Thomas Carew,* [by] The Book Worm, no. vii, [in] The European Magazine, June 1821, p. 514. [Headed by an extract :]

> If that olde bokes were awaie,
> Ylorne were of remembrance the key ;
> Wel ought us then honouren and beleve
> These bokes.—CHAUCER.
>
> [*Legend of Good Women*, Prologue, 25-8, Text B.]

[*See* also below, *c.* 1833, Haslewood, J., *Collections for the Lives of English Poets.*]

1821. Unknown. *Obituary Notice of Edward Gatacre,* [in] The Gentleman's Magazine, Sept., vol. xci, p. 281.

The late gentleman married his lady at Qual in 1767, from Dudmaston, late the seat of Lady Wolryche, with whom he became possessed of . . . several valuable memorials . . . From this source the original painting of Geoffrey Chaucer on board, at Gatacre, a valuable relick of that reverend poet, was doubtless obtained.

1821. Unknown. *Review* of Scott's *Rob Roy . . . Heart of Midlothian, etc.,* [in] The Quarterly Review, Oct., vol. xxvi, p. 116.

But when the author paints a peasant, a cowfeeder, or a queen, he takes from a class with which the reader is so little acquainted, that, if the figure be but spirited and consistent, and contain nothing obviously incompatible with its supposed situation, we are willing, indeed we are forced, to take its resemblance upon trust. And perhaps the author's consciousness of the reliance of his reader is even more valuable to him than that reliance itself. . . . He has the same advantage which Dryden translating Chaucer had over Dryden translating Virgil.

1821. [Wainewright, Thomas Griffiths.] *Exhibition of the Royal Academy,* [in] The London Magazine, July, 1821, p. 67. (Essays and Criticisms, by Thomas Griffiths Wainewright, 1880, p. 138.)

[p. 138] I have an utter distaste for Pope, and a most marvellous clinging to Chaucer's fragrant lusty descriptions of *May Scenery.*

1821. [**Wainewright,** Thomas Griffiths.] *C. Van Vinkbooms, his Dogmas for Dilettanti,* [in] The London Magazine, Sept. 1821, p. 285. (**Essays** and Criticisms, 1880, p. 165.) [Quotations from The Book of the Duchesse, ll. 398–404, 414–20, 424–6, 443–9.]

1821. Wordsworth, William. *Ecclesiastical Sonnets,* Part II, No. **xxxi,** *Edward VI.* (Poetical Works, ed. W. Knight, 1896, 8 vols., vol. vii, p. 59.)

> " Sweet is the holiness of Youth "—so felt
> Time-honoured Chaucer speaking through that Lay
> By which the Prioress beguiled the way,
> And many a Pilgrim's rugged heart did melt.
> Hadst thou, loved Bard! whose spirit often dwelt
> In the clear land of vision, but foreseen
> King, child, and seraph, blended in the mien
> Of pious Edward kneeling as he knelt
> In meek and simple infancy, what joy
> For universal Christendom had thrilled
> Thy heart! what hopes inspired thy genius, skilled
> (O great Precursor, genuine morning Star)
> The lucid shafts of reason to employ,
> Piercing the Papal darkness from afar !

[The *Ecclesiastical Sonnets*—previously *Ecclesiastical Sketches*—were, with some exceptions, written at Rydal Mount in 1821, and printed in 1822.]

1822. Poetical Works of Chaucer, [vols. i–v of] The British Poets, in one hundred volumes, Chiswick.

[The apocryphal pieces, included in vol. v, are *Cuckow and Nightingale, Court of Love, Chaucer's Dream, and Flower and Leaf.* For the life by S. W. Singer *see* below.]

1822. Canterbury Tales of Chaucer. To which are added, an essay upon his language and versification; an introductory discourse and notes. In four volumes. [A re-issue of Tyrwhitt's edn. of 1775–78, with his glossary added in a fifth volume.]

1822–35. Booth, David. *An Analytical Dictionary of the English Language,* 1835, Introduction, pp. xiii, cxvi, cxx, cxxiii, clix, clxii, clxvi, clxxx, clxxxvi, clxxxvii.

[The references in the Introduction are brief allusions to words and grammatical forms in Chaucer. Booth's *Introduction to an Analytical Dictionary of the English Language,* 1806, contains only two slight references.]

1822. Bullar, John. *Selections from the British Poets, commencing with Spenser . . . with . . . short biographical notices,* pp. 103–5 [Dryden].

[p. 103]   [Quotes Hazlitt's saying that "Dryden and Pope are the great masters of the artificial style of poetry in our language, as Chaucer, Spenser, Shakespeare, and Milton, were of the natural," *q.v.* above, 1818.]

[p. 104]   The Good Parson [extract from Dryden's Prologue].

1822. Digby, Kenelm Henry. *The Broad Stone of Honour, or Rules for the Gentlemen of England,* Additional Appendix, pp. 370–2.

[Quotation of Chaucer's description of the Knight, in illustration of the Age of Chivalry.]

1822. [Irving, Washington.] *Bracebridge Hall, or the Humourists: a Medley, by Geoffrey Crayon, Gent.,* New York, 2 vols, vol. i, pp. 46, 97 ; vol. ii, pp. 115–20. (Works, Geoffrey Crayon edition, [1880–83,] vol. iii, pp. 38, 79, 403–7.)

[p. 38]   [Chapter heading :]

> She was so charitable and pitious
>
> [to]
>
> Or if man smote them with a yard smart.
>
> [Prol., ll. 143–9.]

[p. 403]   The good Squire's remarks brought to mind a visit which I once paid to the Tabard Inn, famous for being the place of assemblage, from whence Chaucer's pilgrims set forth for Canterbury. It is in the borough of Southwark, not far from London bridge, and bears, at present, the name of "the Talbot." It has sadly declined in dignity since the days of Chaucer, being a mere rendezvous and packing place of the
[p. 404] great wagons that travel into Kent . . . An inscription over the gateway proclaimed it to be the inn where Chaucer's pilgrims slept on the night previous to their departure, and at the bottom of the yard was a magnificent sign, representing them in the act of sallying forth. I was pleased too at noticing, that though the present inn was comparatively modern, yet the form of the old inn was preserved. There were galleries round the yard, as in old times, on which opened the chambers of the guests . . .
[p. 405]   My fancy peopled the place with the motley throng of Canterbury pilgrims. [Here follows a description of the pilgrims, with quotations from the Prologue, concluding with

[p. 406] " the ancient host of the Tabard, giving them his farewell
God-send to Canterbury"; Irving having apparently forgotten that the host accompanied the pilgrims, and that he is
not described by Chaucer as old.]

1822. [**Laing**, David.] *Select Remains of the Ancient Popular Poetry of
Scotland.* [The book is without pagination. There are various
Chaucer references in the Introductions by Laing : Prefatory
note to *The Pystyll of Swete Susan.* On northern poets' use of
alliteration ; Laing quotes Chaucer's 'rum, ram, ruf,' *Parson's
Prol.*, l. 43, and also Gascoigne's reference to it, *q.v.* above, 1575,
vol. i, p. 110.] No. 12 : *The Tale of Colkelbie Sow*, p. 1 *n.* For
the reference in the text of *Colkelbie Sow*, (ll. 852-3) *see* above
[1440 ?], vol. i., p. 44. Appendix, p. 14.

1822. **Nares**, Robert. *A Glossary . . . of words . . . in the works of
English authors.* Preface, p. vi.

I have carefully abstained from inserting the words and
phrases of an earlier period than the reign of Elizabeth, except
where the writers of her time at all affected the phraseology
of Chaucer ; which affectation, in my opinion, is almost the
only blemish of the beautiful poems of Spenser. My reason
was this ; that, to complete the rational view and knowledge
of our language, a separate dictionary must be required, for
the works of Chaucer, Gower, Lydgate, Occleve, and all those
writers who can properly be called English ; that is, who
wrote when the language was no longer Saxon. [A Saxon
and a British Dictionary would complete the historical view
of the language.]

1822. **P.** *Chaucer's Monument*, [in] The Gentleman's Magazine, Sept.,
vol. cxii, p. 221.

On my visit to Westminster Abbey, in July last, I was
much disappointed at the slight shown to the monument of
my old favourite Poet, Geoffrey Chaucer, the father of English
Poesy. I did expect, among other repairs and *restorations*, to
have seen this tomb noticed, at least the inscription made
legible, and the figure of the old Bard restored, which have
long been nearly obliterated ; but it is at present merely
coloured black, probably the restoration will follow ; decency
demands something should be done. [The inscription on
Chaucer's tomb is then given ; with a mistake in the third
line of " mortis " for " vitae."]

1822. Scott, Sir Walter. *The Fortunes of Nigel*, 3 vols., vol. iii, ch. xii, p. 330 *n.* (Border edition, ed. Andrew Lang, 1893, 2 vols., vol. ii, chap. **xx**, p. 331 *n.*)

Chaucer says, there is nothing new but what it has been old.

1822. Scott, Sir Walter. *Peveril of the Peak*, 4 vols., vol. ii, ch. ix, pp. 226–7 ; vol. iv, ch. vi, p. 122. (Border Edition, ed. Andrew Lang, 1893, 3 vols., vol. ii, chap. vii, pp. 108–9, vol. iii, ch. **xi**, p. 165.)

[vol. ii, p. 108] "A dainty dame, and dangerous, is the miller's wife," said the stranger, looking at Peveril. "Is not that old Chaucer's phrase ? "

" I—I believe so," said Peveril, not much read in Chaucer, who was then even more neglected than at present . . .

" Yes," answered the Stranger; "I see that you, like other young gentlemen of the time, are better acquainted with Cowley and Waller than with 'the well of English undefiled.' I cannot help differing. There are touches of nature about the old bard of Woodstock that, to me, are worth all the turns of laborious wit in Cowley, and all the ornate and artificial simplicity of his courtly competitor. The description, for instance, of his country coquette,—

Wincing she was, as is a wanton colt,
Sweet as a flower, and upright as a bolt.

Then again for pathos, where will you mend the dying scene of Arcite ?

Alas, my heartis queen ! alas, my wife !
Giver at once, and ender of my life.
What is this world ?—what axen men to have ?
Now with his love—now in his cold grave
Alone, withouten other company.

But I tire you, sir; and do injustice to the poet, whom I remember but by halves."

[vol. ii, p. 109] "On the contrary, sir," replied Peveril, "you make him more intelligible to me in your recitation, than I have found him when I have tried to peruse him myself."

"You were only frightened by the antiquated spelling, and 'the letters black,'" said his companion. "It is many a scholar's case, who mistakes a nut, which he could crack with

a little exertion, for a bullet, which he must needs break his
teeth on . . ."

[vol. iii,   Our impatient friend [Geoffrey Hudson] scrambled, with
p. 165]   some difficulty, on the top of the bench intended for his seat;
and there, " paining himself to stand a-tiptoe," like Chaucer's
gallant Sir Chaunticlere, he challenged the notice of the
audience.

1822. **Singer,** Samuel Weller. *Life of Chaucer,* [prefixed to] Poetical
Works of Chaucer, The British Poets, one hundred vols., 1822
[*q.v.* above, p. 136], vol. i, pp. v–xxx.

[*The Testament of Love, Complaint of The Black Knight,
Court of Love, Flower and Leaf,* and *Chaucer's Dream* (*Isle of
Ladies*) are all accepted as genuine, and the biography, based
to some extent on Speght, contains the usual incorrect account
of the exile and imprisonment of the poet. The traditions are
mentioned of his living at Woodstock and buying Donnington
Castle. A brief account of the great editions of Chaucer closes
the Life.]

1822. **Thurlow,** Edward Hovell, Lord. *Arcita and Palamon after the
Excellent Poet Geoffrey Chaucer,* Preface, pp. v, vi ; Arcita and
Palamon, pp. 1–113.

[p. v]   I did not lay down to myself any precise rule in the
manner of making my version : but the sense, which I had,
of the great beauties of the Original, would not allow me far
to wander from it. . . .

[The rendering begins :]

> In the old time, as the old stories say,
> A duke in Athens, did the sceptre sway,
> His name was Theseus, and of mighty state,
> And such a victor in his time and date,
> Under the bright sun there was none more great. . . .

1822. **Unknown.** *Astrology and Alchemy,* [in] The Quarterly Review,
vol. xxvi, pp. 201, 202.

[p. 201]   From the relation, it is equally evident that the Baron of
Chaos [Richterhausen, a quack] practised one of the juggling
tricks of the " elvish craft " which have been so well described
by Dan Chaucer. [Quotation from *Canon's Yeoman's Tale,*
ll. 705–29.]

1822. Unknown. *Review of Nares' Glossary*, [in] The Gentleman's Magazine, Dec., vol. xcii, p. 524.

[For Nares, *see* above, 1822.]

There are three works which exhibit the state of our language at three æras, in a very satisfactory form. The first is Robert of Gloucester . . . He is, generally speaking, more intelligible than Chaucer, there being only a few mixtures of Norman-French.

The next author is Chaucer. In "Tyrwhitt's Essay on the Language and Versification of Chaucer," annexed to the fourth volume of his "Canterbury Tales," we have all the changes of the language minutely particularized.

1823. Brayley, Edward Wedlake. *The History and Antiquities of the Abbey Church of St. Peter, Westminster. . . illustrated by John Preston Neale*, 1818–23, vol. ii (1823), pp. 33 n., 265, 267.

[p. 33, note] The *View in Poet's Corner*, Plate XL [on the left of p. 33], gives a complete idea of the south-east part of this (south) Transept. It shows, also, the situations and forms of the following Monuments, commencing from the left: 1, Dr. Anthony Horneck; 2, Mrs. Martha Birch; 3, the Poet Cowley; 4, John Roberts, Esq.; 5, Sir Geoffrey Chaucer; . . . 8, Michael Drayton, Esq.; . . . 10, the immortal Shakespeare. . . .

[p. 265] Chaucer, the "Father of English Poetry," if that appellation be not more justly due to his contemporary Gower, died in October 1400 [etc., detailed description of his tomb, his epitaph quoted, the portrait which used to be beside it mentioned, of which not a vestige is left]. On the ledge of the Tomb were these lines :

> Si rogitas qvis eram, forsan te fama docebit,
> Quod si fama negat, mvndi qvia gloria transit,
> Hæc Monvmenta Lege.

From Camden's words—"*Musarum nomine hujus ossa transtulit*,"—it would seem that Chaucer's ashes were removed to the new tomb. Dart [*q. v.* above, vol. i, p. 363] states that his gravestone was taken up when Dryden's Monument was erected, and sawn in pieces to mend the pavement !

1823. [De Quincey, Thomas.] *Letters to a Young Man whose Educa-*
tion has been Neglected, by the Author of The Confessions of an
English Opium-Eater, [in] The London Magazine, Jan., March,
vol. vii, pp. 89, 329. (Collected Writings of Thomas De Quincey
. . . ed. David Masson, Edinburgh, 1890, vol. x, pp. 18, 42.)

[p. 18]   He [Coleridge] should adopt as his motto (which I make
it my pride to have done from my earliest days) the simple
grandeur of that line in Chaucer's description of *his* scholar :
        " And gladly would he learn and gladly teach."

1823. D'Israeli, Isaac.   *Curiosities of Literature,* 7th edn., 5 vols.,
1823, vol. i, p. 183, vol. ii, pp. 101, 103, 104, 105, 106, 107, vol. iii,
p. 204, vol. iv, pp. 7, 139, 157.   (14th edn., 3 vols., 1849, vol. i, pp.
108, 249, 250, vol. ii, pp. 30, 109, 120, vol. iii, p. 487.)

[For an earlier edn. *see* above, 1807.]

[14th edn.   *The Progress of old age in New Studies.*   Chaucer's Canter-
vol. i,
p. 108]   bury Tales were the composition of his latest years ; they
were begun in his fifty-fourth year, and finished in his sixty-
first.

[p. 249]   *Anecdotes of Fashion.*   Chaucer has minutely detailed in "The
Persone's Tale " the grotesque and costly fashions of his day ;
and the simplicity of the venerable satirist will interest the
antiquary and philosopher.   Much, and curiously, has his
caustic severity or lenient humour descanted on the "moche
superfluitee," and "wast of cloth in vanitee," as well as "the
disordinate scantnesse."   In the spirit of the good old times, he
calculates "the coste of the embrouding or embroidering ; . . .
the costlewe furring in the gounes ; so much pounsoning of
chesel to maken holes (that is punched with a bodkin) ; so
moche dagging of sheres (cutting into slips) ; with the superfluitee in length of the gounes trailing in the dong and in the
myre . . ." [His Parson also is bitter against the "horrible
disordinat scantnesse of clothing," etc.]

[p. 250]   [Prevalence of French fashions in Chaucer's time.]   In the
Prologue to the Prioresse [*sic*] Chaucer has these humorous
lines :—
        Entewned in her voice full seemly [etc.]
[Prol. ll. 123–6.]

[vol. ii,   *Origin of the Materials of Writing.*   Table books written
p. 30]   upon with styles were not entirely laid aside in Chaucer's
time, who describes them in his Sompners tale :—
        His fellaw had a staffe tipp'd with horne
    [and four following lines (32–6)].

[vol. ii, p. 109] *Poetical Imitations and Similarities.* Gray in his Elegy has—

> " Even in our ashes live their wonted fires."

From the following lines of Chaucer, one would imagine Gray caught the recollected idea. The old Reve, in his prologue, says of himself, and of old men,

> " For what we may not don than wol we speken ;
> Yet in our *ashen* cold is *fire* yreken."
> —Tyrwhit's Chaucer, vol. i, p. 153, v. 3879.
> [For this comparison *see* above, 1782, vol. i, p. 465.]

[vol. ii, p. 120] " The laughing air." Dryden has employed this epithet boldly in the delightful lines, almost entirely borrowed from his original, Chaucer :—

> " The morning lark, the messenger of day,"
> [and three following lines].
> —Palamon and Arcite, B. ii

[vol. ii, p. 487] *Poets*—Ronsard, the French Chaucer.

1823. F., G. *On Ancient House Signs,* [in] The Gentleman's Magazine, vol. xciii, pt. 1, Suppl., p. 601.

We are told by an inscription over the Talbot Inn-yard, in the Borough, that Geoffrey Chaucer and twenty-nine pilgrims rested there on their journey to Canterbury, in 1489. Its present title is a corruption of Tabard, the name given " to a jacket or sleeveless coat."

The witty poet of " olden time" notices at length the accommodation afforded in " Southwerk, at the Tabard."

[Quotations, Prol., ll. 24–5, 28–9, 718–21 (*i. e.* 716–19).]

1823. [Haslewood, Joseph. (Hood, Eu., pseud.).] *A Note on the habit of payment of money at Chaucer's Tomb,* and a print of an Elegie upon the death of the auncient English poetts [*see above,* vol. i, 1596, p. 143, Caesar, 1614, p. 188, Freeman], [in] The Gentleman's Magazine, vol. xciii, part 1, p. 226. [*See* below, c. 1833, where a similar note is quoted.]

Vol. xciii, part 2, pp. 109–10. Inscription on Fly-leaf of an imperfect copy of Chaucer's Works. [*See* above, vol. i, p. 425, 1764, Gough, Richard ?]

1823. H[azlitt], W[illiam]. *My first acquaintance with Poets,* [in] The Liberal, vol. ii, p. 32. (Collected Works of William Hazlitt, ed. Waller and Glover, 1902–6, 13 vols., vol. xii, p. 265.)

The scholar in Chaucer is described as going

> ——' Sounding on his way.'

So Coleridge went on his.

[For a note on Hazlitt's quotations of this *see* below, 1825, p. 156.]

1823. Hunt, James Henry Leigh. *The First Canto of the Squire's Tale of Chaucer, modernized,* [in] The Liberal, No. iv, vol. ii, pp. 317–31.

[The modernization, which is very free in rendering, begins :]

> At Sarra, in the land of Tartary,
> There dwelt a king, the best beneath the sky :
> In prime of life he was a valiant man,
> And Cambus was he called, the noble Khan.

[At the end, p. 330, where Leigh Hunt adds a good deal of his own, there is this allusion to Chaucer :]

> Wake much, if life go right : if it go wrong,
> Learn how to dream with Chaucer all day long.

[For Leigh Hunt's second version of this, *see* below, 1841, and for his preface to the reprint of it, *see* below, 1855.]

1823. [**Hunt**, James Henry Leigh ?] *The Book of Beginnings,* [a poem, in] The Liberal, vol. ii, pp. 98, 114, 115, 117–18 *n.*, 122 *n.*, 124–5 *n.*

[p. 117]   [Note] *Where the cold waters lull old Sleep to sleep.*—See *Chaucer's Dream* [i. e. *The Book of the Duchesse*], beginning

> I have great wonder, by this light,
> How I live :—

for there is another [poem] under the same title : [*i. e.* the non-Chaucerian *Isle of Ladies*]. The poem in question is full of the deepest imagination and sentiment. The beginning conveys some touching information respecting the poet himself. . . .

[p. 122]   Among other poets, who begin small compositions in a spirited and enjoying manner, I must not omit Theocritus and Chaucer. . . .

[p. 124]   I have gone a great way from Chaucer, but it is always easy to return to him. His exquisite series of portraits, at the beginning of the Canterbury Tales, may be accounted a string of happy exordiums. But see also the dream referred to in note 6, The ·Complaint of Mars and Venus, The Flower and the Leaf, etc., never forgetting the exordium of the Wife of Bath's Tale, in which he jokes the friars so happily upon their succeeding to the ubiquitous privileges of the fairies. Readers of taste, who have suffered themselves to be dismayed by the imaginary difficulties of Chaucer's language, are astonished when they come to find how melodious, as well as easy to read, is this "rude old poet" as some have called him.—The syllables, it is to be observed, that form the plural terminations, are to be pronounced,—motès, burghès, etc., as they are to this day in many instances among the uneducated classes of the Metropolis; and it is a pity we ever left off pronouncing them, our consonants being at all times too ready to crowd together, and thrust out their softer neighbours, like fellows in a pit at the theatre. The final *e* also in many words must be humoured, as it still is in French poetry, the common ancestor of our own.

In oldè dayès of the King Artoùr

[and 23 following lines : Wife of Bath's Tale, ll. 857–80].

1823. Hunt, James Henry Leigh. *My Books,* [in] The Literary Examiner, July 5th and 12th 1823. (Indicator and Companion, 1834.) [Reprinted for the first time in complete form in *Essays of Leigh Hunt,* edited by Richard Brimley Johnson, Dent's Temple Edition, 1891, pp. 181, 186, 189, 195, 198, 199, 200.]

[p. 181] Sitting last winter, among my books . . . I looked . . . on my left side at my Chaucer, who lay on a writing desk ; and thought how natural it was in C[harles] L[amb] to give a kiss to an old folio, as I once saw him do to Chapman's Homer. . . .

[p. 186] It [Charles Lamb's library] looks like what it is, a selection made at precious intervals from the bookstalls :—now a Chaucer at nine and twopence; now a Montaigne or a Sir Thomas Browne at two shillings. [For Lamb's library *see* below, 1823.] . . .

[p. 189] The books I like to have about me most are, Spenser, Chaucer, the minor poems of Milton, the Arabian Nights, Theocritus, Ariosto, and such old good-natured speculations as Plutarch's Morals. . . .

[pp.194–5] It is true that it is not at all necessary to love many books, in order to love them much. The Scholar, in Chaucer, who would rather have —

At his beddes head
A twenty Bokes, clothed in black and red,
Of Aristotle and his philosophy
Than robes rich, or fiddle, or psaltry,

doubtless beat all our modern collectors in his passion for reading. . . .

[p. 198] I take our four great English poets to have all been fond

of reading.   Milton and Chaucer proclaim themselves for hard
sitters at books. . . .

[p. 199]   Chaucer's account of himself must be quoted, for the delight
and sympathy of all true readers :—

> And as for me, though that I can but lite,
> On bookès for to rede I me delite,
> [to]
> Farewell my book and my devociön.
> *The Legend of Good Women.*
> [ll. 29–38.]

And again in the second book of his "House of Fame"
where *the eagle* addresses him.

> —Thou wilt make
> At night full oft thine head to ake,
> [to]

[p. 200]   Till fully dazed is thy looke.   [ll. 631–58.]

1823. **[Kent, —, Miss.]**   *Flora Domestica . . . with . . . illustrations
from the works of the poets*, The Daisy, pp. **121–4, 127.**

[Chaucer's love of the daisy, with quotations, Legend of
Good Women, ll. 36–65, 103–24, 171–87, 212–25, 508,
510–19, 531–4 ; Assembly of Ladies, ll. 57–63 (quoted as
Chaucer's).]

1823. **Laing,** David. *The Buke of the Howlat by Holland*, ed. D. Laing,
Bannatyne Club, pp. **xvi, xxii, 5.**

[For Laing's print of Alexander Thomson's MS. Critique
on the *Howlat, see* above, *a.* 1803, Thomson.]

1823. **Lamb,** Charles. *Letter to Mr. Ainsworth*, [dated] Dec. 9, 1823.
(The Works of Charles and Mary Lamb, ed. E. V. Lucas, 1903–5,
7 vols, vol. vii, p. 631.)

I have not a Blackletter book among mine, old Chaucer
excepted, and am not Bibliomanist enough to like Blackletter.

[Mr. Lucas gives the following in his list of Lamb's Books
(Life of Charles Lamb, 1906, 2 vols., vol. ii, App. iii, p. 314),
with a quotation from the above letter :
    Chaucer (Geoffrey). *The Works of our Ancient and
Learned English Poet*, and *Lidgate's Story of Thebes*.
Speght's edition.   Lond., 1598.   Black-Letter. Folio.
    MS. notes and extracts on the fly-leaves.]

1823. Montgomery, Gerard. *La Belle Tryamour,* [in] Knight's
Quarterly Magazine, June, pp. 162–3, 173.

[p. 162]   . . . a beauteous and majestic Maid,
In a fair garden taking her diversion,
Like Emily in Chaucer, when her far sight
Captured the captive Palamon and Arcite.

[p. 163]   I wish I could describe, like that same Chaucer,
Or sweeter Spenser in his Bower of Bliss;
And then I'd tell you all King Arthur saw, Sir,
Of the bright beauties of that dainty Miss; . . .

[p. 173]   Forth on the road to Holyhead they pass'd,
A goodly party—Lords and Knights and Squires,

.   .   .   .

Monks, tailors, mountebanks, and such small deer,
Jumbled like Chaucer's pilgrims, closed the rear.

1823. Skelton, Joseph. *Engraved Illustrations of the Principal Antiquities of Oxfordshire,* from Original Drawings by F. Mackenzie,
pp. 3, 8, 23.

[p. 3]   [*Ewelme Hundred.*] Coeval with the de la Poles was the
family of the Chaucers in Ewelme, descended from the venerable poet sir Geoffrey, whose son Thomas had considerable
possessions in these parts, and who, in right of his wife Maud,
the daughter and coheiress of sir John Burghurst, became
lord of the manors of Ewelme and Donnington, Berks., in
1431.

[p. 8]   [*Wootton Hundred.*] The manor of Kidlington formerly
belonged to Thomas Chaucer, the son of Geoffrey the poet, of
whom more will be found in the account of Ewelme church
in the Hundred of Ewelme.

[p. 23]   [*Ibid.*] The town of Woodstock was, according to Kennet
[*Parochial Antiquities,* 1695], graced with the birth, and it
certainly was long a principal residence, of Geoffrey Chaucer,
the ancient learned poet; of whom Warton, in his History
of English Poetry, informs us, that he procured a portrait
on pannel from an old quadrangular stone house at Woodstock, where it had been preserved: the last remains of
this building, chiefly consisting of what was called Chaucer's
bedchamber, with a carved oaken roof, were demolished about
twenty-five years before Warton's publication appeared [in
1774, 1778, 1781, *see* above, vol. i, pp. 439, 454, 464]. That,

and the one in the Bodleian library, appear to have been taken from the painting which accompanies the epitaph on him by his scholar Occleve, in MS. in the royal library, British Museum, marked 17.D.V.I. copied in a Harleian MS. written in Occleve's time, No. 4866, fol. 91, and again in one in the Cotton library, marked Otho, A. XVIII. Occleve mentions the drawing in his " Consolatio servilis."

[Various biographical facts follow.]

1823. Thurlow, Edward Hovell, Lord. *The Flower and the Leaf after Geoffrey Chaucer*, London, J. Warwick, Brooke St., Holborn, 1823, 8°.

[There is a notice of this book in A Bibliographical Catalogue of privately printed books, by John Martin, 2nd edn., 1854, p. 313 ; a reference is given to Catalogue of the Sale of P. A. Hanrott's Library, 1823, part iv, p. 28, No. 541—" Thurlow's [Lord] Select Poems, *Chiswick*, 1821, Odes to Anacreon, by Lord Thurlow, 1823, *The Flower and the Leaf*, 1823, 3 vols. in 1, all privately printed."]

1823. Unknown. *Footnote* [to] *Review* of Rose's *Orlando Furioso*, [in] The Quarterly Review, vol. xxx, p. 51.

Had the reformation extended to Italy, Ariosto would have been reckoned one of its early promoters in that country, as Langlande and Chaucer were in our own.

1823. W., C. *Sonnet to Chaucer*, [signed C. W., printed in] *The Poems of Geoffrey Chaucer modernized*, ed. R. H. Horne, 1841, p. cxlvii.

ENGLISH CHAUCER ! oft to thy glory old—
Thy sire-ship in poesy, thy fame,
Dull'd not by dusty Time (which aye will hold
Thy name up, banner high, bright as a flame
That burns on holy altar)—have my ears,
Like portals, wide been openéd. Great fears
And worldly cares were on me ; but a hand
Power-fraught with this rich gift, hath gently fann'd
My sorrow'd spirit to a ripe zeal fine.
Now gaze I like young Bacchus on his wine,
And own no check from sorrow's hollow frown,
Full-hearted that the wrestler is down ;
Strong as an eagle gone up to the sun,
Dull earth I quit, and stray with CHAUCER on !

C. W. 1823.

1823. Wordsworth, William. *Letter to Allan Cunningham,* [dated]
Rydal Mount, Nov. 23, 1823. (Letters of the Wordsworth Family,
ed. W. Knight, 1907, 3 vols., vol. ii, pp. 209–10.)

Do not say I ought to have been a Scotchman.   Tear me
not from the country of Chaucer, Spenser, Shakespeare, and
Milton.

**1824. Chaucer's Canterbury Tales, and other Poems, with
Glossary.**   2 vols.

[There is no copy of this edition in B.M.   The dealer's list from which this entry is
taken described it as illustrated with a portrait and engravings in Bewick's style.]

1824 Chalmers, George.   *The Poetic Remains of some of the Scottish
Kings, now first collected by George Chalmers,* pp. 19, [Footnotes]
24, 43, 45–8, 52, 70, 97, 102, 137–44, 146, 148, 149, 151–69,
171–6.

1824. [Chalmers, George.] *Preface and Notes* [to] *Robene and Makyne,
and The Testament of Cresseid, by Robert Henryson,* Bannatyne
Club, pp. v–vi, 1–10.

[The *Testament* printed with Chaucer's Works, 1532;
Kynaston, pp. v–vi; illustrative quotations in the notes to
Robene and Makyne, pp. 1–10.]

1824. De Quincey, Thomas. *False Distinctions,* No. 1.   That Women
have more Imagination than Men, [in] The London Magazine, June
1824, vol. ix, p. 643.   (The Collected Writings of Thomas de
Quincey . . . ed. D. Masson, Edinburgh, 1890, vol. x, p. 442.)

Where is the female rival of Chaucer, of Cervantes, of
Calderon?   Where is *Mrs.* Shakespeare?

1824. Dibdin, Thomas Frognall.   *The Library Companion,* 2 vols.,
vols. ii, pp. 246, 265–77 and notes.

[A gossiping account of early editions of Chaucer, and
of the copies then extant of some.   The following are
mentioned—

   (1) Canterbury Tales, Caxton ed. 1; King's, Merton Coll.,
       Spencer, Wentworth House, Ham House.
   (2) Canterbury Tales, Caxton ed. 2; St. John's Coll., Camb.,
       Pepys, Heber, Spencer.
   (3) Book of Fame; reference to Typographical Antiquities,
       vol. i, p. 313.
   (4) Troilus and Cressida; Grenville and Towneley, with
       the remark that "copies of it will be found in
       distinguished private and public libraries."   Quota-
       tation from the Complaint of Chaucer unto his
       Empty Purse.]

(5) Canterbury Tales, Pynson's ed. 1 ; Spencer.
(6) Canterbury Tales, Pynson, 1526 ; Roxburghe, West.
     Edns. of Canterbury Tales by Wynkyn de Worde,
     1495, Pynson, 1520 and 1522, are apocryphal.
(7) Troilus and Cressida, Wynkyn de Worde, 1517 ;
     Wilbraham, Roxburghe.
(8) Works, Godfray, 1532 ; Douce, Heber, Utterson,
     Towneley (Dibdin's own).
(9) Works, Bonham, Kele, Toy, Petit, 1542.
(10) Works, 1561 ; Nassau.
(11) Works, 1597.
(12) Works, 1602 ; Nassau.
(13) Ed. Urry, 1721.
(14) Canterbury Tales, ed. Tyrwhitt, 1775–8 (with high
     praise of the editor).

Reference to Todd, 1810, for MSS. ; Stafford (now Ellesmere) and Roxburghe-Devonshire MSS. mentioned.]

1824. Drake, Nathan. *Montchensey, a Tale of the Days of Shakspeare,*
[in] Noontide Leisure, by Nathan Drake, vol. i, p. 40, vol. ii,
p. 51.

[Montchensey finds in Shakspeare's study portraits of
Chaucer and Spenser.]

1824. Drake, Nathan. *Observations Critical & Miscellaneous, on the
First Book of the Anonymous Version of "Les Jardins,"* par
M. l'Abbé de Lille, [in] Noontide Leisure, by Nathan Drake,
vol. i, p. 111.

[A quotation from the prefatory address of the translator.
See above, Powell, 1789, vol. i, p. 489.]

1824. Hazlitt, William. *Select British Poets, or new Elegant Extracts
from Chaucer to the present time, with critical remarks,* pp. ii, iii,
v, 1–34. (Collected Works of William Hazlitt, ed. Waller and
Glover, 1902–6, 13 vols., vol. v, pp. 366–71.)

Frontispiece [portrait of Chaucer] ; Preface, pp. ii, iii, v.
[A short critical account of Chaucer. Chaucer is in the first
class of poetry, the *natural ;* in invention he has not much to
boast ; but the masterly execution is his own. He has little
fancy, but he has great wit, humour, strong manly sense,
power of description, perfect knowledge of character, occasional sublimity. Extracts, pp. 1 34. Prologue to *Canterbury Tales, The Squieres Tale, The Prioresses Tale, The
Floure and the Leafe,* part of *The Knightes Tale, The Wif
of Bathes Prologue, Similes from Chaucer.*]

1824. Hazlitt, William.   *Sketches of the Principal Picture-Galleries in England.*   (Collected Works of William Hazlitt, ed. Waller and Glover, 1902–6, 13 vols., vol. ix, p. 74.)

[Speaking of the Cupid and Psyche by Titian at Blenheim :] Did ever creature of mortal mould see any thing comparable to the back limbs of the Psyche, or conceive or read anything equal to it, but that unique description in the Troilus and Cressida of Chaucer ?

1824. Lamb, Charles.   *Letter* to Bernard Barton, [dated] May 15, 1824. (The Works of Charles and Mary Lamb, ed. E. V. Lucas, 1903–5, 7 vols., vol. vii, p. 643.)

His [Blake's] Pictures—one in particular, the Canterbury Pilgrims (far above Stothard's)—have great merit, but hard, dry, yet with grace.   He has written a Catalogue of them with a most spirited criticism on Chaucer, but mystical and full of Vision.

1824. [Park, Thomas.]   *Editor's Preface* [to] Warton's History of English Poetry, new [3rd] edn., 4 vols, vol. i, pp. 46–9 [Chaucer and Fairies], 65–6 [Chaucer and Minstrels], 105.   [Also additional notes throughout by Park, Ritson, Ashby, Douce, etc.]

1824. [Procter, Bryan Waller ("Barry Cornwall").]   *Effigies Poeticæ : or the Portraits of the British Poets, illustrated by notes, etc.,* 2 vols., vol. i, no. 1, Chaucer, no. 2, Gower, no. 3, Lydgate, no. 4, James I of Scotland, no. 5, Occleve, pp. 7–9, 11, 13, 15, vol. ii, p. 12, Dryden.

[to face p. 7] [Portrait *"from a Limning in Occleve's* De Regimine Principis, *preserved in the Harleian Library,"* engraved by W. Finden.]

[p. 7] Our collection opens with the head of the venerable CHAUCER.   He had been called the patriarch of our poetry ; yet he left no posterity behind him . . . Chaucer was a prodigy, considering the age in which he lived.   He was beyond doubt the greatest spirit that preceded Shakespeare . . .

The head now offered to the public is a likeness of the poet in his age.   It has nothing of his wit or humour, nothing of the flash of genius which would probably have [p. 8] illuminated the features of his youth ; but his sweet and sedate expression, his grave good sense, his deep observation and pathos, have been well caught by the artist . . . Chaucer was rather a portrait-painter than an imaginative artist . . . and accordingly, in the place of the fantastic attitude or the

soaring eye, we have a staid and gentle aspect, a steady
glance, and that particular expression about the mouth which
almost invariably denotes an observing man.

1824. Roscoe, William.   *The Works of Alexander Pope, Esq.* [with]
. . . occasional remarks by William Roscoe. Vol. i, The Life of
Alexander Pope, pp. 42–3, 48 ; vol. ii, Estimate of the Poetical
Character and Writings of Pope, pp. x, xi, xiii ; Notes, pp. 252,
253, 254, 255, 297, 301, 302, 303–311, 315, 339, 340, 341, 342,
357, 358.

[vol. i,   These pieces [the modernizations of *January and May*,
p. 42]
and *Wife of Bath's Prologue*] are executed with a degree of
freedom, ease, and spirit, and at the same time with a judgment and delicacy, which not only far exceed what might
have been expected from so young a writer, but which leave
nothing to be wished for in the mind of the reader.   The
[p. 43] humour of Chaucer is transfused into the lines of Pope, almost
without suffering any evaporation.

[vol. ii,   Of English authors those to whom Pope stands the nearest
p. x]
related in genus and poetical character, are Chaucer and
Dryden . . . Chaucer may be said to be, like Pope, a general
poet.   His excellence was not confined to any particular
department . . . In this respect Chaucer is unrivalled by any
of his successors, except Shakespeare and Pope, both of whom
[p. xi] resemble him also in that moral and contemplative character
which delights in comparing and illustrating the phenomena
of the moral and physical world . . .

1824. S., W.   *Letter* [in] The Gentleman's Magazine, May, vol. xciv,
pp. 411–12.

> Whan hys lotte was to wake a night
> [to]
> . . . *horne pipis* of *Cornewayle.*
>
> [Rom. Rose, ll. 4243–50.]

[Chaucer probably mistook *Cornouaille*, the *Corneil* or wild
cherry tree, for *Cornewaille*—Cornwall. This occurs in the
non-Chaucerian portion of the Romance of the Rose. See
Skeat's note on the line.]

1824. Scott, Sir Walter.   *An Essay on Romance,* [in] Supplement to
the Encyclopædia Britannica, vol. vi, pp. 436, 442, 454. (Scott's
Miscellaneous Prose Works, Edinburgh, 1834-71, 30 vols, vol. vi,
pp. 132–3, 158, 209.)

[p. 132]   Chaucer, unable to sleep during the night, informs us that,
in order to pass the time,

"Upon my bed I sate upright,
And bade one rechin me a boke,
A Romaunce, and he it me took
To read and drive the night away."

[*Book of the Duchesse,* ll. 46–9.]

The book described as Romance contained, as we are
[p. 133] informed,

"Fables
That clerkes had, in old tyme,
And other poets, put in rhyme."

[*ib.,* ll. 52–4.]

And the author tells us a little lower,
"This boke ne spake of but such things
Of Queens' lives and of Kings'."

[*ib.,* ll. 57–8.]

The volume proves to be no other than Ovid's *Metamorphoses;*
and Chaucer, by applying to that work the name of Romance,
sufficiently establishes that the word was, in his time, correctly
employed under the modern acceptation . . .

[p. 158]   Chaucer also in his Ryme of Sir Thopas, assigns to the
minstrels of his hero's household the same duty of reciting
romances . . .

"Do cum," he sayed, "my minestrales [to]
And eke of love-longing."

[*Sir Thopas,* ll. 134–9.]

[p. 209]   It is certain, and is proved by the highest authority, that
of Chaucer himself, that even in his time these rhyming
Romances had fallen into great contempt. The *Rime of Sir
Thopas,* which that poet introduces as a parody, undoubtedly,
of the rhythmical Romances of the age, is interrupted by
mine host Harry Bailly with the strongest and most energetic
expressions of total and absolute contempt.

1824. Unknown. *The Works of Chaucer,* [in] The Retrospective
Review, vol. ix, pp. 173–206.

[Researches into old writers very creditable to modern taste,
especially where, as in English, the language has undergone
considerable changes. This may be carried to excess, and
imitation be substituted for research.]

There is no reason, however, why the treasures of their wit
should not be among the objects of our study and research.
. . . They are the beacons and landmarks of our language, to
which our eyes should occasionally be turned. . . . The
wisdom that is preserved in a language that is obsolete, is a

treasure buried in the earth, which we know not where to delve for.

[p. 174]   In treasures of this description [*i.e.* of instruction and delight] the neglected glebe of Chaucer is particularly affluent. As a fabulist and a poet, Dryden gives him the decided preference over Ovid : though Dryden, as we shall hereafter shew, was not capable of appreciating all his beauties. But there are other reasons for recommending him to the attention of the English student.

To the philologist, he is a classic of the first order : for he is pre-eminently the most conspicuous of the makers and methodizers of the language : the first who taught it to flow in expressive harmony, and gave to it consistency and energy. Not that he invented and introduced a verbiage and idiom of his own, or compounded, as some have supposed, a *melange* of imported phraseology ; but because, (as will be obvious to those who consult his contemporaries, Lydgate, Gower, Hocleve, Scogan, &c.) he selected and methodized from the unsettled idioms then in use, what was fittest and most con-
[p. 175] gruous, and gave consistence and solidity to that foundation, upon which the polished structure of our present language has gradually risen.

Even in point of rhythmical harmony, the obligations of our language to Chaucer are not less decisive than in phraseology and structure, and . . . in his versification are to be found, not only the less rigid models of our present septasyllabic and octosyllabic measures, but the exemplars also, which Spenser has acknowledged, and of which Milton has availed himself, of that heroic metre, to which the former gave so much sweetness, and the latter such majestic sublimity : . . . But it is not only to the philologist and the prosodist that the memory of Chaucer should be dear. He has other claims upon our admiration and gratitude, or he could never have had these. . . .

That Chaucer had the soul, as well as the voice of poesy, is sufficiently evinced in the admiration he has excited in those who were neither familiar with his language, nor in possession of the clue that would unravel the harmony of his numbers : nay, who could not, from the defective transcripts they consulted, or by their mode of pronunciation, make out even the numerical proportion of his feet.

[p. 176]   It is not merely in a literary point of view, as works of
[p. 177] amusement and effusions of a poetical imagination, that the
writings of Chaucer are entitled to particular attention.   They
are pregnant with instruction of a higher order.   They are an
essential portion of the authentic history of his country ; . . .
of the history of the national mind . . . The works of
Chaucer, his *Canterbury Tales* in particular, . . . bring the
genuine picture of society alive and breathing before us. . . .
The imaginative historian, who adorns his record with names
of his own creation, and selects the character he assigns to his
[p. 178] imaginary agents from the great book of nature, . . . may use
with freedom the genuine colours of truth, and delineate man
as he really is, with all the modifications of morals, manners,
and characteristics, which the institutions, the necessities, and
the habitudes of the age have imposed upon him.   Whoever
does this is, in fact, an historian of the highest order : an historian, instructive, not to the statesman and politician only,
but to all who may peruse his record.   And such an historian
is the great father of our English poetry—the venerable
Geffrey Chaucer.

[Here follows the life of Chaucer and some further criticism
of his poetry.]

1824. Unknown.   *The Literary History of the Provençals,* [in] Knight's
Quarterly Magazine, vol. iii, p. 131.

Chaucer, in one or two of his smaller poems, appears to
have followed the style of the later Troubadours; and Dryden,
in the preface to his Fables, has borrowed from Rymer the
remark, that the Provençal was in that age the most cultivated
of modern languages, and that Chaucer profited by it to adorn
and enrich the English.

1824. Wordsworth, William.   *Letter to Alaric Watts,* [dated] November 16, 1824, [printed in] Letters of the Wordsworth Family,
ed. W. Knight, 3 vols., 1907, vol. ii, p. 228.

"I am disposed strenuously to recommend to your habitual
perusal the great poets of our own country who have stood
the test of ages.   Shakespeare I need not name, nor Milton,
but Chaucer and Spenser are apt to be overlooked.   It is
almost painful to think how far these surpass all others."

[This paragraph is reprinted as it stands from Professor Knight's text.   From the
stops and quotation-marks Wordsworth seems to be quoting, but from what is
not clear; nor has the passage any relation to the paragraphs that precede and
follow it.]

1825. Collier, John Payne. *The Poet's Pilgrimage*, pp. iv [preface], 118, 120 [notes 2, 3, 18 ; quotations from the Assemble of Foules, the Floure and the Lefe, Wife of Bath's Tale, and Troilus].

1825. Cunningham, Allan. *The Songs of Scotland*, vol. i, pp. 12, 13, 51, 59, 73, 77, 82 ; vol. ii, pp. 35, 156.

[Slight references.]

1825. D., W. C. *On the Pronunciation of Heard, etc.*, [in] The Gentleman's Magazine, Sept. 1825, vol. xcv, pp. 219–20.

[Reply to J. S. H., *q.v.* below.]

[Concerning the changes in English grammar and pronunciation, with several references to Chaucer, and quotations from his poems.]

1825. Elmes, James. *The Arts and Artists*, London, 1825, vol. iii, pp. 70, 71. [The Occleve and Phillips portraits of Chaucer.]

1825. H., J. S. *Critical Disquisition on the words " Heard," "Read," etc.*, [in] The Gentleman's Magazine, vol. xcv, part i, suppl., pp. 584–5.

[For a reply *see* above, D., W. C.]

[Quotations from the Bible ; and from Chaucer (fifteen) as examples.]

1825. Hazlitt, William. *The Spirit of the Age : or Contemporary Portraits.* (Collected Works of William Hazlitt, ed. Waller and Glover, 1902–6, 13 vols., vol. iv, pp. 210, 214, 225, 244, 276, 285, 326.)

[p. 210]   [William Godwin.]   His *Life of Chaucer* would have given celebrity to any man of letters possessed of three thousand a year, with leisure to write quartos : . . .

[p. 214]   [S. T. Coleridge.]   He . . . ' goes sounding on his way ' in eloquent accents uncompelled and free !

[Hazlitt is fond of this quotation, though he is hazy in his recollection of it and confuses two passages in Chaucer's Prologue. *See* above, 1818 and 1823. In ' My First Acquaintance with the Poets ' (1823) he says the scholar in Chaucer is described as going ' sounding on his way,' and in his ' Lectures on the English Poets ' (1818) he says the ' merchant as described in Chaucer went on his way " sounding always the increase of his winning." ' The two passages are Prol. l. 275 and l. 307 (not ' sounding on his way ' but ' Souninge in moral vertu was his speche ').]

[p. 225]   [The Rev. Edward Irving.] . . . he might have defied
the devil and all his works, and by the help of a loud voice
and strong-set person—

> ' A lusty man to ben an Abbot able.'
>
> [Prol. l. 167.]

[p. 244]   What is there (in his [Scott's] ambling rhymes) of the deep
pathos of Chaucer ?

[p. 276]   Chaucer is another prime favourite of his [Wordsworth's],
and he has been at the pains to modernize some of the
Canterbury Tales.

[p. 285]   [Sir James Macintosh.]   ' And gladly would he learn, and
[Prol.
l. 368] gladly teach.'

[p. 326]   [Lord Eldon.]   We are apt to conclude from so fair an
outside, that

> ' All is conscience and tender heart '
>
> [Prol. l. 150.]

within also, and that such a one would not hurt a fly.   And
neither would he without a motive.

1825. [**Hunt**, James Henry Leigh ?]   *My Books*, Part ii, *Originality of
Milton's harmonious use of Proper Names*, [in] The New Monthly
Magazine, New Series, vol, xiv, p. 392.

[Not in R. B. Johnson's edn. of Leigh Hunt's Essays.]

   Chaucer, though he had a finer ear than some of his imitators have been willing to acknowledge, does not think it
necessary to have recourse to it [melody] when he comes to a
set of names.   He takes no more heed of a list in poetry,
than he would have taken of an Abbey roll.

1825. Jeffrey, Francis.   *Review* of Braybrooke's edn. of *Pepys' Diary*,
[in] The Edinburgh Review, Nov., no. lxxxv, p. 26.   (Jeffrey's
Contributions to the Edinburgh Review, 1853, p. 226.)

   [Passages on the abundant minute record of feudal times in
the tales of Chaucer.]

1825. [**Keble**, John.]   *Review* [of Conder's] *The Star in the East.
See* below, App. A.

1825. Roscoe, Thomas.   *The Italian Novelists*, 4 vols. ; vol. i, Preface,
pp. ii [obligations of English to Italian writers earlier than Chaucer],
xix, xxiii [reference to the *Clerkes Tale*].

[p. xix]   Dioneo and Fiammetta . . . are said to recite together the
adventures of Arcite and Palamon . . . The same adventures,
so beautifully imitated in the poem of our own Dryden, form
the subject of Boccaccio's Tescide.

1825. [**Smith**, Horatio.] *Address to the Orange Tree at Versailles*, [in] Gaieties and Gravities, 3 vols., vol. i, p. 166. (Poetical Works, 1846, 2 vols., vol. i, pp. 17–18.)

> Chaucer, so old a bard that time
> Has antiquated every chime
> And from his tomb outworn each rhyme
>   Within the Abbey :
> And Gower . . . .
>
>   .   .   .   .
>
> Lived in thy time—the first perchance
> Was beating monks[1] . . . .

[1] There is a tradition (though not authenticated) that Chaucer was fined for beating a friar in Fleet Street.

1825. Turner, Sharon. *The History of England during the Middle Ages*, vol. v, pp. 256, 257, 259, 268 ; chap. iv, Life and Poems of Chaucer, pp. 289–333, 334, 335, 336, 341, 343, 347, 348, 350, 391, 392, 393.

[p. 330]   The modern reader . . . . cannot peruse his [Chaucer's] works without perceiving the fewness and the defects of the mental and moral associations which they contain.   He wanted Gower's knowledge and ethical taste, as much as Gower wanted his command of language and poetical power. . . .

[p. 331]   Few poets have written so much [as Chaucer], which so few desire to peruse or attempt to disturb. . . .

[p. 350]   As Chaucer became dissatisfied with Gower, and twice, at least, censures him, we have long since become dissatisfied with Chaucer ; and by the aid of the very lights which they have given us, we have passed far beyond both.

1825. Unknown. *Review* of Roscoe's *Italian Novelists*, [in] The Edinburgh Review, vol. xlii, p. 180.

We cannot agree with Warton that the frame-work of the Canterbury Tales is in its general design superior to that of the Decameron. For though, as Mr. Dunlop [*q. v.* above, 1814], has remarked, Chaucer's plan of a pilgrimage has this advantage, that the subject has thus a natural limitation, while Boccaccio's has no other limit but the imagination of the author, the design of the former seems to us to be liable to a more formidable objection—that tales told on horseback to a party of twenty-nine persons, could never have been heard by them all.

1825. Unknown. *Amorum Troile* [sic] *et Cresseidæ, libri duo priores Anglo-Latine,* per Franc. Kinaston, Oxon., 1635, 4to., [in] The Retrospective Review, vol. xii., article vi, pp. 106, 110.

[p. 106]   Chaucer's *Troilus and Creseide* was the first example of a regular serious narrative poem, on a large scale, in the English language. It may be considered as our oldest epic, to use the word in its common, though sufficiently vague, acceptation; and for a long time, with the exception of the *Knyghtes' Tale* by the same author, it continued to be the only one. Hence, it was held in that value which always attaches to the *first* of any thing, and which adheres to it even for some time after it has been superseded by more beautiful and finished specimens of the same kind. It was reverenced as the earliest work in which the powers of English, as a cultivated language, were developed; its author was regarded as the Virgil of his country; his poem was made the foundation of the fictions of subsequent writers; and, according to a practice common in former ages, when, as a contemporary critic expresses it, " the notion of the perishableness of modern tongues, and of the necessity of preserving works worthy to last, by embalming them in the immortal language of Rome," was not yet exploded, it was thought expedient, upwards of two centuries after its publication, to translate it into Latin. . . .

[p. 110]   [Kynaston's version more universally intelligible than the original.] Considering the difficulties of his task, Sir Francis must be allowed to have acquitted himself with much dexterity; and he deserves praise for the fidelity with which he adheres to his original, in spite of the temptations afforded by so ornamental a language as the Latin.

[For Kynaston, *see* above, 1635, vol. i, p. 207.]

1825. Unknown. *Poetry,* [in] The Edinburgh Review, vol. xlii, pp. 48, 49.

[p. 48]   Chaucer . . . raised poetry from the dust. He has been likened to 'the spring,' and has been called the 'morning star' of English poetry. He was so; or rather, he was a sun whom no star preceded,—who rose above our literary horizon, dissipating the wandering lights and sullen vapours which hung about it; and who, by a power independent of accident or the time, threw out a dazzling splendour, which showed at once his own lustre, and the wastes by which he was surrounded.

1825. Unknown. *Pope's Works and Character,* [a review of] Roscoe's *Works of Alexander Pope,* [in] The Quarterly Review, vol. xxxii, pp. 275, 290–3.

[p. 292]   Had the 'Temple of Fame' been entirely an original composition, it would have approached nearer, though not have attained, to an equality with these [Thomson's *Seasons,* and *Castle of Indolence*]; but so much of the ingenuity of the allegory, and so many of the images are Chaucer's, that, with all its beauty of versification, brilliancy of expression, and variety of added congenial beauty, it still wears the livery of a master.   Pope, accordingly, with his usual candour, premises in the advertisement, that 'whenever any hint is taken from Chaucer, the passage itself shall be set down in the marginal notes': and Mr. Bowles, with *his* wonted candour, observes, 'Pope seems unwilling to confess *all* he owes to Chaucer' (*Bowles,* [edn. of Pope's Works, 1806,] vol. ii, [p. 293] p. 107). . . . But this and other imitations from Chaucer, as well as all his minor translations, were done 'as exercises,' in extreme youth; and we cannot, therefore, wonder either at occasional failures in execution, or injudicious selections.

1826. Barrett, afterwards **Browning,** Elizabeth Barrett. *Notes* on proof sheets of a work by Uvedale Price, [printed in] *Elizabeth Barrett Browning, Hitherto Unpublished Poems and Stories,* Bibliophile Society, Boston, 1914, 2 vols., vol. ii, pp. 67–8.

It has appeared to me that a trochee introduced before the last foot (supposing the last foot to be an iambus) produces an agreeable relief from the monotony of the usual heroic structure.   The following examples from Chaucer's Knight's Tale are among the most melodious I can recollect—

"And sŏlĭtāire hĕ wās ēvĕr ălōne
And wāilĭng āll thĕ nīght mākĭng hĭs mōne."

1826. Dallaway, James. *Anecdotes of Painting in England* . . . *by* . . . *Horace Walpole, with* . . . *additions by the Rev. James Dallaway,* vol. i, pp. 56, 57 *n.* ; vol. v, pp. 304–5 [list of Vertue's Works, in the Catalogue of Engravers, *q.v.* above, vol. i, 1763, p. 424].

[vol. i, pp. 56, 57 *n.*]   This portrait of Chaucer [on his tomb at Westminster] could not have afforded any specimen of painting in the reign of Henry IV., for it was copied from some known miniature of him, when Nicholas Bingham [*sic*] erected a monument

to his memory in Westminster Abbey, in 1550, as the
inscription proves, at which time it was painted against the
wall.   No trace is now visible.   A miniature of Chaucer,
on horseback, as he represents himself journeying with the
pilgrims to Canterbury, is preserved in a MS. of his poems,
belonging to the Marquis of Stafford [the Earl of Ellesmere],
which has been engraved in *Todd's Illustrations of Gower
and Chaucer*, 8vo, 1810.   Other MSS. have his portrait, but
usually of half length only.

[For Walpole's original edn. *see* above, vol. i, 1762, p. 423.]

1826. Digby, Kenelm Henry. *The Broad Stone of Honour*, Book I,
Godefridus, 1829 edn. [1st of the enlarged version in B.M.], p. 167.

It is always men who are impious and obscene, like our
' reverend' Chaucer, who have the most bitter sarcasm for
expressing the impiety and vice of others.

[For a reference in the first and short version of the book *see* above, 1822.
According to D.N.B., the 1st edn. of this enlarged version appeared in 1826-7.]

1826. Hazlitt, William.   *Of Persons One Would Wish to Have Seen*,
[in] The New Monthly Magazine, Jan., new series, vol. xvi, p. 35.
(Reprinted in Winterslow, 1839, pp. 41-3 ; Collected Works of
William Hazlitt, ed. Waller and Glover, 1902-6, 13 vols., vol. xii,
pp. 29-30.)

Some one then inquired of B—— [Charles Lamb] if we
could not see from the window the Temple-walk in which
Chaucer used to take his exercise; and on his name being
put to the vote, I was pleased to find that there was a general
sensation in his favour, in all but A—— [William Ayrton,
the musician], who said something about the ruggedness of
the metre, and even objected to the quaintness of the orthography.   I was vexed at this superficial gloss . . . and asked
if he did not think it would be worth while to scan the eye
that had first greeted the muse in that dim twilight and
early dawn of English literature, . . . to watch those lips that
" lisped in numbers, for the numbers came "—as by a miracle,
or as if the dumb should speak !   Nor was it alone that he had
been the first to tune his native tongue (however imperfectly
to modern ears) ; but he was himself a noble, manly character,
standing before his age and striving to advance it ; a
pleasant humourist withal. . . .

B—— put it to me if I should like to see Spenser as well as
Chaucer ; and I answered without hesitation, " No " ; for that

his beauties were ideal, visionary, not palpable or personal, and therefore connected with less curiosity about the man.

1826. Hunt, James Henry Leigh. *Specimens of a Dictionary of Love and Beauty*, [in] The New Monthly Magazine, July, New Series, vol. xvii, pp. 49–50.

Chaucer's modulation is not among the least of his beauties; nor is there any passage in his writings, in which it is more delicately turned, than in this description of the Prioress . . . It is she that tells the beautiful story of the little boy that went through Jewry singing *Alma Redemptoris* . . . [quotes *Prol.* ll. 118–21.]

Then follows a good-natured banter of the poet's upon the mode of singing service in nunneries, their boarding-school French, and, what appears to have been no great part of politeness in those days, the importance they attached to nicety of behaviour at dinner . . . [quotes *Prol.* ll. 137–150.]

This last line [l. 150] has become a favourite quotation. The poet proceeds to say that she was finely grown, and concludes with the lines about the Crowned A and the motto . . . The device, though taken from Ovid, is meant to be religious . . . *Love conquers all things*, quoth Ovid. *Love conquers all things*, repeats the fair nun; and raises her eyes to heaven, swimming with all the pieties of heaven and earth.

1826. Landor, Walter Savage. *Imaginary Conversations;* Johnson and Tooke, pp. 220, 245, 253, 258. (Works, ed. by Charles G. Crump, 6 vols., 1891, vol. iii, pp. 413, 426, 430, 433, 436.)

[The Chaucer references do not occur in the first edition; the dialogue was again expanded and broken in two in the ed. of 1846; a few references appear there for the first time. For other dialogues see 1828, 1829, 1837, 1842, 1846, 1853, 1861.]

[p. 426] *Johnson*. Who would read Chaucer and Spenser for their language?

Tooke. Spenser I would not, delightful as are many parts of his poetry; but Chaucer I would read again and again both for his poetry and his language.

[p. 433] *Johnson*. I recollect no expression in Chaucer worth retaining and not retained.

Tooke. What think you of *Swough*, the long continued sound of wind?

" A swough
As thof a storme should brasten every bough."
                                        Palamon and Arcite.

Johnson. It sounds grandly . . .

1826. Lytton, Edward Bulwer, Lord. *Sketch of the Progress of English Poetry.* [Of the MS. of this, which was written in 1826 and which was never printed, nearly forty pages are devoted to an enquiry, "how far did Chaucer and Langlande contribute by their works to the Reformation in England?" (Life of Edward Bulwer Lord Lytton, by his son, 1883, vol. ii, p. 99.)]

1826. Nicolas, Sir Nicholas Harris. *Testamenta Vetusta,* 2 vols., vol. i.

[(Preface) pp. 2–3; (Preliminary Observations: Nicolas promises that "the very accurate and picturesque descriptions given by Chaucer of the habiliments, jewels, and furniture peculiar to his own age, will be sometimes quoted") iv; (Notes: quotations as promised, to illustrate the jewels, etc., mentioned in the wills) xix–xxi, xxvi, xxix, xxxi–ii, xxxiv–vi; (Text: Philippa Duchess of York appoints Thomas Chaucer executor of her will, dated 1430 and proved 1431) 219.]

1826. Scott, Sir Walter. *Journal,* Jan. 11, 1826, Edinburgh, 1890, 2 vols., vol. i, p. 79.

James [Ballantyne] is in an awful stew, and I cannot blame him; but then he should consider the hyoscyamus which I was taking and the anxious botheration about the money market. However, as Chaucer says :—

"There is na workeman
That can bothe worken wel and hastilie;
This must be done at leisure parfitly."

[*Marchantes Tale,* ll. 9706–8, slightly altered.]

1826. Scott, Sir Walter. *Woodstock, or the Cavalier,* 3 vols., vol. i, title page, ch. i, p. 8; vol. ii, chap. iv, pp. 98–100. (Border Edition, ed. Andrew Lang, 1894, vol. i, ch. i, pp. 4–5, ch. xvi, pp. 278–80.)

[Motto, Title page (omitted in later editions) :]
He was a **very** perfect gentle knight.

[Vol. i, pp. 4–5.] With these grave seniors sate . . . their pretty daughters, whose study, like that of Chaucer's physician, was not always in the Bible. . . .

[vol. ii, p. 278] "Dreams, dreams, dreams, my simple Colonel," said Bletson . . . "Old Chaucer, sir, hath told us the real moral on't—He was an old frequenter of the forest of Woodstock, here—"

"Chaser?" said Desborough; "some huntsman belike, by his name—Does he walk, like Hearne at Windsor?"

[p. 279] "Chaucer," said Bletson, "my dear Desborough, is one of those wonderful fellows, as Colonel Everard knows, who live many a hundred years after they are buried, and whose words haunt our ears after their bones are long mouldered in the dust."

"Ay, ay! well [answered Desborough, to whom this description of the old poet was unintelligible, (*later edd.*)], I for one desire his room rather than his company—one of your conjurers, I warrant him. But what says he to the matter?"

"Only a slight spell, which I will take the freedom to repeat to Colonel Everard," said Bletson; "but which would be as bad as Greek to thee, Desborough.—Old Geoffrey lays the whole blame of our nocturnal disturbances on superfluities of humours [quotes Nonne P. T., ll. 109–116].

While he was thus declaiming . . . Everard saw a book sticking out from beneath the pillow . . . "Is that Chaucer?" he said, making for the volume—I would like to look at the passage—"Chaucer," said Bletson, hastening to interfere:
[p. 280] "No, that is Lucretius . . . [Everard finds it to be the Bible, and tells Bletson it may "serve him in better stead than Lucretius or Chaucer either."]

1826. Unknown. *Notice* of *Gillies's German Stories*, [in] Blackwood's Edinburgh Magazine, Dec. 1826, vol. **xx**, p. 849.

In the Canterbury Tales, the Man of Law's Tale, the Knight's Tale, and that of the Lady Abbess [Prioress], might be transferred to any language which was capable .of doing them justice; for they depend upon nature and universal passion. But in the comic part of the same work, (as the Miller's Tale, the Reeve's, etc.) the exquisite colouring of English life with which Chaucer has invested them would be an effectual bar to their translation.

[The mistake of "the Lady Abbess," which reappears the next year in *Murder as a Fine Art*, also in Blackwood's (*q.v.* below, 1827), and again in 1848 (*q.v.*), might suggest that this article is by De Quincey, though it does not occur in any collection of his writings. But Leigh Hunt is found making the same mistake (*q.v.* below, 1834).]

1826. Unknown. [*Review* of various editions of Chaucer, in] The Retrospective Review, vol. **xiv**, pp. 305–57.

[The article contains severe criticism of modernized versions of Chaucer.]

1827. Adolphus, J. L. *Memoranda*, [in] J. G. Lockhart's Memoirs of Sir Walter Scott, Edinburgh, 1838, vol. **vii**, pp. 56–7. (Ed. A. W. Pollard, 1900, vol. **v**, p. 130.)

The chief ornament in Scott's study] was the print of

Stothard's Canterbury Pilgrims, which hung over the chimneypiece, and, from the place assigned to it, must have been in great favour, though Sir Walter made the characteristic criticism upon it, that, if the procession were to move, the young squire who is prancing in the foreground would in another minute be over his horse's head.

1827. [**De Quincey**, Thomas.] *On Murder considered as one of the Fine Arts,* [in] Blackwood's Edinburgh Magazine, Feb. 1827, p. 202. (Collected Writings, ed. D. Masson, Edinburgh, 1889–90, 14 vols., vol. xiii, p. 20.)

Indeed, the Jewish School [of the Art of Murder] was always respectable, even in the dark ages, as the case of Hugh of Lincoln shows, which was honoured with the approbation of Chaucer, on occasion of another performance from the same school, which, in his Canterbury Tales, he puts into the mouth of the Lady Abbess.

[For another reference of De Quincey to the *Prioresses Tale, see* below, 1848 ; *see* also above, 1826. Unknown, in Blackwood's.]

1827. Hood, Eu., pseud. [i. e. **Haslewood**, Joseph]. *Notes* on *Mayster of the Game,* by Edmond de Langley, fifth son of Edward III, (Fly Leaves no. xxxvii), [in] The Gentleman's Magazine, April, 1827, p. 309.

[" Eu. Hood" is identified with Haslewood l y his album of these Fly Leaves (B.M., 1077. g. 26).]

Alauntz, or *Mastiff.* [Quotation, *Knightes Tale,* l. 1290.]

1827. Johnstone, John. *Specimens of Sacred and Serious Poetry, from Chaucer to the Present Day,* pp. 175–87.

[The Prioresses Tale and Character of a Good Parson, modernised, with a brief account of Chaucer prefixed.]

1827. Laing, Malcolm. *The Knightly tale of Golagrus and Gawane, and other ancient poems. Printed at Edinburgh by W. Chepman and A. Myllar in the year MDVIIJ,* ed. by M. Laing.

[Poem No. viii is *The Maying or Disport of Chaucer, i. e. The Complaint of the Black Knight* (by Lydgate). On p. 14 of the Introduction, Laing has a note on the poem, merely stating that it is included in all the editions of Chaucer's works.]

1827. Lamb, Charles. *Letter to B. R. Haydon,* March, 1827, [in] The Works of Charles and Mary Lamb, ed. by E. V. Lucas, 1903–5, vol. vii, Letters, p. 725.

I think I have hit on a subject for you, but can't swear it was never executed—I never heard of its being—" Chaucer beating a Franciscan Friar in Fleet Street." Think of the old dresses, houses, etc. [Lamb then quotes from Speght's Life, 1598.]

1827. Lamb, Charles. *A Death-bed, in a Letter to R. H., Esq., of B——.* (The Works of Charles and Mary Lamb, ed. by E. V. Lucas, 1903--5, 7 vols., vol. ii, pp. 246–7.)

[p. 246]   Lettered he was not; his reading scarcely exceeded the obituary of the old Gentleman's Magazine . . . Yet there was the pride of literature about him from that slender [p. 247] perusal . . . Can I forget the erudite look with which, having tried to puzzle out the text of a Black lettered Chaucer in your Corporation Library, to which he was a sort of Librarian, he gave it up with this consolatory reflection— "Jemmy," said he, "I do not know what you find in these very old books, but I observe, there is a deal of very indifferent spelling in them."

[The hero of this story was Randal Norris, Sub-Treasurer of the Inner Temple. It is very slightly altered from a letter which Lamb wrote to Crabb Robinson on Jan. 20, 1827 (ed. Lucas, vol. vii, p. 721). For a note on the Essay *see* Lucas, vol. ii, pp. 452–3.]

1827. Neele, Henry. *Lectures on English Poetry. Delivered at the Russell Institution in* . . . 1827, [in] The Literary Remains of the late Henry Neele, 1829. (3rd edn., 1839, pp. 3, 6–10, 19–20, 39, 48, 49–51, 70.)

[The Lectures on English Poetry were reprinted separately. The third edition, 1839, is the earliest in B.M.]

[In the introductory lecture Neele describes Chaucer's genius as 'vast, versatile, and original,' p. 7. His attainments, both in learning and knowledge of human nature, he declares, were profound. He follows Tyrwhitt's lead in his brief remarks on Chaucer's language, p. 8 :]

[p. 8]   Chaucer's versatility was most extraordinary. . . . His humour and wit are of the brightest and keenest character; but then his pathos is tremendous, and his descriptive powers are of the highest order. . . .

[p. 49]   Chaucer's outlines are more spirited and graceful; but Spenser is the finer colourist. Chaucer I should compare to Raffaelle, Spenser to Rubens; but then Chaucer combined with all his elegance and beauty, many laughing graces . . . I should say that Chaucer was Raffaelle and Teniers united : Raffaelle, perhaps, a little lowered from his pinnacle of dignity and elegance, and Teniers certainly much elevated above his vulgarity and grossness.

1827. Taylor, George Watson. *Misreading,* [in the transcript of] *Poems, written in English, by Charles Duke of Orleans,* [from MS. Harleian, 682, producing a supposititious reference to Chaucer], Roxburghe Club, 1827, p. 17.

[MS. Harl. 682 is a very clear, well-written fifteenth-century text, and the original poem in it, fol. 8, reads :

> When y am leyd to slepe as for a stound
> To haue my rest y can in no manere
> For all the nyght myn hert aredith round
> As in the romaunce of pleasaunt pancer,

this being, so far as the last line is concerned, an exact translation of line 4, Ballade viii, in Charles of Orleans' French *Poème de la Prison* (ed. d'Héricault, Paris, 1874, tome i, p. 21), which reads

> Car toute la nuit mon cueur lit
> Ou Rommant de Plaisant Penser.

It is scarcely conceivable that Mr. Taylor, the editor of the Roxburghe Club print, read the "pancer" of the MS. as "Chaucer," but, at any rate, he renders (without comment) the above passage as follows :

> For all the nyght myn hert aredith round
> As in the romaunce of plesaunt chaucer,—

thus, with no foundation in the manuscript, turning the passage into a Chaucer reference. This is misleading for those readers who are not able to examine the MS.; see, for instance, the conjecture of Dr. H. N. MacCracken in Publications of the Modern Language Association of America, vol. xxvi, pp. 150–1, that William de la Pole, Duke of Suffolk, may, in translating the poems, have inserted this Chaucer reference.]

1827. Unknown. *Chaucer, Sir Geoffrey,* [in] Encyclopædia Edinensis, 1827, vol. ii, pp. 254–5.

[A short article, beginning with a cautious biography, in which nothing is stated as certainty except the birth-date 1328, Chaucer's promotions in 1389, and death-date.]
Chaucer was not only the first, but also one of the best English poets. He was great in every kind of poetry, and displays every kind of excellence, excepting melody and accuracy of measure, defects which are to be ascribed to the imperfect state of the language . . . [Dryden quoted. *The Court of Love,* Chaucer's first poem, followed by *Troilus and Criseyde.* Many of the poems are allegories ; the Dream (*i. e.* the Isle of Ladies) and the *Flower and the Leaf* mentioned,

as well as *The Book of the Duchesse, Romaunt of the Rose*
and *Hous of Fame.*]

The Canterbury Tales . . . are alone sufficient to transmit
his name to posterity. . . . In his delineation of character he
is not considered inferior to Shakespeare himself.

1827. Unknown. *Magaziniana,* [in] The London Magazine, vol. vii,
Jan. 1827, new series, vol. vii, pp. 139–40.

[A modernization of Chaucer's poems much needed ; Dryden
departs too much from his text. A version of the Friar from
the *Prologue* (ll. 223–26) is given as a "very fair specimen
of what is wanted."]

> The penance he imposed was never hard—
> Whereby he gained a plentiful reward ;
> And in such cases an abundant gift
> Was proof enough of an effectual shrift [etc.].

1828. Allen, Thomas. *The History and Antiquities of London,* vol. iv,
pp. 117, 525-6.

[p. 117]   The monument of Geoffrey Chaucer . . . is now much defaced,
and is often only very slightly glanced at. Geoffrey Chaucer
. . . was the son of Sir John Chaucer, a citizen of London.

[pp. 525-6]   [Passages on the Tabard Inn and the pilgrims, with
quotations from *Prologue.*]

1828. Angelo, Henry. *Reminiscences of Henry Angelo,* 2 vols., 1828–
30, vol. i, pp. vi, 8.

[p. 8]   I remember being at Hampton many years before he
[Garrick] left the stage [i.e. *c.* 1770 ; *see* above, vol. i, p. 436],
and after supper, to amuse us boys, his reading Chaucer's Cock
and the Fox.

1828. Drake, Nathan. *Mornings in Spring or Retrospections,* [Paper]
No. xiii, *Chaucer, Dunbar, and Burns Compared,* vol. ii, pp. 1–17,
297 [quotation of Lady Pembroke's letter to Selden, *q.v.* below,
App. A., 1649].

[Drake fills a good deal of the space devoted to Chaucer
with appreciation of the poet's descriptions of nature—among
the landscapes selected for praise being those in the spurious
Flower and Leaf and *Complaint of the Black Knight.*]

1828. Gorton, John G., *A General Biographical Dictionary,* 2 vols.,
vol. i, pp. 473–4.

[The article on Chaucer is abridged from Aikin's General
Biography, *q.v.* above, 1801.]

1828. Hazlitt, William. *A Farewell to Essay-Writing,* [in] The London Weekly Review, March 29. (Collected Works of William
Hazlitt, ed. Waller and Glover, 1902–6, 13 vols, vol. xii, p. 327.)

[Praise of "Chaucer's *Flower and Leaf.*"]

1828. Hunt, James Henry Leigh. *Fine Days in January and February,*
[in] The Companion, Jan. 30, 1826, pp. 26–7. (Indicator and Examiner, 1834 ; Essays, 1891, p. 27–9.)

We think we see him [Chanticleer], as in Chaucer's home-
stead :

He looketh as it were a grim leoun

[and 4 following lines, *Nonne Prestes Tale,* ll. 4369–73].

[p. 28]   . . . As fine, considered as mere music and versification, as
the description is pleasant and noble :

His combe was redder than the fine corall

[and 5 following lines, ll. 4049–54].

Hardly one pause like the other throughout, and yet all
flowing and sweet. . . . The accent, it is to be observed, in
those concluding words, as *coral* and *colour,* is to be thrown
on the last syllable.

1828. Hunt, James Henry Leigh. *Lord Byron and Some of his Contemporaries,* pp. 376, 398–9 [also a few passing references].

[p. 376]   Chaucer, one of my best friends, I was not acquainted with
till long afterwards [*i. e.* after his schooldays].

[p. 398]   It is to him [Mr. Bell] the public are indebted for the small
edition of the Poets that preceded Cooke's, and which, with
all my predilections for that work, was unquestionably superior
to it. Besides, it included Chaucer and Spenser. The omission of these in Cooke's edition was as unpoetical a sign of the
times, as the existing familiarity with their names is the
[p. 399] reverse. . . . He knew nothing of poetry. . . . Yet a certain
liberal instinct, and turn for large dealing, made him include
Chaucer and Spenser in his edition; he got Stothard to adorn
the one, and Mortimer the other.

1828. Johnstone, John. *Specimens of the Lyrical, Descriptive and
Narrative Poets of Great Britain, from Chaucer to the Present Day,*
pp. 6, 12, 25–58.

[There are no extracts from Chaucer in the text, which
begins with Surrey; but the earlier history of English poetry
is told in the introduction, and here a very appreciative
account is given of Chaucer, with extracts from *Troilus and
Criseyde,* the *Prologue* and the *Knightes Tale.* Readers are

exhorted to master the few difficulties of his language, and modernisers are criticised; but Wordsworth's version of the *Prioresses Tale* receives praise.]

1828. Landor, Walter Savage. *Imaginary Conversations:* Landor, English Visiter and Florentine Visiter, [in] Imaginary Conversations, vol. iii, 1828, p. 427. (Ed. C. G. Crump, 1891, 6 vols., vol. vi, p. 446.)

[p. 446] [Verses to Keats :]

> Yet I would dream to meet thee at our home
> With Spenser's quiet, Chaucer's livelier ghost.

[Printed in first and second editions only ; given in the appendix of Crump's edition.]

[1828 ?] Moore, Thomas. *Note* [to] *Song of the Departing Spirit of Tithe.* (Poetical Works, ed. A. D. Godley, 1910, p. 613.)

Chaucer's Plowman complains of the Parish rectors, that

> ' For the tithing of a duck,
> Or an apple or an aye (egg),
> They make him swear upon a boke ;
> Thus they foulen Christ's fay.'

[*The Plowman's Tale,* author unknown, ll. 861-64. We have not been able to trace the first appearance of this piece. In Moore's *Poetical Works,* collected by himself, 1840-41, 10 vols., it appears (vol. ix., pp. 17-21) between pieces dated 1828, and immediately following those published in Odes on Corn, Cash and Catholics, 1828. It is not found in Palmer's Index to the Times for 1828. The note containing the Chaucer reference may have been added by Moore in 1841.]

1828. Scott, Sir Walter. *St. Valentine's Eve, or, The Fair Maid of Perth,* 3 vols., vol. ii, ch. x, p. 300, vol. iii, ch. iv, p. 61. (Border edition, ed. Andrew Lang, 1894, vol. ii, chap. v, p. 84, chap. x, p. 147.)

[p. 84]   " How now, Sir Leech ! " said the Dominican. " Do you call prayers for the dead juggling tricks ? I know that Chaucer, the English maker, says of you mediciners that your study is but little on the Bible." [*Prologue,* l. 438.]

[p. 147]   [Chapter Heading]
"This Austin humbly did."—" Did he ? " quoth he.
" Austin may do the same again for me."
Pope's Prologue to the Canterbury Tales from Chaucer.

1828. Scott, Sir Walter. *On Landscape Gardening,* [review of] *The Planter's Guide* . . . by Sir Henry Steuart, [in] The Quarterly Review, March, vol. xxxvii, p. 311.

The ancient English poets, Chaucer and Spenser in particular, never luxuriate more than when they get into a forest; by the accuracy with which they describe particular trees, and from their noticing the different characters of the different species, and the various effects of light and darkness upon the walks and glades of the forest, it is evident that they regarded woodland scenery not merely as associated with their favourite sports, but as having in itself beauties which they could appreciate.

1828. Smith, John Thomas. *Nollekens and his Times.* vol. i, p. 179 [conversation between Nollekens and Catling in Westminster Abbey; a short note on Chaucer's tomb]; vol. ii, pp. 467–71 [an account of Blake's quarrel with Cromek and Stothard; *q.v.* above, 1808 and 1809. *See* Notes and Queries, 1st ser., ii, 420].

1828. Southey, Robert. *Letter to Grosvenor C. Bedford,* dated Keswick, Nov. 28, 1828. (Life and Correspondence of Southey, 1850, vol. v, p. 332.)

[Southey says if he were confined to twelve English books his] library . . . would consist of Shakespeare, Chaucer, Spenser and Milton; Lord Clarendon; Jackson, Jeremy Taylor, and South; Isaac Walton, Sidney's Arcadia, Fuller's Church History, and Sir Thomas Brown.

1828. Tytler, Henry William. *Miscellanies,* Calcutta. [Modernizations of the Clerk's Tale and the Tale of Gamelyn. Not in B.M., Bodleian, etc., or Watt, Allibone, English Catalogue, etc. *See* Chaucer, by E. P. Hammond, 1908, p. 229.]

1828. Unknown. *Critique* of *Woman's Love; or, the Triumph of Patience* (played at Theatre Royal, Covent Garden, Dec. 17, 19, 23, 1828), [in] The Times, Dec. 18, p. 2, col. 3.

[Quotation from *Clerkes Tale.* The play was a dramatisation of the Griselda story. Kemble played the leading part, Andrea, Duke of Saluzzo. The playbill gives no author.]

1828. Unknown. *The Worthies of the United Kingdom; or Biographical Accounts of the Lives of the most illustrious Men, in Arts, Arms, Literature, and Science, connected with Great Britain.*

[No. 4. Geoffrey Chaucer, the Father of English Poetry, pp. 73–82, with engraved portrait, to face p. 73, dated June 1, 1827. A Life (with the old mistakes), and a short account of his Works. His language not obsolete.]

The Canterbury Tales is the great basis of the fame of Chaucer. . . . The . . . Tales are certainly one of the most extraordinary monuments of human genius. . . . The Prologue . . . is a copious and extensive review of the private life of the fourteenth century in England.

1829. Hartshorne, Charles Henry. *The Book Rarities in the University of Cambridge*, pp. 135–6 [Some Minor Poems of Chaucer, Lydgate and others, Caxton, n.d.], 138 [The Book of Fame, Caxton, n.d.], 149 [Troylus and Creseyde, 1517], 202 [Troylus and Creseyde, 1526], 211 [The Workes of Geffray Chaucer, Godfray, 1532], 232 [The Book of the Tales of Caunterburye, 1st edn.], 297 [Chaucer's Works, n.d., fol. The first three are in the University Library, the fourth and fifth in the King's College Library, the sixth in the Pepysian Library, and the seventh in the Trinity College Library.]

1829–30. Hazlitt, William. *Conversations of James Northcote, Esq.,* Conversation the Fifteenth. (Collected Works of William Hazlitt, ed. Waller and Glover, 1902–6, 13 vols., vol. vi, pp. 378, 418, 466, 523.)

[This Conversation probably appeared first in the Atlas, 1829, of which the B.M. has only one no.]

Northcote . . . said, 'Sir Richard Phillips . . . came here once with Godwin to shew me a picture which they had just discovered of Chaucer, and which was to embellish Godwin's *Life* of him. I told them it was certainly no picture of Chaucer, nor was any such picture painted at that time.'

1829. Hood, Thomas. *A Widow,* [in] The Gem, p. 26.

Are the traditional freaks of a Dame of Ephesus, or a Wife of Bath, or a Queen of Denmark to cast so broad a shadow over a whole sisterhood?

[This paper is a parody of Lamb by Hood, and is signed "C. Lamb." *See* Works of Charles and Mary Lamb, ed. E. V. Lucas, 1903–5, vol. vii, pp. 785–6.]

1829. Jameson, Anna. *The Loves of the Poets,* 2 vols., vol. i, pp. 133–60. [Reprinted in 1837 as *Romance of Biography* (same pagination).]

[Chaucer and Philippa Picard.]

1829. Landor, Walter Savage. *Imaginary Conversations,* 5 vols., 1824–9 ; vol. iv, 1829, pp. 209–76 ; *Works,* 1846, vol. i, pp. 402–18. (Imaginary Conversations, ed. C. G. Crump, 1891, 6 vols., vol. iv. pp. 66–108.)

[There are various changes in the language between the editions of 1829 and 1846. In the opening speech, for instance, after '*Decameron,*' the 1829 edition reads "which I shewed to you in his manuscript, you expressed so ardently your admiration," &c. The speech of Petrarca (p. 403), in reply to Chaucer's remarks on the cataract of Terni, is a later addition.]

CHAUCER, BOCCACCIO, AND PETRARCA.

[p. 66]   *Petrarca.* You have kept your promise like an Englishman,
[p. 67] Ser Geoffreddo : welcome to Arezzo. This gentleman is
Messer Giovanni Boccaccio, of whose unfinished *Decameron,*
which I opened to you in manuscript, you expressed your
admiration when we met at Florence in the spring.

Boccaccio. I was then at Certaldo, my native place, filling
up my stories, and have only to regret that my acquaintance
with one so friendly and partial to me has been formed so
late. How did Rome answer your expectation, sir?

Chaucer. I had passed through Pisa ; of which city the
Campo Santo, now nearly finished, after half a century from
its foundation, and the noble street along the Arno, are
incomparably more beautiful than anything in Rome.

Petrarca. That is true. I have heard, however, some of
your countrymen declare that Oxford is equal to Pisa, in the
solidity, extent, and costliness of its structures.

Chaucer. Oxford is the most beautiful of our cities : it
would be a very fine one if there were no houses in it.

Petrarca. How is that?

Chaucer. The lath-and-plaster white-washed houses look
despicably mean under the colleges.

Boccaccio. Few see anything in the same point of view.
It would gratify me highly, if you would tell me with all
the frankness of your character and your country, what struck
you most in "*the capital of the world*" as the vilest slaves
in it call their great open cloaca.

Chaucer. After the remains of antiquity, I know not
whether anything struck me more forcibly than the superiority
of our English churches and monasteries. . . .

[p. 68]   *Boccaccio.* We can not travel in the most picturesque
and romantic regions of our Italy, from the deficiency of
civilisation in the people.

Chaucer. Yet, Messer Giovanni, I never journeyed so far
through so enchanting a scenery as there is almost the whole
of the way from Arezzo to Rome, particularly round Terni
and Narni and Perugia.

Our master Virgil speaks of dreams that swarm upon the
branches of one solitary elm. In this country more than
dreams swarm upon every spray and leaf ; and every murmur
of wood or water comes from and brings with it inspiration.

Never shall I forget the hour when my whole soul was carried away from me by the cataract of Terni, and when all things existing were lost to me in its stupendous waters. The majestic woods that bowed their heads before it; the sun that was veiling his glory in mild translucent clouds over the furthest course of the river; the moon, that suspended her orb in the very centre of it, seemed ministering Powers, themselves in undiminished admiration of the marvel they had been looking on through unnumbered ages. What are the works of man in comparison with this? What indeed, are the other works of Nature?

Petrarca. Ser Giovanni! this, which appears even too great for Nature, was not too great for man. Our ancestors achieved it. Curius Dentatus, in his consulate, forbade the waters of the Velinus to inundate so beautiful a valley, and threw them down this precipice into the Nar. . . .

[p. 69]   *Chaucer.* I was not forgetful that we heard the story from our guide; but I thought him a boaster: and now for the first time I learn that any great power hath been exerted for any great good. Roads were levelled for aggression, and vast edifices were constructed either for pride or policy, to commemorate some victory, to reward the Gods for giving it, or to keep them in the same temper. There is nothing of which men appear to have been in such perpetual apprehension, as the inconstancy of the deities they worship.

Many thanks, Ser Francesco, for reminding me of what the guide asserted, and for teaching me the truth. I thought the fall of the Velinus not only the work of Nature, but the most beautiful she had ever made on earth. My prevention, in regard to the country about Rome, was almost as great, and almost as unjust to Nature, from what I had heard of it both at home and abroad. In the approach to the eternal city, she seems to have surrendered much of her wildness, and to have assumed all her stateliness and sedateness, all her awfulness and severity . . . . .

[p. 70]   *Boccaccio.* If Ser Geoffreddo felt in honest truth any pleasure at reading my Decameron, he owes me a tithe at least of the stories it contains: for I shall not be so courteous as to tell him that one of his invention is worth ten of mine, until I have had all his ten from him: if not now, another day.

Chaucer. Let life be spared to me, and I will carry the
[p. 71] tithe in triumph through my country, much as may be shed

of the heavier and riper grain by the conveyance and the handling of it. And I will attempt to show Englishmen what Italians are; how much deeper in thought, intenser in feeling, and richer in imagination, than ever formerly: and I will try whether we can not raise poetry under our fogs, and merriment among our marshes. We must first throw some litter about it, which those who come after us may remove.

Petrarca. Do not threaten, Ser Geffreddo! Englishmen act.

Boccaccio. Messer Francesco is grown melancholy at the spectre of the tribune. Relate to us some amusing tale, either of court or war.

Chaucer. It would ill become me, signors, to refuse what I can offer: and truly I am loth to be silent, when a fair occasion is before me of adverting to those of my countrymen who fought in the battle of Cressy, as did one or two or more of the persons that are the subjects of my narrative.

Boccaccio. Enormous and horrible as was the slaughter of the French in that fight, and hateful as is war altogether to you and me, Francesco! I do expect from the countenance of Ser Geoffreddo, that he will rather make us merry than sad.

Chaucer. I hope I may, the story not wholly nor principally relating to the battle.

[Here Chaucer tells the story of Sir Magnus Lucy of Charlecote.]

[p. 97]   Now Messer Francesco, I may call upon you, having seen you long since throw aside your gravity, and at last spring up alert, as though you would mount for Picardy.

Petrarca. A right indeed have you acquired to call upon me, Ser Geoffredo; but you must accept from me the produce of our country. . . .

[p. 98]   *Boccaccio.* Well, go on with him.

Petrarca. I do think, Giovanni, you tell a story a great deal more naturally; but I will say plainly what my own eyes have remarked, and will let the peculiarities of men appear as they strike me, whether they are in symmetry with our notions of character, or not.

Chaucer. The man of genius may do this: no other will attempt it. He will discover the symmetry, the relations, and the dependencies, of the whole: he will square the strange problematic circle of the human heart. . . .

[p. 108]   After this narration, Messer Francesco walked toward the high altar and made his genuflexion: the same did Messer

Giovanni, and, in the act of it, slapped Ser Geoffreddo on the shoulder, telling him he might dispense with the ceremony, by reason of his inflexible boots and the buck-skin paling about his loins. Ser Geoffreddo did it nevertheless, and with equal devotion. His two friends then took him between them to the house of Messer Francesco, where dinner had been some time waiting.

1829. Ritson, Joseph. *Ancient Songs and Ballads from the Reign of King Henry the Second to the Revolution*, 2 vols., vol. i, pp. xi [women "tomblesteres" in the time of Chaucer], xxii ["timbestere" and "tymbres" in *Romaunt of the Rose*], xxviii–ix, xlv–vi [vocal melody in the age of Chaucer], xlvi n., xlvii, li n. ["hornpipes of Cornewaile" in *Romaunt of the Rose*], lvii, [harp], lvii n., lix [the rote], lx n., lxi [giterne], lxi n, lxxii n., lxiii ["joly Absolon," and the lute], lxiv [the symphonie], lxv [Chaucer's Miller plays the bagpipe], lxvi [floite and liltying horne, pipes, trompes, nakeres and clariounes], 68 ; vol. ii, p. 3.

1829. Scott, Sir Walter. *Memoir of George Bannatyne*, [in] Memorials of George Bannatyne, Bannatyne Club, Edinburgh, 1829, p. 14. (Miscellaneous Prose Works of Sir Walter Scott, Edinburgh, 1834–71, 30 vols, vol. xxx, pp. 82–83.)

This darling of the Scottish Muses [Dunbar] has been justly raised to a level with Chaucer by every judge of poetry, to whom his obsolete language has not rendered him unintelligible . . . In the pathetic Dunbar is Chaucer's inferior, and accordingly in most of his pieces he rather wishes to instruct the understanding, or to amuse the fancy, than to affect the heart.

1829. Scott, Sir Walter. *Tales of a Grandfather*, 2nd series, vol. i, pp. 37–8. (Miscellaneous Prose Works of Sir Walter Scott, Edinburgh, 1834–71, 30 vols., vol. xxiii, p. 238.)

The Queen [Elizabeth] . . . told the preacher [the Bishop of St. David's] to keep his admonitions to himself, since she plainly saw the greatest clerks . . . were not the wisest men.

[For other references by Scott to Queen Elizabeth's quotation of this line *see* also above, 1820, *The Monastery*, and 1821, *Kenilworth*.]

1829. Wordsworth, William. *Liberty.* (The Poetical Works of William Wordsworth, 1896, vol. vii, p. 219.)

Is there a cherished bird (I venture now
To snatch a sprig from Chaucer's reverend brow)—

Is there a brilliant fondling of the cage,
Though sure of plaudits on his costly stage,
Though fed with dainties from the snow-white hand
Of a kind mistress, fairest of the land,
But gladly would escape ; and, if need were,
Scatter the colours from the plumes that bear
The emancipated captive through blithe air
Into strange woods, where he at large may live
On best or worst which they and Nature give ?

[This is from the sequel to the *Gold and Silver Fishes in a Vase*, written in 1829, printed in 1835.]

1830. Campbell, Thomas.   *Chaucer,* [in] Brewster's Edinburgh Encyclopædia, vol. v, pt. ii, pp. 756–62.

[A long and very appreciative article, echoing in parts the author's *Essay* of 1819, *q. v.* above. The earlier and biographical part is careful, and describes Godwin's *Life* as "a series of suppositions," but the story of Chaucer's exile and imprisonment is treated as certain. Campbell notes that the inscription and figures on Chaucer's tomb were at the time of writing almost obliterated.

Chaucer found English poetry in the rudest state ; he introduced the heroic iambic line. *The Court of Love,* "his first poem," noticed at length. *Troilus and Criseyde,* his next poem, analysed ; its anachronisms.]

[P. 760]   Next to the length of the poem, the greatest obstacle to our interest in it is an inconsistency between the strength and tenderness, and the lawlessness and secrecy of Troilus's passion. The poet represents no sufficient cause to prevent the Trojan from marrying Cresseide. . . . This is a departure from nature and probability, the more remarkable in a poet whose characteristic merit is generally adherence to both. Yet this tale of Troy divine, which Sir Philip Sydney adored, and which was once regarded as an ornament to our language, did not fascinate our forefathers without a reason. As an ancient novel in verse, it reminds us very frequently of the minute touches and pathos of Richardson. [The confession of Criseyde and the grief of Troilus (as in 1819).]

[The *Dream (Isle of Ladies), Book of the Duchesse, Parlement of Foules, Romaunt of the Rose, Flower and the Leaf, Hous of Fame.* The *Canterbury Tales* the work of his old age ; the plan from Boccaccio ; the naturalism of the characters, and the dramatic contrasts between them. Chaucer's other virtues inferior to this; his incongruities, *e. g.* the "cooke scalded for all his longe ladle." The great architect of our versification, but not an importer of French words. His prolixity, like his coarseness, a fault of his time.]

[p. 762]   [The beauties] of Chaucer may be compared to flowers which we collect in a long journey, numerous in the sum, but collected widely asunder. This expression may appear irreverend to those who are enamoured of old English and obsolete spelling, merely because it is old and obsolete; but the reader who sits down to Chaucer, expecting wonders in every page, will find, that though there is much to reward his patience, there is also something to exercise it.

1830. Moore, Thomas. *Letters and Journals of Lord Byron, with Notices of his Life by Thomas Moore*, 2 vols, vol. i, p. 30. (1 vol. ed. 1908, pp. 15, 49, 123, 391.) [*See* above, Byron, 1807, 1811, 1819.]

[Moore quotes Dr. Glennie, Byron's schoolmaster at Dulwich:] His reading in history and poetry was far beyond the usual standard of his age, and in my study he found many books . . . among others, a set of our poets from Chaucer to Churchill, which I am almost tempted to say he had more than once perused from beginning to end.

1830. Murray, Sir Charles Augustus. *Memorandum*, [dated June, 1830, printed in] Goethes Gespräche, Gesamtausgabe, neu herausgegeben von Flodoard Frhr. von Biedermann, 1909–11, 5 vols., vol. iv, p. 286. (The Hon. Sir Charles Murray, K.C.B., a memoir, by . . . Sir Herbert Maxwell, 1898, p. 75.)

After a few minutes general conversation he [Goethe] pointed to a large volume lying before him on the table, and said—

"It is curious that when your visit was announced to me, I was engaged in making a few notes on your Old English literature. Is that a subject that has ever engaged your attention?" To this I was fortunately able to make an affirmative reply, as I had not long before, when at Oxford, spent some time in the study of Anglo-Saxon, and was, moreover, well up in Chaucer, which enabled me to elucidate a few old words and phrases which he had marked as requiring explanation.

1830. Nicolas, Sir Nicholas Harris. *Privy Purse Expenses of Elizabeth of York.* Index and Notes, [Illustrative quotations under] Grayling, p. 198; Housell, p. 202; Pardon, p. 214; Purfle, p. 217; Stations, p. 224; Combe Coverchiefs, pp. 241-2.

1830. Robson, Thomas. *The British Herald or Cabinet of Armorial Bearings of the Nobility and Gentry of Great Britain and Ireland,* vol. i.

[Note, under *Chaucer,* on his coat-of-arms.]

1830. Scott, Sir Walter. *Letters on Demonology and Witchcraft,* John Murray's edition, 1830, pp. 173-75, 178; Reprint in Morley's Universal Library, 1884, pp. 144-5, 148. (Miscellaneous Prose Works, Edinburgh, 1834-71, 30 vols., vol. xxix, pp. 168-70, 173.)

[*Wife of Bath's Tale,* ll. 1-25; Chaucer ascribes the exile of fairies to the prayers of the "limitours" and "freres."]

1830. Scott, Sir Walter. *The History of Scotland,* [in] The Cabinet Cyclopædia, conducted by the Rev. Dionysius Lardner, vol. i, pp. 333, 351.

[References to Dunbar as "the Scottish Chaucer."]

1830. Scott, Sir Walter. *Introduction to The Monastery,* dated Nov. 1, 1830, [in] Introductions . . . to the Novels, Tales and Romances of the Author of Waverley, 3 vols. 1833, vol. ii, p. 117. (Border Edition, ed. Andrew Lang, 1893, vol. i, pp. xxii, xxiii.)

[p. xxii] There are evenings when the spectator might believe, with Father Chaucer, that the—

[p. xxiii]
Queen of Faery,
With harp, and pipe, and symphony,
Were dwelling in the place.

[Sir Thopas, ll. 2004-6.]

1830. Unknown. *Review of Sotheby's Specimens of a New Version of Homer,* [in] The Edinburgh Review, July 1830, vol. li, p. 464.

Of all the British poets, the two most Homeric in *spirit,* however different in *style,* both from the Grecian bard and from each other, are Shakespeare and Scott; but Chaucer, behind all three in fancy and invention, comes nearest to Homer in manner and expression. *He* might have given an English Homer, in which the few, who would in the present day have read it, would have recognised the character and bearing of the great original.

In delivering his rule for a narrator, Chaucer has at least

prescribed a law equally incumbent upon all who aspire to translate the Homeric poems :—

" Whoso shall telle a tale after a man . . .   [to]
     All speke he never so rudely and so large."

[*Prologue*, ll. 731–4.]

1830. Warner, Richard. *Literary Recollections,* 2 vols., 1830, vol. i, pp. 141–2.

[p. 141]   He himself [the Rev. Henry Richman] has frequently told me, that in early manhood, he had written a sequel to Chaucer's Canterbury Tales, which (as I have been informed by a competent judge, who perused them) breathed much of the spirit, style, and diction, of the venerable bard.   But of this

[p. 142] work I never could obtain a sight.   He always declined permitting his friends to peruse it, upon the principle, that the levity of such compositions, was inconsistent with the decorum of the clerical character.

[For Richman, *see* above, p. 49.]

1830. Wordsworth, William. *Letter to Alexander Dyce,* May, 1830, [in] Letters of the Wordsworth Family, ed. W. Knight, 1907, 3 vols., vol. ii, p. 419.

The poetic genius of England, with the exception of Chaucer, Spenser, Milton, Dryden, Pope, and a very few more, is to be sought in her drama.

1831. Bentley, Samuel. *Excerpta Historica,* or *Illustrations of English History.* Issue of Katherine Swynford, pp. 148, 155, 205–7, 210, 230–1, 239, 253, 353.

[p. 155]   The following document and other notices will throw some light on the subject · and as the Swynfords, besides being closely connected with the blood-royal, were, according to the poet's biographers, though the fact is very questionable, nearly allied to Chaucer, this article may be deemed to possess more interest than is generally found in genealogical statements.

Sir Payne Roelt, a Knight of Hainault, and Guienne King-of-Arms, had, it is said, two daughters and co-heirs, Philippa and Katherine.   No particulars of his pedigree have been discovered ; his arms, in allusion to his name, were Gules, three Katherine wheels Or.

Philippa, his eldest daughter, is stated to have been the maid of honour to Philippa Queen of Edward the Third who by the name of "Philippa Pycard" obtained a grant of one hundred shillings per annum on the 28th January

1370, and married Geoffrey Chaucer, to whom, in consequence, it is supposed, of this connection, the Duke of Lancaster granted the Castle of Dodington [*sic*]. Of John of Gaunt's connection with Chaucer, however, no *proof* has been found ; and the circumstance of the lady assigned to him for his wife being styled " Philippa Pycard," instead of Roelt, renders the assertion, that she was the sister of the Duchess of Lancaster, extremely doubtful.

[p. 353]   *Letters relating to the Stonor Family.*

The following . . . deserve insertion as illustrative of the private history of the family. The first is a letter from Alice, Duchess of Suffolk, wife of William de la Pole, Duke of Suffolk, to William Stonor. The Duchess, as being the grand-daughter of Geoffrey Chaucer, is an object of interest. The poet's eldest son is said to have been Thomas Chaucer, who became Speaker of the House of Commons, and was a very eminent person in the reigns of Henry the Fifth and Sixth. His only child, Alice, married William de la Pole, Earl, Marquess, and Duke of Suffolk ; but her issue became extinct in the reign of Henry the Eighth, when all the descendants of Geoffrey Chaucer failed. Their son, John de la Pole, Duke of Suffolk, had a natural daughter, Johanna, who married Thomas Stonor, and had issue by him Sir William, Thomas (from whom descended the Stonors of Stonor), and two other sons who died without issue.

1831. Collier, John Payne. *The History of English Dramatic Poetry to the time of Shakespeare ; and Annals of the Stage to the Restoration,* 3 vols, vol. i, p. 12 ; vol. ii, pp. 124 *n.*, 134 *n.*, 147, 150 [Chaucer's allusions to Miracle Plays], 189 *n.*, 237 *n.*, 285 [note on the phrase " lefe on linde "], 291 *n.*; vol. iii, p. 103 *n.* [the mention of Chaucer by Edward Guilpin in *Skialetheia,* 1598, *q.v.,* above, vol. i, p. 157].

1831. Hallam, Arthur Henry. *Oration on the Influence of Italian Works of Imagination on the same class of Composition in England.* Delivered in Trinity Coll. Chapel, Dec. 16, 1831, [in] Remains in Verse and Prose of Arthur Henry Hallam, 1834, pp. 159, 178–181.

[Chaucer influenced by Italian study.]

1831. [Hunt, James Henry Leigh ?] [*Extracts from Chaucer,* modernised, in] The Tatler, June 30, July 6, 9, 1831, vol. ii, p. 1027, vol. iii, pp. 18, 31.

[vol. ii, p. 1027]   In the passages we propose to extract out of this great Poet

from time to time, the spelling will be modernized, and the
lines (with all humility) new framed on occasion ; so as to
accommodate general readers, and warrant the insertion where
obsoleteness of language might otherwise be complained of.
[Three short extracts ; the first begins :]

> At mortal battles had he been fifteen,
> And foughten for the faith at Tramisene . . . [etc.]
> > [*Prologue*, ll. 60–74.]

1831. [**Peacock,** Thomas Love.]   *Crotchet Castle*, chap. iii., p. 39. (Ed.
Richard Garnett, 1891, p. 39.)

The Reverend Doctor Folliott having promised to return to
dinner, walked back to his vicarage, meditating whether he
should pass the morning in writing his next sermon, or in
angling for trout, and had nearly decided in favor of the
latter proposition, repeating to himself, with great unction,
the lines of Chaucer :

> And as for me, though that I can but lite,
> On bokis for to read I me delite,
> . . . . . [to]
> Farewell my boke and my devocion.
> > [*Legend of Good Women*, Prol., ll. 29–39.]

1831. Ritson, Joseph.   *Fairy Tales*, pp. 26–8 [Dissertation on Fairies],
89 [Tale viii, Drayton's Nymphidia, *q.v.*, above, 1627, vol i, p. 201].

[pp. 26-7]   [Fairies or elves peculiar to the British Isles ; *Wife of Bath's
Tale*, ll. 1–16, quoted.]

[p. 27]   [Chaucer] knew nothing, it would seem, of *Oberon, Titania,*
or *Mab*, but speaks of :

> " Pluto, that is the King of Faerie,
> And many a ladie in his compagnie,
> Folwing his wif, the quene Proserpina, &c."

[p. 28]   Mr. Tyrwhitt " cannot help thinking that his *Pluto* and
Proserpina were the true progenitors of *Oberon* and *Titania*."

In the progress of *The wif of Bathes tale*, it happed the
knight

> " ——in his way . . . to ride
> In all his care, under a forest side
> Whereas he saw upon a dance go
> Of ladies foure-and-twenty, and yet mo . . . [to]
> Yvanished was this dance, he wist not wher."

These *ladies* appear to have been *fairies*, though nothing is
insinuated of their size.

1831. Scott, Sir Walter. *Introduction* to *The Abbot*, dated 1 Jan. 1831, [in] Introductions . . . to the Novels, Tales, and Romances of the Author of Waverley, 3 vols., 1833, vol. ii, p. 173. (Border edition, ed. Andrew Lang, 1893, vol. i, pp. xxii–iii.)

[p. xxii]   I looked round my library and could not but observe, that, from the time of Chaucer to that of Byron, the most popular authors had been the most prolific.

1831. Southey, Robert. *Select Works of the British Poets, from Chaucer to Jonson, with biographical Sketches by Robert Southey,* 1831, Preface ; biography of Chaucer, p. 1, poems, pp. 2–60.

[The selected poems of Chaucer are : *The Prologue to the Canterbury Tales,* the *Knightes,* the *Man of Law's,* the *Clerkes* and the *Squieres Tales, The Parlement of Foules, The Cuckoo and the Nightingale* (not by Chaucer), *The Flower and the Leaf* (not by Chaucer), *Good Counsail of Chaucer,* and *To His Empty Purse.* The biography is a short summary of the facts as then known or assumed, based on the *Testament of Love* and the *Court of Love,* &c. The following are the principal critical remarks :]

Chaucer is not merely the acknowleged father of English poetry, he is also one of our greatest poets. His proper station is in the first class, with Spenser, Shakspeare, and Milton ; and Shakspeare alone has equalled him in variety and versatility of genius. In no other country has any writer effected so much with a half-formed language : retaining what was popular, and rejecting what was barbarous, he at once refined and enriched it ; and though it is certain that his poetry is written rhythmically rather than metrically, his ear led him to that cadence and those forms of verse, which, after all subsequent experiments, have been found most agreeable to the general taste, and may, therefore, be deemed best adapted to the character of our speech. In some of his smaller pieces, he has condescended to use the ornate style which began to be affected in his age ; but he has only used it as if to show that he had deliberately rejected it in all his greater and better works . . . his original works are distinguished by a life, and strength, and vivacity, which nothing but original genius, and that of the highest order, can impart. Whoever aspires to a lasting name among the English poets must get the writings of Chaucer, and drink at the well-head. . . . [Then follow the selected poems, as above.]

[For a more expanded expression of Southey's opinion that Chaucer's verse is rhythmical rather than metrical, *see* below, 1833–6. For Nott, *see* above, 1815–16.]

1831. Southey, Robert. *Essay*, [in] *Attempts in Verse, by John Jones,* with an introductory essay on the . . . lives of our uneducated poets, p. 38.

[John Taylor, the Water Poet] has imitated Chaucer in a catalogue of birds, which . . . has some sweet lines in it.

1831. Wordsworth, William. *Letter to John Kenyon,* [dated] Rydal Mount, Sept. 13, 1831, [in] Letters of the Wordsworth Family, ed. W. Knight, 1907, 3 vols, vol. ii, p. 455.

Our Summer . . . has been . . . a brilliant one. . . . Our Youths and Maidens, like Chaucer's Squire, "have slept no more than doth the nightingale."

1831. Wordsworth, William. *Letter to J. K. Miller,* dated Rydal Mount, Dec. 17, 1831, [in] Letters of the Wordsworth Family, collected and edited by W. Knight, 1907, 3 vols., vol. ii, p. 476.

I am no ready master of prose writing. . . . This last consideration will not weigh with you; nor would it have done with myself a few years ago; but the bare mention of it will serve to show that years have deprived me of courage, in the sense the word bears when applied by Chaucer to the animation of birds in Spring time.

1832. Boucher, Jonathan. *Glossary of Archaic and Provincial Words. A Supplement to the Dictionaries of the English Language,* 1832, edited by the Rev. Joseph Hunter and Joseph Stevenson, pp. vii, xviii–xx, xxxi–ii, xl, xli, xlv, xlvi, li, liii–iv, lvi. [Words from Chaucer on nearly every page. *See* above, 1804, Boucher.]

1832. Collier, John Payne. *An Old Man's Diary,* privately printed, 1871–2; 2 vols., vol. i, part i, pp. 12–13; part ii, p. 57.

[p. 12] Where is Cressida spoken of as a widow? I find two or three passages in Chaucer's first book of *Troylus* that seem more than to intimate it, and even that she may have had children. Thus:

[p. 13] "And as a widowe was she, and al alone,
And nyst to whom she might make her mone".

[*Troilus,* bk. i, ll. 97–8.]

[Further reference to her "widowes habit" (l. 170) and "blacke wede" (l. 177).]

I must look to *Filostrato* and the old romance. Shakespeare does not represent her as a widow.

[For vol ii *see* below, 1833.]

1832. Fitzgerald, Edward. *Letter to John Allen,* [dated] London, Nov. 21, 1832. (Letters and Literary Remains of Edward Fitzgerald, ed. W. A. Wright, 1889, vol. i, p. 10.)

I have read some Chaucer too, which I like.

1832. Hunt, James Henry Leigh. *Preface* [to the] *Poetical Works of Leigh Hunt,* pp. viii, xv, xxxii–vi.

[p. xxxii] To return to double rhymes. They are as old in our language as Chaucer, whose versification is as unlike the crabbed and unintentional stuff it is supposed to be, as possible, and has never had justice done it. The sweet and delicate gravity of its music is answerable to the sincerity of the writer's heart. Take a specimen of his character of the " Good Priest," including some double rhymes :—

" Benigne he was, and wonder diligent . . . [to]
[p. xxxiii]   He was a shepherd, and no *mercenarie*."

[Prot., ll. 483–90, 507–14.]

[pp. xxxv–vi] [Chaucer's practice of ending a paragraph in the middle of a couplet a musical one and ' very fit to be revived'; passages from *Squieres Tale* and *Knightes Tale* quoted in illustration.]

1832. Hunter, William. *An Anglo-Saxon Grammar, and Derivatives; with Proofs of the Celtic Dialects being of Eastern Origin; and an Analysis of the Style of Chaucer, Douglas and Spenser.*

[The examination of the style of Chaucer consists: 1. Of a discussion of parts of speech, with examples from Chaucer; 2. of a very brief biographical account of Chaucer, pp. 62–9, including some remarks on his versification, and some extracts showing the pronunciation of genitive and plural endings.]

1832. [Irving, David.] *Preface* [to] *The Moral Fables of Esope, compyled by Robert Henryson,* Maitland Club, p. v [" Henryson's Tale of Sire Chauntecleire and the Foxe evidently borrowed from Chaucer's Nonnes Preestes Tale "], and *n.,* vi–vii and *nn.* [the *Testament of Cresseid* a sequel to Chaucer's poem, and formerly attributed to him ; neither drawn from classical sources ; quotations from Kynaston and from the *Hous of Fame*], viii–ix [anachronisms in Henryson's *Testament of Cresseid* as in Chaucer's *Troilus*].

1832. Le Bas, Charles Webb. *The Life of Wiclif,* pp. 211–12.

[Wiclif's zeal and charity] have given occasion to the conjecture that he may have been the real original of Chaucer's celebrated picture of the Village Priest.

[Prol. ll. 477–528 quoted.]

1832. Nicolas, Sir Nicholas Harris. *The Scrope and Grosvenor Controversy* [edited by Sir N. H. Nicolas], 2 vols., vol. i, p. 178 [Chaucer's deposition], vol. ii, pp. 404–412 [a biography of Chaucer, based on the documents, and ignoring his works. For a fuller account, fresh documents having meanwhile been discovered, *see* Nicolas's Life of Chaucer, prefixed to Chaucer's Poetical Works, 1845].

[The publication by Godwin of Chaucer's deposition in 1386 (*q.v.* above, vol. i, p. 8, vol. ii, 1803) that he was 'del age de xl ans & plus,' first led to a redating of his birth (1340 instead of 1328). Sir Harris Nicolas himself (vol. ii, p. 405) seems to lean to about the year 1331.]

1832. Scott, Sir Walter. *Castle Dangerous*, chap. ii, pp. 265–6, [in] Tales of my Landlord, 4th series, vol. iii, 1832. (Border edn., ed. Andrew Lang, 1894, ch. ii, p. 34.) [For the "modest as a maid" and "*élève*" of the first edition, later editions read "meek as a maid" and "pattern."]

As to the first [his looks] he [Aymer de Valence] was mild, gentle, and "modest as a maid," and possessed exactly of the courteous manners ascribed by our father Chaucer to the young *élève* of chivalry whom he describes upon his pilgrimage to Canterbury.

[*n.a.* 1832.] Scott, Sir Walter. *Library Catalogue.* (Catalogue of the Abbotsford Library, by J. G. Lockhart, Maitland Club, 1838, pp. 41, 154–5,172, 185, 190, 239.)

[Scott possessed the following editions, etc. : Works, [1561], 1602 (Speght), 1721 (Urry), 1810 (English Poets), Canterbury Tales, 1798 (Tyrwhitt), Canterbury Tales (Ogle's modernisation), 1741 ; Godwin's Life of Chaucer, 1803 ; Todd's Illustrations, 1810.

Under Godwin, Lockhart gives a reference to Scott's review (Prose Works, vol. xvii), and under the [1561] and 1602 Works to Scott's "Poetical Works, passim."]

1832. Tennyson, Alfred. *A Dream of Fair Women*, stanzas 1–4, [in] Poems, 1833 [1832], pp. 123–4. (Works, 1895, pp. 56–7.)

> I read, before my eyelids dropt their shade,
>   '*The Legend of Good Women*,' long ago
> Sung by the morning star of song, who made
>   His music heard below ;
>
> Dan Chaucer, the first warbler, whose sweet breath
>   Preluded those melodious bursts that fill
> The spacious times of great Elizabeth
>   With sounds that echo still.
>
> And, for a while, the knowledge of his art
>   Held me above the subject, as strong gales
> Hold swollen clouds from raining, tho' my heart,
>   Brimful of those wild tales,
>
> Charged both mine eyes with tears. . . .

1832. Unknown. *Chaucer's House of Fame,* [in] The Penny Magazine, August 11, 1832, vol. i, pp. 190-1.

[A short notice on the *Hous of Fame,* more particularly in reference to its value as giving a picture of the learning and opinions of the latter part of the fourteenth century.]

1832. Wordsworth, William. *Letter to John Kenyon,* [dated] Jan. 26, 1832, [in] Letters of the Wordsworth Family, ed. W. Knight, 1907, 3 vols, vol ii, p. 484.

He [Hogarth] reminds me both of Shakespeare and Chaucer ; but these great poets seem happy in softening and diversifying their views of life, as often as they can, by metaphors and images from rural nature.

1833. Clarke, Charles Cowden. *Tales from Chaucer in Prose* [*i.e. The Prologue, The Knightes Tale, The Man of Law's Tale, The Wife of Bath's Tale, The Clerkes Tale, The Squieres Tale, The Pardoneres Tale, The Prioresses Tale, The Nonne Prestes Tale, The Chanouns Yemannes Tale,* and *The Tale of Gamelyn*]. Designed chiefly for the use of young persons. [Second edition, revised, 1870.]

1833. Collier, John Payne. *An Old Man's Diary,* privately printed, 1871-2, 2 vols., vol. ii, part i, pp. 38-9, 85 ; part ii, 45-6, 106.

[pp. 38-9] [Discussion on Sleep. Chaucer's Shipman's Tale quoted. . . . Question whether Chaucer was more gross than his age " voted in the affirmative."]

[For vol. i *see* above, 1832.]

[c. 1833.] Haslewood, Joseph, and **Bliss,** Philip. *Notes and Newspaper Cuttings* in an interleaved copy of William Winstanley's *Lives of the English Poets,* 1687 [B.M., C. 45. d. 13].

[At the beginning, no pagination, cutting of advertisement of] Part I of A Series of Portraits of the British Poets, from Chaucer to Cowper and Beattie . . . published by C. & H. Baldwin, Newgate Street.

[On next page, advertisement of] a new edition of the British Poets, in 100 vols., commencing with Chaucer, Dec. 1821. [*See* above, 1822.]

[MS. list of poets cited, and another of those omitted, in England's Parnassus, 1600 ; Chaucer's name in the second.]

[To face p. 18] [Newspaper cutting from] *The Daily Courant,* March 4, 1731. Essay against law proceedings being in English. [*See* above, 1731, vol. i, p. 373.]

[To face
p. 23]   [Quotations from the following in Haslewood's writing :]

(1) The Art of Poetry, 1715 [*q.v.* below, App. A].

(2) The Debates . . between the Heraudes of England
and France by Tho. Coke, 1550 [*q.v.* vol. i, p. 90].

(3) The British Warrior, a poem addressed to Lord Cutts,
1706 [*q.v.* vol. i, p. 293].

(4) Inscription on Fly-leaf of imperfect copy of Chaucer's
Works. [*See* above, 1764 [Gough ?], vol. i, p. 425,
and Hood, 1823.]

[To face
p. 24]   (5) Procter's Preface to 'Of the Knowledge and Conduct
of War, 1578 ' [*q.v.* vol. i, p. 116].

[To face
p. 25]   [Newspaper cutting of] Notice of Publication of the works
of Chaucer by J. Urry, Feb. 1722. [*See* above, 1721,
vol. i, p. 353.]

[To face
p. 26]   An Elegie upon the death of the auncient English
poetts. [*See* above, 1823, Hood.]

[To face
p. 27]   [Quotations in Haslewood's hand from]

(1) Wesley's Epistle on Poetry, 1700 [*q.v.* vol. i, p. 289].

(2) Verses and Small Poems by Sir A. Cokain, 1658 [*q.v.*
vol. i, p. 235].

[To face
p. 28]   (3) Ancient State . . . of the Court of Requests, 1596
[*q.v.* vol. i, p. 143, on the payment of money at Chaucer's
tomb ; to which Haslewood adds the following MS. note]:

Q. The nature of this payment, and if Chaucer's tomb was
not nominally legalized as a place for fixed payments, after the
manner that there is usually inserted in Mortgage Securities
Lincolns Inn Hall, or other similar place, for the purpose of
alledging a certain default.   Money tendered does not I conceive mean any public gift at the tomb whereto Richard
Puttenham became entitled by way of perquisite.   Rob.
Cheynie I consider to have been the Trustee upon the marriage
and the name of Spencer inserted for legal form.

This construction is added at the time of copying without
referring to see if any authority notices the Tomb as an
appointed place for any purpose here required. [*See* also a
similar note by Haslewood (' Eu. Hood ') in Gentleman's
Magazine, 1823.]

[p. 32]   [A note that in Winstanley's *Select Lives of England's
Worthies* is a Life of Chaucer almost verbatim with this.]

[To face
pp. 56, 57]   [Cutting of] Surrey's Excellent Epitaffe of Syr Thomas
Wyat [*c.* 1542, *q.v.* above, vol. i, p. 84].

[The last sheet inserted in this volume is an extract,

probably from a publisher's catalogue, giving] Proposals for
Macklin's British Poets . . . particularly . . . Chaucer, Skelton,
etc. [The date is given in MS. as 1792, *q.v.* below, App. A.]

[c. 1833.] Haslewood, Joseph, and **Reed**, Isaac. *Notes and Newspaper
Cuttings* in interleaved copy of Theophilus Cibber's *Lives of the
Poets*, 1753 [B.M., 10854. a. 1].

[Newspaper cutting from Daily Advertiser, 2 Jan. 1753, of
the publisher's advertisement of Cibber's *Lives*, immediately
before title-page of vol. i. *See* 1753, Unknown, vol. i,
p. 407. Another before contents.]

[To face p. 10] [Newspaper cutting:] An account of Chaucer, translated
from the French. [*See* 1777, Unknown, *Morning Post* above,
vol. i, p. 449.]

[Cutting from a book (?) page 23. A notice of Gower and
Chaucer:] *Johannes Gower*, Anglorum Poeta [a picture of
Gower prefixed to this cutting] Taken from his monumental
effigy in St. Mary Overie's Church, Southwark. . . . Gower,
who with Chaucer, helped to refine the English language
has ever been esteemed the next in merit to him of his
contemporary poets.

[c. 1833.] Haslewood, Joseph. *Collections for the Lives of the English
Poets* [B.M., C. 45. d. 9–11].

[vol. i, pp. 5–8] [Newspaper cutting:] Observations on the Rise & Progress
of English Poetry, [from] Whitehall Evening Post. Jan. 7,
1769 [*q.v.* vol. i, p. 432, Unknown.]

[p. 71] A Familiar Epistle from the Shades below . . . from a
Collection of Poems . . . by Jemmy Copywell, [from] Lloyd's
Evening Post. April 11, 1760 [*q.v.* vol. i, p. 371, 1730,
Unknown].

[pp. 98–9] [Cutting from the *British Bibliographer*, on the projected
Bibliotheca Critica. *See* above, 1810, Brydges.]

[p. 204] [Cutting from] The Grub Street Journal, 3 Sept., 1730 [*q.v.*
above, vol. i, p. 373, Unknown].

[p. 216] [Cutting, headed by a quotation from Chaucer, from] The
European Magazine for June, 1821, vol. lxxix, p. 514 [*q.v.*
above].

[p. 217] [Notice of publication of an edition of Urry's Chaucer
(price bound one guinea) quoting Dryden's praise in the
Preface to his Fables, and giving date in MS. 5 Jan. 1753,

but not name of paper. No edition of this year is known, and probably the date is an error.]

[p. 354] [Magazine cutting, without name, but dated Sep. 1752, and numbered pp. 420, 421, 422 :] *The* Life *of* JOHN DRYDEN, *Esq. With his Head neatly engraved.* [A reference to Dryden's modernizations of Chaucer.]

[vol. ii, p. 447] [Cutting from] The Monthly Miscellany for June 1774 [*q.v.* above, vol. i, p. 438, Unknown].

[pp. 459–468] [Cutting from] The British Bibliographer, by Sir Egerton Brydges and J. Haslewood, vol. ii, 1812, *q.v.* above. No. VI, Memoirs of Gower & Chaucer.

[vol. iii, p. 817] [Cutting from] The Edinburgh Magazine for April 1801, Remarks on the Writings of Allan Ramsay [*q.v.* above].

1834. Coleridge, Samuel Taylor. *Table Talk*, March 15, 1834. (The Table Talk and Omniana, ed. T. Ashe, 1884, pp. 276–7.)

[p. 276] I take unceasing delight in Chaucer. His manly cheerfulness is especially delicious to me in my old age. How exquisitely tender he is, and yet how perfectly free from the least touch of sickly melancholy or morbid drooping! The sympathy of the poet with the subjects of his poetry is [p. 277] particularly remarkable in Shakspeare and Chaucer; but what the first effects by a strong act of imagination, and mental metamorphosis, the last does without any effort, merely by the inborn kindly joyousness of his nature. How well we seem to know Chaucer! How absolutely nothing do we know of Shakspeare!

I cannot in the least allow any necessity for Chaucer's poetry, especially the Canterbury Tales, being considered obsolete. Let a few plain rules be given for sounding the final *è* of syllables, and for expressing the termination of such words as *ocëan*, and *natiön*, etc., as dissyllables,—or let the syllables to be sounded in such cases be marked by a competent metrist.

This simple expedient would, with a very few trifling exceptions, where the errors are inveterate, enable any reader to feel the perfect smoothness and harmony of Chaucer's verse. As to understanding his language, if you read twenty pages with a good glossary, you surely can find no further difficulty, even as it is; but I should have no objection to see this done :—Strike out those words which are now obsolete, and I will venture to say that I will replace every one

of them by words still in use out of Chaucer himself, or
Gower his disciple.

I don't want this myself; I rather like to see the significant
terms which Chaucer unsuccessfully offered as candidates for
admission into our language; but surely so very slight a
change of the text may well be pardoned, even by black-
letterati, for the purpose of restoring so great a poet to his
ancient and most deserved popularity.

1834. D'Israeli, Isaac. *Curiosities of Literature,* 9th edn., 1834, 6 vols.,
vol. vi, p. 68. (Edn. 1849, **3** vols., vol. iii, p. 321.)

[For other edns. *see* above, 1807 and 1823.]

Dreams at the Dawn of Philosophy.

[p. 321]   But that they [enchantments] were not unknown to Chaucer,
appears in his " Frankelein's Tale," where, minutely describing
them, he communicates the same pleasure he must himself
have received from the ocular illusions of the "Tregetoure"
or "Jogelour." Chaucer ascribes the miracle to "a natural
magique," in which, however, it was as unsettled, whether the
" Prince of Darkness " was a party concerned.

" For I am siker that there be sciences "

[and twelve following lines, *Frankeleyns Tale,* ll. 411–23].

1834. Hunt, James Henry Leigh.   *Fairies,* [in] Leigh Hunt's London
Journal, Oct. 8, 1834, p. 217. [Reprinted in **A Day by the Fire,**
1870, pp. 98–9.]

Chaucer's notion of Fairies was a confused mixture of elves
and romance-ladies, and Ovid and Catholic diablerie. . . .
His Lady Abbess [*sic*] wears a broach exhibiting a motto out
of Virgil. Elves, therefore, and Provençal Enchantresses, and
the Nymphs of the Metamorphoses, and the very devils of
the Pope and St. Anthony, were all fellows well met, all
supernatural beings, living in the same remote regions of
fancy, and exciting the gratitude of the poet. He is angry
with the friars for making more solemn distinctions, and dis-
placing the little elves in their walks; and he runs a capital
jest upon them, which has become famous.

In olde dayes of the Kinge Artour
[and **23** following lines].

In another poem, we meet with Pluto and Proserpine as
the King and Queen of Faerie; where they sing and dance

about a well, enjoying themselves in a garden, and quoting Solomon.

1834. Laing, David. *The Poems of William Dunbar . . . with Notes and a Memoir of His Life by David Laing.* Memoir, vol. i, p. 19, 22, 35, 36, 47–50, 56, 61 ; vol. ii, Notes, pp. 213 [quotation from Hailes], 214, 216, 221, 222 [quotation from Warton], 223 [quotation from Drake], 224, 234, 247, 259 [268, 269, 271], 273, 283, 308, 331, 339 [340, 342], 349, 357 [374, 375, 376, 377, 383, 385, 401], 450 [451, 458].

[The references in square brackets are quotations given by Laing from other authors mentioning Chaucer.]

1834. Lowndes, William Thomas. *The Bibliographer's Manual of English Literature,* 4 vols., vol. i, pp. 216–17, 246, 395–8.

[List of editions, etc., with bibliographical notes and sale prices.]

1834. Planché, James Robinson. *History of British Costume,* pp. 94, 96, 102 *n.,* 113, 125, 148–9, 151, 154–5, 156–7, 161, 162, 163, 165, 166, 167, 181, 229.

[p. 94] [Queintise, in *Rom. Rose.*]

[p. 96] [Shoes " decoped with lace," *Rom. Rose.*]

[p. 113] [Quotations from G. de Lorris on *surquayne,* and mention that Chaucer translates it *rockette. Rom. Rose,* 1240.]

[p. 125] The apron is seen upon a female figure of this date [Edward II]. It is afterwards mentioned by Chaucer as the *barme,* or *lap-cloth.* [*Milleres T.,* 50.]

[p. 148] [Quotation of *Knightes T.,* 2026, *Troilus,* i, 109, &c. on mourning garments.]

[p. 151] Chaucer, who wrote his " Canterbury Tales " towards the close of this reign [Richard II], puts a two-fold lamentation into the mouth of the parson concerning the " sinful costly array of clothing . . ." [*Persones Tale,* 415.]

[pp. 154–7] [Descriptions of the dress of the Richard II period, with Chaucer quotations.]

[pp. 161–3] [Description of knightly accoutrements, with quotations from *The Knightes Tale,* etc.]

[pp. 165–7] [Description of ladies' dress of the reign of Richard II, with quotations from the *Canterbury Tales.*]

[n. a. 1834.] Stothard, Thomas. *Paintings, etc., illustrating Chaucer. See* below, App. A.

1834. Unknown. *Review* of *Clarke's Tales from Chaucer,* [*q.v.* above, 1833, in] The Gentleman's Magazine, August 1834, new series vol. ii, pp. 173–4.

[Although agreeing that by this prose rendering, "some idea of Chaucer's spirit is imparted to the multitude," the critic advocates rather the mere modernization of Chaucer's spelling, and gives a specimen from the *Knightes Tale*, which he contrasts with Dryden's translation and Clarke's paraphrase.]

1834–6. Unknown. *Bibliotheca Heberiana.* *Catalogue of the Library of Richard Heber, Esq.,* 13 pt.

[Different auctioneers take the parts. Edns., etc., of the 18th and 19th centuries are omitted here.]

[Pt. iv, Dec. 1834 ; lots 119, Conusance d'amours (Chaucer reference quoted); 160, Bradshaw, Lyfe of St. Werburge, 1521 (Chaucer reference quoted); 290, Chaucer's Ghoast, 1672; 3[4]7, Assemble of Foules, 1530 (unique, now at Britwell); 742, Feylde's Contrauersye bytwene a louer and a Jaye (Chaucer reference quoted); 808, Works, 1532; 809, Works, Toye; 810, Works, Kele; 811–12, Works, 1542; 813, Works, 1598; 814, Works, 1602; 815, Cant. Tales, imperf., Caxton edn. 1; 816, Cant. Tales, imperf., Caxton edn. 2; 817, Cant. Tales, Pynson; 818, Plowman's Tale; 819, Troylus and Creseyde, etc., Pynson; 1383, Love and Complayntes bytwene Mars and Venus, J. Notary; 1563, Mylner of Abington, with note: " It is similar to Chaucer's Reve's Tale, and both are derived from the same original, Boccaccio."]

[Pt. vii, May–June, 1835; lots 1271–2, Works, 1561, 1602.]
[Pt. viii, Feb.–March, 1836; lots 396, Jack Upland; 458–9, Kynaston (2 copies); 783, Works, Toye ; 784, Cant. Tales, Pynson, imperf., Works, frag. ; 785–6, Works, 1532 ; 788, Works, 1561, imperf.; 789, Works, 1602, imperf.; 790, Works, 1561, etc.; 791, Works, 1598, imperf. ; 792, Works, imperf. ; 793, Cant. Tales, Pynson, 3 copies, imperf. ; 794, Glossary to Urry's edn., with MS. additions.]
[Pt. ix, April, 1836 ; lot 682, Works, 1561.]
[Pt. x, May–June, 1836 ; lot 750, Works, 1602, imperf.]
[Pt. xi, MSS., Feb. 1836 ; lots 495, Cant. Tales, 14th cent.; 495*, item, 15th cent. ; 496, Speght's MS. of the ' Dream,' *i. e.* Isle of Ladies; 1088, Spelman's MS. containing Troilus and Criseyde; 1163, Occleve MS., with note of Occleve's allusions to Chaucer; 1333, MS. containing the Clerkes Tale; 1334, MS. of poems by Chaucer, Lydgate, etc.]
[J. T. Payne had Part iv reprinted, with purchaser's names and prices, also further notes by J. P. Collier, as ' A Catalogue of Heber's Collection of Early English Poetry.']

1834. Unknown. *The King's Library, British Museum,* [in] The Gentleman's Magazine, Jan., March, 1834, new ser., vol. i, pp. 18, 243.

[The various early editions of Chaucer in the King's Library.]

1834. Willmott, Robert Aris. *Lives of Sacred Poets*, 2 vols, 1834, Introduction, vol. i, pp. 1–91; vol. ii, pp. 48, 73, 78, 306, 364. (2nd edn., 1839, vol. i, pp. 2–3, 5–9, 24, 27–8, 77; vol. ii, as in 1st edn.)

[vol. i. It should never be forgotten, in speaking of Chaucer, that p. 1] he was among the first to resort to that precious fountain which his contemporary Wickliffe had opened, and that he drank of the " water springing up to everlasting life."

[In the 2nd edition of this work (2 vols, 1839), the remarks on Chaucer—which are of a general and appreciative kind— are amplified; and the above sentence appears as follows :—

[p. 6] " Though accommodating himself to the popular spirit, he was not altogether uninfluenced by that graver and more solemn train of thought which . . . Wicliffe subsequently diffused . . .

[p. 7] The serious vein of sentiment has not been unobserved by Thomson [who is quoted, *q.v.* 1744, vol. i, p. 391.] . . . We may find religion in the faith of a Constance; in the purity . . . of Grisildis; in the lamentation of Mary Magdalene; in the legend of Hew of Lincoln, and in that most beautiful . . . story of the Christian martyr, related by the Prioress."]

1835. Clarke, Charles Cowden. *The Riches of Chaucer*, in which his impurities have been expunged; his spelling modernized; his rhythm accentuated; and his obsolete terms explained; also have been added a few explanatory notes, and a new memoir of the poet.

[These are selections from the poems, prefaced by a life of Chaucer, pp. 1–57. The book was re-edited, in 1870, with a new short prefatory note, the life of Chaucer remaining un- altered, in which the *Court of Love, the Plowman's Tale, Jack Upland*, the *Testament of Love* and other spurious poems are ascribed to him, and the fictitious story of his exile and imprisonment is given in full.]

1835. Cunningham, George Godfrey. *Lives of Eminent and Illustrious Englishmen*, Glasgow [1835–7], 8 vols., vol. i, pp. 299, 301, 303, 305, 420 [Chaucer a member of Wyclif's party], 458, 459–63, 465–473 [Life of Chaucer, with portrait engraved by S. Freeman from that in the Sloane collection], 473–5, 477, 478, 481. [An edition of 1863–68 is entitled *The English Nation, or a History of England in the Lives of Englishmen*.

[p. 299] The names of Chaucer and Gower, with some of minor note, as those of Richard Hampole and Robert Langlande, afford ample proof of this commencement of a new era.

[The Critical Biography of Chaucer abounds in all the usual errors due to the acceptance as Chaucer's of the *Testament of Love*, etc. Tyrwhitt, Godwin and Thynne are drawn upon. In the controversy upon Chaucer's metre, which took a new turn on the publication of Nott's edition of the poems of Surrey and Wyatt, Cunningham sides with Tyrwhitt against Nott, whom he calls 'Scott' throughout.]

1835. [De Quincey, Thomas.] *Sketches of Life and Character; from the Autobiography of an English Opium-Eater: Oxford,* [in] Tait's Edinburgh Magazine, Aug. 1835, p. 542. (Collected Writings, ed. D. Masson, 1890, 14 vols., vol. ii, p. 58.)

In Chaucer, though acquainted as yet only with part of his works, I had perceived and had felt profoundly those divine qualities which, even at this day, are so languidly acknowledged by his unjust countrymen.

1835. Emerson, Ralph Waldo. *Journal.* (Works, Centenary Edition, 1903, 12 vols., vol. vii, p. 361 [note].)

Poetry to be sterling must be more than a show, must have or be an earnest meaning. Chaucer, Wordsworth,—per contra, Moore and Byron.

1835. Gray, William. *Origin and Progress of English Prose Literature* Oxford, [Motto :] "For out of the old fieldes as men saieth " [and three following lines], pp. 29, 36–45, 54, 61, 64, 92, 97.

[A general account of Chaucer, with special reference to his prose, including the *Testament of Love.* The author does not dispute that Chaucer owed the conception of the *Canterbury Tales* to the *Confessio Amantis,* and says that the *Man of Law's Tale* was certainly purloined from Gower.]

1835. Hunt, James Henry Leigh. *Characteristic Specimens of the English Poets,* [in] Leigh Hunt's London Journal, nos. 63–8, 70, 72, June 13, 20, 27, July 4, 11, 18, Aug. 1, 15, 1835, pp. 180–1, 187–8, 195–6, 218–9, 228, 250–1, 268. [Reprinted in The Seer, 1840, pp. 55-66.]

[Copious extracts from Chaucer, given in Cowden Clarke's modern-spelling text, interspersed with comments, and preceded by a brief biography and criticism. The former retails the story of Chaucer's exile, imprisonment, and release on condition of abandoning his associates.

The criticism : Chaucer one of the four great English poets; his youth and freshness, consistent with maturity of mind ; his width of sympathy ; "his gaiety equal to his gravity, and his sincerity to both "; "his graphic faculty, and his healthy sense of the material "; "he was at once the Italian and the Flemish painter of his time; his faults coarseness and prolixity, both of the time. Chaucer not only a smooth but a powerful and various versifier; still doubtful whether his prosody was always correct in the modern sense.

The 5 nos. are apportioned as follows: 1, biography and criticism, *Prologue*; 2, physical life and movement, *Knightes Tale*; 3, pathos, *Knightes* and *Man of Law's Tales*; 4, Griselda; 5, "further specimens" of his pleasantry and satire, *Wife of Bath's Tale, Nonne Prestes Tale*, etc.; 6, description, portrait painting, and fine sense; [7] omission from the preceding no., a long extract from the *Flower and the Leaf.*]

1835. Hunt, James Henry Leigh. *Review* [of] *Three New Books*, [including Cowden Clarke's *Riches of Chaucer*, in] Leigh Hunt's London Journal, March 25, 1835, p. 89.

We have also to express a doubt, whether Chaucer's versification is so invariably regular in its construction as Mr. Clarke supposes; a doubt which we express with the less willingness, because we have done something in our day towards spreading the contrary notion. But we must own, it now appears to us, that although the divine old bard, generally speaking, is as correct in his prosody as he is instinctively melodious, his lines are now and then short, or superfluous, of a syllable or so, and his time marked only by quantity . . . Here is a sample in Chaucer, from the very first page that we have opened at random—

> "The hand was knowen that the letter wrote,
> And all the venom of this cursed deed,
> But in *what wise* certainly I n'ot:"—

that is, "know not." Now on these two syllables, "what wise," the voice lingers by reason of their natural emphasis and thus makes the two serve the purpose of three; for in this verse there is a syllable wanting. Mr. Clarke, however, has made a present to the reading world, which they ought to seize with joy. He has put an end to the old bugbear of "difficulty" by modernising the spelling of Chaucer, without hurting the spirit of his poetry; and if it is to be regretted that he has put too gratuitous a faith in the far too gratuitous conclusions of Mr. Godwin's otherwise valuable life of the poet, his fault in that respect, as in others, is still a fault of faith, and leaves him a character for *bonhommie*, [sic] not unbecoming a recommender of childlike and loving genius

[Then follows the account of Keats writing his Sonnet on *The Flower and the Leaf* in Cowden Clarke's Chaucer, *q.v.* above, 1817.]

1835. Hunt, James Henry Leigh. *The Streets of the Metropolis*, Supplement to Leigh Hunt's London Journal, 1835, pp. iii, xviii–xix, xxxi. [Republished as *The Town*, 1848; ed. 1859, pp. 19, 38, 103, 106–7, 173.]

[p. 103] The oldest mention of the Temple as a place for lawyers has been commonly said to be found in a passage of Chaucer, who is reported to have been of the Temple himself. [Quotes Chaucer's character of the Manciple, *Prol.*, ll. 566–575.] *

[pp. 106-7] [Discussion of Chaucer's connection with the Temple. Quotes Francis Thynne's " Animadversions," *q.v.* above, 1598, vol. i, p. 154.]

[Leigh Hunt's Note.] * We quote no edition, because, where we could, we have modernized the spelling; which is a justice to this fine old author in a quotation, in order that nobody may pass it over.

1835. Longfellow, Henry Wadsworth. *Outre-Mer*, 2 vols., vol. ii, p. 84. [This chapter is not in the first edition of 1833.] (Works, Riverside Edition, [1886,] 11 vols., vol. i, p. 182–3.)

One holyday, when mass was said and the whole village was let loose to play, we made a pilgrimage to the ruins of this old Moorish alcazar. Our cavalcade was as motley as that of old,— the pilgrims "that toward Canterbury wolden ride;" for we had the priest, and the doctor of physic, and the man of laws [*sic*], and a wife of Bath, and many more whom I must leave unsung.

1835. Strickland, Agnes. *The Pilgrims of Walsingham*, 3 vols., vol. i, pp. i, iii, 23, 34, 56, 216, 274, [Notes] 307–8.

[p. i] Geoffrey Chaucer (the Sir Walter Scott of the thirteenth [*sic*] century) . . .

[p. iii] Each of the votaries to the shrine of our Lady of Walsingham, in this work, like Chaucer's Canterbury Pilgrims, is pledged to relate a tale.

[pp. 34, 56, 216, 274] [Chapter-heading quotations from Chaucer.]

[pp. 307-8] As to the rhyming chronicler, Robert of Gloucester, he assuredly fills the same place, in English poetry, that is attributed to Chaucer, for amidst the ruggedness of his constructions, may now and then be perceived a line that rises into beauty.

1835. T., W. I. *The Court Magazine in the Fourteenth Century,*
[in] The Court Magazine, vol. vi, pp. 254–57.

[p. 254]   [The writer entering Westminster Abbey, notices one present:]
The individual who excited this interest in me was of
middle stature, somewhat inclined to corpulency, and expensively attired in a robe of deep purple. His countenance was
placid and benevolent; his eyes, which were large and mild,
were kept constantly upon a richly illuminated missal which
he held in his hand, with the contents of which, however, he
seemed not so deeply busied but that some fleeting and not
very grave thoughts had power ever and anon to diffuse a
satirical but good-natured smile over his face. His complexion was fair, his forehead broad and smooth, his hair thin
and of silvery whiteness, as was likewise his graceful and
becoming beard.

At length the service concluded, and I took the opportunity
of inquiring of my companion whether he knew the individual
who had so arrested my attention.

"Know him indeed," quoth Master Scrope, "Marry do I—
and so shalt thou too." . . .

[After the service the writer and Scrope follow Chaucer
to the house adjacent:]

[p. 255]   "Give you good even, Master Geoffrey," said Scrope, "I
have brought a friend with me who loveth the Muse, and
would fain hold a little converse with her favourite son,
Master Geoffrey Chaucer."

Master Geoffrey Chaucer! How the words rang in my
ears—I could scarce return thanks for the kindly welcome
with which the great bard greeted me, so intense was the
delight I experienced at finding myself thus suddenly and
agreeably confronted with him. There before me sat he
whose muse I had so long and so earnestly admired.

.   .   .   .

[Chaucer provides wine, and proceeds:]

" When I have done my reckonings in the Exchequer, I have
gotten a copy of verses to write for my good Lord of Vere, or
my Lady Blanche. Let alone his Majesty himself, who is
ever and anon crying out, 'Is your muse turned sluggard,
Master Geoffrey, that we hear nought of her faith [*sic*, for
" i' faith "] !' I believe they wish me to write every week
a poem as long as the siege of Troy. So my scribe Adam

Scrivener and myself have taken council, and here is our resolve."

Here he handed to Scrope and myself a slip of parchment, on which was written as follows :—

"KNOW ALL MEN BY THESE PRESENTS : ON THE 1ST OF JANUARY IN THE YEAR OF OUR LORD 13— AND IN THE — YEAR OF THE REIGN OF OUR MOST GRACIOUS SOVEREIGN, KING RICHARD THE SECOND—WE, GEOFFREY CHAUCER, PURPOSE, BY THE ASSISTANCE OF OUR TRUSTY SCRIBE, ADAM SCRIVENER, TO INDITE A GOODLY VOLUME, CONTAINING SUNDRY AND DIVERS POEMS, SONGS, AND BALLADES BY US THE SAID GEOFFREY CHAUCER, OUR TRUSTY FRIEND JOHN GOWER, AND OTHERS OF HIS MAJESTY'S LIEGES ; AND WE PURPOSE TO INDITE A SIMILAR VOLUME UNDER THE TITLE OF

THE COURT MAGAZINE,

EDITED BY

GEOFFREY CHAUCER,

ON THE FIRST DAY OF EVERY MONTH, UNTIL FURTHER NOTICE. COPIES OF THE SAID VOLUME MAY BE PROCURED OF ADAM SCRIVENER AT OUR HOUSE ABUTTING ON THE ABBEY OF ST. PETER, WESTMINSTER, AT REASONABLE CHARGES.—GOD SAVE THE KING."

"Now my masters, to-morrow is the first of January, and I am going to present my book to his Majesty as a New Year's Gift—and as Adam Scrivener—plague on him !—is very apt to make my verses halt like Dame Jukket's dog, I must needs con over the manuscript before I hand it over to my royal master."

[Chaucer shows them the volume :]

Imprimis, was an address to His Majesty on the New Year, followed by a translation by Chaucer himself of Petrarch's Sonnet "*S'amor non è*," and which if my memory serves me rightly, ran much in this strain :—

> If no love is, O God what fele I so?
> And if love is, what thing and whiche is he? . . .
> [*Troilus*, i. 400, and two following stanzas.]

"By the blessed Virgin, Master Geoffrey," said Scrope, "but thou has rendered the Italian poesy into very delectable

English. Thou encounteredst Master Francis Petrarch, didst not, when thou wentest on the embassy to Genoa?"

Chaucer's answer was in the affirmative and was a long one, for it related the history of the interview between the learned inhabitant of Arqua and Geoffrey Chaucer, poet of Britain, which interview our readers shall have fully described on some future occasion.

A French '*ballade*,' by the " Moral Gower," of which the ' burthen' was

" En toutz errours amour se justifie,"

was the next piece recited by our host, in a style which showed that his acquaintance with the French language had not been acquired " at Stratford-le-Bow."   When Chaucer had finished it, he said—

" A book a month is much to do, and I have been fain to beg for the assistance of my friends, and they have, as you see, kindly given it to me.   Master Gower's is to my fancy a very choice piece of verse, and this "*Dit du Marguerite*," by the gallant French knight Sir John Froissart, is likewise in good sooth much to my mind.   You must come and crack a bowl with Sir John—he's a merry man, and learned withal. Oh!—but King Richard will be well pleased to-morrow, for Sir John's new year's gift to his Majesty will be those chronicles of the affairs of our times, which he has so long busied himself in compiling."

"I met Sir John in France," said Scrope, " when I was with the Count de Foix—but had no converse with him ; he stayed but one night. . . .

" Master Froissart is a good friend of mine," said Chaucer, "and even now I have just gotten from him a goodly poem, which has so delighted me, that I purpose putting it into English rhyme for the amusement of our court dames."   So saying he rose from his chair, and reached from a shelf whereon stood more than

Twenty bokes clothed in blake or red,

a beautifully written manuscript, the title of which he recited as follows :—

" ' *Le Roman de Thesée, ou d'Arcite et Palemon, l'un et l'autre de Thebes, de royal sang extraits, lesquels etant cousins-germains, par superflue amour de la belle Emilie, eurent ensemble question et débat, l'un desquels à cette occasion perdit*

la vie, et l'autre vint à son intencion.' It is indeed a piteous
story, but if I translate it I think I shall make it somewhat
different and somewhat shorter.   But it is a long job, and the
' Romaunt de la Rose ' I found a somewhat tedious undertaking. . . .

[The writer recites a spurious verse, and asks who composed it :]

" By my troth, I know not who composed it. . . . Let him
translate the beautiful Romance of *" Le Chevalier au Lion,"*
which is making such a coil even now.   I showed my copy of
it to a gallant high German knight, who was lately travelling
in these parts, one Master Hartman von der Oue (what outlandish names they have in the countries over sea), and he
was so greatly charmed with it, that he straightways made a
copy thereof, and is going incontinent to turn it into his
mother tongue.   You shall read a bit of the French poem ; it
is a dainty work, by my faith."

The glorious old bard reached down a huge folio from the
shelves which we have already described : and, like all lovers
of poetry, himself read the passages which he had proposed I
should have read.   While he was turning over the leaves of
the manuscript, a slip of paper fell from it. . . . I found that
Chaucer himself had commenced the task he so earnestly
recommended to another.   By his permission, I read the few
lines which he had already executed : they were from the commencement of the Poem*.

> Almightie God that made mankyn,
> He schilde his servandes out of syn,
> And mayntene tham, with might and mayne
> That herkens Swayne [*sic*] and Gawayne :
> Thai war knightes of the tabyl rownde,
> Tharfore listens a lytel stownde.

[And so for 26 lines further.   The dreamer then awakes.]

* Is this the long lost *" Book of the Lion " ?*—W. I. T.

1835. Wordsworth, William.   *Postscript to the Poetical Works.* (Prose
Works, 2 vols., 1896, vol. ii, p. 364.)

How agreeable to picture to one's self, as has been done by
poets and romance-writers, from Chaucer down to Goldsmith,
a man devoted to his ministerial office, with not a wish or a
thought ranging beyond the circuit of its cares !

1835. **Wordsworth, William.** *MS.*, dated 1835, describing his tour with Dorothy Wordsworth to Scotland in 1831, quoted by Prof. W. A. Knight as a note to *Bothwell Castle*. (Poetical Works, 1896, 8 vols., vol. vii, p. 301 *n.*)

These rude warriors cared little, perhaps, about either [sea or rivers] ; and yet if one may judge from the writings of Chaucer, and from the old romances, more interesting passions were connected with natural objects in the days of chivalry than now ; though going in search of scenery, as it is called, had not then been thought of.

1836. **[Bandinel, Bulkeley.]** *Catalogue of Early English Poetry . . . collected by Edmond Malone, Esq., and now preserved in the Bodleian Library,* Oxford, p. 7.

CHAUCER (Geffrey)
The ploughman's tale . . . 1606 [*q.v.* above, vol. i, p. 177].

1836. **Brayley**, Edward Wedlake, and **Britton**, John. *The History of the Ancient Palace and late Houses of Parliament at Westminster,* pp. 275–6.

[The appointment of Chaucer, on July 13th, 1389, as Clerk of the Works at Westminster, the Tower, and the Mews near Charing Cross ; with a lengthy biographical note based on Godwin and the *Testament of Love.*]

1836. **[Browning, Robert ?]** *Life of Strafford*, Browning Soc., 1892, pp. 129, 196–7 *n.*

Chaucer and Dr. Donne appear to have been Wentworth's favourite poets. Chaucer indeed, to the court readers of that day, was as Shakespeare in our own. It is clear too, from the frequent use of peculiar expressions in his dispatches, that the lord deputy was not unacquainted, and that intimately, with the great dramatist, though he never, as with Chaucer and Donne, quotes connected passages. [Passages from letters of and to Strafford, *q.v.* below, App. A., 1635, 1637, Wentworth, 1636, Conway.]

[c. 1836–40.] **Campbell**, Thomas. *Chaucer and Windsor*, [in] The Pilgrim of Glencoe and other Poems, 1842, pp. 100–1. (Poetical Works, ed. J. Logie Robertson, Oxford, 1907, p. 307.)

[Mr. Robertson places this poem between poems of 1836 and of 1840.]

Long shalt thou flourish, Windsor . . .
But, should thy towers in ivied ruin rot,
There's one, thine inmate once, whose strain renowned
Would interdict thy name to be forgot ;
For Chaucer loved thy bowers and trode this very spot.

Chaucer ! our Helicon's first fountain stream,
Our morning star of song—that led the way
To welcome the long-after coming beam
Of Spenser's light, and Shakespeare's perfect day.
Old England's fathers lived in Chaucer's lay,
As if they ne'er had died. He grouped and drew
Their likeness with a spirit of life so gay,
That still they live and breathe in Fancy's view,
Fresh beings fraught with truth's imperishable hue.

1836. [Carey, William ?] *Reminiscences of Stothard,* [in] Blackwood's Edinburgh Magazine, **May** and June, 1836, vol. **xxxix.** pp. 681-4, 753-7, 759. [References to Stothard's painting, *The Canterbury Pilgrims.*]

[p. 681]   So little conscious was he [Stothard] of the pecuniary value of his talents, that I believe I speak perfectly true when I say that he received but £200 for the Canterbury Pilgrims ; a picture which was afterwards exhibited by itself, at one shilling a head, in all the great towns of England ; was engraved . . . and had the most extensive sale of any thing of the kind published within the last century.

[p. 753]   [No artist had previously attempted to illustrate Chaucer so fully and elaborately. Indeed Chaucer had been most undeservedly neglected both by artists and readers. Stothard's Canterbury Pilgrims owe their existence to Mr. Cromek, the engraver, who told the writer that he always wished to see a picture of Chaucer's pilgrims on the road, travelling in company together. But he saw that the great objection to such a picture would be the monotonous uniformity of a procession. Who could hope to make anything of it ? There follows a close account of Stothard's picture, and the several figures in it (pp. 753–6), with a quotation from Hoppner's letter, *q.v.* above, 1807.]

[p. 759]   [A reference to Stothard's] beautiful little picture of the Cock and the Fox, from Chaucer.

[These articles are most probably written by William Carey, the picture dealer, as they closely resemble much in his pamphlet, *q.v.* above, 1808.]

1836. Dale, Thomas. *Lecture on Chaucer. See* below, Ruskin.

1836. Dibdin, Thomas Frognall. *Reminiscences of a Literary Life,* 2 vols., vol. i, pp. 119-20, 235, 237, 241, 273, 387, 390, 416, 497 ; vol. ii, pp. 788-9, 905.

[vol. ii, p. 788]   When Blake entered the arena with *Stothard*, as a rival
[vol. ii, p. 789] in depicting the *Dramatis Personæ* of Chaucer's Canterbury

Tales he seems to have absolutely lost his wits; his pencil was as inferior to that of the former, as his burin was to that of *Cromek*, who engraved Stothard's immortal picture.

[Stothard's picture was published by Cromek, but engraved by Schiavonetti.]

1836. Dunham, Samuel Astley. *Chaucer*, [in Lardner's] Cabinet Cyclopædia (Lives of the most eminent literary and scientific men of Great Britain.—Early Writers), pp. 125–172, 188, 205, 215, 298–9, 312–13, 315, 319, 351.

[p. 125]   [A life of the poet, forty-seven pages, followed by a detailed notice of all his poems; as well as of some not by him.]

[p. 169]   Of the literary and poetical character of Chaucer, it may be remarked, that to no individual, perhaps, has our language been more indebted than to the author of the Canterbury Tales. He found his native tongue a mixed and uncouth dialect of Norman-Saxon, rude, and undigested, and with no writers whom he could consider in any respect as a guide or [p. 170] model. . . . He therefore necessarily turned his eyes to foreign resources; and we find that the greater part of his poetical career was employed in translating . . . from the Latin, French, and Italian. In doing this, however, he enriched his own language with a vast store of verbal wealth . . . and, moreover, moulded what he had taken into a form of such unprecedented beauty and perspicuity, when compared with any previous English poem, that those who immediately succeeded him scarcely ever speak of his style but in terms of enthusiastic rapture. When we consider, indeed, how greatly superior to his contemporaries was the mechanism of his versification, which, though from change of accent unaccommodated to a modern ear, was, in the then construction of the language, beyond all example harmonious and correct . . . the admiration of his disciples, however warmly expressed, seems justly his due. It may, in short, be affirmed, that even now, by him who will take the trouble of becoming familiar with the style of Chaucer, there will often be found, both in his diction and versification, a certain natural sweetness, simplicity, and naïveté, hardly to be met with elsewhere.

If, turning . . . to the consideration of the higher attributes which more immediately constitute the poet, we contrast what he has produced in these departments with the age in which he lived, . . . can we hesitate in pronouncing him one of the most extraordinary men to which his country has given birth ? . . .

[p. 171]	In knowledge of human life, and in the power of delineating it, he has no superior, save Shakspeare, with whom, indeed, in universality of talent, he may justly be compared.

1836. Garnett, Richard, the Elder. *English Dialects,* [in] The Quarterly Review, Feb., 1836, vol. lv, pp. 380–82. (The Philological Essays of R. Garnett, edited by his Son, 1859, pp. 70–72.)

[Chaucer's use of north country dialect in the *Reves Tale,* and especially of the word "lathe," a barn.]

1836. Ruskin, John. *Letter to his father,* from Herne Hill, 25th March. (Works, ed. E. T. Cook and A. Wedderburn, 1903–12, 39 vols., vol. xxxvi, p. 6.)

I sit down to write of I know not what. I intend to commence with our third lecture, English literature [by the Rev. Thomas Dale]. Four lectures on this subject have spoken of four celebrated authors of old time—Sir John Mandeville, Sir John Gower, Chaucer, and Wickliffe. We are made acquainted with their birth, parentage, education, etc. ; the character of their writings is spoken of, and extracts are read as examples of their style. These extracts are always interesting, frequently entertaining, sometimes laughable, although the laugh of the hearer is generally at, not with, the author. The writings of the poets before Chaucer are like—— Lifting my eyes off the paper in search of a simile, they encounter a piece of the sky seen through one of the very large panes of our drawing-room window . . . [there] are long lines of grey cloud, broken away into thin white fleeces, which are standing still in the heavens, for there is no breeze to move them, and between those grey clouds is seen here and there a piece of excessive value, which is not dark, but deep, pure, far away, which the eye seems to plunge into and go on, on, on, into the stillness of its distance, until the grey cloud closes over it and it is gone. That bit of sky is like one of these old poems, cloudy and grey, uninteresting; but ever and anon through the quaintness of his language or uncouthness of expression breaks the mind of the poet, pure and noble and glorious, and leading you away with it into fascination, and then the cloud closes over him and he is gone.

1836. Southey, Robert. *Sketch of the Progress of English Poetry from Chaucer to Cowper,* [in] The Works of William Cowper, with a life of the author by the editor, Robert Southey, 1835–7, 15 vols., vol. ii, 1836, pp. 114–121, 134–5, 148–9, 177.

[vol. ii, p. 114] The first reformation which it [vernacular poetry] underwent was to free it from some gratuitous difficulties, and divest it of the cumbrous ornaments with which it had been overloaded. Chaucer, who is deservedly accounted the Father of English Poetry, effected this . . .

[p. 115] Father Chaucer, throwing off all trammels, simplified our verse. Nature had given him the ear and the eye and the imagination of a poet; and his diction was such as that of all great poets has ever been, and ever will be, in all countries,—neither cramped by pedantic rules . . . nor drooping for want of strength, but rising and falling with the subject, and always suited to it.

The seven-lined stanza of his Troilus and Cresseide [footnote, quoting Sidney's praise in the *Defence of Poesy*] was adopted from the Provenceal [*sic*] poets. I know not whether he had any example of the ten-syllable couplet in the poets of France, Provence, and Italy, but the Hermit of Hampole, Richard Rolle, . . . had shown him the way in this. That the one form of verse was, in his judgement, as well fitted for grave and lofty subjects as the other, is certain, for in such subjects he has employed them both: but it appears that the couplet took its character in common opinion from his lighter pieces, and was supposed to be adapted for nothing better. And while the "Troilus verse," as King James called it, obtained the dignified title of Rhythm Royal, [footnote, quoting Puttenham, *Art of English Poetry,* on the metre of

[p. 116] *Troilus* and "riding rhyme"] the strain in which the knight related his tale of Palamon and Arcite, and in which "the story of Cambuscan bold" had been pitched, was degraded in public estimation, and distinguished by the contemptuous term of *riding rhymes.* [Footnote: Perhaps Shakespeare alludes to this appellation when he describes a still more familiar kind of measure, as the "right butter-woman's rate to market."]

It is a disputed question whether Chaucer's verses be rhythmical or metrical. I believe them to have been written [p. 117] rhythmically, upon the same principle on which Coleridge composed his beautiful fragment of Christabel,—that the number of *beats,* or accentuated syllables in every line should be the same, although the number of syllables themselves might vary. [Footnote, stating that James Boswell (the younger) had impugned that opinion, but that in it Southey had the support of Farmer and Dr. Nott, who, he thought, had established the point. He also quotes Gascoigne in this connexion. *See* above, 1831, and, for Nott, above, 1815–16.] Verse so composed will often be strictly metrical; and because Chaucer's is frequently so, the argument has been raised that it is always so if it be read properly. . . But to suppose that it was written as iambic verse, and that the lines were lengthened or shortened to the required measure by sometimes pronouncing a final syllable, and sometimes letting it [p. 118] remain mute, . . . is supposing that Chaucer took greater liberties with the common pronunciation (which must always be uniform) and relied more on the judgement of the reader, than one who so perfectly understood the character of his mother tongue, and was so well acquainted with the ordinary capacities of men, can be supposed to have done, without impeachment of his sagacity. Be this as it may, it is no slight proof of that sagacity, that he should have pitched the key and determined the length of verse, which . . . have been found to accord best with the genius of the language; and that his "riding rhyme," under the more dignified denomination of the "heroic couplet," should be the measure which Dryden and Pope and their followers have preferred to all others for grave and lofty subjects.

The "ornate style," which is the worst fashion that has ever been introduced into English verse, began in Chaucer's time, and he adopted it in some of his smaller and later pieces; perhaps as an experiment towards the improvement of a language then in a state in which experiments might allowably be tried, ... but unless his faculties were impaired by age, of which there is no proof or indication, it is not possible that he could have approved of it himself. His language was what he had learnt in the country, in the city, and in the court . . . what every one could understand, and every one could feel; it was the language of passion and of real life, and therefore the language of poetry. . . .

[p. 119]   The age after Chaucer was in many respects darker than that which preceded it; his name, however, was held in reverence, and succeeding poets were instructed to look to him as their exemplar.

[p. 120]   From Chaucer's time the line of five feet (whether in couplets or in stanzas) has been the most approved measure.

[p. 121]   Neither the diction of Chaucer, nor of Surrey, . . the
father and the reformer of our poetry, . . could have been more
perfect than it was.   It will not be supposed that because
Surrey is thus named with Chaucer, he is placed in the same
rank with him; for Chaucer stands in the first rank, with
Spenser, Shakespeare, and Milton ; and in variety of power
Shakespeare is his only peer.

[p. 134]   [Reference to Dryden's metre in his modernization of
Chaucer.]

[pp. 148–   [Remarks on the schemes, of 1777, of John Bell and rival
149]   publishers for producing an edition of the Poets of Great
Britain, from Chaucer to Churchill.   Bell's edition comprised
only three writers before Cowley, viz., Chaucer, Spenser and
Donne, and on this point Southey observes:] it is not to the
honour of our country that his collection, which was a mere
bookseller's affair . . . should still contain the only convenient
and most complete edition of the works of the great father
of English poetry.

[p. 177]   In one of his first poems, Mason had in a puerile fiction,
ranked Chaucer and Spenser and Milton below Pope, which is
like comparing a garden shrub with the oaks of the forest.
But he would have maintained no such absurdity in his
riper years.

1836. Unknown. *Chaucer,* [in] The Gentleman's Magazine, new
series, vol. v, pp. 501–4 ; vol. vi, pp. 44–8.

[vol. v,   Few writers are more neglected, less studied, or less known,
p. 501]   though none are more talked of, than Geoffrey Chaucer.   And
yet, whether we consider the richness and diversity of his
genius, the soundness of his feelings, the harmony of his
verse, or, in most instances, the subjects he has chosen, few
poets are less deserving of neglect.   The language, too, after
all, is not so far removed from our own, as to throw much
difficulty in the way even of the general reader. . .

[p. 502]   The neglect which Chaucer has experienced, arises, perhaps,
in a great measure, from the failings of his editors.   [On the
loss of final *e*, destroying the secret of Chaucer's metre, and
the failure of the early printers, except Caxton, to adhere to
the MSS.]

Early in the last century, John Urry, of Christ's [*sic*] Church,
Oxford, first undertook to give a perfect and complete text of
Chaucer's works; and, to judge by the list of manuscripts
which he has left us, he had no reason for complaining of lack
of materials. But, in spite of the encomiums which were
lavished upon him by the editor who finished his edition; in
spite of "his skill in the northern language spoken in the
Lowlands of Scotland," which "qualified him to read this
poet with more ease and pleasure than one altogether bred
be-south the Trent could do, without more than common
application;" still Urry was too ignorant of the language and
spirit of his author, too deficient in correct philological knowledge, to perform, with any degree of success, the task he had
undertaken . . . His list of manuscripts, too, is a mere
parade . . .

[p. 504] [A passage in praise of Tyrwhitt's work, with some remarks
on orthography, and some quotations from Orm, the philological value of whose work Tyrwhitt overlooked.]

[vol. vi,
pp. 44–8] [An attack on Cowden Clarke's *Riches of Chaucer*, followed by eulogy of the Prologue, with extracts, descriptions
of the characters, and quotations from *Piers Plowman*.]

1836. Unknown. *Antiquarian Researches, Society of Antiquaries,*
[in] The Gentleman's Magazine, June 1836, new series, vol. v,
p. 648.

Mr. Limburne exhibited [at the Society of Antiquaries]
a portrait in oil of Chaucer, supposed to be an original from
Harbottle Castle, Northumberland.

1836. Unknown. *Review* of Sir Harris Nicolas's *The Controversy
between Sir Richard Scrope and Sir Robert Grosvenor in the Court
of Chancery,* [*q. v.* above, 1832, in] The Quarterly Review, vol. lvi,
pp. 15, 27–8.

[pp.
27–8] In Chaucer's deposition . . . we think there are traces of
the liveliness and picturesque fancy of the poet. Being asked,
among other questions, if he had ever heard of any interruption
or challenge made by Sir Robert Grosvenor, or his ancestors,
to the use of the arms in dispute by the Scropes, he does not
content himself with saying "No!" but adds the following
anecdote :—

"He was once in Friday-street, London, and walking through

the street he observed a new sign hanging out with these arms thereon, and inquired ' What man that was that had hung out those arms of Scrope ? ' and one answered him, saying, "They are not hung out, Sir, for the arms of Scrope, nor painted there for those arms, but they are painted and put there by a knight of the county of Chester, called Sir Robert Grosvenor ; ' and that was the first time that he had ever heard speak of Sir Robert Grosvenor, or his ancestors, or of any one bearing the name."

[1836.] **Wordsworth**, William. *MS. Note* on a remark of Hazlitt's in *The Spirit of the Age*, [printed in] The Academy, Dec. 23, 1905, p. 1334, col. 1.

[Barron Field, in his (unpublished) *Critical Memoirs on the Life and Poetry of William Wordsworth*, quotes Hazlitt's remark in the *Spirit of the Age*, 1825 : " Chaucer is a prime favourite of his [Wordsworth's], but we do not think he has any cordial sympathy with Shakespeare." Opposite to this Wordsworth wrote, in his note on Barron Field's MS. :]

This is monstrous. I extol Chaucer, and others ; because the world at large knows little, or nothing, of their merits. Modesty, and a deep feeling how superfluous a thing it is to praise Shakespeare have kept me often—and almost habitually —silent on that subject. Who thinks it necessary to praise the Sun ?

[The article in the *Academy* is by Prof. W. Knight.]

1836. **Wordsworth**, William. *Letter to Thomas Noon Talfourd*, [dated] Nov. 28, [1836, in] Letters of the Wordsworth Family, ed. W. Knight, 1907, 3 vols., vol. iii, p. 115.

I cannot help catching at the hope that, in the evening of life, you may realize those anticipations which you throw out. Chaucer's and Milton's great works were composed when they were far advanced in life.

1837. **Burrowes**, Amyas Deane. *The Modern Encyclopædia*, vol. iii, pp. 190–1 ; vol. v, pp. 627–8 ; vol. vii, p. 201.

[The Chaucer and Lydgate articles are reprinted from the *Encyclopædia Britannica, q.v.* above, 1778, vol. i, pp. 452–4.]

1837. **Collier**, John Payne. *A Catalogue, Bibliographical and Critical, of Early English Literature*, forming a portion of the Library at Bridgewater House, pp. 58–9, 93, 118, 144, 179, 250, 268, 286, 304, 327.

[Works, 1561 and 1602 (pp. 58–9). Full literary as well as bibliographical accounts are given of the books, from which

the following Chaucer allusions are quoted: Davy, 1596
(p. 93); Fairfax anticipated by Chaucer in his account (from
Tasso) of the singing of birds (p. 118); Feylde, 1509 (p. 144);
'Fortune' printed in various editions of Chaucer, and also in
the "Proverbs" of Lydgate (p. 179); 'Remedy for Sedition,'
1536 (p. 250); Rowlands, 1620 (p. 268); Guilpin, 1598
(p. 286); Taylor, 1620 (p. 304); Warner, 1606 (p. 327);
q. v. above, vol. i, under the various dates here given.]

1837. [Craik, George Lillie, and **Macfarlane**, Charles.] *The Pictorial
History of England* [published by Charles Knight and, with The
Pictorial History of England during the reign of George the Third,
4 vols. 1841–4, commonly called " Knight's Pictorial History of
England"], 4 vols., 1837–41, vol. i, 1837, pp. 604, 812, 850-1, 862,
865–6, 868–71, 873, 880; vol. ii, pp. 203–4, 206, 209–10, 217–18,
222, 824, 837–9.

[vol. i,
p. 851] [Chaucer distances Langland, and compared with his productions all that precedes is barbarism: he is the founder
of our language and literature.   Only Shakespeare surpasses
his range of qualities, fancy and observation, tenderness and
humour.   His sources as diverse as his qualities.   The Canterbury Tales mentioned as his crowning work and as comprehend-
ing all his powers.]

[vol. ii,
p. 209] [Occleve's portrait of Chaucer.]   Occleve repeatedly speaks
of Chaucer as his master . . . All that Occleve appears to
have gained, however, from his admirable model, is some
initiation into that smoothness and regularity of style of which
Chaucer's writings set the first great example.

[p. 218] [Specimens of Chaucer from *Prologue* and *Persones Tale.*]
[p. 839] [Chaucer, in spite of contentions to the contrary, as regular
as Surrey in syllabic as well as accentual metre; Surrey
merely restored the art that had been lost since Chaucer.]

1837. Devon, Frederick. *Issues of the Exchequer . . . from King
Henry III. to King Henry VI.*

Pp. 203 [allowance to Philippa Chaucer, 27 Nov. 1376],
210 [payment of £12. 13s. on account of Chaucer's pension,
24 May, 1379], 214 [payment of £14 on account of his
wages and expenses in going upon the King's message to
Lombardy, 28 Nov. 1380], 215 [gift of £22 by Richard II.
to Chaucer for going to France in the time of Edward III.,
6 March, 1381], 239 [payment to Chaucer, as Clerk of the
Works, of £66. 13s. 4d., 7 Oct. 1389].   [*See* above, vol. i,
pp. 3–4 (6 July 1374), 1–2 (6 Nov. 1367), 6, 9 (14 and
22 July 1389).]

1837. Emerson, Ralph Waldo. *The American Scholar,* an oration delivered . . . August 31, 1837. (Works, Centenary Edition, 1903, 12 vols., vol. i, p. 91.)

We read the verses of the great English poets, of Chaucer, of Marvell, of Dryden, with the most modern joy,—with a pleasure, I mean, which is in great part caused by the abstraction of all *time,* from their verses.

1837. Hallam, Henry. *Introduction to the Literature of Europe,* 4 vols., vol. i, pp. 47, 62–5, 72, 170–1, 366, 592–5; vol. ii, pp. 305, 328, 333; vol. iv, p. 436. (4th edn., 1854, 3 vols., vol. i, pp. 34, 46–9, 54–5, 125, 262, 311n, 427–9; vol. ii, pp. 121–2, 138–42; vol. iii, pp. 486–7.)

[vol. i, p. 62] But our greatest poet of the middle ages, beyond comparison, was Geoffrey Chaucer; and I do not know that any other country, except Italy, produced one of equal variety in invention, acuteness in observation, or felicity of expression. A [p. 63] vast interval must be made between Chaucer and any other English Poet. . . .

[p. 65] [Chaucer's use of French and Latin words.]

[p. 170] That which we sometimes call pedantry and innovation, the [p. 171] forced introduction of French words by Chaucer, though hardly more by him than by all his predecessors who translated our neighbours' poetry, and the harsh latinisms that began to appear soon afterwards, has given English a copiousness and variety which perhaps no other language possesses.

[pp. 592–5] Surrey rarely lays an unnatural stress on final syllables, . . . another usual trick of the school of Chaucer.

[Nott's theory of Chaucer's verse as rhythmical (*q. v.* above, 1815–16) stated and cautiously set aside in favour of the metrical theory established by Tyrwhitt.]

[vol. ii, p. 305] Sackville's Induction forms a link which unites the school of Chaucer and Lydgate to the Faery Queen. It would certainly be vain to look in Chaucer, wherever Chaucer is original, for the grand creations of Sackville's fancy, yet we should never find any one who would rate Sackville above Chaucer.

1837. Hippisley, John Henry. *Chapters on Early English Literature.* Introduction, pp. ix–xii, ch. i, English Language and Literature previous to Chaucer—Character of Chaucer's earlier poems—Literary taste during the reign of Edward III; ch. ii, Reputation of Chaucer in various ages; ch. iii, Remarks on the biography of Chaucer; ch. iv, Observations on some of Chaucer's earlier poems; ch. v, The Canterbury Pilgrimage; ch. vi, Prose Works of Chaucer and his

contemporaries; ch. vii, English Literature from Chaucer to
Spenser; ch. viii, English Literature in the age of Shakespeare
[numerous Chaucer references] ; Appendix, Specimens of Chaucer's
poetry.

[p. ix]   [Chaucer gives the best picture in early literature of contemporary manners and is most valuable to students of the
intellectual and moral conditions of man.]

[p. x]   [Difficulty of Chaucer's language easily surmounted.]

[Chapter II. Admiration for *Canterbury Tales*, which open
to us the true character of his genius, not evinced till comparatively late period doubtless because of the satire they
contain on the Catholic Clergy.]

[p. 42]   But the neglect which this great work experienced at the
hands of critics, extends beyond the period of the Reformation. Fox, the martyrologist, eulogises Chaucer, not for his
comic and satiric powers, but for "his true Wicklevian spirit;"
and, with the exception of Beaumont's apology [1602 edition
of Chaucer], for the ribaldry of the comic tales, and a
passage in Puttenham's Arte of English Poetrie, there is
scarcely any distinct recognition of the poetical merits of the
Canterbury Pilgrimage anterior to Dryden.

[p. 45]   [Chaucer affords a wonderful contrast of pathos and humour
and in neither was he understood previous to the days of
Puttenham and Spenser.]

The earliest successors of Chaucer, John the Chaplain,
[p. 46] Occleve, and Lydgate, in celebrating the praises, or lamenting
the death, of their "greate maister," all harp upon one theme :
the eloquence, or "rhetoricke," as they usually style it, of the
departed poet.

[p. 49]   [Chaucer compared to Petrarch. Leland and Thynne
praise Chaucer for his style and learning, not for his poetry.]

This practical and philosophical view of the merits of
Chaucer continued in force till the latter years of the sixteenth
century. Webbe, in his "Discourse of English Poetry,"
praises the poet in the spirit of Fox, Bale, or the most zealous
Protestants.

Puttenham, a contemporary of Webbe, is the first critic
who seems in any degree to understand either the history of
our author's works, or their poetical merits.

[p. 50]   [Puttenham is then quoted ; *see* above, vol. i, p. 125.]

This passage, though it does not display any very deep
knowledge in literary history, may, considering the age in
which it was written, be regarded as a masterly outline of

the poetical character of our author, and forms a striking
[p. 51] contrast to the vagueness with which Sidney, in his " Defence
of Poesie," characterized the poet, "as seeing clearly in a
mystic [*sic* for ' mystie '] time," and as " beautifying our mother
tongue." . . .

Up to the days of Leland and William Thynne, there was, as
we have seen, but one opinion on this subject.   Chaucer was
the " floure of rhetoricke," the "garnisher of Englishe rude."
Webbe first ventures to hint that " the manner of his style may
seeme blunt and course to many fine English eares at these days."
In the days of which Webbe speaks, the English tongue, besides
the natural polish which it had acquired from the labours of
[p. 52] successive writers, was also affectedly interlarded with artificial
ornaments, borrowed chiefly from the Spanish and Italian
languages.   These " ink-horn terms," as they were called, form
a frequent theme of ridicule in the comedies of Ben Jonson
and Shakspeare. . . . [Prevalence of Euphuism, and Spenser's
preference for Chaucer's speech.]   The genuine English style
of this age lay between the obsolete diction of Chaucer, and
the affectations above-mentioned.   This is accurately felt,
and sensibly pointed out, by an old writer somewhat senior to
Spenser.   [Ashton is then quoted ; *see* above, vol. i, p. 87.]

[p. 53]   Verstegan, in his Restitution of Decayed Intelligence
[*q. v.* above, vol. i, p. 176], and Skinner, in the preface to his
Etymologicon Anglicanum [*q. v.* above, vol. i, p. 243], have
censured Chaucer for what formed the constant argument in
his praise, up to the Elizabethan period of our literature :
namely, for the introduction of French terms into English.

[p. 54] Rymer [*q. v.* above, vol. i, p. 265], in a passage which shows
that he has reaped the full advantage of the philological
labours of our poet, first introduces him to us as a recruiting
officer of our language ; and afterwards, proceeding more
scientifically to explain the chemical process, by which that
tongue was formed, he represents Chaucer as a skilful brewer
of English. . . .

[On the increase of expressions from a foreign tongue, as a
nation becomes more literary.]

Amongst those who first "employed themselves to the
beautifying and bettering of the English tongue" (to use the
words of his oldest editor, William Thynne), was " that noble
and famous clerke, Geffray Chaucer."

[p. 55]   But in the interval which had elapsed between the days of
"Old Dan Geffrey, in whose gentle spright
The pure well-head of poetry did dwell,"
and those of his illustrious successor, who thus characterises
him, the innovations which Verstegan and Skinner charge
solely upon Chaucer, had been so far increased, that his
language had become obsolete; and the adoption of it by
Spenser is only to be justified, on the ground of its being in
harmony with his theme. . . .

[From Spenser to the present day, only Cowley of English
poets did not imitate or extol Chaucer. Spenser's indebtedness
to Chaucer is here pointed out in detail.]

.   .   .   .

[p. 58]   Judging from Spenser's imitations of Chaucer, we might
conclude that his favourite works were The Dutchesse, The
Parliament of Fowles, and The Squier's Tale: but, perhaps,
(as also in the case of Milton's well-known and pathetic
allusion to the latter poem) these imitations are rather to
be received as evidence of the general admiration of Spenser
[p. 59]   for the works of his predecessor, than of his partiality for
any particular passages. . . . It seems, that during the lifetime of Spenser . . . the poetical character of Chaucer was
rather viewed in reference to his pathetic, than to his comic
powers. . . .

[p. 60]   Amongst the pathetic poems, the Knight's Tale, and the
"Troilus and Cresseide" have always maintained a precedency.   The latter especially seems to have been a favourite
in the age of Spenser.   Puttenham and Sidney, the former
in his Art of Poetrie, the latter in his Defence of Poesie,
both select this work as especially worthy of praise: and
Sidney indeed scarcely mentions any other.   With Beaumont
also this was a favourite work.   Shakspeare, although there
can scarcely exist any doubt that he was an admirer of the
beauties of this work, has, in the plot of his Midsummer
Night's Dream, given us yet clearer proof of his acquaintance
with the Knight's Tale. . . .

[The Fairies of Chaucer, Spenser and Shakespeare.]

[p. 72]   From the days of Shakspeare, the comic powers of Chaucer
have been the constant theme of admiration both with critics
and poets.   In allegorical description he may have been
excelled by Spenser, in pathos by Shakspeare, in sublimity by
Milton; but in true comic humour, and more especially in the

delineation of professional characters, he has few equals, no superiors.

[p. 78]   On a general review of the history of Chaucer's reputation, we may say that his language, which seems chiefly to have attracted the notice of his immediate successors, rude

[p. 79]   as it now appears, was with reference to his own age in itself a marvel. How just were the grounds upon which the critics of the days of Henry the Eighth extolled his learning, will be more fully shown in the following chapter. His pathetic powers, which engaged the admiration of the poets and critics of the age of Elizabeth, continue even now to rival his genuine comic humour . . . The vigorous yet finished painting— both of scenes and characters, serious as well as ludicrous —with which his works abound, are still, notwithstanding the roughness of their clothing, beauties of a highly poetical nature. The ear may not always be satisfied,

[p. 80]   but the mind of the reader is always filled; and even the roughness of his verse, which may offend some readers, is in many instances—at least in the case of his earlier poems— rather to be attributed to the errors of transcribers (that mis-writing and "misse-metring" against which he warns his copyists) than to his own negligence.

[p. 111]   [Chapter IV.]   Chaucer, like Ariosto and Spenser, is essentially a descriptive rather than a dramatic poet. . . . But his descriptive powers are of every kind; satirical, pathetic, picturesque . . .

[p. 112]   The most striking instances of the poetical powers of Chaucer, under all the three above-mentioned heads, are certainly to be found in his great work. But, if we take into consideration that of that great work, the general prologue, and the ludicrous tales, are the most original portions, while the serious stories are, without any exceptions, either imitations or translations, perhaps we shall be inclined to admit that the minor or earlier poems of our author, afford the best instances of those of his pathetic or picturesque descriptions which may be strictly called his own. In these poems, the playful satire which, on a general view of Chaucer's works, seems to form the leading characteristic of his mind, scarcely appears at all. . . .

[p. 124]   Chaucer is a picturesque poet in the narrowest and strictest sense of the term. [*The Book of the Duchesse, Parlement of Foules, Complaint of the Black Knight*, etc., instanced.]

[p. 138]   The difference between the earlier poems of Chaucer, and his "Canterbury Pilgrimage," as regards the portraiture of manners, consists in this :—that, in the former, the tastes, habits, and opinions of the court are represented to us : in the latter, the habits of middle and low life.   The total change of theme, spirit, and style, observable in the general prologue, and in the comic portions of Chaucer's principal and later [p. 139] works, is perhaps to be attributed to his political disgraces, by which he must necessarily have been estranged from the court, in which many of his earlier years had been spent, and re-united in habits and interests with those classes of society in which his birth and parentage seem originally to have placed him.

[p. 180]   [Chapter V.] In the choice of the occasion; in the variety and delicate discrimination of the characters, and in the vivacity and dramatic effect with which the whole plot is conducted ; in all these respects, Boccaccio, when compared with Chaucer, is but a mere shadow.   As a lively and agreeable fabulist, the Italian, especially in his serious tales, has the advantage.   Prolixity, a fault common to all our old poets, is one of the principal blemishes of Chaucer's serious productions. . . .

[p. 200]   The interest to be derived from the prose works of Chaucer is twofold : first, as they illustrate his own life, or afford a comment on his poetry ; secondly, as they throw a light upon the spirit and taste of the age.

[There is a long and appreciative review of Hippisley in the Gentleman's Magazine, March 1839, new series, vol. xi, pp. 278–9, *q. v.* below.]

1837. Hunt, James Henry Leigh. *Blue Stocking Revels; or the Feast of the Violets.* Canto III. *Of the supper that Apollo gave his Visitors and with what sort of spectacle and of after Course he amazed them,* [in] The Monthly Repository, 1837, new ser., vol. i, p. 53. (Poetical Works, Boston, 1866, vol. i, pp. 276–7.)

Then Petrarch appear'd

.   .   .   .

Him follow'd, still modestly keeping behind,

.   .   .   .

Boccaccio, with faces a martyr might bless,
Griselda's among them, the patient excess.
Her look was the sweetest that never knew laughter ;
And backward she turn'd tow'rds the shape that came after,

Great Chaucer. As humbly as maiden went he.
Young queens held their diadems of him in fee ;
Young mothers and beauties, clear angels of earth ;
I know not which grac'd them most, sorrow or mirth.

1837. [**Landor,** Walter Savage.] *The Pentameron and Pentalogia,* pp. 213–15, 217–18. (Longer Prose Works, ed. C. G. Crump, 1893, 2 vols., vol. ii, pp. 92–4.)

[p. 92]   *Petrarca.* The English, I remember Ser Geoffreddo[1] telling us, never kill singing birds nor swallows.

Boccaccio. Musick and hospitality are sweet and sacred things with them . . .

[p. 93]   *Petrarca.* Ser Geoffreddo felt more pleasure in the generosity and humanity of his countrymen, than in the victories they had recently won, with incredibly smaller numbers, over their boastful enemy.

Boccaccio. I know not of what nation I could name so amusing a companion as Ser Geoffreddo . . . Richard de Bury was sent Ambassador to Rome by King Edward. . . . This prelate came into Italy attended by Sir Geoffreddo, in whose company we spent, as you remember, two charming evenings at Arezzo . . .

[p. 94]   Ser Geoffreddo is not only the greatest genius, but likewise the most amiable of his nation. He gave his thoughts and took yours with equal freedom . . .

Petrarca. Ser Geoffreddo, I well remember, was no less remarkable for courtesy than for cordiality.

Boccaccio. He was really as attentive and polite toward us as if he had made us prisoners. It is on that occasion the English are most unlike their antagonists and themselves . . .

[1] [Landor's note :] Chaucer.

1837. Landor, Walter Savage. *An Ode* [to Wordsworth], [in] Literary Hours with Various Authors [edited by Joseph Ablett], 1837, p. 163. (Works, Poems, ed. C. G. Crump, 2 vols., 1892, vol. ii, p. 180.)

To learn my lore on Chaucer's knee,
I left much prouder company ;
Thee gentle Spenser fondly led,
But me he mostly sent to bed.

[For another expression of this by Landor *see* below, *n. a.* 1844.]

1837. Macaulay, Thomas Babington, Lord. *Lord Bacon,* [in] The Edinburgh Review, July 1837, vol. lxv, p. 10. (Works, 1898, 12 vols., vol. viii, p. 510.)

In looking round a well-furnished library, how many

English or French books can we find which were extant when Lady Jane Grey and Queen Elizabeth received their education? Chaucer, Gower, Froissart, Comines, Rabelais, nearly complete the list.

1837. Southey, Robert. *Preface* to his Poetical Works, collected by himself, 10 vols., vol. i, pp. viii, 193 *n*.

. . . I took Spenser for my master. I drank also betimes of Chaucer's well. The taste which had been acquired in that school was confirmed by Percy's " Reliques " and Warton's " History of English Poetry," and a little later by Homer and the Bible.

1837. Unknown. *Chaucer,* [in] The Penny Cyclopædia, 1833–58, vol. vii, 1837, pp. 10–11.

[This article is chiefly biographical, and contains the usual incorrect account of Chaucer's education at Oxford and Cambridge, his authorship of the *Court of Love,* the *Black Knight,* and the *Flower and the Leaf,* and his exile and imprisonment. " A little pains would enable any one to master his language and versification, and the pains would be amply rewarded." Quotations from Warton and Godwin.]

1837. Unknown. *Griselda, the Clerke's Tale. Re-made from Chaucer,* [in] Blackwood's Edinburgh Magazine, May, 1837, vol. xli, pp. 655–67.

[This version begins :

In fair Saluzzo, lovely to behold,

Down at the root of Vesulus the cold,

A marquis whilom ruled that pleasant plain, etc.]

1837. Unknown. *Review* of *Hallam's Introduction to the Literature of Europe,* [*q. v.* above, 1837, in] The Quarterly Review, Feb. 1837, vol. lviii, pp. 37, 38.

After Italy, England could boast in Chaucer, the greatest poet of these ages. But Chaucer's excellence lay in fertile and graceful invention; and in the vivid and humorous delineation of manners . . . rather than in the high perfection of language or melody of verse. The foreign element, the French, with which Chaucer, or perhaps the fashion of the time, the Norman blood and the French wars, enriched our language, is not yet blended and harmonized; it lies, as it were, in separate and distinct masses, not yet having passed through the amalgamating process of common usage. The difficulties of Chaucer's versification are perhaps most reason-

ably traced to the uncertain state of pronunciation, or rather
accentuation—the letters or syllables which afterwards became
mute, still retaining their proper sounds, as in French and
in other languages.

1837. Unknown. *Chateaubriand on the Literature of England,* [in] The
Edinburgh Review, Jan., 1837, vol. lxiv, pp. 520-23, 525-6, 528.

[p. 521]   When Chaucer wrote, though borrowing largely from the
[p. 522] early Italian poetry—though not untinctured by the Norman
—it was at once a national poet formed by national circumstances, and appealing to a nation! Though, as we before
said, a scholar and a courtier, it was in Chaucer that the
literary spirit of the English people, vigorous, simple, and
truthful, found its voice. It was an immense encouragement
to the English language that a man so clerkly and so well
with the great, should have given it the preference to the
French. Unquestionably the extraordinary popularity of the
' Canterbury Tales,' and the ' Troilus and Cresseide ' had a
prodigious effect in rendering the language of a conquered
people not only familiar but musical to the conquerors.
Chaucer wrote for the people, but it was in the style of a
gentleman. And he at once familiarized the Anglo-Norman
and refined the Anglo-Saxon genius. The sympathies of
Chaucer are not those of coteries and courts, they are with
common and universal feelings. He has a passionate love of
nature, and his minute and close descriptions are very different
indeed from the pastoral affectations of the *Trouveres* and
Troubadours. He has also that clear and racy power of discriminating and individualizing character, which springs from
an observant eye and a social temper. Chaucer is the earliest
writer in modern literature whose characters are strongly
marked and distinct. His passages are to those of Boccaccio
what Homer's are to those of Virgil; and the study of
Chaucer would, like that of Homer, conduce insensibly to the
Drama. It was, perhaps, his constitutional sympathy with
broad interests and universal feelings, no less than the con-
cession of his reason to the tenets of Wickliff, that made
Chaucer a satirist of monks and priests. He seems to have
had a practical and shrewd philosophy in his easy sarcasms on
these holy men, which is more subtle and thoughtful than
the careless gibes of the Troubadours. The active career of

Chaucer, his keen observation of the natural, whether in men or scenery, tended, perhaps, to make him the great founder of a very remarkable distinction of English literature,—namely, the mixture of the humorous and pathetic—the solemn and the comic. . . .

[P. 523] [Sterility of genius after Chaucer.]

1837. Wade, Thomas. *The Contention of Death and Love,* [printed in] W. R. Nicoll and T. J. Wise's Literary Anecdotes of the Nineteenth Century, 1895, 2 vols., vol. i, p. 132.

[Death speaks of the dying poet :]
> Thinkst thou that I, whose strong decree
> Swept Homer from Ionian air
> When his allotted years were run,
> And Dante from Italia's Sun
> When all his griefs accomplished were,
> Down-looking Chaucer from his theme,
> And Spenser from his Faery dream,
> .   .   .   .
> Thinkst thou that I . . .
> . . . can pause for him ?

1838. [Barham, Richard Harris.] *Grandpapa's Story—The Witches' Frolic* (Family Stories, no. x. By Thomas Ingoldsby), [in] Bentley's Miscellany, 1838, vol. iv, p. 509. (The Ingoldsby Legends, 1st ser., 1840, p. 176 ; Oxford edn., 1905, p. 108.)

> How our ancestors managed to do without tea
> I must fairly confess is a myst'ry to me ;
> Yet your Lydgates and Chaucers
> Had no cups and saucers ;
> Their breakfast, in fact, and the best they could get,
> Was a sort of a *déjeuner à la fourchette* . . .

1838. Chappell, William. *An Essay on the Ancient Minstrelsy of England,* [in] *A Collection of National English Airs,* 1838–40, pp. 12–13.

[Chaucer's references to music.]

[The musical scores were published in a separate vol. in 1840. The Chaucer references are fuller in the much enlarged edn., *The Ballad Literature and Popular Music of the Olden Time,* 1855–9.]

1838–9. [De Quincey, Thomas.] *A Brief Appraisal of the Greek Literature in its Foremost Pretensions,* [in] Tait's Magazine, Dec. 1838, and June, 1839. (The Collected Writings of Thomas de Quincey, Edinburgh, 1889–90, ed. D. Masson, 14 vols., vol. x, pp. 309–313.)

[Chaucer, " a poet worth five hundred of Homer." Dryden's

eulogy of the *Canterbury Tales.* Chaucer and Homer as
narrators. Chaucer superior in the Homeric characteristics of
life, motion, and picturesque simplicity.]

1838. Emerson, Ralph Waldo. *Literary Ethics,* an oration delivered
. . . July 24, 1838. (Works, Centenary Ed., 12 vols. ; vol. i, p. 168.)

Whilst I read the poets, I think that nothing new can be
said about morning and evening. But when I see the daybreak I am not reminded of these Homeric, or Shakespearian,
or Miltonic, or Chaucerian pictures.

1838. Guest, Edwin. *A History of English Rhythms,* 2 vols. ; vol. i,
pp. 25–34, 121, 153, 177, 215, 237 ; vol. ii, pp. 2, 110, 155, 164,
186, 236–41, 255–8, 308, 312, 357–9, 363, 367–8, 417, 429. [Also
brief references and illustrative quotations throughout vol. i.]

[vol. i,   [After an account of *e* final, Guest continues :] Tyrwhitt
p. 34] deserves our thanks for the manly experiment of editing our
oldest classic, and for accumulating a decent share of general
knowledge, to serve for his occasional elucidation. But what
can we say of an editor who will not study the language of
his author?—of one who, having the means of accuracy (at
least to a great extent) within reach, passes them by, and
judges of Chaucer's grammar in the fourteenth century by that
of Pope in the eighteenth?

[p. 121] [Rhyme.] When . . . the verse was lengthened and alliteration banished, we had a fair right to expect greater caution,
and very rarely indeed does Chaucer disappoint us. His rhimes
are, for the most part, strictly correct.

[p. 153] [Middle pause.] It was not till the middle of the fifteenth
century that the dot, which indicated the middle pause, began
to be omitted in our manuscripts, and no edition of Chaucer
or his contemporaries can be perfect without it.

[p. 177] [English rhythms.] Our heroic verse, as it has been called
of late, was formerly known by the more homely appellation
of *riding rhime.* . . .

Chaucer strictly confined this rhythm to five accents, but
certainly allowed himself great freedom in the number of
his syllables. His rhythm, however, always approaches that
of the common measure. . . .

[p. 215] [Verse of five accents. Quotation of *Prol.,* ll. 1–18, from
MSS. Harl. 1758 and 7333, giving the middle and end
stops.]

[p. 237] Webbe [*q. v.* above, 1586, vol. i, p. 129] has laid it down that "the natural course" of English verse "ran upon the Iambicke stroke. . . . He might have been taught sounder doctrine by his contemporary Gascoigne [*q. v.* above, 1575, vol. i, p. 111]. This critic . . . admires "the libertie in feete and measures" used by their Father Chaucer. . .

[vol. ii, p. 237] [Couplet metre.] Loose as is the rhythm of these verses [an extract from Rolle's *Prick of Conscience*], I have seen few *manuscripts* of the Canterbury Tales, which admit of a more definite scansion. The best copies indeed I have *not* seen; and I think it probable that Chaucer at least confined his metre to the verse of five accents; but any more particular definition I dare not venture upon. Before we can understand the nature of his versification—before we can render Chaucer that justice, which his genius so loudly calls for—we have to settle questions that require for their solution the most search-ing . . . investigations. [Untrustworthiness of the MSS.]

That Chaucer was a *master* of English versification no one, that reads him with due care and attention, can well doubt. There are many passages in his works, which, from the agree-ment of MSS. and the absence of all those peculiarities of structure that leave matter for doubt, have, in all probability, come down to us as Chaucer wrote them—and in *these* the [p. 238] versification is as exquisite as the poetry. It needs not the somewhat suspicious apology of Dryden. I am not one of those who assert, that Chaucer has always "ten syllables in a verse, where we find but nine"; but I am as far from believing, that "he lived in the infancy of our poetry," because the scheme of his metre somewhat differs from our own. As far as we have the means of judging, it was not only "auribus istius temporis accommodata," but fulfilled every requisite that modern criticism has laid down, as either essential to the science, or conducive to the beauty of a versification.

The metre of five accents, with couplet-rhyme, may have got its earliest name of "riding rhyme" from the *mounted* pilgrims of the Canterbury Tales. [Quotes Gascoigne and Puttenham, *q. v.* above, 1575 and 1584–8, vol. i, pp. 111 and 125.]

[p. 239] [Blank verse.] The unrhimed metre of five accents, or as it is generally termed *blank verse*, we certainly owe to Surrey. English verse without rhime was no novelty; and the "cadence" of Chaucer comes full as near to the blank verse of five accents, as the loose rhythms of some of our dramatists.

[p. 255]   [Measured prose.] In the House of Fame, Chaucer represents himself as thus addressed,

> Thou—has [*sic*] set thy wit,
> (Although in thy head full little is)
> To maken bookes, songes and dities
> In ryme, *or els in cadence,*
> As thou best canst, in reverence
> Of love—

and Tyrwhitt conjectured, with his usual sagacity, that he
had written in a " species of poetical composition, distinct
from rhyming verses." The Tale of Melibeus has been considered, by some persons, as " blank verse"; but though its
claim to such a title may be questioned, it is certainly a
specimen of cadence. The model, which Chaucer had
floating before him, was clearly his favourite metre of five
accents. . . . The following extract I have endeavoured to
arrange according to its metrical structure . . .

> A yonge | man cal | led : Mel | ibe | us
> Migh | ty and rich | e : begate | upon | his wif |
> That cal | led was Pruden | ce
> A dough | ter which | : that cal | led was Sophi | e.

.   .   .   .

[p. 256]   This | is more wis | dom
> Than | for to we | pe : for | thy frend |
> Which that | thou hast lorne | : for | ther | ein is | no
>   bote | .

[Tale of Melibeus, ll. 2157-83.]

As the Tale proceeds, the rhythmical structure gradually
disappears.

[pp. 357-9]   [Ballet-staves of eight and of seven.]

1838. Madden, Sir Frederic. *The Old English Versions of the Gesta
Romanorum,* Introduction, pp. xii–xiii [the poems of Chaucer
furnish many instances of his familiarity with the *Gesta Romanorum*], xx–xxi [the *Gesta* gave Gower and Chaucer their tale of
Constance (*Man of Law's Tale*)], Notes, p. 519 [Chaucer introduces into his *Sompnours Tale,* ll. 2017–42, from Seneca, the same
story as *Gesta* 58].

1838. Wright, Thomas. *Note* [on] *Alliterative Poem on the Deposition
of Richard II.,* ed. by T. Wright, Camden Soc., p. 53.

P. 7, *l.* 14—*Hurlewaynis Kynne.* The only other instance
of this word that I have observed in early English poetry,

occurs in the prologue to the Tale of Beryn, printed at the end of Urry's Chaucer.

As Hurlewaynes meyne in every hegg that rapes.

Hurlewaynes meyné is the *Maisnie Hellequin* of old French popular superstition, in Latin *familia Harlequini.*

1839. H., H.	*MSS. of Chaucer in the Bodleian Library,* [in] The Gentleman's Magazine, January, 1839, new series, vol. xi, pp. 50–1.

[A letter drawing attention to different readings in the spurious *Cuckoo and Nightingale* in Fairfax 16, and Arch. Seld. B. 24, and to the ending of the *Parlement of Foules* in Arch. Seld. B. 24, the last 11 stanzas of which differ entirely from the 13 stanzas which ordinarily end it.]

1839. Hood, Thomas.	*Up the Rhine,* 1840, pp. 65, 256.	(Works, 1869–73, 10 vols., vol. vii, pp. 56, 207.)

[Likeness of Mrs. Wilmot to Chaucer's Prioress—for her " tender heart " and her " Stratford atte Bowe " French.]

[According to the D. N. B. *Up the Rhine* was begun in 1836 and published in 1839 ; the imprint is dated 1840.]

1839. [Longfellow, Henry Wadsworth.] *Hyperion,* pp. 65–6. (Works, Riverside ed. [1886], 11 vols., vol. ii, p. 51.)

Blot out from England's history the names of Chaucer, Shakespeare, Spenser, and Milton only, and how much of her glory would you blot out with them !

1839. Madden, Sir Frederic.	*Sir Gawayne,* ed. Sir F. Madden, Bannatyne Club, Introd. pp. x n., xxxix, Notes, 301, 321, 358.

[p. xxxix] [Reference to Chaucer's lines on Sir Gawain, *Squieres Tale,* 1. 75, and *Rom. of the Rose,* B. 1. 2209.]

[p. 358] [Bishop Percy considered that Chaucer borrowed the *Wife of Bath's Tale* from *Sir Gawain, see* above, 1765, vol. i, p. 428.]

1839. Unknown.	*Review* of *Chapters on Early English Literature,* by J. H. Hippisley, [in] The Gentleman's Magazine, March, 1839, new series, vol. ii, pp. 278–9.

[For Hippisley, *see* above, 1837.]

[The review begins with a favourable notice of Hippisley's book and concludes with the correction of some errors ; the main part is occupied by an estimate of Chaucer :]

There is in him [Chaucer] that which is not to be found in any preceding or contemporary poet in any modern language—a groundwork or plot of his great poem laid on observation of . . . real life in its different grade and appearances. At all times and in every age, human character must have been a prevailing subject of human observation ; but to draw that out from the recesses of private life and oral communication ; to leave without regret those favourite topics which had so long enchained the muse amid the enchanted bowers of fairyland . . . and to descend to the hostelry and mill . . . this is the distinctive mark of superior genius . . .

Chaucer certainly cannot be placed on an equality with those mighty masters of song who have accompanied the awful career of human passions through the various scenes of well-constructed fable. . . . He had not the height of genius which could have produced an Œdipus or a Hamlet.

1839. Unknown. *Review* of *A Treatise on Wood Engraving . . . by John Jackson,* [in] The Gentleman's Magazine, Aug., 1839, new series, vol. xii, p. 112.

A popular superstition . . . induced people to believe that the day on which they should see an image of St. Christopher, they should not meet with a violent death, or die without confession. . . . It is not unlikely that to his faith in this article of belief, the Squire, in Chaucer's " Canterbury Tales," wore

' A Christofre on his breast, of silver shene.'

1840. [Bandinel, Bulkeley ?] *Catalogue of the Printed Books and Manuscripts bequeathed by Francis Douce, Esq., to the Bodleian Library,* Oxford, pt. i, p. 63, pt. ii [MSS], p. 28.

[pt. i, p. 63] [Works, Pynson, n.d., 1532, 1598, 1602, 1721 (Urry); Canterbury Tales, 1737, 1775 (Tyrwhitt), 1798 ; Canterbury Tales and other poems, n.d., 2 vols., 8° ; Chaucer's ghoast, 1673 ; Chaucer's incensed ghost, in Morgan's Phœnix Britannicus, 1732 ; Kynaston's Troilus and Cressida, specimen, 1796 ; Tales from Chaucer in prose by C. C. Clarke, 1833 ; Chanon's Yeoman's Tale, p. 227 of Ashmole's Theatr. Chem., 1652 ; Life by Singer, n.d.]

[pt. ii, p. 28] [MS. clxx. John Lane's continuation of the *Squieres Tale* *q.v.* above, 1614, vol. i, p. 189.]

1840. Barrett, afterwards **Browning,** Elizabeth Barrett. *Letter to R. H. Horne* [on *Chaucer Modernised,* dated] Dec. 17th, 1840, [in] Letters of E. B. Browning to R. H. Horne, ed. S. R. T. Mayer, 1877, 2 vols., vol. i, pp. 107–10.

[p. 108] Notwithstanding all the merit and the grace, do not some of the poems militate against the principle you set out with [" gracefully and poetically to retain as much of the original language of Chaucer as possible " (p. 100)] ? I venture to think that the re-fashioners stand—some of them, and in a

measure—too far from Chaucer's side—however graceful the
attitude.   You, yourself, and Wordsworth are most devoutly
near.   *Most* of the contributors are so, but not all, for even
Mr. Leigh Hunt is sometimes satisfied in being with Chaucer
in the spirit, and spurns the accidents of body.   But Mr.
Bell's 'Mars and Venus' is too smooth and varnished, and
redolent of the nineteenth century, as appears to me, for spirit
or body.   I think people will say, you might 'keep more
Chaucer. . . .'

1840. **Halliwell**, afterwards **Halliwell-Phillipps**, James Orchard.
The Volvelle, and on Chaucer s Treatise of the Astrolabe, [in]
Archæologia, vol. xxix, 1842, pp. 374–5.   [Communicated to the
Society, 19th March, 1840.]

> [A vellum volvelle exhibited;   its use explained from
> Ashmole MS. 191, The Rewle of the Volvelle;   Chaucer's
> *Astrolabe* a translation ultimately from a Sanscrit original;
> this fact discovered by Reuben Burrow (reference to Professor
> Davies' *History of Magnetical Discovery*, p. 257);   Nicholas
> Strode was tutor to Chaucer's son at Oxford, as shown by
> the colophon to a Cambridge MS. (Dd. iii. 53) of Chaucer's
> *Astrolabe.*]
>
> [We have not been able to trace the reference to Davies.]

1840. **Hanmer**, Sir John (afterwards Baron Hanmer).   *Sonnets,* xvi.
Chaucer.

> . . . .
>
> I bless thee with a kindred heart, Provence:
> For to thy tales, like waves that come and go,
> Sat Chaucer listening with exulting ear;
> And casting his own phrase in giant mould:
> That still had charms for sorrow's gentlest tear,
> Telling the story of Griselda's woe,
> "Under the roots of Vesulus the cold."

1840. **Lawrance**, Hannah.   *Historical Memoirs of the Queens of
England,* 2 vols., 1838–40;   vol. ii, 1840, pp. 9, 22, 24–5, 36, 150,
154–5, 176, 238–41, 254, 264–8, 270–3, 454n.

> [Vol. i, 1838, only contains two unimportant references, on pp. 281, 441.]

[vol. ii, pp. 24–5]   [Beauty of many of Chaucer's female characters.   He must
have seen such women among "the gentle company that
adorned the court of the noble-minded Philippa, and of the
gracious lady . . . Anne of Bohemia."]

[pp.238–41]   [Anne of Bohemia, a friend and patroness of Chaucer;   some
account of him and of his relations to her is given.]

[pp. 264–68]   [An account of Chaucer.   Interesting and admirable though
the *Canterbury Tales* are, full justice cannot be done to his
poetical character unless we turn to his allegorical poems,

Prologue to *Legend of Good Women, Book of the Duchesse,* etc., also the (spurious) *Chaucer's Dream (Isle of Ladies), Flower and the Leaf* and *Complaint of the Black Knight.* His description of natural scenery is highly praised.]

[pp. 270
–8] [Occleve, Lydgate and Chaucer.]

1840-3. Strickland, Agnes and Elizabeth. *Lives of the Queens of England,* 12 vols., 1840–3, vol. ii, pp. 359, 388, 389*n.,* 395*n.* ; vol. iii, pp. 177, 236 ; vol. vi, p. 17*n.*

[vol. ii, p. 359] [Philippa of Hainault, by Elizabeth Strickland. Chaucer Philippa's protégé ; quotation of the lines (described as his) on the maple —

"That is fair and green
Before the chamber windows of the queen
At Woodstock."]

[p. 388] [*Ibid.* On Margaret, fifth daughter of Edward III, "a distinguished patroness of Chaucer."]

[p. 389] [*Ibid.* Philippa Chaucer's patroness, with whom the court favour of the father of English verse expired.]

[vol. iii, p. 177] [Katherine of Valois, by Elizabeth Strickland. A note on the royal minstrel James Stuart, who had been captive in England, was educated at Windsor by Henry IV, wrote poetry, and took Chaucer and Gower for his models.]

[p. 236] [Margaret of Anjou, by Agnes Strickland. An allusion to Alice Chaucer as "the only child and heiress of Geoffrey Chaucer"—corrected in the edition of 1851, vol. ii, p. 178, to "the grand-daughter and heiress," etc.]

[vol. vi, p. 17] [Elizabeth, by Agnes Strickland. A note on Donnington as once belonging to Chaucer.]

[The references in the new and revised edition, eight vols., London, 1851, are: vol. i, pp. 563, 577, 584, 588*n.* ; vol. ii, pp. 83, 132*n*, 178 ; vol. iv, p. 15*n.* One of these, vol. i, p. 577, an allusion to Philippa's patronage of Chaucer, is not in the first edition.]

1840. Wordsworth, William. *Letter to Moxon,* [dated] Feb. 24th, 1840. (Letters of the Wordsworth Family, ed. W. Knight, 3 vols., 1907, vol. iii, p. 193.)

Mr. Powell, my friend, has some thought of preparing for publication some portion of Chaucer modernised, as far and no farther than is done in my treatment of the "Prioress' Tale." That would, in fact, be his model. He will have coadjutors, among whom, I believe, will be Mr. Leigh Hunt, a man as capable of doing the work well as any living writer. I have placed at my friend Mr. Powell's disposal three other pieces which I did long ago, but revised the other day. They are "The Manciple's Tale," "The Cuckoo and the Nightingale," and twenty-four stanzas of "Troilus and Cressida." This

I have done mainly out of my love and reverence for Chaucer
in hopes that, whatever may be the merits of Mr. Powell's
attempt, the attention of other writers may be drawn to the
subject, and a work hereafter produced, by different persons,
which will place the treasures of one of the greatest of poets
within the reach of the multitude, which now they are not.

[For Wordsworth's modernisations *see* above, 1801 ; for *Chaucer Modernised*, and
for Powell, both below, 1841.]

[*n.a.* 1841.] **The Canterbury Tales**, [in] Dove's Classics.

[A cheap reprint, classed with that in Bell's Poets by the anonymous reviewer of
Chaucer Modernised in the Athenæum (*q.v.* below, 1841). Nothing is known of this
series or of the edn. of the Canterbury Tales which formed part of it. The date is
more probably near 1820–25, when there were many cheap series of poets like the
Chiswick.]

1841. Collier, John Payne. *Introduction* [to] *Patient Grissil*, a comedy by Thomas Dekker, Henry Chettle and William Haughton. Reprinted for Shakespeare Soc., 1841, pp. vi, vii.

[p. vi]   [Chaucer's visit to Padua.]

English readers first became acquainted with the story [of
Griselda] by means of Chaucer's beautiful and extended
versification of the incidents; and comparing them with those
[p. vii] in Boccaccio's novel, it may be inferred that Chaucer saw
Petrarch after he had read, if not translated, what Boccaccio
had sent to him.

[There is no reference to Chaucer either in the play itself or by older editors of it.]

1841. [De Quincey, Thomas.] *Homer and the Homeridæ*, [in] Blackwood's Edinburgh Magazine, Dec. 1841, vol. l, pp. 747–9, 751. (Collected Writings, ed. D. Masson, 1889–90, 14 vols., vol. vi, pp. 69–73, 78.)

[p. 69]   Precisely on this very summer day, so bright and brilliant,
of 1841, are the five hundred years completed (less by
forty-five years than the interspace between Homer and Pisis-
[p. 70] tratus) since Chaucer was a stout boy, " alive," and probably
"kicking"; for he was fined about 1341 for kicking a
Franciscan friar in Fleet Street, though Ritson erroneously
asserts that the story was a " hum," invented by Chatterton.
Now, what was the character of Chaucer's diction ? A great
delusion exists on that point. Some ninety or one hundred
words that are now obsolete, certainly not many more, vein
the whole surface of Chaucer ; and thus a *primâ facie* impression is conveyed that Chaucer is difficult to understand :
whereas a very slight practice familiarises his language.
The Canterbury Tales were not made public till 1380 ; but

the composition was certainly proceeding between 1350 and 1380, and before 1360 some considerable parts were *published.* Here we have a space greater by thirty-five years than that between Homer and Pisistratus. And observe— *had Chaucer's Tales enjoyed the benefit of an oral recitation,* were they assisted to the understanding by the pauses in one place, the hurrying and crowding of unimportant words at another, and by the proper distribution of emphasis every-where . . . there is no man, however unfamiliar with old English, but might be made to go along with the movement of his admirable tales, though he might still remain at a loss for the meaning of insulated words.

Not Chaucer himself, however, but that model of language which Chaucer ridicules and parodies, as becoming obsolete in his days, the rhyme of Sir Thopas—a model which may be safely held to represent the language of the two centuries previous—is the point of appeal. Sir Thopas is clearly a parody of the Metrical Romances. Some of those hitherto published by Ritson, &c., are not older than Chaucer ; but some ascend much higher, and may be referred to 1200, or perhaps earlier. Date them from 1240, and *that* places a period of six centuries complete between ourselves and them. Notwithstanding which the greater part of the Metrical Romances, when aided by the connection of events narrated, [p. 71] or when impassioned, remain perfectly intelligible to this hour.

.   .   .   .

[p. 73]   There is also a philosophic reason, why the range of diction in Chaucer should be much wider, and liable to greater changes than that of Homer. Review those parts of Chaucer which at this day are most obscure, and it will uniformly be found that they are the *subjective* sections of his poetry ; those, for instance, in which he is elaborately decomposing a character. A character is a subtle fugacious essence which does, or does not, exist according to the capacity of the eye which is applied to it. In Homer's age, no such meditative differences were perceived. All is *objective* in the descriptions and external.

.   .   .   .

[p. 78]   Chaucer also, whom Dryden in this point so thoroughly misunderstood, was undoubtedly a most elaborate master of metre, as will appear when we have a *really* good edition of him.

1841. D'Israeli, Isaac. *Amenities of Literature,* vol. i, pp. 34, 115*n.*
117–19, 164, 182–3, 191*n.*, 198, 201, 215, 217–18, 236*n.*, 252–82
[article on Chaucer], 286, 291–4, 302–5, 308–12, 314–16*n.*, 320,
347, 369 ; vol. ii, pp. 30–31, 83, 112, 114, 254, 366, 376 ; vol. iii,
pp. 3–4.

[vol. i,
p. 265].   The creative faculty in Chaucer had not broken forth
in his translations, which evidently were his earliest writings.
The native bent of his genius, the hilarity of his temper,
betrays itself by playful strokes of raillery and concealed
satire when least expected.   His fine irony may have sometimes left his commendations, or even the objects of his
[p. 266] admiration, in a very ambiguous condition . . .   Our poet
has stamped with his immortal ridicule the tale told in his
own person—"The Rime of Sir Thopas."

[p. 268]   Yet humour and irony are not his only excellencies, for
those who study Chaucer know that this great poet has
thoughts that dissolve in tenderness ; no one has more skilfully touched the more hidden springs of the heart.

The Herculean labour of CHAUCER was the creation of a
new style.   In this he was as fortunate as he was likewise
unhappy.   He mingled with the native rudeness of our
English, words of Provençal fancy, and some of French and
of Latin growth.   He banished the superannuated and the
uncouth, and softened the churlish nature of our hard Anglo-
Saxon ; but the poet had nearly endangered the novel diction
when his artificial pedantry assumed what he called "the
ornate style" in the "Romaunt of the Rose," and in his
"Troilus and Cressida."

.   .   .   .

[p. 269]   We have, however, a glorious evidence amid this struggle
both with a new and with a false style, of Chaucer's native good
taste ; he finally wholly abandoned this artificial diction ; and
his later productions, no longer disfigured by such tortured
phrases and such remote words, awaken our sympathy in the
familiar language of life and passion.

TYRWHIT has ingeniously constructed a metrical system to
arrange the versification to the ear of a modern reader . . .
He maintained that the lines were regular decasyllables.
But who can read this poet for any length, even the
Canterbury Tales, in the elaborated text of Tyrwhit, without
[p. 270] being reminded of its fallacy ?   Even the E final, on which our
critic has laid such stress, though often sounded, assuredly is

sometimes mute. Dan Chaucer makes at his pleasure words
long or short, dissyllabic or trisyllabic ; and this he has
himself told us—

> " But for the rime is light and lewde,
>   Yet make it somewhat agréable,
>   Though some verse fail in a sylláble."

 . . . The verse of Chaucer seems more carefully regulated
in his later work, the Tales; but it is evident that Chaucer
trusted his cadences to his ear, and his verse is therefore
usually rhythmical, and accidentally metrical.

   .   .   .   .

[p. 272]   Are the works of our great poet to be consigned to the literary
dungeon of the antiquary's closet ? I fear that there is more
than one obstruction which intervenes between the poet's
name, which will never die, and the poet's works, which will
never be read. A massive tome, dark with the Gothic type,
whose obsolete words and difficult phrases, and, for us,
uncadenced metre, are to be conned by a glossary as obsolete
as the text, to be perpetually referred to, to the interruption
of all poetry and all patience, appalled even the thorough-
paced antiquary, Samuel Pegge, as appears by his honest
confession [*q.v.* above, vol. i, p. 502]. Already a practised
bibliosopher proclaims, alluding to the edition by Tyrwhit
of Chaucer's Canterbury Tales, "And who reads any
other portion of the poet ? " Yet the Canterbury Tales
are but the smallest portion of Chaucer's works ! But
some skilful critics have perpended and decided differently ;
even among the projected labours of Johnson was an edition
[p. 273] of Chaucer's works, and Godwin, when diligently occupied on
this great poet, with just severity observed that "a vulgar
judgment had been propagated by slothful and indolent
persons, that the Canterbury Tales are the only part of the
works of Chaucer worthy the attention of a modern reader,
and this has contributed to the wretched state in which his
works are permitted to exist."

   .   .   .   .

[p. 274]   It is true that the language of Chaucer has failed, but not
the writer. The marble which Chaucer sculptured has betrayed the noble hand of the artist ; the statue was finished ;
but the grey and spotty veins came forth, clouding the lucid
whiteness.

For the poet or the poetical, the difficulty of the language may be surmounted with a reasonable portion of everyday patience.

. . . .

[p. 277]   Ogle, with others, attempted to modernise Chaucer; but it is as impossible to give such a version of Chaucer as to translate the Odes of Horace.

1841. Eller, Irvin. *The History of Belvoir Castle*, p. 207.

[The Regent's Gallery.] In a carved oak frame, a *Portrait of Chaucer*, 1400; 9½ inches broad, by 12 inches high. The author of this work would hazard an opinion, that this was painted by Occleve, one of the first of our poets; and who, it is known, was so attached to Chaucer, that he calls him his master, and his father, and affectionately and repeatedly laments him. What renders this opinion more probable, is, that Vertue mentions an illuminated manuscript of Thomas Occleve, in which there is a portrait of Chaucer, painted by Occleve himself.

[An anonymous reviewer in the Gentleman's Magazine, July 1841 new ser. vol. xvi, pp. 57-8, scouts this ascription.]

1841. Emerson, Ralph Waldo. *History*, and *The Over-Soul*, [in] *Essays, First Series*, London, 1841, pp. 25, 238. (Works, Centenary edition, 1903, vol. ii, pp. 29-30, 288.)

[The Essays first appeared at Boston in 1841; the first edn. in B.M. is the London reprint of the same year.]

[p. 29]   The advancing man discovers how deep a property he has in literature . . . One after another he comes up in his private adventures with every fable of Æsop, of Homer, of Hafiz, of Ariosto, of Chaucer, of Scott, and verifies them with his own head and hands.

[p. 288]   Humanity shines in Homer, in Chaucer, in Spenser, in Shakspeare, in Milton.

[1841. Fox, William Johnson.] *Hymns and Anthems used at the Unitarian Chapel, South Place, Finsbury.* No. cxxiii. [Ed. W. J. Fox, published by Chas. Fox, 1841.]

> Britain's first poet,
> Famous old Chaucer,
> Swanlike in dying
>   Sung his last song,
> When at his heartstrings
>   Death's hand was strong.

[Then follows a paraphrase of 'Fle fro the pres.']

[See *Notes and Queries*, June 12, 1852, vol. v, p. 574; also E. Garnett's *Life of W. J. Fox*, 1910, pp. 218-21. The 1845 edn. is the first in B.M.]

1841. Halliwell, afterwards **Halliwell-Phillipps,** James Orchard. *Ludus Coventriæ.* A collection of Mysteries, formerly represented at Coventry on the Feast of Corpus Christi. (Shakespeare Society.) Notes, pp. 407, 416 ; Glossary, pp. 419–21, 423–4, 426–8, 432–4.

[p. 407]   [Chaucer's definition of Tragedy in the *Monkes Tale* quoted.
[p. 416]   Chaucer's reference to the player's "scaffold" in the *Milleres Tale* quoted.

    Glossary. Remarks on Chaucer's use of asmatryk ; belle ; berde ; brayde ; bysmare ; do, don ; fytt ; flem ; herborwe ; lymyd ; nale ; ore ; pillid ; stevene ; upryth ; ȝemanry.]

1841. Horne, Richard Hengist, **Wordsworth,** William, etc. *The Poems of Geoffrey Chaucer modernised.* [Selections from the Canterbury Tales and other works modernized in verse, by R. H. Horne, W. Wordsworth, Leigh Hunt, E. B. Barrett, T. Powell, and R. Bell. Preceded by a life of Chaucer by L. Schmitz. *See,* for an account of this book, above, Introduction, pp. l–lii; for Wordsworth's contributions to it *see* above, 1801 and 1840 ; and, for Powell's, below, 1841.]

[Contents :]

    Title page, with quotation from Drayton's poem, 'To . . . Henry Reynolds' [*q. v.* above, 1627, vol. i, p. 200], wrongly signed 'Wordsworth.'

    Introduction, by R. H. Horne, headed by quotation "For out of the olde fieldés," etc., pp. v–cv.

    Life of Chaucer, by Professor Leonhard Schmitz, pp. cviii, cxxxviii.

    Eulogies on Chaucer, by his contemporaries and others, pp. cxxxix–cxlvii.

    Prologue to the Canterbury Tales, by R. H. Horne, pp. 3–33.

    The Cuckoo and the Nightingale, by William Wordsworth, pp. 37–53.

    The Legends of Ariadne, Philomene, and Phillis, by Thomas Powell, pp. 57–86.

    The Manciple's Tale, by Leigh Hunt, pp. 88–106.

    The Rime of Sir Thopas, by Z. A. Z., pp. 109–123.

    Extract from Troilus and Cressida, by William Wordsworth, pp. 127–135.

    The Reve's Tale, by R. H. Horne, pp. 138–159.

    The Flower and the Leaf, by Thomas Powell, pp. 162–191.

    The Friar's Tale, by Leigh Hunt, pp. 195–209.

    The Complaint of Mars and Venus, by Robert Bell, pp. 213–234.

Queen Annelida and False Arcite, by Elizabeth B. Barrett, pp. 237–257.

The Squire's Tale, by Leigh Hunt, pp. 260–287 [Hunt's second version : for the first *see* above, 1823].

The Franklin's Tale, by R. H. Horne, pp. 290–331.

[From Horne's Introduction, we print the following :]

[p. v]   The present publication does not result from an antiquarian feeling about Chaucer, as the Father of English Poetry, highly interesting as he must always be in that character alone ; but from the extraordinary fact, to which there is no parallel in the history of the literature of nations,—that although he is one of the great poets for all time, his works are comparatively unknown to the world.   Even in his own country, only a very small class of his countrymen ever read his poems. Had Chaucer's poems been written in Greek or Hebrew, they [p. vi] would have been a thousand times better known.   They would have been translated.   Hitherto they have had almost everything done for them that a nation could desire, in so far as the most careful collation of texts, the most elaborate essays, the most ample and erudite notes and glossaries, the most elaborate and classical (as well as the most trite and vulgar) paraphrases, the most eloquent and sincere admiration and comments of genuine poets, fine prose writers, and scholars —everything, in short, has been done, except to make them intelligible to the general reader.

Except in the adoption of a modern typography, Chaucer's poems have always appeared hitherto, under no better auspices for modern appreciation than on their first day of publication, some three centuries and a half ago.   Concerning the various attempts to render several of his poems available to the public, which have been made at intervals by poets and lovers of Chaucer, a few remarks will shortly be submitted.   With whatever reverence or admiration these latter may have been received by the readers of those poets who in- [p. vii] troduced such specimens among their own works, it is certain that they produced no perceptible effect in the popularity of the original author.

Whether there has been a feeling in the public about Chaucer, amounting to a sort of unconscious resentment at the total inability to read his poems without first bestowing the same pains upon his glossary, which has been more willingly

accorded to poetry and prose in the Scottish dialect; or
whether on account of certain passages which in the present
state of refinement appear offensive to a degree that the good
folks of Chaucer's time, as well as the poet himself, could
never have contemplated, it is not necessary to determine.
Such an antipathy to the study of his language does exist ;
and—while we, curiously enough, find Chaucer sometimes
apologizing, with meek humility and *gentilesse,* for using
some expressions which are *now* in common use, but which
were considered very improper in his day—it is undeniable
that various passages and expressions occur here and there,
[p. viii] in his works, which are calculated to startle a modern reader,
and make him doubt his eyes. Howbeit, this great fact is
sufficiently apparent,—that Chaucer is a poet, and a founder
of the language of his country ; (taking rank as such, with
Homer and with Dante, and being the worthy forefather of
Shakespeare, Spenser, and Milton ;) whose poetry is comparatively unread and unknown even in his own country. The
simple statement of such a fact will sufficiently explain the
feeling which, in all sincerity and reverent admiration, has
prompted those who have united in this present undertaking.

From what has been said, it will be readily apprehended,
that this attempt at a translation, or transfusion, of Chaucer
into modern English, is by no means intended for the reading
of those, who, being learned in the black letter, or familiar
with the dialect of the period, can and do read the great poet
with facility and delight. It is expressly intended for all
that vast majority of our countrymen, and of foreigners
acquainted with the English and English literature, who
[p. ix] are unable to do this ; and who, either from indisposition,
or the want of sufficient leisure, have never given the study
requisite for a right appreciation of the author's meaning,
but who, at the same time, having a genuine love for noble
poetry, would rejoice to find such labours superseded by a
faithful version of the great poet, bereft of his obsolete dialect.
The project has already received demonstration of the utmost
sympathy from many high quarters at home and abroad,
while the work was going through the press ; and we have
at present only met with one individual of literary eminence
[Landor, *q.v.* below, 1841], who boldly declared, that he still
wished "to keep Chaucer for himself and a few friends."

The grand obstacle to be surmounted in reading Chaucer

has, of course, been always, that of his obsolete dialect; but one of the main causes of his poems remaining so long without modernizing (for they have hitherto been only paraphrased in a very free manner), is because they are all in rhyme. Here begins the first and most trying difficulty in [p. x] rendering his poems available to the public of the present time. To translate his poems into blank verse, would be losing a characteristic feature of the original; to give the rhymes he uses is often impossible, because the words themselves, or the grammatical structure of the terminations are obsolete; to substitute rhymes of similar quantity and sound can seldom be successfully accomplished, because it has a tendency, when you are struggling to obtain the sense of the passage, to induce a mechanical awkwardness; and to supply new rhymes generally requires that a whole line, if not the couplet, must be changed in rhythm or totally remodelled. In the attempts, therefore, which have been hitherto made (with the exception of two of the Tales, modernized by Lord Thurlow and Mr. Wordsworth) the whole substantial material of Chaucer has been left as it stood, and the leading ideas only being adopted, a new poem has been written with more or less ability and verisimilitude, according to the genius and talent of the individual and the principle on which he proceeded.

The versions of Chaucer which have been given by Dryden [p. xi] and Pope, are elaborate and highly finished productions, reading exactly like their own poems, and not bearing the slightest resemblance to Chaucer. Even his finest lines and couplets which often require little or nothing more than a change in the orthography, have scarcely ever been retained. Everything was paraphrased, made fluent, sounding, and full of "effects"; though it is equally true, that Chaucer occasionally received a very noble present from Dryden, for which nothing more than a suggestion is traceable in the original. Their versions of several of the Canterbury Tales, bearing the dates of 1699 and 1711, were subsequently adopted by Ogle, together with some of his own, and of sundry other writers, and published in three volumes in 1741. The same versions, [p. xii] with additions, were collected by Lipscombe, and published in 1795. As it is impossible to praise these editions for any resemblance to the original, it would be far more agreeable to pass them without further remark; but our readers will naturally expect some proofs in support of the judgment

thus hazarded. It is earnestly requested, however, that the
following brief review may not be understood as given for
the sake of criticism, but solely out of reverence towards
Chaucer, who has not been fairly treated. . . .

[p. xxi] Perhaps the best in execution of these paraphrases (of
course excepting those of Dryden and Pope) are the tales
furnished by Mr. Boyce; at all events they are the most
ambitious. He renders the "Squire's Tale" in stanzas. The
opening, it must be acknowledged, is high and imposing :—

  "Where peopled Scythia's verdant plains extend"

[and six following lines].

Many readers may perhaps admire the lofty tone of this opening stanza—but why associate it with the name of Chaucer?

[pp. xii- [A review in more detail of previous modernisations, in
xxxi] which severe criticism is passed upon the freedoms and the
vulgarisations allowed themselves by many of the modernisers;
but Lord Thurlow's version of *The Flower and the Leaf* is
praised for its fidelity.]

[p. xxxi] There may be several methods of rendering Chaucer in
modern English. It will be sufficient, however, to mention
the two extremes. The advocates of the one argue—that in
order to render Chaucer truly, it must be done in the spirit
rather than in the letter; simply because so much of the
letter, or words, of his period differ both in sound and sense

[p. xxxii]from those now in use. . . . The advocates of the opposite
method argue, that all the substantial material and various
rhythm of Chaucer should be adopted as far as possible. . . .
To retain or preserve the existing substance is the rule; to
rewrite and paraphrase is the exception. . . .

[p. xxxiii] The safest method, as the most becoming, is manifestly that
of preserving as much of the original substance as can be
rendered available. . . .

[pp. [An examination of Chaucer's rhythm, shewing that he
xxxvii-
xciii] "was a most harmonious and melodious poet."]

[pp. [Chaucer's broad sympathy, pathos, graphic power and true
xciii–cv]morality and piety.]

[pp.cvii- [Professor L. Schmitz's "Life of Geoffrey Chaucer," con-
cxxxviii]taining the errors based on acceptance of the Court of Love
and the Testament of Love.]

1841. Hunt, James Henry Leigh. *See* below, 1841, Powell.

[*n.a.* 1841.] **Landor,** Walter Savage. *Letter to Richard Hengist Horne,*
[not published in Landor's letters; partly printed in] Letters of
Elizabeth Barrett Browning addressed to Richard Hengist Horne,
ed. by S. R. Townshend Mayer, 1877, vol. i, p. 99.

[Horne is writing : In answer to an application from Horne to take part in the modernisation of Chaucer, brought out in 1841, Landor first replied that he believed] "as many people read Chaucer" (meaning in the original) "as were fit to read him." As I [*i. e.* Horne] took leave to doubt this, Landor again wrote, saying—"Indeed I *do* admire him, or rather love him. In my opinion, he is fairly worth a score or two of Spensers. He had a knowledge of human nature and not of doll-making and *fantoccini* dressing. . . . Pardon me if I say I would rather see Chaucer quite alone, in the dew of his sunny morning, than with twenty clever gentlefolks about him, arranging his shoe-strings and buttoning his doublet. I like even his *language.* I will have no hand in breaking his dun but rich-painted glass to put in (if clearer) much thinner panes."

[Landor afterwards changed his mind and defended Wordsworth for his share in these modernisations ; *see* below, 1856. For Horne's comment on this letter *see* above, 1841. In the American edition of these letters, with a Preface and Memoir by R. H. Stoddard, New York, 1877, the reference is vol. i, pp. 78–9.]

1841. N[icolas, Sir] N[icholas] H[arris]. *The French of Stratford atte Bowe,* [in] The Gentleman's Magazine, Aug., 1841, new series, vol. xvi, p. 154.

It is evident that the Prioress's French was none of the purest ; but there is some reason for supposing that Chaucer really meant that the Prioress could not speak any French at all. [Quotation from Ferne, *q.v.,* above, 1586, vol. i, p. 129.]

The Prioress's greatest oath was "by St. Loy," which Tyrwhitt has elongated for the sake of the metre to "St. Eloy" ; but for which he says he has no other authority than Urry. It may therefore be as well to remark, that many towns in France are called St. Eloy.

1841. Powell, Thomas [or **Hunt,** James Henry Leigh ?]. *The Nun's Priest's Tale ; or, the Cock and the Fox. Modernised from Chaucer,* [in] The Monthly Chronicle, Feb. 1841, vol. vii, pp. 119–33.

[p. 120]   A widow poor, and bent with age, I wot,
Was whilome dwelling in a little cot,
Beside a grove, within a rustic dale.
This widow, of the which I tell my tale,
In cheerful patience led a simple life,
Since that sad day when she was last a wife [etc.].

[Robert Browning stated in a letter (*q.v.,* below, 1846) that Powell " bought two modernisations of Chaucer—'Ugolino' and another story from Leigh Hunt—and one 'Sir Thopas' from Horne, and printed them as his own."
The Chaucer modernisations printed by Powell are as follows : (i) *The Floure and*

the *Lefe;* (ii) *The Legends of Ariadne, Philomene and Phillis,* from *L.G.W.;* (iii) *The Rime of Sir Thopas;* (iv) *The Nonne Prestes Tale;* (v) *Ugolino of Pisa,* from *The Monkes Tale.*

Of these i–iv are found in Powell's *Poems,* London, 1842, pp. 3–114, and v in his *Poems,* London, 1845, pp. 209–11. Nos. i–iii had already appeared in *Chaucer Modernised,* 1841 (*q.v.,* above, Horne), i and ii under his own name, and iii signed "Z.A.Z."; iv is that to which this note is appended, and for v we have found no appearance other than the 1845 *Poems.*

The versions (i, ii) appearing over Powell's name in *Chaucer Modernised* at least cannot be Horne's or Hunt's; and if, as Browning says, iii be Horne's (though why Horne should sign this version "Z.A.Z.", when he signs others by his own name, it is difficult to see), and v Leigh Hunt's, then the only remaining one of the five to be the second tale bought from Leigh Hunt is iv, this version of *The Nonne Prestes Tale.* Browning says that he helped Powell with his verses, and certainly the modernisations are superior to the original poems, which are very poor in both volumes. That Powell was the instigator of *Chaucer Modernised* is shown by Wordsworth's letter to Moxon (*q.v.* above, 1840).]

1841. Saunders, John. *The Tabard,* [in] London, ed. Charles Knight, 1841–4, 6 vols., vol. i, 1841, pp. 57–72.

[A full and excellent account of the Tabard, with four woodcuts.]

1841. [**Saunders,** John.] *Chaucer's Portrait Gallery,* [in] The Penny Magazine, vol. x, Feb.–Dec., pp. 65–7, 79–80, 93–5, 101–3, 145–6, 171–2, 185–6, 230–32, 245–6, 271–2, 293–4, 322–4, 345–6, 375–6, 393–4, 442–3, 449–50, 460–62, 481–2, 495–6.

[A series of sketches of the Canterbury Pilgrims, with quotations; enlarged and published in 1845 in volume form as *Cabinet Pictures of English Life: Chaucer, q.v.* below. Each sketch has a woodcut; these reappear in the volume.]

1841. **Schmitz,** Leonhard. A *Life of Geoffrey Chaucer,* [in] The Poems of Geoffrey Chaucer Modernised. *See* above, Horne.

1841. **Smith,** John. *The Life, Journal and Correspondence of Samuel Pepys, Esq.,* 2 vols., vol. ii, pp. 254–255n.

[The Editor reprints Dryden's Letter to Pepys of July 14, 1699 (from Scott's *Dryden,* 1808, xviii, 156) and Pepys' answer to Dryden of same date (*q. v.* above, vol. i, pp. 270–71). He adds a few notes to the letters, and in one in vii, 254, to the *Good Parson,* says:]

To Chaucer's other poems Pepys appears to have been attracted. Thus, in Percy's *Reliques,* there is an original ballad by Chaucer, printed for the first time, from an ancient MS. in the Pepysian library, that contains many other poems of its venerable author.

[The 'ballad' is the Roundel of Merciles Beaute, and the MS. Pepys 2006, p. 390. *See* Percy's Reliques, ed. H. B. Wheatley, 1876–7, 3 vols., vol. ii, pp. 14–16.]

1841. **Unknown.** *The Persone of a Toun,* 1370; *his character from Chaucer, imitated and enlarged by Mr. Dryden, now again altered and abridged. Together with the Persones prologue and tale.* By the Persone of a Toun.

[A small tract of 24 pages; the editor says in a prefatory note: " 'The Parson's Tale,' which in Chaucer is a Homily, has been abridged and adapted as a specimen of the doctrines of the 'Holy Chirche' of England, in the olden time (*circa*) 1370." The "Postscript" at the end (p. 22) begins, " The Prologue has been adapted, and the concluding lines metred, from Chaucer: the latter being, in the original, a prayer at the end of his 'Canterbury Tales,' in which he expresses his sorrow and regret at the ribaldry and pollution contained in his writings. An author should never forget, that when he has passed into another world, his works, if calculated to corrupt, may still be doing their mischief, and . . . his crimes may thus be extended . . . through centuries." A few notes follow.]

[*a.* **1841.**] **Unknown.** *The Book of the Poets (Chaucer to Beattie),* pp. xvi–xviii [Essay on English Poetry; enthusiastic praise of Chaucer's poetry], 2 [biographical sketch of Chaucer], 3–7 [Extracts, un-modernized, from the *Knightes Tale, Prologue* and *Sir Thopas,* and the *Good Counsail.* On p. 3 is an engraving of the inter-ruption by Theseus of the duel between Palamon and Arcite. For the serial review by Elizabeth Barrett, *see* below, 1842].

[The "new edition" of this book, 1841, is the first in the English Catalogue; that of 1846, with steel engravings after Corbould, is the first in B.M. The references given above are to this edn.]

1841. Unknown. *Review* of Horne and Wordsworth's *Poems of Geoffrey Chaucer Modernised,* [in] The Athenæum, 6 Feb. 1841, pp. 107–8.

[p. 107]   To extend a taste for this great poet has been the task of the several writers who have united to produce the work before us, which we venture to predict, without much pre-tension to prophecy, will do no more to make Chaucer read, than Ogle, or Lipscombe, Pope, Dryden, or Wordsworth, have done already. To our thinking, the greatest help ever given to Chaucer, has been in the cheap reprint of his 'Canterbury Tales,' in Dove's Classics and Bell's Poets; the low price of the volumes induced purchasers; and if men will only attempt to read, they will soon relish and appreciate, for Chaucer is as much a poet for the many as Shakspeare himself. . . .

Chaucer, in this modern version, is as much like old Geoffrey as Sprat and Flatman are like Pindar. [Much more very severe condemnation of the plan and execution of the book.]

1841. Wordsworth, William. *Letter to Henry Reed of Philadelphia*, [printed in] Memoirs of William Wordsworth, by Christopher Wordsworth, 1851, 2 vols., vol. ii, p. 373–5. (Letters of the Wordsworth Family, ed. W. Knight, vol. iii, p. 218.)

There has recently been published in London a volume of some of Chaucer's tales and poems modernised. This little specimen originated in what I attempted with the ' Prioress's Tale '; and if the book should find its way to America, you will see in it two further specimens from myself. I had no further connection with the publication than by making a present of these to one of the contributors [Powell; *see* above, 1840, Wordsworth]. Let me, however, recommend to your notice the ' Prologue,' and the ' Franklin's Tale '; they are both by Mr. Horne, a gentleman unknown to me, but are, the latter in particular, very well done. Mr. Leigh Hunt has not failed in the ' Manciple's Tale,' which I myself modernised many years ago ; but, though I much admire the genius of Chaucer as displayed in this performance, I could not place my version at the disposal of the editor, as I deemed the subject somewhat too indelicate, for pure taste, to be offered to the world at this time of day. Mr. Horne has much hurt this publication by not abstaining from the ' Reve's Tale '; this, after making all allowance for the rude manners of Chaucer's age, is intolerable, and by indispensably softening down the incidents, he has killed the spirit of that humour, gross and farcical, that pervades the original. When the work was first mentioned to me, I protested as strongly as possible against admitting any coarseness or indelicacy ; so that my conscience is clear of countenancing aught of that kind. So great is my admiration of Chaucer's genius, and so profound my reverence for him as an instrument in the hands of Providence for spreading the light of literature through his native land, that, notwithstanding the defects and faults of this publication, I am glad of it, as a means for making many acquainted with the original who would otherwise be ignorant of everything about him but his name.

1842. [**Barrett**, afterwards **Browning**, Elizabeth Barrett.] *The Book of the Poets*, [a review of the anonymous anthology so named (*q. v.* above [*a.* 1841]), in] The Athenæum, 1842, pp. 497–99, 520–22, 558–60, 706–8, 728–9. [Reprinted (enlarged) in The Greek Christian Poets and the English Poets, 1863.] (Poetical Works, 1890, 6 vols., vol. v, pp. 203–4, 207–17, 226–9, 250–1, 259, 267.)

[p. 498]   But it is in Chaucer we touch the true height, and look

abroad into the kingdoms and glories of our poetical literature,
—it is with Chaucer that we begin our 'Book of the Poets.'
. . . And the genius of the poet shares the character of his
position : he was made for an early poet, and the metaphors
of dawn and spring doubly become him. A morning-star, a
lark's exaltation, cannot usher in a glory better. The " cheerful
morning face," " the breezy call of incense-breathing morn," you
recognize in his countenance and voice : it is a voice full of
promise and prophecy. He is the good omen of our poetry,
the "good bird," according to the Romans, " the best good
angel of the spring," the nightingale, according to his own
creed of good luck, heard before the cuckoo.

> Up rose the sunne, and uprose Emilie,

and uprose her poet, the first of a line of kings, conscious of
futurity in his smile. He is a king and inherits the earth,
and expands his great soul smilingly to embrace his great
heritage. Nothing is too high for him to touch with a thought,
nothing too low to dower with an affection . . . His senses are
open and delicate, like a young child's—his sensibilities
capacious of supersensual relations, like an experienced
thinker's. Child-like, too, his tears and smiles lie at the edge
of his eyes, and he is one proof more among the many, that
the deepest pathos and the quickest gaieties hide together in
the same nature . . . And because his imagination is neither
too " high fantastical " to refuse proudly the gravitation of the
earth, nor too " light of love " to lose it carelessly, he can
create as well as dream, and work with clay as well as cloud,
—and when his men and women stand close by the actual
ones, your stop-watch shall reckon no difference in the beating
of their hearts. He knew the secret of nature and art,—that
truth is beauty,—and saying " I will make ' A Wife of Bath '
as well as Emilie, and you shall remember her as long," we do
remember her as long. And he sent us a train of pilgrims,
each with a distinct individuality apart from the pilgrimage,
all the way from Southwark and the Tabard Inn, to Canterbury
and Becket's shrine ; and their laughter comes never to an end,
and their talk goes on with the stars, and all the railroads
which may intersect the spoilt earth for ever, cannot hush the
" tramp, tramp " of their horses' feet.

[More on Chaucer's versification, the supposed quarrel with
Gower, etc.]

1842. Black, William Henry. *Introduction* [to] *Paraphrase of the Seven Penitential Psalms,* pp. viii [*Ploughman's Tale* sometimes inserted in Canterbury Tales], xiv [anapæsts strange to those used to Chaucer's regular iambic measures], Notes, pp. 55, 57–8, 59, 61, 65, 69–70.

1842. C[larke,] C[harles] C[owden]. *Chaucer,* [in the] *Encyclopædia Britannia,* 7th edition, vol. vi, pp. 336–8.

[This is a new article on Chaucer, the previous one (author unknown) having appeared in all editions of the *E.B.* from 1778.]

[Possibly 1345 is more correct for Chaucer's birth than 1328, usually assigned because of Chaucer's deposition as to his age in Oct. 1386. Account of Chaucer's offices and service abroad; his flight and imprisonment. Short notice of the editions, in which the Complaint of the Black Knight is treated as authentic. Chaucer's chief merit in regard to versification consisted in rendering it more natural, regular and comprehensive, by discarding alliteration, and by reducing the irregular Alexandrine metre to the heroic measure in an uniform and equal number of syllables. But Wicklif contributed far more than Chaucer to the improvement of the English language. There follows a short account of the Canterbury Tales, and a quotation from Campbell's appreciation of Chaucer in Specimens of the British Poets (*q. v.* above, 1819).]

1842–6. Guest, Edwin. [*Philological Papers,* in] *Proceedings of the Philological Society* for 1842–6, vols. i–iv, 1844–6.

[Many quotations from Chaucer throughout.]

1842. Landor, Walter Savage. *Southey and Porson (Second Conversation),* [in] Blackwood's Edinburgh Magazine, Dec. 1842, vol. lii, p. 710. (Works, 1846, vol. i, pp. 80–81; Imaginary Conversations, ed. C. G. Crump, 1891, 6 vols., vol. iii, pp. 250–52.)

[vol. ii, p. 250]

SOUTHEY AND PORSON.

Porson. There is scarcely a poet of the same eminence [as Spenser] whom I have found it so delightful to read in, or so tedious to read through. Give me Chaucer in preference. He slaps us on the shoulder, and makes us spring up while the dew is on the grass, and while the long shadows play about it in all quarters. We feel strong with the freshness round us, and we return with a keener appetite, having such a companion in our walk. Among the English poets, both on this side and the other side of Milton, I place him next to Shakspeare; but the word *next,* must have nothing to do with the word *near.* . . .

[p 251] I like Pietro Perugino a thousand-fold better than Carlo

Maratta, and Giotto a thousand-fold better than Carlo Dolce. On the same principle, the daybreak of Chaucer is pleasanter to me than the hot dazzling noon of Byron.

Southey. . . . His [Byron's] partisans, no one of whom probably ever read Chaucer, would be indignant at your preference. They would wonder, but hardly with the same violence of emotion, that he was preferred to Shakspeare. Perhaps his countrymen in his own age, which rarely happens to literary [P. 252] men overshadowingly great, had glimpses of his merit. One would naturally think that a personage of Camden's gravity, and placed beyond the pale of poetry, might have spoken less contemptuously of some he lived among, in his admiration of Chaucer. He tells us both in prose and verse by implication, how little he esteemed Shakspeare. Speaking of Chaucer he says, " he, surpassing all others, without question, in wit, and leaving our smattering poetasters by many leagues behind him,

'jam monte potitus
Ridet anhelantem dura ad fastigia turbam.'

1842. [**Landor,** Walter Savage.] *Review* of *Theocritus, Bio. et Moschus, ex recog. Aug. Meinekii,* [in] The Foreign Quarterly Review, Oct. 1842, vol. xxx, p. 180. (Longer Prose Works, ed. C. G. Crump, 1893, 2 vols., vol. ii, p. 195, as 'The Idylls of Theocritus.')

Chaucer was born before that epidemic [of conceits] broke out which soon spread over Europe, and infected the English poetry as badly as any.

1842. **Mitford,** Mary Russell. *Letter to Miss Barrett* [E. Barrett Browning. dated] Aug. 18, 1842, [printed in] The Life of Mary Russell Mitford, related in a selection from her letters, ed. by the Rev. A. G. L'Estrange, 1870, vol. iii, p. 157-8.

What you say of Milton is full of truth. But *one* truth you have, I think, not perceived, that the want of distinctive character causes much of the heaviness of character, individuality, the power of identification, which is the salt of all literature from Horace to Scott. It is the one great merit of your own Chaucer.

1842. **Thoreau,** Henry David. *Journal,* Jan. 2, 1842, [printed in] *Winter.* (Writings, Riverside edn., 1894-5, 10 vols., vol. viii, p. 96.)

[Chaucer's regret for the grossness of his early poems very creditable to him.]

1842. Unknown. *Hints for a New Book of Literary Parallels; Dante, Virgil, Chaucer, Milton and Petrarch,* [in] Fraser's Magazine, March, 1842, vol. xxv, pp. 251, 254–5.

[pp. 254-5] [Chaucer compared for his " vivid picturesque of manners " with Homer and Dante, and also, for his (supposed) exile, to the latter.]

1842. Unknown *Review* of *Poems by Alfred Tennyson,* [in] The Quarterly Review, vol. lxx, p. 391.

See how Chaucer exhibits to us all that lay around him, the roughness and ignorance, the honour, faith, fancy, joyousness of a strong mind, and a strong age, both tranquil within bounds which, as large enough for their uses, neither had tried to pass. . . . Of all these peculiarities of character, so blended in that world are strength and unconsciousness, not one ever rises into individuality of principle. In clearness, freedom, fulness, what delineation of our actual life can be at all compared with this? Of this poet how truly may it be said,

> ' O'er Chaucer's blithe old world, for ever new,
> In noon's broad sunbeam shines the morning dew;
> And while tired ages float in shade away,
> Unwearied glows with joy that clear to-day.'

[We have not been able to trace this reference.]

1843. Poetical Works of Chaucer, with an essay on his language, etc. by T. Tyrwhitt ; Moxon. [The Canterbury Tales and essay are reprinted from Tyrwhitt's edition of 1775–8. For an account of this edn., *see Chaucer,* by E. P. Hammond, p. 139.]

1843. Barrett, afterwards **Browning,** Elizabeth Barrett. *Letter to John Kenyon,* [dated] March 25th, 1843, [in] Letters of Elizabeth Barrett Browning, 1897, vol. i, p. 128.

The poetical faculty, which expresses the highest moods of the mind, passes naturally to the highest objects. Who can separate these things? Did Dante? Did Tasso? Did Petrarch? Did Calderon? Did Chaucer? . . . Chaucer, with all his jubilee of spirit and resounding laughter, had the name of Jesus Christ and God as frequently to familiarity on his lips as a child has his father's name.

1843. Barrett, afterwards **Browning,** Elizabeth Barrett. *Letter to Mrs. Martin,* [dated] May 26, 1843, [in] Letters of Elizabeth Barrett Browning, 1897, vol. i, p. 143.

No, you would certainly never recognise my prison if you were to see it. [Here follows description of alterations in her bedroom] . . . And Chaucer's and Homer's busts on guard over those two departments of English and Greek poetry.

1843. Carlyle, Thomas. *Past and Present,* p. 175. (Works, Centenary Edition, 1896–7, 30 vols., vol. x, p. 130.)

Thinkest thou there were no poets till Dan Chaucer? No heart burning with a thought, which it could not hold, and had no word for; and needed to shape and coin a word for,—what thou callest a metaphor, trope, or the like? For every word we have there was such a man and poet.

1843. [Chambers, Robert.] *Chaucer,* [in the] *Cyclopædia of English Literature,* 1844 [preface dated 1843]. *See* below, App. A.

1843. Emerson, Ralph Waldo. *Europe and European Books,* [in] The Dial (Boston), April, 1843, vol. iii, p. 515. (Works, Centenary Edition, 1903, 12 vols., vol. xii, p. 366.)

The poet must not only converse with pure thought, but he must demonstrate it almost to the senses. . . . In the debates on the Copyright Bill, in the English Parliament, Mr. Sergeant Wakley, the Coroner, quoted Wordsworth's poetry in derision, and asked the roaring House of Commons, what that meant, and whether a man should have public reward for writing such stuff. Homer, Horace, Milton and Chaucer would defy the Coroner. Whilst they have wisdom to the wise, he would see that to the external they have external meaning.

1843. Hood, Thomas. *Mrs. Gardiner,* [in] The New Monthly Magazine, 1843, vol. lxviii, pt. ii, p. 151. (Works, 1869–73, 10 vols., vol. viii, p. 341.)

Let the Horticulturists hunt through their Dictionaries, . . . they will never invent such apt and pleasant names as the old English ones, to be found in Chaucer, Spenser, and Shakespeare.

1843. L[aing], D[avid]. *Reliquiæ Antiquæ,* 1841–3, 2 vols., vol. ii, 1843, pp. 11, 58–70.

[p. 11]   Palamon and Ersyte. [A fragmentary poem in dialogue from a MS. at Trinity Coll., Dublin. The speakers are Palamon, Emlyn, and Ersyte.]

[p. 59]   Folio MS. in the Royal Library at Naples, on paper, middle of the fifteenth century, marked on the back "MS. di Poesie

Tedeschi, O 4n6.—12 A. 47." [flyleaf, 'Lingua Tedescha' corrected to 'Inglese.']

[The Chaucer references in the course of the description of the contents are as follow :]

[p. 65]   p. 87–113 [of the MS.]. *Libious Disconious.*

The romance of Sir Libeaux Desconus belongs to the thirteenth century, and is mentioned by Chaucer as a popular romance.

[p. 67]   p. 114–8 [of the MS.]. *Fragment of Sir Isumbras.*

Two copies of this romance of an old date are known : also an edition in black letter. It is usually considered to have been one of this class of compositions ridiculed by Chaucer in his Ryme of Sir Thopas, which is " full of phrases taken from Isumbras and other romances." (v. Tyrwhitt's Chaucer.)

[p. 68]   p. 119–46 [of the MS.]. *Griselde.*

This poem on the subject of Patient Griseldis has no title, but is in fact Chaucer's Griselde, or The Clerke of Oxenfordes Tale, which, as the Clerke declares in his prologue, he learned of Petrark at Padua.

[1843–4.] Nicolas, Sir Nicholas Harris. *Life of Chaucer.* [Prefixed to the Aldine edn. of the Works, 1845, issued separately in 1843, or early in 1844. *See* below, 1845, Works, and for reviews, etc., below, 1844, Palgrave and Unknown.]

1843. Quillinan, Edward. *Letter to Henry Crabb Robinson,* [in] Diary, Reminiscences and Correspondence of H. C. Robinson, 1869, 3 vols., vol. iii, p. 224.

Pope also taught me to read Chaucer and the "Fairy Queen."

1843. Saunders, John. *Westminster Abbey; IV. Poets' Corner,* [in] London, edited by Charles Knight, 1841–4, 6 vols., vol. iv, 1843, pp. 114–17.

[p. 114–51]   [Chaucer's tomb and its history.]

As we pause to gaze on its decayed and blackened front, and to examine, with an interest that finds little to repay it, the remains of the poet's effigy, a kind of melancholy similarity between the fate of Chaucer's reputation and that of his memorial suggests itself : what Spenser calls "black oblivion's rust" has been almost as injurious to the first as to the last, and has caused one of the greatest, and, as far as qualifications

are concerned, most popular of poets, to be the most neglected.
. . There is a rust upon his verses, it is true, that mars,
upon the whole, their original music (such as we find it breaking out at intervals where time has not played his fantastic
tricks with the spelling and pronunciation). . . . He who
devotes one day to *studying* Chaucer will be delighted the
next, and on the third will look back with amazement on his
ignorance of the writer who, all circumstances of time and
position considered, can scarcely be said to have had yet a
superior, unless it be Shakspere. And even he has not
equalled, in some respects, the man who at once made England
a poetical country ; there is nothing in the whole range of
literature that can be compared, for instance, to the pathos of
the story of Griselda. . . . Chaucer, like Shakspere, seems
to have combined in himself all the qualities which are
generally found to belong to different individuals.

1843. Shaw, Henry. *Dresses and Decorations of the Middle Ages*, vol. i.
[No pagination.]

[Vol. i, sig. B4, *b* : Quotations from Prologue. Chaucer's
description of the pilgrims our best authority for dresses in the
time of Richard II. There are various other brief references.
Vol. i concludes with a coloured portrait of Chaucer, from
Additional MS. 5141, and a short article on his life and work.
In vol. ii, engraving no. 62, the Canterbury Pilgrimage, from
MS. Reg. 18 D ii, and references on 2 pp. of letterpress
following.]

[*n. a.* **1843.**] **Southey**, Robert. *Commonplace Book*, ed. J. W. Warter,
1849–51, 4 vols., vol. i, p. 438 [quotes Habington's *Castara*, q. v.
above, 1635, vol. i, p. 216] ; vol. ii, pp. 315–16 [quotations from
Rom. Rose for Primitive Dance, Idilnesse, Yellow Hair, Wall-
Painting, Fastening on of Clothes with a Needle, the Undress of
Avarice, and the Game of Bilbo-Catch, the last with a quotation
from the French original], 333 [*Frankeleyn's Prol.* quoted for
borel] ; vol. iii, pp. 227 [*see* above, *c.* 1810], 544 [Pinkerton proposed to J. Nichols to publish the select works of Chaucer, 1783
(*q. v.* above, vol. i, p. 473)] ; vol. iv, p. 259 [we have no language
into which to translate the early (i. e. the Anglo-Saxon ?) poets;
"that of Chaucer is too rugged, and almost as difficult"], 310
[quotations from Jackson (*q. v.* below, App. A., 1657) : "our posterity within few years will hardly understand some passages in
. . . Chaucer, better known at this day to old courtiers than to
young students "], 322–3 [Malcolm's account of Chaucer, taken
from Stowe (*q. v.* above, 1803), Lane's *Squire's Tale* (*q. v.* above,
1614, vol. i, p. 189), Dryden's account of Cowley's distaste for
Chaucer (*q. v.* above, 1700, vol. i, p. 281, and below, App. A.

[*a*. 1667] Cowley), and other references, quoted], 326 [Ben Jonson, in *The Golden Age Restored*, calls up Gower and Lydgate with Chaucer and Spenser (*q. v.* above, 1615, vol. i, p. 190)], 331 [quotations from the Monthly Review (*q. v.* below, App. A., 1761), that "Spenser, Jonson, Beaumont, Fletcher . . . are now almost as little known or read as Chaucer, Lydgate, Gower . . ."], 634 [Gavin Douglas' reference to Chaucer quoted (*q. v.* above, 1501, vol. i, p. 65)].

1843. Thoreau, Henry David. *Homer, Ossian, Chaucer.* Extracts from a Lecture on Poetry. Read before the Concord Lyceum, Nov. 29, 1843, by Henry D. Thoreau, [printed in] The Dial (Boston), vol. iv, Jan. 1844, pp. 297–303. [Reprinted (revised) in] A Week on the Concord and Merrimack Rivers, 1849, pp. 386–93. (Writings, Riverside Edn., 1894-5, 10 vols., vol. i, pp. 364–5, 417–8, 436, 483–94.)

[p. 48?] What a contrast between the stern and desolate poetry of Ossian, and that of Chaucer. . . . When we come to the
[p. 484] pleasant English verse, the storms have all cleared away, and it will never thunder and lighten more. The poet has come within doors. . . .

[p. 485] Notwithstanding the broad humanity of Chaucer, and the many social and domestic comforts which we meet with in his verse, we have to narrow our vision somewhat to consider him, as if he occupied less space in the landscape, and did not stretch over hill and valley as Ossian does. Yet, seen from the side of posterity, as the father of English poetry, preceded by a long silence or confusion in history, unenlivened by any strain of pure melody, we easily come to reverence him. . . . Chaucer's is the first name after that misty weather in which Ossian lived, which can detain us long. Indeed, though he represents so different a culture and society, he may be regarded as in many respects the Homer of the English poets. Perhaps he is the youthfulest of them all. . . . He is so natural and cheerful, compared with later poets, that we might
[p. 486] almost regard him as a personification of spring. . . . It is still the poetry of youth and life rather than of thought. . . .

[p. 487] Chaucer had eminently the habits of a literary man and a scholar. There were never any times so stirring that there were not to be found some sedentary still. He was surrounded by the din of arms. . . . He regarded himself always as one privileged to sit and converse with books. He helped to establish the literary class. His character as one of the fathers of the English language would alone make his works important, even those which have little poetical merit. He was as simple as Wordsworth in preferring his homely but vigorous Saxon tongue, when it was neglected by the court, and had not yet attained to the dignity of a literature, and rendered a similar service to his country to that which Dante rendered to Italy . . . In the [Prologue to the] Testament of [p. 488] Love he writes, "Let then clerkes enditen in Latin, for they have the propertie of science . . . and let Frenchmen in their French also enditen their queinte termes . . . and let us shewe our fantasies in soche wordes as we lerneden of our dames tonge." He will know how to appreciate Chaucer best who has come down to him the natural way, through the meagre pastures of Saxon and ante-Chaucerian poetry. . . .

[p. 489] There is no wisdom that can take place of humanity, and we find *that* in Chaucer. We can expand at last in his breadth. . . He was worthy to be a citizen of England, while Petrarch and Boccaccio lived in Italy, and Tell and Tamerlane in Switzerland and in Asia, and Bruce in Scotland, and Wickliffe, and Gower, and Edward the Third, and John of Gaunt, and the Black Prince were his own countrymen as well as contemporaries ; all stout and stirring names. . . . On the whole, Chaucer impresses us as greater than his reputation. . . . The affectionate mention which succeeding early poets make of him, coupling him with Homer and Virgil, is to be taken into the account in estimating his character and influence. . . .

p. 490] We admire Chaucer for his sturdy English wit. . . . But though it [the *Prologue*] is full of good sense and humanity, it is not transcendent poetry. . . .

[p. 491] Humor, however broad and genial, takes a narrower view than enthusiasm. To his own finer vein he added all the common wit and wisdom of his time. . . . His genius does not soar like Milton's, but is genial and familiar. . . . The charm of his poetry consists often only in an exceeding naturalness, perfect sincerity, with the behaviour of a child rather than of a man.

Gentleness and delicacy of character are everywhere apparent in his verse. . . . Nor can we be mistaken respecting [p. 492] the essential purity of his character, disregarding the apology of the manners of the age. A simple pathos and feminine gentleness, which Wordsworth only occasionally approaches but does not equal, are peculiar to him. . . .

Such pure and genuine and childlike love of Nature is hardly to be found in any poet. . . .

[p. 493] There are many poets of more taste, and better manners, who knew how to leave out their dullness, but such negative genius cannot detain us long: we shall return to Chaucer still with love.

1843. Wright, Thomas. *A Selection of Latin Stories from manuscripts of the thirteenth and fourteenth centuries,* [in] Early English Poetry, Percy Soc., vol. viii, Notes, pp. 233–4.

[The story "de caeco et ejus uxore," in the Appendix to Aesop and in Adolfus, the source of the *Marchantes Tale.*]

[1838–44.] Barrett, afterwards **Browning,** Elizabeth Barrett. *The Lost Bower,* and *A Vision of Poets,* [in] Poems by Elizabeth Barrett Barrett, 1844, vol. ii, pp ·24, 104, 112–13. [In the preface these poems are said to have been written between 1838 and 1844.]

[vol. ii,   And Chaucer, with his infantine
p. 24]   Familiar clasp of things divine—
           That mark upon his lip is wine.

[p. 104]   . . . If Chaucer had not travelled
           Through a forest by a well,
           He had never dreamt nor marvelled
           At those ladies fair and fell
Who lived smiling without loving, in their island-citadel.

     ·   ·   ·   ·   ·   ·

[p. 112]   If it *were* a bird, it seemëd
           Most like Chaucer's, which, in sooth,
           He, of green and azure dreamëd,
[p. 113]   While it sate in spirit-ruth
On that bier of a crowned lady, singing nigh her silent mouth.

[The reference in the stanza quoted from p. 104 is to the non-Chaucerian *Isle of Ladies.*]

1844–5. Craik, George Lillie. *Sketches of Literature and Learning in England, with Specimens of the Principal Writers,* 6 vols., vol. i, pp. 45, 103, 122, 189, 198–9, 215–16, 233–4, 242–3; vol. ii, pp. 9–90 [Chapter on Chaucer, much of it criticism of the theories of Tyrwhitt and Dr. Nott], 91–2, 96 [Chaucer and Gower], 101, 104, 108, 112–13 [Chaucer and Barbour], 138–146 [Chaucer's prose], 165, 166 [Caxton's edition], 175 [Chaucer and science], 183–4 [Occleve and Lydgate], 191–3 [the Scottish Chaucerians], 227 [English prose after Chaucer], 238 [Dean Colet's study of Chaucer], 248–9 [English poetry after Chaucer; Hawes, Lydgate], 257–8 [Scottish poets of early sixteenth century], 260 [Chaucer and Surrey]; vol. iii, pp. 79, 80, 84, 91 [influence of Chaucer on Spenser], p. 88 [Chaucer mentioned with Homer and Shakespeare]; vol. v, pp. 84–5.

1844. Emerson, Ralph Waldo. *The Poet,* [in] Essays, Second Series, London, 1844, pp. 20, 26. (Works, Centenary edition, 12 vols., London, 1903, vol. iii, p. 31.)

[The Second Series of Essays appeared at Boston in 1844 ; the 1st edn. in B.M. is the London reprint (in the "Catholic Series") of the same year.]

When Chaucer, in his praise of 'Gentilesse,' compares good blood in mean condition to fire, which, though carried to the darkest house betwixt this and the mount of Caucasus, will yet hold its natural office and burn as bright as if twenty thousand men did it behold . . . we take the cheerful hint of the immortality of our essence, and its versatile habit and escapes, as when the gypsies say "it is in vain to hang them, they cannot die."

1844. Horne, Richard Hengist. *Comment,* [in] Letters of Elizabeth Barrett Browning to R. H. Horne, 1877, 2 vols., vol. i, pp. 239–41.

[Horne says that, to console Miss Barrett for his criticism that her Eve travelled too far for a single night, he pointed out to her that Chaucer makes fourteen or fifteen years elapse during the action of the *Knightes Tale.*]

1844. Hunt, James Henry Leigh. *A Jar of Honey from Mount Hybla,* no. ix, [in] Ainsworth's Magazine, vol. vi, Sept., 1844, p. 278. (Ed. 1870, p. 172.)

Chaucer was a courtier and a companion of princes ; nay, a reformer also and a stirrer out in the world. . . . Yet as he was a true great poet in everything, so in nothing more was he so than in loving the country and the trees and fields.

1844. Hunt, James Henry Leigh. *Imagination and Fancy, or Selections from the English Poets,* illustrative of those First Requisites of their Art ; with markings of the best passages, critical notices of the writers. And an Essay in Answer to the Question, "What is Poetry ?", pp. vii, 5–6, 15–17, 32–3, 62–3, 66, 72, 87, 141, 149, 151–2, 186–8, 213, 218–19, 253, 261–2, 278, 335.

[Preface, p. vii]   [The scope of the editor's intentions outlined and a reference to the Balade "Hide, Absolon," in *Legend of Good Women,* Prol.]

.   .   .   .

[p. 5]   [What is Poetry ?]   Nay, the simplest truth is often so beautiful and impressive of itself, that one of the greatest proofs of his [the Poet's] genius consists in his leaving it to stand alone, illustrated by nothing but the light of its own

tears or smiles, its own wonder, might, or playfulness. Hence
[p. 6] the complete effect of many a simple passage in our old
English ballads and romances, and of the passionate sincerity
in general of the greatest early poets, such as Homer and
Chaucer, who flourished before the existence of a "literary
world," and were not perplexed by a heap of notions and
opinions, or by doubts how emotion ought to be expressed.

. . . .

[p. 15] Chaucer, for all he was "a man of this world" as well as
the poets' world, and as great, perhaps a greater enemy of
oppression than Dante, besides being one of the profoundest
masters of pathos that ever lived, had not the heart to con-
[p. 16] clude the story of the famished father and his children, as
finished by the inexorable anti-Pisan.

. . . .

Chaucer's steed of brass, that was
So horsly and so quick of eye,
[*Squieres T.*, l. 186]

is copied from the life. You might pat him and feel his
brazen muscles. Hobbes, in objecting to what he thought
childish, [in his letter prefixed to Gondibert] made a childish
mistake. . . .
[p. 17] Hobbes did not see that the skill and beauty of these
fictions lay in bringing them within those very regions of truth
and likelihood in which he thought they could not exist.
Hence the serpent Python of Chaucer,
[*Maunciples T.*, l. 5]

Sleeping against the sun upon a day,
when Apollo slew him.

. . . .

[p. 32] Fancy, however, is not incapable of sympathy with
Imagination. She is often found in her company; always,
in the case of the greatest poets; often in that of less, though
[p. 33] with them she is the greater favourite. Spenser has great
imagination and fancy too, but more of the latter; Milton
both also, the very greatest, but with imagination predominant; Chaucer, the strongest imagination of real life, beyond
any writers but Homer, Dante, and Shakspeare, and in comic
painting inferior to none; Pope has hardly any imagination,
but he has a great deal of fancy; Coleridge little fancy, but

imagination exquisite. Shakspeare alone, of all poets that ever lived, enjoyed the regard of both in equal perfection.

.   .   .   .

[p. 62]   Next to Homer and Shakspeare come such narrators as the less universal, but still intenser Dante ; Milton, with his dignified imagination ; the universal, profoundly simple Chaucer ; and luxuriant, remote Spenser—then the great second-rate dramatists, unless those who are better acquainted [p. 63] with Greek tragedy than I am, demand a place for them before Chaucer.

.   .   .   .

[p. 72]   [Spenser.] Superfluousness, though eschewed with a fine instinct by Chaucer in some of his latest works, where the narrative was fullest of action and character, abounded in his others.

.   .   .   .

[p. 87]   Upton, one of Spenser's commentators, in reference to the *trickling stream*, has quoted in his note . . . some fine lines from Chaucer, in which, describing the " dark valley " of Sleep, the poet says there was nothing whatsoever in the place, save that,

> A few wells
> Came running fro the clyffes adowne,
> That made a deadly sleeping sowne.
>
> [*B. of the Duchesse*, ll. 160–162.]

.   .   .   .

[p. 145]   [Shakespeare.] He is equal to the greatest poets . . . except in a certain primeval intensity, such as Dante's and Chaucer's.

[p. 151]   Most people would prefer Ariosto's and Chaucer's narrative poetry to his [Shakspeare's] ; the Griselda, for instance, and the story of Isabel,—to the Rape of Lucrece. The intense passion is enough. The misery is enough. We do not want even the divinest talk about what Nature herself tends to petrify into silence. *Curæ ingentes stupent.* Our divine poet had not quite outlived the times when it was thought proper [p. 152] for a writer to say everything that came into his head. He was a student of Chaucer : he beheld the living fame of Spenser ; and his fellow-dramatists did not help to restrain him.

[The references and passages are identical in the second edition, 1845.]

1844. Knight, Charles. *William Caxton, the First English Printer,*
pp. 21, 26, 32–34 [quotations illustrating city life in London],
38–40 [quotation from Caxton's preface to Canterbury Tales, edn.
2], 41–3, 46, 47, 51, 152, 157, 187–8 [Caxton "the devoted printer
of Chaucer"], 214, 216.

[*n.a.* **1844.**] **Landor**, Walter Savage. *Extract from a Letter to a Friend,*
[quoted in] R. H. Horne's New Spirit of the Age, 1844, 2 vols.,
vol. i, pp. 174–5.

> I found the 'Faery Queen' the most delightful book to fall
> asleep upon by the sea-side. Geoffrey Chaucer always kept me
> wide awake, and beat at a distance all other English poets but
> Shakspeare and Milton. In many places Keats approaches
> him.
>
> [*See* also above, 1837, Landor, *An Ode.*]

1844. Milnes, Richard Monckton (Lord Houghton). *From Chaucer,*
[in] *Poems of Many Years*, pp. 274–5.

> [Not in first edn., 1838. The poem is a modernisation of
> 'Truth,' and begins :]
>
> Fly from the world and dwell with Truthfulness ;
> Sufficient be thy wealth, albeit small . . .

1844. Nicolas, Sir Nicholas Harris. *The Wife of Chaucer,* [in] The
Gentleman's Magazine, Feb., 1844, new ser., vol. xxi, p. 160.

> [Nicolas points out that the reviewer in the Jan. no. (*see*
> below, Unknown), mistakenly states that Chaucer married
> Philippa Picard, whereas Nicolas clearly said that he married
> Philippa Roet.]

1844. Palgrave, formerly **Cohen**, Sir Francis. *Fifth Report of the
Deputy Keeper of the Public Records* (March 25, 1844), p. 21.

> For biographical purposes they [the Pell Records] abound
> in information which cannot be found elsewhere ; and by
> their means Sir Harris Nicolas has been enabled to complete
> the collection of all the information which the Records afford
> concerning the Life of Chaucer, and for the composition of
> that very small volume he was compelled to examine from
> 20 to 50 Rolls per diem.
>
> [For Nicolas's *Life of Chaucer, see* below, Works, 1845.]

1844. Patmore, Coventry Kersey Dighton. *Sonnet,* [in] *Poems*, p. 103.

> Rich Spenser, deep-toned Wordsworth, Chaucer green,
> Shakspere, and mighty Milton, sought their fame
> First in their own approval : we have seen
> How the world's followed.

1844. Thoms, William John. *The History of Reynard the Fox,* Percy Soc., Preface, p. i, Introd. p. lxxiii [Chaucer's *Nonnes Prestes Tale* a Reynard history], Notes, pp. 173, 176–8, 180, 182, 184–6, 190–1, 193.

1844. Unknown. *Review* of Sir N. Harris Nicolas's *Life of Chaucer,* prefixed to the Aldine edition of Chaucer's works, [*q. v.* below, 1845, in] The Athenæum, Feb. 10, 1844, pp. 125–7.

[This long review (seven columns, principally a summary of the main events in Chaucer's career) gives full credit to Nicolas for his discovery and use of documents relating to Chaucer's life, and contrasts it favourably with Godwin's speculative theories.]

1844. Unknown. *Review* of Sir N. Harris Nicolas's *Life of Chaucer,* [*q. v.* below, 1845, in] The Gentleman's Magazine, Jan. 1844, new ser., vol. xxi, pp. 3–19.

[This long and careful article gives a good appreciation of Chaucer's work, his 'spirited representations of life and native manners,' his 'rich and quaint humour.' It characterises correctly the 'Lives' by Tyrwhitt and Godwin, and then gives an abridgment of the facts as recorded by Nicolas, pointing out that the exile to Zealand is pure fiction, as there is now proof that Chaucer was in London, personally receiving his pension, from 1380 to 1388. Some space is then given to emphasising the influence of the active life Chaucer led, and of the various offices he filled, upon his poetical work.]

[p. 17]   His various occupations and calls into the world must have been to him the richest volume of information he could open, for he thus enlarged his views of society, and increased his knowledge of the characters of men. . . .

[p. 18]   In truth, every description by Chaucer has a fresh, out-of-door, open-air look with it; it has the light of the sky upon it; to him the market-place was a practical volume of moral philosophy; his embassy to Genoa and Florence, a rich and princely picture-book, filled with the costliest forms of nature and art; and his comptrollership of the customs, an excellent tome of never-ending casuistry.

1844. Wright, Thomas. *Anecdota Literaria* . . . ed. by Thomas Wright, pp. v, vi, 13–27.

[p. v]   I was led to insert a few inedited fabliaux, by the accidental discovery of one [the Miller and the two Clerks, from MS. Berne] which appears to be the immediate original of one of Chaucer's tales, which I have therefore chosen for the purpose of showing how much remains to be done to produce even a tolerable text of Chaucer's works.

[p. 13]   After the fabliau of Dame Siriz, we can scarcely point out a regular English fabliau till the time of Chaucer, who entered more than any other old English writer into the spirit of the French originals. Many of the stories in the Canterbury Tales are translations from French fabliaux. It is singular that a poet of so much talent as Chaucer should have written scarcely a single original poem. I owe to the friendly communication of M. Paulin Paris of the Bibliothèque Royale at Paris, the copy of the following stanzas addressed to Chaucer by his friend and contemporary, the French poet Eustache Deschamps. They . . . are remarkable as stating so strongly his real character of a " great translator." . . .

[Text of Deschamps' ballade ; *q. v.* below, App. B. [1386 ?].]

[pp. 14–   [Chaucer's stories probably not taken from Boccaccio, but
15]   from earlier French fabliaux. The text of the Miller of
[1. 23]   Trumpington, from MS. Berne, no. 354, follows. Tyrwhitt's text very corrupt : "there is perhaps not a single line in Tyrwhitt's edition of the Canterbury Tales which Chaucer could possibly have written . . . all grammar is set at defiance . . . the essay on the versification of Chaucer . . . is a mass of confusion." Chaucer's version of the Tale is
[p. 24]   given from MS. Harl., no. 7334, collated with MS. Lansdowne, no. 861 (a) and MS. Harl., no. 1758 (b). " In almost every one of these variations, Tyrwhitt is wrong."]

1845. Poetical Works of Chaucer, with memoir by Sir N. H. Nicholas [*q. v.* below], 6 vols., Aldine edition of British Poets, vols. xlvii–lii. [Reprinted, 1852, and re-edited, 1866, by R. Morris. The text is Tyrwhitt's for the Canterbury Tales, that of the Chiswick edn., 1822, for the other works.]

1845. Barrett, afterwards **Browning**, Elizabeth Barrett. *Letter*, [dated 12 May, 1845, in] The Letters of Elizabeth Barrett Browning to R. H. Horne, ed. S. R. Townshend Mayer, 1877, 2 vol., vol. ii, pp. 175–6.

[p. 176]   Chaucer wrote on precisely the same principles (eternal principles) [of metre] as the Greek poets did, I believe unalterably ; and you, who are a musician, ought [in *Chaucer Modernised*] to have sung it out loud in the ears of the public.

2063. Chaucer at the Court of Edward III. By FORD MADOX BROWN. B.1821. D.1893.

CHAUCER AT THE COURT OF EDWARD III
BY FORD MADOX BROWN, 1845-51
FROM THE REDUCED VERSION, BEGUN IN 1856 AND CONTINUED 1864-68
Now in the Tate Gallery

1845. Barrett, afterwards **Browning,** Elizabeth Barrett. *Letters to Robert Browning,* [dated] 1845, [printed in] The Letters of Robert Browning and Elizabeth Barrett Barrett, 1899, vol. i, pp. 160, 267, 336–7.

[p. 160]   [13 Aug. 1845.] Does not the old word King Lud's men stomped withal, claim identity with our 'stamping'? The *a* and *o* used to 'change about,' you know, in the old English writers—see Chaucer for it.

[p. 267]   [6 Nov. 1845.] I have considered about Mr. Kenyon and it seems best, in the event of a question or of a remark equivalent to a question, to confess to the visits 'generally once a week' . . because he may hear, one, two, three different ways, . . not to say the other reasons and Chaucer's charge against 'doubleness.' I fear . . I fear that he (not Chaucer) will wonder a little—and he has looked at me with scanning spectacles already and talked of its being a mystery to him how you made your way here. . .

[pp. 336, 337]   [19 Dec. 1845.] And speaking of verse —somebody gave me a few days ago that Mr. Lowell's book you once mentioned to me. [. . .] But these American books should not be reprinted here—one asks, what and where is the class to which they address themselves? [. . .] here, with us, whoever *wanted* Chaucer, or Chapman, or Ford, got him long ago—what else have Lamb, and Coleridge, and Hazlitt, and Hunt and so on to the end of their generations . . what else been doing this many a year?

[The stops, except those in square brackets, are in the original text.]

1845—51. Brown, Ford Madox. *Chaucer at the Court of Edward III.*

[A painting on a large scale, now in the Municipal Gallery, Sydney. It was only finished in time for exhibition at the Academy in 1851, but Brown conceived and began work for it in the autumn of 1845, taking the first suggestion from a passing reference in Sir James Mackintosh's *History of England*. He at once read the life (Godwin's) and the works of Chaucer, apparently for the first time. Chaucer (whose figure was painted from D. G. Rossetti) stands on a daïs and reads at a lectern to the Court assembled below him the lines from the *Tale of the Man of Lawe,* ll. 834–40 :—

Hire litel child lay weping on hire arm . . .
And unto the heven hire eyen up she cast.

See Brown's Diary in *Praeraphaelite Diaries and Letters,* ed. Wm. Rossetti, 1900, *passim,* his own Exhibition Catalogue, 1865, and F. M. Hueffer's *Ford Madox Brown,* 1896, where the picture is reproduced, to face p. 71. The Chaucer is said by W. M. Rossetti (*Dante Gabriel Rossetti; his Family Letters,* 1895, 2 vols, vol. i, p. 170) to be 'a very fair portrait of Rossetti,' in whom, as well as in Morris and R. W. Dixon (*q.v.* below, both 1855), their friends found a resemblance to the Occleve portrait.]

1845. Hunt, James Henry Leigh. *Death and the Ruffians,* [a modernization of the *Pardoneres Tale,* in] The New Monthly Magazine, Aug. 1845, vol. lxxiv, p. 509. [Reprinted, revised, and with a preface in place of the brief note which appeared in 1845, in *Stories in Verse,* 1855, *q.v.*] (Poetical Works, ed. S. A. Lee, Boston, 1866, 2 vols., vol. i, pp. 218–26.)

[The version begins :]

> In Flanders once there liv'd a company
> Of foolish youth, a lawless set of three,
> That, haunting every place of foul repute,
> And giddy with the din of harp and lute,
> Went dancing, and sat dicing, day and night,
> And eat and drank beyond their nature's might,
> And thus upon the devil's own altar laid
> The bodies and the souls that God had made. . .

1845. [**Leigh,** Percival.] *The Lament of the Statues,* [in] Punch, 1845, p. 185.

[Protests of the poets against the proposal in the Report of the Committee of the Royal Commission to erect statues of them in the new Houses of Parliament. (Fourth Report of the Commission, 1845, p. **9.**)

Mr. M. H. Spielmann (*The Portraits of Geoffrey Chaucer,* Chaucer Soc., 1900, p. 17) says that this is by P. Leigh.

Chaucer speaks first :]

> Good sirs, I marvel what we herè maken,
> Gretè folk, certès, be sometimes mistaken,
> We standen in this stound by much errour,
> Ne poet was in Parlement before . . .

[and four more lines ; Spenser, Shakespeare, Milton, Dryden and Pope follow, in more recognizable styles.]

1845. Longfellow, Henry Wadsworth. *The Poets and Poetry of Europe,* Philadelphia, pp. 423–4 [*Rom. Rose,* ll. 21–134], 439 [*La Belle Dame sans Merci,* from Alain Chartier, the translation (really by Sir Richard Ros) given as Chaucer's], 508 [Chaucer's mention of Petrarch, *Clerkes Prol.,* ll. 31–3].

1845. Lowell, James Russell. *Conversations on Some of the Old Poets,* Cambridge, Mass., First Conversation, "Chaucer," pp. 1–121 ; Second Conversation, "The Old Dramatists," pp. 126, 169–70. [Not in the Riverside Edn. of Lowell's works. The quotations are all more or less modernized by Lowell himself ; *see* p. 86.]

[pp. 15 and 16] PHILIP: . . . You must put no faith at all in any idea you may have got of Chaucer from Dryden or Pope. Dryden appreciated his original better than Pope; but neither of them had a particle of his humor, nor of the simplicity of his pathos. . . . Pope was not a man to understand the quiet tenderness of Chaucer, where you almost seem to hear the hot tears falling, and the simple, choking words sobbed out. I know no author so tender as he, not even Shakspeare.

[A comparison of the *Knightes Tale*, ll. 1903–1924, with Dryden's version follows; and while Dryden's version is described as "the sentiment of Giles Scroggins, and the verse of Blackmore," Chaucer's is considered "perfect." After some further discussion Philip continues:]

[p. 21] The recording angel had but little trouble in footing Chaucer's account. The uncleanness of his age has left a smooch here and there upon his poems; but it is only in the margin, and may be torn off without injury to the text. His love of beauty was too sincere not to have made him truly pious. . . .

[p. 22] I love to call him *old* Chaucer. The farther I can throw him back into the past, the dearer he grows; so sweet is it to mark how his plainness and sincerity outlive all changes of

[p. 24] the outward world. . . . His simplicity often reminds me of Homer; but, except in the single quality of *invention*, I prefer him to the Ionian. Yet we must remember that he shares this deficiency with Shakspeare, who scarcely ever scrupled to run in debt for his plots. . . .

[p. 25] There is in him the exuberant freshness and greenness of spring. Everything he touches leaps into full blossom. His gladness and humor and pathos are irrepressible as a

[p. 26] fountain. . . . There is no nebulosity of sentiment about him, no insipid vagueness in his sympathies. His chief merit, the chief one in all art, is sincerity.

[A discussion, with quotations from the *Nonne Prestes Tale*, follows, pp. 29–33, 40–47. Chaucer and Crabbe are compared, p. 35; and the description of the Shipman in the *Prologue* is read. Elizabeth Barrett's lines on Chaucer (*q.v.* above, 1844) cited, p. 38. Chaucer's piety is discussed, p. 58, and the possibility, from the *Clerkes Tale*, of his having been in Italy and met Petrarch, pp. 63–64. The *Clerkes Tale* is next discussed, pp. 65–7. Some of the other references are: *Troilus*, pp. 73, 93, 112; Chaucer's love of nature, p. 77; *Legend of Good Women*, pp, 84, 99; Cowden Clarke's

Riches of Chaucer, p. 86 ; *Knightes Tale*, pp. 88, 100 ; *Book
of the Duchesse*, p. 96 ; Chaucer's early love, p. 98 ; *Man of
Law's Tale*, p. 107 ; *Pardoneres Tale*, p. 108 ; Wordsworth's
modernization of *Troilus*, pp. 86–112.

Second Conversation : p. 126. Chaucer, when in prison,
wrote a treatise on the astrolabe for his son ; pp. 169–70.
Squieres Tale and *Maunciples Tale*, quotations.]

1845. Nicolas, Sir Nicholas Harris. *Memoir of Chaucer* [prefixed to
the Aldine edition of the Works, *q.v.* above], pp. 9–107, Notes,
pp. 119–144.

[This very carefully written memoir is the first ' Life ' of
Chaucer to be based entirely on documentary evidence, and it
is consequently a valuable addition to Chaucer biography.
Nicolas prints many more documents than Godwin had done.
He disposes of the story (built up on the spurious *Testament
of Love*) of Chaucer's flight and exile in 1384, the return to
England in 1386, and imprisonment in the Tower till 1389,
by showing that Chaucer must have been in London from
1380 to May 1388, for during that period he regularly received his pension at the Exchequer with his own hands
(Issue Rolls from Easter, 3 Ric. II to Easter, 11 Ric. II).
Also at the very time when he was supposed to have been
a prisoner, he was sitting in Parliament as a knight of the
shire of Kent. Nicolas, however, does not doubt the authenticity of the *Testament of Love*, but regards it as an allegorical
composition.

This ' Life ' must have been published in 1843, probably
in a limited edition, before it was issued with the Aldine
Poets ; for it is reviewed in the *Athenæum*, Feb. 10, 1844
(as ' about to be published in the Aldine edition '), in the
Monthly Review, March, 1844, and the *Gentleman's Magazine*,
Jan. 1844 ; for the first and last *see* above.]

1845. North, Christopher [*ps.*, i. e. John Wilson]. *Specimens of the
British Critics*, [in] Blackwood's Edinburgh Magazine, April 1845,
vol. lvii, pp. 503, 508 ; May, pp. 617–46 ; June, pp. 771–93 ; July,
vol. lviii, pp. 114–28. [Published in volume form in 1846 ; the
references are : pp. 63–4, 66, 77, 95, 111, 120, 157–266.]

[p. 617]   Nothing is gained by attempting to deny or to disguise a
known and plain fact, simply because it happens to be a dis-
tasteful one—Time has estranged us from Chaucer. Dryden
and Pope we read with easy, unearned pleasure. Their speech,
their manner of mind, and their facile verse, are of our age,
almost of our own day. The two excellent, graceful, and
masterly poets belong, both of them, to THIS NEW WORLD.
Go back a little, step over an imperceptible line, to the con-

temporary of Dryden, Milton, and you seem to have overleaped some great chronological boundary; you have transported yourself into THAT OLD WORLD . . .

We call Chaucer the Father of our Poetry, or its Morning Star. The poetical memory of the country stretches up to him, and not beyond. The commanding impression which he has made upon the minds of his people dates from his own day. The old poets of England and Scotland constantly and unanimously acknowledge him for their master. Greatest names, Dunbar, Douglas, Spenser, Milton, carry on the tradition of his renown and his reign.

In part he belongs to, and in part he lifts himself out of, his age. The vernacular poetry of reviving Europe took a strong stamp from one principal feature in the manners of the times. The wonderful political institution of Chivalry—turned into a romance in the minds of those in whose persons the thing itself subsisted—raised up a fanciful adoration of women [p. 618] into a law of courtly life; or, at the least, of courtly verse, to which there was nothing answerable in the annals of the old world. . . .

This exaggeration of an immense natural power, Love—making, one might almost say, man's worship of woman the great religion of the universe, and which was the "amabilis insania" of the new poetry—long exercised an unlimited monarchy in the poetical mind of the reasonable Chaucer. See the longest and most desperate of his Translations—which Tyrwhitt supposes him to have completed, though we have [p. 619] only two fragments—seven thousand verses in place of twenty-two thousand—the "ROMAUNT OF THE ROSE" . . .

1845. Saunders, John. *Cabinet Pictures of English Life: Chaucer.* [One of "Knight's Weekly Volumes." Revised and enlarged from the Penny Magazine and Knight's *London, q.v.* above, both 1841. This and the same author's *Canterbury Tales from Chaucer (q.v.* below) were reprinted together, revised, in 1889; this volume forms the first half of the reprint.]

[The contents of the volume are:
1. Introduction, with a general discussion of Chaucerian matters, language, versification, and Dryden's criticism.
2. Section I. "A Visit to the Tabard," with notes on the Tabard from without and within, and its locality, and a general description of the pilgrims, with quotations (revised, not from the *Penny Magazine,* but from Knight's *London,* 1841, *q.v.* above).

3. Section II. " Chivalry."—The Knight, Squire and Yeoman.
4. Section III. " Religion,"—The Monk, Friar, Prioress, Sumpnour, Pardoner, and Parson.
5. Section IV. "Domestic Life : Professional Men." The Sergeant at law, Doctor of Physic, Alchemist, Clerk of Oxenford.
6. Section V. " Domestic Life—Agriculture " : The Franklin, Miller, Reeve and Ploughman.
7. Section VI. "Domestic Life : Trade and Commerce." The Merchant, Shipman, Haberdasher, etc., Prentice, Cook, and Wife of Bath.

The book illustrates social and political conditions in Chaucer's times by means of general discussion and the examination of his characters. Each chapter has a woodcut.]

1845. [Saunders, John.] *Chaucer's Canterbury Tales,* [in] The Penny Magazine, vol. xiv, [*Knightes Tale*] pp. 65–7, 81–3, 110–12, 118–20 ; [*Man of Law's Tale*] 137–9, 146–8 ; [*Wife of Bath's Tale*] 185–6, 235–6 ; [*Freres Tale*] 241–2, 258–9 ; [*Clerkes Tale*] 300–2, 310–11, 323–4 ; [*Squieres Tale*] 361–2, 406–7 : [*Frankeleyns Tale*] 437–8, 455–6 ; [*Pardoneres Tale*] 461–2 ; [*Nonne Prestes Tale*] 481–3 ; *Chanouns Yemannes Tale*] 497–8. [Epitomes interspersed with extracts from the Tales. For the revised edn. in 2 vols., *see* immediately below.]

1845-7. Saunders, John. *Canterbury Tales from Chaucer,* 2 vols. Vol. i is one of " Knight's Weekly Volumes " ; vol. ii, 1847, was published by C. Cox. The series which appeared in the *Penny Magazine,* 1845 (*q.v.* immediately above), only contains a few sentences of the preface, and the extracts and prose summaries differ throughout. Of the contents of vol. ii, 1847, only the 1st–4th Tales had appeared in the *Penny Magazine.* For the revised edn. of 1889, *see* above, the same author's *Cabinet Pictures of English Life : Chaucer,* 1845.]

[vol. i,   Three different modes have been adopted by the lovers of
p. 5]   Chaucer in their attempts to popularize his works.

First, they have modernized his poetry ; that is to say, re-written it, as poetry. Now, whenever a man shall arise possessing *exactly* the same powers, views, tastes, and individual characteristics as the great father of our literature, and will undertake to give us a new version of the Canterbury Tales, we have no doubt the task may be satisfactorily accomplished, and not till then. . . .

[p. 6]   Secondly, the *poetical* has been transformed into a *prose* narration ; and thus the story, at least, has been freed from the difficulties and hindrances caused by antiquated words or pronunciations ; but then it has necessarily been relieved at the same time from all the subtler elements of the poetry. . . .

Thirdly, Chaucer's poetry has been presented in its own proper form, with a modernized spelling, and an accented pronunciation. Eventually, perhaps, this will be the method permanently adopted for all popular editions of the poet; but, at present, such books attract neither the student nor the general reader: too lax for the one, they still remain— apparently—too irksome for the other.

In the following pages we have endeavoured to combine the peculiar advantages offered by the two methods last named, and to get rid of their drawbacks. We have proposed to ourselves to make the whole course of the *story* clear by resolving inconvenient or difficult passages of the poetry into prose; but, at the same time, to allow the reader to be

[p. 7] constantly refreshing himself from the " well of English *undefiled*," by leaving all the remainder, including the finest portions of the poetry, in its own nervous and beautiful language. . .

[p. 11] [Specimen of the rendering of the *Knightes Tale :*]

Once, as old stories tell, there was a duke named Theseus, the lord and governor of Athens, and who, in his time, was such a conqueror, that there was not a greater under the sun. He had won many a rich country. With his wisdom and his chivalry, he conquered all the realm of the Amazons that was formerly called Scythia,—

And wedded the freshe queen Hypolita,

and brought her, and also her young sister Emily, home with him to his own country, with much glory and great solemnity.

. . . .

[p. 15] When that this worthy duke, this Theseus, hath slain Creon and won Thebes,

Still in the field he took all night his rest.

[p. 16] And he did as he pleased with all the country. After the battle and discomfiture, the pillers did their business; they ransacked the heap of dead bodies, in order to strip them of their armour and garments. And it so befell that they found in the heap, pierced through with many a bloody grievous wound, two young knights, lying by each other, in the same kind of armour, which was full richly wrought. Of these two, one was named Arcite, the other Palamon,

Not fully quick nor fully dead they were ;
But by their coat armóur, and by their gear,

the heralds knew them well, as those who were of the royal blood of Thebes, and born of two sisters. [&c., &c.]

[Then follow :

The Man of Law's Tale,	The Freres Tale,
The Wife of Bath's Tale,	The Clerkes Tale,

with " Remarks " on each at the end.

Vol. II :

The Squieres Tale,	The Second Nonnes Tale,
The Frankeleyns Tale,	The Chanouns Yemannes
The Pardoners Tale	Tale,
The Prioresses Tale,	The Maunciples Tale,
The Nonne Prestes Tale,	The Phisiciens Tale ;

and selections from :

The Milleres Tale,	The Marchantes Tale,
The Reves Tale,	The Shipmannes Tale.

Concluding remarks on Chaucer's essential morality, with special reference to the *Frankeleyns Tale*, and on his achievement as restorer of learning and founder of our language and literature.]

Each Tale is also followed by " Remarks," and is illustrated by the woodcut which appeared in *The Penny Magazine, q.v.* above, 1845, Saunders.]

1845. [**Saunders**, John.] *Chaucer*, [in] The Cabinet Portrait Gallery of British Worthies, 1845–7, 12 vols., vol. i, pp. 120–144.

[A biographical sketch, without criticism of Chaucer's poetry ; based in the main on the private first issue of Sir H. Nicolas's Life, described as not yet published. *The Court of Love*, the *Complaint of the Black Knight* and, except so far as Nicolas had disproved the story of exile and imprisonment, the *Testament of Love*, are accepted. Reviewed as the work of Saunders, with his *Chaucer* and *Canterbury Tales*, in the *Athenæum*, 1847, *q.v.* below, Unknown.]

[*c.* **1845.**] **Skeat**, Walter William. *See* below, App. A, 1823, Markham.

[**1845.**] **Unknown.** *Griselda*, [in] Ballads and Metrical Tales, selected from Percy, Ritson, etc., pp. 27–37.

[An abridgement, modernised, of the *Clerkes Tale*.]

1845. Unknown. *Glimpses of the Pageant of Literature*, no. 1, [in] Fraser's Magazine, Jan. 1845, vol. xxxi, pp. 27, 29–30.

[pp. 29-30] This is precisely the simple truthfulness of contemporary manners portrayed by our own Chaucer . . . Homer's hero wiping the moisture from his face, and Chaucer's nun letting no particle of food drop into her lap, belong to similar ages of imagination.

1845. Wright, Thomas. *Meeting of the British Archaeological Association at Canterbury,* [in 1844, in] *The Archaeological Album,* 1845, pp. 19–23.

[Account of the Chequer Inn, where the Pilgrims are supposed to have lodged, with quotations from the "supplement" to the *Canterbury Tales* printed by Urry (i. e. the *Tale of Beryn*).]

1846. Chaucer's Romaunt of the Rose, Troilus and Creseide, and the Minor Poems, with the life of the poet, by Sir N. H. Nicolas. Pickering, 3 vols.

[A reprint of vols. iv–vi of Pickering's 1845 Aldine edn., with Nicolas's "Life" only.]

1846. Brewer, Ebenezer Cobham. *Poetical Chronology of Inventions, Discoveries, Battles, and of Eminent Men,* pp. 51–2.

[p. 51]   In Richard's reign SIDE-SADDLES first, came into English use,
And GOWER with merry CHAUCER, too, their rhapsodies produce . . .

[p. 52]   Cannons and Gunpowder disclose their most destructive power ;

Dantè & Petrarch sing their lays with Chaucer & John Gower.

1846. Browning, Robert. *Letter to Alfred Domett,* [dated] New Cross, Hatcham, March 19, 1846, [in] *Robert Browning and Alfred Domett,* ed. F. G. Kenyon, 1906, pp. 124–5.

You received, of course, I trust, the last number [*Dramatic Romances*] with a letter. I don't think that at that time Landor's all too generous lines about it had appeared. . . . The first thing to notice is the kindness, and after, the blindness of such praise; but these acknowledged duly, surely one may remark on the happy epithet "hale" as applied to Chaucer. . . .

[For Landor's poem *see* below, 1846.]

1846. Browning, Robert. *Letters,* [in] *The Letters of Robert Browning and Elizabeth Barrett Barrett,* 1899, vol. i, pp. 393, 429.

[p. 393]   [12 Jan. 1846.] That Mr. Powell . . . When I took pity on him once on a time and helped his verses into a sort of grammar and sense, I did not think he was a *buyer* of other men's verses, to be printed as his own; thus he *bought* two modernisations of Chaucer—'Ugolino' and another story from Leigh Hunt—and one 'Sir Thopas' from Horne, and printed them as his own, as I learned only last week.

[p. 429]   [23 Jan. 1846.]   But when you find Chaucer's graver at his work of 'graving smale seles' by the sun's light, you know that the sun's self could not have been *created* on that day— do you 'understand' that, Ba?

['' Ba '' was Elizabeth Barrett's pet-name.   For Powell's modernizations *see* above, 1841.]

1846. Ellis, Sir Henry.   *Original Letters, Third Series*, vol. i, p. xi, *n.*

[On the cultivation of French in the monasteries: the Prioress's French.]

1846. Fairholt, Frederick William.   *Costume in England:* a History of Dress to the end of the Eighteenth Century, pp. 140–1, 144–6, 167–8, 177, 215, 232, 407–618.   (Third edition, 2 vols., 1885, enlarged and thoroughly revised by the Hon. H. A. Dillon, vol. i., pp. 128–29, 132–33, 154–55, 163, 200–220; vol. ii., Glossary.)

[p. 140]   Chaucer,—the Shakspeare of the middle ages and certainly the most original and extraordinary writer that England up to that period had produced . . . has, in his immortal *Canterbury Tales*, given us the best information connected with the costume of the different grades in English society during this reign.

[p. 141–6]   [Account of costumes described in the *Prologue, Milleres Tale, Persones Tale*, and *Plowmans Tale* (treated as Chaucer's), the last with many quotations.]

[pp. 167 –8]   [Chaucer's description of knightly costume, with quotations from *Sir Thopas*.]

[pp. 407 –618]   [A Glossary of terms used in the description of costume from the early times, contains many allusions to and quotations from Chaucer.]

[The third edition in 2 vols, 1885, by H. A. Dillon, shows no material alteration in the above passages, except that the quotations are in some cases freed from modernization and that here and there Fairholt's text is slightly cut down.]

1846. Hunt, James Henry Leigh.   *Stories from the Italian Poets: with Lives of the Writers*, 2 vols., vol. i, pp. 5, 55, 407n.; vol. ii, pp. 21, 72, 88, 170.

[vol. 1, p. 407 n.]   Chaucer has told the greater part of this story [Ugolino] beautifully in his " Canterbury Tales; " but he had not the heart to finish it.   He refers for the conclusion to his original hight " Dant," the " grete poete of Itaille; " adding, that Dante will not fail his readers a single word—that is to say, not an atom of the cruelty.

Our great gentle-hearted countryman, who tells Fortune
that it was

> " great cruelte
> Such birdès for to put in such a cage,"

adds a touch of pathos in the behaviour of one of the children,
which Dante does not seem to have thought of:

> " There day by day this child began to cry,
>   Till in his father's barme (lap) adown he lay;
>   And said, ' Farewell, father, I muste die,'
>   And *kissed his father*, and died the same day."

1846. Hunt, James Henry Leigh. *Wit and Humour, Selected from
the English Poets.* With an Illustrative Essay, and Critical Comments, pp. 12, 18–19, 63, 73–121.

[p. 12.] Humour . . . deals in incongruities of character and
circumstance, . . . Such is the melting together . . . of
the professional and the individual, or the accidental and the
permanent, in the Canterbury Pilgrims . . .

[pp. 18, 19] [The Cock's address to the Hen:

> For also siker as *in principio* . . .

etc. (*Nonne Prestes Tale*), quoted as an example of irony.]

[p. 63] [Chaucer famous for the humours of nations and classes.]

[p. 74] I wish I could have given more than one comic story out
cf Chaucer; but the change of manners renders it difficult at
any time, and impossible in a book like the present.

.   .   .   .

[p. 75] When Chaucer is free from this taint of his age [*i. e.*
coarseness], his humour is of a description the most thoroughly
delightful; for it is at once entertaining, profound, and good-
natured. If this last quality be thought a drawback by some,
as wanting the relish of personality, they may supply even
that (as some have supplied it), by supposing that he drew
his characters from individuals, and that the individuals were
very uncomfortable accordingly. I confess I see no ground
for the supposition beyond what the nature of the case
demands. Classes must of course be drawn, more or less,
from the individuals composing them; but the unprofessional
particulars added by Chaucer to his characters (such as the
Merchant's uneasy marriage, and the Franklin's prodigal son)
are only such as render the portraits more true, by including

them in the general category of human kind. The gangrene which the Cook had on his shin, and which has been considered as a remarkable instance of the gratuitous, is, on the contrary (besides its masterly intimation of the perils of luxury in general), painfully in character with a man accustomed to breathe an unhealthy atmosphere, and to be encouraging bad humours with tasting sauces and syrups. Besides, the Cook turns out to be a drunkard.

[p. 76]   Chaucer's comic genius is so perfect, that it may be said to include prophetic intimations of all that followed it . . . One of its characteristics is a certain tranquil detection of particulars, expressive of generals; as in the instance just mentioned of the secret infirmity of the Cook. Thus the Prioress speaks French; but it is "after the school of Stratford at Bow." Her education was altogether more showy than substantial. The Lawyer was the busiest man in the world, and yet he "seemed busier than he was." He made something out of nothing, even in appearances.

Another characteristic is his fondness for seeing the spiritual in the material; the mind in the man's aspect. He is as studious of physiognomy as Lavater, and far truer. Observe, too, the poetry that accompanies it,—the imaginative sympathy in the matter of fact. His Yeoman, who is a forester, has a head "like a nut." His Miller is as brisk and healthy as the air of the hill on which he lives, and as hardy and as coarse-grained as his conscience. We know, as well as if we had ridden with them, his oily-faced Monk; his lisping Friar (who was to make confession easy to the ladies); his carbuncled [p. 77] Summoner or Church-Bailiff, the grossest form of ecclesiastical sensuality; and his irritable money-getting Reve or Steward, with his cropped head and calf-less legs, who shaves his beard as closely as he reckons with his master's tenants.

The third great quality of Chaucer's humour is its fair play;—the truth and humanity which induces him to see justice done to good and bad, to the circumstances which make men what they are, and the mixture of right and wrong, of wisdom and of folly, which they consequently exhibit. His worst characters have some little saving grace of good-nature, or at least of joviality and candour. Even the Pardoner, however impudently, acknowledges himself to be a "vicious man." His best people, with one exception, betray some infirmity. The good Clerk of Oxford, for all his simplicity

and singleness of heart, has not escaped the pedantry and
pretension of the college. The Good Parson seems without
a blemish, even in his wisdom; yet when it comes to his turn
to relate a story, he announces it as a "little" tale, and then
tells the longest and most prosing in the book,—a whole
sermonizing volume. . . .

[p. 78]   The only character in Chaucer which seems faultless,
is that of the Knight; and he is a man who has been all over
the world, and bought experience with hard blows. The poet
does not spare his own person. He describes himself as a fat,
heavy man, with an "elvish" (wildish?) countenance, shy,
and always "staring on the ground. . . ."

This self-knowledge is a part of Chaucer's greatness;
and these modest proofs of it distinguish him from every
other poet in the language. Shakespeare may have had as
much, or more. It is difficult to suppose otherwise. . . .
His sonnets are not without intimations of personal and other
defects; but they contain no such candid talking as Chaucer.

[p. 79]   The father of English poetry was essentially a modest man.
He sits quietly in a corner, looking down for the most part
and meditating; at other times eyeing everything that passes,
and sympathising with everything; chuckling heartily at a
jest, feeling his eyes fill with tears at sorrow, reverencing
virtue, and not out of charity with vice. When he ventures
to tell a story himself, it is as much under correction of the
Host as the humblest man in the company; and it is no
sooner objected to, than he drops it for one of a different
description.

[Here follow selections, each with a modernized version
printed below, and notes: Characters of Pilgrims (Prologue).
The Friar's Tale. The Pardoner's way of Preaching. The
Merchant's Opinion of Wives. Gallantry of Translation (Cock
and the Fox). The Disappearance of the Fairies.]

1846. Landor, Walter Savage. *Imaginary Conversations,* [in] Works,
1846, vol. i, pp. 337, 402–8; vol. ii, pp. 164–7, 229. (Imaginary
Conversations, ed. C. G. Crump, 1891, 6 vols., vol. iii, pp. 159,
352, 389, 394; vol. iv, pp. 66–108, 239, 274–5, 283; vol. vi,
p. 45 n.)

[There was no Chaucer allusion in the 1st edn., 1824, and only a very few insig-
nificant ones in the 2nd, 1826; for the 1st edn. of *Chaucer, Boccaccio, Petrarca, see*
above, 1827.]

[vol. vi,   LANDOR, ENGLISH VISITER [*sic*], AND FLORENTINE VISITER.
p. 45 n.]   *Landor.* . . . Since the time of Chaucer there have only

been two poets who at all resemble him; and these two are widely dissimilar one from the other, Burns and Keats. The accuracy and truth with which Chaucer has described the manners of common life, with the fore-ground and back-ground, are also to be found in Burns, who delights in broader strokes of external nature, but equally appropriate. He has parts of genius which Chaucer has not in the same degree; the animated and pathetic. Keats, in his *Endymion*, is richer in imagery than either.

[This passage is not in the 1st edn. of 1829.]

[vol. iv, pp. 66-103] [Chaucer, Boccaccio, and Petrarca, slightly enlarged from the first edition of 1829.]

SOUTHEY AND LANDOR.

[p. 274] *Landor.* . . . Keats is the most imaginative of our poets after Chaucer, Spenser, Shakspeare, and Milton.

Southey. I am glad you admit my favourite, Spenser.

Landor. He is my favourite too, if you admit the expression without the signification of precedency. I do not think him equal to Chaucer even in imagination, and he appears to me very inferior to him in all other points, excepting harmony. Here the miscarriage is in Chaucer's age, not in Chaucer, many of whose verses are highly beautiful, but never (as in Spenser) one whole period. I love the geniality of his temperature : no straining, no effort, no storm, no fury. His vivid thoughts burst their way to us through the coarsest integuments of language. . . . Chaucer first united the two glorious realms of Italy and England. Shakspeare came after, and subjected the whole universe to his dominion. But he mounted the highest steps of his throne under those [p. 275] bland skies which had warmed the congenial breasts of Chaucer and Boccaccio. [Chaucer's and Shakespeare's powers of imagination greater than Spenser's.]

[Some brief remarks follow on Dryden's criticism of Chaucer's metre and his comparison of Chaucer with Boccaccio.]

[p 282 *Southey* [to Landor] . . . It is hard upon Milton, and harder still upon inferior poets, that every expression of his used by a predecessor should be noted as borrowed or stolen. Here in v. 822,

> Will bathe the drooping spirits in delight

is traced to several, and might be traced to more. Chaucer, in whose songs it is more beautiful than elsewhere, writes,

His harte bathed in a bath of blisse.

Probably he took the idea from the bath of knights. You could never have seen Chaucer nor the rest when you wrote those verses at Rugby on Godiva. . . .

1846. Landor, Walter Savage. *To Robert Browning,* [in] Works, 1846, vol. ii, p. 673. (Poems, ed. C. G. Crump, 2 vols., 1892, vol. ii, pp. 194–5.)

> There is delight in singing, tho' none hear
> Beside the singer: and there is delight
> In praising, tho' the praiser sit alone
> And see the prais'd far off him, far above.
> Shakspeare is not our poet, but the world's,
> Therefore on him no speech ! and brief for thee,
> Browning ! Since Chaucer was alive and hale,
> No man hath walkt along our roads with step
> So active, so inquiring eye, or tongue
> So varied in discourse. But warmer climes
> Give brighter plumage, stronger wing : the breeze
> Of Alpine highths [*sic*] thou playest with, borne on
> Beyond Sorrento and Amalfi, where
> The Siren waits thee, singing song for song.

[For Browning's comment on this *see* above, 1846.]

1846. Ruskin, John. *Modern Painters,* vol. ii, 1846, part iii, sec. ii, ch. ii, § 13, p. 149. (Works, ed. E. T. Cook and A. Wedderburn, 1903–12, 39 vols., vol. iv, p. 240.)

[Passing reference in a simile to] The grain upon the tongue of Chaucer's sainted child.

[For the further references in *Modern Painters, see* below, 1854–6.]

1846. Unknown. *Chaucer—His Age and Writings,* [in] The British Quarterly Review, Feb.–May, vol. iii, pp. 105–33.

[In Chaucer's time poetry was conceived to be the metrical dissemination of information. Hence his prolixity and pedantry. Great scale and elaborate detail in his poetry.]

[p. 132] In the age of Chaucer, writers had . . . to drive the plough of their ideas through the stubborn soil of an unformed language. And therefore it is that the word *naïveté* becomes

[p. 133] less applicable to the productions of English writers after the age of Shakespeare; while it continues applicable to those of Scottish writers to a later period.

1847-51. The Canterbury Tales of Geoffrey Chaucer, a new text, 3 vols., printed for the Percy Society, ed. T. Wright, vols. **xxiv–xxvi**.

[Vol. i. Introduction, pp. v–xlii. Text, pp. 1–295 (with the Cokes Tale of Gamelyn).
Vol. ii. Text, pp. 1–386.
Vol. iii. Text, pp. 1–318, with the " Merchauntes Second Tale" (the *Tale of Beryn*).

The edition is annotated at the bottom of the pages. Wright's introduction consists of a sketch of Chaucer's life, based on Sir N. H. Nicolas's "Life"; an examination of the Tales, especially of their unfinished state and arrangement; an account of the editions; and a statement of the "Plan of the present Edition," beginning with some remarks on Chaucerian English, and stating the editor's reasons for the selection of Harleian MS. 7334 as the basis of the text. Reprinted in the Universal Library, 1853, *q. v.* below.]

1847. Deshler, C. D. *Selections from the Poetical Works of Geoffrey Chaucer*. With a concise life of that Poet . . . by C. D. Deshler, London. [Wiley and Putnam's Library of American Books.]

[The volume contains an Introduction, notes on pronunciation, and five chapters of biography and criticism (vitiated through the usual acceptance of the *Court of Love, Testament of Love,* etc.), discussing the condition of the language and Chaucer's effect on it, characteristics of his poetry, estimate of women, omission to celebrate the great personages of his age, &c. The selections which follow are divided into five categories : I. Rural Descriptions ; II. Paintings—Female Characters ; III. Paintings—Masculine Characters ; IV. Narrative Poetry ; V. Miscellaneous. Among these are extracts from the non-Chaucerian *Complaint of the Black Knight, Cuckoo and Nightingale,* &c. An Appendix gives some information on and extracts from Gower, Lydgate, Gavin Douglas, *Story of Cockaygne,* and Herrick.]

1847. Halliwell (afterwards **Halliwell-Phillips**), James Orchard. *A Dictionary of Archaic and Provincial Words,* obsolete phrases, proverbs and ancient customs, from the fourteenth century.

[Contains many words from Chaucer.]

1847. Hare, Julius Charles and Augustus William. *Guesses at Truth, by two Brothers. First Series,* pp. 60, 151; 151–2 [use of *wight* and *folk* in Chaucer]; 171 [use of *you* in Chaucer]; 307 [Chaucer's language] ; 350 [union of grave and light in Chaucer], 371.

[1847-8.] Knight, Charles. *Half Hours with the Best Authors*, 4 vols., vol. i, p. 235 [Flowers]; vol. ii, p. 34 [Griselda]; vol. iii, p. 180 [Chaucer gave our literature a more popular and national character]; pp. 318–23 [Godwin]; vol. iv, pp. 514–17 [" Dryden's Good Parson"].

[vol. i, p. 235]   The exquisite simplicity of our first great poet's account of his love for the daisy may well follow Shakspere's spring-garland. Rarely could he move from his books; no game could attract him; but when the flowers begin to spring,

" Farewell my book and my devotion."

[*L. G. W., Prol.* l. 39.]

Above all the flowers in the mead he loves most

" . . . these flowres white and red . . . [to]
Of it, to doen it all réverence."

[*Ib.,* ll. 42–52.]

1847. Thackeray, William Makepeace ['Titmarsh, Michael Angelo'.] *A Grumble about the Christmas Books*, [in] Fraser's Magazine, Jan. 1847, vol. xxxv, p. 125.

Do you remember the dainty description of the Prioress in Chaucer? It has lately been quoted in Leigh Hunt's charming volume of *Wit and Humour*, and concludes with the account of a certain talisman this delicate creature wore :—

" About hire arm a broche of golde ful shene
On which was first written a crowned **A**
And after *Amor vincit omnia.*"

[*Prol.* ll. 158–62, misquoted.]

The works of the real humourist have always this sacred press-mark, I think.

1847. Unknown. Review of *Canterbury Tales from Chaucer by John Saunders*, [in] The Athenæum, no. 1037, Sept. 11, 1847, p. 950.

[A long review, in the main appreciative of Saunders's work, but the reviewer considers the plan of his *Canterbury Tales* to savour too much of modernisation, which he strongly condemns.]

1847. Wright. Thomas. *On some early Latin Stories, imitated at a later period by Chaucer and Shakespeare*, read Dec. 16th, 1847, [in] Archaeologia, vol. xxxii, 1847, pp. 362–5.

[The *Freres Tale* derived from a lost fabliau, a Latin version of which, "De Advocato et Diabolo," (MS. Cott. Cleopatra, D. viii, f. 110) Wright describes as nearer to Chaucer than that printed in his Percy Society collection of Latin stories.]

1847–51. Wright, Thomas. *Introduction* and *Notes* [in] The Canterbury Tales, Percy Society. *See* above, p. 274.

[*n.a.* **1848.**] **Coleridge,** Hartley. *Chaucer,* [printed in] *Poems,* **1851,** 2 vols., vol. ii, pp. 289–91. (Complete Poetical Works, Muses' Library, [1907,] pp. 317–8.)

[According to information kindly given by Mr. E. H. Coleridge, the copy of Anderson's Poets in which this was written probably did not come into Hartley Coleridge's possession (though nominally given to him by his father in 1803) till the death of his uncle Southey in 1843. These lines must therefore have been written between that year and the end of 1848, as Hartley Coleridge died 6 Jan. 1849.]

How wayward oft appears the poet's fate,
Who still is born too early or too late ! . . .
The fleeting language, to its trust untrue,
Vext by the jarring claims of old and new,
Defeats his beauty, makes his sense the fee
Of a blind, guessing, blundering glossary.
Thus CHAUCER, quaintly clad in antique guise,
With unfamiliar mien scares modern eyes.
No doubt he well invented—nobly felt—
But O ye Powers ! how monstrously he spelt.
His syllables confound our critic men,
Who strive in vain to find exactly ten . . .
His language too, unpolished and unfixt,
Of Norman, Saxon, Latin, oddly mixt—
Such words might please th' uneducated ears
That hail'd the blaring trumpets of Poictiers . . .

Yet, thou true Poet ! let no judgment wrong
Thy rich, spontaneous, many-coloured song ;
Just mirror of a bold, ambitious age
In passion furious, in reflection sage ! . . .
When every beast, and bird, and flower, and tree,
Convey'd a meaning and a mystery ;
And men in all degrees, sorts, ranks, and trades,
Knights, Palmers, Scholars, Wives, devoted Maids,
In garb, and speech, and manners, stood confest . . .
And told their state and calling by their vest.

[*n.a.* **1848.**] **Coleridge,** Hartley. *Notes on Shakespeare,* [written in a copy of Stockdale's edition of the Plays, printed in] Essays and Marginalia, ed. Derwent Coleridge, 1851, p. 189.

It is remarkable that he [Shakespeare] has scarce adopted a single expression from the " Troilus and Cresseide " of Chaucer, the most beautiful diary of love ever written. The work of Lollius is not to be found. I am disposed to think that Chaucer, in disowning the invention of this sweet poem, only followed the common practice of the minstrels.

1848. [**De Quincey**, Thomas.] *Review* of T. N. Talfourd's *Final Memorials of Charles Lamb*, [in] The North British Review, Nov. 1848, vol. x, p. 208. (Collected Writings, ed. D. Masson, 1890, 14 vols., vol. v, p. 253.)

> [Lamb] Being himself a Lincoln man, he treated Sir Hugh of Lincoln, . . . as a true historical personage on the rolls of Martyrdom.
>
> [Author's footnote.] The story which furnishes a basis to . . . the Canterbury Tale of Chaucer's Lady Abbess.

[For another reference by De Quincey to the *Prioresses Tale*, with the same error of 'Abbess' for 'Prioress,' *see* above, 1827.]

1848. [**De Quincey**, Thomas.] *Review* of the *Works of Alexander Pope*, ed. W. Roscoe, [in] The North British Review, Aug. 1848, vol. ix, p. 305. (Collected Writings, ed. D. Masson, 1890, 14 vols., vol. xi, p. 58.)

> At this hour, five hundred years since their creation, the tales of Chaucer, never equalled on this earth for their tenderness, and for life of picturesqueness, are read familiarly by many in the charming language of their natal day, and by others in the modernisations of Dryden, of Pope, and Wordsworth.

1848. **Emerson**, Ralph Waldo. *Shakspeare: or, the Poet*, [in] Representative Men, London, 1850, pp. 145–6, 160. (Centenary Edition, London [1903], vol. iv, pp. 197–8, 216.)

[This essay was read at a lecture in London in 1848, and was published in *Representative Men*, Boston, 1850. The London reprint of the same year is the first edn. in B.M.]

[p. 197] He [the great poet who appears in illiterate times] knows the sparkle of the true stone, and puts it in high place, wherever he finds it. Such is the happy position of Homer perhaps, of Chaucer, of Saadi. . . . The influence of Chaucer is conspicuous in all our early literature ; and more recently not only Pope and Dryden have been beholden to him, but, in the whole society of English writers, a large unacknowledged debt is easily traced. One is charmed with the opulence which feeds so many pensioners. But Chaucer is a huge borrower. Chaucer, it seems, drew continually, through Lydgate and Caxton [*sic, see* below, Notes and Queries, April 9, 1853, and Aug. 12, 1854], from Guido di Colonna, whose Latin romance of the Trojan war was in turn a compilation from Dares Phrygius, Ovid and Statius. Then Petrarch, Boccaccio and [p. 198] the Provençal poets are his benefactors : the Romaunt of the Rose is only judicious translation from William of Lorris and

John of Meung ; Troilus and Creseida from Lollius of Urbino :
the Cock and the Fox from the *Lais* of Marie : the House of
Fame, from the French or Italian ; and poor Gower he uses as
if he were only a brick-kiln or stone-quarry out of which to
build his house. He steals by this apology,—that what he
takes has no worth where he finds it and the greatest where
he leaves it.

1848. [**Garnett**, Richard, the Elder.] *Antiquarian Club-Books,* [in]
The Quarterly Review, March 1848, vol. lxxxii, pp. 323, 339.
[Reprinted in *The Philological Essays of R. Garnett,* edited by
his Son, 1859, pp. 126, 143-4.]

[p. 323] [Seriously questions Thomas Wright's qualifications for editing the Canterbury Tales.]

[p. 339] [Strong resemblance in grammar and idiom between Chaucer,
Orm, and Mannyng. Possibly Chaucer and Wyclif exercised
the same kind of influence in England as Dante and Boccaccio
did in Italy and Luther in Germany.]

1848. Hare, Julius Charles and Augustus William. *Guesses at Truth,*
by two Brothers. Second Series, p. 100.

[On the unwisdom of compressing Chaucer's heroic line into
an octosyllable.]

1848. Landor, Walter Savage. *Letter to Monckton Milnes,* [printed
in] John Keats, by Sidney Colvin, 1917, p. 537.

On my return to Bath . . . I find your valuable present
of Keatses [*sic*] Works. . . . Of all our poets, excepting
Shakespeare and Milton, and perhaps Chaucer, he has most
of the poetical character. . . . There is . . . a freshness such
as we feel in the glorious dawn of Chaucer.

1848. Macaulay, Thomas Babington, Lord. *History of England,*
1849-61, 5 vols., vol. i, pp. 20, 342. (Works, 1898, 12 vols.,
vol. i, pp. 21, 358.)

[Vols. i and ii were published in November 1848 (*D. N. B.*).]

[p. 21] Nor were the arts of peace neglected by our fathers during
that stirring period [the fourteenth century]. . . . A copious
and forcible language, formed by an infusion of French into
German, was now the common property of the aristocracy and
of the people. Nor was it long before genius began to apply
that admirable machine to worthy purposes. While English
warriors, leaving behind them the devastated provinces of
France, entered Valladolid in triumph and spread terror to

the gates of Florence, English poets depicted in vivid tints all the wide variety of human manners and fortunes, and English thinkers aspired to know, or dared to doubt, where bigots had been content to wonder and to believe. The same age which produced the Black Prince and Derby, Chandos and Hawkwood, produced also Geoffrey Chaucer and John Wycliffe.

[p. 358] About a day's journey south of Leeds, on the verge of Shef- a wild moorland tract, lay an ancient manor . . . which field was known by the name of Hallamshire. Iron abounded there; and, from a very early period, the rude whittles fabricated there had been sold all over the kingdom. They had indeed been mentioned by Geoffrey Chaucer in one of his Canterbury Tales. [*Reves T.* l. 13.]

1849. B., N. *Chaucer's Grave,* [in] The Gentleman's Magazine, Dec. 1849, new ser., vol. xxxii, pp. 594–5.

[Was Chaucer's grave desecrated on the occasion of Dryden's interment? Reference to Dart's account, *q.v.* above, 1723, vol. i, pp. 363–6.]

1849. Froude, James Anthony. *The Nemesis of Faith,* p. 151.

The poets, from Chaucer to Milton, were, without exception, on the reforming side.

[*n.a.* **1849.**] **Hunt,** James Henry Leigh. *Sonnet.* [Quoted by C. Day in Notes and Queries, 22 Dec. 1849, vol. i, p. 122.]

> Were I to name out of the times gone by,
> The poets dearest to me, I should say,
> Pulci for spirits, and a fine, free way,
> Chaucer for manners, and a close, silent eye . . .

1849. Notes and Queries, 1st series, vol. i, pp. 81, 122, 126.

Author.	Date.	Reference.	Subject.
Editor.	Dec. 8.	1st S. i, 81.	Contributors of notes resemble Chaucer's Scholar.
Day, C.	Dec. 22.	1st S. i, 122.	Quotation of Leigh Hunt's Sonnet, *q.v.* above [*n.a.* 1849].
Unknown.	Dec. 22.	1st S. i, 126.	Quotation of entry of Caxton's edn. of the Boethius from

Thorpe's catalogue, with extract from Caxton's epilogue, *q.v.* above, 1479, vol. i, p. 58.

[The Chaucer articles and correspondence in *Notes and Queries* have been analysed, and the result of this is given up to 1867, although limits of space make it impossible to print an analysis throughout.]

1849. Ruskin, John.   *The Seven Lamps of Architecture*, Note to chapter ii, § 10, p. 202.   (Works, Library edition, ed. E. T. Cook and A. Wedderburn, 39 vols., 1903–12, vol. viii, pp. 269–70.)

[p. 269]   [On the lines : "It may be perhaps permitted me to assume that true architecture does not admit iron as a constructive material," Ruskin says :]

Except in Chaucer's noble temple of Mars :

" And dounward from an hill under a bent,
    Ther stood the temple of Mars, armipotent . . . [to]
    Was tonne-gret of yren bright and shene."
The Knightes Tale [ll. 1981–94].

[p. 270]   There is, by the bye, an exquisite piece of architectural *colour* just before :

" And northward, in a turret on the wall
    Of alabaster white, and red corall,
    An oratorie riche for to see,
    In worship of Diane of Chastitee."
[ll. 1909–12.]

[This note was reprinted as it stands in the second edition of 1855 ; in the third edition of 1880, however, it was altered somewhat, the spelling of the lines quoted being modernised and explanatory notes added.]

1849. Ticknor, George, *History of Spanish Literature*, New York, 3 vols, vol. i, pp. 22 *n*., 85–6.

[pp. 85–6.]   [Juan Ruiz de Hita, comparable to Chaucer, who wrote a little later in the same century, in his prevailingly natural and spirited tone, in seeking materials in northern French poetry, in the mixture of devotion and immorality, in knowledge of human nature, and in being a reformer of prosody ; he has not, however, " the tenderness, the elevation, or the general power of Chaucer."]

1849. Unknown.   *The Times and Poetry of Chaucer*, by a New Contributor, [in] The Knickerbocker Magazine, New York, Sept. and Oct. 1849, vol. xxxiv, pp. 236–41, 292–98.

[p. 238]   He who shall study the poetry of this father of English verse, will not be a dull, dry, dead piece of humanity ; but if he read with deep attention, he will feel that he is in the presence of a master spirit, who is striking every chord that vibrates in harmony with truth and nature in his soul. . . .

[p. 296]   Few poets have equalled Chaucer in word painting.   In one

bold, though antiquated expression, he shows us the character
of a " Doctour of Phisicke."

> " For gold in phisike is a cordial,
>   Therefore he loved gold in special."
>
> <div align="right">[<i>Prol.</i> ll. 443-4.]</div>

Such are a few samples of his manner of describing his
heroes and heroines : he gives us an outline *cap-à-pie* ; un-
covers the mind and shows us the very heart.   Like Shakspeare
he had an intellect which rose far above all competition in
its power of judging character. . . . For conciseness and energy
united, come to the Tales of Chaucer.

1849. Unknown. *Chaucer,* [in] The North British Review, Edinburgh,
1849, vol. x, pp. 293-328. [A review of Nicolas's edition of the
Works, Saunders' *Cabinet Pictures* and *Canterbury Tales,* Deshler's
Selections, Horne's *Poems Modernised,* and Cowden Clarke's *Tales
from Chaucer* and *Riches of Chaucer.*]

[p. 294]   The first question, as it seems to us which we are bound
at once to ask or to answer, is—belongs he [Chaucer]
to the living or to the dead ; does he or does he not speak
words of living interest to living men ; is he or is he not
an integral part of our existing civilisation ? . . .

. . . So far is his story from being strange and distant to us,
that we believe every one who investigates it for the first
time will feel astonished that it should have been possible
for any one, in the times of Cressy and of Poictiers, to
lead a life in all respects so nearly resembling that of an
accomplished and successful civilian at the present day.

[Here follow an appreciation of recent work on Chaucer,
especially that of Saunders and Nicolas, who are both contrasted favourably with Godwin ; and a life of Chaucer, largely
based on the latter, occupies pp. 299-314.]

.   .   .   .

[p. 324]   In its form it [the speech which Chaucer employed] was
the Saxon of Edward the Confessor, with such flectional
modifications as three centuries of further development had
effected ; and in its substance it had superadded to the great
Saxon substratum such Norman words as the contact of three
centuries had gradually introduced . . .

[p. 325]   A few observations before parting, for the purpose of fixing,
in some measure, the rank that he is entitled to hold among
our poets. . . . We do not venture to equal him to
the two greatest of them.   With Milton, indeed, he can in

no wise be compared, for the difference in kind is so absolute
as to render it impossible to measure the degree ; and by
Shakespeare he is unquestionably surpassed in his own
walk. . . .

As a poet of character—and as such chiefly he must be
viewed, we believe him to come nearer to Shakespeare than
any other writer in the language. There is the same vigour
in all that he pourtrays, the same tone of health belongs to it.
. . . We believe that no writer ever was so healthy as
Chaucer. . . .

[p. 326] Chaucer is essentially the poet of man. Brought up from
the first from among his fellows and discharging to the last
the duties of a citizen, he wandered not,—nor wished to
wander in solitary places. His poetry is that of reality. . . .

[pp. 327-8] . . . In many respects it seems to us that Chaucer resembles
Goethe more than any of the poets of our own country. He
has the same mental completeness and consequent versatility
which distinguish the German ; the same love of reality ;
the same clearness and cheerfulness ; and, in seeming contradiction to this latter characteristic, the same preference for
grief over the other passions, in his poetical delineations. In
minor respects, he also resembles him, and in one, not
unimportant, as marking a similarity of mental organization,
that, namely, of betaking himself at the close of a long life
spent in literature and affairs, to the study of the physical
sciences, as if here alone the mental craving for the positive
could find satisfaction.

1849. Whittier, John Greenleaf. *Margaret Smith's Journal*, Boston,
1859 [not in B.M.]. (Writings, Riverside Edn., 1888–89, 7 vols.,
vol. v, Prose, vol. i, p. 51.)

I think old Chaucer hath it right in his Pardoner's Tale
[ll. 549–55] :—

> A likerous thing is wine, and drunkenness
> Is full of striving and of wretchedness [etc.].

1850. Boker, George Henry. *Letter to R. H. Stoddard*, [dated] Jan. 7,
1850, [quoted in] Recollections . . . by R. H. Stoddard, New
York, 1903, p. 186.

Read Chaucer for strength, read Spenser for ease and
sweetness, read Milton for sublimity and thought, read
Shakespeare for all these things and for something else which
is his alone. Get out of your age as far as you can.

1850. Bright, John. *Speech on abolition of capital punishment.*
The Life and Speeches of John Bright, 2 vols. 1881, by George
Barnett Smith, vol. i, p. 307.

If you wish to teach the people to reverence human nature,
you must first show them that you reverence it yourselves.
An old English writer, Chaucer, says of his " Parson "—

" Christ's lore, and his Apostles twelve
He preached, but first he followed it himself ; "
[*Prol.* ll. 527–8.]

and if we would teach men to reverence the lives of their
fellow-men the first and most powerful step we could take
would be to abandon the halter and the scaffold.

1850. Bruce, John, and **Others.** (Committee for the Repair of the
Tomb of Geoffrey Chaucer.) *Advertisement,* [on the cover of] The
Gentleman's Magazine, Aug. 1850, new ser., vol. xxxiv, also in
Notes and Queries, Feb. 22, and May 10, 1851, 1st ser., vol. iii,
pp. 159, 383.

[The names of the Committee are—

John Bruce, Esq., Treasurer S.A.	Sir Frederick Madden, K.H. John G. Nichols, Esq., F.S.A.
J. Payne Collier, Esq., V.P.S.A.	Henry Shaw, Esq., F.S.A.
Peter Cunningham, Esq., F.S.A.	Samuel Shepherd, Esq., F.S.A.
W. Richard Drake, Esq., F.S.A.	William J. Thoms, Esq., F.S.A.
Thomas W. King, Esq., F.S.A.	

A statement follows that the tomb "is fast mouldering into
irretrievable decay," and that £100 "will effect a perfect
repair ;" with an appeal for this sum.

On pp. 182–3, 293, 632 of vol. xxxiii, and on pp. 75,
280–2, 485 of vol. xxxiv, of *The Gentleman's Magazine,* are
further notes, articles and appeals.]

1850. Collier, John Payne. *Chaucer's Monument and Spenser's Death,*
[in] The Gentleman's Magazine, Nov. 1850, new series, vol. xxxiv,
pp. 485–7.

[Collier argues from a passage in Wm. Warner's *Albion's
England* [*q.v.* above, 1606, vol. i, p. 178] that Spenser was
only accidentally and not designedly buried near Chaucer, the
couplet being :

" Per accidens only interr'd
Nigh venerable Chaucer."]

1850. Dickens, Charles. *David Copperfield,* chap. xxvii, lii, pp. 287,
536. (Works, Gadshill Edition, ed. Andrew Lang, 1892–1908,
36 vols., vol. xiv, David Copperfield 2 vols., vol. i, pp. 487–8 ;
vol. ii, p. 386.)

[p.287] "It was at Canterbury where we last met. Within the
shadow, I may figuratively say, of that religious edifice,

immortalized by Chaucer, which was anciently the resort of Pilgrims from the remotest corners of—in short," said Mr. Micawber, "in the immediate neighbourhood of the cathedral."

[p. 536]　[Mr. Micawber is again speaking :] " So be it ! For myself, my Canterbury Pilgrimage has done much ; imprisonment on civil process, and want, will soon do more."

1850. Hunter, Joseph. *The Seal of Chaucer: copy of the deed to which it is appended : copy of a public instrument notifying to him his removal from his office of Clerk of the King's Works* . . . Read May 14, 1850, [in] Archaeologia, vol. xxxiv, 1852, pp. 42–5.

[With a drawing of the seal and counterseal. The first document is a deed of Thomas Chaucer of Ewelme, dated 20 May, 10 Henry IV (1409), *q.v.* above, vol. i, p. 19, the second is of 17 June, 14 Richard II (1391), (Life Records of Chaucer, p. 300), *q.v.* below, App. A, 1391.]

[c. 1850.] Landor, Walter Savage. *James I of Scotland,* [lines printed in] *Letters and other Unpublished writings of Walter Savage Landor,* ed. Stephen Wheeler, 1897, p. 205.

> James ! I will never call thy fortunes hard,
> A happy lover and unrival'd bard.
> For Chaucer, Britain's firstborn, was no more,
> And the Muse panted after heavy Gower.

[c. 1850.] Noble, T. *Ovid's Art of Love, Remedy of Love and Art of Beauty : to which is added Chaucer's Court of Love* [Maynwaring's version], etc., London, T. Noble.

[A reprint of the original edn. of 1709, *q.v.* above, vol. i, p. 310. The Chaucerian authorship of the *Court of Love* is nowhere questioned in the little book, which is a plain reprint without notes.]

1850. Notes and Queries, 1st Series, vol. i, pp. 155–6, 203, 218, 222, 229, 235, 254, 281, 303, 307, 335, 343. 395, 419–420 ; vol. ii, pp. 27, 31, 108–9, 164, 199, 237, 269, 316, 322–3, 376, 403–4, 420–21, 442, 485, 495.

	Author.	Date.	Reference.	Subject.
1850.	Todd, J. H.	Jan. 5.	1st S. i, 155–6.	' Rehete': Tyrwhitt's glossary quoted.
	Thoms, W. J.	Jan. 26.	1st S. i, 203.	Sonnet written on the opening of the Session, 1847.

It is not mine to commune with the men
[*i.e.* the great Parliamentarians].
Not so when I unfold some favorite book.
Chaucer and I grow boon companions then . . .
Quotation, *Prol.* ll. 293-6.

Author.	Date.	Reference.	Subject.

Corney, Feb. 2. 1st S. i, 218. 'Poke.'
Bolton.

Thoms, Feb. 2. 1st S. i, 222. Sonnet written on the close of
W. J.   the Session, 1849.
Now am I free . . .
Free, and I wish to go a pilgrimage
With Chaucer, my companion long approved . . .
Quotation :
The tyme came that resoun was to ryse.—Chaucer.

Thoms, Feb. 9. 1st S. i, 229. Chaucer's Night Charm in the
W. J. *Milleres Tale* (ll. 3483–6). Has it been met with
elsewhere ?

Editor. Feb. 9. 1st S. i, 235. 'Gibbe our cat' (*Rom. Rose,* C.
6204).

B., E. M. Feb. 16. 1st S. i, 254. 'Dulcarnon' (*Troilus,* iii, 933).

Rock, Mar. 2. 1st S. i, 281. Chaucer's Night Charm. The
D. Pater noster was sometimes used by witches, and
this might be the "white" Pater noster. "Seynte
Petres Soster" refers possibly to the legend of St.
Petronilla, or St. Pernell, said to be the daughter of
St. Peter.

B., J. M. Mar. 9. 1st S. i,   (i) Lollius (*Troilus* and *Hous*
303–4.   *of Fame*); (ii) Trophee (*Monkes*
Tale); (iii) Corinna (for 'Colonna'?); (iv.) 'Friday
weather' (*Knightes Tale*).

Corney, Mar. 9. 1st S. i, 307. 'Beaver hat' (*Prol.* l. 272).
Bolton.

Foss, E. Mar. 23. 1st S. i, 335. 'The Temple, or 'A Temple'
(*Prol.* l. 567).

Editor. Mar. 23. 1st S. i, 343. Preliminary announcement of
the scheme for restoring Chaucer's monument in Westminster Abbey [*q.v.* above, 1850, Bruce].

Editor. April 20. 1st S. i, 395. 'To-break' (*Lenvoy a Scogan,*
l. 1).

R., C. I. April 27. 1st S. i, 419. 'Gourd' (*Manciple's Prol.,* l.
82).

F., P. H. April 27. 1st S. i, 420. 'The Temple,' or 'A Temple.'

Foss, E. June 8. 1st S. ii, 27. 'The Temple,' or 'A Temple.'

B., C. June 8. 1st S. ii, 31. 'Hoppesteris' (*Knightes Tale,*
l. 2017); Chaucer must have read Boccaccio's 'bella-
trici' as 'ballatrici.'

B., C. July 13. 1st S. ii,   'Dulcarnon,' from Arabic *Dhoul*
108–9.   *carnun* = with the two horns.

Y., T. Aug. 10. 1st S. ii, 164. Chaucer quoted on the screech-
owl : "The oule eke that of deth the bode bringeth."

Philo- Aug. 24. 1st S. ii, 199. What is the route of the Can-
Chaucer.   terbury pilgrims ?

H., S. Sept. 7. 1st S. ii, 237. Pilgrim's Road to Canterbury.

Author.	Date.	Reference.	Subject.
Jackson, E. S.	Sept. 21.	1st S. ii, 269.	Pilgrim's Road to Canterbury.
V., R.	Oct. 12.	1st S. ii, 316.	Pilgrim's Road to Canterbury.
Jackson, E. S.	Oct. 19.	1st S. ii, 322–3).	Chaucer's Damascene (*Prol.* l.

Mr. Saunders, in *Cabinet Pictures of English Life,* has confounded Damascenus, the Physician, with Johannes Damascenus Chrysorrhoas, " the last of the Greek Fathers," a voluminous writer on ecclesiastical subjects, but no physician, and therefore not at all likely to be found among the books of Chaucer's Doctour, " Whose studie was but litel on the Bible."

B., J. M.	Nov. 2.	1st S. ii, 376.	Meaning of ' la langue

Pandras' in Deschamps' ballade to Chaucer?

Corney, Bolton.	Nov. 16.	1st S. ii, 403.	Deschamps' ballade.
C., D.	Nov. 16.	1st S. ii, 403-4.	Deschamps' ballade.
S. M. N.	Nov. 23.	1st S. ii, 420.	Chaucer's Monument. Evidence, in Smith's *Life of Nollekens,* vol. i.

p. 179 [*q.v.* above, 1828], that remains of the painted figure of Chaucer were to be seen in Nollekens' time.

An editorial note follows stating that one of the lay vicars of Westminster Abbey said that when he was a boy, some sixty-five or seventy years since, the figure of Chaucer might be made out by rubbing a wet finger over it.

P.	Nov. 30.	1st S. ii, 442.	Chaucer's portrait by Occleve. Is this portrait to be found in *all*

the MSS. of *Egidius de Roma,* and, if so, has it ever been engraved?

D., J. I., Editor, and **P., W.**	Dec. 14.	1st S. ii, 485.	Chaucer's Portrait by Occleve is engraved in—(1) Strutt's *Regal*

and Ecclesiastical Antiquities; (2) *Canterbury Tales,* edited by Tyrwhitt, published by Pickering; (3) in octavo and folio by Vertue. A full-length portrait of Chaucer is given in Shaw's *Dresses and Decorations of the Middle Ages;* another, on horseback, in Todd's *Illustrations of Gower and Chaucer.*

Campkin, Henry.	Dec. 21.	1st S. ii, 495.	" Mercenary preacher"; Chaucer's " Good Parson" quoted to

illustrate the phrase.

[*a.* 1850 ?] **Ruskin**, John. *Letter* on his early poem, *The Last Song of Arion,* to W. H. Harrison. (Works, Library edition, ed. E. T. Cook and A. Wedderburn, 1903–12, 39 vols., vol. ii, p. 123.)

[The editors state that this letter is undated but was probably written before 1850.]

[Writers comparing their mistresses to the sun:] Only one man has done *that* rightly, in the pure way—Chaucer.

' Up rose the Sonne, and up rose Emilie !'

[*Knightes T.,* l. 1415.]

1850. Unknown. *History of the English Language,* [in] The Edinburgh Review, Oct. 1850, vol. xcii, pp. 306, 310, 313–315, 317, 320, 323.

[pp. 313-14] [Chaucer's influence on the language; he introduced a large number of words from the French, and endeavoured, though unsuccessfully, to introduce innovations of accent and pronunciation.

As regards vocabulary; our most idiomatic writers have never admitted more than a tenth that is not Anglo-Saxon; our least never less of Anglo-Saxon than two-thirds.

Even in his translations, Chaucer will more than bear the latter test, and in his original compositions he will more than bear the former.]

[p. 314] Excepting a very few passages in which he makes a large demand on general and abstract nouns (as of ethical qualities), or of terms of art (as of physic or alchemy), his diction is more purely Saxon than that of Swift. In his most graphic descriptions of character and incident, it will be found that all the more vivid and expressive words and phrases—those which are most poetical in their effect—are Anglo-Saxon; as, for example, in his picture of the jovial monk of whom he says that

> ' When he rode, men might his bridle hear
> Gingling in a whistling wind, as clear
> And eke as loud as doth his chapel bell ; '
> [*Prol.,* ll. 169–71.]

and of the poor parson, of whom he writes

> ' That Cristes lore and his apostles twelve
> He taught—but first he followed it himself.'[1]
> [*Prol.,* ll. 527–8.]

[The other references are brief.]

[1] [Author's Note.] The beautiful imitation by Dryden of Chaucer's description of the genuine minister of Christ is decidedly inferior, in simple force and vividness, to the original. Nor have Goldsmith or Cowper, in treating the same theme, equalled the graphic touches of our antique poet.

[n.a. 1850.] **Wordsworth,** William. *Miscellaneous Memoranda,* [in] Memoirs of W. Wordsworth, by Christopher Wordsworth, 1851, 2 vols, vol. ii, p. 470.

[Wordsworth died in 1850.]

When I began to give myself up to the profession of a poet for life, I was impressed with a conviction, that there were four English poets whom I must have continually before me as examples—Chaucer, Shakespeare, Spenser and Milton. These I must study, and equal *if I could ;* and I need not think of the rest.

[This paragraph was communicated to Christopher Wordsworth by Crabb Robinson. The former says (vol. i, p. 27) that in the dining-room at Rydal Mount "are engravings of poets—Chaucer, Spenser, Shakespeare, Ben Jonson and Milton ; " and (vol. i, p. 49) that " the mind of Wordsworth was indeed cheered at Cambridge . . . by visions of the illustrious dead who had been trained in that University—Chaucer, Spenser, Ben Jonson, Milton, Cowley, Dryden."]

PART III

(1851–1900)

1851. Craik, George Lillie. *Outlines of the History of the English Language . . . for Colleges and Schools,* pp. 62, 70, 87–8 [Chaucer did not introduce French diction, the *Testament of Love* quoted as genuine], 95–102, 110–15, 117 [Chaucer's English transitional, many references to Guest's *History of English Rhythms*], 135–6, Illustrative Specimens [from the *Reves T.* and *Persones T.*].

1851. Emerson, Ralph Waldo. *The Conduct of Life,* London, 1860, pp. 5–6 [Essay on Fate, *Knightes Tale,* ll. 1663–72, quoted], 40 [*Hous of Fame,* ll. 43–51, quoted], 116 [Essay on Culture], 182 [Essay on Worship, *Legend of Good Women,* ll. 1037–43, quoted for "Chaucer's extraordinary confusion of heaven and earth in the picture of Dido"]. (Works, Centenary Edition, 1903, 12 vols., vol. vi, pp. 5, 6, 46, 132, 207.)

[Delivered as lectures in 1851, and published at Boston in 1860 ; the London reprint of the same year is the first edn. in B.M.]

1851. Emerson, Ralph Waldo. *Journal* [quoted in notes to Representative Men, Centenary Edition, [1903,] vol. iv, p. 374].

[Emerson notices the absence in Goethe's *Faust* of] the cheerful, radiant, profuse beauty of which Shakspeare, of which Chaucer, had the secret.

1851. FitzGerald, Edward. *Euphranor, a Dialogue on Youth,* pp. 63–6, 70. (Letters and Literary Remains, ed. W. A. Wright, 1902–3, 7 vols., vol. vi, pp. 237–40, 243–4, 246–7.)

[p. 63]   [Quotation of *Prol.,* ll. 79–100 :

' With him there was his Sonn, a yongé Squire. . .
to
' And karft before his Fadir at the table.']

' Chaucer, however,' said Euphranor when he had finished [p. 64] the passage, ' allows his young squire more accomplishments than you would trust him with, Doctor. See, he dances, draws, and even writes songs—quite a *petit maître.*'

' But also,' I added, ' is of "grete strength," " fair y-rides," and had already " born him well in Chivauchie." Besides,' continued I . . . ' in those days, you know, there was scarce any reading, which usurps so much of knighthood now. Men left that to the clergy ; contented, as we before agreed, to follow their bidding to pilgrimages and holy wars. Some gentler accomplishments were needed then to soften manners, just as we want rougher ones to fortify ours. . . .

[p. 65]   'And look at dear old Chaucer himself,' said I, 'how the fresh air of the Kent hills, over which he rode four hundred years ago, breathes in his verses still. They have a perfume like fine old hay, that will not lose its sweetness, having been cut and carried so fresh. All his poetry bespeaks a man of sound mind and body.'

[p. 66]   [Chaucer and Shakespeare men of business.]

[p. 70]   [Tenderness of Chaucer and Shakespeare.]

[In May, 1882, FitzGerald caused to be printed 50 copies of a revised edn. of *Euphranor*. In this the passage on p. 65 of the 1851 edn., quoted above, disappears; while another is inserted, which concludes (p. 50) with the following paragraph :]

"They [Pepys and Parson Adams] were both prefigured among those Canterbury Pilgrims so many years before," said I. "Only think of it ! Some nine-and-twenty, I think, 'by aventure yfalle in feleweship,' High and Low, Rich and Poor, Saint and Sinner, Cleric and Lay, Knight, Ploughman, Prioress, Wife of Bath, Shipman, hunting Abbot-like Fryar, Poor Parson (Adams' Progenitor) — Webster (Pepys') —on rough-riding 'Stot' or ambling Palfrey, marshall'd by mine Host of the Tabard to the music of the Miller's Bag-pipes, on their sacred errand to St. Thomas'; and one among them taking note of all in Verse still fresh as the air of those Kentish hills they travelled over on that April morning four hundred years ago."

[Corresponding to the passing allusion on p. 70 of edn. 1851 to 'the whole familiar tenderness of this very Shakspeare and Chaucer of ours' is (pp. 53–4) the following :]

"Wordsworth ?" said I—a man of the Milton rather than of the Chaucer and Shakspeare type—without humour, like the rest of his Brethren of the Lake."

"Not but he loves Chaucer as much as you can, Doctor, for those fresh touches of Nature, and tenderness of Heart— insomuch that he has re-cast the Jew of Lincoln's Story into a form more available for modern readers."

" And successfully ? "

"Ask Lexilogus — Ah! I forgot that he never read Chaucer . . ."

[On p. 56 is added a comparison of Sir Kenelm Digby, author of *The Broad Stone of Honour,* to Chaucer's Squire in physical strength, and to Chaucer himself in his eye for humours.]

1851. Innes, Henry. *A Lecture on the Genius of Chaucer,* Malta.

[A short sketch of Chaucer's life, followed by stories from the *Canterbury Tales.*]

1851. Meredith, George. *Poems,* p. 22. [The dedication to T. L. Peacock is dated May, 1851.]

The Poetry of Chaucer.

Gray with all honours of age! but fresh featured and
    ruddy
As dawn when the drowsy farm-yard has thrice heard
    Chaunticlere.
Tender to tearfulness—childlike, and manly, and motherly ;
Here beats true English blood richest joyance on sweet
    English ground.

1851. Notes and Queries, 1st Series, vol. iii, pp. 74, 92, 109, 131–3, 156, 158–9, 188, 201–3, 205–6, 235, 252, 258, 263, 297, 300, 306, 308, 315–17, 330, 345–6, 361–3, 368, 383, 385–7, 419–21, 429–30, 434, 450, 473–4, 492–3, 496, 507–8, 515 ; vol. iv, pp. 54, 65, 68, 76, 88, 93, 145–7, 159, 176, 189, 255, 275, 318, 337, 475.

Author.	Date.	Reference.	Subject.
Q., F. S.	Jan. 25.	1st S. iii, 74.	'Pilled' (*Reves Tale*).
Q., F. S.	Feb. 1.	1st S. iii, 92.	'Velouttes blew, in signe of trouth.'
"Good B'ye."	Feb. 8.	1st S. iii, 109.	'By and by' = side by side.
E.	Feb. 22.	1st S. iii, 131–2.	Note on *Knightes Tale.* Chaucer specially mentions the arrival of Palamon and Arcite at Athens on a *Sunday,* and this circumstance is astrologically connected with the issue of the contest.
Anon.	Feb. 22.	1st S. iii, 133.	'Nettle in, dock out' (*Troilus,* iv, st. 66) is the beginning of a Northumbrian charm for a nettle-sting.
Anon.	Feb. 22.	1st S. iii, 158.	Short notice of Wright's *Canterbury Tales,* vol. iii.
Bruce, John, and Others.	Feb. 22.	1st S. iii, 159.	Chaucer's tomb ; *see* above, 1850, and below, May 10.

Author.	Date.	Reference.	Subject.
C. R.	March 8.	1st S. iii, 188.	Chaucer's descendants, if any, might contribute to the repair of his tomb.
B[rae], A. E.	Mar. 15.	1st S. iii, 201–3.	The astrological note on the 24 hours of the day in *Knightes Tale* (Feb. 22) anticipated by Tyrwhitt.
Crossley, Fras., and Editor.	March 15.	1st S. iii, 205–6.	'Nettle in, dock out.'
B[rae], A. E.	Mar. 29.	1st S. iii, 235.	The astronomical allegory contained in Chaucer's *Complaint of Mars and Venus.*
X., A. L.	Mar. 29.	1st S. iii, 252.	Chaucer's 'Fifty Wekes.'—With regard to Chaucer meaning by

this the interval of a solar year; compare it with his original, the *Teseide* of Boccaccio; where (V. 98) Theseus says, appointing the listed fight:

'E TERMINE vi sia a ciò donato
D'UN ANNO INTERO.'

To which the poet subjoins:

'E così fu ordinato.'

B[rae], A. E.	April 5.	1st S. iii, 258, 306.	Further notes on the *Complaint of Mars and Venus.*
B[rae], A. E.	Apr. 26.	1st S. iii, 315–7.	Tyrwhitt's astronomical mistakes in his notes on the opening

lines of the *Prologue* and *Marchantes Tale*, l. 889.

Editor.	April 26.	1st S. iii, 330.	'Span-newe.'
B[rae], A. E.	May 3.	1st S. iii, 345.	Introduction to the Man of Law's Prologue. 'The Arke of

Artificial Day' means the Azimuthal Arch of the horizon included between the point of sunrise and that of sunset.

Editor.	May 10.	1st S. iii, 361–3.	Chaucer's prophetic view of the Crystal Palace, as shown in his

description of the 'temple y-made of Glas' in the *Hous of Fame*. Several extracts pieced together. [For a parallel see below, 1854, Unknown.] The article concludes with an appeal for money towards restoring Chaucer's tomb.

"Arun."	May 10.	1st S. iii, 368.	'Nettle out, dock in.'
Bruce, John, and Others.	May 10.	1st S. iii, 383.	Chaucer's tomb; a fuller appeal, with a woodcut of it as it should be;

" the portrait and the inscriptions have disappeared; the overhanging canopy has suffered damage; the table

Author.	Date.	Reference.	Subject.

is chipped and broken; the base is fast mouldering into irretrievable decay." *See* above, 1850, and Feb. 22, p. 159 in this vol.

B[rae], A. E.   May 17.   1st S. iii, 385–7.   The date of the journey to Canterbury as deduced from the Prologue to the *Man of Law's Tale.* . . . Speaking strictly, this declination would more properly apply to the 17th of April, in Chaucer's time, than to the 18th; but since he does not profess to critical exactness, . . . such MSS. as name the 18th of April ought to be respected; but Tyrwhitt's '28th' . . . . ought to be scouted at once.

[See Skeat's note on 1. 3 of Introduction to the *Man of Law's Tale*, Chaucer's *Works*, vol. v, p. 132.]

With regard to 'Ten on the clokke' in the afternoon observation [*Parson's Prol.*, l. 5], there seems no need to retain a reading 'by which broad sunshine is attributed to ten o'clock at night'! It may be explained in the circumstance that 'ten' and 'four' in horary reckoning were *convertible terms.* The old Roman method of naming the hours, wherein noon was the sixth, was long preserved, especially in conventual establishments: and doubtless the idiomatic phrase 'o'clock' originated in the necessity for some distinguishing mark between hours 'of the clock' reckoned from midnight, and hours of the day reckoned from sunrise or 6 A.M. So that *Ten* was very likely a gloss upon *four* by some monkish transcriber, ignorant perhaps of the meaning of 'o'clock'; since *four* o'clock is the tenth hour of the day reckoning from 6 A.M.

[See Skeat's note, confirming this, to l. 5 of the *Parson's Prologue*, Chaucer's *Works*, vol. v, p. 444.]

B[rae], A. E.   May 31.   1st S. iii, 419–21.   The Star Min Al Auwâ—

'Therewith the mones exaltacioun
In libra, men alawai gan ascende
As we were entrying at a townes end.'

The meaning of these lines is discussed, and it is suggested that Chaucer intended to mark the moon's place by associating her rising with that of a known fixed star; compare, for this same method, ll. 263–5 of the Squire's Tale.

It is very remarkable that the only year, perhaps in the whole of Chaucer's lifetime, in which the moon could have arisen with this star on the 18th of April, should be the identical year to which Tyrwhitt, *reasoning from historical evidence alone*, would fain attribute the writing of the *Canterbury Tales*, i. e. 1388.

"Arun."   May 31.   1st S. iii, 429–30.   Pilgrims' Road to Canterbury.

Author.	Date.	Reference.	Subject.
Editor.	May 31.	1st S. iii, 434.	' Went ' = way.
C., J. H.	June 7.	1st S. iii, 450.	' Hernshaw.'
B[rae], A. E.	June 14.	1st S. iii, 473–4.	The Armorican word ' menez ' (Frankeleyns Tale) = points or summits of rocks.
Thoms, W. J.	June 21.	1st S. iii, 492–3.	Coincidence between Chaucer and Gray. Did Gray owe the

well-known line,

E'en in our ashes live their wonted fires,

to the one in Chaucer's *Reves Prologue*,

Yet in our ashen cold is fire yreken ? (l. 28).

[For this comparison *see* above, 1782 [Dodsley, J. ?], vol. i, p. 465.]

Editor.	June 21.	1st S. iii, 496.	Chaucer's reference (*Nonnes P. T.* ll. 4537–42) to Geoffrey de Vinsauf's lament for Richard Cœur de Lion.
T., H. G.	June 21.	1st S. iii, 507–8.	' Hernshaw.'
B[rae], A. E.	June 28.	1st S. iii, 515.	The Astronomical evidence of the true date of the Canterbury

Pilgrimage. When it is recollected that some at least of the facts recorded by Chaucer must have been theoretical . . . it must be admitted that his near approach to truth is remarkable . . .

Assuming that the true date intended by Chaucer was Saturday the 18th of April 1388, the following particulars of that day are those which have reference to his description. Astronomical particulars are then given.

Chaucer's knowledge of astronomy is most probably the result of real observation at the time named. Probable that he wrote the prologues to his *Canterbury Tales* more as a narration (with some embellishments) of events that really took place, than that they were altogether the work of his imagination.

H[alli-well], J. O.	July 26.	1st S. iv, 54.	Chaucer and Gray (iii, 492.)— Gray himself refers in a note to Petrarch as his original for the line—

'Even in our ashes live their wonted fires.'

Varro.	,,	,,	The thought also occurs in Shakespeare.

Gray's line was originally written—

'Awake and faithful to her wonted fires,'

which has but little to do with Chaucer.

Author.	Date.	Reference.	Subject.
Campkin, Henry.	July 26.	1st S. iv, 65, 68.	'Eisel.'
P., G.	July 26.	1st S. iv, 76.	'Hernshaw.'
Editor.	Aug. 2.	1st S. iv, 88.	'Deal,' ' never a del.'
Editor and others.	Aug. 30.	1st S. iv, 145–7.	Chaucer and Caxton.—Why not repair Chaucer's tomb with the money of the Caxton fund? Nothing would be more agreeable to Caxton himself.
L[aing], D[avid].	Sept. 6.	1st S. iv, 176.	Where is Kinaston's MS. of his Latin version of *Troilus?*
P., J. W.	Sept. 13.	1st S. iv, 189.	'Ruell.'
Laurie, James.	Oct. 4.	1st S. iv, 255.	What was the original pronunciation of the name of the poet Chaucer? Was not the *ch* in his day a guttural? And was not the name *Hawker,* or *Howker?*
Editor.	Oct. 11.	1st S. iv, 275.	'Livery.'
"A Londoner."	Oct. 25.	1st S. iv, 318.	'Cockney.'
"A Londoner."	Dec. 13.	1st S. iv, 475.	'Cockney.'

1851. Turner, Thomas Hudson. *Some Account of Domestic Architecture in England from the Conquest to the End of the Thirteenth Century,* Oxford, 1851, pp. 122, 146. [For the continuation of this work, by J. H. Parker, *see* below, 1853.]

[p. 122] Perhaps the earliest [hostel or tavern] in London was the Saracen's Head in Friday Street, Chepeside, where Chaucer, in his youth, saw the Grosvenor arms hanging out; the poet did not make his acquaintance with the Tabard in Southwark till a later date.

1851. Unknown. *Review* of Wright's *Canterbury Tales,* vol. iii, [in] The Athenæum, March 15, 1851, pp. 294–5.

[A long review, praising Wright's principle of printing from a single MS. and giving the variations of others; surprise is expressed that he had not used the Ellesmere MS., and hope that he would add the other poems, a glossary, and a biography which should, without being diffuse like Godwin's, contain the new facts which have come to light since Nicolas published his.]

1851. Unknown. *Biographical Sketches of Eminent British Poets . . .
intended for teachers,* Dublin, *Geoffrey Chaucer,* pp. 1–11.

[A very brief biography, accepting the events based on *The
Testament of Love,* followed by quotations in praise of Chaucer
from Campbell, Southey, Leigh Hunt, etc.]

[This book was probably intended to be a companion to the *Selections from the
British Poets,* Dublin, 1851, *q.v.* below. Both were published by direction of the
Commissioners of National Education in Ireland.]

1851. Unknown. *Selections from the British Poets, . . . from Chaucer
to the present Time* . . . Dublin, 1851, vol. i, p. 337 [" Truth "] ;
vol. ii, pp. 4–5 [" Spring "], 105–6 [" An April Day "], 210–12
[" The Good Parson "], 253 [" The Daisy "], 365, 399.

[The first four pieces are more or less modernised, the third
so much so that its original cannot be identified. The first
stanza reads :

All day the low-hung clouds have dropt
    Their garner'd fulness down ;
All day the soft grey mist hath wrapt
    Hill, valley, grove and town.

This reappears in several later school anthologies, the latest
we have found being H. C. Bowen's *Studies in English,* 1876.]

1852. Clough, Arthur Hugh. *Lecture on the Development of English
Literature from Chaucer to Wordsworth,* [printed in] Prose Remains
of A. H. Clough, 1888, pp. 333–42.

[p. 334] In commencing such a conspectus [of the mutual reaction of
literature and national character in England], I can have no
hesitation in selecting the first name : English Literature
begins with Chaucer. . . . The picture of all that pertains to
those first exhibitions (for good or for evil, or for both) of our
English genius and temper you may see surviving unfaded in
the lively colouring of the " Canterbury Tales." . . . What,
[p. 335] for example, can be truer to permanent English likings
and dislikings . . . than these lines in description of the
Monk ? [Quotation, *Prol.,* ll. 173–8, 183–8.] Certainly we
may still find in old England ladies — I quote Chaucer —
paining themselves to counterfeit cheer of court, and be
estately of manere, and to be held worthy of reverence ; busy
or busy-seeming lawyers [quotation, *Prol.,* ll. 321–2] ; country
gentlemen, great at the sessions, and greater at the dinner
table ; the tried soldier, silent and unpretending ; the young
[p. 336] soldier, much the reverse ; the merchant, so discreet and
steadfast [quotation, *Prol.,* l. 282] ; religious and laborious
parish-clergymen, and church dignitaries, not very religious,
and not at all laborious.

[p. 342] [Chaucer, by the copious admission of Norman-French elements, completed and transformed 'our homely meagre Semi-Saxon into a civilised and living speech.']

1852. Edgar, Andrew. *Popular Literature,* [in] *Tusculana,* pp. 116, 118–19, 127–8.

[p. 118] We never rise from their perusal [*i. e.* of the Canterbury Tales] without a conviction that, but for their antique
[p. 119] phraseology, their popularity at the present day would be unbounded. . . They present to us men *as they were,* and in truth, as they always will be. . . The masterly narrative of Hume conveys but an imperfect notion of those times, in comparison with what may be derived from the " Canterbury Tales." We are presented with the very form and pressure of the age. . . We are admitted behind the scenes ; we inspect the interior of society. We see causes beginning to operate of which we now enjoy the effects. We see the clergy meeting with the contempt and sneers of wise observers. . . We see the rising influence of the people. . . Then in addition to all this we have fancy and imagination shedding their radiance over all, romance so like truth, poetry so full of nature. Would not a writer of such powers, and such a character, but for the unfortunate drawback to which we have alluded, and which the failure of every attempt has rendered us almost hopeless of ever seeing removed, be likely to find favour in the eyes of a generation who pay such homage to the mirrored life of Shakespeare, and who take such delight in " the pictured page " of Scott ?

[This passage was quoted in extenso by a reviewer in the Gentleman's Magazine, March, 1853, new ser., vol. xxxix, pp. 286–7, and commended as "a little overwrought, but in the main just."]

1852. Mitford, Mary Russell. *Recollections of a Literary Life,* 3 vols. ; vol. i, p. 111; vol. ii, pp. 176, 236 ; vol. iii, pp. 189–91, 194.

[iii. 190] These towers [Donnington] with their battlements, and the deep, arched entrance . . . speak of little but war in its sternest form ; but the little hall, with its beautiful groined roof, and a certain mixture of rude splendour and homely comfort, . . . tells of the genial poet whose healthy, cordial,
[p. 191] hearty spirit must have made him the delight of every board, and most especially of his own.

I was much tempted to extract some passage in harmony

with this feeling; some bright and life-like portrait from the description of the Canterbury Pilgrims, or that inimitable character of the good Parson, which amongst its innumerable merits has none higher than the proof it affords of Chaucer's own love of piety and virtue. . . . I subjoin (taking no other freedom than that of changing the orthography) one of my own favourite bits, . . . full as it seems to me of tenderness, pathos and truth.

[Quotation—*Man of Law's Tale*, ll. 722–875.]

[For Miss Mitford's letter and sonnet on this occasion, *see* above, 1815.

1852-3. N., F. M. *Letters*, [in] The Gentleman's Magazine, Sept. 1852, Jan., Feb., March, 1853, new series, vol. xxxviii, pp. 274-5, vol. xxxix, pp. 52-4, 169-70, 276-7.

[On English etymology, with many examples from Chaucer.]

1852. Notes and Queries, 1st Series, vol. v, pp. 26, 141, 170, 237, 252-3, 267-8, 319, 325-6, 373, 466, 536, 574, 607, 621; vol. vi, pp. 118, 167, 304, 409, 424, 603.

Author.	Date.	Reference.	Subject.
Editor?	Jan. 10.	1st S. v, 26.	Johnson the author of the newspaper announcement of Cibber's *Lives of the Poets*, with Chaucer allusions; *q. v.* above, 1753, vol. i, p. 407.
A., E.	Feb. 7.	1st S. v, 141.	'Buxom.'
B[rae], A. E.	Feb. 21.	1st S. v, 170.	'To do' = to cause.
Warde, H. Corville, and **Editor.**	Feb. 21.	1st S. v, 180.	'Dulcarnon,' still current.
Juvenis.	Mar. 6.	1st S. v, 237.	'Dun is in the mire.'
Singer, Samuel Weller, and **N., A.**	Mar. 13.	1st S. v, 252-3.	'Dulcarnon,' from the Arabic.
Campkin, Henry.	Mar. 20.	1st S. v, 267-8.	Burlesque on Cowley's epitaph, with Chaucer allusions; *q. v.* below, App. A., [1667?].
' Philo-Chaucer.'	April 3.	1st S. v, 319.	Is the copy of Speght's *Chaucer* in existence, in which was a note by Gabriel Harvey on Heywood's Epigrams? [See a note in Warton's *Poetry*, vol. iii, p. 86 (ed. 1840).]

Author.	Date.	Reference.	Subject
Singer, Samuel Weller.	April 3.	1st S. v, 325–6.	'Dulcarnon.' 'Are we never to have an edition of Chaucer worthy of him and creditable to us?'
Benmohel, N. L.	April 17.	1st S. v, 373.	'Rehete.'
'Philo-Chaucer.'	May 15.	1st S. v, 466.	'Soth play quod play' (*Cokes Prol.*, l. 33).
'Eliza.'	June 5.	1st S. v, 536.	Who is the author of the following lines on Chaucer? 'Swan-like, in dying Famous old Chaucer Sang his last song.'
'Jaydee.'	June 12.	1st S. v, 574.	Reference given for the above, *q.v.* above, 1841.
R., J. C.	June 26.	1st S. v, 607.	'Gat-tothed.'
L.	June 26.	1st S. v, 621.	A slight correction in the above.
T., F. W.	Sept. 25.	1st S. v, 304.	'Vernicle.'
M., J. R.	Oct. 30.	1st S. vi, 424.	The Man in the Moon; Henryson's *Testament of Cresseide* quoted as Chaucer's.
B., J. N.	Dec. 25.	1st S. vi, 603.	What authority is there for the statement (made by Aikin) that Chaucer studied law at the Temple?

1852. Smith, Alexander. *A Life Drama*, sc. iv. (Poems, 1853 [1st in B.M., a reissue?], p. 52; Poetical Works, ed. W. Sinclair, 1909, p. 36.)

Breezes are blowing in old Chaucer's verse.

1852. Unknown. *Review* of *The Life of Thomas Stothard, R.A.*, by *Anne Eliza Bray*, [in] The Gentleman's Magazine, Feb. 1852, new ser., vol. xxxvii, pp. 148–50.

[p. 150]   Should Mrs. Bray . . . reprint her life of her famous father-in-law . . . she should certainly refer to the rival Pilgrimage which Blake painted and engraved—a rival only in the co-incidence of its appearance—for it is not only Blake's poorest production, but a most sorry performance itself, while Stothard's fine composition has been happily described by Scott, in his Life of Dryden, as "executed with the genius and spirit of a master, and all the rigid attention to costume that could be expected by the most severe antiquary."

[1853.] The Canterbury Tales; A New Text, with illustrative Notes by T. Wright. Universal Library (Ingram, Cooke and Co.), Poetry, Vol. ii. [Reprinted with additions in 1860.]

[A reprint of Wright's Percy Society edn., 1848–51, *q.v.*]

1853. The Canterbury Tales . . . from the text and with the notes and glossary of T. Tyrwhitt, . . . A new edition. Illustrated by Edward Courbould. (Routledge's British Poets.) [Re-issued in Routledge's Standard Library in 1878, 1882, etc.]

1853. Clough, Arthur Hugh. *Letter to Charles E. Norton,* [dated] Dec. 9, 1853, [printed in] Prose Remains of A. H. Clough, 1888, pp. 221-2.

Tell Child not to be *too* learned about his Chaucer, for my sake ; and above all, to make the verses scan. I hesitate about recommending any indications of the metre in the typography. But a set of simple directions emphatically and prominently given at the outset (*e. g.* for the sounding or silencing of the final e) will, I think, be essential. People won't read Chaucer against their ears.

[Professor F. J. Child abandoned the scheme of editing Chaucer, considering the time unripe. For another letter by Clough on the same subject, *see* below, 1854.]

1853. FitzGerald, Edward. *Six Dramas of Calderon,* freely translated by Edward FitzGerald, pp. 173-4*n.* (Letters and Literary Remains, ed. W. Aldis Wright, 1902-3, 7 vols., vol. v, p. 271*n.*)

[To illustrate —
       . . . give me my staff.

Alas, alas ! and I with no strength left
To wield it, only as I halt along,
Feeling about with it to find a grave,
And knocking at deaf earth to let me in!
         Three Judgments at a Blow.   Act II, scene 1.

FitzGerald quotes in a note :
Ne dethe alas ! ne wolle not [han] my life . . .
Leve moder, let me yn.
         Chaucer's Pardoner's Tale.

A better text of Chaucer's lines has been printed in subsequent editions. For another reference by FitzGerald to this passage, *see* below, 1856.]

1853. Landor, Walter Savage. *Imaginary Conversation, Archdeacon Hare and Walter Landor,* [in] Last Fruit off an Old Tree, pp. 107–8, 124. (Works, ed. C. G. Crump, 1891–3 ; Imaginary Conversations, vol. iv, pp. 407, 426.)

[Landor persuades Hare that Chaucer's spelling is much better than the modern.]

p. 426] Shakespeare and Milton and Chaucer have more imagination than any of those to whom the quality is peculiarly attributed.

1853. Notes and Queries, 1st Series, vol. vii, pp. 38, 69–70, 160–1, 201, 274, 282, 284, 335, 356–7, 391, 392, 397–99, 401, 424, 440, 512, 517–19, 542, 560, 568–9, 584–5, 620, 622, 624 ; vol. viii, pp. 10, 161, 180, 311, 323, 450, 455, 475, 502, 584.

Author.	Date.	Reference.	Subject.
' Tyro.'	Jan. 15.	1st S. vii, 69–70.	Two extracts, (1) from the Life of Chaucer by Sir Harris Nicolas, and (2) from Godwin's Life of Chaucer, giving what authority there is for the assertion that Chaucer studied law at the Temple.
Keight- ley, Thomas.	Feb. 12.	1st S. vii, 160–1.	' Its,' not used by Chaucer, or by any poet earlier than the end of the sixteenth century, a test for Rowley.
S., T. A.	Feb. 26.	1st S. vii, 201.	Inedited Poem on Chaucer, called ' Eulogium Chaucerj,' found in MS. in a black-letter Chaucer [1561], *q.v.* above, vol. i, p. 109.
' Erica.'	Mar. 19.	1st S. vii, 282.	' Rather.'
M.	Mar. 19.	1st. S. vii, 284.	' Rape and renne.'
Singer, Samuel Weller.	April 2.	1st S. vii, 335.	' Seldom-when,' ' selden-time.'
' An Oxford B.C.L.'	April 9.	1st S. vii, 356–7.	Emerson states (*q.v.* above, 1848) that Chaucer's *Hous of Fame* is taken ' from the French or Italian.' Is this so ? and if so, from what sources ?
Crossley, Francis.	April 16.	1st S. vii, 392.	' Rather.'
Bede, Cuth- bert.	April 23.	1st S. vii, 397–9.	A list of the epithets given by British poets to the nightingale ; Chaucer's are : evening, good, heavenly, lusty, merry, new-abashed, shrill, sweet.
Arrow- smith, W. R.	April 23.	1st S. vii, 401.	' More ' = root.
B., J. M.	April 30.	1st S. vii, 425.	' Latin ' = Italian (*Troilus,* ii, Prohem. l. 14).
B., J. M.	April 30.	1st S. vii, 440.	No foreign original has ever been found for Chaucer's *Hous of Fame* . . . We may fairly presume that Emerson never took the trouble to investigate the matter.

Author.	Date.	Reference	Subject.
Anon.	May 21.	1st S. vii, 512.	'Rathe.'
B., J. M.	May 28.	1st S. vii, 517–19.	On Chaucer's knowledge of Italian. Sir Harris Nicolas (in Aldine edn. of Chaucer, 1845) says Chaucer was not acquainted with the Italian language or literature. This is not the case, and many passages from Chaucer's writings are quoted which are either translations or paraphrases from lines in Dante, Petrarch or Boccaccio.
Arrow-smith, W. R.	June 4.	1st S. vii, 542.	'Dare' = lurk or cause to lurk.
G., W. H.	June 11.	1st S. vii, 568–9.	An early satirical poem mentioning Chaucer, *q.v.* below, App. A., [*n.b.* 1506].
M., J.	June 11.	1st S. vii, 584–5.	Chaucer's knowledge of Italian (1st S. vii, 517) upheld by Dr. Nott (in his edn. of Surrey and Wyatt, *q.v.* above, 1815–16).
Editor.	June 25.	1st S. vii, 620.	'Bumble,' used of the bittern
B., E. M.	June 25.	1st S. vii, 622.	'Leden' = Latin, used of the song of birds, etc.
Chever-ells.	June 25.	1st S. vii, 624.	'Parvise.'
Editor.	July 2.	1st S. viii, 10.	'Dissimulate.'
H., T. H. de.	Aug. 13.	1st S. viii, 160–1.	'Unneath.'
R., C. I.	Aug. 20.	1st S. viii, 180.	Lydgate's 'Balade warnynge men to beware of deceitful women,' quoted as Chaucer's.
'Broc-tuna.'	Nov. 5.	1st S. viii, 450.	'Lozenges.'
Editor.	Nov. 5.	1st S. viii, 455.	Brief notice of Routledge's edition of the Canterbury Tales.
Pinker-ton, W.	Nov. 12.	1st S. viii, 475.	Poetical epithets of the nightingale ; Chaucer uses, beside those given in vii, 397–9, 'sely.'
C., B. H	Nov. 19.	1st S. viii, 502.	Black as a mourning colour first alluded to by Chaucer (*Troilus* and *Knightes Tale*) and Froissart.
Whit-borne, J. B.	Dec. 17.	1st S. viii, 584.	Church reves.

1853–9. Parker, John Henry. *Some Account of Domestic Architecture in England,* [vol. ii] by the Editor of "The Glossary of Architecture" [J. H. Parker], Edward I.–Richard II., 1853, pp. 41 48–50, 54, 66 *n.*, 67, 74, 87, 94, 97 *n.*, 98, 116–7, 128, 132, 184 [quotations from Chaucer illustrating the high table, painted chambers, eating utensils, the Squire's carving, minstrelsy at meals, door locks, sleeping chambers, gardens, the cook, sauces and inns], 270 [Chaucer retired to Donyngton Castle, in Berkshire, in the seventieth year of his age, about 1396]; [vol. iii] Richard II.- Henry VIII., 1859, pt. i, p. **47** [the Tabard, its destruction and rebuilding in the reign of Charles II.].

[Vol. i, by T. Hudson Turner, appeared in 1851, *q.v.*]

1854–56 Works of Chaucer, 8 vols., in Bell's Annotated Edition of the English Poets. [The introductions and notes are by Robert Bell. Re-edited in 1878, *q.v.* below.]

[Vol. i contains the Biography and Literary Introduction. The Biography, though the usual apocryphal pieces, except the *Testament of Love,* are accepted, is a good gathering-up of the facts then known, based on Tyrwhitt, Godwin, Nicolas, etc. The residence at Donnington Castle is not accepted. The Introduction deals with Chaucer's learning, language, metre, etc. The various pieces in the text have each an Introduction and notes. The apocryphal pieces include *The Court of Love, Parlement of Foules, Cuckoo and Nightingale, Flour and Lefe,* vol. iv; *Chauceres Dreme (The Island of Ladies),* vol. vi; *Complaint of the Black Knight, Balade de Vilage (= Vissage) sans Peynture, Chaucer's Prophecy, Orisoun to the Virgin, Lamentation of Mary Magdalen, Praise of Women, Eight Goodly Questions, Lines to the King and Knights of the Garter,* vol. viii, the latter four pieces being included in *Poems Attributed to Chaucer.*]

1854–6. Bell, Robert. *Introduction* and *Notes* to the Works of Chaucer [*q. v.* above].

1854 Case, M. P. *Chaucer and his Times,* [in] Bibliotheca Sacra, Andover, Mass., April, 1854, art. viii, 2nd series, vol. xi, pp. 394–416.

[Chaucer "a dim and shadowy figure." An account of the age of Chaucer, Wiclif's religious reform, Edward III and his Queen Philippa, &c.]

[p. 404]   [Remarks on the 'foreign air' of Chaucer's language at a cursory glance.]

The English tongue . . . was a rude mass, *rudis indigestaque moles,* a material the most unpromising possible for genius to find an utterance in. The French had been used by the higher classes, Latin by the learned, and the Saxon by the common people; and during the period of Norman ascendency, for more than two centuries, the Anglo-Saxon had ceased to be a written language. It was only a dialect of slaves, the *patois* of a crushed and despised race . . .

[p. 405]   Rarely, if ever, has the history of letters recorded such a phenomenon as we here behold. A great genius, one of the world's elect bards, arises in a country and in an age where the language is an unfit and an insufficient medium for his utterances, and where he must not only create his forms and conceptions, but, in some sense, the language also, with which to clothe them . . .

[pp. 406–7]   [Remarks on the uncertainty of the chronology of Chaucer's life and writings, followed by a criticism of 'the two capital allegories of Chaucer,' the *Hous of Fame*, and the *Flour and the Lefe*.]

[p. 409]   In the Canterbury Tales, our poet leaves this fanciful region where he had so fondly lingered, and places before us persons and scenes of the most matter-of-fact kind possible. This was his last and greatest work; the labor of his old age.

[pp. 409–14]   [Here follows a detailed criticism of the characters in the *Prologue*.]

[p. 414]   In seeking for Chaucer's prominent characteristics, we recognize at once his great descriptive power. Every scene and every character lives before us. His naturalness, also, is most observable. Nothing is artificial; nature reigns supreme everywhere. He is, in fact, preëminently a poet of nature. He is the poet of spring, of the singing of the birds, of the zephyrs, and the flowers. He is no weak nor lazy copyist; he takes nothing at second hand.

[pp. 414–15]   [Chaucer contrasted with Byron.]

[p. 415]   The popularity of Chaucer has experienced various vicissitudes. In the age of Queen Elisabeth [*sic*], he was truly regarded as the first of English poets; and Spenser, his fond admirer and copyist, when dying, requested, as an especial honor, to be buried near his tomb. At other periods he has not been so generally read. . . .

[Hindrances to his popularity, the grossness of the times, and the obsoleteness of the language; the latter easily surmountable.]

[p. 416]   Whatever the general and popular estimation of his writings may be, he will be read so long as a love for nature and truth shall remain among those who speak the English language. He was worthy to lead off that noble band of British bards, who will long reflect glory on the English name. It is a conspicuous place which he holds among his compeers in that 'House of Fame,' which he has so graphically described to us.

1854. Clough, Arthur Hugh. *Letter to F. J. Child*, [dated] Sept. 2, 1854, [printed in] Prose Remains of A. H. Clough, 1888, p. 228-9.

I hope the Chaucer is going on prosperously. I think you should adopt means to make the metre quite obvious, at any sacrifice of typographical prettiness. Yet I don't like the grave accent, 'When Zephyrus eke with his sotè breth,' and should almost prefer the ˘, sotĕ, but that it seems unmeaning to use a mark of quantity. Yet it is not a case of accent, either. I think I should in one way or another mark every syllable that would not now be pronounced, grevès and levès and Emperourè's daughter—the most correct mark would be ë : Emperourë's ; sotë. And I should prefix to the whole a very plain and short statement of the usage in these points. I suppose there is not much doubt about a few general rules, though Chaucer did not regularly observe them, as, for example, the use of the ĕ in adjectives after definite articles, which it seems to me he omits occasionally, with French adjectives, as if it was a matter of ear rather than rule. So also with such Saxon dissyllables, as tymĕ, which is not invariably a dissyllable, I think. And yet it would be worth while giving a list of such words as are liable to be dissyllables. However, ere this, I daresay you have settled all these preliminaries. I don't quite see what you should do about the Miller's and the Reve's Tales. I think explanation might be
[p. 229] a little retrenched there, so as to leave them in the " decent obscurity of a learned language.

[For another letter by Clough on the same subject *see* above, 1853.]

1854. Lowell, James Russell. *Leaves from my Journal in Italy and Elsewhere*, [in] Graham's Monthly, April-June, 1854 [not in B M. See Bibliography of J. R. Lowell by G. W. Cooke]. (Writings, Riverside Edn., 11 vols., vol. i, p. 184.)

I cannot describe our drive [from Subiaco to Tivoli] . . .

It is not often that we can escape the evil genius of analysis that haunts our modern daylight of self-consciousness . . . and enjoy a day of right Chaucer.

1854. Notes and Queries, 1st Series, vol. ix, pp. 54, 112, 307, 351, 383, 399, 433, 470–1 ; vol. x, pp. 82, 96, 135, 182, 203, 208, 387, 398, 411, 474, 535.

Author.	Date.	Reference.	Subject.
Q.	Jan. 21.	1st S. ix, 54.	'Starve' = die.
Middleton, F. M.	April 1.	1st S. ix, 307.	The chase of the fox in *Nonnes P.T.* the embryo of fox-hunting.
Foss, Edward.	April 22.	1st S. ix, 383.	In the reign of Henry IV, there was a Club called 'La Court de bone Compagnie,' of which Occleve was a member, and probably Chaucer. So also was Henry Somer, who received Chaucer's pension for him.
Editor.	April 29.	1st S. ix, 399.	'Gossip.'
'Zeus.'	May 20.	1st S. ix, 470–1.	'Galoche.'
Riley, H. T.	Aug. 12.	1st S. x, 135.	Chaucer and Emerson (vii, 356). Is an Oxford B.C.L. correct in his quotation from Emerson's *Representative Men?* 'Chaucer, it seems, drew continually, through Lydgate and *Caxton,* from Guido di Colonna,' &c. Surely Mr. Emerson never penned such nonsense as this. [For the passage in Emerson's *Shakespeare,* in *Representative Men, see* above, 1848.]
Riley, H. T.	Sept. 2.	1st S. x, 182.	'Tabard' and 'Talbot.'
B., J. M.	Sept. 9.	1st S. x, 203.	'Jack of Dover.'
G., H. T.	Sept. 9.	1st S. x, 208.	Mention in *Sompnoures T.* of kissing.
P., J.	Nov. 11.	1st S. x, 387.	What are the grounds for the surmise that Chaucer's Parish Priest was sketched from Wiclif in his later days ?
Editor.			This is merely conjectural, probably from the fact that when Wiclif was warden of Canterbury College, Oxford, he is said to have had Chaucer under his tuition. *The Persone of a Town* (1841), [*q.v.* above], and Le Bas, *Life of Wiclif* [*q.v.* above, 1832], quoted.
C , T. Q.	Nov. 18.	1st S. x, 398.	Quotation: *Pardoneres Prol.,* ll. 361–5.

Author.	Date.	Reference.	Subject.
S., J. D.	Nov. 18.	1st S. x, 411.	'Harlot,' applied to males, derived, like varlet, from 'hyran,' to hire.
Q.	Dec. 9.	1st S. x, 474.	'A per se.'
' 'Οὔτις.'	Dec. 30.	1st S. x, 535.	Doubtless the notion of Chaucer having portrayed Wickliff as his "Parish Priest" (x. 387) is of equal authenticity with the tradition that Dryden drew his beautiful exemplification of it from Bishop Ken.

[*c.* **1854.**] **Rossetti**, Dante Gabriel. *Beauty and the Bird,* [a sonnet, in] Poems, 1870 (edn. 2, 1870, 1st in B.M.) p. 278. (Collected Works, ed. W. M. Rossetti, 1897, 2 vols., vol. i, p. 286.)

She fluted with her mouth as when one sips . . .
Till her fond bird, with little turns and dips,
Piped low to her of sweet companionships.
And when he made an end, some seed took she
And fed him from her tongue . . .
And like the child in Chaucer, on whose tongue
The Blessed Mary laid, when he was dead,
A grain,—who straightway praised her name in song :
Even so, when she, a little lightly red,
Now turned on me and laughed, I heard the throng
Of inner voices praise her golden head.

[Placed chronologically in the Collected Works after a poem attributed to about 1854 (see note, vol. i, p. 521).

Mr. W. M. Rossetti (*ib.* vol. i, p. xxvii), after giving a list of poets who influenced D. G. Rossetti, says : " The reader may perhaps be surprised to find some names unmentioned in this list . . . Chaucer, Spenser, the Elizabethan dramatists (other than Shakespeare), Milton, Dryden, Pope, Wordsworth, are unnamed. It should not be supposed that he read them not at all or cared not for any of them ; but if we except Chaucer in a rather loose way . . . they were comparatively neglected."]

1854. Thoreau, Henry David. *Walden*, Boston, p. 228. (Writings, Riverside Edn., 1894–5, 10 vols., vol. ii, pp. 330–31.)

Thus far I am of the opinion of Chaucer's nun, who

Yave not of the text a pulled hen
That saith that hunters ben not holy men.

Prol. ll. 177–8.

[It was, of course, not the nun, but the monk, who held this opinion.]

1854. Unknown. *The Crystal Palace,* [in] Blackwood's Edinburgh Magazine, Sept. 1854, vol. lxxvi, p. 335.

We summon then, our oldest poet, to celebrate as afar off, for coming time, our newest Crystal Palace and its wonders, in

CHAUCER'S DREAM
OF THE CRYSTAL PALACE.

' As I slept I dreamt I was
    Within a temple made of glass . . .
    Of metal that shone out full clear. . . .

[*Hous of Fame*, ll. 119–27, and other passages strung together.]
[For a parallel *see* above, 1851, Notes and Queries, May 10.]

1854. Unknown. *The Beard*, [in] The Westminster Review, July, 1854,
new ser., vol. vi, p. 58.

In Richard II's reign, . . . the beard was "forked," . . .
The venerable authority of Chaucer now comes in ; and what
a glimpse is this he gives us of his " Shipman " :—
    " Hardy he was, and wise I undertake,
        With many a tempest hadde his berd be shake " !
Here is vigour of delineation !
    [The Frankeleyns "white berd" and the Merchantes
" forked berd " also noted.]

1854. Wall, James W. *Early English Poets, Chaucer,* [in] The
Knickerbocker Magazine, New York, May, vol. xliii, pp. 441–50.

[A short life, followed by some notice of the estimation in
which Chaucer was held by his successors (pp. 446–7), ending
with a short account and criticism of the Canterbury Tales.]

1855. Burne-Jones, Sir Edward Coley. *See* below, 1855, Morris.

1855. Chatelain, Jean Baptiste François Ernest de. *La Fleur et la
Feuille :* poème, avec le texte en regard, traduit en vers français
de G. Chaucer par le Chevalier de Chatelain, London. *See* below,
App. B.

1855-8. Clarke, Mary Cowden. *Music among the Poets and Poetical
Writers,* [in] The Musical Times, vol. vi, 1855, Feb. 1, p. 290,
Feb. 5, p. 311, March 15, p. 343, April 1, p. 353, May 1, p. 383 ;
vol. vii, May 15, p. 6, June 15, p. 37, July 1, p. 54, Aug. 1, p. 85 ;
1856, May 1, p. 235, July 1, p. 261, Aug. 1, p. 283, Dec. 1, p. 347 ;
vol. viii, 1857, March 1, p. 6, July 1, pp. 74, 79, Sept 1, p. 106,
Nov. 1, pp. 137–8 ; 1858, Jan. 1, pp. 169–70, Feb. 1, p. 186, March
1, p. 207, June 1, p. 252, Aug. 1, p. 286, Oct. 1, pp. 317–18.

[Quotations with comments, more freely from Chaucer than
from any other poet.]

[*c.* **1855** ?] **Dixon**, Richard Watson. *A Wedding Scene from Chaucer.*

[A painting, the only one of Dixon's that survives, according to H. C. Beeching, *Dict. Nat. Biog.*, 1st Suppl., vol. ii, 1901, p. 139. Dixon was a college friend of William Morris and Burne-Jones, and no doubt shared their readings in Chaucer (*see* below, 1855, Morris). Dean Beeching further notes (*ib.* p. 140) that 'Dixon had a great look of Chaucer as he appears in Hoccleve's portrait, and the resemblance was more than external, reaching to a characteristic and humorous interest in all sorts and conditions of people.' That the same resemblance was also noticed in Morris and in D. G. Rossetti (*q.v.* above, 1845, F. M. Brown) is perhaps only a sign of the enthusiasm of the Pre-raphaelites for Chaucer.]

1855. **Dobell**, Sydney Thompson. *America*, [printed in] Poetical Works, 1875, 2 vols., vol. i, p. 235.

Ye shall be

Lords of an Empire wide as Shakespeare's soul,
Sublime as Milton's immemorial theme,
And rich as Chaucer's speech, and fair as Spencer's dream.

1855. **Hunt**, James Henry Leigh. *Beaumont and Fletcher*, or, The Finest Scenes, Lyrics and other Beauties of those two Poets . . . with . . . notes and . . . preface by Leigh Hunt, pp. 288 *n.*, 294 *n.*

[p. 288]   [The Two Noble Kinsmen.]

Who dost pluck
With arm armipotent, etc.

A most magnificent image. The epithet armipotent is from Chaucer, and employed in a manner not unworthy of that ill-understood master of versification. Chaucer took it from Boccaccio, but turned it from prose into poetry, by putting it in a right place :—

Vide in questa la casa del suo Dio
Armipotente, ed essa edificata
Tutta d'acciajo isplendido e pulio.

Teseide, lib. vii. st. 32.

And downward from an hill, under a bent,
There stood the temple of Mars *armipotent*,
Wrought all of burned stele, etc.

[This example, from *the Two Nobel Kinsmen*, of the use of "armipotent" is not given in the New English Dictionary, one from 'Fairfax's' Tasso, 1600, being given for this period. It is probable that the word has never been used in English without conscious reference to the passage from the *Knightes Tale* quoted by Leigh Hunt above.]

[*c.* **1855.**] **Hunt,** James Henry Leigh. *An Essay on the Sonnet,* [in] *The Book of the Sonnet,* ed. Leigh Hunt and S. Adams Lee, Boston, 1867, vol. i, pp. 65–6.

[For the date, which should be two years later, *see* below, App. A., [*c.* 1857].

[p. 65]   How are we to account for the non-appearance of a Sonnet in the poems of Chaucer?—of Chaucer, who was so fond of Italian poetry, such a servant of love, such a haunter of the green corners of revery, particularly if they were "small,"— of Chaucer, moreover, who was so especially acquainted with the writings of Petrarca's predecessor, Dante, with those of his friend Boccaccio, and who, besides eulogizing the genius of Petrarca himself, is supposed to have made his personal acquaintance at Padua?   Out of the four great English poets, Chaucer is the only one who has left us a sonnet of no kind [p. 66] whatsoever, though he was qualified for every kind, and though of none of the four poets it would seem more naturally to have fallen in the way.

[Three reasons for this are suggested : (1) Chaucer's close connection with France led him to French miscellaneous poetry rather than Italian, (2) the sonnets of Dante and Petrarch were not yet known in England, (3) Chaucer's own propensity to narrative in poetry.]   The second of these reasons, however, I take to have been the chief.   Had Chaucer been familiar with the Sonnets of men whom he so admired, the very lovingness of his nature would hardly have failed to make him echo their tones !

1855. Hunt, James Henry Leigh.   [*Preface to*] *Death and the Ruffians, modernized from Chaucer,* [in] Stories in Verse, pp. 262–3.

[This modernization of the *Pardoners Tale* first appeared, without a preface, in 1845, *q.v.*   It is followed in *Stories in Verse* by *Cambus Khan*, Hunt's second version of part of the *Squiers Tale*, which first appeared in Horne's *Chaucer Modernized*, 1841. *q.v.*]

[p. 262]   The reader will do me great injustice, if he thinks that modernizations like these are intended as substitutes for what they modernize.   Their only plea for indulgence is, that they may act as incitements towards acquaintance with the great original.   Chaucer's stories are all complete of their kind, all interesting in their plots, and surprising in their terminations ; and the satirical stories are as full of amusement, as the serious are of nobleness and pathos. It is therefore scarcely possible to repeat any one of them, in any way, without producing, in intelligent readers, a desire to know more of him ; and so far, and so far only, such ventures as the first of the two following become excusable. I heartily [p. 263] agree with those critics who are of opinion, that no modernizations of Chaucer, however masterly they might be, could do him justice ; for either they must be little else but re-spellings (in which case they had better be wholly such at once, like Mr. Clarke's, and profess to be nothing but aids to perusal), or, secondly, they must be something betwixt old style and new, and so reap the advantages of neither (which is the case, I fear, with the one just mentioned) ; or lastly, like the otherwise admirable versions by Dryden and Pope, they must take leave *in toto* of the old manner of the original, and proceed upon the merits, whatever those may be, of the style of the modernizers ; in which case Chaucer is sure to lose, not only in manner but in matter.

" Conscience," for example, is now a word of two syllables. In Chaucer's time it was a word of three—*Con-sci-ence.* How is a modern hand to fill up the concluding line in the character of the Nun, without spoiling it ?

> " And all was con-sci-ence and tender heart."

" *A* tender heart " would not do at all ; nor can you find any monosyllable that would.

So, still more emphatically, in the use of the old negative *n'as* (was not) in the exquisite couplet about the officious lawyer—

> " No where so busy a man as he there *n'as.*"
> (Pronounce *noz*),
> " And yet he seemèd busier than he was."

Here the capital rhyme with those two smart peremptory monsyllables (*noz* and *woz*) and consequently the perfection of the couplet, and part of the very spirit of the wit, must be lost in the necessity for turning the old words into new.

1855. Milman, Henry Hart. *History of Latin Christianity*, vol. vi, pp. 432, 536, 545–550 ; 3rd edition, 1864, vol. ix, pp. 97, 232–3, 244–50.

[p. 224] [Outlines of Chaucer's biography, with mention of the tradition that he was present at the wedding of Lionel and

Violante Visconti at Milan, and there met Petrarch. Sir Harris Nicolas cited.]

[p. 245] Chaucer was master of the whole range of vernacular poetry, which was bursting forth in such young and prodigal vigour, in the languages born from the Romance Latin. He had read Dante, he had read Petrarch ; to Boccaccio he owed the ground-work of two of his best poems—The Knight's Tale . . . and Griselidis. I cannot but think that he was familiar with the Troubadour poetry of the Langue d'Oc ; of the Langue d'Oil, he knew well the knightly tales of the Trouvères and the Fabliaux, as well as the later allegorical school, which was then in the height of its fashion in Paris.

[References to *Man of Law's Tale, Troilus, Squieres Tale, Knightes Tale, Frankeleyns Tale, Clerkes Tale, Merchantes Tale, Milleres Tale, Reves Tale, Sir Thopas, Nonnes Prestes Tale, Rom. Rose, Hous of Fame.*]

[p. 246] Yet all the while Chaucer in thought, in character, in language is English—resolutely, determinately, almost boastfully English [footnote : quotation from Testament of Love in sup-
[p.247] port of this]. The creation of native poetry was his deliberate aim ; and already, that broad, practical, humorous yet serious view of life, of life in its infinite variety, that which reaches its height in Shakespeare, has begun to reveal itself in Chaucer. The Canterbury Tales, even in the Preface, represent, as in a moving comedy, the whole social state of the times ; they display human character in action as in speech ; and that character is the man himself. . . . There is an example of every order and class of society, high, low, secular, religious. As yet each is distinct in his class, as his class from others. Contrast Chaucer's pilgrims with the youths and damsels of Boccaccio. Exquisitely as these are drawn, and in some respects finely touched, they are all of one gay light class ; almost any one might tell any tale with equal propriety ; they differ in name, in nothing else.

In his religious characters, if not in his religious tales . . . Chaucer is by no means the least happy. In that which is purely religious the poet himself is profoundly religious ; in his Prayer to the Virgin, written for the Duchess Blanche of Lancaster, for whom also he poured forth his sad elegy ; in his Gentle Martyrs, S. Constantia and S. Cecilia : he is not without his touch of bigotry, as has been said in Hugh of

Lincoln.   But the strong Teutonic good sense of Chaucer had
[p. 248] looked more deeply into the whole monastic and sacerdotal
system.   His wisdom betrays itself in his most mirthful, as in
his coarsest humour.   He who drew the Monk, the Pardoner,
the Friar Limitour, the Summoner, had seen far more than the
outer form, the worldliness of the Churchmen, the abuse of
indulgences, the extortions of the friars, the licentiousness of
the Ecclesiastical Courts, of the Ecclesiastics themselves; he
had penetrated into the inner depths of the religion.   Yet his
wisdom, even in his most biting passages, is tempered with
charity.   Though every order, the Abbot, the Prioress, the
Friar, the Pardoner, the Summoner, are impersonated to the
life, with all their weaknesses, follies, affectations, even vices
and falsehoods, in unsparing freedom, in fearless truth, yet none
or hardly one, is absolutely odious. . . . The Summoner, whose
[p. 249] office and the Archdeacon's Court in which he officiated seem to
have been most unpopular, is drawn in the darkest colours, with
his fire-red cherubim's face, lecherous, venal, licentious.   Above
all, the Parish Priest of Chaucer has thrown off Roman mediæval
sacerdotalism ; he feels his proper place ; he arrays himself
only in the virtues which are the essence of his holy function.
This unrivalled picture is the most powerful because the most
quiet, uninsulting, unexasperating satire.   Chaucer's Parish
Priest might have been drawn from Wycliffe . . . not at
Oxford . . . but the affectionate and beloved teacher of his
humble flock. . . . [The rest of the Chaucerian passage refers
to incidents and subjects connected with Chaucer only by the
acceptance of the *Testament of Love* as his.]

1855. Morris, William, and **Burne-Jones,** Sir Edward Coley.   *Reading*
of Chaucer at Oxford [recorded in] *The Life of William Morris,* by
J. W. Mackail, 2 vols., 1901, vol. i, p. 61.

[" During this year (1855) he (Morris) and Burne-Jones read
through Chaucer.   He found, in the poet whom he afterwards
took for his special master, not merely the wider and sweeter
view of life which was needed to correct the harsh or mystical
elements of his own mediævalism, but the conquest of English
verse as a medium boundless in its range and perfect in its
flexibility."   Of Morris in 1854, Mr. Mackail says (*ib.* p. 39),
"The two books, which afterwards stood with him high and
apart beyond all others, Chaucer and Malory, were as yet

unknown to him." See also *Memorials of Edward Burne-Jones*, by G. B.-J., 2 vols., 1904, vol. i, p. 104.

Morris is said (like D. G. Rossetti, *see* above, 1845, Brown, and like R. W. Dixon, *q.v.* 1855) to have resembled the Occleve portrait of Chaucer at this time.]

1855. Notes and Queries, 1st Series, vol. xi, pp. 82–3, 213, 280, 334, 356, 434, 440, 454 ; vol. xii, pp. 58, 70–1, 123, 140–1, 244, 308.

Author.	Date.	Reference.	Subject.
S., H.	Feb. 3.	1st S. xi, 82.	The man in the moon (*Troilus*).
Aveling, J. H.	Feb. 3.	1st S. xi, 83.	A note about the mutilation of Chaucer in a lecture *On Desultory and Systematic Reading*, by Sir James Stephen, where

ll. 193–4 of the Prologue are quoted thus :

> " I saw his sleeves *perfumed* at the hand
> With *grèase*, and that the finest in the land."

Perfumed for *purfiled* = worked on the edge, and *grease* for *gris* = a species of fur.

Warwick, Eden.	Mar. 17.	1st S. xi, 213.	' Wodewale.'
F.	April 28.	1st S. xi, 334.	' Te-he.'
Bede, Cuthbert.	June 2.	1st S. xi, 434.	Dr. Davy's *Observations on Mr. Fox's Letter to Mr. Grey* (on the *merry* note of the nightingale and Chaucer's use of the word).
Y.	June 9,	1st S. xi, 440.	Survival of Chaucerian expressions in the Lowlands of Scotland.
Denton, W.	June 9.	1st S. xi, 454–5.	Nuns acting as priests (the Prioress's nun-chaplain).
Singer, Samuel Weller.	July 28.	1st S. xii, 58.	Quotes *Testament of Love* as Chaucer's.
Denton, W.	July 28.	1st S. xii, 70–1.	Trees and flowers ; quotations from Chaucer.
Dukes, Leopold.	Aug. 18.	1st S. xii, 123.	A note on "win of ape," the expression used by Chaucer in *Manciple's Prol.*, l. 44.

> " I trow that ye have dronken *win of ape*."

Philo-Chaucer.	Aug. 25.	1st S. xii, 140–1.	Inedited Poem by Chaucer. The ' Orisonne to the Holy Virgin,' preserved in a MS. of John de Irlandia, Opera Theologica, 1490 [*q.v.* above, vol. i, p. 64].[1]

[1 This poem deceived even Dr. Furnivall, who printed it in his Parallel-Text edition of Chaucer's Minor Poems (Part II, No. vi, Mother of God), 1878, and again in 1880, in No. lxi, "A One-Text Print of Chaucer's Minor Poems," Part II. It had been previously printed by Dr. R. Morris in his Aldine edition of *Chaucer's Poetical Works*, 1866. In a note to the Parallel-Text edition, Dr. Furnivall says, "No one can suppose that poor Hoccleve had the power of writing his Master's *Mother of God*."—Notwithstanding this, it has now been definitely decided that the poem is undoubtedly by Hoccleve, and it has been printed by Dr. Furnivall amongst Hoccleve's Works (E.E.T.S., 1892, pp. 52–6). *See also* Ten Brink's History of English Literature, 1895, vol. ii, p. 216 ; vol. iii, Appendix, p. 272   *Also* John Koch *in* Anglia, iii, 183 f. ; iv, Anz., 101 ; vi, 104 f.]

Author.	Date.	Reference.	Subject.
'A Racket Player.'	Sept. 29.	1st S. xii, 244.	'Racket.'
White, A. Holt.	Oct. 20.	1st S. xii, 308.	'Racket' (*Troilus, Testament of Love*, cited as Chaucer's).

1855. **Stanley**, Arthur Penrhyn. *Historical Memorials of Canterbury*, pp. 104*n*., 118, 146, 164–77, 184–7, 189, 206.

[The second and third Essays, which originally appeared in 1853 and 1852, contain only passing references.]

[p. 165]   [Canterbury Tales.]   In the first place we may observe that
[p. 166] every element of society except the very highest and lowest was represented . . . These no doubt are selected as the types of the classes who would ordinarily have been met on such an excursion. . . .
[p. 167]   And further, though the particular plan laid out in his prologue, and the regulation of the whole by the host, is evidently the poet's own creation ; yet the practice of telling stories on the journeys to and from Canterbury must have been common in order to give a likelihood to such a plan.   It was even a custom for the bands of pilgrims to be accompanied by hired minstrels and story-tellers. . .

[These marvellous tales gave rise to the proverbial expression 'a Canterbury Tale,' probably now extinct in England, but surviving in America in the exclamation 'What a Canterbury !'

The tales were in other cases probably related at the halts ; but in this instance on the road, those of the party who were distant thus hearing nothing—' a circumstance which to some extent palliates the relation of the coarser stories in a company which contained the prioress, the nuns, the parson, and the scholar.'

Remarks follow on the auspicious start in spring-time giving 'the colour to Chaucer's whole poem'; on the topographical details of the route, the Tabard, and the approach to the city. There are many other minor allusions.]

1855. Trench, Richard Chenevix. *English Past and Present,* pp. 33–6, 46, 56, 79, 84, 86–7, 97–8, 101, 103. 110–13, 118, 121, 138–9, 143, 152, 159.

[pp. 33–6] [Trench believes, with Tyrwhitt, that Chaucer's influence in introducing French words into the language has been much exaggerated; he only furthered a tendency already existing. Yet his diction is much more French than Wycliffe's; some of his French-derived words failed to retain their place in English.]

1855. Unknown. *English Surnames,* [in] The Edinburgh Review, vol. ci, p. 355.

Camden, in a list of names of occupations, inserts that of the great father of English poetry, *Chaucer*, adding by way of necessary explanation, ' id est *Hosier.*' . . .

The *Chaussure*, commonly used in England when surnames were first adopted by the commonalty, was of leather, covered both the foot and the leg, and appears to have been called *Hose.** *Hosier* therefore is the same with *Chaucier*, which comes from the Latin *Calcearius.*†

* Hose occurs as a surname *Hosatus,* etc., in the Close Rolls.
† Adelung, Wörterbuch, under *Hose* and *Schuster;* Du Cange, v. *Ossa;* and Gesenius, *Dissertatio Grammatica de Lingua Chauceri,* p. 4.

1855. Unknown. *The Genius of Dryden,* [in] The Edinburgh Review, July, 1855, vol. cii, pp. 1, 3, 6, 9, 14, 26.

[p. 14] The early versification of Dryden is as superior to that of Fairfax and Sandys as the versification of Fairfax and Sandys is superior to that of Chaucer.

1855. Unknown. *Review* of *Kingsley's Novels and Poems,* [in] The National Review, July 1855, vol. i, pp. 126–7.

[Thousands who only know Roger Bacon in connection with his brazen head are familiar with the bright and living word-pictures of Chaucer. History and records go but a little way in helping common minds towards the conception of bygone manners and institutions.] But the *poet* comes, and not an intelligent artisan nowadays but can ride with him and his four and twenty [*sic*] in a company from the Southwark Tabard that bright May morning on their pilgrimage to the shrine of Thomas à Beckett. [Chaucer was familiar with the speculations of his day, but shows his knowledge in characters and tales, not in discourses.]

1855. Wiseman, Nicholas Patrick Stephen, Cardinal. *On the Perception of Natural Beauty*, (a lecture, delivered 10 Dec., 1855), 1856, pp. 5–8, 24.

[p. 5]   This intense love [of Nature] is to be found in the father of our poetry, Chaucer. Narrow as was the limit of his
[p. 6] knowledge, or the range of his observation, he had those instinctive perceptions which affection always bestows. His descriptions of every aspect of nature . . . have not been surpassed by any modern poet.

[pp. 6–8] [Comparison of passages from the *Parlement of Foules* (ll 190–96 and 176–82) with Spenser, *F. Q.*, Bk. ii, c. 1 and 2 ; reference to the *Flour and the Lefe.*]

[p. 8] But before leaving these authors, I cannot but express a natural regret, that in both too much, but I think exclusively in the later one, every rich description of natural beauty is connected with wantonness, voluptuousness, and debauchery . . .

[p. 24]   [The idea that May is the month of the Virgin Mary is as old as Chaucer ; quotes *Man of Law's Tale*, ll. 848–54.]

[For Leigh Hunt's criticism on the passage from p. 8, *see* below, 1859.]

1856. Emerson, Ralph Waldo. *English Traits.* Universities, p. 113, Literature, pp. 131–2, 144. (Works, Centenary edn., 1903, vol. v, pp. 200, 233–4, 256.)

[p. 233] A taste for plain strong speech, what is called a biblical
[p. 234] style, marks the English. . . . Chaucer's hard painting of his Canterbury pilgrims satisfies the senses.
[p. 256] We want the miraculous ; the beauty we can manufacture at no mill, can give no account of ; the beauty of which Chaucer and Chapman had the secret.

[1856.] **FitzGerald**, Edward. *Salámán and Absal*, p. v, Prefatory Letter to Professor E. B. Cowell. (Letters and Literary Remains, ed. W. Aldis Wright, 1902–3, 7 vols., vol. vii, pp. 191, 210.)

[p. 191] As for the much bodily omitted—it may readily be guessed that an Asiatic of the 15th Century might say much on such a subject that an Englishman of the 19th would not care to read. Not that our Jámí is ever *licentious* like his contemporary Chaucer, nor like Chaucer's Posterity in Times that called themselves more civil.

[p. 210]   [In later editions of *Salámán and Absal*, on the lines

Yearn, as is likely, to my Mother Earth,

Upon whose bosom I shall cease to weep,

And on my Mother's bosom fall asleep.

FitzGerald added the note :] The same figure is found in Chaucer's "Pardoner's Tale," and, I think, in other Western poems of that era.

> [FitzGerald quoted this passage from the Pardoner's Tale in his Calderon, *q.v.* above, 1853.]

1856. Knight, Charles. *The Popular History of England.* 8 vols. 1856–62; vol. i, 479–83, 489 ; vol. ii, pp. 11–13.

[vol. i, pp. 479–83]   [Social classes in the fourteenth century illustrated by the Statute of Apparel, 1363, and Chaucer's pilgrims ; quotations from *Prol.*]

[vol. ii, pp. 11–13]   [Chaucer a contributor to and a symptom of the spread of knowledge in his day.]

1856. Landor, Walter Savage. *On Orthography.* [Letter] *To the Rev. Augustus Jessopp,* [in] Fraser's Magazine, Feb. 1856, vol. liii, p. 244.

I much commend the late publisher of Milton's works for observing his authography [*sic*]. The same had been done by the judicious Tyrwhitt in his edition of Chaucer . . .

I do not join you in your reprehension of Wordsworth for modernizing Chaucer; because there are many who cannot comprehend that admirable poet's versification, in which the mute *e*, as in the French, is prolonged and sounded. Wordsworth is a poet of high merit, but neither of the same kind nor of the same degree as Chaucer. He could no more have written the *Canterbury Tales,* nor any poetry so diversified, than he could have written the *Paradise Lost* . . .

> [Cf. Landor's letter, declining to take part in Horne's modernization, above, 1841.]

1856. Lloyd, William Watkiss. *Critical Essay on Troilus and Cressida,* [in] The Dramatic Works of William Shakespeare, ed. S. W. Singer, 10 vols., vol. vii, pp. 316–9. [Reprinted in "Critical Essays on the Plays of Shakespeare," 1875, pp. 322–4.]

[p. 316]   Chaucer's Troilus and Cressida, in five long books, is a work remarkable for more than its length ; it is exceedingly full and diffuse, a mere modicum of incident furnishes the simplest skeleton to the large bulk, yet slowly as the story moves, it is [p. 317] always moving, minute as are its details, they are ever touched with liveliness; and archness and mock simplicity, irony most delicate in grain is [*sic*] thrown over the whole, and gives a fanciful glow to descriptions of otherwise literal nature. . . .

[p. 318]   There is some flatness perhaps in the last book both of Chaucer and Boccaccio, from the falsehood of Cressida being conveyed to Troilus at second-hand, by hearsay, cold letters, and conclusively only by his love tokens being captured with the equipments of Diomed. Shakespeare relieved this by carrying him personally to the Greek tents.

The actual conclusion of Chaucer's poem is replete with spirit generally in both conception and execution, but in no point more so than in the compensation allotted to Troilus, less it must be said for his merit, than for his simplicity and suffering. It is after his troubles are over with his life that he rises superior to the false loves and poor passions and pride of a low world, and beholds the better end of existence.

[These Essays are reprinted from an edition of Shakespeare, of the same year, edited by W. W. Lloyd; there are further Chaucer allusions in the footnotes to this.]

1856. Maurice, Frederick Denison. *The Friendship of Books*, [a lecture delivered in 1856, printed in] The Friendship of Books, and other lectures, 1874, p. 16.

I might have spoken of the time of our Edward III., and have given you some proofs that our first poet, Chaucer, was a cordial, genial, friendly man, who could tell us a great many things which we want to know about his own time, and could also break down the barrier between his time and ours.

1856. Notes and Queries, 2nd Series, vol. i, pp. 52, 234, 357, 401, 414, 426, 451; vol. ii, pp. 3, 9, 70, 236, 277, 285, 338, 391, 420, 429.

Author.	Date.	Reference.	Subject.
T., B.	Jan. 19.	2nd S. i, 52.	The name of Walter le Chaucer (1292 and 1293) is to be found

in Kirkpatrick's *History of the Religious Orders and Communities, and of the Hospitals and Castle of Norwich*, and he is not mentioned in the list given by Sir Harris Nicolas of all known persons bearing the poet's name. Might not further search in the records in the Guildhall at Norwich reveal farther traces of the family?

Author.	Date.	Reference.	Subject.
Sartor.	Mar. 22.	2nd S. i, 234.	'Vernage.'
D[en-ton?], **W.**	May 17.	2nd S. i, 401.	*Complaint of the Black Knight* quoted as Chaucer's.
B., G.	May 24.	2nd S. i, 414.	'Ribible,' 'ribibe.'
Denton, **W.**	May 31.	2nd S. i, 426.	Proverbs from Chaucer (also *Testament of Love*, etc., quoted as his).

'A De- June 7.   2nd S. i,   A Word for Chaucer. A plea
sultory   451.   that Chaucer's name should be
Reader.' classed with that of Cervantes as coming nearest to
Shakespeare as a painter of human nature.

Keight-ley, **Thomas.**	July 5.	2nd S. ii, 3.	'Merry.'
Collier, **John** **Payne.**	July 5.	2nd S. ii, 9.	Barnfield's *Poems in divers humors*, 1598, *q.v.* above, vol. i, p. 156.
P., T. H. **Editor.**	July 26.	2nd S. ii, 70.	Chaucerian oaths.
S., S. S.	Sept. 20.	2nd S. ii, 236.	'Kalends.'
Bede, **Cuth-bert.**	Oct. 4.	2nd S. ii, 277.	Dr. Davy and the merry nightingale.'

R., E. G., Oct. 25.   2nd S. ii,   'Medlar;' I have heard it so
                      338.   called [*i. e.* by Chaucer's name
for it, *Reves Prol.* l. 17] by old men in Norfolk.
The Reve is described by Chaucer as a Norfolk man. . .
And more than one instance of Norfolk dialect may be
found in his language.

Wilkin-son, **J. B.**	Nov. 29.	2nd S. ii, 429.	'Squaimous.'

1856. Ruskin, John. *Modern Painters*, 1854–6, Volume iii, 1856,
Part iv, Chapter vii, § 19, Chapter xiv, § 33. (Works, Library
edn., ed. E. T. Cook and A. Wedderburn, 1903–12, 39 vols.,
vol. v, pp. 127, 273–4.)

[p. 127]   Finally, as far as I can observe, it is a constant law that
the greatest men, whether poets or historians, live entirely in
their own age, and that the greatest fruits of their work are
gathered out of their own age. Dante paints Italy in the
thirteenth century; Chaucer, England in the fourteenth;

Masaccio, Florence in the fifteenth ; Tintoret, Venice in the sixteenth : all of them utterly regardless of anachronism and minor error of every kind, but getting always vital truth out of the vital present.

.   .   .   .

[p. 273]   It is quite true that this [horror of a forest] is partly a characteristic, not merely of Dante, or of mediæval writers, but of *southern* writers; for the simple reason that the forest, being with them higher upon the hills, and more out of the way than in the north, was generally a type of lonely and savage places ; while in England, the ' greenwood,' coming up to the very walls of the towns, it was possible to be 'merry in the good greenwood,' in a sense which an Italian could not have understood. Hence Chaucer, Spenser, and Shakspere send their favorites perpetually to the woods for pleasure or meditation ; and trust their tender Canace, or Rosalind, or Helena, or Silvia, or Belphœbe, where Dante would have sent no one but a condemned spirit.

1856. Ruskin, John. *The Harbours of England*, [Illustrative text to Turner's drawings,] pp. 6–8. (Works, Library edn., ed. E. T. Cook and A. Wedderburn, 39 vols., 1903–12, vol. xiii, pp. 20–23.)

[p. 20]   It is very interesting to note how repugnant every oceanic
[p. 21]   idea appears to be to the whole nature of our principal English mediæval poet, Chaucer. Read first The Man of Lawe's Tale, in which the Lady Constance is continually floated up and down the Mediterranean, and the German Ocean, in a ship by herself ; carried from Syria all the way to Northumberland, and there wrecked upon the coast ; thence yet again driven up and down among the waves for five years, she and her child ; and yet, all this while, Chaucer does not let fall a single word descriptive of the sea, or express any emotion whatever about it, or about the ship. He simply tells us the lady sailed here and was wrecked there ; but neither he nor his audience appear to be capable of receiving any sensation, but one of simple aversion, from waves, ships, or sands. Compare with his absolutely apathetic recital, the description by a modern poet of the sailing of a vessel, charged with the fate of another Constance :

> " It curled not Tweed alone, that breeze—
> For far upon Northumbrian seas

It freshly blew, and strong;

. . . [to] The merry seamen laughed to see
Their gallant ship so lustily
Furrow the green sea foam."
[Marmion, ii. 1.]

Now just as Scott enjoys this sea breeze, so does Chaucer
the soft air of the woods; the moment the older poet lands,
he is himself again, his poverty of language in speaking of
the ship is not because he despises description, but because
he has nothing to describe. Hear him upon the ground in
Spring :

" These woodes else recoveren greene,
That drie in winter ben to sene,

[p. 22]   [to] Through which the ground to praisen is."
[Rom. Rose, ll. 57-70.]

In like manner, wherever throughout his poems we find
Chaucer enthusiastic, it is on a sunny day in the " good
greenwood," but the slightest approach to the seashore makes
him shiver; and his antipathy finds at last positive expression,
and becomes the principal foundation of the Frankeleine's Tale,
in which a lady, waiting for her husband's return in a castle
by the sea, behaves and expresses herself as follows :—

" Another time wold she sit and thinke,

[to] ' Why han ye wrought this werk unresonable ? ' "
[Frankeleyns T., 129-44.]

The desire to have the rocks out of her way is indeed severely
punished in the sequel of the tale; but it is not the less
[p. 23] characteristic of the age, and well worth meditating upon, in
comparison with the feelings of an unsophisticated modern
French or English girl among the black rocks of Dieppe or
Ramsgate.

[*n.b.*1856.] **Smith**, Alexander.   *Sydney Dobell*, [in] Last Leaves,
1868, p. 179.

[Written after the publication (in 1856) of Dobell's *England in Time of War.* Smith
died in 1867.]

Chaucer and Spenser are the fountain-heads of all succeeding English poetry. Chaucer is the father of the humorous,
kindly, dramatic, genially-lyrical men; Spenser of the intense,
allegorical, didactic, remote, and, by comparison, unsocial men.

Shakespeare, Dryden, Burns, Byron, Browning, draw descent from Chaucer. Milton, Young, Wordsworth, Shelley, and Tennyson from Spenser.

1856. Unknown. *Review* of *Poetical Works of Geoffrey Chaucer,* ed. Robert Bell, [in] The Christian Remembrancer, Oct. 1856, vol. xxxii, new series, pp. 327–56.

[A general account and welcome of Bell's edition, with references to previous editions. The treatment of *The Testament of Love* for biographical purposes is new. The writer does not pretend "to trace all the particulars of his [Chaucer's] life in *The Testament of Love,* or to distinguish what is purely fictitious from what is intended to relate to real events": though he cannot help thinking that in one sentence Chaucer intended to convey his love for his birthplace. *The Court of Love* is considered genuine, much space is devoted to it, and there is some speculation as to Chaucer's life at the University. *The Cuckow and Nightingale* and *Flour and Lefe* are likewise accepted. The possibilities of Chaucer's adventures in Italy and the effect of his journeys on his work are dwelt upon, pp. 344–5. There is a long account and examination of the *Hous of Fame,* pp. 347–50,— "one of the most admirable burlesque poems in the English language,"—"which has not attracted so much attention as, in our opinion, it deserves." The review contains much quotation from Chaucer, and the main pieces are examined in some detail.]

1856. Unknown. *Review* of *Poetical Works of Geoffrey Chaucer,* ed. Robert Bell, [in] Fraser's Magazine, April, vol. liii, pp. 461–72.

[p. 462]   As regards Chaucer, indeed, there is some excuse for the comparative neglect of his writings by his countrymen. In spite of all that has been written about the harmony of his verse, and his portraiture of life, manners and nature, his language is beset with no ordinary difficulties. As a language, indeed, it is almost anomalous. It is not a foreign tongue, neither is it our own. . . .

[pp. 463–4]   [The area of, and public for, written English very limited in Chaucer's time; that for his new art still more so.]

[p. 465]   [The biographies; inadequacy of all before Nicolas's.]

[pp. 466–70]   [An account of Chaucer's life.]

[p. 470]   From the circumstances of his position, Chaucer therefore enjoyed the most abundant means of studying and representing the character of his fellow-countrymen. And he had not only the fairest opportunity for studying, but also a genius and disposition peculiarly suited to the task. His powers of observation were most keen and catholic; his sympathy with every form of humanity intense; his curiosity was indefatigable. . . .

[p. 471]   Our age moves onward with such rapidity that we cannot hope for any looking back to our elder literature as to a general source of amusement or instruction. . . . It would

[p. 472] accordingly be rash to predict, or even to hope, that Chaucer will ever resume his station as a popular favourite. All that we can claim for him is, therefore, the recognition of his surpassing worth as an adjunct to the historian.

1856. Unknown. *Review* of *Poetical Works of Geoffrey Chaucer*, ed. Robert Bell, [in] Bentley's Miscellany, March 1856, vol. xxxix, pp. 252–9.

[pp. 252–4]   [Quotations from Byron, Berington, Denham, North, Tennyson, and Knight on Chaucer. Reference to the modernizations published by Horne, 1841. On this work, following Bell, the writer says:]

[p. 255]   Wordsworth's Chaucer Wordsworthises. Leigh Hunt's Chaucer is Leigh Huntish. Mrs. Browning's Chaucer indulges in Elizabeth Barrettisms. A reader acquainted with the Lyrical Ballads, with the Story of Rimini, and with the Vision of the Poets, has little difficulty, when conning these several versions of the old bard, to discriminate between this and that " eminent hand," and distribute unhesitatingly *suum cuique.*

[p. 256]   [Praise of Bell's edition, as making the true Chaucer known to popular readers, with an account of Chaucer's versification and language and a reprint of an accented passage from Bell.]

[pp. 256–9]   [Further quotations from De Quincey, Alexander Smith, Camden, Elizabeth B. Browning, Coleridge, Dryden, Fitz-Gerald, Knight, Hippisley, and Bell, with a running commentary on the *Canterbury Tales, Troilus* and certain of the minor poems. *Chaucer's Dream (The Isle of Ladies)* is considered genuine.]

1856. Unknown. *Chaucer, Geoffrey,* [in] *The English Cyclopædia* . . . conducted by Charles Knight, Biog. vol. i, coll. 209–10.

[A life of Chaucer containing all the old legends, and attributing to him the supposititious works, except the *Testa-*

ment of Love, Nicolas's rejection of which is quoted. Few can read him with ease, and none without a dictionary ; yet his language can be mastered with a little pains, which would be amply rewarded.]

1857-60. Chatelain, Jean Baptiste François Ernest de. *Contes de Cantorbéry,* traduits en vers français, 9 tom, London. [*See* below, App. B., and *Chaucer devant la Critique,* par C. F. E. Spurgeon, Paris, 1911, p. 316.]

1857-9. Child, Francis James. *English and Scottish Ballads,* 8 vols., vol. i, pp. 80, 131 ; vol. ii, p. i ; vol. iii, p. 137 ; vol. iv, p. 207 ; vol. v, p. 38 ; vol. viii, p. 152.

[vol. i, p. 131] [Guy of Warwick mentioned by Chaucer among 'romances of pris.'

[vol. ii, p. 1] [Glasgerion.]

[vol. iii, p. 137] HUGH OF LINCOLN. The exquisite tale which Chaucer has put into the mouth of the Prioress exhibits nearly the same incidents as the following ballad.

1857. Furnivall, Frederick James. *MS. Notes, Illustrations of the Prologue to Chaucer's Canterbury Tales,* dated " Working Men's College, 1857." [The Notes consist of passages copied from different books in illustration of the various characters in the Prologue, and were used for lectures at the Working Men's College in 1857-8. See Biography of Furnivall by John Munro in *Frederick James Furnivall,* 1911, p. xxxvi. The original note-book is in the possession of the present Editor. The contents are as follows.]

[p. 2] " The Fat Friar." Extract from *Piers Plowman's Creed,* l. 435 (ed. Wright, 1856), beginning—

> " Than turned I ayen
> Whan I hadde all y-toted,
> And fond in a freitoure
> A frere on a benche," etc.

[p. 3] " The Ploughman." Paraphrase of long passage from the *Creed,* l. 475 [or rather 831], etc.

[p. 6] " The Ploughman's Diet and Work—recommended for the Friars." Extract from *Creed,* l. 1553, etc., and a note. " See Vis. [vol.] i, [p.] 134."

[p. 9] " The Friars' Laziness, Greediness and Selfishness, and want of kindness to one another." Extract from *Creed,* ll. 1437–82.

[p. 13] " Priests—their residing in London." Extract from *Piers Plowman,* Prol. ll. 163–72.

[p. 17]   "Knight." Extract from Leland, *Itinerary* (Somersetshire), vol. II, fol. 53–4, vol. iii, 91 (of original).

[pp. 26, 27, 28 and inserted leaves]

"The Assault of Massoura (*Excerpta Historica*, Bentley, 1831, p. 64)." The valour of Longespee fighting the Saracens.

[p. 30]   " Franklins." Extract from Fortescue, *de Laudibus Legum Angliae*, cap. 29, temp. Hen. VI, 1422–61.

[p. 31]   Extract from W. Lambarde, *Perambulation of Kent*, 1570, published 1576, copied from edn. 1826, p. 8. Note on the " Franklyns and Yeomen of England."

[p. 32]   " Doctor of Phisic." "For a first-rate skit on 'thes fisisiens that helpeth men to dye' see 'A Poem on the Times of Edward II,' ed. Hardwick (Percy Society), stanzas 39–44, pp. 18–21."

Extract from *Piers Plowman*, [vol.] I, [p.] 133 :—
"For murtheris are many leches," etc.

[p. 39]   "The Merchant, as to his selling scheeldes."

Extract from *Piers Plowman*, C, vii, l. 278 :—
" And if I sente over see
My servaunt₃ to Brugges," etc.

[B. v, 392 ; C. vii, 278.]

[p. 41]   " Sergeant₃ (at law)."

Extract from *Piers Plowman*, i, 418 :—
" Yet hoved there an hundred
In howves of selk," etc.

[pp. 42–3] "Sergeant." "Pervise." Selden's note in *Fortescue de laudibus Legum Angliae*, cap. 51.

[p. 43]   Extract from *Songs and Carols, 15th Century*, ed. Wright, for Percy Society, p. 36 :
" If thou have out tò do with the law to plete," etc.,
and from notes, p. 100 : " The Parvis or portico of St. Paul's, in London, was the common place of consultation among the Lawyers." " See Victor Hugo's *Notre Dame* as to the Parvise there, in Paris."

[End pages of book, an index of personages (such as Ancres, Bachelers, Bishop, Clerks, etc.) mentioned in *Piers Plowman*, under heads of " Church," " State and Household," and " Trades and Professions."]

1857. Kingsley, Charles. *Two Years Ago*, 3 vols., vol. i, chapter vii, p. 168 [quotation of the beginning of *Prol.*, perverted to suit the context] ; vol. iii, chapter iii, p. 112 [reference to " Chaucer's house of fame "]. (Works, 1880–85, 28 vols., vol. viii, chapter vii, p. 105, chapter xxi, p. 386.)

1857. Maurice, Frederick Denison. *Milton considered as a School-master*, [a lecture delivered in Jan. 1857, printed in] The Friendship of Books, and other Lectures, 1874, p. 273.

Geoffrey Chaucer was probably born in London. He was Comptroller of the Petty Customs in the port of London. He fell into disgrace with the Court by the part he took in the election of a Lord Mayor. We have reason to remember these facts; for if we owe "the Testament of Love" and the "Legend of Fair Women" to the knowledge which he acquired in Courts, or while on foreign embassies, we should never, I conceive, have had the "Canterbury Tales," but for the acquaintance with homely English life which he learned as a London citizen.

1857. Notes and Queries, 2nd Series, vol. iii, pp. 49, 152-3, 170, 193, 216–7, 228, 253, 264, 268, 299, 329, 352–3, 376, 389–90, 419, 435, 465, 471, 509, 511; vol. iv, pp. 82, 199, 297, 383, 397, 407-8, 436, 450, 505, 509-10.

Author.	Date.	Reference.	Subject.
N., G.	Jan. 17.	2nd S. iii, 49.	*The Wife of Beith* (the ballad).
O., J.	Feb. 21.	2nd S. iii, 152–3.	*The Wife of Beith* and *The Wanton Wife of Bath.*
T., W. H. W.	Feb. 28.	2nd S. iii, 170.	'Carrenare.'
Taylor, Henry W. S.	Mar. 7.	2nd S. iii, 193.	'Lollard,' 'loller.'
W., B.	Mar. 14.	2nd S. iii, 217.	'Carrenare' = 'carnerie.' (charnel house).
C., G. R.	Mar. 21.	2nd S. iii, 228.	Has any attempt been made to identify Chaucer's Canterbury Pilgrims? The writer thinks he has identified the Host, Harry Bailly. In the Parliament held at Westminster, in 50th Edw. III, Henry Bailly was one of the representatives for that borough. And he was again returned to the Parliament held at Gloucester 2nd Richd II. In the Subsidy Rolls, 4 Richard II, in Southwark, occurs the name of— "Henr' Bayliff, Ostyler, Xpian Ux eius. . ij ˢ." Can Roger the Coke be identified? What was a Jack of Dover? [*Cokes Prol.*, ll. 21–23.]
K., H. C.	Mar. 28.	2nd S. iii, 253.	'Bane' and 'bale.'
Anon.	April 11.	2nd S. iii, 299.	'Carrenare' = careening-dock (Spanish 'carenero').

Author.	Date.	Reference.	Subject.
F.,	April 25.	2nd S. iii, 329.	Blue the colour of truth (*Court of Love*, l. 246, quoted as Chaucer's).
Boys, Tho-mas.	May 2.	2nd S. iii, 352–3.	'Jack of Dover' = the stock-fish called 'Poor John'; in Chaucer's time there were Priors of Dover named John.
Leo, F. A.	May 16.	2nd S. iii, 390.	'Watling Street'= the Milky Way (*Hous of Fame*, ii. 427).
Norman, Louisa Julia.	May 30.	2nd S. iii, 435.	Chaucer's reminiscence of Dante's 'nessun maggior dolore' in *T. & C.* iii.
Mat-thews, Wil-liam.	June 13.	2nd S. iii, 471.	'Maze.'
Allen, R. James.	June 27.	2nd S. iii, 509–10.	'Persoun' or 'Persone,' and 'Parson'; 'Parishens.'
Shep-pard, John.	June 27.	2nd S. iii, 511.	'Tabard,' recently corrupted to 'Talbot.'
East-wood, J.	Oct. 10.	2nd S. iv, 297.	'Scarcely' = temperately.
Boys, Tho-mas.	Nov. 14.	2nd S. iv, 397.	'Envelope' (Chaucer, 'envo-lupe') from Italian 'inviluppo.'

„   Nov. 21. 2nd S. iv, 407–8.   CHAUCER DIFFICULTIES.—'The shippes hopposteries.' Is '*hopposteres*' an old form of the word *upholsteries?* *op* for *up* is Dutch—the '*h*' is a little out of place, but there are other instances of this in Chaucer.

Ships' *hopposteres* would then mean the dockyards or arsenals where the ships are refitted.

| **East-wood.** J. | Nov. 28. | 2nd S. iv, 436. | Early satirical poem (cf. 1853, vii, 569). |

Boys, Thos.   Dec. 5. 2nd S. iv, 450.   CHAUCER DIFFICULTIES (2). 'Broken harm' (*Marchantes Tale*, l. 181). The reading:

'So moch *el-broken harm,* is suggested, el-brooken = *illbrooked;* therefore *harm not easily brooked.* 'A Cristofre' (*Prol.*, l. 115). Did this not mean something bearing a cross or crucifix? The yeman would be allowed to wear a silver Cristofre (in spite of Stat. 37 Edw. III) because it was a sacred emblem or badge, not an ornament.

Author.	Date.	Reference.	Subject.
Stein-metz, Andrew.	Dec. 26.	2nd S. iv, 505.	'A mouse's hert.'

| **Boys,** Thos. | Dec. 26. | 2nd S. iv, 509–10. | CHAUCER DIFFICULTIES (3). 'Rewel-bone' (*Sir Thopas*, l. 167). |

Might this not be *whalebone? Rewel bone = Revel bone, i.e.* bone from *Revel*, one of the Hanse Towns? 'Madrian' (*Monk's Prol.*, l. 4). Does this not stand for *Madre Anna,* Anna the mother of the Virgin Mary?

1857. Pauli, Reinhold. *Confessio Amantis of John Gower,* edited and collated . . . by Dr. R. Pauli, 3 vols., vol. i, Introductory Essay, pp. vi, xiii–xvi, xxix, xxxii, xxxv–vi, xxxviii, xliii.

[pp. xiii–xv] [Gower's relations with Chaucer ; the evidence for a breach in their friendship insufficient.]

1858. Bagehot, Walter. *Article* on *Charles Dickens* [in] *The National Review,* Oct. 5, 1858, p. 462. (Reprinted in *Literary Studies,* 1879, p. 188.)

[The symmetry of Chaucer's mind, his healthy sagacity and ordered comprehension.] *The Prologue to the Canterbury Tales* is in itself a series of memorial tablets to mediæval society ; each class has its tomb, and each its apt inscription.

1858. Burne-Jones, Sir Edward Coley. *The Prioresses Tale.*

[A painting in oils on a cabinet belonging to William Morris, representing the Virgin placing the grain on the " little clergeon's " tongue. Burne-Jones began a replica of this picture in 1869, which was only completed and exhibited in 1898. See *Sir Edward Burne-Jones,* by Malcolm Bell, 1899, pp. 40, 70. See also the list of Burne-Jones's works by J. P. Anderson in O. G. Destrée, *Les Préraphaélites,* Bruxelles, [1895].]

1858. Clough, Arthur Hugh. *Letter to Professor F. J. Child,* [dated] April 10, 1858, [printed in] Prose Remains of Arthur H. Clough, 1888, p. 241.

Do you see that the Frenchman [de Chatelain] who trans-lated 'the Canterbury Tales' has found at Paris the original of the 'Squire's Tale,' 30,000 lines? I wonder if it is like Spenser's in any respect.

1858. Cust, Katherine Isabella. *Introduction* [to] *The Ancient Poem of Guillaume de Guileville entitled le Pèlerinage de l'Homme, compared with the Pilgrim's Progress of John Bunyan; edited* [by K. I. Cust] *from Notes collected by the late Mr. Nathaniel Hill*, pp. ix, xi, 3–9, 11, 38–9, 41–2, appendix p. xxxv.

[p. ix.] [Quotation from a translation in a hand of *c.* 1630 from Pits (*q.v.* below, App. A., *a.* 1616) in MS. Harl. 4826, on Lydgate.]

[pp. 5–6] [Chaucer's *A.B.C.*; three stanzas of the English text, side by side with De Guileville's French.]

[p. 7] [Chaucer's imitation at the end of *The Book of the Duchesse*, "Right thus me mett, as I you tell," etc., of De Guileville's description (also quoted) of being waked by the convent-bell,—

> Ce me sembla en ce moment
> Si que de lespouentement
> Esueille et desdormy fu [etc.].

[pp. 8–9] [Quotation from Lydgate's *Pilgrimage* of the passage excusing himself from translating the *A.B.C.*, already translated by Chaucer, with the proofs that the translation of the *Pilgrimage* from De Guileville in MS. Cotton Vitellius, C. xiii, was by Lydgate.]

[pp. 38–9] [On the Dream Prologue in O.F. literature, with extracts from De Guileville's Pèlerinage and Chaucer's *Book of the Duchesse*.]

[pp. 41–2] [On the "Go little book" formula with which early poets and dreamers sent forth their books, with quotation from "Chaucer's" *Flour and the Lefe*.]

1858. De Vere, Aubrey Thomas. *Select Specimens of the English Poets with Biographical Notices*, &c., ed. Aubrey de Vere, pp. 1–3 [biographical and critical notice of Chaucer] ; pp. 3–8 [extracts from *Canterbury Tales*, ll. 43–164, 2765–808, 5240–96], 20–1, 131. [Reprinted in *The Household Poetry Book, an Anthology of English-speaking Poets from Chaucer to Faber*, 1893 (same pagination).]

1858. Emerson, Ralph Waldo. *Persian Poetry* [in] The Atlantic Monthly, April, 1858, vol. i, p. 729, [reprinted in] Letters aud Social Aims, 1875, p. 226 [ed. 1876, the first in B.M.]. (Works, Centenary Edition, 1903, 12 vols., vol. viii, p. 252.)

The law of the *ghaselle*, or shorter ode, requires that the poet insert his name in the last stanza. . . . We remember but two or three examples in English poetry: that of Chaucer, in the "House of Fame" . . . .

1858. H. *Chaucer's Monument,* [in] The Gentleman's Magazine, new series, vol. iv, Feb. 1858, p. 83.

[A letter complaining that Chaucer's tomb was still not restored and was moreover " entirely hemmed in by umbrella stands."]

1858. Holmes, Oliver Wendell. *The Autocrat of the Breakfast Table,* ch. iv, v, [in] The Atlantic Monthly, Feb., March, 1858, vol. i, p. 462, 619 ; 1st vol. edn., Boston, 1858, pp. 92, 125. (Writings, 1891, 13 vols., vol. i, pp. 82–3, 110.)

[pp. 82-3] Men often remind me of pears in their way of coming to maturity. . . . Rich, juicy, lively, fragrant, russet-skinned old Chaucer was an Easter-Beurré ; the buds of a new summer were swelling when he ripened.

[p. 110]	As the one word " moi " revealed the Stratford-atte-Bowe-taught Anglais . . .

1858. Hunt, James Henry Leigh. *The Tapiser's Tale, attempted in the manner of Chaucer,* [in] Fraser's Magazine, Feb. 1858, vol. lvii, pp. 160–3.

[The Tale is that of the miracle of the Field of Flowers, from Mandeville, and is preceded by an introductory note, and by a prologue, in which " occasion has been taken to suppose that the Carpenter has just been telling a tale, which his hearers have found tedious . . . and that the Host . . . feels himself warranted in rebuking the narrator."
The Prologue begins :]

The Carpenter, whan that his tale was done,
Which sette us nigh on sleepyng everych one . . .
Lookèd as big and highe, as thof his lore
Gaf him Saint Joseph for his auncestor . . .

1858. Landor, Walter Savage. *Old-fashioned Verse,* [in] *Dry Sticks,* p. 44.

In verse alone I ran not wild
When I was hardly more than child,
Contented with the native lay
Of Pope or Prior, Swift or Gay . . .
Then listened I to Spencer's strain,
Till Chaucer's Canterbury train
Came trooping past, and carried me
In more congenial company.

Soon my soul was hurried o'er
This bright scene : the " solemn roar "
Of organ, under Milton's hand,
Struck me mute . . .

1858–9. Marsh, George Perkins.   *Lectures on the English Language,*
New York, 1860, pp. 18. 22 and *n.*, 30, 49–50, 71, 103, 111–3,
168–9, 174–7, 180, 252 *n.*, 257–8, 323 and *n.*, 391, 415, 424, 432–3,
468, 473, 500–1, 526–8, 530, 534 *n.*, 539, 546, 603, 625, 675–6.

[These lectures were delivered in 1858-9, and the Congress copyright entry is
dated 1859. An edn. of 1860, is in Bodl. ; edn. 4, London, 1863, is the first in B.M.
For Marsh's second series of lectures *see* below, 1862.]

[p. 22]   In original power, and in all the highest qualities of poetry,
no Continental writer of that period, with the single exception
of Dante, can, for a moment, be compared with Chaucer, who,
only less than Shakespeare, deserves the epithet, myriad-
minded.

[p. 168]   There are few instances . . . where a single writer has
exerted so great . . . an influence on the language of his time
as Chaucer. . . . Gower and Chaucer, writing for ladies and
cavaliers, used the phraseology most likely to be intelligible
and acceptable to courtiers. . . . Wycliffe and his associates,
[p. 169] in their biblical translations, use few foreign words . . . but
in their own original writings, they employ as large a proportion of Romance vocables as occurs in those of Chaucer's
works where they are most numerous.   In the Squires Tale,
nine per cent. of the words are of Continental origin, in the
Nonne Prestes Tale the proportion falls to seven, while in the
prose Persones Tale . . . it rises to eleven. . . . It is the
selection of his vocabulary, and the structure of his periods,
that mark his style as his own, and it is a curious fact, that of
the small number of foreign words employed by him and by
Gower, a large share were in a manner forced upon them by
the necessities of rhyme ; for while not less than ninety parts
in a hundred of their vocabularies are pure Anglo-Saxon,
more than one-fourth of the terminal words of their verses are
Latin or French.

1858. Notes and Queries, 2nd Series, vol. v, pp. 22, 24–5, 123, 166–7,
225, 229–30, 271, 290–91, 309–10, 337–8, 359, 362, 375, 387,
392, 402–3, 432–3, 453, 471, 511–2, 521 ; vol. vi, pp. 18,
37–8, 45, 57, 77, 108, 120, 199, 229–30, 314, 335, 356, 371,
416, 428, 437, 521, 534.

Author.	Date.	Reference.	Subject.

Madden, Jan. 9. 2nd S. v,   John Shirley, his lines on
Sir Frederic.   22   Chaucer (*q.v.* above, _[c. 1450]
vol. i, p. 49) quoted.

Boys, Jan. 9. 2nd S. v, CHAUCER DIFFICULTIES (4).
Thos.   24–5. 'Whipultre' (*Knightes T.*, l. 2065).
May not this be the "willow-palm" or palm-sallow?
'Poudre Marchant' (*Prol.*, l. 381). Is not *poudre*
a *verb*, not a *noun*, meaning here, *to season* the three
following things, viz. marchant, tart and galingale?

Boys, Feb. 13. 1st S. v, CHAUCER DIFFICULTIES (5).
Thos.   123.   'Marchant' (*Prol.*, l. 381). This is
a name for *waterfowl*, in German *merchente*, properly
the *Mergus albellus*, but here probably used in a generic
sense.
'Gnof' (*Milleres Tale*, l. 2). This appears to be a
word of Jewish-German origin = a *thief*. From the
Hebrew the Jews have *gannov*, a thief. The meaning
might change from *extortioner* to *miser*.

Boys, Feb. 27. 2nd S. v, CHAUCER DIFFICULTIES (6).
Thos.   166.   'Tidifies' (*Squieres Tale*, l. 648)
= *sea-mews* (*tide-wives*).

White, Mar. 13. 2nd S. v,   'Whipultre' (2nd S. v, 24).
A. Holt.   225.   The writer believes this to be
the *wild apple tree*, or crab. It is nearly the only tree
Chaucer has omitted that was in his day known in
England. 'Whippletree' still used in Essex for the
bar by which a pair of horses a-breast draw the plough,
now generally made of ash.

N., H. F. Mar. 13. 2nd S. v,   Might not this be the *Horn-*
225. *bean* [*sic*], or whip-pulling tree
not otherwise mentioned by Chaucer?

Boys, Mar. 20. 2nd S. v, CHAUCER DIFFICULTIES (7).
Thos.   229.   'Eclympasteire' (*Book of the
Duchesse*, l. 167). The writer suggests that this stands
for *Death*, and is a very anomalous derivative from
the Gr. ἐκλιμπάνω, which is nearly equivalent to ἐκλείπω,
which sometimes signifies *to die*.[1]
'Parodie' (*Troilus*, v. 1548). The more modern
editions have *jeopardie* for *parodie*. But the writer
thinks Tyrwhitt is right, and that it is parodie, to be
understood here in the sense of *episode*.[2]

[1] See Skeat, *Chaucer's Complete Works* (1894), vol. i, p. 468.
[2] See Skeat, *ibid.*, vol. ii, p. 502.

Boys, April 3. 2nd S. v, CHAUCER DIFFICULTIES (8).
Thos.   271.   'Cost.'
"That nedes-cost he most him selven hide"
(*Knightes Tale*, l. 619).
The writer would understand by "nedes cost" the
O.Fr. *ne discoste*, meaning not far off, near.

Author.	Date.	Reference.	Subject.

Boys, April 2nd S. v, CHAUCER DIFFICULTIES (9).
Thos. 10. 290. 'Blake beried' (*Pardoner's Prol.*, l. 78). Might this mean the poorest kind of funeral, a *black bier* ?

See Skeat, *Chaucer's Complete Works*, vol. v, p. 272. Also *N. & Q.*, 4th S. x, 222 ; xii, 55.

Boys, April 2nd S. v, CHAUCER DIFFICULTIES (10).
Thos. 17. 309. 'Blake beried.'
1. *beried* = bier'd, *i. e.* carried on a bier.
2. *blake* = black, *i. e.* a bier with the ordinary covering of a black cloth.
3. *a* may = *in*, *i. e. in black*,
or (preferably) *a* may = the auxiliary *have.*

μ. April 2nd S. v, 'Cost or nedescost' (2nd S. v,
24. 337–8. 271). The writer takes it to mean *of necessity, necessarily.* It is the genitive *nedes* plus *cost*, manner, way, and is equivalent to "by way of necessity." Many examples from M.E. texts quoted.

This meaning is confirmed by Prof. Skeat, *Chaucer's Works*, vol. v, p. 71.

B., T. May 1. 2nd S. v, 'Wade.'
359.

Rock, D. May 1. 2nd S. v, Separation of the sexes in
362. churches ; *Prol.*, ll. 449–50 quoted.

Berry, May 8. 2nd S. v, 'Blake beried.' Is not *blake* an
M. E. 387. old word meaning *naked?* See Elisha Coles' *English Dictionary*, edit. 1677, for the meaning of "black beried."
'Eclympasteyre.' Coles gives this word: *Eclympastery*, son to Morpheus, the god of sleep.

Crossley, May 8. 2nd S. v, 'Blake beried.' Surely the
Fran. 387. meaning of this passage is "Though their souls go a black berrying ;" *i. e.* "go gathering blackberries." In this sense we have the full force of the reckless speech of the Pardoner.

White, May 8. 2nd S. v, The Harleian MS. No. 7334
A. Holt. 387. reads "black bered."

Boys, May 15. 2nd S. v, CHAUCER DIFFICULTIES (11).
Thos. 392. 'Gat-toothed' (*Wife of Bath's Prol.*, 603). This clearly = goat-toothed. The goat was an animal sacred to Venus.

Boys, May 15. 2nd S. v, 'Nedes cost.' A reply to 2nd S.
Thos. 402. v, 337, defending the argument that this expression comes from O.Fr. *ne discoste.*

White, May 15. 2nd S. v, On the analogy of *needs must*,
A. Holt. 403. why should this not = *need is caused* ?

Author.	Date.	Reference.	Subject.
Boys, Thos.	May 29.	2nd S., v, 432.	CHAUCER DIFFICULTIES (12). 'Spiced conscience' = 'salved.' 'Cankedort' = 'kinkèd ort' or *vulg.* 'fix'?
R., C. J.	June 5.	2nd S. v, 453.	MS. of *Troilus* in Bishop Cosin's Library, Durham.
Carring- ton, F. A.	June 5.	2nd S., v, 465.	'Gat-toothed.'
Boys, Thos.	June 12.	2nd S., v, 471.	Suggests other difficulties for others to settle, *e.g.* 'Fortenid crese,' 'Limote,' 'Ballenus,' 'Farewell feldefare,' 'Wades bote.'
D., C. de.	June 12.	2nd S., v, 487.	'Blake beried.'
K., H. C.	June 26.	2nd S., v, 511–2.	CHAUCER DIFFICULTIES. — 1. 'Farewel feldefare.' 2. 'Fortenid crese.' 3. 'Hawebake.' 4. 'Wades bote.'
Thoms, W. J.	June 26.	2nd S., v, 521.	'Whipultre.'
Sansom, J.	July 3.	2nd S. vi, 18.	'Dives' as a proper name, *Sompnoures Tale,* l. 1877.
Rock, D.	July 10.	2nd S., vi, 37.	CHAUCER DIFFICULTIES.—'Carrenare' = Quarentena?
H., F. C.	July 10.	2nd S., vi, 38.	'Whipultre' = holly (whip pole tree)?
Mackin- tosh, J.	July 17.	2nd S., vi, 57.	'Whipultre'; confirming the last.
Boys, Thomas.	July 24.	2nd S. vi, 77.	'Carrenare'; interpretation a careening dock defended.
Anon.	Aug. 7.	2nd S. vi, 120.	Sale of the MS. of Kynaston's *Troilus,* the property of S. W. Singer and formerly of Dean Aldrich.
A., A.	Sept. 4.	2nd S. vi, 199.	'Gat-toothed' = gap-toothed.
"Silver- stone."	Sept. 18.	2nd S. vi, 229–30.	Annotations, dated 1577, copied from the flyleaf of a copy of *The Vision of Pierce Plowman,* 1561; *see* below, App. A., 1577.
Picton, J. A.	Oct. 16.	2nd S. vi, 314.	'Roam.'
Buck- ton, T. J.	Oct. 23	2nd S. vi, 335.	'Some'; 'all and some' in Chaucer = all and *total.*
R., A. B.	Nov. 6.	2nd S. vi, 371.	Chaucer's *Balade of Gode Counsaile;* 'prees' in l. 4 = pre-eminence (præesse)?
Rock, D.	Nov. 20.	2nd S. vi, 416.	Separation of the sexes in churches; the Wife of Bath.

Author.	Date.	Reference.	Subject.
β.	Nov. 27.	2nd S. vi, 428.	Dr. Darrell's satire on Browne Willis, *q.v.* above [*a.* 1760], vol. i, p. 417.
R., E. G.,	Nov. 27.	2nd S. vi, 437.	'Bedstaff'; *Reves Tale*, ll. 4292–6, quoted.
β.	Dec. 25.	2nd S. vi, 521.	Popularity of hot condiments in Chaucer's time :—

'Woe was his cook, but that his sauces were Poinant and sharp.'

1858-9. Unknown. *The Arms, Armour and Military Usages of the Fourteenth Century*, [in] The Gentleman's Magazine, Jan. 1858—April, 1859, new ser., vol. iv. pp. 3–18, 123–38, 235–51, 347–55, 459–67, 575–92 ; vol. v, pp. 3–19, 99–114, 211–27 ; 323–39 ; 435–51, 547–63 ; vol. vi, pp. 3–21, 111–23, 227–43, 339–55.

[Quotations from Chaucer throughout.]

1859. B. *Geoffrey Chaucer*, [in] The Dublin University Magazine, March, 1859, vol. liii, pp. 272–87.

[p. 272] [An account of Chaucer's seven chief biographers and commentators—Leland, Thomas Speght, Thomas Fuller, Urry, Tyrwhitt ("a gentlemanlike and learned dryasdust"), and Sir Harris Nicolas :]

The copious Godwin closes the roll in his quartette of four volumes, octavo. Doctor Johnson has no life of Chaucer, as he has none of Shakspeare, or of Spenser. At times he celebrates the owls, and passes by the eagles. There is a very full and agreeable little book published . . . in 1841, entitled "Chaucer Modernized." It is a highly Philo-Chaucerian and chivalric small volume, and sets out like Don Quixote . . . bent on righting wrongs on behalf of its poet against every translator who had ventured to meddle with the ark of the antique text, or the sacredness of the Saxon ; and thus he casts out of the saddle Messrs. Ogle, Lipscombe, and Boyce . . . and runs a tilt against Henry Brooke . . . and is only half pleased with Lord Thurlow, who revised and published "The Knight's Tale " ; also " the Flower and Leaf," which is the most beautiful and pure of all Chaucer's works . . .

[p. 278] Beyond all doubt his works are not known in proportion to their great merit. The early English must be learned before they can be enjoyed ; . . . the tongue of Chaucer has passed away, except from the pages of works as old as his own. Yet to his intense admirers, the difficulties of his language are regarded as producing a kind of esoteric sacredness which involves the text with a mystery akin to the Books of the Sibyl . . . His unintelligible obsoleteness, to minds so framed, resembles the high flavour of an antique Stilton or the taste of an æruginous coin ; and one connoisseur [Landor, *q.v.* above, 1841] has gone so far as to say " he would wish to keep Chaucer for himself and a few friends."

[A life of the poet is given, containing the old inaccuracies, due to acceptance of the apocryphal pieces.]

1859. Braune, George Martin.	*The Persone of a Toun.*

[A poem (92 pp.) in imitation of the style and stanza of Spenser, 'as a mean between the times of Chaucer and our own,' but owing no more than the suggestion to Chaucer's Parson.]

1859. FitzGerald, Edward.	*Letter to George Crabbe,* Oct. 4, 1859, [printed in] More Letters of Edward FitzGerald, with Preface by W. Aldis Wright, 1901, p. 50.

Chaucer I don't want : and am glad you should take to him.	I told you of the Tales I thought would please you : The Clerk of Oxford (Griseldis), the Pardoners, and the Knight and Squire.	Read also all the Prologue Narrative between the Tales.	One must feel Chaucer is akin to Shakespeare, in his Humour, Sympathy and Activity of Life, but he has not Sounded such Depths of Thought and Feeling.

1859. Hunt, James Henry Leigh.	*English Poetry versus Cardinal Wiseman,* [in] Fraser's Magazine, Dec., vol. lx., pp. 749–53, 755, 760–2.

[A defence of Chaucer and Spenser against the charge of associating natural beauty with " wantonness, voluptuousness, and debauchery."]

[Cardinal Wiseman's opinions, here controverted, were expressed in his lecture "On the Perception of Natural Beauty," *q.v.* above, 1855. Hunt had announced his intention of replying in *Fraser's Magazine. See* his letters to Edmund Peel and B. W. Proctor (Barry Cornwall) of 4 Nov. and 5 Dec. 1858 (Correspondence, 1862, vol. ii, pp. 240, 264).

1859. Notes and Queries, 2nd Series, vol. vii, pp. 21, 66. 89, 96, 218, 229, 440, 465, 500 ; vol. viii, pp. 257, 276, 283–4, 338, 351, 360, 439, 444, 474–5.

Author.	Date.	Reference.	Subject.
Thoms, William John.	Jan. 8.	2nd S. vii, 21.	Chaucer's debt to Italy ; did he owe anything to Germany or the Low Countries? Was his *Book of the Lion* a translation of Hartman von Aue's *Ritter mit der Löwe?*

Author.	Date.	Reference.	Subject.
Wonfor, T. W.	Jan 22.	2nd S. vii, 66.	'Nesh'; *Court of Love* quoted as Chaucer's.
Libya.	Jan. 29.	2nd S. vii, 89.	Achilles' spear; references by Fielding, Bishop Earle, and Chaucer (*Squieres Tale*, l. 239); a classical reference asked for.
Wonfor, T. W.	Jan. 29.	2nd S. vii, 96.	'Coverchief.'
μ.	Mar. 12.	2nd S. vii, 218.	From what text is the Aldine Ed. taken?
β.	Mar. 19.	2nd S. vii, 229–30.	Clogie's attribution of The Shepherd's Tale, 'conceived in the old dialect of Tusser and Chaucer,' to Bishop Bedell impossible. *See* below, App. A., [1605, Bedell?] and [c. 1675–6], Clogie.
Blades, William.	May 28.	2nd S. vii, 440.	Discovery at St. Albans of fragments of books printed by Caxton, including the *Assemble of Fowls* (14 leaves).
Eastwood, J.	June 18.	2nd S. vii, 500.	'Silk.'
W., H.	Sept. 24.	2nd S. viii, 257.	'Pill-garlick'; Prol. *Merchant's 2nd Tale*, quoted as Chaucer's.
Eastwood, J.	Oct. 1.	2nd S. viii, 276.	The grotesque in churches; hatred, etc., are painted on the outside of the garden wall of the Rose in Chaucer's *Rom. Rose*.
Myers, Gustavus A.	Oct. 8.	2nd S. viii, 282–3.	'To tote'; *Plowman's Tale* quoted; doubtful authorship admitted.
M., J.	Oct. 8.	2nd S. viii, 284.	Notice of Sandras's *Étude sur Chaucer* (q. v. below, App. B., 1859).
Thompson, Pishey.	Oct. 22.	2nd S. viii, 338.	'To tote.'
Eastwood, J.	Oct. 29.	2nd S. viii, 351.	Origin in *Perceval le Galois* of the last stanza of *Sir Thopas*.
Boys, Thomas.	Oct. 29.	2nd S. viii, 360.	'Smalle' = 'semle,' similar?
„	Nov. 26.	2nd S. viii, 439.	'Undermele.'
C., H. C.	Nov. 26.	2nd S. viii, 444.	'Eclympasteire'; Sandras's comparison of Froissart's 'Enclimpostair.'
Eastwood, J.	Dec. 10.	2nd S. viii, 474-5.	'In hie' or 'on hie' = in haste.

1859. Riley, Henry Thomas. *Munimenta Gildhallæ Londoniensis* (Rolls Ser.), vol. i, 1859, Liber Albus, p. 553.

Dimissio Portæ de Algate facta Galfrido Chaucer.

[For this lease *see* above, 1374, May 10, vol. i, p. **3.** The entry given here is translated in Riley's *Liber Albus*, 1860, p. 475, and the lease itself is translated in his *Memorials of London and London Life,* 1868.]

1859. [Riley, Henry Thomas ?]. *Lease of the 'mansio' over Aldgate to Chaucer,* extracted from Guildhall, Letter Book G., in] The *Gentleman's Magazine,* March 1859, new ser., vol. vi, p. 243.

[*See* above, 1374, May 10, vol. i, p. **3.**]

[1859.] Starkey, Alfred. *The Prioress' Tale, and other Poems.*

[Not in B.M.; Bodl. 280. s. 229 ; information kindly given by Miss K. M. Pogson.]

[The title-poem, which is in sixty-two *sesta rima* stanzas, is stated in the preface to be " founded on the same subject as Chaucer's of the same name. I do not think," the author adds, " that I can justly be accused of plagiarism. . . It is something, however, to have trodden, ever so vaguely, near the footsteps of a great genius." The tale is " protestantized," *e. g.* such details as the " Alma Redemptoris Mater " are omitted.]

1859. Unknown. *Review* [of] *The Poetical Works of Geoffrey Chaucer,* edited by Robert Bell . . . 1855, [in] The London Review, July 1859, vol. xii, pp. 285–303.

[pp. 285–291] [A short sketch of Chaucer's life, noting the rejection by Nicolas of the episodes dependent on the *Testament of Love,* and laying stress on the substantial nature of the patronage Chaucer received.]

[p. 292] All that is peculiar, all that seems now so distant and unattainable, in the poetry of Chaucer, arises from the one great typical fact, that it is always nothing more nor less than the telling of a story . . .

We must conceive of the people of the Middle Ages as children in their love of stories, and in their adoration of those who could tell them. . . Hence originated a poetical complexion or turn, which everything seems to have assumed, and the passionate cultivation of poetry by all classes. It seems incredible to us, but it was undoubtedly the case, that in the Middle Ages poetry formed the chief delight of the people. [Evidence of this in Chaucer: *Troilus* and *Book of the Duchesse* quoted.]

[p. 293] He [Chaucer] cares not at all for the praise of originality or invention . . . he cares for nothing but his story. Hence he is quite content to become a translator, if he has seen a good story in a foreign tongue. [Contrast in this between the age of Chaucer, like all great periods, and the unpoetical and would-be original nineteenth century. Explanation of the cause : loss of enjoyment. "To our forefathers every old thing was really a new thing : every new thing is an old thing to us." The cure, a study of such as Chaucer.]

[p. 298] We come then to discuss the great distinguishing marks of the mind and power of Chaucer. They seem to be four in number : dramatic fearlessness and breadth, workmanlike directness, comparatively non-intellectual character, and sense [p. 299] of beauty. [Expansion of these four points.]

1859. Vaughan, Robert. *Revolutions in English History,* 3 vols., vol. i, pp. 479–81, 563–5.

[p. 479] Poet of manners as he is, the compass of subject included in his works is a conspicuous fact . . . Chaucer appears to have the power of understanding the pleasures of the most ethereal virtue, and those found in the most free and riotous indulgence of the sensuous passions. The comedy and tragedy of earth, the hell in it, and the heaven above it, were open to him.

[pp. 480-1] [Chaucer's material partly derived from literature, partly from the world about him.]

[p. 564] [The *Canterbury Tales* shew grossness side by side with simple faith :] The clerk and the monk, the prioress and the nun, are all among the listeners to these impure stories.

1860. Canterbury Tales of Chaucer, to which are added, An Essay on his language and versification, and an Introductory Discourse, together with notes and a glossary, by T. Tyrwhitt, F.R.S., with memoir and critical dissertation by the Rev. G. Gilfillan, Edinburgh, 3 vols.

[The glossary is arranged in the margin. Gilfillan's memoir and dissertation, "The Genius and Poetry of Chaucer," precede the second and third vols. respectively.

The memoir contains all the old mistakes, based on the *Court of Love* and *Testament of Love,* and is very flamboyantly written ; *e. g.* Chaucer's position was at best that "of a pensionary dependent, nourished on the rinsings of the royal cellar." Doubtful whether he died " a Papist or a Protestant."

The Dissertation is written in the same style and contains many allusions to Chaucer's "ruggedness," and to his Wycliffite views.]

1860. Bulwer, Edward, 1st Lord Lytton. *Letter to his son,* [printed in] The Life of Edward Bulwer, by his grandson, 1913, 2 vols., vol. ii, pp. 419–20.

I am amazed at his [Chaucer's] wonderful accuracy of rhythm ; according to his own accentuation, there are as few lines with a defective foot as there are in Dryden. His metre, too, is extremely artful. As a general rule, he always has his stop at the end of a couplet, does not break into verses as blank verse does. But he makes his pause of the ultimate sense, by a preference so marked that he must have arrived at it by a rule of art, at the end of a first line. . . The effect of this is both [*sic*] surprise, and with him it is music ; the relief from the rhyme has a melody.

1860. Gilfillan, George. *See* above, Canterbury Tales.

[*a*. 1860.] Irving, David. *The History of Scottish Poetry,* by David Irving . . . edited by John Aitken Carlyle [from the MS. which Irving left unpublished at his death in 1860], Edinburgh, 1861, pp. 37*n*., 52, 68*n*., 70*n*., 73, 85, 95, 102*n*., 107–9, 134*n*., 136*n*., 141–2, 170, 173, 175*n*., 187, 193, 212–14, 218, 219*n*., 221, 231–2, 239, 242*n*., 244, 267–8, 272, 283*n*., 298, 310*n*., 326, 341. [Some of the references are almost identical with those in the Lives of the Scottish Poets, 1804. Some chapters, including that on Barbour, had appeared as articles in the *Encyclopædia Britannica.*]

[p. 95] [Reference to Barbour as the contemporary and in some respects the rival of Chaucer.]

[p. 107] [Comparison, by quotation of passages in Barbour's *Bruce* and Chaucer's *Romaunt.*]

[Many other brief references, with quotations from Tyrwhitt and Nott on versification, language, &c.]

1860. J., J. C. *MS. of Chaucer's Minor Poems,* [letter, in] The Gentleman's Magazine, Dec. 1860, new ser., vol. ix, pp. 642–5.

[The Sion Coll. MS. of the *A.B.C.* The writer comments severely on Bell's text.]

1860. Notes and Queries, 2nd Series, vol. ix, pp. 51, 83, 107, 141, 240, 251, 350, 435, 441, 479 ; vol. x, pp. 135, 227, 302, 358, 403–4, 453, 459, 499, 510, 523.

Author.	Date.	Reference.	Subject.
Thompson, P.	Jan. 21.	2nd S. ix, 51.	'Quishen.'

Author.	Date.	Reference.	Subject.
Offor, George. Editor.	Feb. 4.	2nd S. ix, 83.	'Soote' = sweet.
Eastwood, J.	Feb. 11.	2nd S. ix, 107.	'Marish.'
Eastwood, J.	Feb. 25.	2nd S. ix, 141.	'Whippletree.'
L.	Mar. 31.	2nd S, ix, 240.	'Hackney.'
Buckton, T. J.	Mar. 31.	2nd S. ix, 251.	'Boll.'
Eastwood, J.	May 5.	2nd S. ix, 350.	
'Ache.'	June 2.	2nd S. ix, 435.	'The kinges note' (*Milleres T.*, l. 3217) = the 'Anthem of the Three Kings of Colon'?
T., C.	June 9.	2nd S. ix, 441.	'Cole,' 'cole-blake.'
Tennent, J. E.	June 23.	2nd S. ix, 479.	'Vermelet,' vermilion.
Para- thina.	Sept. 22.	2nd S. x, 227.	Tubal's invention of music (*Book of the Duchesse*, ll. 1162–6); why was Chaucer's couplet called 'riding-rhyme'?
C., T. Q.	Sept. 22.	2nd S. x, 227.	'Hoppesteres' = 'hoppesterres' or meteors?
Keight- ley, Thomas.	Oct. 20. Nov. 24.	2nd S. x, 302. 2nd S. x, 403–4.	The *Tale of Melibeus* and the *Persones Tale* are in blank verse, as are all the 'prose' passages of the dramatists.
Nichols, W. L. **Collins,** Mortimer.	Dec. 8.	2nd S. x, 453.	Confute the preceding by printing extracts from his articles as blank verse.
C., W.	Dec. 8.	2nd S. x, 459.	Curate and Vicar (*Parson's Prol.*, ll. 22–3).
Keightley, Thomas.	Dec. 22.	2nd S. x, 499.	Chaucer intended his 'metric prose' for verse, writing it continuously to save paper.
Q.	Dec. 29.	2nd S. x, 510.	Chaucer at King's Lynn.
R., E. G.	Dec. 29.	2nd S. x, 523.	Doubts explanations of 'hoppesteres' as 'female dancers' and 'St. Elmo's fires.'

1861-2. Arnold, Matthew. *On Translating Homer,* and *Last Words on Translating Homer,* lectures delivered at Oxford, 1861-2. (Works, 1903–4, 15 vols., vol. v, pp. 186, 222, 274, 276, 278–9.)

'To translate Homer suitably,' says Mr. Newman, 'we need

a diction sufficiently antiquated to obtain pardon of the reader for its frequent homeliness.' . . . Antiquated !—but to whom ? . . . The diction of Chaucer is antiquated ; does Mr. Newman suppose . . . that Homer's diction seemed antiquated to Sophocles, as Chaucer's diction seems antiquated to us ? . . .

[p. 222]   It is in didactic poetry that the ten-syllable couplet has most successfully essayed the grand style. In narrative poetry this metre has succeeded best when it essayed a sensibly lower style, the style of Chaucer, for instance ; whose narrative manner, though a very good and sound manner, is certainly neither the grand manner nor the manner of Homer.

[p. 274]   And another [of Mr. Newman's readers] says : ' Doubtless Homer's dialect and diction were as hard and obscure to a later Attic Greek as Chaucer to an Englishman of our day ' . . .

[p. 278]   When language is antiquated for that particular purpose for which it is employed,—as numbers of Chaucer's words, for instance, are antiquated for poetry,—such language is a bad representative of language which, like Homer's, was never antiquated for that particular purpose for which it was employed. . . . When Chaucer, who uses such [antiquated] words, is to pass current amongst us, to be familiar to us, as Homer was familiar to the Athenians, he has to be modernised, as Wordsworth and others set to work to modernise him . . .

[p. 279]   Chaucer's words, the words of Burns, great poets as these were, are yet not thus an established possession of an Englishman's mind, and therefore they must not be used in rendering Homer into English.

1861–3. Blades, William. *The Life and Typography of William Caxton,* 2 vols.. vol. i, pp. 48n., 73, 80, 151–2, 173–4, 278 ; vol. ii, pp. xviii, xxxvi, lviii, 45–7, 51–2, 61–71, 138, 162–7, 169–70, 254, 260, 263, 265–77, 281–8, 290–91, plates xiv, xvii, xlii.

[Descriptions of and references to Caxton's editions of Chaucer.]

1861. Burne-Jones, Sir Edward Coley. *Cupid's Forge.*

[A painting in water-colour, illustrating the opening of the *Parlement of Foules. See* M. Bell, *Sir E. Burne-Jones,* 1894, pp. 30, 31 ; and for Chaucer's influence on Burne-Jones, which was very great, see *ibid.,* pp. 86–89.]

1861. Craik, George Lillie. *A Compendious History of English Literature and of the English Language,* 2 vols., vol. i, pp. vii, viii, 98*n*.,
107, 170–1, 191, 207–8, 227, 245–306 [a chapter on Chaucer], 307–8,
316–7, 319, 321, 324–5, 342–7, 360–1, 367, 378–9, 382, 385–6, 410–1,
425, 432–4, 441, 488–9, 493, 495, 497 ; vol. ii, p. 102.

[The chapter on Chaucer is largely devoted to a refutation
of Nott's theory that Chaucer's verse is rhythmical, shewing
both by old tradition and by the evidence of the changes in
the language, that Chaucer was a metrist, and the introducer
into English of iambic metre (pp. 247–69).   Chaucer a great
poet and "the Homer of his country" (pp. 269–72).   His
sources.   Specimens from *Rom. Rose, Hous of Fame,* and
Canterbury Tales.   Some non-Chaucerian pieces are quoted as
genuine.]

1861. De Vere, Aubrey Thomas.   *Chaucer,* and *Spenser,* [in] *The
Sisters, Inisfail, and other Poems,* pp. 64–5, 100.

[p. 65]   In Spring, when the breast of the lime-grove gathers
              Its roseate cloud, when the flush'd streams sing,
            And the mavis tricks her in gayer feathers ;
              Read Chaucer then ; for Chaucer is spring !

            On lonely evenings in dull Novembers . . .
            Read Chaucer still !

[p. 100]   [" Spenser " : brief reference to "the well-head of Chaucer."]

1861. Edman, L. E.   *A Specimen of Chaucer's Language,* with Explanatory Notes, a Philological Essay, Upsala.

[Introduction with short life of Chaucer and analysis of the
Canterbury Tales, followed by a specimen of the first 100 lines
of the Prologue, then 58 pages of notes on the language of
those lines.]

1861. Landor, Walter Savage.   *Letter to A. de N. Walker,* [dated]
Florence, August, 1861, [printed in] Letters and other Unpublished
Writings of Walter Savage Landor, ed. Stephen Wheeler, 1897, pp.
123, 171.

It would be worth a scholar's while to trace the different
spellings of the same words from Chaucer down to the present day.   Many are spelt better by him than by any author
since.   He avoids the reduplication of vowels *ea* etc., and
ends the word with *e.*

[Landor expresses the same opinion in a letter to the
Athenæum (April 20, 1861, pp. 529–30), remarking that he
has read Chaucer attentively several times.   *See* also above,
1856, and immediately below.]

[c. 1861.] Landor, Walter Savage. *Chaucer.*

[An unpublished prose fragment of some 50 lines, the autograph MS. of which was sold by Messrs. Maggs, Catalogue no. 340, 1915, no. 1789].

[Messrs. Maggs have very kindly given us the following note : "The little MS. was not dated, but judging from our remembrance of the handwriting, we should think it would be of a rather late date in his career." Internal evidence confirms this. *See* immediately above.]

There is no poet excepting Homer whom I have studied so attentively as Chaucer. They are the ablest of their respective countries. It may be doubted, and must be whether the language in the Iliad and Odyssee was exactly as we find it now . . .

The learned Pisistratus and his sons collected all they found. . . Chaucer by the care of studious and learned men remains as we find him, even in spelling. This is worthy of notice and thankfulness. We find many words in his Canterbury Tales spelt better than we spell them now. Several of these I have noted in my Imaginary Conversations and elsewhere . . .

Chaucer was the builder of our language . . .

1861. Landor, Walter Savage. *Milton and Marvel,* [in] The Athenæum, May 18, 1861, p. 661. (Imaginary Conversations, ed. C. G. Crump, 1891, 6 vols., vol. v, p. 34.)

Milton. Frequently do I read the *Canterbury Tales*, and with pleasure undiminished.† They are full of character and of life. You would hardly expect in so early a stage of our language such harmony as comes occasionally on the ear; it ceases with the verse, but we are grateful for it, shortly as it stays with us.

† [Landor's note :] A Bachelor of Arts, a Mr. Pycroft, without any authority, classes W. S. Landor with Byron and Wordsworth, as holding Chaucer cheap. Let this *Conversation* indicate the contrary. There is one art—namely, the *ars poetica*—in which the Bachelor is unlikely to take his Master's degree.

[For a further allusion to Pycroft by Landor *see* below, 1863.]

1861. Notes and Queries, 2nd Series, vol, xi, pp. 11, 99–100, 150, 161, 181, 239, 371, 417, 433, 474, 493 ; vol. xii, pp. 45, 151, 172, 235–6, 239, 286–8, 325, 360, 373–4, 434, 482.

Author.	Date.	Reference.	Subject.
R., E. G.	Jan. 5.	2nd S. xi, 11.	'Melle' is Chaucer's form for mill, the Suffolk pronunciation now ; perhaps Chaucer intended his Reeve to speak the Icenian, as it is admitted that the two scholars speak a Northern, dialect.

Author.	Date.	Reference.	Subject.
Editor.	Feb. 2.	2nd S. xi, 100.	Brief notice of Chatelain's *Contes de Cantorbéry,* tom. iii.
P., H. T.	Feb. 23.	2nd S. xi, 150.	Enquires for information as to any MSS. of Chaucer not mentioned by Tyrwhitt or Todd, as he desires to make a complete list.
[Yeowell, James.]	March 9.	2nd S. xi, 181.	Extract from W. Oldys' *Adversaria,* on the Occleve portrait of Chaucer ; *see* below, App. A., [*a.* 1735.]
C., W.	March 23.	2nd S. xi, 239.	' Barm-cloth ' = bosom - cloth (*Milleres T.,* l. 3236).
Editor.	May 11.	2nd S. xi, 371.	St. Thomas Wattering, 'the watering of Seint Thomas' (*Prol.,* ll. 825-7).
H., E. C.	June 22.	2nd S. xi, 493.	' Antem' (*Prioresse T.,* ll. 1849–50).
Jebb, John.	Aug. 24.	2nd S. xii, 151.	' Antem' from antiphona.
' **Queen's** Gardens.'	Sept. 21.	2nd S. xii, 235-6.	The Canterbury Pilgrims depicted (by Stothard ?) riding Flemish cart-horses.

A parody of the Canterbury Pilgrims, published soon after Queen Victoria's marriage, shewing the Queen, Prince Consort and retinue riding to Dunmow. [This is really no. 669-70 of H. B.'s *Political Sketches,* "Stothard's admired picture of 'The Procession of the Flitch of Bacon' (i.e. " The ceremony of the Dunmow Flitch ") somewhat metamorphosed," drawn in 1841, and, except for a similarity of composition, has nothing to do with the Canterbury Pilgrims.]

Aurelian.'	Sept. 21.	2nd S. xii, 239.	The seven planets (*Chanouns Yemannes T.,* ll. 825-9).
Mewburn, Fra.	Oct 12.	2nd S. xii, 286.	' Daffe ' (*Reves T.,* l. 288).
'Ithuriel.'	Oct. 12.	2nd S. xii, 287–8.	Copy of the writ of Nov. 11, 1373, to pay Chaucer £25 6*s.* 8*d.* for his journey to Genoa and Florence (*q.v.* above, vol. i, p. 3), not noticed by Godwin.
T., J.	Oct. 26.	2nd S. xii, 325.	Was the Tabard really burnt down in the reign of Charles II., as stated in Parker's *Domestic Architecture?*
Corner, George R.	Nov. 9.	2nd S. xii, 373–4.	Evidence from various sources of the destruction of the Tabard in 1676.
Keightley, Thos.	Nov. 30.	2nd S. xii, 434.	To what was Addison referring in his Chaucer quotation, Spectator no. 73 (*q.v.* above, 1711, vol. i, p. 314) ?

Author.   Date.   Reference.   Subject.
P., W.   Dec. 14.   2nd S. xii,   The document communicated
                          482.   by Ithuriel (xii, 287–8) is in Sir
               Harris Nicolas's *Life of Chaucer.*

1861. Pauli, Reinhold. *Pictures of Old England,* translated by E. C.
Otté, 1861. [The German original was published at Gotha,
1860.]

1861. Peacock, Thomas Love. · *Gryll Grange,* capp. viii and xxxiv,
pp. 59 *n.*, 296. (Ed. 1896, introd. by G. Saintsbury, pp. 53 *n.*, 273).

[Cap. viii : quotation from *Cook's Prologue,* A, ll. 4347–8
(Jakke of Dover). Cap. xxxiv : quotation from *Prologue,*
ll. 731–6.]

1861. Reynolds, Samuel Harvey. *Dante and his English Translators,*
[in] The Westminster Review, January, 1861, vol. xix, pp. 203,
229. [Reprinted in Studies in Many Subjects, 1898, pp. 3, 34.]

[p. 34]   It would hardly be untrue to say that there is more of
Dante's influence traceable in Chaucer's poems—more genuine
evidence that Dante had been read and loved—than in the
whole body of English literature (Milton's writings alone
excepted) from Chaucer's time to our own.

1861. Ruskin, John. *Tree Twigs,* [a lecture delivered at the Royal
Institution, April 19, 1861, printed in] The London Review, April
27, 1861, pp. 476–7. (Works, ed. E. T. Cook and A. Wedderburn,
1903–12, 39 vols., vol. vii, p. 474.)

[p. 474]   The main function of the flower, therefore, is accomplished
only in its death ; that of the leaf depends on prolonged work
during its life.

This difference in the operation of the flower and leaf has
attracted the attention of all great nations, as a type of the
various conditions of the life of man. Chaucer's poem of
the Flower and the Leaf, in which the strongest knights and
noblest ladies worship the goddess of the leaf in preference to
the goddess of the flower, is perhaps the clearest expression of
the feeling of the middle ages in this respect.

1861. Unknown. *Review* of *Bell's Annotated Series of British Poets,*
[in] The Quarterly Review, Oct. 1861, vol. cx, pp. 436–8, 440, 442,
449.

[p. 437]   The Anglo-French dialect of Chaucer, interspersed with
Latinisms, which, like Milton, he failed to naturalize, was not
aptly described as a " well of English undefiled." It is rather

such chivalric English as Froissart might have employed, and within a century it was obsolete. Except in the rare passages of humour and vivid description, which in style belongs to no special age, the substance of his bulky volume refers as closely [p. 438] to the mediæval times, as Homer's to the heroic. Chaucer's longest production is his translation of the once-famous " Roman de la Rose." . . . He seems to have been wanting in a certain lightness of touch, conciseness, and melody ; and hence the lyrical manner of the Troubadours and of the early poets of Italy and Swabia is unrepresented in his collection. But, this excepted, he has given admirable specimens of every form of poetical literature then practised ; closing in his old age with that magnificent Prologue to the Pilgrimage, which gives intimations of a vast advance in nature and invention. . . . His poems neither were, nor could be, precursors or models in any strict sense for the poets of modern England. Chaucer is the Hesperus of what, in absence of a better term, we must call our Feudal Ages.

1861. Wright, Thomas. *Essays on Archæological Subjects*, 2 vols., vol. ii, pp. 45, 57–60, 75–6, 259.

[vol. ii, p. 57] [While nearly all the obsolete words in the other writers are Anglo-Saxon, the great proportion in Chaucer are French : hence he is easier to read.]

[pp. 75–6] [Chaucer (*Boke of the Duchesse*, ll. 434–42, quoted) shews that Arabic numerals were not yet in general use.]

[vol. ii, p. 259] [The fabliaux of the thirteenth century, with all their spirit and satire, and much of their objectionable characteristics, took an English form in the hands of Chaucer.]

1862. Arnold, Thomas. *A Manual of English Literature*, pp. 47–58, 60–1, 63, 65, 68, 270–7, 279, 290, 412.

[In the first, historical, section of the book is a short biography (pp. 47–55), in which the *Court of Love* and *Testament of Love* are accepted as genuine, followed by a chronological table and account of the periods of his work. The second half is divided into accounts of the various genres, and under Narrative Poetry an account is given of the *Canterbury Tales.* This very jejune work was frequently revised and reprinted, in 1867, 1873, 1885, 1888, and 1897.]

1862. Borrow, George. *Wild Wales—Its People, Language and Scenery*, 3 vols., vol. i., pp. 216–7.

[On a miller's man shewing a knowledge of Taliesin and Huw Morris :]

"What a difference," said I to my wife, after we had departed, "between a Welshman and an Englishman of the lower class. What would a Suffolk miller's swain have said if I had repeated to him verses out of Beowulf or even Chaucer, and had asked him about the residence of Skelton?"

1862. Burne-Jones, Sir Edward Coley. *Designs to illustrate "The Legend of Good Women."*

[Some of these were executed in glass in 1864 by Morris, and are at Peterhouse, Cambridge, as also is a portrait of Chaucer, designed by Burne-Jones in 1874. *See* M. Bell, *Sir E. Burne-Jones*, 1899, p. 32.]

1862. Child, Francis James. *Observations on the Language of Chaucer* [in the] Memoirs of the American Academy, new ser., vol. viii, 1863, pp. 445–502. [Rearranged and reprinted by A. J. Ellis in *Early English Pronunciation*, 1869–75, *q.v.*, below.]

[This is the first minute and scholarly analysis of Chaucer's language, and it marks an epoch in the study of the poet, for it made possible the full solution of the question of the right scansion of the Canterbury Tales. It consists of classified lists of Chaucer's vocabulary and grammatical forms, and is preceded by an introductory note:]

[pp. 445-6] [Wright's edn. of the *Canterbury Tales* employed, as being based on a single good MS. and fairly accurate. The prevalent ignorance of the English language of that period.]

[p. 446] We are a long way off from a knowledge of the English of the fourteenth century, and still further from a satisfactory edition of Chaucer.

Indeed, there is reason to doubt (and the editors may find some comfort in the thought) whether there ever was an accurate copy of a poem by Chaucer, except his own, or a manuscript corrected by his hand. Certainly this would not be an absolutely extravagant inference from what he says "unto his own Scrivener."

Adam Scrivener was only the first in a long line of corrupters . . . Adam may have been heedless and stupid, but . . . he might justly plead the unsettled state of the language in part excuse. It was undoubtedly very hard for an humble scribe to remember and observe all the nice differences between

[p. 447] the courtly style of his patron and the vulgar dialect... Chaucer thought the prospect of his verses being preserved as he wrote them very unpromising and he expresses his apprehension thus . . . [*Troilus*, v, 1793–6].

This anxiety of Chaucer about the writing and reading of his verses was a thousand times justified by the course of events. [The copyists and editors. Tyrwhitt's textual principle his weak point. A new edition undesirable until an editor arises who will make thorough work with the MSS. Bell's edition likely to block the way for a good while.]

[p. 449] That diversity in English which made Chaucer apprehensive of damage to his verses may have been so considerable, that we could not be sure of restoring them to perfect purity, even if we had several manuscripts of the date 1400 before us. But by far the larger part of the irregularities and corruptions with which the text is now loaded are undoubtedly of later origin, and there is no reason why, (if we are allowed only to take for granted that Chaucer had an ear, and meant to write good metre,‡) by taking pains enough, by a patient comparison of [p. 450] apparently uncorrupted verses, followed by a collation of good contemporary manuscripts, and of the forms of earlier and contemporary authors, we should not at last obtain a text approximately correct.

[p. 449 n.] ‡ [Child's note.] Of course, unless Chaucer wrote good metre, there is an end to all inquiry into the forms of his language. Nothing can be more absurd than Dr. Nott's theory upon this point . . . or more [p. 450 n.] just than Tyrwhitt's remarks . . . Is it not surprising . . . that a man of sense and taste should write as follows? " At the same time, many of his lines evidently consist . . . of ten syllables only ; and such a construction of verse, for ordinary purposes, is become so much more agreeable to modern usage and taste, *that his poetry had better be so read whenever it can be done, even at the cost of thereby somewhat violating the exactness of the ancient pronunciation.*"—Craik's Hist. Eng. Lit. i. 249.

1862. Furnivall, Frederick James. *Preface* [to] Robert of Brunne's *Handlyng Synne* (Roxburghe Club), pp. iv, xxii, xxv, 435, 447.

[p. iv] So far as narrative power and versification are concerned, he [Brunne] seems to me the worthiest forerunner of Chaucer,— the cheery dear old man, who so loved women, and the " glad light green" of spring [from the *Flour and the Lefe*], and made his verse instinct with the grace and brightness that he saw in the objects of his love.

[p. xxii] The MS. [of *Handlyng Synne*] was accordingly copied, and then came the question as to how much of the text was Robert's own, and how much translated from Wadington.

The only way to answer this was by printing Wadington's text opposite Brunne's—a course I had often desired to see taken with Chaucer and his originals, so-called.

1862. Kent, William Charles Mark. *Chaucer at Woodstock,* [in] *Dreamland, with other Poems,* pp. 10–16.

[A poem describing Chaucer basking in the sun in his garden, and seeing his Canterbury Pilgrims pass by as in a vision.]

1862. Lytton, Edward Bulwer, Lord. *Essay* on *the Influence of Love upon Literature and Real Life,* [first printed in Miscellaneous Prose Works, 1868, 3 vols., vol. ii, p. 371–2; and reprinted in Works, Knebworth edn., Quarterly Essays, 1875, pp. 351–2.]

[p. 351]   Chaucer receives him [Love] from the Provençal and the Italian, as they had received him from the Saracen and the Arab.   Where Chaucer, however, appears to write most from his own Anglo-Norman inspiration, love is not very serious. . . .

[p. 352] We may doubt whether Chaucer experienced in his own life more of actual love than a chivalrous fantasy, or a light intrigue.

1862. Marsh, George Perkins. *Origin and History of the English Language* [based on lectures delivered at Boston, U.S.A., in 1860–61], London, 1862, pp. 10, 17, 19, 134–6, 138, 147, 196–8, 215–6, 284, 286–7, 297, 303, 315–7, 335, 365, 372; Lecture IX, *Chaucer and Gower,* pp. 379–453, 454, 455, 456, 458, 463, 465, 482–5, 506, 511, 566, 569–70.

[For Marsh's earlier series of lectures *see* above, 1858–9.]

[Lecture ix begins with a general account of the English language at Chaucer's birth, pp. 379–81.]

[p. 381]   Chaucer did not introduce into the English language words
[p. 382] which it had rejected as aliens before, but out of those which had been already received he invested the better portion with the rights of citizenship, and stamped them with the mint mark of English coinage. . . .

Of the Romance words found in his writings, not much above one hundred have been suffered to become obsolete, while a much larger number of Anglo-Saxon words employed by him have passed altogether out of use.

[Linguistic conditions ready for Chaucer, p. 385.   Chaucer's introduction of Romance words less than is supposed; the translation of the Romaunt is used in evidence, pp. 390–1.

Chaucer not an historical poet, pp. 393–5. Chaucer's sources and his acknowledgments : contents of books common property in the middle ages, pp. 395–99. His Italian sources, pp. 400–1. Discussion of the *Romaunt*, pp. 401–7.]

[p. 413]   It cannot be said that the poem [*Troilus*] is essentially improved by the changes of the translator, though, in some passages, great skill in the use of words is exhibited, and the native humour of Chaucer pervades many portions of the story. . . .

[*The Flour and the Lefe* discussed, pp. 414–6. General account of the *Canterbury Tales*, pp. 417–31.]

[p. 419]   He is essentially a dramatist, and if his great work does not appear in the conventional dramatic form, it is an accident of the time.

1862.   **Notes and Queries**, 3rd Series, vol. i, pp. 99, 193, 199, 260, 322, 484 ; vol. ii, pp. 48, 165, 190, 204, 218, 319, 327, 347, 376 7, 400, 461, 463–4, 479, 507.

Author.	Date.	Reference.	Subject.
W. S.	Feb. 1.	3rd S. i, 99.	Chaucer's Tabard Inn and Fire of Southwark, 1667 and 1676.
Corner, G. R.	March 8.	3rd S. i, 193.	
East- wood, J.	March 8.	3rd S. i, 199.	' Nockynge and Dowell money ' (*Prol.* ll. 507–11 quoted).
Allport, Douglas.	March 29.	3rd S. i, 260.	' Tabard ' ; Chaucer's Plowman described as wearing one ; the Southwark inn perhaps named in compliment to Kentish farmers.
Collier, J. P.	Ap. 26.	3rd S. i, 322.	Entry by A. Jeffes, 1592, of Chaucer's Works, in the Registers of the Stationers' Company.
W., W. Editor.	July 19.	3rd S. ii, 48.	' Citryne eyes ' (*Knightes Tale*, l. 2162).
Mayhew, A. L.	Sept. 6.	3rd S. ii, 190.	' mystery ' = craft.
Hazlitt, W. C..	Sept. 13.	3rd S. ii, 204.	Some copies of the *Works*, 1561, purport to be printed by Henry Bradsha or Bradshaw.
Mewburn, Fra.	Nov. 1.	3rd S. ii, 347.	The Yeoman's (or rather Frankelein's) bake-meats (*Prol.* ll. 343–4).
Work- ard, B.	Nov. 8.	3rd S. ii, 377.	' Forthink.'

Author.	Date.	Reference.	Subject.

Keight-   Dec. 13.   3rd S. ii,   All English prose from Chaucer
ley, T.   463–4.   to Dryden is written in rhythmical lines of five beats ; Chaucer perhaps introduced this,
as he did the five-foot verse-line.

'Chess-   Dec. 13.   3rd S. ii,   'Forthink'; identification of
borough.'   479.   an edition of 1560 (really 1561)
asked for.

1862. Peacock, Thomas Love. *Letter to Lord Broughton,* [dated] Feb.
22, 1862, [printed in] A Biographical Notice by his grand-daughter
Edith Nicolls, p. xlvii. (Works, ed. Cole, 1875, vol. i, p. xlvii.)

I have more pleasure in reading through books which I
have read and admired before than in reading anything new.
The three last old works which I have so gone through were
"Rabelais," Chaucer's "Canterbury Tales," and the "Morgante
Maggiore."

1862–3. Ruskin, John. *Munera Pulveris,* chapters iii, v, vi, *Coin-
keeping, Government* and *Mastership,* and Appendix vi, [first
published as *Essays on Political Economy,* in] Fraser's Magazine,
Dec. 1862, vol. lxvi, p. 749*n.,* April, 1863, vol. lxvii, pp. 446*n.,*
457, 462 ; 1st vol. ed., 1872 (as *Munera Pulveris*), in Works, 1871–
80, 11 vols., vol. ii, pp. 84, 126*n.,* 162–3*n.,* 186. (Works, ed.
E. T. Cook and A. Wedderburn, 1903–12, 39 vols., vol. xvii, pp.
208, 244, 273, 292.)

[p. 208]   [Chaucer, like Plato, Dante, Shakspere, etc., spoke in
enigmas.]

[p. 244]   [Quotation from *Romaunt of the Rose,* ll. 177–80.]

[p. 273]   [Chaucer's feeling respecting birds.]

[p. 292]   [Appendix vi: Quotation from *Romaunt of the Rose,* ll.
1142–3.]

1862. Smith, Alexander. *Geoffrey Chaucer,* [in] The Museum, Jan.
1862, vol. i, pp. 459–66. [Reprinted, much revised, in Dreamthorp, 1863, pp. 211–45.]

[p. 459]   Chaucer is admitted on all hands to be a great poet, but by
the general public, at least, he is not frequently read.   He is
like a cardinal virtue, a good deal talked about, a good deal
praised, a good deal admired, but very seldom practised.
[Reasons for this :] He is an ancient . . . He is garrulous,
homely and slow-paced . . . He does not dazzle by sentences ;

[p. 460] he is not quotable. [His kindliness ; visible in his face.
Inadequacy of the modernizers :] Dryden and Pope did not
translate Chaucer, or modernize Chaucer; they committed
assault and battery upon him . . .

[p. 461] [Chaucer's clearness of outline justifies Hazlitt's epithet 'intense.' Colour and gaiety of his world. The *Canterbury Tales* a gathering up of tales written at different times. Observation shewn in the *Prologue;* dramatic variety of the tales; pathos of the tale of Constance.]

[In *Dreamthorp* the passage on the modernizers is replaced by a contrast between Chaucer and Spenser, which is extracted from an article, *Edmund Spenser,* in *The Museum,* July, 1862, vol. ii, p. 151. The latter part of the essay is practically rewritten, and concludes with prose summaries of the *Knightes* and *Man of Law's Tales.*]

1862. Unknown. *Mediæval English Literature: Chaucer,* [in] The National Review, Jan. 1862, vol. xiv, pp. 1–37.

[The book nominally reviewed is Bell's edn. of the Poetical Works of Chaucer, in 8 vols., 1854–56. Chaucer's literary character and genius is reviewed as influenced by his age and its limitations; hence he is often careless and prolix, and he lacks historical perspective (p. 8). His genius, though of the rarest kind, was not of the highest order (p. 9). The essential characteristic of it is a strong sense of the real (p. 12). Some account follows of Chaucer's life and reading (pp. 14–16), and his works are then reviewed in some detail, arranged in six divisions: Grave Stories; Comic Stories; Pieces of sufficient extent to stand alone; Allegorical and Personal Poems; Miscellaneous Pieces; Prose Works.]

1862. Weymouth, Richard Francis. *Bishop Grosseteste's " Castle of Love,"* [a paper, read Nov. 13, 1862, printed in] Transactions of the Philological Society, 1862–3, [1864,] p. 59.

Chaucer . . . has generally preferred a five-fold ictus in his Canterbury Tales, though the number of his syllables varies from eight to twelve : see for instance, in his description of the Friar, the second and fourth of these lines [*Prol.*, ll. 246–50],—

> It is not honest, it may not avaunce,
> For | to de|len with | such | poraile,
> But al with riche and sellers of vitaille.
> And óver|al thér e|ny pro|fyt schulde | arise,
> Curteys | he was | and lowle of | servise.

1862. Wright, Thomas. *History of Domestic Manners and Sentiments in England during the Middle Ages,* (reprinted, with additions, as *The Homes of Other Days, a History,* etc., 1871), pp. 133–4, 139, 142, 155, 171–2, 188, 210–1, 217, 242, 248–9, 279, 281, 284–6, 288–9, 313, 315, 319–22, 325, 335, 372, 395–8, 405, 419, 439.

[pp. 133–4] [Details of houses in *Milleres T., T. of Gamelyn, Sompnoures T., Nonne Prestes T.*]

1863. Arnold, Matthew, *Maurice de Guérin,* [in] Fraser's Magazine, Jan. 1863, vol. lxvii, p. 48. [Reprinted in *Essays in Criticism,* 1865, p. 83, and as a preface to the *Journal of Maurice de Guérin,* 1867.] (Works, 1903–4, 15 vols., vol. iii, p. 91.)

For English poetical production on a great scale, for an English poet deploying all the forces of his genius, the ten-syllable couplet was, in the eighteenth century, the established, one may almost say the inevitable, channel.   Now this couplet, admirable (as Chaucer uses it) for story-telling not of the epic pitch, and often admirable for a few lines even in poetry of a very high pitch, is for continuous use in poetry of this latter kind inadequate.

1863. [Blanchard, Edward Litt Leman. ("Francisco Frost.")] *Harlequin and Friar Bacon; or great grim John of Gaunt, and the enchanted lance of Robin Goodfellow: an entirely new . . . pantomime,* (Astley's Pantomime, 1863–4), [1864].

[Scene II shews Chaucer, the Host, and the rest of the Pilgrims at the Tabard ; Scene III shews them on the road. Chaucer has a speaking part, but no attempt at archaism is made.   The text is followed by a note on the Tabard Inn. For the authorship, *see The Life and Reminiscences of E. L. Blanchard,* by Clement Scott and Cecil Howard, 1891, 2 vols., vol. i, p. 285.]

1863–64. Chambers, Robert. *The Book of Days,* a Miscellany of Popular Antiquities in connection with the Calendar, edited by R. Chambers, 2 vols. ; vol. i, 1863, pp. 53, 220, 339, 472 ; vol. ii, 1864, pp. 493–4.

[vol. i, p. 53] [Chaucer's allusion to the Man in the Moon, *Troilus,* i, 1024.]

[p. 220] In the middle ages, solemn betrothal by means of the ring often preceded matrimony, and was sometimes adopted between lovers who were about to separate for long periods.   Chaucer, in his *Troilus and Cresseide,* describes the heroine as giving her lover a ring, upon which a love-motto was engraved, and receiving one from him in return.

[p. 472] [Reference made to Chaucer being often called poet-laureate, to the offices held by him, and to several curious grants of which he was the recipient.]

[vol. ii, pp. 493–4] [Biographical notice.]

1863. Landor, Walter Savage. *Heroic Idylls, with additional Poems,*
pp. 142-3, 181, 224, 270.

To Chaucer.

[p. 142]

Chaucer, O how I wish thou wert
Alive and, as of yore, alert !
Then, after bandied tales, what fun
Would we two have with monk and nun.
Ah, surely verse was never meant
To render mortals somnolent.
In Spenser's labyrinthine rhymes
I throw my arms o'erhead at times,
Opening sonorous mouth as wide
As oyster shells at ebb of tide. . .
No bodyless and soulless elves
I seek, but creatures like ourselves. . .
Thou wast content to act the squire
Becomingly, and mount no higher,
Nay, at fit season to descend
Into the poet with a friend,
Then ride with him about the land
In lithesome nut-brown boots well tann'd . . .
    The lesser Angels now have smiled
To see thee frolic like a child,
And hear thee, innocent as they,
Provoke them to come down and play.

    [Squibs, crackers, serpents, etc. . .]

[p. 181]

I leaving good old Homer, not o'erlong,
Enjoy the merriment of Chaucer's tales.

    [Wrongs have I suffered . . .]

[p. 224]

Wrongs have I suffered, great and many,
Insufferable never any
Like that prepensely murderous one
An Oxford hang-dog rogue has done,
Who shoved me on a bench with men
Biting the point of Chaucer's pen.
Chaucer I always loved, for he
Led me to woo fair Poesie.
He of our craft the worthy foreman
Stood gallantly against the Norman,

> And in good humour tried to teach
> Reluctant churls our native speech.
> Now I must mount my cob and hurry
> To join his friends at Canterbury,
> A truly English merry party,
> Tho' none so jocular and hearty.

[James Pycroft's Ways and Works of Men of Letters, 1861, pp. 79, 379, is here referred to. *See* above, 1861, Landor.]

[p. 270] ON THE WIDOW'S ORDEAL, BY WASHINGTON IRVING.

> Chaucer I fancied had been dead
>   Some centuries, some four or five;
> By fancy I have been misled
>   Like many; he is yet alive.

> *The Widow's Ordeal* who beside
>   Could thus relate? Yes, there is one,
> He bears beyond the Atlantic wide
>   The glorious name of Washington.

1863. Notes and Queries, 3rd Series, vol. iii, pp. 2, 17, 77, 95, 134, 137, 243, 371, 389, 427–8, 432–3, 453–5, 476–8, 496–7; vol. iv, pp. 18, 26, 158, 359, 365–6, 423.

Author.	Date.	Reference.	Subject.
Collier, John Payne.	Jan. 3.	3rd S. iii, 2.	Entry by Islip on 20 Dec., 1594, in the Register of the Stationers' Company, of Speght's edition of Chaucer's Works. *See* below, App. A., 1594.
Workard, J. J. B.	Jan. 3.	3rd S. iii, 17.	'Forthink'; editions of Chaucer. Reply to 'Chessborough' (3rd S. ii, 377, 479).
A., A.	Jan. 24.	3rd S. iii, 77.	'Hoppesteres' = hopping, disabled, on the analogy of 'tomblesteres' = tumblers.
A., A.	Jan. 31.	3rd S. iii, 95.	'Hackney' (*Rom. Rose*, A. 1137); origin of the word?
B., N.	Feb. 14.	3rd S. iii, 134.	'Hackney.'
Burn, John S.	Feb. 14.	3rd S. iii, 137.	'Rood coat'; *Plowman's Tale.* quoted as Chaucer's.
Pinkerton, William.	Mar. 28.	3rd S. iii, 243.	Lydgate's *Story of Thebes* printed by William Thynne, at the end of Chaucer's *Works*, 1561, as an additional Canterbury Tale.
Editor.	May 9.	3rd S. iii, 371.	Shakespeare's 'Patience on a monument' imitated from Chaucer (*Parl. Foules*, ll. 242–3).

Author.	Date.	Reference.	Subject.
'Her-mentrude.'	May 16.	3rd S. iii, 389.	Griselda; origin of the tale? Chaucer's and Edwin Arnold's versions; modernisation of the former in Blackwood's, 1838 [*q.v.*].
'Daniel.'	May 30.	3rd S. iii, 427–8.	'Dan Chaucer'; meaning of 'Dan'?
'Tweed-side.' Editor.	May 30.	3rd S. iii, 432–3.	Ralph Strode, the friend of Chaucer and praised by him for his philosophy.
'Chess-borough.'	June 6.	3rd S. iii, 453–5.	Reply to W. Pinkerton and J. J. B. Workard; further enquiry for evidence of a 1560 edition of Chaucer.
East-wood, J. Buck-ton, T. J.	June 13.	3rd S. iii, 476–7.	'Dan' is from 'dominus.'
Addis, John.	June 13.	3rd S. iii, 478.	*Troilus*, i. 108, quoted in reference to the phrase 'A.1.'
Work-ard, J. J. B.	June 20.	3rd S. iii, 496–7.	'Chessborough's' '1560' copy of Chaucer's Works probably of one of Speght's editions.
Pinker-ton, William.	June 20.	3rd S. iii, 497.	'Chessborough's' Chaucer; Warton records the insertion of Lydgate's Story of Thebes by William Thynne in the 1561 edition.
'Juxta Turrim.'	July 4.	3rd S. iv, 18.	Thynne, who died in 1546, could not have edited the 1561 Chaucer.
Camp-bell, J. D.	July 11.	3rd S. iv, 26.	'Wailed.'
Buckton, T. J.	Aug. 22.	3rd S. iv, 158.	'Fast' (*Chanouns Yemannes Prol.*, ll. 127–30, quoted).
"	Oct. 31.	3rd S. iv, 359.	'Rochette' (*Rom. Rose*, B. 4754, referred to).
'Juxta Turrim.'	Nov. 7.	3rd S. iv, 365–6.	An account of William Thynne, the editor of Chaucer.
Editor.	Nov. 21.	3rd S. iv, 423.	Longfellow's *Tales of a Wayside Inn*; the introductions, as in the *Canterbury Tales*, are the best part.

n. a. 1863.] **Smith**, Alexander. *William Dunbar*, [in] *Dreamthorp*, 1863, pp. 67–72, 81.

[p. 68]   Chaucer . . . appeared at a time when the Saxon and Norman races had become fused. . . . He was the first great

poet the island produced; and he wrote for the most part in
the language of the people. . . . In his earlier poems he was
under the influence of the Provençal Troubadours, and in his
"Flower and the Leaf" and other works of a similar class, he
riots in allegory. . . . He lived in a brilliant and stirring
time; he was connected with the court; he served in armies;
he visited the Continent; and, although a silent man, he
carried with him, wherever he went, and into whatever
[p. 69] company he was thrown, the most observant eyes perhaps that
ever looked curiously out upon the world. . . . And so it was
that, after mixing in kings' courts, and sitting with friars in
taverns, and talking with people on country roads, and travelling in France and Italy, and making himself master of the
literature, science, and theology of his time, and when perhaps
touched with misfortune and sorrow, he came to see the depth
of interest that resides in actual life. . . . It is difficult to
define Chaucer's charm. He does not indulge in fine sentiments; he has no bravura passages; he is ever master of himself and of his subject. The light upon his page is the light
[p. 70] of common day. . . . It is his shrewdness, his conciseness, his
ever-present humour, his frequent irony, and his short homely
line—effective as the play of the short Roman sword—which
strikes the reader most. [Chaucer and Fielding compared in
their common-sense and English relish for fact.] Chaucer was
a Conservative in all his feelings; he liked to poke his fun at
the clergy, but he was not of the stuff of which martyrs are
made . . .
[p. 71]   Chaucer was born about 1328, and died about 1380.

[Probably reprinted from a review. Irving's *History of Scottish Poetry* (1860) is
spoken of (p. 75) as "published the other day."]

1864. Works. [Projected editions.]

[In 1864 Professor Earle, W. Aldis Wright and Henry
Bradshaw undertook to edit for the Clarendon Press a standard
library edition of Chaucer. Work on it was in progress in
1866 and 1867. In 1870 Professor Earle gave up the editor-
ship-in-chief, and, after refusals by Aldis Wright and Skeat,
Bradshaw accepted it, but soon found that he had not the
time.

Also in 1864 Alexander Macmillan proposed to Bradshaw a
small edition in the Globe series. So late as 1879, in con-
junction with Furnivall, Bradshaw had some specimen pages

printed, but no more came of it. *See* for these schemes, G. W. Prothero, *A Memoir of Henry Bradshaw*, 1888, pp. 108–9, 223–5, and, for Bradshaw's Chaucer studies in general, *ib.*, pp. 14, 122, 143, 212–23.]

1864. The Prologue to the Legend of Good Women. [The text of the earlier version, privately printed from the Cambridge MS. for Henry Bradshaw. *See* Hammond, *Chaucer*, p. 381. No copy in B.M. or University Library, Cambridge.]

1864. Bradshaw, Henry. *See* above, *Works*, and *The Prologue to the Legend of Good Women.*

1864. Burne-Jones, Sir Edward Coley. *The Dream of Good Women.* [A stained glass window, at Peterhouse, Cambridge.]

1864. Dickens, Charles. *Our Mutual Friend,* 2 vols., 1864–5, vol. i, chap. iii, x, pp. 13, 89. (Works, Gadshill edition [1897–1908], 36 vols., vol. xxiii, pp. 21, 145.)

[p. 21] Mortimer looked at the boy, and the boy looked at the bran-new pilgrims on the wall, going to Canterbury in more gold frame than procession, and more carving than country.

[p. 145] Veneering shoots out of the study wherein he is accustomed, when contemplative, to give his mind to the carving and gilding of the Pilgrims going to Canterbury [*i. e.* probably the print after Stothard].

1864. Earle, John. *See* above, *Works.*

1864–7. Morley, Henry. *English Writers,* vol. i, pp. 21–2 [Chaucer's debt to Italy], 771–5 [his debt to France; his life, without the apocryphal episodes, the *Testament of Love* being treated as a genuine but purely imaginative work]; vol. ii, pp. 1–5 [Chaucer the first fully English writer]: 39–43 [Petrarch and Boccaccio], 66–9, 107–8, 135–6, 138–9 [Gower]; 140–338 [chapters iv–vii, devoted to Chaucer; p. 140, his character sociable and free from bitterness; pp. 141–65, his life; *The Court of Love* treated as genuine; pp. 165–335, his works described and analysed in a chronological order (*Troilus* being compared at some length with the *Filostrato*, and Chaucer's refinements on Boccaccio pointed out, pp. 237–43); pp. 335–6, cause of his greatness; pp. 336–7, his verse regular; pp. 337–8, his English]; 425, 429–32 [Lydgate]; 434 [Occleve].
[In the revised and enlarged edn., 11 vols., 1887–95, chapters vi–xiii, pp. 83–347, of vol. v (1890) are devoted to Chaucer; many brief passages relating to him are scattered up and down the whole work.]

1864. Notes and Queries, 3rd Series, vol. v, p. 53 ; vol. vi, pp. 125,
200, 259, 284, 288, 432, 464–5.

Author.	Date.	Reference.	Subject.
Heath, R. C.	Jan. 16.	3rd S. v, 53.	Neglect of the swallow by Chaucer, perhaps owing to its lack of song.
' **Chaucer.**'	Aug. 13.	3rd S. vi, 125.	No allusion to Chaucer beyond the signature.
Congreve, H.	Sept. 10.	3rd S. vi, 200.	*The Squieres Tale* derived from an Eastern original, perhaps *The Enchanted Horse,* in *The Arabian Nights,* by way of the thirteenth century romance *Cleomades and Claremond.*
Henderson, John.	Sept. 24.	3rd S. vi, 259.	' Raines,' ' cloth of raines' (*Book of the Duchesse,* ll. 251–5), derived by Tyrwhitt from Rennes.
Dixon, J.	Oct. 8.	3rd S. vi, 284.	Strange that Milton accented Cambuscan differently from his original.
„	Nov. 26.	3rd S. vi, 432.	' Dun is in the mire '; doubts whether ' dun ' = donkey.
Carey, Stafford.	Dec. 3.	3rd S. vi, 464–5.	Milton's misaccentuation of ' Cambuscan,' though not without sonorous grandeur, shews how imperfectly our earlier poets were understood in the latter half [*sic*] of the seventeenth century. Dryden, with all his veneration for Chaucer, had no adequate conception of the beauties of his versification. Long quotation from the preface to the *Fables,* 1700, *q.v.* above, vol. i, p. 276–7.

1864. O'Hagan, John. *Chaucer,* [in] The Afternoon Lectures on
Literature and Art, delivered in the Theatre of the Museum of
Industry, St. Stephen's Green, Dublin, 1863–9, 5 series, ser. ii,
1864, pp. 247–77.

[pp. 247–50] [Chaucer's language having very soon become obsolete, he
never could nor can be a popular favourite; even Dryden's
[pp. 250–53] excellent imitations are as much Dryden as Chaucer. Chaucer's
life, with no mention of the *Testament of Love* or the episodes
[pp. 253–4] founded on it. His versification ; the final vowel and the
[pp. 254–7] French element in the pronunciation. *The Court of Love*
' Chaucer's earliest work.' *The Canterbury Tales ;* the
[pp. 257–77] characters and their stories. Chaucer's coarseness inexcusable
and also dramatically inartistic. His vivid pictures of society
in the fourteenth century.]

[*n. a.* **1864 ?**] **Pater**, Walter Horatio. *Conversation with Mr. Richard C. Jackson,* [in] The Life of Walter Pater, by Thomas Wright, 1907, 2 vols., vol. ii, pp. 267–8.

[p. 268] One day, when Pater and Mr. Jackson were visiting an acquaintance, Pater chanced to take up a rather rare little book called *Chaucer Modernised*. He remarked that he had never seen it before, and frankly admitted that he was entirely ignorant of the literature connected with Chaucer; that, more-over, of Chaucer himself and his work he knew very little. " Of course," he added, " I have heard of the *Canterbury Tales,* but I did not know that they were considered of sufficient importance to be modernised."

[Mr. Jackson exclaims upon Pater's ignorance of English literature, which however he finds natural in "a Tutor of Oxford," and offers to shew him a work in his library which cannot fail to open his eyes.]

Pater duly presented himself early one morning, and Mr. Jackson placed before him the magnificent Black Letter Chaucer above described [ed. Speght, 1598]. Opening the book, Pater gave an exclamation of wonder and delight, and all that day he sat poring over its pages, scarcely saying a word.

[In the evening he made severe observations on the neglect of English in education, concluding :]

"Books like this or *facsimiles* of them ought to be in all schools and colleges." . . . Then pointing to the portrait of Chaucer he said : "This portrait, dight with heraldry, has as much within it as a vast number of the so-called commentaries of the Bible."

[It is obvious from the phrasing alone that this story is untrue as it stands. The whole book is full of equal and even greater absurdities. But it may be based on some real expression of regret on Pater's part at his ignorance of Chaucer, and is perhaps worth quoting on that account.

If Pater was "a Tutor of Oxford" at the time, it must have been in or after 1864, when he took his Fellowship at Brasenose.

Mr. Jackson had inherited Charles Lamb's library, and this may have been the copy mentioned above, 1823. He also (Wright, vol. ii, p. 180) owned, and shewed to Pater, Blake's original oil-sketch for the Canterbury Pilgrims.]

1864. **Ruskin**, John. *Sesame and Lilies,* Lecture ii, *Of Queen's Gardens.* [Delivered 14 Dec., 1864,] 1st vol. ed., 1865, p. 138. (Works, ed. E. T. Cook and A. Wedderburn, 1903–12, 39 vols., vol. xviii, pp. 118–19.)

Now I could multiply witness upon witness of this kind

[of the queenly power of women] upon you if I had time.
I would take Chaucer and show you why he wrote a Legend
of Good Women; but no Legend of Good Men.

1864. Tennyson, Alfred, Lord.   *Letter to the Duke of Argyll,* [printed
in] Tennyson ; a Memoir by his Son, 1897, 2 vols., vol. ii, p. 3.

One cannot exactly say of him [Garibaldi] what Chaucer
says of the ideal knight, "As meke he was of port as is a
maid." He is more majestic than meek.

[Tennyson enjoyed reading Chaucer aloud more than any poet except Shakespeare
and Milton. *See Tennyson: a Memoir,* vol. ii, pp. 83, 284.]

1864. Wright, William Aldis.   *See* above, *Works.*

1865. Bradshaw, Henry.   [*Advertisement* of] *An Attempt to Ascertain
the State of Chaucer's Works, as they were left at his death, with
some notices of their subsequent history.*

[The advertisement, inserted by Macmillan on the front page
of Notes and Queries, Aug. 12, 1865, begins with the words
" Shortly will be published," but Bradshaw did not advance
far into the work, of which only the introductory pages were
found after his death.   The *Skeleton of Chaucer's Canterbury
Tales* summed up his results ; *see* below, 1867.]

1865. Burne-Jones, Sir Edward Coley.   *Chaucer's Dream.*

[A water-colour, illustrating the non-Chaucerian *Isle of
Ladies.* Burne-Jones painted a larger and much altered
version in 1871. For other Chaucerian subjects painted by
him *see* above, 1858, 1861, 1862, 1864. He also painted, in
1874 and succeeding years, a series of scenes from the
Romaunt of the Rose. See M. Bell, *Sir E. Burne-Jones,* 1899,
and O. G. Destrée, *Les Préraphaélites* [1895].]

1865. Collier, John Payne.   *A Bibliographical and Critical Account of
the Rarest Books in the English Language,* vol. i, pp. viii*, xii*,
xli*, xliv*, 87, 97–8, 128-9, 147, 191, 200, 227, 255, 267, 280, 338,
400, 526 ; vol. ii, pp. 92, 101–2, 145, 178, 183, 238, 295, 378, 418,
424, 427–8, 440, 464, 477, 485–6, 546.

[Editions of Chaucer and allusions to him in old literature.]

[p. xli*] We do not know that it has been observed upon, but it is a
fact, that no less a poet than Chaucer was the earliest introducer of classical measures into our language.   He commences

his prose version of Boethius with these two hexameter
lines . . .

" Alas, I wepyng am constrayned to begin verse of sorowful
mater,
That whilom in flourisshyng studye made delytable verses."

1865. Furnivall, Frederick James. *The Wright's Chaste Wife*, by
Adam of Cobsam, ed. F. J. Furnivall, E.E.T.S., Preface, p. vii.

Would that we knew as much of Adam of Cobsam as of
our White-Rose king.   He must have been one of the Chaucer
breed. . . .
[To this a footnote was added in ed. 2, 1869, on Chaucer's
Carpenter and the *Milleres T.*]

1865. [Furnivall, Frederick James ?] [*Article* in] The Reader, May 27,
1865, p. 598.

[No thorough testing of Chaucer MSS. ever yet carried out.]
It may be that a further testing of the two texts [the Harleian,
used by Wright, and the Ellesmere] will establish the superiority of the " Ellesmere " MS. in readings, though it is later
in date, and may necessitate its being taken as the basis of the
new Oxford edition, should the University Press proposal for
one ever be carried into effect. . . . It is clear to any eye that
these illustrations [*i. e.* those of the Ellesmere MS.] are much
later than the MS. (which is about 1430 A.D.) . . . and have
thus unfortunately thrown discredit on the MS. itself.   On
the question of which of the two schemes—Professor Child's,
of printing the six or eight texts, or the Oxford one, of printing one and collating the others—is the more deserving of
support, we can only say that we wish well to both,
though we fear the Oxford one, if carried out first, might
prevent the success of Professor Child's.   The true way would
be for the Oxford Press delegates to take both schemes in
hand, to print the six or eight texts as material for their
editor, or better, their editors, and then issue their one text,
without collations, which are always a bother. . . . They
would be producing a book worthy of their own reputation,
and of our own bright poet of the dawn.

1865. Furnivall, Frederick James. *Chaucer and Arthur,* [review of *Thynne's Animadversions,* ed. Kingsley, and *Morte Arthure,* ed. Perry (E.E.T.S.), in] The Reader, 18 November, 1865, pp. 565–6.

We put Chaucer before Arthur, for we care more about him; the more we read him the more we love him, sunning ourselves in the bright sheen of his humour, and sniffing the fragrance of his verse, as on a bright spring day on his own Kent downs. The old man is the foremost and most glowing figure of all the troop of our early writers; and, of all, he is the one we can take closest home to ourselves, for he has written himself in his books, if ever writer has, and we know the man from soul to skin.

1865. Hook, Walter Farquhar. *Lives of the Archbishops of Canterbury,* 1860–76, 12 vols., vol. iii, 1865, pp. 37*n.,* 40–1, 47, 67, 69*n.*

[p. 67]   [Against Chaucer's evidence of the demoralisation of the clergy of his time must be set his picture of a parish priest.]

[p. 69]   [Identification of Chaucer's good priest with Wyclif impossible; if intended by Chaucer, it must have been as a masked sarcasm. Robert Bell quoted. Further improbability " that the gay and licentious poet should have been intimate with the reformer."]

1865. Kingsley, George Henry. *Chaucer. Animaduersions . . . by Francis Thynne . . .* edited by G. H. Kingsley, Early English Text Soc., pp. iv, vi, viii, ix, xi, xii.

[p. xi]   The old story of Chaucer's having been fined for beating a Franciscan friar in Fleet Street is doubted by Thynne, though hardly, I think, on sufficient grounds. Tradition (when it agrees with our own views) is not lightly to be disturbed, and remembering with what more than feminine powers of invective " spiritual " men seem to be not unfrequently endowed, and also how atrociously insolent a Franciscan friar would be likely to be (of course from the best motives) to a man like Chaucer, who had burnt into the very soul of monasticism with the caustic of his wit, I shall continue to believe the legend for the present. If the mediæval Italians are to be believed, the cudgelling of a friar was occasionally thought necessary even by the most faithful, and I see no reason why hale Dan Chaucer should not have lost his temper on sufficient provocation.

[A review of Kingsley in the *Saturday Review* led to a strong denunciation of the reviewer by Furnivall in *The Reader*, Feb. 3, 1866, *q.v.* below. The second edition, 1875, edited by F. J. Furnivall, with a new preface by Kingsley, and hindwords by Furnivall, contains other Chaucer references.]

1865. Laing, David. *The Poems and Fables of Robert Henryson*, ed. David Laing, pp. xix, xxi–ii, xxv–ix [*The Testament of Cresseid* and Chaucer's *Troilus*. Also numerous references to Chaucer, chiefly quotations from Chalmers, in the notes.]

1865. Maurice, Frederick Denison. *On Books*, [a lecture delivered Nov. 1865, printed in] The Friendship of Books and other Lectures, 1874, pp. 76–7.

[pp. 76-7] Chaucer was possibly the friend of Wycliffe—certainly shared many of his sympathies and antipathies. He loved the priest, or, as he was called, the secular priest, who went among the people, and cared for them as his fellow-countrymen; he intensely disliked the friars, who flattered them and cursed them, and in both ways governed them and degraded them. His education had been different from Wycliffe's, his early poetical powers had been called forth by the ladies and gentlemen of the court. He mingled much French with his speech, as they did; he acquired from them a kind of acquaintance with life which Wycliffe could not obtain in the Oxford schools. Had he remained under their influence he might have been merely a very musical court singer; but he entered into fellowship with common citizens. He became a keen observer of all the different forms of life and society in his time—a keen observer, and, as all such are, genial, friendly, humorous, able to understand men about him by sympathising with them, able to understand the stories of the past by his experience of the present. Without being a reformer like Wycliffe, he helped forward the Reformation by making men acquainted with themselves and their fellows, by stripping off disguises, and by teaching them to open their eyes to the beautiful world which lay about them. Chaucer is the genuine specimen of an English poet—a type of the best who were to come after him; with cordial affection for men and for nature; often tempted to coarseness, often yielding to his baser nature in his desire to enter into all the different experiences of men ; apt through this desire, and through his hatred of what was insincere, to say many things of which he had need to repent, and of which he did repent ; but never losing his loyalty to what was pure, his reverence for what was divine. . . . The English books which live through ages are those which connect themselves with human life and action. His other poems, though graceful and harmonious, are only remembered, because in his "Canterbury Tales" he has come directly into contact with the hearts and thoughts, the sufferings and sins, of men and women, and has given the clearest pictures we possess of all the distinctions and occupations in his own day.

1865. Notes and Queries, 3rd Series, vol. vii, pp. 268, 279, 345, 436, 486, 492 ; vol. viii, pp. 13, 63, 77, 104, front cover of no. for Aug. 12, pp. 145, 164, 221–2, 260, 348, 360, 367–8, 419, 459, 483, 532.

Author.	Date.	Reference.	Subject.
Burn, J. S.	Apr. 1.	3rd S. vii, 268.	'Dagon' = remnant.
N., N.	Apr. 8.	3rd S. vii, 279.	'Dalfe,' 'dolven,' not 'delved,' the past of 'delve' in Chaucer.
T., C.	Apr. 29.	3rd S. vii, 345.	'Cole' = charcoal.
Furnivall, F. J.	June 3.	3rd S. vii, 436.	Verses by Roger North in the Ellesmere MS. of the *Canterbury Tales.*
A. A.	June 17.	3rd S. vii, 486.	'Chevisaunce.'
Norgate, F.	June 17.	3rd S. vii, 486.	Adam's *Description of King's Lynn (q.v.* above, [1676?], vol. i, p. 272) claiming Chaucer as a native.
'Hermentrude.'	June 24.	3rd S. vii, 492.	Extracts from the Issue Rolls, including life-records of Chaucer.
Dixon, J.	July 1.	3rd S. viii, 13.	Improbabilities in the framework of the *Canterbury Tales ;*

the pilgrims never halt; between Boughton and the "litel town" there is only time for one short tale, the *Chanouns Yemannes ;* but, between the "litel town" and Canterbury come *four* tales, the *Manciples,* the *Prestes,* the *Cokes,* and the *Plowmans,* all told while they are riding a mile and a half. Is it possible, by any rearrangement of the order of the tales, to adapt them to the time of the journey with probability ? Can this be done by a careful collation of MSS. ?

Author.	Date.	Reference.	Subject.
'Hermen-trude.'	July 22.	3rd S. viii, 63.	Extracts from the Issue Rolls, including life-records of Chaucer.
Jacobson, P. à.	July 22.	3rd S. viii, 77.	'Fonne,' to be foolish.
Brad-shaw, Henry.	Aug. 12.	front cover.	Announcement of Bradshaw's *Attempt to Ascertain the State of Chaucer's Works, as they were left at his death, q.v.* above, Bradshaw, 1865.
'Schin.'	Aug. 19.	3rd S. viii, 145.	Difficulties of Chaucer: an explanation of 'Wades Bote' in "They connen so moch craft on Wades bote" (*Marchantes Tale*, l. 180).
„	Aug. 26.	3rd S. viii, 164.	Difficulties of Chaucer: 'fortened crese' (*Rom. Rose*, B., l. 4875); an emendation to 'forten decrese' = further decrease, is suggested.
H., A.	Sept. 16.	3rd S. viii, 221-2.	An appeal for preventing the demolition of the Tabard Inn, with an extract to the same effect from the *London Review*, Aug. 26.
Editor.	Sept. 23.	3rd S. viii, 260.	References for 'Wades bote.'
Addis, John.	Oct. 28.	3rd S. viii, 360.	Meeting eyebrows considered a blemish by Chaucer (*Troilus*, quoted).
'Hermen-trude.'	Nov. 4.	3rd S. viii, 367-8.	Extracts from the Issue Rolls, including life-records of Chaucer.
Hahn, J. C.	Nov. 18.	3rd S. viii, 419.	'Yeoman'; quotations from *Prol.*
P., J. A.	Dec. 2.	3rd S. viii, 459.	'By and by'; quotations from *Rom. Rose* and *Knightes Tale*.
'Verb Sap.' Wright, W. Aldis.	Dec 9.	3rd S. viii, 483.	'Let make.'
Editor.	Dec. 23.	3rd S. viii, 532.	Brief notice of G. H. Kingsley's E.E.T. Soc. edn. of Thynne's *Animadversions*.

1865. **Ruskin**, John. *The Cestus of Aglaia*, Chapter iii, *Patience*, [in] The Art Journal, April, 1865, vol. iv, pp. 101–2: [revised and enlarged in] On the Old Road, 1885, vol. i, pt. ii, pp. 468, 471–2. (Works, ed. E. T. Cook and A. Wedderburn, 1903–12, 39 vols., vol. xix, pp. 82–6.)

[p. 82]   " Dame Paciencë sitting there I fonde,
With facë pale, upon an hill of sonde."

[*Parlement of Foules*, ll. 242-3.]

[p. 84] I should like truly to know what Chaucer means by his sand-hill. . . . Sometimes I would fain have it to mean the ghostly sand of the horologe of the world. . . . Sometimes I like to think that she is seated on the sand because she is herself the Spirit of Staying, and victor over all things that pass and change. . . . And sometimes I think, though I do not like to think (neither did Chaucer mean this, for he always meant the lovely thing first, not the low one), that she is seated on her sand-heap as the only treasure to be gained by human toil. . . .

But of course it does not in the least matter what it means. All that matters specially to us in Chaucer's vision, is that, next to Patience (as the reader will find by looking at the context in the *Assembly of Foules*), were " Beheste " and " Art ";—Promise, that is, and Art : and that although these visionary powers are here waiting only in one of the outer courts of Love, and the intended patience is here only the long-suffering of love ; and the intended beheste, its promise; and the intended art, its cunning,—the same powers companion each other necessarily in the courts and ante-chambers of every triumphal home of man.

1866. The Poetical Works of Geoffrey Chaucer. Aldine edition, ed. R. Morris, 6 vols.

[With Sir N. H. Nicolas' Life, and Tyrwhitt's Essay and Discourse, and a glossary. To the Essay are appended some sections on Chaucer's metres by W. W. Skeat. The *Court of Love* and the *Cuckow and the Nightingale, Chaucer's Dream* (*The Isle of Ladies*) and the *Flour and the Lefe* are included in the text.]

[Preface, p. v] In this edition of Chaucer's poetical works Tyrwhitt's text has been replaced by one based upon manuscripts . . .

No better manuscript of the Canterbury Tales could be found than the Harleian manuscript, 7334, which is far more uniform and accurate than any other I have examined ; it has, therefore, been selected and faithfully adhered to throughout [pp. vi-viii] as the text of the present edition. [MS. Lansdowne 851 and the MSS. employed by Tyrwhitt also used to check MS. Harl. Examples of successful emendations introduced, and of the final *e*. A list of the poems included and of the MSS. used.]

1866. Arnold, Matthew. *The Study of Celtic Literature,* part iv, [in] The Cornhill Magazine, May 1866, p. 541, and July 1866, p. 113. (Works, 1903–4, 15 vols., vol. v, p. 79.)

German schools have the good habit of reading and commenting on German poetry, as we read and comment on Homer and Virgil, but do *not* read and comment on Chaucer and Shakespeare.

1866. Bond, Sir Edward Augustus. *New Facts in the Life of Geoffrey Chaucer,* [in] The Fortnightly Review, Aug., 1866, vol. vi, pp. 28–35.

[Essay on the two parchment leaves which had been pasted down to the covers of MS. Add. 18,632, and were found to be fragments of the Household Accounts of the Duchess of Clarence. The name of Geoffrey Chaucer is met with three times, the period covered being the regnal years 30, 31, 32, and 33—evidently of Edward III.—corresponding with the years 1356 to 1359. The record shows that Chaucer, at the outset of his career, was closely connected with the court and its functions. See above, vol. i, p. 1.]

1866. Chatelain, Jean Baptiste François Ernest de. *L'Hostellerie du Tabard,* 1866, [in] *A travers Champs,* London, 1867.

[The Chevalier de Chatelain lived and wrote in England ; this poem is noticed in *Notes and Queries,* March 16, 1867, 3rd ser., vol. xi, p. 227.]

1866. Dickens, Charles. *Letter to Sir James Emerson Tennent,* [dated] Aug. 20th, 1866, [in] Letters of Charles Dickens, 1880–2 [1879–81], 3 vols., vol. ii, pp. 259–60.

Chaucer certainly meant the Pardonere to be a humbug, living on the credulity of the people. After describing the sham reliques [*sic*] he carried, he says :
> But with these relikes whawne [*sic*] that he found
> [and five following lines.]

And the worthy Watts (founder of the charity [the Refuge for Poor Travellers]) may have had these very lines in his mind when he excluded such a man.

1866. Eastwood, Jonathan, and **Wright,** William Aldis. *The Bible Word-Book.* [Many quotations from Chaucer or poems then attributed to him.]

1866. Green, Henry. *Obsolete Words in Whitney, with parallels chiefly from Chaucer, Spenser and Shakespeare,* [in] *Whitney's "Choice of Emblems"* (1586) . . . ed. H. Green, pp. 253–65.

[Agaste, amisse, annoy, bale, bane, boorde, carle, carpes, create (= created), deface, defame, fardle, feare (= terrify), fonde, gate, let, mislike, moe, mowes, newfanglenes, nones, pill, roome, shamefastnes, sield (= happy), sithe, stithe, teene, unrest, ure, wonne, worlde.]

1866. Hazlitt, William Carew. *Remains of the Early Popular Poetry of England* . . . edited . . . by W. C. Hazlitt (Library of Old Authors), 4 vols., 1864–6, vol. iii, 1866, pp. 98–9 [Introduction to *The Mylner of Abington*].

[p. 99]   In an artistic and constructive point of view, the *Mylner of Abington* is superior to its predecessor [Chaucer's *Reves Tale*], and while it is quite as entertaining, it is much less gross.

[J. R. Lowell singled out this judgment as evidence that Hazlitt was "an editor without taste, discrimination or learning." (Review of the Library of Old Authors, in Works, Riverside Edn., 1890, 11 vols., vol. i, p. 320.)]

1866. Maurice, Frederick Denison. *On the Representation and Education of the People,* pp. 57–9, 67.

[p. 57]   Chaucer appears certainly to have been concerned in the insurrection of John of Northampton.

[p. 58]   [Chaucer, as essentially the English citizen, the link between the literature of Court and Commons. His wide appreciation of English life.]

He has been called a Wycliffite. He is not that. He is simply an Englishman. He hates Friars, because they are not English and not manly.

[p. 59]   [Becket's shrine had acquired a national sanctity, of the origin of which Chaucer was not critical.]

1866. Morris, Richard. *See* above, *The Poetical Works,* ed. R. Morris.

1866. Notes and Queries, 3rd series, vol. ix, pp. 10, 47, 57, 198, 264–5, 306, 327, 409, 414-5, 483 ; vol. x, pp. 49, 104, 297, 307, 356, 390, 400, 414, 430, 442, 485, 508–9, 518.

Author.	Date.	Reference.	Subject.
A., A.	Jan. 6.	3rd S. ix, 10.	'Husbands at the Church door' *(Wife of Bath's Prol.).* Hus-

bands endowed their wives with their goods at the Church door ; does this passage mean that the Wife of Bath's husbands were all men of property ?

Author.	Date.	Reference.	Subject.
Skeat, W. W.	Jan. 13.	3rd S. ix, 47.	' Duresse.'
Chate- lain, Chev. de.	Jan. 20.	3rd S. ix, 57.	' A Plea for Chaucer,' *i. e.* for the preservation of the Tabard Inn.
W., T.	April 14.	3rd S. ix, 306.	' Night-spell.'
Sandys, Wm.	April 21.	3rd S. ix, 327.	' Baggepipe.'
Foss, E.	April 21.	3rd S. ix, 383.	Henry Somer, who received Chaucer's pension for him.
D., A. **Editor.** }	May 19.	3rd S. ix, 414-5.	' A Canterbury story ' ; quotation from an unspecified book

of 1737, *q.v.* above, vol. i, p. 383.

Author.	Date.	Reference.	Subject.
Skeat, W. W.	June 9.	3rd S. ix, 483.	Chaucer on daisies.
Atkinson, J. C.	July 21.	3rd S. x, 49.	The lapwing (*Parlement of Foules,* l. 347, quoted).
' **Este.** '	Oct. 13.	3rd S. x, 297.	The 'Scheffield thwitel' *Reves T.,* l. 13).
A., A.	Oct. 20.	3rd S. x, 307.	' Wardrobe ' (*Prioresses T.,* l. 120).
Editor.	Nov. 3.	3rd S. x, 356.	' Ambes-as ' (*T. of the Man of Lawe,* l. 26).
Beisly, S.	Nov. 17.	3rd S. x, 390.	Evidence of tooth sealing in Chaucer's lines,

In witness that this is sooth
I bite the wax with my wang tooth.

[This couplet is not by Chaucer; nor is it in the *Chaucerian Pieces* edited by Skeat.]

Author.	Date.	Reference.	Subject.
Skeat, W. W.	Nov. 17.	3rd S. x, 400.	' Whittle ' (*Reves T.,* l. 13).
Williams, W. H.	Nov. 24.	3rd S. x, 414.	' Murder will out ' (*Nonne Prestes T.,* l. 232).
Larwood, Jacob.	Dec. 29.	3rd S. x, 508.	' Levesell ' (*Reves* and *Persones Tales*) = lattice ?
' **Filius** Ecclesiæ.'	Dec. 29.	3rd S. x, 509.	' Joly,' first used in English by Chaucer ?
Fishwick, H.	Dec. 29.	3rd S. x, 518.	' Murder will out ' (*Wife of Bath's Prol.*—in error for *N.P.T.,* l. 232).

1866. **Skeat,** Walter William. *See* above, *The Poetical Works,* ed. R. Morris.

1866. Swinburne, Algernon Charles.   *William Blake,* 1868, pp. 50, 58, 61, 89*n.,* 137.   (New edn., 1906, pp. 55, 64, 67, 97–8*n.,* 152.)

[Entered here in error ; the first edn. appeared in 1868.]

[pp. 97–8*n.*] [A long note on " Chaucer's " *Court of Love,* his " most beautiful of young poems," calling attention to the paganism of its tone, and comparing it in this respect with *Aucassin and Nicolette.*]

[p. 152]   Mixed with this [Blake's] fervour of desire for more perfect freedom, there appears at times an excess of pity (like Chaucer's in his early poems) for the women and men living under the law, trammelled in soul or body.

1866. Unknown. *Chaucer—His Position, Life, and Influence,* [in] The Westminster Review, July, 1866, vol. xxx, pp. 184–200.

[A long and appreciative article of a general nature, with a good deal about Chaucer's life and times, and something on his language, and on the text of the *Canterbury Tales* in recent editions.]

[p. 184]   Chaucer . . . may be read with comparative ease.   There are a few of his phrases obscure; a few of his endings silent; a few of his words obsolete.   But we require neither grammar nor glossary to understand and enjoy him.

[p. 199]   Not much has yet been done to make Chaucer's works more popular or more intelligible.   [There are great difficulties, his text is uncertain, often obscure.   Tyrwhitt has done a great deal to remove obscurities, though he] often unnecessarily and pretentiously displays his abstruse and curious learning. [But in spite of his pedantry, Tyrwhitt's text of the C. Tales in 1755 [*sic*], seems as good as that of Wright, in 1847. The worst features of Tyrwhitt's edn. reappear in that of Routledge [1863], where " none of Tyrwhitt's mistakes are corrected nor his defects supplied."   Robert Bell's edn. 1854, is the best, by this editor nearly everything which can explain or illustrate his author has been skilfully condensed.]   But it is not likely that all Chaucer's writings— consisting, as they mostly do, of translations,—can ever become popular.   We still require an edition of the " Canterbury Tales " in which the obsolete words, opinions and customs will be explained, and the obsolete pronunciation indicated.

1866. Unknown. *Catalogue of the First Special Exhibition of National Portraits . . . on Loan to the South Kensington Museum, April 1866, pp. 3, 193.*

[These portraits are Spielmann's nos. VI and VII.]

[p. 3]　　8. GEOFFREY CHAUCER. Lent by Bodleian Library, Oxford.

Poet; b. in London; believed to have been partly educated at Cambridge; was in the service of King Edward III; patronised by John of Gaunt; married Philippa Rouet, daughter of a knight of Hainault; imprisoned on occasion of the persecution of the Lollards; d. 25th Oct. 1400; bu. in Westminster Abbey.

Three-quarters miniature, looking to r., white head-covering and dress; inscribed "Caucer, 1400." Panel, 1 ft. 2 in. × 10½ in.

9. GEOFFREY CHAUCER. [Lent by] Mr. J. P. Seddon.

. . . To waist, small life-size, face three-quarters to r.; dated 1400. Panel, 19 × 14 in.

Stated to have been preserved for more than three centuries in the family of Stokes of Llanshaw Court, Gloucester; given in 1803 to Benjamin Dyke.

[p. 193]　[Quotation from the *Athenæum*, Ap. 14, 1866, *q.v.* immediately below.]

1866. Unknown. *National Portrait Exhibition* (see last entry), [in] The Athenæum, April 14, 1866, p. 502, col. 2.

In the two portraits of Chaucer (7 and 8) [a mistake for 8 and 9] we see reproductions of that which Occleve painted from memory (Harleian MS. 4866) treated by different hands, of which those which produced No. 8 [meaning No. 9] were by far the more skilful.

1867. Chaucer. The Prologue, the Knightes Tale, the Nonne Prestes Tale, from the Canterbury Tales, edited by R. Morris, Oxford. (Clarendon Press Series.)

[Introduction, pp. v–xlviii. The *Court of Love, Complaint of the Black Knight, Chaucer's Dream (Isle of Ladies)*, the *Flower and the Leaf*, and all the *Roman de la Rose*, are certainly, the *Testament of Love* hesitatingly, allowed to be genuine. A brief biography, based on the facts then known, followed by analyses of the *Prologue* and two Tales included in this volume, a summary of Chaucerian grammar and metre, and a table of contemporary events.]

1867. The Clerk's Tale, edited by W. Aldis Wright, from MS. D. 4. 24. in the University Library, Cambridge. Privately printed, Cambridge.

1867–71. Bradshaw, Henry. *The Skeleton of Chaucer's Canterbury Tales: an attempt to distinguish the several fragments of the work as left by the author* (Memoranda, no. iv), preface dated 1867, title page 1868, and postscript 1871. (Collected Papers, 1889, pp. 102–48.)

[This is the only printed result of Bradshaw's Chaucer work, which was largely the cause of the foundation of the Chaucer Society. For the editions of the Works projected by him *see* above, 1864, *Works.* In 1865 "An attempt to ascertain the state of Chaucer's works as they were left at his death, with some notices of their subsequent history" was advertised as shortly to be published (*q. v.* above, 1865); of this the introductory pages alone were found among his papers (*see* G. W. Prothero, *A Memoir of Henry Bradshaw*, 1888, p. 347). This memorandum was, it seems, printed as a tentative preparation for the larger work. But in the postscript of 1871 Bradshaw bids farewell to Chaucer work, the Library claiming his time.

He divides the *Canterbury Tales* into twelve fragments, and prints the beginnings and ends of these and of his subdivisions of them. The MSS. are classified by their arrangement of the Tales, which corresponds with their classification by textual value. Not only mentions of time and place occurring in the 'links' are used, but orthographical and rhyme tests. *Gamelyn* is retained, in Frag. 1.]

1867. Collier, John Payne. *General Introduction* [to] *Seven English Poetical Miscellanies*, 7 vols., vol. i [Tottell], pp. i–iii.

[Godfray's 1532 edn. of Chaucer's Works really the first English miscellany. *The Testament of Love*, which appears there first, is one of the non-Chaucerian pieces. This a new point, in the writer's belief, for Warton and later biographers, including Sir Harris Nicolas, attribute it to Chaucer, though the last notices the contradiction it seems to give to the tradition of Chaucer's committal to the Tower, etc. Quotation from the end of *The Testament of Love*, in which *Troilus* and its author are highly praised; an impossibility for Chaucer to have written this. Thus all that the book contains as to the author's share in the tumults in the city and his imprisonment does not apply to Chaucer. This conclusion supported by a comparison of style. *The Testament of Love* probably written by some admiring imitator of Chaucer's translation of Boethius.]

See also below, *Notes and Queries*, 1867, Collier.

1867. Furnivall, Frederick James. *Early English Text Society, Third Annual Report of the Committee,* Jan. 1867, pp. 2, 5–6.

[p. 2] Two other events the Committee also allude to with pleasure : 1. The publication of an accurate Text from the best MS. of each of Chaucer's Poetical Works by Mr. Richard Morris (though, unfortunately, without the collation and notes that the editor desired to add) ; and, 2, The undertaking to edit Bishop Percy's long-hidden folio MS.

[p. 5] [In a list of 32 Texts that *can* be produced this year, if funds enough are supplied :]

Chaucer. The Household Accounts of Elizabeth, wife of Prince Lionel, in which Chaucer is mentioned ; with the other documents relating to the Poet. To be edited by E. A. Bond, Esq., Keeper of the MSS. in the British Museum.

[p. 6] Chaucer's Prose Works. To be edited from the MSS., with an Essay on the Dialect of Chaucer, by R. Morris, Esq. ; and a Treatise on the Poet's Pronunciation, by Alexander J. Ellis, Esq., F.R.S. . . .

A glance at the List above will show what important and interesting contributions will be made to our Literature if only the first twenty of these books can be produced this year : a new Romance . . . traces of CHAUCER (with a discussion of his dialect and pronunciation).

1867. Furnivall, Frederick James. *The Early English Text Society,* [an announcement of the Extra Series, to begin with an edition of Chaucer's prose works, and an appeal for more support, in] The Gentleman's Magazine, Aug. 1867, new ser., vol. iv, p. 213.

1867. Furnivall, Frederick James. *A New 'Envoy' of Chaucer's,* in The Athenæum, no. 2081, Sept. 14, 1867, p. 333.

[A copy of 'Fle fro the pres,' from MS. Add. 10,340 (Boethius), then being copied for the E.E.T.S. ; the best and completest text known, the envoy not having been printed before.]

1867. Furnivall, Frederick James. *The Chaucer Society,* [the Society's Manifesto, in] The Gentleman's Magazine, Dec. 1867, new ser., vol. iv, pp. 782–3.

This Society has been founded in order to do honour to Chaucer, and to let the lovers and students of him see how far the best unprinted manuscripts of his works differ from the

printed texts. It will deal with the works of no other man—
except so far as may be found necessary for the illustration of
Chaucer—and will be dissolved as soon as all the good manuscripts of the poet's works, and all matter wanted for their
illustration, are in type. It is not intended to interfere with
any edition of Chaucer's works, past or future, but to supplement them all, and afford material for the improvement of
his text. Eight or ten years will suffice, if the Society be well
supported, to finish its work.

If men said it was well done for Lord Vernon to reprint the
first four printed texts of Dante's " Divina Commedia "—if we
know it is well done of the Early English Text Society to
print the three versions of Chaucer's great contemporary's
work, William Langland's " Vision of Piers Ploughman "—it
cannot be ill done of us to print all the best MSS. of him who
is allowed to be the greatest among our early men. . . . It is
hardly too much to say that every line of Chaucer contains
points that need reconsideration. Our proposal then is to
begin with "The Canterbury Tales," and to give of them (in
parallel columns in royal 4to) six of the best unprinted manuscripts known, and to add in another quarto the six next best
MSS., if 300 subscribers join the Society. The first six MSS.
to be printed will probably be, The Lansdowne (Brit. Mus.),—
The best Ashburnham (if Lord Ashburnham will consent to its
publication ; if not, the best Sloane),—The Ellesmere,—The
Hengwrt,—The best Oxford (probably the Corpus MS.),—The
best Cambridge (Univ. Libr.).

In securing the fidelity of the texts, Mr. Richard Morris,
Mr. J. W. Hales, myself, and others (who will form the
Committee of the Society) will take part. The first essay in
illustration of Chaucer's works that will be published by
the Society will be, " A detailed Comparison of Chaucer's
' Knight's Tale ' with the ' Teseide ' of Boccaccio," by Henry
Ward, Esq., of the MS. Department of the British Museum . . .

The Society will begin its work on the 1st of January,
1868. Professor Child gives 50*l.* to start it . . .

Members' names and subscriptions may be sent *pro tempore*
to yours, &c.

FREDK. J. FURNIVALL,

3, *Old Square, Lincoln's Inn, W.C.*

P.S. — An honorary secretary who cares enough for

Chaucer to take some trouble in working the Society is wanted . . .

[This letter, or manifesto, appeared also in the Athenæum in an earlier and slightly shorter form (no. 2108, 1867, vol. ii, p. 467), and was heralded by a brief announcement in the preceding no., p. 435. Various modifications in the plan outlined above were made. In the Six-Text Print the Petworth and not a Sloane MS. was substituted for the Ashburnham, and Dr. Ward's study of the *Knightes Tale* and the *Teseide* never appeared.]

1867. [**Furnivall**, Frederick James ?]   *See* below, Unknown.

1867. Hazlitt, William Carew.   *Handbook to the Popular, Poetical and Dramatic Literature of Great Britain from the Invention of Printing to the Restoration*, pp. 96–9.

[A list of editions of Chaucer, with notes of some copies.]

1867. Longfellow, Henry Wadsworth.   *Notes* [to] *The Divine Comedy of Dante Alighieri*, translated by H. W. Longfellow, 1867, [reprinted in] Writings, Riverside edn., 11 vols., [1886], vol. ix, pp. 187, 203 ['perse,' *Prol.*, l. 441], 208 [gluttony, *Persones Tale*], 218 [avarice, *ib.*], 222 [wrath, *ib.*], 223, 242 [Theseus, *Knightes Tale*, ll. 1–16], 244 [Deianire, *Monkes Tale*], 248 [description of a wood, *Inferno* xiii, compared with *Knightes Tale*], 252, 274 [Jason, *L.G.W.*], 276 [simony, *Persones Tale*], 287 [reference to Henryson's *Testament of Creseida* as Chaucer's], 293, 332–3, 342–3, 347 ; vol. x, pp. 171, 214 [Chaucer's quotation from *Purg.* vii, 121, etc. in *Wife of Bath's Tale*, ll. 269–76], 230 [the sculptures on the wall of Purgatory (*Purg.* x, 29, etc.) compared with the temples of Venus, Mars and Diana in *Knightes Tale*], 275 [Fortuna Major, *Troilus*, iii, 1415–20], 306 ['vernage,' *Merchantes Tale*, l. 563], 308 [reference to the *Complaint of the Black Knight* as Chaucer's] ; vol. xi, pp. 168–9 [quotations from *Hous of Fame, Anelida*, and (Lydgate's) *Ballade in commendation of Our Lady*], 212 [Demophoön, *L.G.W.*, ll. 2441–51], 250 [*Testament of Love* quoted as Chaucer's], 252, 254, 258 [imitation in *Troilus*, v, 1863–5, of *Paradiso*, xiv 28–30], 264, 277, 289–90 [*Troilus*, iv, 995–1043, with the original passage on foreknowledge from Boethius, quoted], 341, 382 [the invocation to the Virgin, *Second Nonnes Tale*, ll. 36–56, quoted to illustrate the opening of *Paradiso*, xxxiii].

1867. Mackay, Charles.   *A Thousand and One Gems of English Poetry, selected and arranged by Charles Mackay*, Introduction, p. iii. [On pp. 1 and 2 are the following extracts from Chaucer :] Praise of Women, The Young Squire [*Prol.* ll. 79–100], Arcita's Dying Address [*Knightes T.*, ll. 2771–2780], Good Counsel of Chaucer.

1867. Morris, Richard.   *Specimens of Early English* . . . A.D. 1250– A.D. 1400, with grammatical introduction, notes and glossary, Oxford.   (Clarendon Press Series.)

[Various references to Chaucer in the Grammatical Introduction.

The specimens from Chaucer (pp. 345–366) are the

Pardoneres Tale, and the *Prioresse Tale.* In the preface
(p. vii) the editor says : " the extracts from Chaucer's Canterbury Tales are limited to two short narratives, because a more
extended selection, by the present editor, is in the press " (*i. e.*
the Prologue, etc., *q.v.* above).]

1867. Morris, William. *The Life and Death of Jason,* Book xvii, ll. 5–24,
pp. 317–8.

Would that I
Had but some portion of that mastery
That from the rose-hung lanes of woody Kent
Through these five hundred years such songs have sent
To us, who, meshed within this smoky net
Of unrejoicing labour, love them yet.
And thou, O Master !—Yea, my Master still,
Whatever feet have scaled Parnassus' hill,
Since like thy measures, clear, and sweet, and strong,
Thames' stream scarce fettered drave the dace along
Unto the bastioned bridge, his only chain.—
O Master, pardon me, if yet in vain
Thou art my Master, and I fail to bring
Before men's eyes the image of the thing
My heart is filled with : thou whose dreamy eyes
Beheld the flush to Cressid's cheeks arise,
As Troilus rode up the praising street,
As clearly as they saw thy townsmen meet
Those who in vineyards of Poictou withstood
The glittering horror of the steel-topped wood.

[This is taken from the final edition as printed in Works, with introductions by
his daughter, May Morris, 1910, vol. ii, pp. 259–60. The only difference in the 1867
version is that line 14 there reads—
  'Thames' stream scarce fettered bore the bream along.']

1867. Notes and Queries, 3rd series, vol. xi, pp. 47, 65, 67, 144, 146,
161, 227, 284, 287, 337–8, 352, 384–5, 403, 466, 504 ; vol. xii, pp.
18, 58, 107, 114, 119, 140, 249, 300, 303–5, 391, 422, 424–5, 462,
491.

Author.	Date.	Reference.	Subject.
W., C. A.	Jan. 12.	3rd S. xi, 47.	" Murder will out" probably a colloquial saying, not original in Chaucer.
A., A.	Jan. 19.	3rd S. xi, 65.	' Levesell ' = a tavern-bush.

Author.	Date.	Reference.	Subject.
Addis, John, jun.	Jan. 19.	3rd S. xi, 67.	'Jolly' earlier in English than Chaucer.
Skeat, W. W.	Feb. 16.	3rd S. xi, 144.	'Callabre,' the physician's dress (*Prol.* ll. 439–40).
Editor.	Feb. 16.	3rd S. xi, 146.	Notice of the Aldine (Morris's) edn. of Chaucer's Works (*q.v.* above, 1866).
Shaw, J. B.	Feb. 23.	3rd S. xi, 161.	'Jolly.'
Editor.	Mar. 16.	3rd S. xi, 227.	Notice of the Chevalier de Chatelain's *A travers Champs : Flâneries,* containing a poem on the destruction of the Tabard Inn, *q.v.* above, 1866.
Skeat, W. W.	April 6.	3rd S. xi, 284.	'Levesell,' an overgrown trellised porch.
Baily, J.	April 6.	3rd S. xi, 287.	The original idea of a song on the creation of Eve, quoted vol. xi, pp. 96, 163, to be found in the *Persones Tale,* § 79.
Skeat, W. W. **Bouchier, J.** 'St. Swithin.'	April 27.	3rd S. xi, 337–8.	'Gab.'
Skeat, W. W.	May 4.	3rd S. xi, 352.	'Christ-cross'; quotation from the *Astrolabe.*
P., J. A.	May 11.	3rd S. xi, 384–5.	'Caitiff' and 'mock.'
Skeat, W. W.	May 18.	3rd S. xi, 403.	'Atone.'
Peacock, E.	June 8.	3rd S. xi, 466.	'Pair of beads' (*Prol.,* l. 159).
Bede, Cuthbert.	June 22.	3rd S. xi, 504.	Quotation from *The Cuckoo and the Nightingale* as Chaucer's.
Skeat, W. W.	July 20.	3rd S. xii, 58.	'Butterfly' (*N.P.T.,* ll. 453–5).
Addis, J.	Aug. 10.	3rd S. xii, 114.	'Beauty unfortunate' (*Words of the Host,* following *Phisiciens T.,* ll. 293–300).
"	Aug. 10.	3rd S. xii, 119.	'Butterfly' (*Marchantes T.,* ll. 259–60, and *Prol. N.P.T.,* l. 24).
"	Aug. 17.	3rd S. xii, 140.	'Algate' (*T. & C.,* bk. v, l. 1071).

Author.	Date.	Reference.	Subject.
Editor.	Oct. 12.	3rd S. xii, 300.	Notice of the formation of the Chaucer Society.
Collier, J. P.	Oct. 19.	3rd S. xii, 303–4.	Doubts whether the *Testa....nt of Love* can be by Chaucer, especially in view of the passage on himself and his *Troilus* (*see* above, 1867, Collier).
Fish-wick, H.	Nov. 23.	3rd S. xii, 422.	'Laund.'
Addis, J.	Nov. 23.	3rd S. xii, 424–5.	'No fors.'
Butler, T.	Dec. 7.	3rd S. xii. 462.	Yemanrie (*Reves T.*, ll. 22–9).

1867. Part, William A. *Spenser,* [a letter, in] The Gentleman's Magazine, April, 1867, new ser., vol. iii, pp. 501–2.

[Lancashire words used by Chaucer.]

1867. Ruskin, John. *On the Present State of Modern Art.* [A lecture, delivered June 7, 1867; first printed in full in] Works, ed. E. T. Cook and A. Wedderburn, 1903–12, 39 vols., vol. **xix,** pp. 207–8.

[p. 207]   This first cartoon is a sketch for tapestry, from Chaucer, of Love bringing in Alcestis. . . . In Chaucer the Spirit of Love which leads her is only that of perfect human passion :—

> " Yclothed was this mighty God of Love
> In silk, embroudered full of red rose leaves—
> The freshest since the world was first begun—
> And his gilt hair was crowned with a sun
> Instead of gold;
> And in his hand methought I saw him hold
> Two fiery darts, as the coals red;
> And angel-like his wings I saw him spread.[1]

[p. 208]   But in this design the painter has gone farther into the meaning of the old Greek myth, and he has given the Spirit of the Love that lives beyond the grave. . . .

Then this second cartoon, also from the Legend of Good Women, is of the two wives of Jason—Hypsipyle and Medea.

[1] [Editor's note]: "From the Prologue to the *Legende of Goode Women.* Chaucer wrote, after the first line—
> 'In silke embrouded, ful of grene greves
> In which a fret of rede rose leves.'
The fifth line continues, 'for hevynesse and wyghte'; and then Ruskin omits two lines. The last line but one is, in the original, 'Two firy dartes, as the gledes rede.' The sketches (by Burne-Jones) are Plates VI, VII, in vol. xix.]

1867. Ruskin, John.   *Time and Tide by Weare and Tyne,* Letter XVII, *Difficulties,* [dated] April 3, 1867, [in] Leeds Mercury, [and in] Manchester Daily Examiner and Times, April 13, 1867. (2nd vol. ed., 1868, [1st in B.M.], p. 104. (Works, ed. E. T. Cook and A. Wedderburn, 1903–12, 39 vols., vol. xvii, p. 402.)

Shakespeare and Chaucer,—Dante and Virgil,— . . . all the men of any age or country who seem to have had Heaven's music on their lips, agree in their scorn of mechanic life.

1867. Swinburne, Algernon Charles.   *Review* of Morris's *Life and Death of Jason,* [in] The Fortnightly Review, July, 1867, new ser., vol. ii, pp. 22–3, 26, 28.

[p. 22]   " Jason " is a large and coherent poem, completed as conceived ; the style throughout on a level with the invention. In direct narrative power, in clear forthright manner of procedure, not seemingly troubled to select, to pick and sift and winnow, yet never superfluous or verbose, never straggling or jarring ; in these high qualities it resembles the work of Chaucer.   Even against the great master his pupil may fairly be matched for simple sense of right, for grace and speed of step, for purity and justice of colour.   In all the noble roll of our poets there has been since Chaucer no second teller of tales, no second rhapsode comparable to the first, till the advent of this one.

[p. 23]   The romance poets have never loved the sea as have the tragic poets ; Chaucer simply ignores it with a shiver ; . . .

1867. Unknown.   *Early English Texts,* [in] The Edinburgh Review, Jan. 1867, vol. cxxv, pp. 225, 231–2, 244, 251.

[Criticism of the chauvinism of French critics, especially Sandras and Le Clerc (*q.v.* below, App. B., 1859, 1862) for their attempt to class Chaucer with the trouvères.]

1867. Unknown.   [Furnivall, Frederick James ?]   *Note,* [in] The Athenæum, no. 2094, Dec. 14, 1867.

A new and interesting testimony to Chaucer's worth turns up unexpectedly in the Courtesy poem of 'Lytil Johan,' in the Balliol MS. . . . The writer, a disciple of Lydgate, is telling his Little Jack what to read, and, like a wise man, names the best poets of the day, Gower, Chaucer, Occleve, Lydgate, and thus apostrophizes Chaucer.   [Quotes stanzas 48–50.   *See* above, 1477, vol. i, p. 57.]

1867. Wright, William Aldis.   *See* above, *The Clerk's Tale.*

1868–77. A Six-Text Print of Chaucer's Canterbury Tales in Parallel Columns from the following MSS. : 1. The Ellesmere; 2. The Hengwrt 154 ; 3. The Cambridge Univ. Libr. Gg. 4. 27 ; 4. The Corpus Christi Coll., Oxford ; 5. The Petworth; 6. The Lansdowne 851. Edited by F. J. Furnivall. Chaucer Society, 8 parts, 1868–77, oblong 8vo.

[The six-text edition contains when complete :—

(1) The Dedication : To Prof. Francis James Child, etc.

(2) Specimens of the two chief moveable Prologues in the Canterbury Tales when they are moved from their right places, and of some of the substitutes for them (pp. i*–xx*) :

> I. Specimens of the *Man of Law's End-Link*, the real *Shipman's Prologue*, when moved from its right place.
>
> II. Specimens of the *Spurious Prologue* to the *Shipman's Tale*.
>
> III. Specimens of the *Squire's End-Link* (which should head the *Franklin's Tale*), when the *Franklin's Tale* is moved from its right place, and the Squire's End-Link is used as the *Merchants' Prologue*.
>
> IV. Specimens of the *False Prologues* to the *Franklin's Tale* when it is moved from its right place after the *Squire's Tale*.

(3) Trial-Tables (now superseded) of the Groups of Tales, and their order in Chaucer's "Canterbury Tales," according to the *Edited Manuscripts* and Tyrwhitt. (pp. xxi*–xxiii*.)

(4) Drawings of the 23 tellers of the 24 Canterbury Tales, copied from the Ellesmere MS., and cut on wood, by Mr. W. H. Hooper, and coloured after the originals, under his direction, (9 leaves, bound at the end of vols. i and ii—pts. iii and iv— in the B.M. copy.)

(5) The Texts of the Tales from the six MSS. (pp. 1–685), and including, (5) Appendix to Group A. The Spurious Tale of Gamelyn (with its spurious Head-Links) from the following 6 MSS.:—Royal MS. 18. C. ii. ; Harleian 1758 ; Sloane, 1685 ; Corpus MS. (Oxford); Petworth MS. ; Lansdowne MS. 851 (pp. xxv–lxxvii.)

(6) Ryme-Index to the Ellesmere Manuscript of Chaucer's Canterbury Tales. By Henry Cromie, M.A., 1875. [pp. 1*–255*,—or in oblong triple pages, i†–lxxxv† : and including the Notes and Corrections for the Ryme-Index, i†–lxxxviii† ; 1st ser. 45 and 46.]

[In 1868 Dr. Furnivall published separately (2nd ser. 3):
*A Temporary Preface to the Six-Text Edition of Chaucer's
Canterbury Tales, attempting to shew the true order of the
Tales, and the days and stages of the pilgrimage, etc., etc.*]

[See Skeat's *Evolution of the Canterbury Tales* for a study
of the sequence of the Tales as set forth in the Six-Text
edition. Each of the texts constituting the Six-Text edition
was printed separately, for editorial use, 1868–77: Child
himself had conceived the idea of printing a six or eight-
text *Chaucer*. See the notice of a note on the subject in the
Reader, under 1865, Furnivall (?)]

[Later publications of the Chaucer Society have for the most part been omitted,
as being generally accessible and known to members of the Society.]

1868–70. Morris, William. *The Earthly Paradise*. Prologue: The
Wanderers, Part i, 1868, p. **3**; L'Envoi, Part iv, 1870, pp. **439–442.**

> Forget six counties overhung with smoke,
> Forget the snorting steam and piston stroke,
> Forget the spreading of the hideous town ;
> Think rather of the pack-horse on the down,
> And dream of London, small, and white and clean,
> The clear Thames bordered by its gardens green ;
> Think, that below bridge the green lapping waves
> Smite some few keels that bear Levantine staves,
> Cut from the yew wood on the burnt-up hill,
> And pointed jars that Greek hands toiled to fill,
> And treasured scanty spice from some far sea,
> Florence gold cloth, and Ypres napery,
> And cloth of Bruges, and hogsheads of Guienne ;
> While nigh the thronged wharf Geoffrey Chaucer's pen
> Moves over bills of lading—mid such times
> Shall dwell the hollow puppets of my rhymes.

[p. 439]   [L'Envoi.   The poet addresses his book :]

> Nay, let it pass, and hearken !   Hast thou heard
> That therein * I believe I have a friend,
> Of whom for love I may not be afeard ?
> It is to him indeed I bid thee wend . . .

> Well, think of him, I bid thee, on the road,
> And if it hap that midst of thy defeat,
> Fainting beneath thy follies' heavy load,

* *i.e.* in " The Land of Matters Unforgot. "

CHAUCER'S LONDON, 'SMALL AND WHITE AND CLEAN'
THE TOWER, WITH LONDON BRIDGE IN THE BACKGROUND
From a late 15TH Century MS. of the poems of Charles d'Orléans
MS. Roy. 16. F. ii, f. 73 (British Museum)

My Master, GEOFFREY CHAUCER, thou do meet,
Then shalt thou win a space of rest full sweet;

[p. 440]   Then be thou bold, and speak the words I say,
The idle singer of an empty day !

"O Master, O thou great of heart and tongue,
Thou well mayst ask me why I wander here
In raiment rent of stories oft besung !
But of thy gentleness draw thou anear,
And then the heart of one that held thee dear
Mayst thou behold ! " . . .

[p. 441]   O Master, if thine heart could love us yet,
Spite of things left undone, and wrongly done,
Some place in loving hearts then should we get,
For thou, sweet-souled, didst never stand alone,
But knew'st the joy and woe of many an one—
—By lovers dead, who live through thee, we pray,
Help thou us singers of an empty day ! "

Fearest thou, Book, what answer thou mayst gain
Lest he should scorn thee, and thereof thou die ?
Nay, it shall not be.—Thou mayst toil in vain
And never draw the House of Fame anigh ;
Yet he and his shall know whereof we cry,
Shall call it not ill-done to strive to lay
The ghosts that crowd about life's empty day.

1868. Swinburne, A. C.   *William Blake.*   See above, 1866.

1868. Waller, John Green.   [*A Painted Window,* designed by J. G.
Waller, with medallions of Chaucer and Gower, and with scenes
from Chaucer's life and poems, placed over Chaucer's tomb in
Westminster Abbey as the gift of Dr. Rogers.]

1869. Browne, Matthew.   [pseud., i.e. **Rands,** William Brighty.]
Chaucer's England, 2 vols.

[Chapters on "The Poet of the Canterbury Tales," and " The
Story and the Pilgrims," followed by others on various aspects of
mediæval life.   Diffuse and inaccurate but not without merit.]

1869-89. Ellis, Alexander James.   *On Early English Pronunciation,
with especial reference to Shakspere and Chaucer.*   Including a
rearrangement of Prof. F. J. Child's memoirs on the language of
Chaucer and Gower [*q.v.* above, 1862], Parts i and ii, London,
Chaucer Society and E.E.T. Soc., 1869 ; Part iii, 1871 ; Part iv,
1875 ; Part v, 1889.

[The parts directly concerning Chaucer's language are:

Part i, chap. i, pp. 26–30, summary of the method of
investigation used in chap. iv, and comparative table of
the pronunciation of Chaucer, Spenser, Dryden and
Goldsmith ; chap. iv, ' On the pronunciation of English during
the 14th century, as deduced from an examination of the
rhymes in Chaucer and Gower,' pp. 241–416 : Principles of
the investigation (no real faulty rhymes in Chaucer), pp.
241–57 ; The Vowels, pp. 258–307 ; The Consonants, pp.
308–17 ; On the pronunciation of *e* final in the 14th
century [its use proved by rhymes from the Harl. MS. ;
table of rules, p. 342], pp. 318–42 ; F. J. Child's Observations on the language of Chaucer and Gower [*q.v.* above,
1862], pp. 342–97 ; Chaucer's pronunciation and orthography [with a table of probable sounds of the letters],
pp. 397–404. Part iii, 1871, chap. vii, ' Illustrations of
the Pronunciation of English during the 14th century,'
pp. 633–742 : Chaucer, pp. 633–725 : Critical text of
Prologue [illustrating the previous conclusions, the text from
the seven MSS. on the versos, and the phonetic transcript
on the rectos], pp. 680–725 [prefaced by notes on] :
Pronunciation of long *u* and of *ay, ey*, as deduced from
a comparison of the orthographies of seven MSS. of the
Canterbury Tales [the Society's six texts and MS. Harl.
7334], pp. 634–56 ; Treatment of final *e* in the critical
text, pp. 646–8 ; Metrical peculiarities of Chaucer, pp. 648–9 ;
Chaucer's treatment of French words, pp. 650–1 ; Penn-
sylvania German the analogue of Chaucer's English, pp.
652–63 ; F. W. Gesenius on the language of Chaucer,
pp. 664–71 ; M. Rapp on the pronunciation of Chaucer,
pp. 672–7 ; Instructions for reading the phonetic transcript
of the Prologue, pp. 677–9.]

1870. [**Baynes,** Thomas Spencer.] *The Text of Chaucer,* [in] the Edinburgh Review, July, 1870, vol. cxxxii, pp. 1–45.

    [Information as to the authorship of this article was kindly supplied by the
Editor of the *Edinburgh Review.*]

[p. 1]   It is a national reproach that after the lapse of nearly five
hundred years we are still without a critical and illustrative edition of Chaucer's poetical works. Excepting
Shakspeare, no English poet so thoroughly requires and
[p. 2]   deserves careful editing as Chaucer; and, in the essential
characteristics of his genius, no English poet comes nearer
to Shakspeare.

[pp. 2, 3]   [Chaucer's dramatic insight, love of nature, wide human
interest, and felicity of expression.]

GEOFFREY CHAUCER   [·D·M·DCCCCI·]

STAINED GLASS WINDOW PLACED OVER CHAUCER'S TOMB
IN WESTMINSTER ABBEY IN 1868
WITH SCENES FROM CHAUCER'S LIFE AND POEMS
DESIGNED BY J. G. WALLER

[p. 3]   These excellences have justly made Chaucer not only the
father of English poetry, the greatest of our dramatists before
the rise of the regular drama, but one of the most delightful
and habitually read of all English poets. The many eulo-
gistic references to him by later writers both in prose and
verse, down to the close of the Elizabethan period, show how
constantly he was studied during the two centuries after his
death.

[Lydgate, Occleve, Douglas, Wilson, Puttenham, Ascham,
Fox, Camden, Sidney, Spenser, Milton, among his admirers.]

Dryden, again, did his utmost to popularise the more
striking of the ' Canterbury Tales,' and has left, perhaps,
the best critical estimate of their author we possess. During
the eighteenth century there were several elaborate attempts
to make English readers better acquainted with Chaucer,
whose language had by that time become too archaic for
the effortless enjoyment of ordinary readers. And in our
own day, notwithstanding the obstacles interposed by a
grammar and vocabulary partially obsolete, Chaucer has
reappeared in a greater number of forms, and is, perhaps,
more generally read and studied, than any of the great
Elizabethan poets except Shakspeare.

These circumstances render it the more surprising, and,
we may add, the more discreditable to our national scholar-
ship, that no complete critical edition of Chaucer's poetical
works should yet have been produced. The reproach is one
of old standing, and many suggestions have from time to
time been made with the view of wiping it away.

[Quotation of Dr. Johnson's note on his projected edition.
A correct edition called for by Godwin and Todd.]

[p. 5]   The truth is, that until the last few years the greater part
of Chaucer's poetical works have never, strictly speaking,
been edited at all. ' Troilus and Cressid,' a story nearly as
long as the 'Æneid,' the ' Romaunt of the Rose,' the ' House
of Fame,' the ' Legend of Good Women,' and the minor
poems, collected and published together for the first time
by Thynne in 1532, were printed from defective and imperfect manuscripts without any critical oversight or correction; and from that time to our own day they have been
reprinted from the black-letter folios without any attempt

at systematic critical revision. The 'Canterbury Tales' have, indeed, fared somewhat better, having been more than once carefully edited by critics in many respects well qualified for the task.   But much still remains to be done for the text of Chaucer's greatest work; and still more, perhaps, for the adequate explanation of its language and allusions.   We have as yet no satisfactory and authoritative text even of the 'Canterbury Tales'; and the best published text, that recently revised by Mr. Morris, to which we shall presently refer in detail, is without note or comment of any kind. The work which Johnson projected, and which a succession of eminent scholars and critics have so earnestly desiderated, still remains, therefore, to be done.

In these circumstances the formation of a Chaucer Society, mainly for the purpose of printing the best existing manuscripts of the poet's works, ought to be matter of hearty congratulation to all lovers of English literature.   Our public and private libraries are rich in Chaucer manuscripts, and the best of these must be available for critical use before an authoritative, complete and satisfactory text of Chaucer can be produced.   But the only way of placing these manuscripts within the reach of English scholars is by printing them; and, if done at all, this must obviously be the work of a special Society.   With this end in view, the Chaucer Society was accordingly founded two years ago.

[p. 7]   [Account of the Chaucer Society's aims and publications. Value of the latter to students.   Only seventy subscribers in England, and thirty in the United States.   Readers recommended to subscribe.]

[p. 8]   From what we have said it will be seen that the publications of the Chaucer Society are preparing the way for a complete edition of Chaucer's works in the twofold direction of text and commentary.   The requirements of such an edition are an authoritative text based on a comparison of the best manuscripts, and an adequate explanation in the shape of notes and commentary of Chaucer's learning and literary studies, his allusions, language and versification. The first point is the text; and, in order to estimate fairly the work the Chaucer Society is doing in this respect, it is necessary to glance at the history of the printed texts down to the present time. Caxton printed the 'Canterbury Tales' twice, the first time from a very corrupt manuscript, and the second time from a much better one. 'Troilus and Cressid,' 'The House of Fame,' 'The Assembly of Fowls,' and some minor pieces, were printed by Caxton's coadjutors and successors, Wynken de Worde and Pynson. The first edition of Chaucer's poetical works was that published in 1532, and edited by W. Thynne. In his curious dedication to Henry VIII, Thynne claims to have corrected, by comparison with the manuscripts, those parts of the poet's works already printed, and to have published the rest for the first time. [Thynne quoted; *see* above, 1532, vol. i, p. 79].

As may be surmised from this extract, Chaucer did not benefit much from Thynne's supervision, his text of the 'Canterbury Tales' being in some respects inferior to that of Caxton's second reprint, while the minor poems are crowded with verbal corruptions. Stowe, the next editor, added little to Thynne's work, except some miscellaneous poems, 'now imprinted for the first time,' which fill twenty pages of his massive folio. These poems are of doubtful authority, being more in Lidgate's manner than Chaucer's; but the longest of them, 'The Court of Love,' has kept its place in the subsequent editions of the poet's works. The third chief edition published during the sixteenth century is [p. 9] that edited by Speight, and in many respects he may fairly be regarded as the first editor, strictly so called, of Chaucer. Thynne and Stowe paid but little attention to the text; and neither of them attempted anything in the way of illustration or commentary. Speight attended in a manner to both these departments of an editor's duty; and, though his alterations in the text are comparatively few and unimportant, they are still in the main improvements. But his claims as an editor rest mainly on his explanations of Chaucer's language. He is the first that attempted any detailed explanation of archaic words and phrases; and his glossary, with all its imperfections, entitles him to the grateful remembrance of Chaucer students. . . . Speight's compact folio, first published in 1598, again in 1602, with some improvements, and a third time in 1687, with a few trifling additions, continued to be the standard edition of Chaucer throughout the whole of the seventeenth century. Down to the beginning of the eighteenth century, indeed, the collected works of our more celebrated poets generally appeared in the folio form, and the folio belongs to the pre-critical period of our literary history. Urry's ambitious work, which appeared in 1721 and has the distinction of being the tallest of all the Chaucer folios, is certainly no exception. The licentious alterations of the text, in which Urry habitually indulged, have simply made it perversely corrupt in every part. . . .

[p. 10]   The first editor of any part of Chaucer's works who displayed anything like the spirit and power of genuine criticism was undoubtedly Dr. Thomas Morell, best remembered perhaps by his learned ' Thesaurus ' . . . Dr. Morell was, however, an English as well as a classical scholar, having edited Spenser, and commenced the publication of the ' Canterbury Tales ' on a thoroughly complete and satisfactory plan. The only matter of regret is that he did not carry out his admirable scheme and finish the work he had so well begun. The first volume of the projected work, and we believe the only one ever issued, appeared in 1737, and was entitled ' The Canterbury Tales of Chaucer in the original, from the most authentic manuscripts, with references to authors ancient and modern, various readings, and explanatory notes.' This volume contains the ' Prologue ' and the ' Knight's Tale,' a modern version of each being appended to the original text. Tyrwhitt refers to it in terms of high but just praise; and it appears from his reference to have been the only part of the work that had been published. . . . This part is, however, quite sufficient to show that in undertaking to edit Chaucer Dr. Morell took a just and comprehensive view of the work to be done, and that he possessed many of the higher qualities essential to its successful execution. His plan includes minute attention both to text and commentary; and in dealing with the text ' he set out,' says Tyrwhitt, ' upon the only rational plan, that of collating the best manuscripts and selecting from them the genuine readings.' [Then follow comments and quotations on Morell and Urry's views of Chaucer's versification.]

[p. 12]   Tyrwhitt comes next as an editor of Chaucer, and his

edition of the 'Canterbury Tales' is so well known that it
is needless to specify its merits and defects in detail.   In
our judgment, the merits of the work far outweigh its defects,
although in the present state of our knowledge the text
must no doubt be regarded as seriously defective.   Still on
the whole Tyrwhitt has done more for Chaucer than any
other single editor.   It is no doubt true that he was unacquainted with the niceties of Chaucer's grammar, and their
intimate connexion with the mechanism of his verse; and
[p. 13] Mr. Wright, in the introduction to his edition of the 'Canterbury Tales,' has emphasized these deficiencies in somewhat
sweeping terms.   But Tyrwhitt was a sagacious critic, possessing great literary knowledge, taste, and industry; and
he brought all his powers and acquirements to the illustration
of his favourite author, often with the happiest results. . . .

The next step in the history of Chaucer texts is the publication of this manuscript—the Harleian—by Mr. Wright in
1847.   This publication represents something like a revolution
in the plan of editing Chaucer, and at once raises the whole
question as to the best method of dealing with the text.   At
first sight Mr. Wright seems to make out a strong case for his
own plan.   After noticing that the grammatical forms of the
fourteenth century underwent a considerable change about the
middle of the fifteenth, and that copyists of this date usually
employed the language of the time rather than of the author
they are copying, he contends that the only satisfactory plan
of editing Chaucer is to select the oldest and best manuscript,
and to adhere to it faithfully throughout.   The opposite plan,
which had hitherto been usually followed, he condemns
indeed in no very measured terms :—

'It is evident, therefore,' he says, ' that the plan of forming
the text of any work of the periods of which we are speaking
from a number of different manuscripts, written at different
times and different places, is the most absurd plan which it
is possible to conceive.   Yet this was the method professedly
followed by Tyrwhitt in forming a text of the " Canterbury
Tales " of Chaucer.'

And after pointing out Tyrwhitt's special disqualifications
as a student of manuscripts, he adds :—

' Under these circumstances it is clear that to form a satisfactory text of Chaucer, we must give up the printed editions, and fall back upon the manuscripts; and that instead of bundling them altogether, we must pick out one best manuscript which also is one of those nearest to Chaucer's time. The latter circumstance is absolutely necessary, if we would reproduce the language and versification of the author. At the same time it cannot but be acknowledged that the earliest manuscript might possibly be very incorrect and incomplete, from the ignorance or negligence of the scribe who copied it. This, however, is not the case with regard to Chaucer's [p. 14] " Canterbury Tales." The Harleian manuscript, No. 7334, is by far the best manuscript of Chaucer's " Canterbury Tales " that I have yet examined, in regard both to antiquity and correctness. The handwriting is one which would at first sight be taken by an experienced scholar for that of the latter part of the fourteenth century, and it must have been written within a few years after 1400, and therefore soon after Chaucer's death and the publication of the " Canterbury Tales." Its language has very little, if any, appearance of local dialect; and the text is in general extremely good, the variations from Tyrwhitt being usually for the better.'

This reasoning seems, as we have said, sufficiently conclusive, and it has very naturally determined the course of subsequent editors, both Mr. Bell and Mr. Morris having followed Mr. Wright's plan, and adopted the text he had selected. But the publication of the Chaucer Society six-text edition of the ' Prologue' and ' Knight's Tale' has very much destroyed the force of Mr. Wright's plea in favour of adhering strictly to a single text. A comparison of the Harleian text with the six now publishing by the Society, will show that there are numberless points of grammar, metre, or sense in which it may be improved by careful collation, and that the old plan must still be followed before we can hope to secure a satisfactory and authoritative text. . . .

[p. 15]   The latest text of Chaucer's poetical works, that edited by Mr. Morris, and substituted for Tyrwhitt's in the new issue of the Aldine Series, is undoubtedly also the best. Mr. Morris is one of our most accurate and accomplished early English scholars, and no better editor of a mediæval text could possibly be found. After examining several manuscripts of the

'Canterbury Tales,' he agreed with Mr. Wright in thinking the Harleian text the best, and it has accordingly been selected and faithfully adhered to throughout. Clerical errors and corrupt readings were corrected by collation with other manuscripts, especially the Lansdowne, and a careful examination of Mr. Morris's text will show how painstaking he has been in this part of his work. The rest of the poems have been edited from the manuscripts where they existed, and the result is the best text of Chaucer that has yet appeared. . . .

A comparison of Mr. Morris's text of the 'Prologue' and the 'Knight's Tale' with the texts of the Society, has, however, convinced us that the question as to possible improvement must be answered decisively in the affirmative. Knowing beforehand the excellence of the Harleian text, and the general agreement of the six other manuscripts, we have [p. 16] been surprised indeed at the number of emendations of greater or less importance they afford. In the 'Prologue' alone there are, in our judgment, upwards of fifty lines that may be improved by collation either in sense or metre, while in the 'Knight's Tale' the better readings are in proportion to its length even more numerous and important. These better readings affect mainly the metre, the meaning, or the poetical expressiveness of the existing text. Some, again, effect marked improvements in minutiæ of grammar, emphasis, and spelling.

[pp. 16–33] [Examples are given and various readings discussed.]

[p. 33]   Quite as much still remains to be done for the illustration as for the text of Chaucer's poetical works. There are in his writings almost innumerable points of philological, literary, or historical interest that require to be elucidated. Chaucer was not only familiar with every phase of contemporary life, but profoundly read in all existing literature. He knew by intimate personal experience the tastes and habits, the pursuits and recreations, the superstitions and beliefs, of all ranks and classes amongst his own countrymen; and his public employments had enlarged the field of his observation so as to include almost every country in Europe. He had seen active military service abroad, and had taken part in splendid public ceremonials at home; had lived habitually

in courts, camps and great cities, as well as in the congenial
[p. 34] retirement of country life. The whole world of nature and
human experience was in this way mirrored in his sunny
intellect, while the higher influences of both had melted
serenely into the quiet depths of his curiously meditative
and observant mind.   As a natural result there is a mellowed
fulness in his maturer delineations; a joyous animation, a
living truth, a variety and completeness of detail in his pictures
of life that obscure at first the purely literary or academical
accomplishments of his mind; or rather, perhaps, it would be
more correct to say that in his later works the learning and
knowledge of life are so fused by imaginative sympathy into
a new poetical whole, that there is at first no distinct consciousness of the separate elements. . . .   On closer examination, however, the range and minuteness of Chaucer's
learning becomes clearly apparent. He employed materials
derived from all existing literatures home and foreign; not
only the early English chronicles and stories, the Norman-
French romances and fables, the new epic and lyrical poetry
of Italy, and the whole range of Latin literature, including
not only the classics proper, as well as the science and art,
the history and philosophy of the time, but also Byzantine
legends and brilliant fragments of Eastern romance, that
had passed into Europe in the wake of the returning
Crusaders. The adequate illustration of Chaucer thus requires, in addition to a minute acquaintance with the state
of the language in his day, a full knowledge of contemporary literature and history. No single editor has as
yet united these requirements. Tyrwhitt, who studied with
some care the literature and history of the fourteenth
century, was comparatively ignorant of Chaucer's language;
while recent editors, such as Mr. Wright and Mr. Morris,
who are well acquainted with Chaucer's language, have
attempted hardly anything in the way of literary or historical
illustration.

But the primary requirement of all expository criticism
of Chaucer is undoubtedly the full interpretation of his
language. . . . There is still, however, a great deal to be
done for the elucidation of Chaucer's language; and, unfortunately, Mr. Morris, who of living scholars is in many

respects best qualified for the work, has confined his labours
in this direction to a revision of previous glossaries. . . .
[An examination of Morris's Glossary follows.]

[p. 40]   This [comparison with *Piers Plowman*] points to an important means of interpreting Chaucer's language which has not
as yet been turned to anything like adequate account. We
refer to the critical examination of the writings of his contemporaries and immediate successors. The more carefully
the early literature of the fourteenth century is studied, the
more clearly will it appear that Chaucer's additions to the
vocabulary of the language are far less numerous than is
commonly supposed. He has been charged with adulterating
the English speech of his time by the wholesale importation
of foreign, and especially of Norman-French, words. In his
early translations and paraphrases from Norman-French he
occasionally, it is true, transfers words mainly for the convenience of their rhymes. But with these exceptions his
importations are comparatively few. His real superiority
lies in the admirable taste and judgment displayed in the
[p. 41] selection of his vocabulary, the natural reflex of his keen and
exquisite sensibility to the latent significance of language.
The perfection of his art lies in his subtle insight into the
deeper meaning of words, and his power of combining them
in the most felicitous manner. He is not fond of verbal
novelties for their own sake, and his obscurities of phrase
and diction may generally therefore be explained by a
reference to the literature of the fourteenth and fifteenth
centuries. The works of Gower and Lidgate, especially the
latter, are of essential service in this respect.

1870. Brae, Andrew Edmund. *The Treatise of the Astrolabe of Geoffrey
Chaucer,* edited by A. E. Brae, with notes and illustrations.

[The volume contains seven illustrations of Chaucer's Astrolabe, with a text of his treatise, an Appendix reprinting
essays on the astronomy of the *Canterbury Tales*; and a
series of notes on Chaucer's astronomy.]

1870. Courthope, William John. *The Paradise of Birds,* pp. 9, 122-3.

[Man has exterminated all the feathered tribes, and the
insect is becoming the lord of creation. Maresnest, the
scientific theorist, and Windbag, the romantic poet, come to

the Paradise of Birds to beg two eggs of every species. They
are tried by a jury of birds, and plead the "kindliness of
men to birds," giving as examples Aristophanes, Chaucer,
Gilbert White, etc.]

[p. 9] The Bird has thoughts like Man, but while he lives,
Each to one feeling various utterance gives,
Even in this life the grammar of the tree
Was by our Chaucer learned, and Canace.

[p. 122] If Man's good work may cancel Man's ill deed,
For us let English Chaucer intercede.
Think with what rhymes, what measures old and quaint,
He sings your love-day, and exalts your saint!

[p. 123] Think how he rose from bed betimes in spring,
To hear the Nightingale and Cuckoo sing!

NIGHTINGALE

O flower of the prime ! O fountain of rhyme !
O lover of daisies ! O poet of May !
Thy boon and my debt if I ever forget,
Let my heart have forgotten her lay.

Thou did drive from my view " the lewd Cuckoo ";
And I was thy singer that whole May long,*
Time since has grown grey, but I love thee to-day,
And I solace my soul with thy song.

[The illustrated edition of 1889 has a picture of Chaucer in
the woods.]

* The Cuckoo and the Nightingale, ll. 226–30.

1870. Lowell, James Russell. *Chaucer*, [in] the North American
Review, July 1870, vol. cxi, pp. 155–198. [Reprinted, revised
and enlarged, in *My Study Windows*, 1871.] (Riverside edition
of Works, 10 vols., 1890–91, vol. iii, pp. 290–366.)

[Passages between †† did not appear in the *North American Review*.]

[p. 293] It is good to retreat now and then beyond earshot of
the introspective confidences of modern literature, and to lose
ourselves in the gracious worldliness of Chaucer. Here was
a healthy and hearty man, so genuine that he need not ask
whether he were genuine or no, so sincere as quite to forget
his own sincerity, so truly pious that he could be happy in
the best world that God chose to make, so humane that he
loved even the foibles of his kind. Here was a truly epic

poet, without knowing it, who did not waste time in considering whether his age were good or bad, but quietly taking it for
granted as the best that ever was or ever could be for *him*,
has left us such a picture of contemporary life as no man ever
painted.   † 'A perpetual fountain of good sense,' Dryden calls
him, yes, and of good humor, too, and wholesome thought.†

[p. 300]   It is not the finding of a thing, but the making something
out of it after it is found, that is of consequence.   Accordingly, Chaucer, like Shakespeare, invented almost nothing.

[p. 322]   † Chaucer . . . drew from the South a certain airiness of
sentiment and expression, a felicity of phrase, and an elegance
of turn hitherto unprecedented and hardly yet matched in
our literature, but all the while kept firm hold of his native
soundness of understanding, and that genial humour which
seems to be the proper element of worldly wisdom.   With

[p. 323] Dante, life represented the passage of the soul from a state
of nature to a state of grace ; . . . With Chaucer, life is a
pilgrimage, but only that his eye may be delighted with the
varieties of costume and character.   There are good morals
to be found in Chaucer, but they are always incidental.
With Dante the main question is the saving of the soul, with
Chaucer it is the conduct of life.†

[p. 324–5] Chaucer is the first who broke away from the dreary
traditional style, and gave not merely stories, but lively
pictures of real life as the ever-renewed substance of poetry.
He was a reformer, too, not only in literature, but in morals.
But as in the former his exquisite tact saved him from all
eccentricity, so in the latter the pervading sweetness of his
nature could never be betrayed into harshness and invective.
. . . There is no touch of cynicism in all he wrote.
Dante's brush seems sometimes to have been smeared with
the burning pitch of his own fiery lake.   Chaucer's pencil is
dipped in the cheerful colour-box of the old illuminators, and
he has their patient delicacy of touch, with a freedom far
beyond their somewhat mechanic brilliancy.

[p. 336]   One of the world's three or four great story tellers, he was
also one of the best versifiers that ever made English trip and
sing with a gayety that seems careless, but where every foot
beats time to the tune of the thought.   By the skilful arrangement of his pauses he evaded the monotony of the couplet,

and gave to the rhymed pentameter, which he made our
heroic measure, something of the architectural repose of
blank verse.   He found our language lumpish, stiff, unwilling,
too apt to speak Saxonly in grouty monosyllables; he left it
enriched with the longer measure of the Italian and Provençal
poets.

[p. 353]   [Chaucer is a great narrative poet.]   The power of diffusion
without being diffuse would seem to be the highest merit of
narration, giving it that easy flow which is so delightful.
Chaucer's descriptive style is remarkable for its lowness of
tone—for that combination of energy with simplicity which
is among the rarest gifts in literature. . . .

Not that Chaucer cannot be intense, too, on occasion; but
it is with a quiet intensity of his own, that comes in as it
were by accident. . . .

Pandarus, looking at Troïlus,

> 'Took up a light and found his countenance
> As for to look upon an old romance.'

With Chaucer it is always the thing itself and not the
description of it that is the main object.   His picturesque bits
are incidental to the story, glimpsed in passing; they never
stop the way.   His key is so low that his high lights are never
obtrusive.

[p. 356]   Chaucer never shows any signs of effort, and it is a main
proof of his excellence that he can be so inadequately sampled
by detached passages—by single lines taken away from the
connection in which they contribute to the general effect.
He has that continuity of thought, that evenly prolonged
power, and that delightful equanimity, which characterize
the higher orders of mind.   There is something in him of the
disinterestedness that made the Greeks masters in art.   His
[p. 357] phrase is never importunate.   His simplicity is that of
elegance, not of poverty.   The quiet unconcern with which he
says his best things is peculiar to him among English poets,
though Goldsmith, Addison, and Thackeray have approached
it in prose.

When Chaucer describes anything, it is commonly by one
of those simple and obvious epithets or qualities that are so
easy to miss.   Is it a woman?   He tells us she is *fresh*, that

she has *glad* eyes. . . . Sometimes he describes amply by the merest hint, as where the Friar, before setting himself softly down, drives away the cat.   We know without need of more words that he has chosen the snuggest corner.

[p. 360]   Chaucer seems to me to have been one of the most purely
[p. 361] original of poets, as much so in respect of the world that is about us as Dante in respect of that which is within us. There had been nothing like him before, there has been nothing since.   He is original, not in the sense that he thinks and says what nobody ever thought and said before, and what nobody can ever think and say again, but because he is always natural; because, if not always absolutely new, he is always delightfully fresh, because he sets before us the world as it honestly appeared to Geoffrey Chaucer, and not a world as it seemed proper to certain people that it ought to appear.

[p. 365]   In spite of some external stains, which those who have studied the influence of manners will easily account for without imputing them to any moral depravity, we feel that we can join the pure-minded Spenser in calling him 'most sacred, happy spirit.'   If character may be divined from works, he was a good man, genial, sincere, hearty, temperate of mind, more wise, perhaps, for this world than the next, but thoroughly humane, and friendly with God and men.   I know not how to sum up what we feel about him better than by saying (what would have pleased most one who was indifferent to fame) that we love him more even than we admire.

1871. Brooke, Stopford Augustus.   *The Descriptive Poetry of Chaucer,* [in] Macmillan's Magazine, Aug. 1871, vol. **xxiv**, pp. 268–79.

[p. 269]   The landscape of Chaucer is sometimes taken from the Italian and sometimes from the French landscape. It possesses almost always the same elements, differently mixed up in different poems : a May morning—the greenwood, or a garden—some clear running water—meadows covered with flowers—some delectable place or other with an arbour laid down with soft and fresh-cut turf.   There is no sky, except in such rapid allusions as this, " Bright was the day and blue the firmament ;" no cloud studies ; no conception of the beauty of wild nature.

His range, therefore, is extremely limited ; but within the

limits his landscape is exquisitely fresh, natural, and true in spite of its being conventional.

[p. 272] [Chaucer's love of colour.] But of all the colours which Chaucer loved in nature, he loved best the harmony of white and green in one of his favourite daisied meadows. . . .

It may be in an age when colours in art had each their peculiar religious significance, that Chaucer, a man who had travelled in Italy and who had himself the instinct of sym-[p. 273] bolism, had some spiritual meaning in the constant association of these two colours of white and green. Green, the hue of spring, signified hope, and particularly the hope of Immortality ; white was the emblem, among other things, of light and joy. . . .

Still dwelling on Chaucer's colour, it is curious the number of concentrated pictures which are to be found in his poems, pictures so sharply drawn in colour that they might be at once painted from the description. He looks in and the arbour is full of scarlet flowers, and down among them, sore wounded, "a man in black and white colour, pale and wan," is lying, bitterly complaining. Scarlet, black, white, one sees that, "flashing upon the inward eye," not in outline, nor in detail, but in colour, and that is the test whether a poet is a good colourist or not. It is no common excellence. . . .

There is a splendid study of colour, unequalled in its way in our literature, in Chaucer's picture of the cock in the "Nun's Priests Tale." The widow keeps in her yard a famous stock of poultry,

> "In which she had a cock, hight Chaunticlere [to]
> And lik the burnischt gold was his colour."

[p. 274] This simple childlikeness and intensity of Chaucer . . . are the first necessity of a poetic nature, . . . This is the first of those elements of his poetry which make his landscapes impossible to be painted.

Of two other unpaintable things the landscape is also full— of the scent of flowers, and the songs of birds, and now and then of the noise of water.

1871-2. Eliot, George. *Chapter headings*, [in] *Middlemarch*, 1871-2, 4 vols.

Chap. xii, vol. i, p. 180 [*Milleres Tale*, ll. 3774–5] ; chap. xxi, vol. i, p. 369 [*Phicisiens Tale*, ll. 50–52] ; chap. l, vol. iii, p. 108 [*Shipmannes Prol.*, ll. 15–20] ; chap. lxv, vol. iv, p. 49 [*Wife of Bath's Prol.*, ll. 440–442].

1871–3. Furnivall, Frederick James. *Trial-Forewords to my " Parallel-Text Edition of Chaucer's Minor Poems," for the Chaucer Society* (with a try to set Chaucer's works in their right order of time, 1871).—Corrections and Additions, 1872.—Further Corrections and Additions, 1873. (Chaucer Society.)

1873. Furnivall, Frederick James.	*Recent Work at Chaucer*, [in] Macmillan's Magazine, March, 1873, vol. xxvii, pp. 383–93.

[p. 383]	Taking it . . . for granted that the study of Early English has revived and is spreading, though miserably slowly, in England and elsewhere, let us ask what that study has done for Chaucer, that tenderest, brightest, most humourful sweet soul, of all the great poets of the world, whom a thousand Englishmen out of every thousand and one are content to pass by with a shrug and a sneer.

[pp.383–7]	[The gradual settling of the Chaucer canon which had been confused by Stowe and other early editors. Tyrwhitt's contribution to this. Nicolas and the biographical facts. Bradshaw's and ten Brink's work on the text ; the rhyme-tests. The French and Italian periods first distinguished by ten Brink.]

[p. 387]	[The *Compleynte to Pite* the key to Chaucer's early sad poetry, telling of his own unhappy love.]

[pp.388–9]	[A suggested chronological list of the works in four periods, and an order of dates for the *Canterbury Tales* " not yet quite fully worked out. Thus far had one got when Mr. Hales supplied the generalization wanted—' Power of characterization is the true test. . . . The Tales too that take half-views of life, like the Clerk's . . . the Man of Law's . . . must be before the best time too.' "]

[p. 389]	With this guide every reader can work out the succession of the Tales for himself, and mix them with the Minor Poems as ranged above. He will then see Chaucer, not only outwardly as he was in the flesh—page, soldier, squire, diplomatist, Custom-house officer, Member of Parliament, then a suppliant for protection and favour, a beggar for money ; but inwardly as he was in the spirit—clear of all nonsense of Courts of Love, etc.—gentle and loving, early timid and in despair, sharing others' sorrow, and, by comforting them,

losing part of his own; yet long dwelling on the sadness of
forsaken love, seeking the "consolation of philosophy,"
watching the stars, praying to the "Mother of God"; studying
books, and, more still, woman's nature; his eye open to all
the beauties of the world around him, his ear to the "heavenly
harmony" of birds' song; at length becoming the most
gracious and tender spirit, the sweetest singer, the best
pourtrayer, the most pathetic, and withal the most genial
and humourful healthy-souled man that England had ever
seen. Still, after 500 years, he is bright and fresh as the
glad light green of the May he so much loved; he is still
second only to Shakespeare in England, and fourth only to
him and Dante and Homer in the world. When will our
Victorian time love and honour him as it should? Surely, of
all our poets he is the one to come *home* to us most.

[p. 389] [Contrast between Chaucer and Tennyson.]

[pp. 389
-90] [The change in Chaucer marked by the development of
humour.]

[pp. 390
-3] [The work of the Chaucer Society; the Six-text Edition; a
comparison of the MSS. made the Tales fall into their proper
places in the pilgrimage, and prepared the way for a real
edition. The Society's other texts and studies. An appeal
for support.]

[Dr. Furnivall's copy of his article with important additions
and alterations, is in the possession of the editor. One of
Dr. Furnivall's additions reads thus:]

One may fairly claim then, for the Chaucer Society the
credit of having, with Mr. Bradshaw's and Prof. ten Brink's
help, done the best work at and for Chaucer that has been
done since his death. It has explained the secret of his early
life, cleared his memory from the reproach of having written
many unworthinesses, and of having muddled his greatest
work; it has laid the sure foundations for a fitting edition of
one of the greatest poets of mankind, and has made plainer to
modern English ears the music, to modern English eyes the
sunny soul, that cheered our ancestors in Wicliffe's day.

1873, etc. Furnivall, Frederick James, and **others.** *Notices of Chaucer
Discoveries, Notes, Correspondence, etc.,* [in] The Athenæum [and]
The Academy.

[In 1873 Dr. Furnivall contributed a series of notices of
recent Chaucerian discoveries to the *Athenæum*, and later he

and others published notes, etc., frequently in the *Academy*
and less frequently in the *Athenæum.*]

1873. Hales, John Wesley. *Chaucer and Shakespeare,* [in] the Quarterly
Review, Jan. 1873, vol. cxxxiv, pp. 225–255. (Reprinted in *Notes
and Essays on Shakespeare,* by John W. Hales, 1884, pp. 56–104.)

[p. 226]   [An account of the Chaucer Society and the work of
Furnivall.]

[p. 227]   Chaucer and Shakespeare have much in common. However diverse the form of their greatest works, yet in spirit
there is a remarkable likeness and sympathy. Their geniuses
differ rather in degree than in kind. Chaucer is in many
respects a lesser Shakespeare. [Immaturity of the drama
as a literary form in Chaucer's day] . . . Chaucer stands in
relation to the supreme Dramatic Age in a correspondent
position to that held by Scott. Chaucer lived in the morning
twilight of it, Scott in the evening. There can be little
doubt that both would have added to its lustre—that England
would have boasted one more, and Scotland at least one
great dramatist had they been born earlier and later
respectively. . . .

[p. 230]   Probably it was these piteous, but seemingly not inevitable or reproachless, distresses [embarrassments due to
attachment to a court party] that impeded the completion
of the " Canterbury Tales.' The original design, indeed,
is in itself too vast for realisation. Chaucer commits the
same error in this respect as Spenser does.

[p. 231]   We have said that his genius exhibits a remarkable affinity
to that of Shakespeare—a closer affinity, we think, than that
of any other English poet. To Chaucer belongs in a high
measure what marks Shakespeare supremely—a certain
indefinable grace and brightness of style, an incomparable
archness and vivacity, an incessant elasticity and freshness,
an indescribable ease, a never faltering variety, an incapability
of dulness. . . .

For skill in characterization who can be ranked between
Chaucer and Shakespeare ? Is there any work, except the
' theatre ' of Shakespeare, that attempts, with a success
in any way comparable, the astonishing task which Chaucer
sets himself ? He attempts to portray the entire society
of his age from the crown of its head to the sole of its foot—

from the knight, the topmost figure of mediæval life, down
to the ploughman and the cook; and the result is a gallery
of life-like portraits, which has no parallel anywhere, with
one exception, for variety, truthfulness, humanity. [This
is elaborated.] . . .

[p. 232]   We ask, who among our poets, except Shakespeare, shall
be placed above Chaucer in this domain of art ? In our
opinion there is not one of the Elizabethans that deserves
that honour. . . .

[p. 234]   [Chaucer's pathos contrasted with Sterne's and Shakespeare's.]

[pp. 236-7] [Chaucer's irony.]

[p. 237]   It is because his spirit enjoyed and retained this lofty
freedom that it was so tolerant and capacious. He, like
Shakespeare, was eminently a Human Catholic, no mere
sectary. He refused to no man an acknowledgment of
kindred. . . .

[pp. 238-9]   There is just one point of personal likeness between Chaucer
and Shakespeare that we wish to notice. Of each man, as
his contemporaries knew him, the chief characteristic was
a wonderful loveableness of Nature. [Quotations from
Jonson, Occleve, Lydgate, &c. on this point.]

[pp. 240-2]   [On Shakespeare's probable knowledge of Chaucer's work,
a subject not yet sufficiently investigated; with remarks
on Chaucer's fame and accessibility in Shakespeare's time.
The Two Noble Kinsmen considered, and the reason for no
mention of him in *Richard II* and *Henry IV* thought to be
that he would, as a poet, have seemed out of place in an
historical setting. Shakspere's acquaintance with the
Knight's Tale and *Troylus* to be seen in *Midsummer-Night's
Dream, Two Noble Kinsmen, Venus and Adonis, Tarquin and
Lucrece, Troilus and Cressida, Romeo and Juliet ;* while in
As You Like It is seen knowledge of *Gamelyn.* Parallel
passages are quoted, and the subject is further discussed.]

1873. Rossetti, William Michael. *Chaucer's Troylus and Cryseyde
compared with Boccaccio's Filostrato,* Prefatory Remarks, pp. iii–ix.
(Chaucer Soc.).

[pp. iii, iv]   The most important point of absolute difference between
the Italian and the English poets—the most important
both in subject-matter and in scale of treatment—is in the
incidents which lead up to the actual amour between Troilus

and Chryseis. . . . Chaucer has invented an entirely new series of preliminaries; far more elaborate, and such as almost to leave his Cryseyde in the position of a modest and chaste-minded woman, even after the amour is in full career. . . . The English poet neither schemes nor affects (if I do not misapprehend) to invent an essentially different character: but he leads up to the crisis by a more artful and more sympathetic course of incident. . . .

[A study of the two Pandaruses, the sources, etc., follows.]

1873. Unknown. *The Cycle of English Song*, II, [in] Temple Bar, vol. xxxviii, June–July, pp. 308–324, 458, 460–1.

[p. 311]   He talked, a child, to children—the biggest, oldest, wisest, cleverest child of the company—and so he amused them
[p. 312] incessantly. . . . In a sense, ordinary persons now alive may be said to have overtaken him, just as extraordinary persons have far outstripped him. In the early dawn of English poetry it required a man of the highest genius to feel what nearly everybody now feels, and to put the feeling into words which have almost passed into commonplace, and which would indeed have done so but for the musical and cunning fashion in which they are arranged. . . . In a word, it is the childhood
[p. 313] of poetry. . . . Nor is it nature only that he treats in this childish, simple, superficial, non-artificial way. Men and women, and all that men and women do, say, eat, drink, and wear, he views and describes in the same plain, matter-of-fact, exact, truthful fashion. . . . Who are they? Where do they come from? What are their names? . . . [Chaucer's prolixity
[p. 315] typical of childhood.] Neither must it be supposed, in anticipation of the criticism of later times . . . that he is so long-winded . . . from the very depth and subtlety of his art, and from a conviction that this is the only way of making people see the things you want them to see. For it is not the only way, nor yet the best way. Indeed, it is the worst and lowest way of all the ways that do achieve the object. It is the earliest way, the childish way; and Chaucer employed it because he knew no other.

1874. Green, John Richard. *A Short History of the English People,* pp. 163–4, 212–6, 229, 231, 248–9, 287–90.

[p. 214]   If with the best modern critics we reject from the list of his genuine works the bulk of the poems which preceded " Troilus and Cressida," we see at once that, familiar as he was with the literature of the Trouvères, his real sympathies drew him not to the dying verse of France, but to the new and mighty upgrowth of poetry in Italy. . . . But even while changing, as it were, the front of English poetry, Chaucer preserves his own distinct personality. If he quizzes in the rime of Sir Thopaz the wearisome idleness of the French romance, he retains all that was worth retaining of the French temper, its rapidity and agility of movement, its lightness and brilliancy of touch, its airy mockery, its gaiety [p. 215] and good humour, its critical coolness and self-control. The French wit quickens in him more than in any English writer the sturdy sense and shrewdness of our national disposition, corrects its extravagance, and relieves its somewhat ponderous morality. If, on the other hand, he echoes the joyous carelessness of the Italian tale, he tempers it with the English seriousness. As he follows Boccaccio, all his changes are on the side of purity; and when the Troilus of the Florentine ends with the old sneer at the changeableness of woman, Chaucer bids us " look Godward," and dwells on the unchangeableness of Heaven.

But the genius of Chaucer was neither French nor Italian, whatever element it might borrow from either literature, but English to the core.

[p. 216] It is the first time in English poetry that we are brought face to face not with characters or allegories or reminiscences of the past, but with living and breathing men, men distinct in temper and sentiment as in face or costume or mode of speech; and with this distinctness of each maintained throughout the story by a thousand shades of expression and action. It is the first time, too, that we meet with the dramatic power which not only creates each character, but combines it with its fellows, which not only adjusts each tale or jest to the temper of the person who utters it, but fuses all into a poetic unity. . . . He has received his training from war, courts, business, travel—a training not of books, but of life. And it is life that he loves—the delicacy of its sentiment, the breadth of its farce, its laughter and its tears, the tenderness of its Grisildis or the Smollett-like adventures of the miller and the schoolboy. It is this largeness of heart, this wide tolerance, which enables him to reflect man for us as none but Shakspeare has ever reflected it [*sic*], but to reflect it with a pathos, a shrewd sense and kindly humour, a freshness and joyousness of feeling, that even Shakspeare has not surpassed.

[pp. 229 -31] [Chaucer's satire on the clerics.]

[p. 248]   Nothing brings more vividly home to us the social chasm which in the fourteenth century severed the rich from the poor than the contrast between the " Complaint of Piers the Ploughman " and the " Canterbury Tales." The world of wealth and ease and laughter through which the courtly Chaucer moves with eyes downcast as in a pleasant dream is a far-off world of wrong and of ungodliness to the gaunt poet of the poor.

[The passages on Chaucer were re-handled in Green's *History of the English People*, 1877–80.]

1874. Minto, William. *Characteristics of English Poets from Chaucer to Shirley*, Edinburgh, pp. vii, 1–58 [Chapter 1 : Geoffrey Chaucer], 59–66, 70–7, 81–2, 90, 91, 96, 99, 101–2, 105, 111–2, 122–6, 129–30, 133–4, 143, 146, 149, 151, 153, 170–1, 177, **213**, 219–20, 300–1, 316, 392, 416, 453.

[The biography of Chaucer is based on the latest discoveries of Furnivall and other scholars, as well as on the older material. Minto thinks the idea of Chaucer's " hopeless passion " in early life (based on the *Complaint of Pity*, etc.) has been made too much of. A comparison between Chaucer and Shakespeare in their knowledge of men is made, p. 17. Ten Brink's division of Chaucer's work into three periods is rejected, as it seems to Minto that from first to last Chaucer had more affinity with the French than with the Italians; and he adds : " I can distinguish no change either in his methods or in his spirit that is fairly attributable to Italian influence," p. 19. The work of ten Brink, Bradshaw and Furnivall in proving the non-Chaucerian character of the *Testament of Love, Assembly of Ladies, Lamentation of Mary Magdalene, Court of Love, Flower and Leaf,* and *Chaucer's Dream*, is described. As the chief argument is the *y-ye* rhyme, and as this is found in the *Romaunt*, the whole question, according to Minto, depends largely on this poem. Minto argues for the genuineness of the *Court of Love*. He remarks :]

[p. 21]   It is simply incredible that these poems could have been written by a poet whose name has perished. If he had written before Chaucer, which could hardly be seriously maintained, he could not but have become famous; and the probability is that Chaucer would have mentioned him as [p. 22] the model of his seven-line stanza. If he had written after Chaucer, he would certainly have mentioned Chaucer in his list of masters, according to the universal habit of the time. The idea of deliberate forgery is out of the question; and if the " Court of Love " had been the work of a forger or an imitator, the artificial restriction of rhyme was precisely the sort of thing he would labour to observe. Finally, the " Court of Love " is unmistakably imitated in the ' King's Quhair ' of James I, whose captivity in England began only five years after Chaucer's death, and yet he mentions no master except Chaucer, Gower and Lydgate. That makes it quite clear that James attributed the " Court of Love " to Chaucer; and what need is there for further evidence ?

[Subsequent sections of the Chaucer portion are, II. His Language, Metres and Imagery. III. The Chief Qualities of his Poetry. IV. His Delineation of Character.]

1875. Longfellow, Henry Wadsworth. *The Masque of Pandora, and other Poems,* pp. 95–6, 140. (Writings, Riverside edn., vol. v, pp. 195, 196, 200, 217.)

[*A Book of Sonnets :*]

CHAUCER.

[p 200]   An old man in a lodge within a park ;
      The chamber walls depicted all around
      With portraitures of huntsman, hawk, and hound,
    And the hurt deer.   He listeneth to the lark,
    Whose song comes with the sunshine through the dark
      Of painted glass in leaden lattice bound ;
      He listeneth and he laugheth at the sound,
    Then writeth in a book like any clerk.
    He is the poet of the dawn, who wrote
      The Canterbury Tales, and his old age
      Made beautiful with song ; and as I read
    I hear the crowing cock, I hear the note
      Of lark and linnet, and from every page
      Rise odors of ploughed field or flowery mead.

1876. Haweis, Mary Eliza.   *Chaucer for Children* . . . illustrated
with eight coloured pictures, and numerous woodcuts by the
Author, 1877.

[Published late in 1876.]

[With a preface "To the Mother" on the reading and
pronunciation of Chaucer, followed by a biographical sketch,
"Chaucer the Tale Teller." Abridged stories from *Prol.,
Knightes, Friers, Clerkes, Frankeleyns* and *Pardoneres Tales,
Complaint to his Purse, Two Rondeaux* (*Your yën two* and
Sin I fro Love), *Virelai* and *Good Counsel,* follow in original
and modernised form with connecting summary.]

1876. Minto, William.   *Chaucer,* [in] Encyclopædia Britannica,
ninth edition.   *See* above, 1778, Unknown, vol. i, p. 452.

1877. Fleay, F. G.   *Guide to Chaucer and Spenser.*   [One of Collins'
School and College Classics.]

[The section given to Chaucer occupies pp. 1–72, and in
this short space is contained a summary of the latest critical
knowledge of his life, sources, language, works and their
chronology, arrangement of the *Tales* (in two days instead of
four), etc.   Fleay rejects the rhyme-test of *y, ye,* and the
conclusions as to authenticity of poems founded on it,
retaining e.g. ' *Chaucer's Dream* ' (*the Isle of Ladies*), and also
disbelieves in Chaucer's early unhappy love, interpreting his
' sickness ' as married life.]

[p. 10]   Of the practicability of acquiring it [a sound acquaintance
with Chaucer] at the age of thirteen or thereabouts, I have
had many proofs among my own pupils, from the time when
I first introduced English literature as a specific subject of
education in our grammar schools, now twenty years ago.
The methods I was then almost, if not quite, alone in using,
are now in general practice.

1877. Green, John Richard.   *Letters to Dr. F. J. Furnivall,* [the first
undated, the second dated] March 12, 1877 [in the possession of
Mr. Percy Furnivall].

[1] Anent the Chaucer, I hope our talk cleared your mind
into hopefulness and a practical view of things. What we
really want (' we ' being the would-be-intelligent-readers-of-
Chaucer) is simply (1) Sketch of Early English poetry afore
him to bring out the great step he made.   (2) His life
with what pictures of men's ways and manners in his day

you like. (3) An account of his poems one by one in as chronological an order as is possible, what each is, whence it came, peculiarities of it, necessary information about it, and the like. (4) *If you like*, a chapter on Chaucer influence on later poetry—And (5) another on Chaucer bibliography.

These are what occur to me. You may perhaps think of other fitting topics. But anyhow—if you will do a Division-Sum, and divide 140 pages by the various topics to be thus treated—you will see how briefly and simply each will have to be treated—and how *simple and easy your work would be*. Do the Life first, in 30 pages or so—then the series of works—and leave the head and tail of the book till the last. But *do* write it.

[2] I am as hungry as ever for your ' Chaucer.' *Do* let me have it.

[The book on Chaucer referred to was to form one of the series of primers brought out by Green ; the Chaucer one was eventually written, in 1893 (*q.v.* below), by A. W. Pollard.]

1877. Meredith, George. *On the Idea of Comedy, and of the Uses of the Comic Spirit*, [in] The New Quarterly Magazine, vol. viii, April, 1877, p. 35. (Works, 1897–8, 34 vols., vol. xxxii, p. 72.)

The Comic spirit is not hostile to the sweetest songfully poetic. Chaucer bubbles with it : Shakespeare overflows.

1877. Unknown. *Chaucer's Love-Poetry*, [in] the Cornhill Magazine, March 1877, vol. xxxv, pp. 280–97.

[p. 281]   Before going further, it may be as well to point out how very small a portion of Chaucer's work decides the special impression of him which now is historically transmitted from generation to generation.

If it were possible to take away only a little more than a tenth part of the poet's voluminous writings, there would be left a mass of outlandish recital having nothing whatever to do with anything we now know of English tastes. Instead of appearing a broad humourist, with an overpowering love of nature, painting persons and scenes with exact reality, there would then seem to be no English poet so artificial, so romantic, so lackadaisical as Chaucer. The truth is, that the literary associations for which the mention of his name is the cue, belong to the *Canterbury Tales* only. . . . If the match-less Introduction had not been written, or had been different, and if he had not included in the list two or three of the stories, or not given prologues to the others, Chaucer could not have survived in our literature. Of course there is a historical explanation for it all. . . . Put at its briefest the explanation is this : his object was to give Englishmen a literature bodily, instantly as it were, by transferring into our tongue, such as he found it and made it, the famous achievements of the great foreign writers. . . .

[p. 282]   Our business here is instantly to narrow all we have been saying into the statement, that with the above exceptions, Chaucer's writings are a lackadaisical exaggeration of one feeling—Love, and that in them the passion is taken in its weakest, vainest form of sentimentality. He is, and for ever will remain, the chief erotic poet of our language.

1878. Poetical Works of Chaucer, with poems formerly printed with his, or attributed to him. Edited, with a Memoir, by R. Bell. Revised edition. . . . With a preliminary essay by W. W. Skeat. 4 vols. [A revised edition of that of 1854–6, *q.v.* above.]

[The introductory essay (vol. i, pp. 1–12) is concerned with the Chaucer canon. *The Testament of Love, Rom. Rose, Complaint of the Black Knight, Cuckoo and Nightingale, Flower and the Leaf, Chaucer's Dream (Isle of Ladies), Court of Love, Virelai,* etc., are declared to be spurious. They are printed in this edition at the end of the genuine works.]

1878. Skeat, Walter William. *See* above, *Poetical Works.*

1878. Storr, Francis (the Younger), and **Turner,** Hawes. *Canterbury Chimes, or Chaucer Tales retold for Children.* Illustrated by woodcuts from the Ellesmere MS.

[A very free rendering, in simple modern English, of *Prol.,* and an abridgment of the *Knightes, Man of Law's, Nonne Prestes, Squieres, Frankeleyns* and "*Chaucer's*" *Tales* (the last = *Gamelyn,* which is purposely inserted instead of *Sir Thopas,* as being more suitable ; see Preface, p. vi).]

1879–80. The Poetical Works of Chaucer, to which are appended poems attributed to Chaucer, edited by Arthur Gilman, 3 vols., Boston, 1880.

[Gilman's edition of Chaucer is the first considerable use made, by way of an edition, of the work of Furnivall and the Chaucer Society. In the case of the *Canterbury Tales,* the text was based on the Ellesmere MS., which was collated with others. It was considered advisable " not to burden the volume with the various readings." The line-numbers of Tyrwhitt's edition are given in parentheses every fiftieth line, and in the prose tales every tenth break in the six-text edition is indicated. The greatest praise and thanks are given to the Chaucer Society. The edition is also indebted to the labours of Child, Skeat, Morris, Bradshaw and ten Brink.

The Biography entitled *The Times and the Poet* is by the editor, and is divided into sections : i. The Outer Life; ii. The Social Life; iii. The Poet's Life; iv. The Poet's Works; v. The Poet's Genius. A Section *On Reading Chaucer* follows with information on pronunciation, stress and scansion. Sections on *Astrological Terms* and *Biblical References* follow. The Tales are divided into four days' recital.

The apocryphal pieces include : *Proverbe of Chaucer, Balade de Visage*, etc., *Court of Love, Flower and Leaf, Cuckow and Nightingale, Praise of Women, Chaucer's Dream, Virelai* (Alone walkyng," etc.), *Chaucer's Prophesy* and *Go Forth King.*

The biography is dated 1879; the volumes were published in 1880.]

1879–80. Gilman, Arthur. *See* above, *Poetical* Works of Chaucer, edited by A. Gilman.

1879–80. Lanier, Sidney. *Shakspere and his Forerunners*, London, 1902, vol. i, pp. xiv, 32, 56–62 [Chaucer's treatment of Nature in *The Flour and the Lefe*], 89, 93–4, 113, 137 [Chaucer's praise of wifehood], 140, 146–59 [*The Clerkes Tale*, copious extracts], 162–5 [the enormous error of calling Chaucer a ' well of English undefiled '], 192 [Chaucer's pronunciation], 202, 277, 287 ; vol. ii, pp. 19–21 [Chaucer's testimony as to English love of music], 27, 34n., to f. p. 102 [pictures of ' A Poticary and a Pardoner' from the Ellesmere MS.], 188, 221, 298–300 [*Knightes Tale* and *Midsummer Night's Dream*], 306, 316–7. [These lectures, printed in 1902, were delivered in Baltimore during the winter of 1879–80 ; *see* Preface.]

[p. 56]   Chaucer's poem *The Flower and the Leafe.* . . . I do not hesitate to pronounce a far finer poem than any of the *Canterbury Tales*—in fact, to my thinking, worth all the *Canterbury Tales* put together.

1879. Ward, Sir Adolphus William. *Chaucer.* (English Men of Letters.)

[p. 146]   One very pleasing quality in Chaucer must have been his modesty. In the course of his life this may have helped to

recommend him to patrons so many and so various, and to make him the useful and trustworthy agent that he evidently became for confidential missions abroad. . . . To us, of course, this quality of modesty in Chaucer makes itself principally manifest in the opinion which he incidentally shows himself to entertain concerning his own rank and claims as an author. Herein, as in many other points, a contrast is noticeable between him and the great Italian masters, who were so sensitive as to the esteem in which they and their poetry were held.   Chaucer again and again disclaims all boasts of
[p. 147] perfection, or pretensions to pre-eminence, as a poet. . . . He acknowledges as incontestable the superiority of the poets of classical antiquity.
[p. 179]   Closely allied to Chaucer's liveliness and gaiety of disposition, and in part springing from them, are his keen sense of the ridiculous and the power of satire which he has at his command.   His humour has many varieties, ranging from the refined and half-melancholy irony of the *House of Fame*
[p. 180] to the ready wit of the sagacious uncle of Cressid, the burlesque fun of the inimitable *Nun's Priest's Tale,* and the very gross salt of the *Reeve,* the *Miller,* and one or two others. . . . Concerning, however, Chaucer's use of the power which he in so large a measure possessed, viz. that of covering with ridicule the palpable vices or weaknesses of the classes or kinds of men represented by some of his character-types, one assertion may be made with tolerable safety.   Whatever may have been the first stimulus and the ultimate scope of the wit and humour which he here expended, they are *not* to be explained as moral indignation in disguise.   And in truth Chaucer's merriment flows spontaneously from a source very near the surface; he is so extremely diverting, because he is so extremely diverted himself.

Herein, too, lies the harmlessness of Chaucer's fun.   Its harmlessness, to wit, for those who are able to read him in something like the spirit in which he wrote. . . .
[p. 181]   But the realism of Chaucer is something more than exuberant love of fun and light-hearted gaiety.   He is the first great painter of character, because he is the first great observer of it among European writers. . . . More especially with regard to the manners and ways of women, which

often, while seeming so natural to women themselves, appear so odd to male observers, Chaucer's eye was ever on the alert.

[p. 187] His descriptions of nature are as true as his sketches of human character; and incidental touches in him reveal his love of the one as unmistakably as his unflagging interest in the study of the other. Even those May-morning *exordia*, in which he was but following a fashion—faithfully observed both by the French *trouvères* and by the English romances translated from their productions and not forgotten by the author of the earlier part of the *Roman de la Rose*—always came from his hands with the freshness of natural truth.

[Chap. IV, Epilogue, giving a sketch of the influence of Chaucer.]

1880. Arnold, Matthew. *The Study of Poetry,* [the General Intro- duction to *The English Poets,* 1880, edited by T. H. Ward], pp. xxxi–xxxvi, xliv, xlv. [Reprinted in *Essays in Criticism,* 2nd ser., 1888, pp. 26–34, 49–51.]

[p. xxxi] But in the fourteenth century there comes an Englishman nourished on this poetry [French romance-poetry], taught his trade by this poetry, getting words, rhyme, metre from this poetry; for even of that stanza which the Italians used, and which Chaucer derived immediately from the Italians, the basis and suggestion was probably given in France. Chaucer (I have already named him) fascinated his contemporaries, but so too did Christian of Troyes and Wolfram of Eschenbach. Chaucer's power of fascination, however, is enduring; his poetical importance does not need the assistance of the historic estimate; it is real. He is a genuine source of joy and strength, which is flowing still for us and will flow always. He will be read, as time goes on, far more generally than he is read now. His language is a cause of difficulty to us, but so also, and I think in quite as great a degree, is the language of Burns. In Chaucer's case, as in that of Burns, it is a difficulty to be unhesitatingly accepted and overcome.

If we ask ourselves wherein consists the immense supe- riority of Chaucer's poetry over the romance poetry—why it is that in passing from this to Chaucer we suddenly feel ourselves to be in another world, we shall find that his

[p.
xxxii] superiority is both in the substance of his poetry and in the
style of his poetry. His superiority in substance is given by
his large, free, simple, clear yet kindly view of human life,—
so unlike the total want, in the romance-poets, of all intelligent command of it. Chaucer has not their helplessness; he
has gained the power to survey the world from a central, a
truly human point of view. We have only to call to mind
the Prologue of *The Canterbury Tales.* The right comment
upon it is Dryden's 'It is sufficient to say, according to the
proverb, that *here is God's plenty.*' And again: 'He is a
perpetual fountain of good sense.' It is by a large, free,
sound representation of things, that poetry, this high criticism
of life, has truth of substance.

Of his style and manner, if we think first of the romance-
poetry and then of Chaucer's divine liquidness of diction, his
divine fluidity of movement, it is difficult to speak temperately.
They are irresistible, and justify all the rapture with which
his successors speak of his "gold dewdrops of speech."
Johnson misses the point entirely when he finds fault with
Dryden for ascribing to Chaucer the first refinement of our
numbers, and says that Gower can also show smooth numbers
and easy rhymes. The refinement of our numbers means
something far more than this. A nation may have versifiers
with smooth numbers and easy rhymes, and yet may have
no real poetry at all. Chaucer is the father of our splendid
English poetry; he is our 'well of English undefiled,' because
by the lovely charm of his diction, the lovely charm of his
movement, he makes an epoch and founds a tradition. In
Spenser, Shakespeare, Milton, Keats, we can follow the
tradition of the liquid diction, the fluid movement, of
Chaucer; at one time it is his liquid diction of which in these
poets we feel the virtue, and at another time it is his fluid
movement. And the virtue is irresistible.

[p.
xxxiii] . . . I must yet find room for an example of Chaucer's
virtue. . . . I feel disposed to say that a single line is enough
to show the charm of Chaucer's verse; that merely one line
like this—

'O martyr souded [1] in virginitee!'

has a virtue of manner and movement such as we shall not

[1] [Arnold's note :] The French *soudé;* soldered, fixed fast.

find in all the verse of romance-poetry;—but this is saying
nothing. The virtue is such as we shall not find, perhaps, in
all English poetry, outside the poets whom I have named as
the special inheritors of Chaucer's tradition. A single line,
however, is too little if we have not the strain of Chaucer's
verse well in our memory; let us take a stanza. It is from
The Prioress's Tale, the story of the Christian child murdered
in a Jewry—

> ' My throte is cut unto my nekké-bone
> Saidè this child, and as by way of kinde
> I should have deyd, yea, longè time agone [etc.].

Wordsworth has modernised this Tale, and to feel how delicate
and evanescent is the charm of verse, we have only to read
Wordsworth's first three lines of this stanza after Chaucer's—

> ' My throat is cut unto the bone, I trow,
> Said this young child, and by the law of kind
> I should have died, yea, many hours ago.'

The charm is departed. It is often said that the power of
liquidness and fluidity in Chaucer's verse was dependent
upon a free, a licentious dealing with language such as is now
impossible; upon a liberty, such as Burns too enjoyed, of
making words like *neck, bird*, into a dissyllable by adding to
[p. xxxiv] them, and words like *cause, rhyme*, into a dissyllable by sound
sounding the *e* mute. It is true that Chaucer's fluidity is
conjoined with this liberty, and is admirably served by it;
but we ought not to say that it was dependent upon it. It
was dependent upon his talent. Other poets with a like
liberty do not attain to the fluidity of Chaucer; Burns himself does not attain to it. Poets, again, who have a talent
akin to Chaucer's, such as Shakespeare or Keats, have known
how to attain to his fluidity without the like liberty.

And yet Chaucer is not one of the great classics. His
poetry transcends and effaces, easily and without effort, all
the romance-poetry of Catholic Christendom; it transcends
and effaces all the English poetry contemporary with it, it
transcends and effaces all the English poetry subsequent to it
down to the age of Elizabeth. Of such avail is poetic truth
of substance, in its natural and necessary union with poetic
truth of style. And yet, I say, Chaucer is not one of the

great classics. He has not their accent. What is wanting to him is suggested by the mere mention of the name of the first great classic of Christendom, the immortal poet who died eighty years before Chaucer,—Dante. The accent of such verse as

"In la sua volontade è nostra pace . . ." [1]

is altogether beyond Chaucer's reach ; we praise him, but we feel that this accent is out of the question for him. It may be said that it was necessarily out of the reach of any poet in the England of that stage of growth. Possibly ; but we are to adopt a real, not a historic, estimate of poetry. However, we may account for its absence, something is wanting, then, to the poetry of Chaucer, which poetry must have before it can be placed in the glorious class of the best. And there is no doubt what that something is. It is the σπουδαιότης, the high and excellent seriousness which Aristotle assigns as one of the grand virtues of poetry. The substance of Chaucer's poetry, his view of things and his criticism of life, has largeness, freedom, shrewdness, benignity ; but it has not this high seriousness. Homer's criticism of life has it, Dante's has it, Shakespeare's has it. It is this chiefly which gives to our spirits what they can rest upon ; and with the increasing demands of our modern ages upon poetry, this virtue of giving us what we can rest upon will be more and more highly esteemed. A voice from the slums of Paris, fifty or sixty years after Chaucer, the voice of poor Villon out of his life of riot and crime, has at its happy moments (as, for instance, in the last stanza of *La Belle Heaulmière*) more of this important poetic virtue of seriousness than all the productions of Chaucer. But its apparition in Villon, and in men like Villon, is fitful ; the greatness of the great poets, the power of their criticism of life, is that their virtue is sustained.

[p. xxxv]

To our praise, therefore, of Chaucer as a poet there must be this limitation ; he lacks the high seriousness of the great classics, and therefore an important part of their virtue. Still, the main fact for us to bear in mind about Chaucer is his sterling value according to that real estimate which we

---

[1] So quoted by Arnold ; the original (*Paradiso*, iii, 85) reads : E la sua volontate . . .

firmly adopt for all poets. He has poetic truth of substance though he has not high poetic seriousness, and corresponding to his truth of substance he has an exquisite virtue of style and manner. With him is born our real poetry. . . .

The age of Dryden, together with our whole eighteenth century which followed it, sincerely believed itself to have produced poetical classics of its own, and even to have made advance, in poetry, beyond all its predecessors. Dryden regards as not seriously disputable the opinion 'that the sweetness of English verse was never understood or practised by our fathers.' [1] Cowley could see nothing at all in Chaucer's poetry. Dryden heartily admired it, and, as we have seen, praised its matter admirably; but of its exquisite manner and movement all he can find to say is that 'there is the rude sweetness of a Scotch tune in it, which is natural and pleasing, though not perfect.' Addison, wishing to praise Chaucer's numbers, compares them with Dryden's own. And all through the eighteenth century, and down even to our own times, the stereotyped phrase of approbation for good verse found in our early poetry has been, that it even approached the verse of Dryden, Addison, Pope and Johnson. . . .

[p. xliv] Burns, like Chaucer, comes short of the high seriousness of the great classics. . . . Yet we may say of him [Burns], as of Chaucer, that of life and the world, as they come before [p. xlv] him, his view is large, free, shrewd, benignant,—truly poetic, therefore; and his manner of rendering what he sees is to match. But we must note, at the same time, his great difference from Chaucer. The freedom of Chaucer is heightened in Burns, by a fiery, reckless energy; the benignity of Chaucer deepens, in Burns, into an overwhelming sense of the pathos of things;—of the pathos of human nature, the pathos, also, of non-human nature. Instead of the fluidity of Chaucer's manner, the manner of Burns has spring, bounding swiftness. Burns is by far the greater force, though he has perhaps less charm. The world of Chaucer is fairer, richer, more significant than that of Burns.

---

1 [Note (unpublished) added by Dr. Furnivall:] We must recollect that, till Tyrwhitt, no decent edition of the *Canterbury Tales* was accessible, and till Richard Morris, none of the Minor Poems. So long as printers and editors disregarded Chaucer's final *e* and printed as his, pieces that he never wrote, it was impossible for any readers to appreciate his poetic powers.—F. J. F.

1880. Swinburne, Algernon Charles. *Short Notes on English Poets,* Chaucer, Spenser, the Sonnets of Shakespeare, Milton, [in] The Fortnightly Review, 1880, pp. 708–10. [Reprinted in *Miscellanies,* 1886, pp. 2–6, 88, 150, 152, 175.]

[Mr. W. Rossetti, in his *Lives of Famous Poets,* has selected four of our poets " as composing the supreme quadrilateral of English song."]

[p. 2] It is through no lack of love and reverence for the name of Chaucer that I must question his right, though the first narrative poet of England, to stand on that account beside her first dramatic, her first epic, or her first lyric poet. But, being certainly unprepared to admit his equality with Shakespeare, with Milton, and with Shelley, I would reduce Mr. Rossetti's mystic four to the old sacred number of three. Pure or mere narrative is a form essentially and avowedly inferior to the lyrical or the dramatic form of poetry ; and the finer line of distinction which marks it off from the epic marks it also thereby as inferior.

Of all whose names may claim anything like equality of rank on the roll of national poets—not even excepting Virgil— we may say that Chaucer borrowed most from abroad, and did most to improve whatever he borrowed. I believe it would be but accurate to admit that in all his poems of serious or tragic narrative we hear a French or Italian tongue speaking with a Teutonic accent through English lips. It has utterly unlearnt the native tone and cadence of its natural inflections ; it has perfectly put on the native tone and cadence of a stranger's ; yet it is always what it was at first—*lingua romana in bocca tedesca.* It speaks not only with more vigour but actually with more sweetness than the tongues of its teachers ; but it speaks after its own fashion no other

[p. 3] than the lesson they have taught. Chaucer was in the main a French or Italian poet, lined thoroughly and warmly throughout with the substance of an English humourist. And with this great gift of specially English humour he combined, naturally as it were and inevitably, the inseparable twin-born gift of peculiarly English pathos. . . . Dante represents, at its best and highest, the upper class of the dark ages not less than he represents their Italy ; Chaucer represents their middle class at its best and wisest, not less than he represents their England ; Villon represents their lower class at its worst and its best alike, even more than he represents their France. And of these three the English middle class, being incomparably the happiest and wisest, is indisputably, considering the common circumstances of their successive times, the least likely to have left us the highest example of all poetry then possible to men. And of their three legacies, precious and wonderful as it is, the Englishman's is accordingly the least wonderful and the least precious. The poet of the sensible and prosperous middle class in England had less to suffer and to sing than the theosophic aristocrat of Italy, or the hunted and hungry vagabond. . . .

[p. 5]   But in happy perfection of manhood the great and fortunate Englishman almost more exceeds his great and unfortunate fellow-singers than he is exceeded by them in depth of passion and height of rapture, in ardour and intensity of vision or of sense. With the single and sublimer exception of Sophocles, he seems to me the happiest of all great poets on record ; their standing type and sovereign example of noble and manly happiness.

[p. 152]   [Comparison between Chaucer and Wordsworth. Chaucer superior in breadth of human interest, in simplicity of varied sympathies, in straightforward and superb command of his materials as an artist, in warmth and wealth of humour, in consummate power of narrative and in childlike manfulness of compassionate or joyous emotion; but Wordsworth's sublimity . is worth all the rest put together.]

[This last paragraph was added in 1886.]

1881. Braddon, Mary Elizabeth (Mrs. Maxwell). *Asphodel*, 3 vols.

[Miss Braddon took all the chapter headings of this novel from Chaucer.]

[" The reason of these quotations was this. Miss Braddon's ' *Vixen* ' came out serially ; and week by week in the dull London winter brought the beautiful wilful heroine hunting in the New Forest and loving her horses and hounds as a fresh bright scene to one reader, F. J. Furnivall. He delighted in the book, and told Mrs. Maxwell so with enthusiasm. She asked him to visit her at Richmond, and afterwards, meaning to please him, a Chaucer and Shakspere man, put the above Chaucer headings to the chapters in her next novel, and laid several of its scenes by Avonside near Stratford. When the work was published, she sent a copy to Dr. Furnivall, and he, not knowing the kind intent of it, was shocked to find its charming heroine Daphne, made to commit suicide at the end. So, in his letter of thanks to the generous authoress, he accused her of being a murderess, for killing his favourite character. Then Mrs. Maxwell heaped coals of fire on his head by telling him how she had tried to please him, and how he ought to have seen from the first that Daphne's sad end was inevitable, and was prepared for from her first appearance. Whereupon he repented, and apologized." F. J. F.]

1881. Poole, Henry. *Westminster Abbey: A Study on Poets' Corner,* [in] The Antiquary, October 1881, vol. iv, pp. 137, 139.

[p. 139]   Having alluded to the probability that the table-tomb of Chaucer was once against the screen of St. Benedict's Chapel, it may not be inopportune here to follow out the probable story of it.

The tomb proper is evidently due to the period of the death of Chaucer. Its quatre-foils bear his shield of arms, and around at least three of the sides with [*sic*] the verge moulding, which probably bore a painted inscription. In 1556, there was perhaps some necessity for totally removing the tomb, of which advantage was taken by Chaucer's admirer, Nicholas Brigham, to place it where it now is, and add to it a handsome, though debased, canopy of Purbeck marble, and also a similar marble slab, with a new inscription in Latin, that of the marble table having become decayed and illegible. This slab has undergone great decay and disintegration, so much so as to almost totally obscure the inscription, as reported by Neale in 1823 [or rather by E. W. Brayley in his *History and Antiquities of the Abbey Church of St. Peter, Westminster,* illustrated by J. P. Neale, 1818–23, vol. ii, 1823, *q.v.* above]. Fifty years' more disintegration followed with still further obscuration, when the writer closely scrutinized and cleansed the slab, discovering traces of all the letters but four. Without any attempt to strengthen the engraving, the lettering was developed by painting all the remaining traces with gold-coloured paint, and with the same pigment reproducing the four absent letters ; and now the inscription of 1558 is quite distinct and perfectly durable.

The table of the tomb has lately been fully cleansed of dirt and adhesions, beneath which the moulding, as well as much of the surface, was found still to retain its original polish, which the adhesion had preserved. Now the table displays a fine specimen of the best Purbeck marble, which need never become dull again.

1883. Coote, Henry Charles. *Chaucer's Ten-Syllable Verse,* [in] The Antiquary, July 1883, vol. viii, pp. 5–8.

[p. 5]   Chaucer's *Troilus* was not only the first heroic poem and the first real display of poetic genius in the language of mediæval England, but was the starting-point and departure

from which English metre took its best and still prevailing
form. . . .

[p. 7]   At the very threshold of his task [that of rendering the
Filostrato into English] he had a problem to solve. . . .
There was no English verse at all fit for the transfer of the
Italian. He must accordingly invent a new one. . . .

He knew of two metres only, always excepting those used for
ballads and such like, which were of course out of the question
here. Of these two metres, one was too short as the other was
too long for his taste. I mean, of course, the eight-syllabled
distichs of himself and Gower, and the popular twelve-syllable
[p. 8]   verse such as is exhibited in the rough tale of Gamelin. . . .

He therefore elected to invent for the nonce an entirely new
metre of his own, and to apply it to his new task. There was
a mean between eight and twelve, viz. ten. He accordingly
invented a verse of ten syllables with varying and appropriate
cæsuræ ; and utilized his new invention by translating the
Filostrato into it ; and posterity ratified his choice by adopting
it as the only verse to be employed upon themes either great
or graceful. . . .

The consequences of this invention of the ten-syllable metre
it is impossible to exaggerate or over-estimate. The obvious
outcome of it is simply this and no other : without it we
should have had no Shakespeare, Milton, Dryden, or Pope, in
the sense in which we now have these great masters. To
convince us of this, we have only to imagine *Othello* and
Hamlet, not as we now have them through the remote leader-
ship of Chaucer in a verse framed upon his model, but told
either in the lilting measure of Calderon, or the drawling
Alexandrines of France. . . . Of course Milton must have
been better than Cædmon, and Pope would have done his best
to surpass Butler even in his own light measure, but that is all.

From all this Chaucer saved English literature and the
English race. . . .

1883. Fagan, Charles G. *Chaucer in Oxenforde*, [in] The Oxford
Magazine, Feb. 14, 1883, vol. i, pp. 66–7.

At Oxenforde I sawe in that citee
Of yongë clerkes a ful gret compagnie,
and I wol nowe you tellen everich on
hir wone and eke of hir condicion.

An aesthete was there as I schell you tell,
that hadde of artë lernèd every del ;
of Michael-Ange and Raffael and Giote
he couldë glosen of hem al by rote.

.   .   .   .

A Schipman was there eke, a bote captáin
that woldë souffre mochel toil and payne
teachand the freschë clerkes howe to rowe,
[etc.].

1883. Koch, John.   *A Critical Edition of some of Chaucer's 'Minor Poems,'* Berlin.

[An introduction treating of the orthography, etc., of the early MSS. of Chaucer's Works is followed by a collated text of I. *An ABC.*   II. *Chaucers Wordes vnto Adam, his owen Scriveyn.*   III. *The Former Age.*   IV. *Fortune.*   V. *Truth.* VI. *Gentilesse.*   VII. *Lack of Stedfastnesse.*   VIII. *Lenvoy de Chaucer a Bukton.*   IX. *Lenvoy de Chaucer a Scogan.* X. *La Compleinte de Chaucer a sa Bourse Voide* ; followed by notes on each.]

1884. à Beckett, Gilbert Arthur, and **Stanford,** Sir Charles Villiers. *The Canterbury Pilgrims,* Opera in 3 Acts, written by Gilbert à Beckett, composed by C. Villiers Stanford.

[The scene of the 1st Act is the exterior of the Tabard Inn, Southwark, at close of the 14th century.   The characters include Sir Christopher Synge, a knight of the shire, Geoffry Blount, the Host of the Tabard, his wife and daughter and apprentice, two other apprentices and Hal o' the Chepe. In Act i, sc. 3, the Pilgrims enter in twos and threes slowly assembling, the Merchant, Clerk, Doctor of Physick, etc., all with appropriate music.

This opera, written for the Carl Rosa Company, was first performed at Drury Lane, on Wednesday, April 23rd, 1884.]

1884. Pitt-Taylor, Frank.   *The Canterbury Tales;* being selections from the Tales of Geoffrey Chaucer rendered into Modern English with close adherence to the Language of the Poet.

[Brief Preface, followed by modernizations of the Prologue and Tales by the Knight, Man of Law, Prioress, Monk, Nun's Priest, Doctor, Pardoner, Wife of Bath, Clerk, Second Nun, Canon's Yeoman and Manciple, with occasional omission of various passages.   The Prologue begins :]

When April with its sweet refreshing rain,
After the drought of March, hath reached again
The roots, and bathed each vein with gentle shower,
Of which virtue engendered is the flower;
When, too, the Zephyr, with her sweetest breath,
Inspiréd hath in every grove and heath
The tender crops, and when the youthful sun. . . .

1884. Swinburne, Algernon Charles. *A Midsummer Holiday*, iii, *On a Country Road*, pp. 9–11. (Poems, 1904, 6 vols., vol. vi, pp. 9–10.)

[p. 9]　　Along these low pleached lanes, on such a day,
So soft a day as this, through shade and sun,
With glad grave eyes that scanned the glad wild way,
And heart still hovering o'er a song begun,
And smile that warmed the world with benison,
Our father, lord long since of lordly rhyme,
Long since hath haply ridden, when the lime
Bloomed broad above him, flowering where he came.
Because thy passage once made warm this clime,
Our father Chaucer, here we praise thy name.

　　　·　　·　　·　　·　　·　　·　　·　　·

[p. 10]　　Each turn of the old wild road whereon we stray,
Meseems, might bring us face to face with one
Whom seeing we could not but give thanks, and pray
For England's love our father and her son
To speak with us as once in days long done
With all men, sage and churl and monk and mime,
Who knew not as we know the soul sublime,
That sang for song's love more than lust of fame.
Yet, though this be not, yet, in happy time,
Our father Chaucer, here we praise thy name.

Friend, even as bees about the flowering thyme,
Years crowd on years, till hoar decay begrime
Names once beloved; but, seeing the sun the same,
As birds of autumn fain to praise the prime,
Our father Chaucer, here we praise thy name.

1885. Collins, John Churton. *The Predecessors of Shakespeare*, [in] The Quarterly Review, Oct. 1885, vol. clxi, p. 338. [Revised and enlarged in *Essays and Studies*, 1895, pp. 106–7.]

The verdict of the age which immediately succeeds them

[p. 107] [prose writers] is, as a rule, final. . . . How different has been the fate of poets! Take Chaucer. In 1500 his popularity was at its height. During the latter part of the sixteenth century it began to decline. From that date till the end of William III's reign—in spite of the influence which he undoubtedly exercised over Spenser, and in spite of the respectful allusions to him in Sidney, Puttenham, Drayton, and Milton—his fame had become rather a tradition than a reality. In the following age the good-natured tolerance of Dryden was succeeded by the contempt of Addison and the supercilious patronage of Pope. Between 1700 and 1782 nothing seemed more probable than that the writings of the first of England's narrative poets would live chiefly in the memory of antiquarians. In little more than half a century afterwards we find him placed, with Shakespeare and Milton, on the highest pinnacle of poetic renown.

1887. Marshall, Isabel, **Porter,** Lela, and **Skeat,** Walter William. *Ryme Index to the Manuscript Texts of Chaucer's Minor Poems.* By Miss I. Marshall and Miss L. Porter. With an introduction and an appendix of ryme-indexes to some spurious poems . . . by W. W. Skeat.

[For use with the Parallel-Text edition, Chaucer Society, and reissued in 1889 for use with the One-Text edition.]

1887. Morris, William. *Feudal England,* [in] The Commonweal, nos. 84–87. [Reprinted, with slight alterations (as Lecture 3), in *Signs of Change,* 1887, pp. 73–5.]

[No. 87. p. 282] [The central period of the Middle Ages in England] has a literature of its own too, somewhat akin to its art, yet inferior to it, and lacking its unity, since there is a double stream in it. On the one hand the Court poet, the Gentleman, Chaucer, with his Italianizing metres, and his formal recognition of the classical stories; on which, indeed, he builds a superstructure of the quaintest and most unadulterated mediævalism, as gay and bright as the architecture which his eyes beheld and his pen pictured for us, so clear, defined and elegant; a sunny world even amidst its violence and passing troubles, like those of a happy child, the worst of them are amusement rather than a grief to the onlookers; a world that scarcely needed hope in its eager life of adventure and love, amidst the sunlit blossoming meadows, and green woods and white begilded manor-houses. A kindly and human muse is Chaucer's, nevertheless, interested in and amused by all life, but of her very nature devoid of strong aspirations for the future; and that all the more, since, though the strong devotion and fierce piety of the ruder Middle Ages had by this time waned, and the Church was more often lightly mocked than either feared or loved, still the *habit* of looking on this life as part of another yet remained : the world is fair and full of adventure; kind men and true and noble are in it to make one happy; fools also to laugh at, and rascals to be resisted, yet not wholly condemned; and when this world is over we shall still go on living in another which is a part of this. Of this picture, note all and be as merry as you may, never forgetting that you are alive and that it is good to live.

That is the spirit of Chaucer's poetry; but alongside of it existed yet the ballad poetry of the people . . . [and what] you may call Lollard poetry, the great example of which is William Langland's " Piers Plowman." It is no bad corrective to Chaucer, and in *form* at least belongs wholly to the popular side.

[For Skeat see below, 1888.]

1887. Stevenson, Robert Louis. *A Portrait*, [in] *Underwoods.* (Works, Edinburgh Edition, 1894–8, 28 vols., vol. xiv, p. 123.)

I am " the smiler with the knife ". . .

1888. Furnivall, Frederick James. *Note*, [in] The Academy, Dec. 22, 1888, Notes and News, vol. xxxiv, p. 403.

Dr. Furnivall writes :

" May I appeal through you for two volunteer editors for the Chaucer Society ? . . . I want (1) somebody with access to a large library, to compile ' The Praise of Chaucer '—all allusions to him from his own day to (say) Dryden, and the chief ones since; and (2) a history and record man to write an ' England in Chaucer's Time ' (1300–1400)—a better Godwin. . . . The ' England in Chaucer's Time ' would form a good foundation for an after ' History of England in the Fourteenth Century '—a book much wanted."

[The present work attempts to fulfil, and in some respects exceeds, the first of these ideals laid down by Dr. Furnivall.]

1889. Bright, James W. Review of *Chaucer's Minor Poems*, ed. **W. W.** Skeat (1888), [in] Modern Language Notes, Baltimore, June 1889, vol. iv, pp. 359–63.

[p. 359] Dr. Furnivall has made an appeal for "somebody with access to a large library to compile 'The Praise of Chaucer'— —all allusions to him from his own day to (say) Dryden, and the chief ones since " [*Academy*, Dec. 22, 1888]. This appeal, it is hoped, will soon find a fitting response ; for a history of opinion relating to Chaucer as a poet, which would be made possible by such a collection of evidence, would con- stitute a novel and important adjunct to the history of English Poetry.   Just as the characteristics of the dramatists of the Restoration Period may be understood by their treatment of the plays of Shakespeare, so the repute of Chaucer at any given time will serve to reveal much of the culture and of the poetic fashions of that time.

[For Dr. Furnivall's appeal, to which the present work is a response, *see* immediately above, 1888.]

1890. Koch, John. *The Chronology of Chaucer's Writings, &c.* (Chaucer Soc., 2nd series, 27.)

[A carefully reasoned argument, carrying forward the researches of ten Brink, Morley and Skeat.   At the end are notes by Skeat on some doubtful points.]

1890. Manly, John Matthews. *Observations on the Language of Chaucer's Legend of Good Women*, [in] Harvard Studies and Notes in Philology and Literature, 1893, vol. ii, pp. 1–120.

[Part of a dissertation prepared in 1890 ; modelled on Professor G. L. Kittredge's similar study of Troilus, then (1893) in the press, *q.v.* below, 1894.   Based on the Cambridge MS. Gg. 4. 27].

1891. [To Rosemounde.]

[Professor Skeat discovered the text of the balade *To Rosemounde* in MS. Rawlinson Poet. 163, and contributed it to the Athenaeum, April 4, 1891 ; he also had it privately printed in a double leaflet at about the same time, but we have not been able to see this. *See* Hammond, *Chaucer,* p. 460.]

1891. Butler, Samuel. *The Wife of Bath,* [Note, dated 1891, in] The Notebooks of Samuel Butler, 1912, p. 262.

There are Canterbury Pilgrims every Sunday in summer who start from close to the old Tabard, only they go by the South-Eastern Railway and come back the same day for five shillings. And, what is more, they are just the same sort of people. If they do not go to Canterbury they go by the *Clacton Belle* to Clacton-on-Sea. There is not a Sunday the whole summer through but you may find all Chaucer's pilgrims, man and woman for man and woman, on board the *Lord of the Isles* or the *Clacton Belle.* Why, I have seen the Wife of Bath on the *Lord of the Isles* myself. She was eating her luncheon off an *Ally Sloper's Half Holiday,* which was spread out upon her knees.

1891. K[er], W[illiam] P[aton]. *Of Chaucer's Rosemounde, Balade to yᵉ Makeres,* [in] The Oxford Magazine, April 29, 1891, vol. ix, p. 305.

[Occasioned by Professor Skeat's discovery of *To Rosemounde.*]

Maisters that in the goodly sees divyne
the brighte Apolo with the laurer grounde,
we thanken yow that of youre hye ingyne
on erthe yit the crommes ben yfounde :
loo Aristotle in Egipte under grounde
that of Athenes wroot the governaunce,
and Chaucer thy balade of Rosemounde
of joye encresing oure inheritaunce.

.   .   .   .

L'Enuoy.

Go litel lewede rimes cercling rounde,
loketh ye be nat blamed of bobaunce
ther sortil [sic] lore is and the craft profounde
of joye encresing our inheritaunce.

1891. Lounsbury, Thomas Raynsford. *Studies in Chaucer: His Life and Writings.* In three volumes, New York, 1891. [The London issue, 1892, is in B. M.].

[The eight chapters or " monographs " which make up the book are as follows :]

Vol. I. Chapter   I.—The Life of Chaucer.
   „   Chapter II.—The Chaucer Legend.
   ,,   Chapter III.—The Text of Chaucer.

[Vol. iii, p. 439] I have sought to show that Chaucer was not only a great artist, but that he became so at the cost of time and labour; that in him, standing at the fountain-head of English literature, the critical spirit was as highly developed as the creative. . . . If we need further confirmation, we can find it in one marked change that took place in his literary methods. In his earlier work he introduces constantly characters that are merely personifications of qualities or acts or sentiments. In so doing he followed the practice of his immediate predecessors. As he advanced in knowledge and taste he shook himself free from the trammels of this temporary fashion. He abandoned almost entirely the field of abstractions in which the men of his time delighted, and in which his contemporary Langland was contented to remain. For the shadowy beings who dwell in the land of types he substituted living men and women; for the allegorical representations of feelings and beliefs, the direct outpourings of passion. Changes of method such as these are not the result of freak or accident. Chaucer, accordingly, must stand or fall not merely by our opinion of what he did, but by our knowledge that what he did was done consciously. . . .

It is impossible to take final leave of the poet without some notice of what is on the whole the most pronounced character-[p. 441] istic of his style. This is the uniformly low level upon which he moves. There is no other author in our tongue who has clung so closely and so persistently to the language of common life. Such a characteristic appealed strongly to the men who led the revolt against the artificial diction that prevailed in the poetry of the last century. It attracted in particular the attention of Wordsworth. The course of his predecessor he cited as an authority for the one which he himself adopted. . . .

There have been many men of genius who have been able to say grand things grandly. To the fewest of the few is reserved the achievement of the far harder task of discoursing of mean things without discoursing meanly; of recounting the prosaic events of life without becoming prosaic one's self; of narrating them in the plainest terms, and yet investing them with a poetic charm. It is in the power of genius only to accomplish this at all; but it is by no means in the power of all genius.

[p. 442] It is because he stayed so persistently on these low levels that Chaucer was enabled to combine with apparent ease characteristics and methods that are often deemed incompatible. His words are the more effective because their very simplicity makes upon the mind the impression of understatement. The imagination of the reader fills in and exaggerates the details which have been left half-told. It is owing to this restraint of expression that whatever he says is not only at all times and in all places free from literary vulgarity, it never loses the dignity that belongs, as well in letters as in life, to consummate high-breeding. There is an exquisite urbanity in his manner which gives it attractiveness as pervasive and yet as indefinable as that which the subtle evanescent flavour of arch allusion imparts to his matter. I do not mean by this to convey the idea that Chaucer abounds in ornate and brilliant passages, or that he is constantly saying remarkable things in a remarkable way. It is simply that in dealing with the common he is never common-place. . . . As a further result of this absolute naturalness, he is enabled to pass from the gravest to the lightest topics without giving the reader the

[p. 443] slightest sensation of shock. . . . His freedom, indeed, verges at times upon audacity. In the Knight's tale, for illustration, following close upon the high-wrought description of the great tournament comes the recital of the methods taken by the physicians to save the life of the victor in the struggle. The failure they meet with is told in the simplest terms. Their efforts were fruitless because they received no help from nature. Suddenly the poet interposes his own comment on the uselessness, under such conditions, of the medical art in words like these :—

> " And certainly there nature will not wirche
> Farewell, physic!   Go! bear the man to church!"

With this quaint expression of personal opinion, he passes at
once to the pathetic parting-scene between the dying lover
and the woman for whom he is about to die. Yet these rapid
transitions do not produce upon the mind any effect of inap-
propriateness or incongruity. Tears and laughter stand side
by side in Chaucer's verse as they do in life . . .

[p. 444]   I am not claiming for Chaucer that he is one of the few
supremest poets of the race. His station is near them, but he
is not of them. Yet, whatever may be the rank we accord
him among the writers of the world's chief literatures, the
position he holds in his own literature is one that can no
longer be shaken by criticism or disturbed by denial. . . . To
one alone among the writers of our own literature is he
inferior. Nor even by him has he been surpassed in every
way. There are characteristics in which he has no superior,
and, it may be right to add, in which he has no equal. . . .
There is one particular in which his merits in reference to the
literature are transcendent. He overcame its natural tendencies
to a dull seriousness which could sometimes be wrought into
vigorous invective, but had little power to fuse the spiritual
element of poetry with the purely intellectual. Into the stolid
English nature, which may be earnest, but evinces an almost
irresistible inclination towards heaviness, he brought a lightness, a grace, a delicacy of fancy, a refined sportiveness even
upon the most unrefined themes which had never been known
[p. 445] before save on the most infinitesimal scale, and has not been
known too much since.

Nor is this the only distinctive characteristic in which
Chaucer excels. There is no other English author so absolutely
free, not merely from effort, but from the remotest suggestion
of effort. Shakspeare mounts far higher; yet with him
there are times when we seem to hear the flapping of the
wings, to be vaguely conscious that he is lashing his imagination to put forth increased exertions. But in Chaucer no
slightest trace of strain is to be detected. As on the lower levels
the line never labours, so on the higher he never makes the
impression that he is trying to make an impression. It is the
absolute ease with which he rises that often prevents our perceiving how rapidly he has risen. . . . Nor is it alone for the
naturalness and ease which result from this union of strength

and simplicity that the greatest of his successors have delighted
to honour the poet.   Full as willingly have they paid homage
to the qualities of character displayed in his works as to those
of intellect; in perfect serenity of spirit as well as in perfect
sanity of view; in the large-hearted toleration which could
[p. 446] not speak bitterly even of the vicious; in the gracious worldliness which never hardened into the callousness of insensibility;
in the manly tenderness which never degenerated into sentimentality; in the repose of conscious strength which never
wearied itself or worried itself in striving for effect;—in all
these characteristics the royal line of English poets has never
refused to acknowledge the supremacy of him whom it
recognizes as its founder.

1892. Kittredge, George Lyman.   *The Authorship of the English
Romaunt of the Rose,* [in] Harvard Studies and Notes in Philology
and Literature, Boston, Mass., 1892, vol. i, pp. 1–65.

[A detailed examination and rejection of Lounsbury's claim
that the M. E. *Romaunt* is Chaucer's, in his *Studies in Chaucer*,
q.v. above, 1891.   Professor Kittredge says in conclusion :]

[p. 65]   The affirmative evidence brought forward by Mr. Lounsbury,
when reduced to its lowest terms, we have found to be
entirely consistent with the belief that the translation is not
by Chaucer, but by an imitator.   The negative evidence, on
the other hand, from dialect, grammar, and metre, if it does
not show conclusively that Chaucer and the translator were
two persons, still creates the strongest kind of probability in
favour of that supposition.   We must therefore be allowed to
prefer the theory that is in accordance with all the facts to the
theory that is strongly opposed to the most significant of them,
and to believe that the *Romaunt* is not Chaucer's, with the
possible exception of the first seventeen hundred lines.

1893. Pollard, Alfred William.   *Chaucer,* [one of the] *Literature
Primers,* edited by J. R. Green.

[Dr. Furnivall was originally invited to write the Primer
on Chaucer for this series: *see* above, Green, 1877.   In the
little book, as finally written by Mr. Pollard, the chapters
are: Introduction; Chaucer, the King's Servant; Chaucer,
the Student; The Contents and Order of Chaucer's Writings
(also the Canon); Poems of Chaucer's First Period; Poems
of Chaucer's Second Period—Chaucer at work on Italian

Models; The Canterbury Tales; Later Minor Poems—Chaucer's rank as a Poet (a comparison with Shakespeare); Appendix—Chaucer's Metre and Versification—Spurious and Doubtful Works.   The author, while summarising the best knowledge, offers throughout much fresh and suggestive criticism.]

[p. 75]   It was by service in the King's Court, on diplomatic missions, and at the Custom House, that a living had to be earned and a substantial position won; and it is to these objects, trivial in his case as we may now think them, that
[p. 76] Chaucer appears to have devoted the best years of his life. . . . If Shakspere had died in his thirtieth year he would have been remembered as a botcher of a few poor plays, and the author of *Venus and Adonis*, the *Midsummer Night's Dream*, and *Richard III.*   Where Shakspere botched Chaucer translated, and the charm of a few hundred lines in the *Death of Blaunche* and the pathos of the stories of *Grisilde* and *Constance* are the chief titles to remembrance of all the work he did on the younger side of forty.   From the very first he is distinguished from his contemporaries by the music of his verse; but the humour, the insight into character, the knowledge of life, the entire mastery of words, the essential qualities, that is, which we now connect with his name, all came to Chaucer exceptionally late.

[p. 116]   The portraits [in the *Prologue*], we should note, are all such as one traveller might draw of another.   There is no attempt to show that the best of the pilgrims had their weak points, and the worst their good ones.   For the best Chaucer has hearty admiration, for the worst a boundless tolerance, which yet only thinly cloaks the keenest satire.   One and all he views from his holiday standpoint, building up his descriptions with such notes as he would naturally gather as he rode along with them on his pilgrimage—notes of dress, of speech, of manner, of their talk about themselves and their doings, until we can see his fellow-pilgrims as clearly as if we too had mounted our rouncies and ridden along with them.

1894. Chaucer's Canterbury Tales, edited with notes and introduction by Alfred W. Pollard. 2 vols. (In Macmillan's " Eversley Series.")

[The text is preceded by an Introduction in which, after a statement as to the history of the edition and its relation to the projected Library Edition and as to the treatment of the text, the editor outlines Chaucer's progress from slavish translation in the early *Second Nonnes Tale*, through the *Clerkes Tale*, *Troilus* and *Knightes Tale*, to complete freedom from his source or analogue in his latest work, such as the *Prioresses*, *Reves* and *Pardoneres Tales*.]

1894-97. The Complete Works of Geoffrey Chaucer. Edited . . . by . . . W. W. Skeat, 7 vols.

[The chief contents are: Vol. I, Life of Chaucer, etc.; Romaunt of the Rose and Minor Poems, with introductions and notes. (See also vol. iv below, for additions to Minor Poems.)

Vol. II: Boethius and Troilus, with introductions and notes.

Vol. III: House of Fame; Legend of Good Women; Astrolabe, with introductions and notes. An Account of the Sources of the Canterbury Tales.

Vol. IV: The Canterbury Tales, in groups A to I, with the Tale of Gamelyn as an appendix; Introduction on the MSS. and the plan of the Tales adopted. The Introduction contains also three Minor Poems additional to those in vol. i.

Vol. V: Notes to the Canterbury Tales, with an Introduction on the Chaucer Canon; the earlier editions; the Text of the Canterbury Tales; Chaucer's scansion, accentuation and pronunciation; with rules for reading and a note on modernised spelling.

Vol. VI: General Introduction, discussing the texts of the various pieces; the editor's obligations to others; the dialect of Chaucer; his Kenticisms; pronunciation; scansion and accents; open and close *o* and *e*, etc.; rime; assonances; final *y* and *ye*; metres and forms of verse; analysis of Chaucer's language and grammar; versification; his authorities. Glossaries, indices, etc.

Vol. VII (Supplementary Volume), *Chaucerian and other Pieces*, contains:

Introduction on the (selected) apocryphal pieces, generally and individually, and the texts as follows, concluding with indices, etc.:

    I. Testament of Love (Usk).
    II. Plowman's Tale.
    III. Jack Upland.
    IV. Gower's Praise of Peace.
    V. Hoccleve's Letter of Cupid.

    VI. To the Kinge's most noble Grace
        To the Lordes and Knightes of the }Hoccleve.
        Garter
    VII. Scogan's Moral Ballade.
   VIII. Lydgate's Complaint of the Black Knight.
     IX. Lydgate's Flour of Curtesye.
      X. Lydgate's Balade in Commendation of our Lady.
     XI. To my Soverain Lady (Lydgate).
    XII. Ballad of Good Counsel (Lydgate).
   XIII. Beware of Doubleness (Lydgate).
   XIV. Balade Warning Men to Beware of Deceitful
        Women (Lydgate).
    XV. Three Sayings (Lydgate).
   XVI. Ros's La Belle Dame sans Mercy.
  XVII. Henryson's Testament of Cressid.
 XVIII. Clanvowe's Cuckoo and Nightingale.
   XIX. Envoy to Alison.
    XX. Flower and Leaf.
   XXI. Assembly of Ladies.
  XXII. Goodly Balade (Lydgate).
 XXIII. Go Forth, King (Lydgate).
 XXIV. Court of Love.
  XXV. A Virelai.
 XXVI. Prosperity (John Walton).
XXVII. Leaulte vault Richesse.
XXVIII. Sayings printed by Caxton.
 XXIX. Balade in Praise of Chaucer.

[vol. vi. p. ix] In the first place, my endeavour has been to produce a
thoroughly sound text, founded solely on the best MSS. and
the earliest prints, which shall satisfy at once the requirements
of the student of language and the reader who delights in
poetry. In the interest of both, it is highly desirable that
Chaucer's genuine works should be kept apart from those
which were recklessly associated with them in the early
editions, and even in modern editions have been but imperfectly suppressed. It was also desirable, or rather absolutely
necessary, that the recent advances in our knowledge of middle-
English grammar and phonetics should be rightly utilized,
and that no verbal form should be allowed to appear which
would have been unacceptable to a good scribe of the
fourteenth century.

I have also provided a large body of illustrative notes, many
of them gathered from the works of my predecessors, but

enlarged by illustrations due to my own reading during a long course of years, and by many others due to the labours of the [p. x] most recent critics. The number of allusions that have been traced to their origin during the past fifteen years is considerable; and much additional light has thus been thrown upon Chaucer's method of treating his originals. . . .

[p. xviii] As regards the texts, my chief debt is to the Chaucer Society, which means, practically, Dr. Furnivall, through whose zeal and energy so many splendid and accurate prints of the MSS. have been produced, thus rendering the actual readings and spellings of the scribes accessible to students in all countries. It is obvious that, but for such work, no edition of Chaucer could have been attempted without an enormous increase of labour and a prodigal expenditure of time.

1894. Kittredge, George Lyman. *Observations on the Language of Chaucer's Troilus*, Chaucer Society, 1894 [issue for 1891]. (Also issued as vol. iii of Harvard Studies and Notes in Philology and Literature, Boston, 1894.)

[A detailed and most valuable linguistic study, based on the readings of four MSS.: Campsall, Harl. 2280; Camb., Gg. 4, 27; and Harl. 3943, all as edited for the Chaucer Society by Dr. Furnivall. It consists of (1) a Grammatical Chapter in which the forms occurring in *Troilus* are recorded and analysed; and (2) a Metrical Chapter, with special reference to final *e*.]

1894. Pollard, Alfred William. *See* above, *Chaucer's Canterbury Tales.*

1894–7. Skeat, Walter William. *See* above, *The Complete Works of Geoffrey Chaucer.*

1895. Ker, William Paton. *The Poetry of Chaucer*, [*review of*] *The Complete Works of Geoffrey Chaucer*, edited by the Rev. Walter W. Skeat, [in] The Quarterly Review, April, 1895, vol. clxxx, pp. 521–48. [The greater part of this article, that which is more directly concerned with Chaucer's poetry, *i.e.* pp. 534–47, is reprinted, with slight verbal changes and omissions, in *Essays on Medieval Literature*, by W. P. Ker, 1905, pp. 76–100.]

[The importance of Skeat's edition. Its supreme merit is that it has cleared the poems of Chaucer from blunders of language and rhythm, which in former editions interrupted the flow of the verse, pp. 521–2. Chaucer's art and versification, with especial reference to Dryden's criticism, pp. 522–3.]

[p. 522]   With regard to some of the strongest parts of Chaucer's poetry, no later writer has been able to add anything essentially new to the estimate given by Dryden. 'Here is God's plenty' is still the best criticism ever uttered on the 'Canterbury Tales.'

[There is some justification for Dryden's censure of Chaucer's verse, p. 523. Decay of metrical ability after Chaucer, and Skeat's method in adopting readings, pp. 524–5. Examples of Skeat's emendations and readings, pp. 525–6. Account of the contents of the volumes, with the comment that "the Clarendon Press has done little to relieve the general aspect of sobriety, much at variance with the demeanour of the contents, and very unlike the appearance of the illuminated books from which the poems are copied," pp. 526–7. Complaint of the over-insistence on Dr. Furnivall's classification of the groups of the Canterbury Tales, pp. 527–8. On Skeat's introductions, his metrical symbols, his remarks on Chaucer's vowels and Kentish forms and knowledge of Old French verse—any possible flaws in which do not prejudice his handling of the texts, pp. 528–31. The texts of the *Romaunt*, *Troylus* and the *Legende* acknowledged and praised, p. 532. Skeat's abstention from literary criticism, and reference of the reader to Lowell's essay, deprecated, p. 533. Comparison of Chaucer and Dante in their use of mediæval habit and fashion, pp. 534–5. Historical commentary on Chaucer inevitable and useful, pp. 535–6. On Skeat's statement of the debt in the *Hous of Fame* to Dante, and the general independence of Chaucer's poem, p. 537. How much of Chaucer's genius can be seen outside the *Canterbury Tales*, pp. 537–8.]

[p. 538]   It is difficult to speak moderately of Chaucer's "Troilus." It is the first great modern book in that kind where the most characteristic modern triumphs of the literary art have been won; in the kind to which belong the great books of Cervantes, of Fielding, and of their later pupils—that form of story which is not restricted in its matter in any way, but is capable of taking in comprehensively all or any part of the aspects and humours of life. No other mediæval poem is rich and full in the same way as "Troilus" is full of varieties of character and mood. It is a tragic novel, and it is also strong enough to pass the scrutiny of that Comic Muse who detects the impostures of inflated heroic and romantic poetry. More than this, it has the effective aid of the Comic Muse in that alliance of tragedy and comedy which makes an end of all the old distinctions and limitations of narrative and drama.

[*Troilus* and the *Filostrato*, pp. 538–9. The dignity, beauty and proportion of *Troilus*, pp. 539–40. The *Knightes Tale* and the *Teseide*, pp. 540–1. Chaucer's different handling of the *Troilus* and *Knightes Tale* themes, pp. 541–3. Chaucer's changes of handling throughout his works, p. 543. The *House of Fame* an indulgence in mediæval vanities, pp. 544–5. Contradictions and problems of the *Canterbury Tales*, pp. 544–7.]

1896. The Works of Geoffrey Chaucer, now newly imprinted. Edited by F. S. Ellis ; ornamented with pictures designed by Sir Edward Burne-Jones, and engraved on wood by W. H. Hooper. Printed by me, William Morris, at the Kelmscott Press, Hammersmith, 1896.

[The great folio ' Kelmscott Chaucer.' It took three years and four months to prepare and execute, the printing alone occupying a year and nine months. It has 87 pictures by Burne-Jones ; and, in addition, a full page woodcut title, 14 large borders, 18 borders for the pictures, and 26 large initial words, as well as ornamental initial letters, all designed by William Morris. See The Life of William Morris, by J. W. Mackail, 1899, vol. ii, chaps. xx, xxi.]

1896. Morris, William ; **Ellis,** F. S. ; **Burne-Jones,** Sir Edward ; **Hooper,** W. H. *See* supra : *The Works of Geoffrey Chaucer* (' Kelmscott Chaucer ').

1898. The Works of Geoffrey Chaucer, edited by Alfred W. Pollard, H. Frank Heath, Mark H. Liddell, W. S. McCormick. (The Globe Edition.)

[p. ix] [Preface by A. W. Pollard.]

In the division of labour . . . I have myself remained responsible for the *Canterbury Tales*, the *Legende of Good Women*, the Glossary, and the General Introduction ; Professor Liddell has taken the *Boece*, the *Treatise on the Astrolabe*, and the *Romaunt of the Rose ;* Professor McCormick, *Troilus and Criseyde ;* Dr. Heath, the *Hous of Fame, Parlement of Foules*, and all the shorter pieces. . . . We [the editors] all believe that in the present state of our knowledge the most conservative treatment, consistent with the necessities of common sense and the known rules of Chaucerian usage, is also the best.

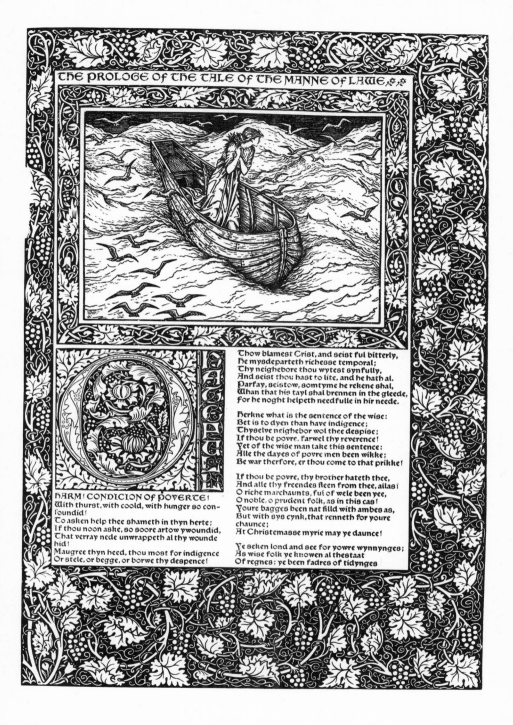

THE PROLOGE OF THE TALE OF THE MANNE OF LAWE.

HARM! CONDICION of POVERTE!
With thurst, with coold, with hunger so confoundid!
To asken help thee shameth in thyn herte;
If thou noon aske, so soore artow ywoundid,
That verray nede unwrappeth al thy wounde hid!
Maugree thyn heed, thou most for indigence
Or stele, or begge, or borwe thy despence!

Thow blamest Crist, and seist ful bitterly,
He mysdeparteth richesse temporal;
Thy neighebore thou wytest synfully,
And seist thou hast to lite, and he hath al.
Parfay, seistow, somtyme he rekene shal,
Whan that his tayl shal brennen in the gleede,
For he noght helpeth needfulle in hir neede.

Herkne what is the sentence of the wise:
Bet is to dyen than have indigence;
Thyselve neighebor wol thee despise;
If thou be povre, farwel thy reverence!
Yet of the wise man take this sentence:
Alle the dayes of povre men been wikke;
Be war therfore, er thou come to that prikke!

If thou be povre, thy brother hateth thee,
And alle thy freendes fleen from thee, allas!
O riche marchauntz, ful of wele been yee,
O noble, o prudent folk, as in this cas!
Youre bagges been nat filld with ambes as,
But with sys cynk, that renneth for youre chaunce;
At Christemasse myrie may ye daunce!

Ye seken lond and see for yowre wynnynges;
As wise folk ye knowen al thestaat
Of regnes: ye been fadres of tidynges

THE PROLOGUE OF THE TALE OF THE MANNE OF LAWE
KELMSCOTT CHAUCER, 1896, P. 43

[Mr. Pollard in the Preface gives an account of the genesis and history of the edition, its abortive undertaking by Henry Bradshaw (*see* above, 1864, *Works*), Aldis Wright, Skeat, and Furnivall, and its relation to the "library edition," ultimately edited by Skeat in 1894 (*q.v.*). The Introduction consists of a cautious biography setting out only the known external facts of Chaucer's life, followed by a more tentative chronological account of his writings. Special introductions by the various responsible editors then precede the text.]

1898. Pollard, Alfred William ; **Heath,** Sir Henry Frank ; **Liddell,** Mark Harvey ; **McCormick,** Sir William Symington. *See* supra : *The Works of Geoffrey Chaucer* (Globe edition).

1900. Skeat, Walter William. *The Chaucer Canon,* with a discussion of the works associated with the name of Geoffrey Chaucer.

[The argument starts from the admitted genuineness of the *Canterbury Tales;* Chaucer's grammatical practice in the *Squieres Tale,* and that of the *Ormulum* and the metre and rhyme-tests of the *Tales* are analysed ; the conclusions are applied to the poems of whose genuineness there is external testimony, and then in succession to the non-Chaucerian pieces printed by Thynne, Stowe, Speght, Urry, etc.]

[p. v]   Much that is here said is necessarily repeated from what I have already advanced in my six volume edition of Chaucer and in the supplementary volume entitled Chaucerian Pieces ; but, [with other new matter] . . . the account here given of the striking parallel between Chaucer's grammatical usages and the regular employment of various grammatical suffixes in the unassailable text of the Ormulum is, to the best of my belief, wholly new, and adds much firmness and certainty to the whole argument. . . .

The argument which I adduce is briefly this. The extreme regularity of the metre of the Ormulum enables us to deduce

[p. vi]   with certainty the circumstances under which grammatical inflexions are employed in it. Precisely similar inflexions occur in the genuine works of Chaucer, but not (speaking generally) in works which have erroneously been connected with his name.

Further, the genuine works, and these only, satisfy various rime-tests which are duly explained, and are all deducible from the Canterbury Tales ; and in this way the true Chaucer Canon can be established.

1900. S[keat], W[alter] W[illiam]. *In Honorem F. J. F.*, [issued separately, and inserted in] *An English Miscellany presented to Dr. Furnivall on his 75th birthday*, Oxford, 1901.

IN HONOREM F. J. F. (A.D. 1900).

(From MS. Harl. 7334, fol. 999, back.)

A Clerk ther was of Cauntebrigge also,
That unto rowing haddè longe y-go.
Of thinnè shidès wolde he shippès makè,
And he was nat right fat, I undertakè.
And whan his ship he wrought had attè fullè,
Right gladly up the river wolde he pullè,
And eek returne as blythly as he wentè.
Him rekkèd nevere that the sonne him brentè,
Ne stinted he his cours for regn ne snowè;
It was a joyè for to seen him rowè !
Yit was him lever, in his shelves newè,
Six oldè textès, clad in greenish hewè,
Of Chaucer and his oldè poesyè
Than ale, or wyn of Lepe, or Malvoisyè.
And therwithal he wex a philosofre;
And peynèd him to gadren gold in cofre
Of sundry folk; and al that he might hentè.
On textes and emprinting he it spentè;
And busily gan bokès to purveyè
For hem that yeve him wherwith to scoleyè.

.   .   .   .

Souning in Erly English was his spechè,
" And gladly wolde he lerne, and gladly techè."

CAMBRIDGE : PRINTED BY W. LEWIS AT THE UNIVERSITY PRESS